SOMETHING ABOUT THE AUTHOR®

Something about
the Author *was named
an "Outstanding
Reference Source,"
the highest honor given
by the American
Library Association
Reference and Adult
Services Division.*

ISSN 0276-816X

something ABOUT THE AUThOR®

**Facts and Pictures about Authors
and Illustrators of Books for Young People**

volume 194

GALE
CENGAGE Learning™

Detroit • New York • San Francisco • New Haven, Conn • Waterville, Maine • London

GALE
CENGAGE Learning™

Something about the Author, Volume 194

Project Editor: Lisa Kumar

Editorial: Dana Ferguson, Amy Elisabeth Fuller, Michelle Kazensky, Jennifer Mossman, Joseph Palmisano, Mary Ruby, Marie Toft

Permissions: Margaret Abendroth, Timothy Sisler, Sara Teller

Imaging and Multimedia: Leitha Etheridge-Sims, John Watkins

Composition and Electronic Capture: Amy Darga

Manufacturing: Drew Kalasky

Product Manager: Janet Witalec

For product information and technology assistance, contact us at
Gale Customer Support, 1-800-877-4253.
For permission to use material from this text or product,
submit all requests online at **www.cengage.com/permissions.**
Further permissions questions can be emailed to
permissionrequest@cengage.com

Gale
27500 Drake Rd.
Farmington Hills, MI, 48331-3535

LIBRARY OF CONGRESS CATALOG CARD NUMBER 62-52046

ISBN-13: 978-1-4144-2166-7
ISBN-10: 1-4144-2166-4

ISSN 0276-816X

This title is also available as an e-book.
ISBN-13: 978-1-4144-5740-6
ISBN-10: 1-4144-5740-5
Contact your Gale sales representative for ordering information.

Printed in the United States of America
1 2 3 4 5 6 7 13 12 11 10 09

Contents

Authors in Forthcoming Volumes

Below are some of the authors and illustrators that will be featured in upcoming volumes of *SATA*. These include new entries on the swiftly rising stars of the field, as well as completely revised and updated entries (indicated with *) on some of the most notable and best-loved creators of books for children.

Mary Blair ❚ Considered a significant influence within modernist 1950s animation, Blair's concept art—the paintings that mapped out the look of each scene for film animators—defined the unique look of such classic Walt Disney Company films as *Peter Pan, Cinderella,* and *Alice in Wonderland.* In addition to appearing in film, Blair's concept art for Disney has been adapted for the picture-book format in *Walt Disney's Cinderella,* with text by Cynthia Rylant, and *Walt Disney's Alice in Wonderland,* with a story by Jon Scieszka. Prior to her death in the late 1970s, Blair also designed the characters for Disneyland's popular "It's a Small World" exhibit.

*Judy Blume ❚ Since she published her first book in 1969, Blume has become one of the most popular authors for children. Her accessible, humorous style and direct, sometimes explicit treatment of youthful concerns have won her many fans—as well as critics who sometimes seek to censor her work. The author of *Are You There God? It's Me, Margaret, The Pain and the Great One, Fudge-a-Mania, Forever,* and *Blubber,* Blume continues to produce works that are, according to critics, both entertaining and thought-provoking.

John Fardell ❚ Fardell, a Scottish writer, illustrator, and cartoonist, is the author of the highly regarded fantasy novels *The Seven Professors of the Far North* and *The Flight of the Silver Turtle.* Praised for his fast-paced stories and vivid settings, Fardell is also the creator of the comic strips "The Modern Parents," "The Critics," and "Hanover Square," and his work appears regularly in the adult comic magazine *Viz.*

*Sharon M. Draper ❚ An award-winning teacher and writer, Draper is the author of the novels *Forged by Fire, Romiette and Julio, Darkness before Dawn,* the Coretta Scott King Award-winning *Copper Sun,* and the easy-reading "Ziggy and the Black Dinosaurs" mystery series. In addition to addressing the challenges faced by African-American young people—particularly black males—in white society, Draper's books also explore African-American families and communities. Her stories, which are often set in her native Cincinnati, Ohio, feature resilient characters and fast-moving plots that frequently involve solving a mystery.

Gordon C. James ❚ A successful painter in oils whose work has been widely exhibited, James also creates artwork for children's books. His detailed, light-filled paintings are inspired by the work of such romantic artists as John Singer Sargent. James's images are a feature of Patricia C. McKissack's "Scraps of Time" chapter-book series, which focuses on several generations of an African-American family, and also serve as a highlight of David A. Adler's biography *Campy: The Story of Roy Campanella.*

*Patricia McKissack ❚ McKissack is a prolific writer and former educator who creates historical fiction and biographies for children. Her awards include a Newbery Honor Book designation for the short-story collection *The Dark Thirty* as well as several Coretta Scott King awards. Fiction by McKissack, which features illustrations by Jerry Pinkney, Kyrsten Brooker, and other talented artists, includes the picture book *The All-I'll-Ever-Want Christmas Doll* and *Precious and the Boo Hag.* Working with husband Fredrick L. McKissack, she also produces books focusing on little-known aspects of African-American history, among them *Red-Tail Angels: The Story of the Tuskegee Airmen of World War II, Black Diamonds: The Story of the Negro Baseball Leagues,* and *Black Hands, White Sails: The Story of African-American Whalers.*

Jimmy Pickering ❚ Pickering, a painter and designer who has worked at such film companies as Walt Disney and Universal Studios, also provides artwork for children's books. His distinctive work, which is slyly macabre, appears in *Vampire Brat* by Angie Sage, *Halloween Night* by Elizabeth Hatch, and *Sloop John B: A Pirate's Tale,* the last a picture book with text by Beach Boys cofounder Alan Jardine. Pickering has also authored several self-illustrated children's books, and he counts the quirky picture book *Skelly the Skeleton Girl* among these original works.

Thomas E. Sniegoski ❚ Sniegoski is a popular and prolific novelist, comic-book writer, and journalist. Working in the comics industry for more than two decades, Sniegoski has contributed to several series, including "Batman" and "Star Trek: The Next Generation," as well as numerous original titles such as novels in his "Fallen" quartet. He also works with collaborators such as Christopher Golden, with whom he created the popular "Outcast" fantasy novel series for young adults.

*James Stevenson ❚ Known for his antic touch and light humor, Stevenson is the creator of such beloved characters as the irascible Worst—a grandfather who is anything but lovable—and the more endearing Grandpa, who enjoys telling tall tales and whoppers to his gullible grandchildren. Sharing his upbeat view of life with readers, Stevenson's gently humorous, animated stories include *Clams Can't Sing, Wilfred the Rat,* and *Higher on the Door.* The sketchy, high-spirited drawing style he uses in illustrating his own tales has also brought to life texts by such notable children's authors as Dr. Seuss, Else Holmelund Minarik, Charlotte Zolotow, and Jack Prelutsky.

Peter Yarrow ❚ A singer and songwriter, Yarrow gained fame in the mid-twentieth century as the founder of the popular folk trio Peter, Paul, and Mary. In the years since, Yarrow has combined his musical career with his work as an activist, while also entertaining younger audiences with a picture-book version of his popular song *Puff the Magic Dragon.*

Introduction

Something about the Author (*SATA*) is an ongoing reference series that examines the lives and works of authors and illustrators of books for children. *SATA* includes not only well-known writers and artists but also less prominent individuals whose works are just coming to be recognized. This series is often the only readily available information source on emerging authors and illustrators. You'll find *SATA* informative and entertaining, whether you are a student, a librarian, an English teacher, a parent, or simply an adult who enjoys children's literature.

What's Inside *SATA*

SATA provides detailed information about authors and illustrators who span the full time range of children's literature, from early figures like John Newbery and L. Frank Baum to contemporary figures like Judy Blume and Richard Peck. Authors in the series represent primarily English-speaking countries, particularly the United States, Canada, and the United Kingdom. Also included, however, are authors from around the world whose works are available in English translation. The writings represented in *SATA* include those created intentionally for children and young adults as well as those written for a general audience and known to interest younger readers. These writings cover the entire spectrum of children's literature, including picture books, humor, folk and fairy tales, animal stories, mystery and adventure, science fiction and fantasy, historical fiction, poetry and nonsense verse, drama, biography, and nonfiction. Obituaries are also included in *SATA* and are intended not only as death notices but also as concise overviews of people's lives and work. Additionally, each edition features newly revised and updated entries for a selection of *SATA* listees who remain of interest to today's readers and who have been active enough to require extensive revisions of their earlier biographies.

Autobiography Feature

Beginning with Volume 103, many volumes of *SATA* feature one or more specially commissioned autobiographical essays. These unique essays, averaging about ten thousand words in length and illustrated with an abundance of personal photos, present an entertaining and informative first-person perspective on the lives and careers of prominent authors and illustrators profiled in *SATA*.

Two Convenient Indexes

In response to suggestions from librarians, *SATA* indexes no longer appear in every volume but are included in alternate (odd-numbered) volumes of the series, beginning with Volume 57.

SATA continues to include two indexes that cumulate with each alternate volume: the Illustrations Index, arranged by the name of the illustrator, gives the number of the volume and page where the illustrator's work appears in the current volume as well as all preceding volumes in the series; the Author Index gives the number of the volume in which a person's biographical sketch, autobiographical essay, or obituary appears in the current volume as well as all preceding volumes in the series.

These indexes also include references to authors and illustrators who appear in *Gale's Yesterday's Authors of Books for Children, Children's Literature Review,* and *Something about the Author Autobiography Series.*

Easy-to-Use Entry Format

Whether you're already familiar with the *SATA* series or just getting acquainted, you will want to be aware of the kind of information that an entry provides. In every *SATA* entry the editors attempt to give as complete a picture of the person's life and work as possible. A typical entry in *SATA* includes the following clearly labeled information sections:

PERSONAL: date and place of birth and death, parents' names and occupations, name of spouse, date of marriage, names of children, educational institutions attended, degrees received, religious and political affiliations, hobbies and other interests.

ADDRESSES: complete home, office, electronic mail, and agent addresses, whenever available.

CAREER: name of employer, position, and dates for each career post; art exhibitions; military service; memberships and offices held in professional and civic organizations.

MEMBER: professional, civic, and other association memberships and any official posts held.

AWARDS, HONORS: literary and professional awards received.

WRITINGS: title-by-title chronological bibliography of books written and/or illustrated, listed by genre when known; lists of other notable publications, such as plays, screenplays, and periodical contributions.

ADAPTATIONS: a list of films, television programs, plays, CD-ROMs, recordings, and other media presentations that have been adapted from the author's work.

WORK IN PROGRESS: description of projects in progress.

SIDELIGHTS: a biographical portrait of the author or illustrator's development, either directly from the biographee—and often written specifically for the *SATA* entry—or gathered from diaries, letters, interviews, or other published sources.

BIOGRAPHICAL AND CRITICAL SOURCES: cites sources quoted in "Sidelights" along with references for further reading.

EXTENSIVE ILLUSTRATIONS: photographs, movie stills, book illustrations, and other interesting visual materials supplement the text.

How a *SATA* Entry Is Compiled

SATA editors examine a wide variety of published sources to gather information for an entry. Biographical and bibliographic sources are consulted, as are book reviews, feature articles, published interviews, and material sometimes obtained from the biographee's family, publishers, agent, or other associates. Whenever possible, the author or illustrator is sent a copy of the entry to check for accuracy and completeness.

Entries that have not been verified by the biographees or their representatives are marked with an asterisk (*).

Contact the Editor

We encourage our readers to examine the entire *SATA* series. Please write and tell us if we can make *SATA* even more helpful to you. Give your comments and suggestions to the editor:

Editor
Something about the Author
Gale, Cengage Learning
27500 Drake Rd.
Farmington Hills MI 48331-3535

Toll-free: 800-877-GALE
Fax: 248-699-8070

Something about the Author Product Advisory Board

The editors of *Something about the Author* are dedicated to maintaining a high standard of excellence by publishing comprehensive, accurate, and highly readable entries on a wide array of writers for children and young adults. In addition to the quality of the content, the editors take pride in the graphic design of the series, which is intended to be orderly yet inviting, allowing readers to utilize the pages of *SATA* easily and with efficiency. Despite the longevity of the *SATA* print series, and the success of its format, we are mindful that the vitality of a literary reference product is dependent on its ability to serve its users over time. As literature, and attitudes about literature, constantly evolve, so do the reference needs of students, teachers, scholars, journalists, researchers, and book club members. To be certain that we continue to keep pace with the expectations of our customers, the editors of *SATA* listen carefully to their comments regarding the value, utility, and quality of the series. Librarians, who have firsthand knowledge of the needs of library users, are a valuable resource for us. The *Something about the Author* Product Advisory Board, made up of school, public, and academic librarians, is a forum to promote focused feedback about *SATA* on a regular basis. The nine-member advisory board includes the following individuals, whom the editors wish to thank for sharing their expertise:

Eva M. Davis
Youth Department Manager,
Ann Arbor District Library,
Ann Arbor, Michigan

Joan B. Eisenberg
Lower School Librarian,
Milton Academy,
Milton, Massachusetts

Francisca Goldsmith
Teen Services Librarian,
Berkeley Public Library,
Berkeley, California

Susan Dove Lempke
Children's Services Supervisor,
Niles Public Library District,
Niles, Illinois

Robyn Lupa
Head of Children's Services,
Jefferson County Public Library,
Lakewood, Colorado

Victor L. Schill
Assistant Branch Librarian/Children's Librarian,
Harris County Public Library/Fairbanks Branch,
Houston, Texas

Caryn Sipos
Community Librarian,
Three Creeks Community Library,
Vancouver, Washington

Steven Weiner
Director,
Maynard Public Library,
Maynard, Massachusetts

Something About the Author

ABRAHAMS, Peter 1947-

Personal

Born June 28, 1947; married Diana Gray (a teacher), 1978; children: Seth, Ben, Lily, Rosie. *Education:* Williams College, B.A., 1968.

Addresses

Home—Cape Cod, MA. *E-mail*—pa@cape.com.

Career

Writer. Worked as a spear fisher in the Bahamas, 1968-70; Canadian Broadcasting Corporation, Toronto, Ontario, Canada, radio producer.

Awards, Honors

Edgar Allan Poe Award nomination for best novel, Mystery Writers of America, 1994, for *Lights Out;* Edgar Allan Poe Award nomination, and Agatha Award for best children's/young-adult fiction, both 2006, both for *Down the Rabbit Hole.*

Writings

JUVENILE NOVELS; "ECHO FALLS MYSTERY" SERIES

Down the Rabbit Hole, Laura Geringer Books (New York, NY), 2005.

Behind the Curtain, Laura Geringer Books (New York, NY), 2006.
Into the Dark, Laura Geringer Books (New York, NY), 2008.

ADULT NOVELS

The Fury of Rachel Monette, Macmillan (New York, NY), 1980.
Tongues of Fire, M. Evans (New York, NY), 1982.
Hard Rain, Dutton (New York, NY), 1988.
Pressure Drop, Dutton (New York, NY), 1989.
Revolution Number 9, Mysterious Press (New York, NY), 1992.
Lights Out, Mysterious Press (New York, NY), 1994.
The Fan, Warner Books (New York, NY), 1995.
A Perfect Crime, Ballantine Books (New York, NY), 1998.
Crying Wolf, Ballantine Books (New York, NY), 2000.
Last of the Dixie Heroes, Ballantine Books (New York, NY), 2001.
The Tutor, Ballantine Books (New York, NY), 2002.
Their Wildest Dreams, Ballantine Books (New York, NY), 2003.
Oblivion, William Morrow (New York, NY), 2005.
End of Story, William Morrow (New York, NY), 2006.
Nerve Damage, William Morrow (New York, NY), 2007.
Delusion, William Morrow (New York, NY), 2008.

OTHER

Red Message, 1986.

(With Sidney D. Kirkpatrick) *Turning the Tide: One Man against the Medellin Cartel* (nonfiction), Dutton (New York, NY), 1991.

Contributor to anthologies, including *666,* Scholastic (New York, NY), 2007; and *Up All Night,* Laura Geringer Books (New York, NY), 2008.

Adaptations

The Fan was adapted for film by Frank Darabont and Phoef Sutton and released by TriStar, 1996. The "Echo Falls" novels have been adapted for audiobook by HarperAudio, beginning 2006.

Sidelights

Peter Abrahams is the author of critically acclaimed crime novels that include *Nerve Damage, Oblivion, End of Story,* and *Lights Out,* the last which was nominated for the Mystery Writers of America's coveted Edgar award. Turning to a younger readership, the Massachusetts-based novelist and father of four is also the creator of the "Echo Falls" mystery novels, which includes the award-winning *Down the Rabbit Hole* and *Behind the Curtain.* Commenting on his books to Kay Longcope in the *Boston Globe,* Abrahams stated: "I'm interested in putting ordinary people into extraordinary situations, as [British film director] Alfred Hitchcock did, rather than making James Bond-type superheroes and putting them in life and death situations. You can generate a lot more dread. I want to directly attack the imagination, to ensnare it. That's the way a good book works for me."

In *Down the Rabbit Hole* readers meet thirteen-year-old Ingrid Levin-Hill, a middle-school student living in small-town Connecticut. A fan of famous literary sleuth Sherlock Holmes, Ingrid is also a likeable eighth grader with a love of soccer. When a woman the girl has met is found murdered, Ingrid recognizes that their brief friendship makes sleuthing an obligation. As the mystery surrounding the woman's death thickens, the girl develops a useful friendship with Joey, the son of the town's chief of police. She also manages to keep up with the clues while studying and rehearsing the title role in a stage version of *Alice in Wonderland.* Calling *Down the Rabbit Hole* "good, smart entertainment," Claire Rosser praised Abraham's novel for its realistic setting and for a heroine who "acts in ways most of us readers wouldn't dare to attempt."

In *Behind the Curtain* Ingrid and Joey team up to prove the truth of her allegations about a local drug ring that may be selling steroids to her older brother Ty. Meanwhile, Grampy is hoping to keep his farm from greedy land developers and Ingrid's father seems preoccupied with worries about his job. With its focus on the steroid crisis among young athletes, Abrahams's novel addresses "a timely issue [that] gives this mystery a 'ripped from the headlines' flavor," according to Connie Fletcher in *Booklist.* Noting Ingrid's similarity to teen sleuth Sammy Keyes in the mystery series by Wendelin Van Draanen, *Kliatt* contributor Rosser called the novel "entertaining and well constructed." In *School Library Journal* Denise Moore dubbed *Behind the Curtain* "a fast-paced mystery with well-defined characters," and in *Kirkus Reviews* a critic concluded that Abraham's "wonderfully realized" young sleuth shines in "a deliciously plotted, highly satisfying adventure."

The "Echo Falls" series continues with *Into the Dark,* which Rosser deemed "the best [installment] of all." Here the mystery centers on a murder committed on Grampy's farm, and Grampy is arrested as the suspected killer. When the elderly man refuses to give police an alibi, Ingrid decides to come to his rescue and follows the mystery back into Grampy's experiences during World War II. Praising the suspense that builds throughout *Into the Dark, School Library Journal* contributor Sheila Fiscus added that "Ingrid's ability to not only think through the crime but also solve it is impressive." Noting that "the hallmark of this series is the author's revealing of clues to readers ahead of Ingrid," a *Kirkus Reviews* contributor described the teenage sleuth as "intrepid."

One of Abrahams' early adult thrillers, *Lights Out,* focuses on Eddie Nye. Finally released from prison on trumped-up drug charges, Eddie is quickly plunged into dangerous intrigue while investigating the circumstances of his frame-up. Also adapted as a feature film starring Robert DeNiro and Wesley Snipes, *The Fan* focuses on Gil Renard, a divorced and down-and-out traveling salesman, and Bobby Rayburn, an arrogant and successful baseball player. Renard, a baseball fanatic who has slid into committing petty crimes, is obsessed with Rayburn. He manages to become caretaker on Rayburn's estate while also planning to murder the star athlete on the playing field. According to a *Publishers Weekly* critic, in *Lights Out* Abrahams presents readers with "a fascinating and memorable character" in Eddie, making the book "consistently interesting and suspenseful." In *Booklist,* Wes Lukowsky called *The Fan* a "first-rate thriller," and *Library Journal* reviewer Marylaine Block termed it an "excellent novel."

A complex marriage is at the heart of another thriller, *A Perfect Crime.* Here Roger Cullingwood is in an unhappy marriage, and his employment situation has not been the best for months. The man's idyllic perception of his life is finally shattered when he learns that his wife, Francie, is romantically involved with a well-known local psychologist. Determined to restore his enormous ego, Roger engineers a complex plan to kill his wife but loses control of the scheme after enlisting the help of a convicted murder. In *Booklist* Thomas Gaughan cited the novel's "complex and compelling" plotting and "sharp and almost flawless" dialogue. *A Perfect Crime* "is fast-paced, tense, even witty as it careens to its bloody conclusion," noted Karen Anderson in her *Library Journal* review.

What will a middle-class kid from a small Colorado town do to pay for a prestigious university education in New England? Abrahams presents one possible scenario in *Crying Wolf,* "a suspense novel built around kidnapping, extortion and youthful stupidity," according to a *Publishers Weekly* reviewer. Nat, a high school valedictorian, uses his $2,000 essay-contest winnings to help his mother cover the tuition for his freshman year at Inverness. When his mom loses her job, Nat decides to subsidize his education by kidnapping, hatching his "victimless" scheme with the help of wealthy twin friends from school.

The title character in Abrahams' thriller *The Tutor* was likened by a *Publishers Weekly* contributor to the Hitchcock character Norman Bates of *Psycho* fame: an apparently ordinary and pleasant fellow who gradually emerges as a sinister threat to an entire family. Hired by the suburban Gardner family to prepare son Brandon for his Scholastic Aptitude Test, tutor Julian Sawyer manages to penetrate the weaknesses of the family members, guiding each toward a personalized, destructive objective. It is up to Brandon's teenaged sister Ruby to unravel the emerging clues and save her family from danger. "Once again this author finds menace in dailiness," the *Publishers Weekly* reviewer observed, and a *Kirkus Reviews* critic viewed the plot of *The Tutor* as "the familiar laced with lingering irony."

In *End of Story,* Abrahams "solidifies his reputation as one of the best contemporary thriller writers around," proclaimed a *Publishers Weekly* contributor. This novel takes readers to upstate New York as they follow protagonist Ivy Seidel. Trained as a writer but finding it difficult to find work, Ivy eventually gets a job at Dannemora Prison, teaching writing to inmates. When a poem by one of her incarcerated students professes innocence, Ivy decides to clear the man's name, her efforts recounted by Abrahams in what *Booklist* contributor Keir Graff described as "prose [that is] "cool and vivid, [and] keeps the focus . . . on the story."

A sculptor with only months to live is the focus of *Nerve Damage.* Here Abrahams' "succinct prose" conveys the mystery surrounding the untimely death of the ill man's wife's in a helicopter accident, using "more than enough substance . . . to keep readers . . . engrossed," according to *Booklist* critic Thomas Gaughan. In another thriller, *Delusion,* a tropical storm leaves in its wake a formerly hidden videotape that sheds new light on the murder of Nell Jarreau's boyfriend twenty years before. Now married to the chief of police, Nell is haunted by the crime and fascinated by the now-released convict, who she may have incorrectly identified as the murderer. In *Booklist,* Stephanie Zvirin praised the thriller's complex characters, concluding that in *Delusion* "readers catch a glimpse of how betrayal and loyalty can be equally deadly."

In *Oblivion* Abrahams moves into the detective genre. Private investigator Nick Petrov is trying to locate a missing teen, but the memory loss and mental confu-

sion he experiences due to a cerebral hemorrhage slows and then halts his investigation. The challenges both in Nick's career and his personal life soon entwine in what *New Yorker* critic Joyce Carol Oates referred to as "a Dali landscape of baffling clues, memory lapses, and visual hallucinations." As Abrahams' story unwinds, the psychological fear associated with Nick's amnesia inspires fear: The fragmented clues available to him cause him to question his own integrity. Could he himself be a criminal—even a murderer? Oates called *Oblivion* "gratifyingly attentive to psychological detail, richly atmospheric, [and] layered in ambiguity."

Biographical and Critical Sources

PERIODICALS

Armchair Detective, spring, 1990, William J. Schafer, review of *Pressure Drop,* p. 238.

Booklist, August, 1992, Peter Robertson, review of *Revolution Number 9,* p. 1998; February 1, 1994, Wes Lukowsky, review of *Lights Out,* p. 996; January 15, 1995, Wes Lukowsky, review of *The Fan,* p. 868; July, 1998, Thomas Gaughan, review of *A Perfect Crime,* p. 1827; August, 1999, Karen Harris, review of *A Perfect Crime,* p. 2075; January 1, 2000, Vanessa Bush, review of *Crying Wolf,* p. 833; March 1, 2006, Keir Graff, review of *End of Story,* p. 43; May 1, 2006, Connie Fletcher, review of *Behind the Curtain,* p. 47; February 15, 2007, Thomas Gaughan, review of *Nerve Damage,* p. 37; February 1, 2008, Stephanie Zvirin, review of *Delusion,* p. 5.

Boston Globe, February 22, 1988, interview by Kay Longcope.

Bulletin of the Center for Children's Books, September, 2006, review of *Behind the Curtain,* p. 4.

Entertainment Weekly, April 21, 1995, Gene Lyons, review of *The Fan,* p. 49; March 15, 2007, Jennifer Reese, review of *Nerve Damage,* p. 72.

Kirkus Reviews, May 1, 2002, review of *The Tutor,* p. 588; June 15, 2003, review of *Their Wildest Dreams,* p. 817; December 15, 2004, review of *Oblivion,* p. 1151; February 15, 2006, review of *End of Story,* p. 143; April 1, 2006, review of *Behind the Curtain,* p. 341; August 1, 2007, review of *666;* February 15, 2008, review of *Delusion;* March 1, 2008, review of *Into the Dark.*

Kliatt, March, 2005, Claire Rosser, review of *Down the Rabbit Hole;* May, 2006, Claire Rosser, review of *Behind the Curtain,* p. 4; March, 2008, Claire Rosser, review of *Into the Dark,* p. 6.

Library Journal, August, 1980, Samuel Simons, review of *The Fury of Rachel Monette,* p. 1655; April 15, 1982, review of *Tongues of Fire,* p. 823; December, 1987, A.M.B. Amantia, review of *Hard Rain,* p. 126; May 1, 1991, review of *Turning the Tide: One Man against the Medellin Cartel,* p. 89; July, 1992, Michele Leber, review of *Revolution #9,* p. 119; February 1, 1994, Dan Bogey, review of *Lights Out,* p. 109; February 1,

1995, Marylaine Block, review of *The Fan,* p. 97; August, 1998, Karen Anderson, review of *A Perfect Crime,* p. 128; December, 1998, Danna Bell-Russel, review of *A Perfect Crime,* p. 173.

Los Angeles Times Book Review, June 27, 1982, Raymond Mungo, review of *Tongues of Fire,* p. 10; January 17, 1988, Charles Champlin, review of *Hard Rain,* p. 10.

New Republic, September 9, 1996, Stanley Kauffmann, review of *The Fan,* p. 37.

New York, July 5, 1982, Rhoda Koenig, review of *The Fury of Rachel Monette,* p. 103.

New Yorker, April 4, 2005, Joyce Carol Oates, review of *Oblivion,* p. 94; April 2, 2007, review of *Nerve Damage,* p. 79.

New York Times Book Review, February 21, 1988, William J. Harding, review of *Hard Rain,* p. 20; October 11, 1998, Marilyn Stasio, review of *A Perfect Crime,* p. 28.

Publishers Weekly, June 27, 1980, review of *The Fury of Rachel Monette,* p. 79; April 9, 1982, Barbara A. Bannon, review of *Tongues of Fire,* p. 43; November 6, 1987, Sybil Steinberg, review of *Hard Rain,* p. 58; September 29, 1989, review of *Pressure Drop,* p. 60; April 19, 1991, review of *Turning the Tide,* p. 54; June 1, 1992, review of *Revolution Number 9,* p. 50; January 10, 1994, Sybil Steinberg, review of *Lights Out,* pp. 43-44; January 23, 1995, review of *The Fan,* pp. 58-59; July 20, 1998, review of *A Perfect Crime,* p. 206; January 10, 2000, review of *Crying Wolf,* p. 42; July 1, 2002, review of *The Tutor,* p. 55; August 4, 2003, review of *Their Wildest Dreams,* p. 56; April 4, 2005, review of *Down the Rabbit Hole,* p. 60; February 27, 2006, review of *End of Story,* p. 34; January 15, 2007, review of *Nerve Damage,* p. 32; February 18, 2008, review of *Delusion,* p. 136.

Quill and Quire, February, 1990, Paul Stuewe, review of *Pressure Drop,* p. 27.

School Library Journal, May, 2005, Susan W. Hunter, review of *Down the Rabbit Hole,* p. 120; April, 2006, Denise Moore, review of *Behind the Curtain,* p. 133; March, 2008, Sheila Fiscus, review of *Into the Dark,* p. 193.

Spectator, January 30, 1982, Harriet Waugh, review of *The Fury of Rachel Monette,* pp. 22-23.

Tribune Books (Chicago, IL), August 2, 1992, Richard Martins, review of *Revolution Number 9,* p. 5.

West Coast Review of Books, July, 1982, review of *Tongues of Fire,* p. 33.

Voice of Youth Advocates, June, 2005, Cyndi Gueswel, review of *Down the Rabbit Hole,* p. 124; April, 2006, Barbara Johnston, review of *Behind the Curtain,* p. 37.

ONLINE

HarperCollins Web site, http://www.harpercollins.com/ (October 15, 2008), "Peter Abrahams."

Peter Abrahams Home Page, http://www.peterabrahams. com (October 15, 2008).

WritersBreak Web site, http://www.writersbreak.com/ (October 15, 2008), Jennifer Minar, interview with Abrahams.*

AFFABEE, Eric
See STINE, R.L.

* * *

BABBITT, Natalie 1932-

Personal

Born July 28, 1932, in Dayton, OH; daughter of Ralph Zane (a business administrator) and Genevieve Moore; married Samuel Fisher Babbitt (a university administrator), June 26, 1954; children: Christopher Converse, Thomas Collier II, Lucy Cullyford. *Education:* Smith College, B.A., 1954. *Politics:* Democrat. *Hobbies and other interests:* Needlework, piano, word puzzles.

Addresses

Home—Providence, RI.

Career

Author and illustrator.

Member

Authors Guild, Author's League of America, PEN (American Center).

Awards, Honors

Best Book for children ages nine to twelve, *New York Times,* 1969, for *The Search for Delicious;* Notable Book, American Library Association (ALA), 1970, Newbery Honor Book designation, ALA, 1971, and Honor Book citation, *Horn Book,* all for *Kneeknock Rise;* Children's Spring Book Festival Honor Book designation, *Book World,* 1971, Children's Book Showcase, Children's Book Council, Best Books designation, *School Library Journal,* and Edgar Allan Poe award runner-up, Mystery Writers of America, all 1972, all for *Goody Hall;* Notable Book designation, ALA, Best Books designation, *School Library Journal,* Honor Book citation, *Horn Book,* and National Book Award finalist, American Academy and Institute of Arts and Letters, all 1975, and Parents' Choice Award (story book category), Parent's Choice Foundation, 1987, all for *The Devil's Storybook;* Best Books designation, *New York Times,* 1975, Notable Book designation, ALA, Honor Book citation, *Horn Book,* Christopher Award for juvenile fiction, The Christophers, all 1976, Children's Choice selection, International Reading Association, U.S. Honor Book citation, Congress of the International Board on Books for Young People (IBBY) citation, and Lewis Carroll Shelf Award, all 1978, all for *Tuck Everlasting;* Notable Book designation, ALA, 1977, for *The Eyes of the Amaryllis;* Recognition of Merit Award, George C. Stone Center for Children's Books, 1979, for body of work; Hans Christian Andersen Medal nomination, IBBY, 1981; Best Books desig-

Natalie Babbitt (Reproduced by permission.)

nation, *New York Times,* 1982, for *Herbert Rowbarge;* Children's Literature Festival Award, Keene State College, 1993, for body of work; Blue Ribbon Book, *Bulletin of the Center for Children's Books,* 1998, Notable Book designation, ALA, 1999, and Audie Award, 2001, all for *Ouch! A Tale from Grimm.*

Writings

SELF-ILLUSTRATED VERSE

Dick Foote and the Shark, Farrar, Straus (New York, NY), 1967.

Phoebe's Revolt, Farrar, Straus (New York, NY), 1968.

SELF-ILLUSTRATED FICTION

The Search for Delicious, Farrar, Straus (New York, NY), 1969.

Kneeknock Rise, Farrar, Straus (New York, NY), 1970.

The Something, Farrar, Straus (New York, NY), 1970.

Goody Hall, Farrar, Straus (New York, NY), 1971.

The Devil's Storybook, Farrar, Straus (New York, NY), 1974.

Tuck Everlasting, Farrar, Straus (New York, NY), 1975.

The Eyes of the Amaryllis, Farrar, Straus (New York, NY), 1977.

Herbert Rowbarge, Farrar, Straus (New York, NY), 1982.

The Devil's Other Storybook, Farrar, Straus (New York, NY), 1987.

Nellie: A Cat on Her Own, Farrar, Straus (New York, NY), 1989.

Bub; or, The Very Best Thing, HarperCollins (New York, NY), 1994.

Elsie Times Eight, Hyperion (New York, NY), 2001.

Jack Plank Tells Tales, Michael di Capua Books (New York, NY), 2007.

ILLUSTRATOR

Samuel Fisher Babbitt, *The Forty-ninth Magician,* Pantheon (New York, NY), 1966.

Valerie Worth, *Small Poems,* Farrar, Straus (New York, NY), 1972.

Valerie Worth, *More Small Poems,* Farrar, Straus (New York, NY), 1976.

Valerie Worth, *Still More Small Poems,* Farrar, Straus (New York, NY), 1978.

Valerie Worth, *Curlicues: The Fortunes of Two Pug Dogs,* Farrar, Straus (New York, NY), 1980, published as *Imp and Biscuit: The Fortunes of Two Pugs,* Chatto & Windus (London, England), 1981.

Valerie Worth, *Small Poems Again,* Farrar, Straus (New York, NY), 1986.

Valerie Worth, *Other Small Poems Again,* Farrar, Straus (New York, NY), 1986.

Valerie Worth, *All the Small Poems,* Farrar, Straus (New York, NY), 1987.

Valerie Worth, *All the Small Poems and Fourteen More,* Farrar, Straus (New York, NY), 1994.

Valerie Worth, *Peacock and Other Poems,* Farrar, Straus (New York, NY), 2002.

OTHER

(Reteller) *Ouch!: A Tale from Grimm,* illustrated by Fred Marcellino, HarperCollins/Michael di Capua Books (New York, NY), 1998.

Contributor to *Redbook, Publishers Weekly, Horn Book, New York Times Book Review, Cricket, School Library Journal, USA Today,* and *Washington Post Book World.*

Babbitt's books have been translated into several languages.

Adaptations

Kneeknock Rise was made into a filmstrip, Miller-Brody Productions, 1975, and recorded on audiocassette, American School Publishers, 1987; *The Search for Delicious* was recorded on audiocassette, Listening Library; *Ouch!* was recorded on audiocassette with teacher's guide, Live Oak Media, 2000. *Tuck Everlasting* was recorded on audiocassette, Audio Bookshelf, 1995, and adapted as a motion picture, Walt Disney Productions, 2002.

Sidelights

Primarily known as a children's book writer, Natalie Babbitt is also appreciated as a gifted storyteller by adult readers. In entertaining narratives, her characters confront many basic human necessities, including the need for love and acceptance, the need to grow and make independent decisions, the need to overcome fears, and the need to believe in something unexplainable. Her originality, sense of humor, and challenging themes have earned her acclaim as a children's author. Babbitt's 1975 work, *Tuck Everlasting,* garnered numerous awards and honors when it was first published, and in the years since it has been deemed a masterpiece of children's literature. "Babbitt has made a special place for herself in the world of children's literature," concluded a contributor to the *St. James Guide to Children's Writers.*

Babbitt's mother encouraged the author's early interest in art and reading. Genevieve Moore read children's books aloud to her two daughters, and the three decided that Natalie would become an artist and her sister a writer. Impressed with Spanish artist Luis de Vargas's airbrushed figures of glamorous women, which were popular during World War II, young Babbitt imitated them using colored pencils. Discouraged by the difference between Vargas's finished drawings and her own, she was then inspired by Sir John Tenniel's illustrations in *Alice in Wonderland* and decided to work with pen and ink, which became her specialty.

While taking a summer fashion illustration course at the Cleveland School of Art, Babbitt realized that she enjoyed creative drawing more than sketching alligator handbags. Later, in art classes at Smith College, where she competed with other artists for the first time in her life, she saw that success as an illustrator required more than just creativity. In an essay for *Something about the Author Autobiography Series* (SAAS), Babbitt explained: "It was an invaluable lesson, the best lesson I learned in four years of college: to wit, you have to work hard to do good work. I had always done what came easily, and what came easily had always been good enough. It was not good enough at Smith, and would never be good enough again."

While at Smith, she met Samuel Babbitt, whom she married in 1954. She kept busy working and raising a family of three children while her husband, an aspiring author, wrote a novel. The many solitary hours spent working on the novel did not suit him, however, and he went back to work as a college administrator. Babbitt's sister also produced a comic novel, for which Babbitt supplied illustrations, but the project was abandoned when an editor asked for a substantial rewriting. "I learned three valuable things from observing what happened to my mother, sister, and husband with their forays into the writer's world," she said in her autobiographical essay. "You have to give writing your full attention, you have to like the revision process, and you have to like to be alone. But it was years before I put any of it to good use." After reading Betty Friedan's *The Feminine Mystique,* Babbitt realized that while her life as a homemaker had been successful, it was time to

try to develop her talents. Discussions with other women making similar discoveries led to her decision to pursue a career as an illustrator.

In 1966, *The Forty-ninth Magician,* illustrated by Babbitt and written by her husband, was published with the help of Michael di Capua at Farrar, Straus & Giroux. Di Capua encouraged Babbitt to continue producing children's books even after her husband became too busy to write the stories. She began by writing *Dick Foote and the Shark* and *Phoebe's Revolt,* two picture books in which the stories are told in rhyming poetry.

Another original work, *Goody Hall,* is a Gothic mystery set in the English countryside. A large Victorian house decorated with ornate woodcarvings belongs to Midas Goody, whose disappearance spurs a young tutor to investigate. His encounters with an empty tomb, a gypsy, a rich youngster and his unusual mother, and other surprises lead to a happy ending when the Goody family is reunited. Although Babbitt's plot, like the old house with its hints of secret passageways and hidden closets, can frighten and bewilder, "in the end we feel the way the Goodys did about their house," Jean Fritz observed in the *New York Times Book Review.*

In *The Devil's Storybook,* Babbitt's title character is a trickster who is fooled as often as he tries to fool others. For example, he gives the power of speech to a goat who then annoys him with his constant complaining. In another story, the Devil sneaks into the bedroom of a pretty lady who outwits him. Babbitt's devil is middle-aged and potbellied and often fails to attain his goal of causing trouble for others. "The stories are delightful in their narrative fluency," declared Paul Heins in *Horn Book.* Others noted Babbitt's humorous illustrations: "Neatly framed pen sketches of beefy peasants and roguish inmates of Hell add folktale flavor and provide further proof of this Devil's fallibility," noted Jane Abramson in a *School Library Journal* review of *The Devil's Storybook.*

Tuck Everlasting features a family who, upon discovering a secret spring that imparts immortality, finds out that living forever without ever growing or changing is not very pleasant. This also becomes clear to a ten-year-old girl who discovers the family by accident and decides to try to help them. Tuck's explanation of the role of death in the cycle of nature "is one of the most vivid and deeply felt passages in American children's literature," *Ms.* reviewer Michele Landsberg declared. In *Children's Books and Their Creators,* Eden Edwards remarked of *Tuck Everlasting:* "The writing is economical, straightforward, and unassuming, like the Tucks, yet the result is a mysterious, subtle evocation of emotion for this family and their fate. Here, as in most of Babbitt's fiction, sophisticated ideas are presented with simplicity." Since its publication, *Tuck Everlasting* has become a classic of children's literature and has also been adapted for film. "I think, a century from now, that *Tuck* will still have something essential to say about the human condition," Tim Wynne-Jones remarked in *Horn Book.* "And how well it does so, with flawless style, in words that are exact and simple and soothing and right."

Babbitt's *The Eyes of the Amaryllis,* features a seafaring family haunted by a tragic accident. After her grandmother breaks an ankle, eleven-year-old Jenny Reades must go to the ocean shore and help the elderly woman recover. Forbidden from visiting the sea by her father, Jenny looks forward to finally seeing the strong waves of the Atlantic. During the summer, the young protagonist begins to understand her grandmother's habit of searching the beach after every high tide, looking for remnants of the missing ship her long-lost husband captained over thirty years before. Strangely, a piece of the lost ship surfaces during Jenny's stay, beginning a life-threatening series of events. Praising the use of the sea both "as an impelling atmospheric force and as an effective protagonist," *Booklist* reviewer Barbara Elleman claimed that in *The Eyes of the Amaryllis* "Babbitt wastes nary a word, deftly carving characters and events into a gripping tale." Writing in *Horn Book,* Mary M. Burns credited the book's success to "a well-wrought narrative in which a complex philosophic theme is developed through the balanced, subtle use of symbol and imagery."

Completed after a twenty-five-year break from novel writing, Babbitt's *Jack Plank Tells Tales* is an "enchanting story about telling stories," observed Paula Rohrlick in *Kliatt. Jack Plank Tells Tales* centers on a pirate who has lost his taste for plundering and is let go by his crew. Arriving in the Caribbean town of Saltwash, Jack Plank takes a room at Mrs. Delfresno's boardinghouse, where he is assisted in his job search by the landlady's young daughter, Nina. Unfortunately, Jack finds a reason to turn down every prospective employer, recalling experiences from his seafaring days that have soured him on farming, fishing, and other respectable forms of work. "These stories spin out, one each for eight days, at the end of which, the resourceful Nina comes up with the perfect job," noted *School Library Journal* critic Susan Hepler. According to Long, audiences will be charmed "by the author's sweetly ironical voice—colloquial, studded with deliciously unexpected words, and exquisitely honed."

Not limiting her efforts to novels for children, Babbitt entered the genre of picture books with *Nellie: A Cat on Her Own,* which she both wrote and illustrated. Created by an old woman from wood, string, and broom straws, Nellie is a marionette who thinks she cannot dance without the old woman's help. After the woman dies, Big Tom the cat encourages Nellie to dance on her own. At a midnight gathering of other cats, Nellie finds inspiration in the moonlight and learns to find joy in dancing just to please herself. Describing the picture book as a "small tale, charmingly rendered," *Horn Book* contributor Ann A. Flowers insisted that "this tale of independence achieved . . . is enhanced by delicate wa-

N A T A L I E   B A B B I T T

F R E D   M A R C E L L I N O

Cover of Natalie Babbitt's **Ouch!,** *which features artwork by Fred Marcellino.* (Michael Di Capua Books, 1998. Illustration copyright © 1998 by Fred Marcellino. Used by permission of HarperCollins Publishers.)

tercolors of the dubious Nellie and competent Big Tom." Praising Babbitt's theme, Ilene Cooper wrote in a *Booklist* review that in *Nellie* "Babbitt subtly yet surely weaves a strong message about self-reliance into this charming fantasy."

In *Bub; or, The Very Best Thing,* a picture book fantasy, a young king and queen argue about what is the very best thing for their young son. Pursuing an authoritative answer, the king and his advisors look into books, while the queen, accompanied by the child, his toy dragon, and a dog dressed as a court jester, traverse the castle, polling everyone they encounter. Finally, the cook's daughter suggests that they ask the child himself, and he replies "bub," which the girl interprets for adults as "love." "It's a fine book for new parents, whose point of view it reflects entirely," remarked Betsy Hearne in the *Bulletin of the Center for Children's Books.* In a *Horn Book* review, Hanna B. Zeiger declared of *Bub* that the author's "elegant writing style and the totally engaging characterizations in her illustrations combine to create a memorable picture book."

In *Elsie Times Eight,* Babbitt portrays what happens when a hard-of-hearing fairy godmother goes into action. She clones eight Elsies, and havoc ensues as the girl's parents try to cope. Eventually they locate the godmother, who puts things to rights. Among the book's enthusiasts was Joanna Rudge Long, who in *Horn Book* praised Babbitt's "lively compositions" and "cheerful narration, with its funny, unexpected turns," while a *Kirkus Reviews* contributor predicted that the book's premise is "sure to appeal to youngsters." Grace Oliff, writing in *School Library Journal,* likened Babbitt's pastel watercolors to those of classic Mother Goose tales and complimented her "inimitable prose style." In *Booklist,* Ilene Cooper complimented Babbitt for her energetic and "edgy" telling and her ink-and-watercolor illustrations, which contain some "delightful moments."

After her husband stopped writing, Babbitt gave up illustrating for others, with the exception of the poetry books of Valerie Worth. Published as *Small Poems, More Small Poems,* and so forth, the collection reached nine volumes in 2002 with *Peacock and Other Poems,* a volume published after Worth's death. "The earlier works have been widely praised, for good reason," remarked Nancy Vasilakis in a *Horn Book* review of *All the Small Poems and Fourteen More,* adding that the fourteen new poems are "every bit as worthy as their predecessors." Babbitt's illustrations for this book were praised by Hazel Rochman in *Booklist,* who wrote that the artist's "small ink drawings embody the realistic and make us imagine much more." Reviewing *Peacock and Other Poems, Horn Book* contributor Mary M. Burns described Worth and Babbitt as "kindred spirits,"

Cover of Babbitt's award-winning **Jack Plank Tells Tales,** *which describes the life of a disheartened pirate.* (Illustration copyright © 2007 by Natalie Babbitt. Reproduced by permission of Scholastic, Inc.)

and *School Library Journal* critic Nicole Lindsay applauded the illustrator's contributions, stating that her pictures "face each poem with quiet detail that draws readers into the words."

Babbitt has also written texts that have been illustrated by other artists, including her retelling *Ouch!: A Tale from Grimm,* featuring artwork by Fred Marcellino. In this story, a young man named Marco, born with a crown-shaped birthmark, grows up to marry a princess. Unfortunately, her evil father insists that Marco descend to Hell and steal three golden hairs from the devil's head, a deed the young man convinces the devil's grandmother to commit. Marco, meanwhile, returns to the kingdom to exact revenge on his evil father-in-law. "Babbitt rewrites the classic story in a casual voice infused with wry wit," wrote a reviewer in *Publishers Weekly,* concluding that "readers will likely lap up [her] intelligent retelling, mixed with a dash of sly humor."

Babbitt once commented, "I write for children because I am interested in fantasy and the possibilities for experience of all kinds before the time of compromise. I believe that children are far more perceptive and wise than American books give them credit for being." In an interview on the *Scholastic* Web site, she described her writing style as "wordy," adding: "I like words, and words are the tools that writers use, just like paint is the tool that artists use. I think words are fun, and I have a lot of fun using them." Asked if her background as an illustrator has influenced her prose, Babbitt replied, "I think my writing style and my pictures come out of the same place—they're mutually informed by what I see in my head. When you're writing a story, it's like watching a movie—you describe what you're seeing in your head. And illustrating is the same thing—you draw what you see in your head."

Looking back on her published work, Babbitt recognizes that many of her own childhood memories are woven into her stories. These childhood experiences remain meaningful into adulthood, according to Anita Moss in the *Dictionary of Literary Biography,* and it is this quality that makes her books enjoyable for readers of all ages. "While much of children's literature presents moral dilemmas that are easily resolved," Moss wrote, "many of Babbitt's best works indicate that neat solutions to the baffling paradoxes of the human situation are unattainable. Her books in fact are notable for introducing complex issues and for exploring these issues from multiple points of view. Yet for all the seriousness of the themes she explores, Babbitt's treatment is apt to be humorous and deftly handled."

Biographical and Critical Sources

BOOKS

Babbitt, Natalie, essay in *Something about the Author Autobiography Series,* Volume 5, Gale (Detroit, MI), 1988.

In Babbitt's detailed watercolors, she draws readers back to medieval times in **Bub; or, The Very Best Thing.** (Michael di Capua Books, 1994. Illustration © 1994 by Natalie Babbitt. Used by permission of HarperCollins Publishers.)

Children's Books and Their Creators, edited by Anita Silvey, Houghton Mifflin (Boston, MA), 1995.

Children's Literature Review, Volume 53, Gale (Detroit, MI), 1999.

Dictionary of Literary Biography, Volume 52: American Writers for Children since 1960: Poets, Writers, Illustrators, and Non-Fiction Authors, Gale (Detroit, MI), 1987.

St James Guide to Children's Writers, 5th edition, St. James Press (Detroit, MI), 1999.

PERIODICALS

Booklist, November 15, 1977, Barbara Elleman, review of *The Eyes of the Amaryllis,* p. 546; October 15, 1989, Ilene Cooper, review of *Nellie: A Cat on Her Own,* pp. 447-448; January 15, 1995, Hazel Rochman, review of *All the Small Poems and Fourteen More,* p. 933; November 15, 1998, review of *Ouch!: A Tale from Grimm,* p. 582; March 15, 1999, review of *Ouch!,* p. 1302; November 15, 2001, Ilene Cooper, review of *Elsie Times Eight,* pp. 579-580; August, 2002, Carolyn Phelan, review of *Peacock and Other Poems,* p. 1963; April 1, 2007, Carolyn Phelan review of *Jack Plank Tells Tales,* p. 48.

Bulletin of the Center for Children's Books, June, 1994, Betsy Hearne, review of *Bub; or, The Very Best Thing,* pp. 312-313; November 15, 1998, Stephanie Zvirin, review of *Ouch!,* p. 582; September 15, 1999, Elaine

Hanson, review of *Bub,* p. 275; December, 2001, review of *Elsie Times Eight,* p. 129.

Horn Book, October, 1974, Paul Heins, review of *The Devil's Storybook,* p. 134; February, 1978, Mary M. Burns, review of *The Eyes of the Amaryllis,* pp. 42-43; May, 1988, Selma G. Lanes, "A Second Look: The Devil's Storybook," pp. 329-331; September, 1988, Natalie Babbitt, "Metamorphosis," pp. 582-589; March, 1989, Anita Silvey, "A Rare Entity," pp. 133-134; January-February 1990, Ann A. Flowers, review of *Nellie,* p. 48; May-June, 1994, Hanna B. Zeiger, review of *Bub,* p. 305; March-April, 1995, Nancy Vasilakis, review of *All the Small Poems and Fourteen More,* p. 212; January, 1999, review of *Ouch!,* p. 73; March, 2000, Betsy Hearne, "Circling Tuck: An Interview with Natalie Babbitt," p. 153; July, 2000, review of *Tuck Everlasting,* p. 425; November, 2000, Tim Wynne-Jones, review of *Tuck Everlasting,* p. 720; January-February, 2002, Joanna Rudge Long, review of *Elsie Times Eight,* p. 66; July-August, 2002, Mary M. Burns, review of *Peacock and Other Poems,* p. 481; July-August, 2007, Joanna Rudge Long, review of *Jack Plank Tells Tales,* p. 389.

Kirkus Reviews, February 1, 1994, review of *Bub,* p. 137; November 1, 1998, review of *Ouch!,* p. 1596; August 15, 2001, review of *Elsie Times Eight,* p. 1206; March 1, 2002, review of *Peacock and Other Poems,* p. 349; April 15, 2007, review of *Jack Plank Tells Tales.*

Kliatt, May, 2007, Paula Rohrlick, review of *Jack Plank Tells Tales,* p. 6.

Library Journal, October, 1974, Jane Abramson, review of *The Devil's Storybook,* p. 102; November 1, 2001, review of *Tuck Everlasting,* p. 160.

Ms., May 11, 1990, Michele Landsberg, review of *Tuck Everlasting,* p. 74.

New York Times Book Review, November 16, 1975, p. 32; November 1, 1987, Laurel Graeber, review of *The Devil's Other Story Book,* p. 36; June 19, 1994, review of *Bub,* p. 28; March 14, 1999, review of *Ouch!,* p. 31; January 20, 2002, review of *Elsie Times Eight,* p. 15.

Publishers Weekly, April 19, 1993, Steve Sherman, "Babbitt Has Strong Words for 'Star System,'" p. 24; February 21, 1994, Amy Meeker, "Natalie Babbitt: The Gifted Writer of Children's Books Has Returned to Her First Love—Illustrating Them," pp. 229-230; November 2, 1998, review of *Ouch!,* p. 80; October 1, 2001, review of *Elsie Times Eight,* p. 60; February 11, 2002, review of *Peacock and Other Poems,* p. 184; April 9, 2007, review of *Jack Plank Tells Tales,* p. 54; April 16, 2007, Sue Corbett, "Natalie Everlasting: Newbery Honor Author Natalie Babbitt Writes Her First Novel in 25 Years," p. 19.

School Library Journal, October, 1974, Jane Abramson, review of *The Devil's Storybook,* p. 102; May, 2000, "A Timeless Classic," p. 17; November, 2001, Grace Oliff, review of *Elsie Times Eight,* p. 110; May, 2002, Nicole Lindsay, review of *Peacock and Other Poems,* p. 145; May, 2007, Susan Hepler, review of *Jack Plank Tells Tales,* p. 84.

Washington Post Book World, April 3, 1994, Michael Dirda, review of *Bub,* p. 10; November 1, 1998, review of *Ouch!*, p. 8; December 9, 2001, review of *Elsie Times Eight*, p. 8.

ONLINE

Scholastic Web site, http://www2.scholastic.com/ (September 20, 2008), interview with Babbitt.

OTHER

"A Visit with Natalie Babbitt," *Tuck Everlasting*, DVD special feature, Walt Disney Home Video, 2003.*

* * *

BAILEY, Peter 1946-

Personal

Born 1946, in India; father a British railroad worker, mother a museum attendant; married; wife's name Sian (an illustrator). *Education:* Attended Brighton School of Art (now University of Brighton).

Addresses

Home—Wirral Peninsula, Merseyside, England.

Career

Freelance illustrator. Liverpool Art School (now Liverpool John Moores University), Liverpool, England, instructor in illustration until 1997. *Exhibitions:* Work exhibited in Cardiff, Wales, 1983.

Writings

SELF-ILLUSTRATED

A Scary Story, Scholastic Children's Books (London, England), 1993.

ILLUSTRATOR

Sylvia Haymon, *Bonnie Prince Charlie*, Macdonald (London, England), 1969.

Ronald Blythe, *Akenfield: Portrait of an English Village*, Allen Lane (London, England), 1969.

Joan Aiken, *A Harp of Fishbones and Other Stories*, Jonathan Cape (London, England), 1972.

Carolyn Sloan, *Victoria and the Crowded Pocket*, Longman Young Books (London, England), 1973.

Margaret Mahy, *Watch Me!*, Dent (London, England), 1975.

Ernest Dudley, *The Badgers of Blind Dog Farm*, Hart-Davis Educational (St Albans, England), 1978.

Jane Cox, *Hit the Word!*, Nelson (Sunbury-on-Thames, England), 1979.

Forts and Castles, Silver Burdett (Morristown, NJ), 1980.

Philip Pullman, *Count Karlstein*, Chatto & Windus (London, England), 1982.

Joan Aiken, *Fog Hounds; Wind Cat; Sea Mice*, Macmillan Children's (London, England), 1984.

Jonathan Swift, *Gulliver's Travels*, Armada (London, England), 1987.

Alexander McCall Smith, *Akimbo and the Elephants*, Mammoth (London, England), 1990.

Alexander McCall Smith, *Akimbo and the Lions*, Methuen (London, England), 1992.

Kit Wright, *Tigerella*, Scholastic (New York, NY), 1993.

Pat Thomson, compiler, *A Stocking Full of Christmas Stories*, Corgi (London, England), 1993.

Chris Powling, compiler, *Faces in the Dark: A Book of Scary Stories*, Kingfisher Books (New York, NY), 1994, published as *The Kingfisher Book of Scary Stories*, Kingfisher (London, England), 1994.

Kit Wright, *Dolphinella*, Andre Deutsch Children's Books (London, England), 1995.

Philip Pullman, *The Firework-maker's Daughter*, Doubleday (London, England), 1995.

(With Chris Fisher) Jean Ure, *Skinny Melon and Me*, Collins (London, England), 1996.

Gordon Snell, *Lottie's Letter*, Orion Children's (London, England), 1996.

John Mole, *Hot Air: Poems*, Hodder Children's (London, England), 1996.

Susan Dickinson, compiler, *The Sea-Baby, and Other Magical Stories to Read Aloud*, Collins (London, England), 1996.

Philip Pullman, *Clockwork; or, All Wound Up*, Doubleday (London, England), 1996.

Robert Hull, *Stargazer*, Hodder Children's (London, England), 1997.

Gregory Evans, *Owl in the House*, Mammoth (London, England), 1997.

Joan Aiken, *The Jewel Seed*, Hodder Children's (London, England), 1997.

Philip Pullman, *Mossycoat*, Scholastic (London, England), 1998.

Tony Mitton, *Plum*, Scholastic (London, England), 1998.

Dick King-Smith, *The Crowstarver*, Doubleday (London, England), 1998.

Philip Pullman, *I Was a Rat: or, The Scarlet Slippers*, Doubleday (London, England), 1999.

Carol-Ann Duffy and others, *Five Finger-Piglets: Poems*, Macmillan Children's (London, England), 1999.

Pat Posner, *Animal Stories That Really Happened*, Hippo (London, England), 1999.

Linda Newbery, *Star's Turn*, Corgi Pups (London, England), 1999.

Geraldine McCaughrean, *Too Big!*, Corgi Pups (London, England), 1999.

Rose Impey, reteller, *Bad Boys and Naughty Girls*, Orchard Books (London, England), 1999.

Rose Impey, reteller, *Ugly Dogs and Slimy Frogs*, Orchard Books (London, England), 1999.

Rose Impey, reteller, *Silly Sons and Dozy Daughters*, Orchard Books (London, England), 1999.

Rose Impey, reteller, *Cinderella; and, The Sleeping Beauty,* Orchard Books (London, England), 2000.

Dick King-Smith, *Spider Sparrow,* Crown Publishers (New York, NY), 2000.

Tony Mitton, *The Red and White Spotted Handkerchief,* Scholastic (London, England), 2000.

Adélè Geras, *Peas in a Pod,* Corgi Pups (London, England), 2000.

(With Chris Fisher) Jean Ure, *Skinny Melon and Me,* Henry Holt (New York, NY), 2000.

Pat Thomson, compiler, *A Cauldron of Magical Stories,* Corgi (London, England), 2000.

Andrew Matthews, reteller, *Thumbelina; and, The Tin Soldier,* Orchard Books (London, England), 2000.

Andrew Matthews, reteller, *The Emperor's New Clothes; and, The Tinder Box,* Orchard Books (London, England), 2000.

Andrew Matthews, reteller, *Hans Christian Andersen's The Little Mermaid; and, The Princess and the Pea,* Orchard Books (London, England), 2000.

Andrew Matthews, reteller, *The Little Matchgirl; and, The Wild Swans,* Orchard Books (London, England), 2000.

Patricia Finney, *I, Jack,* Corgi Yearling (London, England), 2000, HarperCollins (New York, NY), 2004.

Julie A. Stokes, *The Secret C: Straight Talking about Cancer,* foreword by HRH the Prince of Wales, Winston's Wish/Macmillan Cancer Relief (London, England), 2000.

Pat Thomson, compiler, *A Dungeon Full of Monster Stories,* Corgi (London, England), 2001.

Claire Llewellyn, *What's Creepy and Crawly?,* Frances Lincoln (London, England), 2001.

Tony Mitton, *Pip,* Scholastic (London, England), 2001.

Adrian Mitchell, *Zoo of Dreams: Poems by Adrian Mitchell and Daisy,* Orchard Books (London, England), 2001.

Paul May, *Cat Patrol,* Corgi Pups (London, England), 2001.

Rose Impey, reteller, *Hansel and Gretel; and, The Princess and the Pea,* Orchard Books (London, England), 2001.

Rose Impey, reteller, *Jack and the Beanstalk; and The Three Wishes,* Orchard Books (London, England), 2001.

Rose Impey, reteller, *Rapunzel; and, Rumpelstiltskin,* Orchard Books (London, England), 2001.

Claire Funge, *The War Monkey,* Oxford University Press (Oxford, England), 2001.

Francis Bryan, *Jim Hawkins and the Curse of Treasure Island,* Orion (London, England), 2001.

Jill Bennett, *Peace Begins with Me: A Collection of Poems,* Oxford University Press (Oxford, England), 2001.

Pie Corbett, *Write Your Own—Thrillers,* Belitha (London, England), 2001.

Pie Corbett, *Write Your Own—Chillers,* Belitha (London, England), 2001.

Margaret Mahy, *Wonderful Me!,* Dolphin (London, England), 2002.

Richard Kidd, *The Tiger Bone Thief,* Corgi Yearling (London, England), 2002.

Patricia Finney, *Jack and Police Dog Rebel,* Corgi Yearling (London, England), 2002, published as *Jack and Rebel, the Police Dog,* HarperCollins (New York, NY), 2007.

John Foster, compiler, *Moondust and Mystery: Magic Poems,* Oxford University Press (Oxford, England), 2002.

Adèlé Geras, *The Gingerbread House,* Barrington Stoke (Edinburgh, Scotland), 2002.

Allan Ahlberg, *The Improbable Cat,* Puffin (London, England), 2002, Delacorte Press (New York, NY), 2004.

Fiona Waters, compiler, *The Kingfisher Treasury of Magical Stories,* Kingfisher (Boston, MA), 2003.

Margaret Mayo, reteller, *The Giant Sea Serpent; and, The Unicorn,* Orchard Books (London, England), 2003.

Margaret Mayo, reteller, *The Fiery Phoenix; and, The Lemon Princess,* Orchard Books (London, England), 2003.

Margaret Mayo, reteller, *The Magical Mermaid; and, Kate Crackernuts,* Orchard Books (London, England), 2003.

Margaret Mayo, reteller, *Pegasus the Proud Prince; and, The Flying Carpet,* Orchard Books (London, England), 2003.

Margaret Mayo, reteller, *The Daring Dragon; and, The Kingdom under the Sea,* Orchard Books (London, England), 2003.

Margaret Mayo, reteller, *Unanana and the Enormous Elephant; and, The Feathered Snake,* Orchard Books (London, England), 2003.

Margaret Mayo, reteller, *The Incredible Thunderbird; and, Baba Yaga Bony-Legs,* Orchard Books (London, England), 2003.

Margaret Mayo, reteller, *The Man-eating Minotaur; and, The Magic Fruit,* Orchard Books (London, England), 2003.

Brian Patten, *Ben's Magic Telescope,* Puffin (London, England), 2003.

Margaret Mahy, *Wait for Me!,* Orion Children's Books (London, England), 2003.

Richard Kidd, *The Last Leg,* Corgi Yearling (London, England), 2003.

Tony Mitton, *The Tale of Tales,* David Fickling Books (Oxford, England), 2003, David Fickling Books (New York, NY), 2004.

Philip Pullman, *The Scarecrow and His Servant,* Doubleday (London, England), 2004.

(With others) *Once upon a Poem: Favourite Poems That Tell Stories,* foreword by Kevin Crossley-Holland, Chicken House (Frome, England), 2004.

John Betjeman, *John Betjeman: Selected Poems,* edited by Alan Powers, Folio Society (London, England), 2004.

Pie Corbett, *Write Your Own—Fantasy,* Chrysalis Children's Books (London, England), 2004.

John Mole, *Back by Midnight,* Puffin (London, England), 2004.

Heather Dyer, *The Girl with the Broken Wing,* Scholastic (New York, NY), 2005.

Sally Gardner, *Lucy Willow,* Orion's Children's Books (London, England), 2006.

Jamila Gavin, *Grandpa Chatterji,* Egmont (London, England), 2006.

Jamila Gavin, *Grandpa Chatterji's Third Eye,* Egmont (London, England), 2006.

Alexander McCall Smith, *Akimbo and the Snakes,* Bloomsbury Children's (London, England), 2006.

Michael Morpurgo, *Singing for Mrs. Pettigrew: A Story-Maker's Journey,* Walker (London, England), 2006.

Paul Dowswell, *Battle Fleet,* Bloomsbury Children's Books (New York, NY), 2008.

Paul Kieve, *Hocus Pocus: A Tale of Magnificent Magicians and Their Amazing Feats,* Scholastic Press (New York, NY), 2008.

Sidelights

For more than three decades, Peter Bailey has been illustrating stories by some of the United Kingdom's most popular and well-respected authors. "Today, however, fewer and fewer children's novels have illustrations," Joanna Carey noted regretfully in the London *Guardian,* "and the very specific art of black and white line drawing seems to be in decline. But one artist who has never given up on it is Peter Bailey." Although Bailey occasionally works in color, most of his illustrations are simple yet effective pen-and-ink renderings that use line and shadow to envision and extend the story.

Bailey was born in India, where his father worked for a British railway company, but at age four his family returned to England and established a new home in London. His father took a job at the Victoria & Albert Museum, the world's largest museum devoted to decorative arts and design. Now young Bailey had special access to the collections, as well as to the museum's storage rooms and cellars, which held a treasure trove of art that included ceramics, glass, textiles, costumes, jewelry, furniture, sculpture, and art prints. He was particularly intrigued by the art students who came to the museum to practice drawing; soon he was sketching pictures in his own sketchbooks.

After studying illustration at the Brighton School of Art, Bailey worked as a freelance illustrator for five years before taking a job as an instructor in illustration at the Liverpool School of Art. While working there, he also began illustrating children's books on occasion, including his original self-illustrated picture book *A Scary Story.* In 1997 he left teaching to focus on his own work, and he has created artwork for dozens of texts in the years since.

Some of Bailey's first projects were illustrating texts by such respected children's authors as Joan Aiken and Margaret Mahy. In 1982, he illustrated *Count Karlstein,* the first story for children written by Philip Pullman, the award-winning author best known for the "His Dark Materials" fantasy trilogy. Further collaborations with Pullman include five other original fairy tales. For the British edition of *Clockwork; or, All Wound Up,* he employs crosshatching and other texturing techniques to underscore the sinister plot of Pullman's tale. "The tussle between good and evil certainly inspired me to see just how far I could push the extremes of dark and light," Bailey explained to Carey in the *Guardian.* As a result, the artist's "ink drawings have a finely etched quality that cunningly reflects the intricacy of Pullman's narrative machinery," Carey remarked.

In Pullman's *The Scarecrow and His Servant,* Bailey's illustrations help portray the adventures of a scarecrow

Peter Bailey's stylized artwork brings to life Kit Wright's magical story in Tigerella. (Illustration copyright © 1993 by Peter Bailey. All rights reserved. Reproduced by permission of Scholastic, Ltd.)

brought to life by a bolt of lightning. The book's line drawings are a charming counterpart to the tale," Deirdre F. Baker noted in *Horn Book,* while *School Library Journal* contributor Sharon Grover observed that Bailey's illustrations "provide just the right feeling of long ago that every good fairy tale deserves." The illustrator also creates an appropriately spooky atmosphere in his work for Allan Ahlberg's *The Improbable Cat,* the story of a sinister feline who takes over a family. A *Publishers Weekly* critic observed that Bailey's "cross-hatch pen-and-inks nicely dramatize the enigmatic developments" of Ahlberg's story.

Bailey has also illustrated two books by Heather Dyer that involve fantastic creatures. *The Fish in Room 11* involves a boy who discovers a mermaid living near the seaside hotel where he works. Here the artist's "spidery ink sketches of the pointy-nosed cast, about three per chapter, are as captivating as the story," Karin Snelson remarked in *Booklist.* A *Publishers Weekly* critic observed that "Bailey's pen-and-inks make the most of the comic moments." In Dyer's *The Girl with the Broken Wing,* an angel named Hilary befriends two children. Here Bailey "illustrates the animated goings-on in cheery pen-and-inks that effectively depict Hilary straddling both land and skies," a writer for *Publishers Weekly* wrote. Gillian Engberg concluded in *Booklist* that "Bailey's ink illustrations hit just the right notes of humor and old-fashioned whimsy."

Bailey shows a range of techniques in his illustrations for Tony Mitton's *The Tale of Tales.* When Monkey sets off to Volcano Valley to hear the Tale of Tales, he meets several animals along his journey who share stories of their own. Bailey used silhouettes to illustrate the story of the journey, while line drawings depict the animals' tales-within-the-tale. "Bailey's excellent pen-and-ink illustrations, silhouettes, and motifs decorate each page of this elegantly designed collection," Susan Hepler remarked in *School Library Journal.* "Bailey's striking illustrations will invite repeated viewings," a *Publishers Weekly* critic noted, resulting in "a book that looks and reads much like a treasure from grandmother's attic."

Discussing his work as an illustrator with Carey, Bailey noted: "I like to leave something to the imagination, and to make use of shadow and tonality rather than specific, over-representational images." Line drawing remains his favorite technique and a fine-point ink pen his tool of choice. "I like the simplicity of it, and the economy," he noted. "I like the feeling that I can sit here and create a little world with just that one fine point."

Biographical and Critical Sources

PERIODICALS

Booklist, April 15, 2004, Hazel Rochman, review of *The Tale of Tales,* p. 1443; June 1, 2004, Karin Snelson, review of *The Fish in Room 11,* p. 1726; Nov 1, 2005, Gillian Engberg, review of *The Girl with the Broken Wing,* p. 52.

Guardian (London, England), September 10, 2005, Joanna Carey, "Hatching Plots."

Horn Book, September-October, 2005, Deirdre F. Baker, review of *The Scarecrow and His Servant,* pp. 586-587.

Publishers Weekly, March 22, 2004, review of *The Tale of Tales,* pp. 85-86; May 3, 2004, review of *The Fish in Room 11,* p. 192; August 9, 2004, review of *The Improbable Cat,* p. 251; August 1, 2005, review of *The Scarecrow and His Servant,* p. 65; October 24, 2005, review of *The Girl with the Broken Wing,* p. 58.

School Library Journal, April, 2004, Susan Hepler, review of *The Tale of Tales,* p. 140; August, 2004, Susan Hepler, review of *The Improbable Cat,* p. 115; September, 2005, Sharon Grover, review of *The Scarecrow and His Servant,* p. 210.*

*   *   *

BEAN, Jonathan 1979-

Personal

Born March 23, 1979; son of John and Pauline Bean. *Education:* Messiah College (PA), B.A., 2001; School of Visual Arts (New York, NY), M.F.A., 2005. *Hobbies and other interests:* Hiking, bird watching, landscape drawing.

Addresses

Home—New York, NY.

Career

Author and illustrator. Dimensions, Reading, PA, staff artist; illustrator for *New York Times* and *Cricket* magazine. Messiah College, Grantham, PA, adjunct instructor in art, 2008.

Awards, Honors

Boston Globe/Horn Book Award for best picture book, 2008, and Charlotte Zolotow Award Honor Book designation, Cooperative Children's Book Center, both 2008, both for *At Night;* Ezra Jack Keats New Illustrator Award, New York Public Library/Ezra Jack Keats Foundation, 2008, for *The Apple Pie That Papa Baked* by Lauren Thompson.

Writings

SELF-ILLUSTRATED

At Night, Farrar, Straus & Giroux (New York, NY), 2007.

Our House, Farrar, Straus & Giroux (New York, NY), 2009.

ILLUSTRATOR

Lynne Jonell, *Emmy and the Incredible Shrinking Rat,* Henry Holt (New York, NY), 2007.

Wendy Orr, *Mokie and Bik,* Henry Holt (New York, NY), 2007.

Lauren Thompson, *The Apple Pie That Papa Baked,* Simon & Schuster (New York, NY), 2007.

Lynne Jonell, *Emmy and the Home for Troubled Girls,* Henry Holt (New York, NY), 2008.

Wendy Orr, *Mokie and Bik Go to Sea,* Henry Holt (New York, NY), 2008.

Sidelights

Jonathan Bean grew up in Pennsylvania, the second of four children who were all homeschooled by their parents. He had an interest in art and illustrated books from a young age. "I grew up with my mom reading me Virginia Lee Burton books and later I discovered Wanda Gag," he told Shannon Maughan in *Publishers Weekly,* referring to the author-illustrators of the childhood classics *Mike Mulligan and His Steam Shovel* and *Millions of Cats* respectively. During high school, Bean took weekly drawing classes with Myron Barnstone of Barnstone Studios, where he studied basic techniques, practiced them over and over, and explored how great artists incorporated them into their works. As a senior, he wrote an essay exploring form in artworks from ancient Greece to modern times.

After graduating with a degree in fine arts illustration from Pennsylvania Messiah College, Bean worked as staff artist for a company that created craft and paint-by-number patterns. During the day, he helped transform artworks—sometimes his own—into cross-stitch patterns, while at night he worked on his own illustrations. Attending graduate school in New York City, Bean focused on children's-book illustration and developed a portfolio to show to publishers. One of his graduate projects developed into his first picture book, and by the time he received his master's degree in 2005, Bean was getting steady work as an illustrator for magazines, including *Cricket.*

In 2007, Bean's illustrations appeared in four separate children's books, including one he had also authored. His work included drawings for a flip-book incorporated in writer Lynne Jonell's novel *Emmy and the Incredible Shrinking Rat,* as well as crosshatch-style illustrations for Wendy Orr's chapter book *Mokie and Bik. Booklist* reviewer Carolyn Phelan called Bean's work in the latter "often graceful and always appealing," and *School Library Journal* contributor Carole Phillips likewise observed that Bean's drawings for *Mokie and Bik* "capture the exuberant spirit of the [characters] and splendidly match their energetic adventures."

Bean also produced artwork for Lauren Thompson's picture book *The Apple Pie That Papa Baked,* a clever reworking of "The House That Jack Built." Bean's illustrations, in tones of gold, red, cream, and black, impressed many critics. "The art tells its own story," Jennifer Brabander observed in *Horn Book,* adding that Bean's work has "an old-fashioned sensibility" reminiscent of Gag and Burton. In *Booklist* Ilene Cooper similarly noted that "Bean uses the best of old and new in artwork that harkens back to the works of Lois Lenski, Robert McClosky, and especially Wanda Gag." "This tribute to the artists of an earlier age should take its place among bedtime favorites," a *Publishers Weekly* writer concluded, and a *Kirkus Reviews* critic dubbed Bean "someone to watch." The New York Public Library and the Ezra Jack Keats Foundation agreed, awarding Bean the Ezra Jack Keats New Illustrator Award for 2008 for *The Apple Pie That Papa Baked.*

Bean's artistic talent also enhanced his first original picture book, *At Night,* an award-winning bedtime story about a girl who makes a comfortable bed on a rooftop during a hot summer night in the city. "The plot is so quiet it would escape a lesser writer," a *Publishers Weekly* writer observed, but Bean "creates almost magical rhythms in this pitch-perfect story." *Booklist* reviewer Gillian Engberg similarly observed that Bean's "spare sentences have a lulling rhythm," while his illustrations "add a quiet drama." The artist's watercolor images "perfectly depict the shadows, darkness, and light of the slumbering city," Ieva Bates wrote in *School Library Journal.* A *Kirkus Reviews* writer dubbed Bean's "sweet, gentle story . . . perfectly constructed and balanced." *At Night* has "a modest text that quietly lets the art take center stage," Jennifer M. Brabander remarked in *Horn Book,* the critic concluding that Bean's debut is "perfect reading for a warm night."

To other aspiring artists, Bean offered the following advice: "Once you think you have the skill and the talent, don't give up," as he told Howard Richman of *Pennsylvania Homeschoolers.* "Make the most of every opportunity, of every professor you have, and of every connection. I sent out work for four or five years before I really found work that paid. At first I was just piecing together a living, rather than making a living. I envied some of my fellow students who were employed by others. But if you can stick at it long enough, you can really have something solid. Don't give up. Continue to work away at it."

Biographical and Critical Sources

PERIODICALS

Booklist, June 1, 2007, Carolyn Phelan, review of *Mokie and Bik,* p. 82; July 1, 2007, Gillian Engberg, review of *At Night,* p. 60; August, 2007, Ilene Cooper, review of *The Apple Pie That Papa Baked,* p. 68.

Bulletin of the Center for Children's Books, October, 2007, Deborah Stevenson, review of *At Night,* pp. 73-74.

Horn Book, September-October, 2007, Jennifer M. Brabander, review of *At Night,* p. 556; January-February, 2008, Jennifer M. Brabander, review of *The Apple Pie That Papa Baked,* p. 80.

Kirkus Reviews, July 15, 2007, review of *At Night.*

Publishers Weekly, August 27, 2007, reviews of *At Night* and *The Apple Pie That Papa Baked,* p. 88; December 24, 2007, Shannon Maughan, "Flying Starts," p. 16.

School Library Journal, July, 2007, Carole Phillips, review of *Mokie and Bik,* p. 82; September, 2007, Ieva Bates, review of *At Night,* p. 157, and Catherine Callegari, review of *The Apple Pie That Papa Baked,* p. 177.

ONLINE

Jonathan Bean Home Page, http://www.jonathanbean.com (October 14, 2007).

Pennsylvania Homeschoolers Web site, http://www.pahomeschoolers.com/ (summer, 2005), Howard Richman, "Jonathan Bean Succeeding as an Illustrator."*

*   *   *

BEDDOR, Frank

Personal

Born in Minneapolis, MN; children: Luc.

Addresses

Office—Automatic Pictures, 5225 Wilshire Blvd., Ste. 525, Los Angeles, CA 90036.

Career

Film producer, actor, executive, and writer. Chief executive officer, Automatic Pictures, Los Angeles, CA. Freestyle skiing champion; stuntman in motion pictures, including *Hot Dog: The Movie,* 1984, and *Better Off Dead,* 1985. Producer of motion pictures, including *There's Something about Mary,* 1998, and *Wicked,* 1998; actor in television and motion pictures, including *Remote Control,* 1987, *Made in USA,* 1987, *Amazon Women on the Moon,* 1987, *Nightbreaker,* 1989, and "Smoke Gets in Your Thighs," *L.A. Law,* 1990.

Writings

The Looking Glass Wars (novel), Dial Books (New York, NY), 2006.

Sidelights

A glimpse of an incomplete deck of handmade, illuminated playing cards in the British Museum inspired film producer Frank Beddor to write the novel *The Looking Glass Wars,* the first in a planned trilogy of books that revisits the world of *Alice in Wonderland.* While Lewis Carroll's original masterpiece, produced in Victorian England, examined the dream-fantasies of a preadolescent girl, Beddor approaches the story in a very different way. For him, Alice Liddell is actually Alyss Hart, the rightful queen of Wonderland. Her throne has been usurped by her aunt Redd, who relies on terror, assassination, and intimidation to maintain her grip on power. Alyss escapes from her aunt's clutches via a looking glass and arrives in nineteenth-century London, where she is adopted by the Liddell family. She winds up telling her story to Charles Dodgson, who wrote the narrative down using the pseudonym Lewis Carroll, presenting it as a dream-tale. Over time, Alyss despairs of ever returning to Wonderland and suppresses her memories of the realm. Finally she is tracked down by Hatter Madigan, her former bodyguard, who has also escaped Wonderland and has located her through Carroll's time-honored classic. "It is now up to Alyss," explained a *Kirkus Reviews* contributor, "to rally her troops, drive out the usurper and claim her throne."

Beddor's novel aroused fierce controversy among critics, mostly because of the way it treats Carroll's original story. "Throughout *The Looking Glass Wars* there are twisted mirror images of Dodgson's story," Caroline Horn stated in the *Bookseller,* "including Generals Doppel and Ganger, a white albino professor with big ears, and Hatter Madigan, who does a special line in deadly hats." "Beddor makes ample use of Carroll-esque humor and wit," wrote a *Publishers Weekly* reviewer, "so much so that the thought of an entire trilogy is somewhat daunting." Some reviewers had grave reservations about Beddor's novel, among them Barbara Scotto, who wrote in *School Library Journal* that the author "has usurped the characters and setting and changed them for his own purposes, keeping only the story's flame." Others, however, found it exciting and intriguing. "An entertaining cross between [Gregory] Maguire's *Wicked* and Steven Spielberg' Peter Pan movie, *Hook, The Looking Glass Wars* launches a promised trilogy about Alyss's new adventures," Brian Farrey wrote on *TeenReads.com.* "Beddor grabs the imagination and refuses to let go until the reader is pulled as deeply into the adventure as Alyss herself."

Biographical and Critical Sources

PERIODICALS

Booklist, September 1, 2006, Krista Hutley, review of *The Looking Glass Wars,* p. 109.

Bookseller, May 21, 2004, Caroline Horn, "Through a Glass Darkly: Frank Beddor's Debut Novel Offers a Twisted Take on the Story of Alice in Wonderland," p. 33.

Kirkus Reviews, August 15, 2006, review of *The Looking Glass Wars,* p. 835.

Kliatt, September, 2006, Donna Scanlon, review of *The Looking Glass Wars,* p. 6.

Publishers Weekly, August 14, 2006, review of *The Looking Glass Wars,* p. 206.

School Library Journal, October, 2006, Barbara Scotto, review of *The Looking Glass Wars,* p. 148; February, 2007, Francisca Goldsmith, review of *The Looking Glass Wars,* p. 63.

ONLINE

Comic World News, http://www.comicworldnews.com/ (April 1, 2007), Caleb Gerard, "The Frank Beddor/Looking Glass Wars Interview."

TeenReads.com, http://www.teenreads.com/ (April 1, 2007), Brian Farrey, review of *The Looking Glass Wars.**

* * *

BLACKER, Terence 1948-

Personal

Born February 5, 1948, in Suffolk, England; married (divorced); children: Xan, Alice. *Education:* Attended Cambridge University. *Hobbies and other interests:* Reading, playing guitar with his group Something Happened, wildlife.

Addresses

Home—Norfolk, England. *E-mail*—terblacker@aol.com.

Career

Novelist and author of children's books.

Awards, Honors

Teenage Book of the Year award, for *Homebird;* writing fellowship, University of East Anglia, 1994; Angus Award, 2004, for *Boy2Girl.*

Writings

FOR CHILDREN

If I Could Work, illustrated by Chris Winn, Lippincott (Philadelphia, PA), 1988.

Henry and the Frights, illustrated by Adriano Gon, Piccadilly (London, England), 1989.

Herbie Hamster, Where Are You?, illustrated by Pippa Uwin, Random (New York, NY), 1990, published as *Houdini, the Disappearing Hamster,* Andersen (London, England), 1990.

Homebird (novel), Macmillan (London, England), 1991, Bradbury, 1993.

The Surprising Adventures of Baron Münchausen, illustrated by William Rushton, Knight, 1991.

The Great Denture Adventure, illustrated by John Eastwood, Pan (London, England), 1992.

Nice Neighbours/Nasty Neighbours, illustrated by Frank Rodgers, Macmillan (London, England), 1992.

The Transfer (novel), Macmillan (London, England), 1998.

The Angel Factory (young-adult novel), Macmillan (London, England), 2001, Simon & Schuster (New York, NY), 2002.

You Have Ghost Mail, illustrated by Adam Stower, Macmillan (London, England), 2002.

Boy2Girl, Farrar, Straus (New York, NY), 2004.

Parentswap, Farrar, Straus (New York, NY), 2005.

Contributor of short fiction to anthologies, including *Silent Night: Ten Tales of the Supernatural,* Scholastic (London, England), 2002, and *My Dad's a Punk: Twelve Stories about Boys and Their Fathers,* edited by Tony Bradman, Kingfisher (Boston, MA), 2006.

Author's works have been translated into Welsh.

"HOTSHOTS" SERIES; FOR CHILDREN

Pride and Penalties, Pan Macmillan (London, England), 1997.

Shooting Star, Pan Macmillan (London, England), 1997.

On the Wing, Pan Macmillan (London, England), 1997.

Dream Team, Pan Macmillan (London, England), 1997.

"MS WIZ" SERIES; FOR CHILDREN

Ms Wiz Spells Trouble, illustrated by Toni Goffe, Piccadilly (London, England), 1988, Marshall Cavendish (Tarrytown, NY), 2008.

In Stitches with Ms Wiz, Piccadilly (London, England), 1989, Marshall Cavendish (Tarrytown, NY), 2008.

You're Nicked Ms Wiz, illustrated by Toni Goffe, Piccadilly (London, England), 1989.

In Control, Ms Wiz?, illustrated by Kate Simpson, Piccadilly (London, England), 1990.

Ms Wiz Goes Live, illustrated by Toni Goffe, Piccadilly (London, England), 1990.

Ms Wiz Banned!, illustrated by Kate Simpson, Piccadilly (London, England), 1990.

Time Flies for Ms Wiz (also see below), illustrated by Kate Simpson, 1992.

Power-crazy Ms Wiz (also see below), illustrated by Tony Ross, Piccadilly (London, England), 1992.

Ms Wiz Loves Dracula (also see below), illustrated by Kate Simpson, Piccadilly (London, England), 1993.

You're Kidding, Ms Wiz, illustrated by Tony Ross, Macmillan (London, England), 1996.

Ms Wiz Supermodel, illustrated by Tony Ross, Macmillan (London, England), 1997.

Ms Wiz Smells a Rat, illustrated by Tony Ross, Piccadilly (London, England), 1998.

Ms Wiz and the Sister of Doom, illustrated by Tony Ross, Piccadilly (London, England), 1999.

Ms Wiz Goes to Hollywood, illustrated by Tony Ross, Piccadilly (London, England), 2000.

Ms Wiz, Millionaire, illustrated by Tony Ross, Piccadilly (London, England), 2001.

The Secret Life of Ms Wiz, illustrated by Tony Ross, Piccadilly (London, England), 2002.

The Amazing Adventures of Ms Wiz (includes *Time Flies for Ms Wiz, Power-crazy Ms Wiz,* and *Ms Wiz Loves Dracula*), illustrated by Tony Ross, Macmillan (London, England), 2003.

Totally Spaced, Ms Wiz (includes *Ms Wiz and the Dog from Outer Space* and *Ms Wiz Banned!*), illustrated by Tony Ross, Piccadilly (London, England), 2008.

Fangtastic, Ms Wiz (includes *Ms Wiz Spells Trouble* and *Ms Wiz Loves Dracula*), illustrated by Tony Ross, Piccadilly (London, England), 2008.

The "Ms Wiz" books have been compiled in several omnibus volumes.

FOR ADULTS

Fixx (novel), Bloomsbury (London, England), 1989.

The Fame Hotel (novel), Bloomsbury (London, England), 1992.

Reverence (novel), Bloomsbury (London, England), 1996.

(Editor, with William Donaldson) *The Meaning of Cantona,* Mainstream (Edinburgh, Scotland), 1997.

Kill Your Darlings (novel), Weidenfeld & Nicolson (London, England), 2000, St. Martin's (New York, NY), 2001.

You Cannot Live as I Have Lived and Not End Up like This: The Thoroughly Disgraceful Life and Times of Willie Donaldson, Ebury (London, England), 2007.

Contributor of biweekly column to London *Independent.* Contributor to periodicals, including London *Sunday Times.*

Blacker's books have been translated into eighteen languages.

Adaptations

Parent Swap was adapted as an audiobook, BBC Audiobooks America, 2006.

Sidelights

In addition to writing such well-received young-adult novels as *Homebird, The Angel Factory,* and *Boy2Girl,* Terence Blacker is well known on both sides of the Atlantic for his picture books and his popular "Ms Wiz" series of middle-grade novels. His "Hotshots" series, also for younger readers, recounts the trials and tribulations endured by members of a girls' soccer team. In addition to earning legions of young fans in his native England through his writing, Blacker is known to adult readers as the author of the novels *Fixx* and *Kill Your Darlings,* as well as for the highly praised biography *You Cannot Live as I Have Lived and Not End Up like This: The Thoroughly Disgraceful Life and Times of Willie Donaldson.*

"I've heard many authors say that they had always known, from a very early age, that they wanted to write," Blacker noted in an online interview for Englishonline.co.uk. "Not me. I enjoyed reading when I was a child and used to write stories—but no more than most children. I didn't come from a very bookish family and the idea that one day I could earn a living from writing stories never occurred to me." Following college, Blacker worked with race horses as an amateur jockey, and then moved to a job at a bookstore. After a decade spent in publishing in London, he turned to writing. "Looking back, I can see that I was edging my way nervously towards writing over many years," he explained, "but it took a long time to realise that it was what I really wanted to do. I wish I'd seen it earlier."

In *Homebird,* Blacker tells the story of a teenager who flees from boarding school after meeting with violence from a vicious bully. As a runaway, the hero encounters a host of memorable individuals, including a thief, a drug dealer, and a prostitute, and he finds himself framed for robbery. The novel ends with the youth returned home, though he still suffers from nightmares involving the cruel classmate. A *Voice of Youth* reviewer deemed *Homebird* "short but potent," and Jacqueline Rose praised it in *School Library Journal* as a "riveting" novel that generates "plenty of action and suspense." Similarly, *Horn Book* critic Ellen Fader cited the novel's "can't-put-it-down quality" and "fast-paced action," and a *Publishers Weekly* critic concluded that Blacker's "wisecracking . . . narrative" helps render *Homebird* "an ideal book for reluctant readers."

The Transfer, another novel for teen readers, focuses on a fanatical soccer fan who magically transforms himself into a computer-generated player capable of saving a professional team from relegation to a lower division. The boy's plans go horribly awry, however, after he loses the magical device necessary for his extraordinary play. Further exacerbating matters, the hero discovers that his own teacher has become infatuated with his alter-ego. *Books for Keeps* reviewer Andrew Kidd stated that "this comic fantasy really hits the target" due to Blacker's "high quality writing." Another critic, Linda Saunders, wrote in *School Librarian* that *The Transfer* "offers action, humour and a few lessons about life," and Geoff Fox declared in the *Times Literary Supplement* that the novelist "plays wittily with ideas and language."

Blacker turns to science fiction in *The Angel Factory,* which introduces a British preteen who discovers that he is adopted and his parents are actually extraterrestrials. With the help of friend Gip, Thomas Wisdom learns about his parents' mission: to transform humanity so that human society becomes more stable and individuals more compliant. With this knowledge—and the realization that the aliens intend to use him to further their aim—Thomas is left to decide whether the fate of humankind under the sway of the alien "angels" is for good or ill. *The Angel Factory* was compared positively by *Booklist* contributor Ilene Cooper to Lois Lowry's classic novel *The Giver,* while a *Publishers Weekly* critic dubbed Blacker's story a "riveting futuristic tale" that "masterfully constructs an intriguing world of remarkable possibilities and chilling consequences."

Boy2Girl follows the experiences of a California transplant when his twelve-year-old British cousin Matthew Burton schemes to use him to infiltrate a gang of girls at his London private school. With his long hair and laid-back, West coast manner, Sam Lopez can pass for a girl, and when he comes to live with Matthew's family after his mom is killed, the California preteen willingly agrees to his cousin's scheme of attending his new school in drag. However, when "Samantha" is embraced by the school's all-girl gang, Sam realizes that his temporary role as the new girl is one he does not want to give up. Blacker organizes his novel as a collection of brief narratives by many characters, resulting in what *Booklist* critic Todd Morning described as "a fast-paced story" that explores "the ever-complicated world of sex roles." Noting that *Boy2Girl* "uses gender bending to explore the dynamics between adolescents of both sexes," *Kliatt* critic Michele Winship praised the book's "characters, complications, and comedic chaos."

Another young teen makes personal discoveries when given the opportunity to create a new identity in *Parent Swap.* Here thirteen-year-old Danny Bellingham is a daydreamer because life in his dysfunctional family gives him no real opportunity to experience life. When he decided to employ the services of a company that helps kids transfer into a new family, Danny becomes suspicious that the ParentSwap company is up to something fishy due to their insistence on hidden video cameras. Blacker's "humorous and ultimately tender" novel points up "the sense of powerless" teens experience "in a world . . . controlled by adults," wrote *School Library Journal* contributor Amy S. Pattee. In *Kirkus Reviews,* a critic dubbed *Parent Swap* "a satisfying, entertaining spoof on both a common teenage desire and reality show culture."

In addition to his novels, Blacker is also the author of a series of tales featuring Ms Wiz, a plucky witch who works as a teacher. The woman's spunky and imaginative nature is brought to life in cartoon art by Tony Ross and her lighthearted adventures play out in series installments such as *Ms Wiz Smells a Rat, Ms Wiz and the Sister of Doom,* and *Ms Wiz Goes to Hollywood.* Pamela Cleaver, writing in *Books,* called Ms Wiz "cool and clever," and Chris Stephenson, in a *School Librarian* assessment, dubbed Blacker's fictional witch "dashing."

In addition to the "Ms Wiz" stories, Blacker has written such children's books as *If I Could Work,* wherein a boy imagines himself in jobs ranging from firefighter to film actor. Nancy A. Gifford, writing in *School Library Journal,* contended that the book "just doesn't work,"

Cover of Terence Blacker's young-adult novel **The Angel Factory,** *which posits a frightening future.* (Aladdin Paperbacks, an imprint of Simon & Schuster, Inc., 2001. Cover insert photo copyright © by Darren Robb/FPG International. Reproduced by permission.)

but a *Booklist* critic deemed it "a good choice for preschool story hours." Another tale, *Henry and the Frights,* concerns a boy who overcomes his nighttime fears with the aid of kindly nocturnal creatures. Jill Bennett, in her *Times Educational Supplement* analysis, called *Henry and the Frights* "appealing and accessible."

A more demanding book, *Herbie Hamster, Where Are You?*—published in England as *Houdini, the Disappearing Hamster*—features illustrations where the main character is hidden; readers are instructed to find the hamster in various settings. *Booklist* reviewer Denise Wilms proclaimed the volume "a fun exercise," Cliff Moon noted in *School Librarian* that the book calls for "rapt attention," and Pearl Herscovitch reported in *School Library Journal* that "children are challenged" by Blacker's hide-and-seek tale.

Blacker's writing for younger children also include *The Surprising Adventures of Baron Münchausen,* a recounting of the German folk hero's preposterous exploits. A *Books for Keeps* reviewer recommended the book as "irrepressible fun." Similarly, *The Great Denture Adventure*—wherein a grandmother accidentally expels her false teeth, thus sending them on a series of unlikely but amusing travels—impressed a *School Librarian* critic as "entertaining and enjoyable."

The first of Blacker's adult novels, *Fixx* concerns a deceitful opportunist who gets a job as an arms dealer at the behest of British Prime Minister Margaret Thatcher. After entering high society via a marriage made through coercion and blackmail, Jonathan Fixx becomes an arms dealer and eventually engages in espionage on behalf of both the British and Soviet governments. Jane Dorrel, in a *Books* analysis, hailed *Fixx* as a "chilling and witty account," and John Melmoth wrote in the *Times Literary Supplement* that Blacker's novel is "flawless and funny."

In *The Fame Hotel* Blacker relates the police investigation that ensues following the fetishistic murder of a ghost writer whose journal provides unappealing insights into the lives of various public figures. A *Books* reviewer deemed the novel "beautifully written" and a "sheer delight from start to finish," while Ruth Pavey wrote in the London *Observer* that *The Fame Hotel* offers readers "plenty of opportunities for laughing."

In *Reverence* Blacker relates events in a small village plagued by the ghost of a woman who suffered rejection from her lover. Since being jilted by poet John Skelton, who died in 1529, the ghost troubles various citizens, including a child molester and several promiscuous teens. Patrick Skene Catling, writing in the *Spectator*, proclaimed *Reverence* a "very funny" novel in which "Blacker writes realistically, establishing believable ordinariness to maximise the impact of an outbreak of the extraordinary." In *New Statesman & Society* Laurie Taylor called the novel a "hectically enjoyable fantasy," and *Times Literary Supplement* reviewer Roz Kaveney deemed *Reverence* "an intelligent novel."

Kill Your Darlings tells of an unproductive writing teacher who drives a promising student to suicide, then appropriates his manuscript with intentions of assuming authorship. In *Booklist* Emily Melton summarized Blacker's novel as "literate, clever, and entertaining," citing its "witty digs at the world of the literary glitterati." A London *Times* critic noted "the scythe [Blacker] wittily takes to the fads of the book world," while Hugo Barnacle concluded in *New Statesman* that the story's "perverse humour exerts a horrible fascination." Sheila Riley, writing in *Library Journal*, commented that in *Kill Your Darlings* Blacker "delves . . . deeply and convincingly into the pit of narcissism, mayhem, and soul-destroying Faustian bargains," while a *Kirkus Reviews* critic concluded that the novel "reveals far more than anyone should know about a writer's inner and outer lives."

Biographical and Critical Sources

PERIODICALS

Booklist, June 1, 1988, review of *If I Could Work,* p. 1672; August, 1990, Denise Wilms, review of *Herbie Ham-* *ster, Where Are You?,* p. 2169; November 1, 2001, Emily Melton, review of *Kill Your Darlings,* p. 461; December 1, 2001, Anna Rich, review of *Ms Wiz Supermodel,* p. 64; August, 2002, Ilene Cooper, review of *The Angel Factory,* p. 1945; March 1, 2005, Todd Morning, review of *Boy2Girl,* p. 1151.

Books, March, 1989, Jane Dorrell, review of *Fixx,* p. 22; October, 1989, Pamela Cleaver, reviews of *Ms Wiz Spells Trouble, In Stitches with Ms Wiz,* and *You're Nicked Ms Wiz,* p. 22; September, 1992, review of *The Fame Hotel,* p. 27; October, 1997, review of *The Meaning of Cantona,* p. 17.

Books for Keeps, July, 1990, review of *In Stitches with Ms Wiz,* p. 10; March, 1992, review of *The Surprising Adventures of Baron Münchausen,* p. 10; July, 1993, review of *Time Flies for Ms Wiz,* p. 13; May, 1994, review of *Ms Wiz Loves Dracula,* p. 12; November, 1996, review of *You're Kidding, Ms Wiz,* p. 9; May, 1998, Andrew Kidd, review of *The Transfer,* p. 27.

Books for Your Children, spring, 1991, C. Haydn Jones, review of *You're Nicked Ms Wiz,* p. 21.

Bulletin of the Center for Children's Books, January, 2003, review of *The Angel Factory,* p. 189; March, 2005, Deborah Stevenson, review of *Boy2Girl,* p. 281; October, 2006, Loretta Gaffney, review of *Parent Swap,* p. 57.

Children's Book Service Review, October, 1990, review of *Herbie Hamster, Where Are You?,* p. 13.

Horn Book, July-August, 1993, Ellen Fader, review of *Homebird,* p. 464.

Junior Bookshelf, October, 1989, review of *Henry and the Frights,* p. 210.

Kirkus Reviews, October 1, 2001, review of *Kill Your Darlings,* p. 1378; August 1, 2002, review of *The Angel Factory,* p. 1122; February 1, 2005, review of *Boy2Girl,* p. 174.

Kliatt, March, 2005, Michele Winship, review of *Boy2Girl,* p. 6; July 15, 2006, review of *Parent Swap,* p. 720.

New Statesman, July 10, 2000, Hugo Barnacle, review of *Kill Your Darlings,* p. 57; April 9, 2007, Alexander Larman, review of *You Cannot Live as I Have Lived and Not End Up like This,* p. 60.

New Statesman & Society, February 17, 1989, Sean French, "First-Person Thatcherism," p. 39; January 19, 1996, Laurie Taylor, review of *Reverence,* p. 40.

Observer (London, England), February 12, 1989, John Spurling, review of *Fixx,* p. 50; August 30, 1992, Ruth Pavey, review of *The Fame Hotel,* p. 50.

Publishers Weekly, April 5, 1993, review of *Homebird,* p. 79; October 15, 2001, review of *Kill Your Darlings,* p. 44; July 22, 2002, review of *The Angel Factory,* p. 180; January 15, 2005, review of *Boy2Girl,* p. 56; August 7, 2006, review of *Parent Swap,* p. 61.

School Librarian, February, 1989, Chris Stephenson, review of *Ms Wiz Spells Trouble,* pp. 19-20; August, 1990, Shona Walton, review of *In Control, Ms Wiz?,* p. 106; November, 1990, Cliff Moon, review of *Houdini, the Disappearing Hamster,* p. 141; May, 1993, Katherine Moule, review of *The Great Denture Adventure,* p. 53; August, 1993, Chris Stephenson, review of *Ms Wiz Loves Dracula,* p. 105; summer, 1998, Linda Saunders, review of *The Transfer,* p. 76.

School Library Journal, August, 1988, Nancy A. Gifford, review of *If I Could Work,* p. 78; November, 1990, Peal Herscovitch, review of *Herbie Hamster, Where Are You?,* p. 85; April, 1993, Jacqueline Rose, review of *Homebird,* p. 140; August, 2002, Sharon Rawlins, review of *The Angel Factory,* p. 182; March, 2006, Rhona Campbell, review of *Boy2Girl,* p. 206; August, 2006, Amy S. Pattee, review of *Parent Swap,* p. 114.

Spectator, February 17, 1996, Patrick Skene Catling, "Let Me Go, Lover," p. 32.

Times (London, England), October 28, 2001, Trevor Lewis, review of *Kill Your Darlings,* p. 46.

Times Educational Supplement, June 2, 1989, Jill Bennett, "Means of Escape," p. B8; April 18, 1997, reviews of *Pride and Penalties, On the Wing,* and *Shooting Star,* p. 12; October 31, 1997, Geraldine Brennan, "Wild and Wonderous Witchery," p. 8; February 27, 1998, Geoff Fox, "Call of the Wild," p. 10; June 8, 2001, review of *The Angel Factory,* p. 20; January 17, 2003, "You Have Ghost Mail," p. 26; July 29, 2005, Michael Thorn, review of *The Parent Swap,* p. 26.

Times Literary Supplement, May 5, 1990, John Melmoth, "Up and on the Make," p. 483; October 2, 1992, Mark Sanderson, "Trash by the Tranche," p. 21; February 2, 1996, Roz Kaveney, "Little Local Difficulties," p. 23; July 21, 2000, Sam Gilpin, "Creative Writing," p. 22.

Voice of Youth Advocate, August, 1993, Eleanor Klopp, review of *Homebird,* p. 148; October, 2002, review of *The Angel Factory,* p. 292; April, 2005, Ed Goldberg, review of *Boy2Girl,* p. 35.

ONLINE

English Online Web site, http://www.englishonline.co.uk/ (October 15, 2008), interview with Blacker.

Independent Online, http://www.independent.co.uk/ opinion/ (October 10, 2008), "Terence Blacker."

Terence Blacker Home Page, http://terenceblacker.com (December 5, 2008).

*   *   *

BLUE, Zachary
See STINE, R.L.

*   *   *

BORGO, Lacy Finn 1972-

Personal

Born 1972.

Addresses

Home—Montrose, CO.

Career

Teacher and author.

Writings

Big Mama's Baby, illustrated by Nancy Cote, Boyds Mills Press (Honesdale, PA), 2007.

Sidelights

Growing up in Texas with a family who liked to tell stories, Lacy Finn Borgo discovered a love for books and writing at a young age. She recalled to *Montrose Daily Press* reporter Lisa Huynh that her first work of fiction was a murder mystery inspired by "too much '70s television." As an author and teacher, Borgo now enjoys inspiring younger children to write stories of their own.

Borgo indulges in a little silliness in her first published picture book, *Big Mama's Baby.* In a story brought to life in Nancy Cote's art, the "baby" of the title is a Black Angus bull that is fed from a bottle by an elderly woman known as Big Mama. While the bull is small, Baby sleeps nicely next to Big Mama's bed and spends its days in her Texas yard. As the bull grows bigger, however, the neighbors start to complain about its grazing as well as its manure. However, when Baby goes missing, the neighbors help a worried Big Mama search and they eventually find the bull happily grazing on a ranch with other cattle. A *Kirkus Reviews* critic predicted in a review of *Big Mama's Baby* that children will "recognize the joy and affection" in the owner-pet relationship. To this simple and universal theme, "Borgo adds a touch of narrative tension when the neighbors get into busy-body mode," the critic added.

The best way to create writers, according to Borgo, is to read and recite stories to children. "You can't write from nothing," she commented. "You fill up their tanks and when given the opportunity, children will write when they have a story to tell." The best thing about writing, Borgo tells her own students, is that anything can happen. "Sometimes, things that happen in books are silly," she said. "The great thing with books is that you can do what you want to do."

Biographical and Critical Sources

PERIODICALS

Bulletin of the Center for Children's Books, October, 2007, Deborah Stevenson, review of *Big Mama's Baby,* pp. 74-75.

School Library Journal, August, 2007, Ieva Bates, review of *Big Mama's Baby,* p. 77.

Kirkus Reviews, August 1, 2007, review of *Big Mama's Baby.*

ONLINE

Montrose Daily Press Online (Montrose, CO), http://www.montrosepress.com/ (March 8, 2008), Lisa Huynh, "Letting Imagination Spill onto the Pages of a Book."*

BOWE, Julie 1962-

Personal

Born June 19, 1962, in WI; daughter of a cabinet maker and sheep farmer; married; children: one daughter, one son. *Education:* Luther College (Decorah, IA), bachelor's degree; Luther Seminary (St. Paul, MN), M.A.

Addresses

Home—WI. *Agent*—The Chudney Agency, 72 N. State Rd., Ste. 501, Briarcliff Manor, NY 10510.

Career

Author and editor. Augsburg Fortress Publishers, Minneapolis, MN, curriculum writer and editor. Has also worked as a youth director and camp program director.

Member

Society of Children's Book Writers and Illustrators.

Writings

My Last Best Friend, Harcourt (Orlando, FL), 2007.
My New Best Friend, Harcourt (Orlando, FL), 2008.

Sidelights

Julie Bowe grew up on a farm in Luck, Wisconsin, in a close-knit family that celebrated their Danish heritage. She was interested in writing from a young age, and turned to creating stories for children after her second child was born. Her first novel, *My Last Best Friend,* tells the story of Ida May, a girl who finds it hard to face fourth grade now that her best friend has moved away. Ida May hopes to befriend new girl Stacey, although to do so she will have to overcome the bullying of popular classmate Jenna. "Like Ida," Bowe told *SATA,* "I loved to read and draw when I was a kid, and hoped to be an artist someday. I still love to read and I like to think that I make pictures with my writing. I guess I grew up to be an artist after all!"

In *Booklist,* Stephanie Zvirin observed that *My Last Best Friend* is filled with "comedy and important growing-up issues" that "meld in a strong debut, just right for the age group." "Delightful details enhance this friendship story that develops realistically," Debbie Stewart Hoskins similarly noted in *School Library Journal.* A *Kirkus Reviews* writer observed that "Ida's humorous outlook is engaging, and the situation is realistic," and recommended the book for reluctant readers. "If the book's resolution is a little too tidy, Bowe's characters emerge fully formed," a *Publishers Weekly* critic commented, concluding that in *My Last Best Friend* "Ida embodies the universal longing to connect with a kindred spirit."

A sequel to Ida May's story, *My New Best Friend* finds friends Ida May and Stacey hoping to form a "Secret Mermaid Club." When the club gets out of hand in acting against Jenna, Ida May must find a way to calm things down while still preserving her friendship with Stacey. In *School Library Journal* contributor Maryann H. Owen remarked that "various family situations are well represented and lend credence to the characters' behaviors" in *My New Best Friend.* "Bowe is spot-on with Ida May's feelings," a *Kirkus Reviews* critic commented, concluding that "fans of Ida May will be overjoyed to read this new installment."

Biographical and Critical Sources

PERIODICALS

Booklist, September 1, 2007, Stephanie Zvirin, review of *My Last Best Friend,* p. 114.
Kirkus Reviews, March 15, 2007, review of *My Last Best Friend;* July 1, 2008, review of *My New Best Friend.*
Publishers Weekly, April 23, 2007, review of *My Last Best Friend,* p. 51.

Cover of Julie Bowe's young-adult novel **My Last Best Friend,** *featuring artwork by Jana Christy.* (Illustration copyright © 2007 by Jana Christy. Reproduced by permission of Houghton Mifflin Harcourt Publishing Company.)

School Library Journal, May, 2007, Debbie Stewart Hoskins, review of *My Last Best Friend,* p. 85; October 1, 2008, Maryann H. Owen, review of *My New Best Friend.*

ONLINE

Julie Bowe Home Page, http://www.juliebowe.com (October 15, 2008).

*   *   *

BRANDE, Robin

Personal

Married. *Education:* Earned J.D. *Hobbies and other interests:* Backpacking, watching movies, reading.

Career

Full-time writer. Has also worked as a trial lawyer, entrepreneur, community college instructor, yoga instructor, and insurance agent.

Awards, Honors

Best Books for Young Adults citation, American Library Association (ALA) Young Adult Library Services Association division (YALSA), Amelia Bloomer List inclusion, ALA Feminist Task Force, and Notable Children's Trade Books in the Field of Social Studies citation, National Council of Social Studies/Children's Book Council, all 2008, all for *Evolution, Me, and Other Freaks of Nature.*

Writings

Evolution, Me, and Other Freaks of Nature, Knopf (New York, NY), 2007.

Adaptations

Evolution, Me, and Other Freaks of Nature was adapted as an audiobook, Random House Audio.

Sidelights

Robin Brande's first novel, *Evolution, Me, and Other Freaks of Nature,* explores what happens when a teenager is forced to reconcile her faith, her sense of what is right, and her growing interest in science. Fifteen-year-old Mena has been kicked out of her church for taking a stand on bullying, and she enters high school feeling like an outcast. When a science unit on evolution inspires controversy once again, Mena explores what she believes and learns to stand up for her beliefs.

"I grew up in a church like Mena's, and I, too, was kicked out right before high school—although it was for a really bizarre and stupid reason, not at all as noble

as Mena's," Brande explained in an online interview for *Becky's Book Reviews.* As she read news stories about the fight over teaching evolution in schools, "the more I wondered how a girl like me would have dealt with that fight in her own school. I wanted to explore how—or whether—a person of faith could reconcile her religious beliefs with her belief in science." As she noted on the Random House Web site, one of the benefits of writing her novel was "articulating for myself what it is I believe about God and evolution. It's something I never really threw light on until I had to put it in the mouths and the heads of the various characters in this book."

Critics praised *Evolution, Me, and Other Freaks of Nature* for its insightful yet humorous exploration of faith, conformity, and everyday teen problems. "Brande's buoyant story thoughtfully takes on debates both time-worn and current," a *Kirkus Reviews* writer stated. "The . . . slow revelation of the back story will hook readers from the start," predicted a *Publishers Weekly* critic, the reviewer adding that while the creationist characters are somewhat one-dimensional, Brande's "fluid storytelling offers thought-provoking situations and ideas." In

Robin Brande focuses on a teen's efforts to reconcile science with a strong religious faith in her young-adult novel Evolution, Me, and Other Freaks of Nature. *(Copyright © 2007 by Robin Brande. Photograph on front © by John Drysale/Corbis. Used by permission of Alfred A. Knopf, an imprint of Random House Children's Books, a division of Random House, Inc.)*

Booklist John Peters noted of *Evolution, Me, and Other Freaks of Nature* that "readers will appreciate this vulnerable but ultimately resilient protagonist," as well as the novel's "unusually appealing supporting cast." Mena's "heartfelt struggle to reconcile her belief in God and in science is portrayed with grace, humor, and humility," a *School Library Journal* reviewer concluded.

Biographical and Critical Sources

PERIODICALS

Booklist, June 1, 2007, John Peters, review of *Evolution, Me, and Other Freaks of Nature,* pp. 55-56.

Horn Book, September-October, 2007, Patty Campbell, review of *Evolution, Me, and Other Freaks of Nature,* pp. 567-568.

Kirkus Reviews, July 15, 2007, review of *Evolution, Me, and Other Freaks of Nature.*

Kliatt, March, 2008, Susan Allison, review of *Evolution, Me, and Other Freaks of Nature,* p. 42.

Publishers Weekly, August 6, 2007, review of *Evolution, Me, and Other Freaks of Nature,* p. 190.

School Library Journal, April, 2008, "A Question of Faith," p. 61.

ONLINE

Becky's Book Reviews, http://blbooks.blogspot.com/ (February 4, 2008), interview with Brande.

Edge of the Forest Online, http://www.theedgeoftheforest.com/ (September 1, 2007), Kelly Herold, interview with Brande.

Random House Web site, http://www.randomhouse.com/ (October 14, 2008), "Author Spotlight: Robin Brande."

Robin Brande Home Page, http://robinbrande.com (October 14, 2008).*

*   *   *

BUCHMANN, Stephen L. 1955(?)-

Personal

Born c. 1955, in Rockford, IL. *Education:* California State University, Fullerton, B.S., 1974, M.S., 1975; University of California at Davis, Ph.D., 1978. *Hobbies and other interests:* Photography, Macintosh computing, simulation games, cyberspace surfing.

Addresses

Office—The Bee Works, 1870 W. Prince Rd., Ste. 16, Tucson, AZ 85705.

Career

Research entomologist and author. University of Arizona, Tucson, research associate in Department of Ecology and Evolutionary Biology at Carl Hayden Bee Research Center, 1979—, then adjunct associate professor in Department of Entomology. Bee Works (independent research organization), Tucson, founder and researcher, beginning 1999. Arizona-Sonora Desert Museum, Phoenix, research associate; American Museum of Natural History, research associate.

Awards, Honors

Los Angeles Times Book Prize nomination in Science and Technology, 1997, for *The Forgotten Pollinators.*

Writings

(Editor, with Andrew Matheson, with Christopher O'Toole) *The Conservation of Bees* (Linnean Society Symposium series, no. 18; includes "Competition between Honey Bees and Native Bees in the Sonoran Desert and Global Bee Conservation Issues"), Academic Press, 1996.

(With Gary Paul Nabhan) *The Forgotten Pollinators,* illustrated by Paul Mirocha, Island Press/Shearwater Books (Washington, DC), 1996.

How to Keep Stingless Bees in the Yucatan Peninsula (bilingual Spanish/Mayan text), 2004.

Pollinators of the Sonoran Desert: A Field Guide, 2005.

(With Bannign Repplier) *Letters from the Hive: An Intimate History of Bees, Honey, and Humankind,* Random House (New York, NY), 2005.

(With Diana Cohn) *The Bee Tree,* illustrated by Paul Mirocha, Cinco Puntos Press (El Paso, TX), 2007.

Contributor of articles and reviews to periodicals, including *Botanical Gazette, International Journal of Plant Sciences, Quarterly Review of Biology,* and *Journal of Experimental Biology.* Also author of technical papers.

Sidelights

Stephen L. Buchmann is an associate professor of entomology at the University of Arizona in Tucson. He is also an amateur beekeeper and founder of The Bee Works, an environmental company. In addition to technical works and works such as *The Forgotten Pollinators,* one of the first books to raise awareness regarding environmental threats to the pollination cycle, Buchmann channels his fascination for bees into an admiring tribute to the honey bee titled *Letters from the Hive: An Intimate History of Bees, Honey, and Humankind,* and a younger audience in the pages of the picture book *The Bee Tree.*

In *The Forgotten Pollinators* Buchmann examines relationships between plants and their pollinators—not only insects but also birds, reptiles, and mammals. The book highlights the frequently overlooked roles of these animals and plants in producing much of the food people eat. In addition to providing information on bees and

Cover of Stephen L. Buchmann's Letters from the Hive, *a scientist's reflection on his life and work that features artwork by Emile Claus.* (Illustration by Emile Claus/Bridgeman Art Library copyright © 2005. Used by permission of Bantam Books, a division of Random House, Inc.)

ral world surrounding the hive contributes to this small ecosystem, where flower gardens, sunshine, and other insects all play an important role. In addition to cooking recipes, a discussion of the curative power of honey, myths surrounding the honey bee, and an explanation of the bee's place as an inspiring metaphor within literature and art are also covered in Buchmann's book, which ranges from the Australian outback to the Himalayas in its focus. Calling Buchmann "one of the foremost authorities on pollination and pollinators," *Booklist* critic Nancy Bent added that the scientist's "blend of science and passion makes" the book "a lively read." In *Publishers Weekly* a reviewer concluded that *Letters from the Hive* serves readers as "a highly entertaining and informative introduction to the world of the bee."

Featuring artwork by Paul Mirocha, *The Bee Tree* features a text by Buchmann and fellow writer Diana Cohn. The story is set in Malaysia, where thirteen-year-old Nizam is excited to join his grandfather in his clan's annual honey hunt. During the night, the hunters climb up tall tualang trees into the rainforest canopy and mine honey from the extensive hives of aggressive, one-inchlong honeybees. Highlighted by illustrations that bring to life "the lush landscape of the rainforest," *The Bee Tree* "is infused with reverence for the gifts of the forest and respect for the insects" that provide such wealth, wrote *School Library Journal* contributor Kathy Piehl. Dubbing the picture book "wonderful," *Booklist* critic Donna Seaman also commended Buchmann and Cohn for including "a section of amazing facts about Malaysia's rainforests" in their ecology-minded picture book.

Biographical and Critical Sources

PERIODICALS

Booklist, July, 1996, Donna Seaman, review of *The Forgotten Pollinators,* p. 1787; April 1, 2005, Nancy Bent, review of *Letters from the Hive: An Intimate History of Bees, Honey, and Humankind,* p. 1332.
Discover, June, 2005, Zach Zorich, review of *Letters from the Hive,* p. 81.
Kirkus Reviews, February 15, 2005, review of *Letters from the Hive,* p. 206; May 1, 2007, review of *The Bee Tree.*
Library Journal, June 15, 1996, William H. Wiese, review of *The Forgotten Pollinators,* p. 87.
New York Times Book Review, August 18, 1996, review of *The Forgotten Pollinators.*
People Weekly, May 22, 1989, "By Using Bar Coding on Busy Bees, Scientist Stephen Buchmann Becomes an Unstung Hero," p. 105.
Publishers Weekly, May 13, 1996, review of *The Forgotten Pollinators,* p. 63; March 7, 2005, review of *Letters from the Hive,* p. 62.
School Library Journal, April, 1997, Judy McAloon, review of *The Forgotten Pollinators,* p. 167; July, 2007, Kathy Piehl, review of *The Bee Tree,* p. 67.

beekeeping, field research, and a discussion of related scientific disciplines, Buchmann and ethnobiologist Gary Paul Nabhan also describe such contemporary threats to pollinators as the overuse of pesticides and habitat destruction. Terming *The Forgotten Pollinators* an "important addition to the environmental bookshelf," a contributor to *Publishers Weekly* described Buchmann's book as "a disturbing story of disappearing insects and diminishing plant reproduction." In the *New York Times Book Review,* Carol Kaesuk Yoon pointed out that the "most significant" contribution in *The Forgotten Pollinators* is their presentation of "a new view of nature." "More than the species and the land that holds them," Yoon added, *The Forgotten Pollinators* puts forth the coauthors' belief that "the living world to be cherished includes everything that these creatures, plants, and places do . . . [the] biodiversity of relationships."

Coauthored with Banning Repplier, *Letters from the Hive* reveals the rich life of the honey bee, showing that within each small hive exists a bustling community featuring a nursery, a regal court overseen by a powerful queen, and a factory producing golden honey. The natu-

Washington Post Book World, April 17, 2005, Adrian Higgins, review of *Letters from the Hive,* p. 10.

ONLINE

Bee Works Web site, http://www.thebeeworks.com/ (October 13, 2008), "Stephen L. Buchmann."
High Country News Online, http://www.hcn.org/ (March 19, 2007), Brendan Borrell, "Busy as a Buchmann."
University of Guelph Web site, http://www.uoguelph.ca/~iucn/contacts/ (October 13, 2008), "Stephen L. Buchmann."*

* * *

BURKETT, D. Brent

Personal
Male.

Addresses
Home—Springfield, OR.

Career
Painter, video-game artist, and illustrator. Created artwork for games, including *Stellar 7,* Dynamix, 1990; *Nova 9: Return of Gir Draxon,* Sierra, 1991; *Heart of China,* Sierra, 1991; *The Adventures of Willy Beamish,* Dynamix, 1991; *Aces of the Pacific,* Dynamix, 1992; *Betrayal at Krondor,* Sierra, 1993; *Aces over Europe,* Sierra, 1993; *Aces of the Deep,* Sierra, 1994; and *Command: Aces of the Deep,* Sierra, 1995.

Illustrator
Maryl Barker, *Gracie,* Gracemar Productions (Eugene, OR), 1997.
Maryl Barker, *Wild Country Animal Park,* Gracemar Productions (Eugene, OR), 1998.
Maryl Barker, *My Own Backyard,* Gracemar Productions (Eugene, OR), 1999.
Lloyd Alexander, *Dream-of-Jade: The Emperor's Cat,* Cricket (Chicago, IL), 2005.
Eve Bunting, *Reggie,* Cricket (Chicago, IL), 2006.

Sidelights
Oregon-based artist D. Brent Burkett is best known for his oil paintings of Willamette Valley. Video game players might recognize his work on computer games from Sierra or Dynamix, including the computer role-playing game Betrayal at Krondor, based on the work of fantasy writer Raymond Feist. Burkett did not begin illustrating for children until 1997, when he was approached by Maryl Barker of GraceMar Productions, who was looking for an illustrator for a series of books about her dog, Gracie. Burkett illustrated three titles for Barker—*Gracie, Wild Country Animal Park,* and *My Own Back-*

yard—all of which feature full-color illustrations in a realistic style. Most of the illustrations feature the large black Labrador/shar-pei star, but some include more imaginative images, such as gophers around a stove, singing as they prepare a morning breakfast.

Burkett is also the illustrator of *Dream-of-Jade: The Emperor's Cat,* a collection of related short stories by Lloyd Alexander, three of which were originally published in *Cricket* magazine. Set in a fictional setting reminiscent of ancient China, the satiric tales tell how the cat, Dream-of-Jade, becomes a friend to the emperor. The "finely lined, stylish paintings on marbled yellow backgrounds convey the cultural mystique, invoking both richness and absurdity," wrote Julie Cummins in a *Booklist* review of *Dream-of-Jade.* Calling the book "handsome," Miriam Lang Budin noted in *School Library Journal* that Burkett's "graceful pencil-and-watercolor art . . . adds atmosphere." The color illustrations "lavishly capture court life in ancient China as well as Dream-of-Jade's feline essence," wrote a contributor to *Kirkus Reviews.* A *Publishers Weekly* contributor felt that Burkett "humorously illustrates the havoc" brought about by the emperor allowing the cat to advise him, "and captures the growing love between the wise cat and the perceptive Emperor."

Along with picture books, Burkett has also illustrated a book for beginning readers, creating black-and-white drawings for Eve Bunting's novel *Reggie.* Kay Weisman, writing in *Booklist,* noted that the design of the book, as well as the "frequent black-and-white illustrations make for an appealing format," and a *Kirkus Reviews* contributor complimented Burkett's "rich, atmospheric pen-and-ink illustrations."

Biographical and Critical Sources

PERIODICALS

Booklist, September 15, 2005, Julie Cummins, review of *Dream-of-Jade: The Emperor's Cat,* p. 61; October 1, 2006, Kay Weisman, review of *Reggie,* p. 56.
Bulletin of the Center for Children's Books, January, 2007, Elizabeth Bush, review of *Reggie,* p. 204.
Kirkus Reviews, August 15, 2005, review of *Dream-of-Jade,* p. 907; August 1, 2006, review of *Reggie,* p. 782.
Publishers Weekly, September 5, 2005, review of *Dream-of-Jade,* p. 62.
School Library Journal, November, 2005, Miriam Lang Budin, review of *Dream-of-Jade,* p. 82; November, 2006, Debbie Lewis O'Donnell, review of *Reggie,* p. 86.

ONLINE

Gracemar Productions Web Site, http://www.graciedog.com/ (November 2, 2008), profile of Burkett.

Moby Games Web site, http://www.mobygames.com/ (November 2, 2008), profile of Burkett.*

* * *

BUSSE, Sarah Martin

Personal

Born in Mt. Vernon, IA; daughter of Richard (a professor) and Jacqueline Briggs Martin (a writer); married Reed Busse, 1998; children: one child.

Addresses

Home—Madison, WI.

Career

Children's author and poet.

Writings

(With mother, Jacqueline Briggs Martin) *Banjo Granny,* illustrated by Barry Root, Houghton Mifflin (Boston, MA), 2006.

Also author of poetry chapbook *A Blue like Milk,* 2003.

Sidelights

Sarah Martin Busse grew up in a family that loves words. Her mother is a picture-book author, and her father is an emeritus professor of English at Cornell College in Mt. Vernon, Iowa. Such a literary upbringing led Busse to collaborate with her mother on *Banjo Granny,* a folk-tale story featuring artwork by Barry Root. The story follows baby Owen's loving Granny as she treks across the country on foot to visit Owen, after hearing that the youngster loves the high-lonesome twang of bluegrass music. Owen is updated on his Granny's trip by birds, as Granny overcomes obstacles through the use of her banjo. Hazel Rochman noted in *Booklist* that, "part lullaby and part tall tale, this warm picture book is both cozy and exciting." Tamara E. Richman described the book in *School Library Journal* as "an up-to-date story" in which "the narrative's cadence and traditional structure make the tale feel timeless." A *Kirkus Reviews* critic noted of children's reaction to Granny's musical and magical mode of transportation that while some "will be left wondering why Granny didn't hop a plane . . . most will find her modes of transportation delightful and inspirational." In *Publishers Weekly* a critic concluded of *Banjo Granny* that, "with its heartwarming message and visuals," Busse and Martin's tale "is a celebration of the bond between grandparent and child."

Biographical and Critical Sources

PERIODICALS

Booklist, November 1, 2006, Hazel Rochman, review of *Banjo Granny,* p. 58.
Bulletin of the Center for Children's Books, January, 2007, Deborah Stevenson, review of *Banjo Granny,* p. 205.
Kirkus Reviews, November 1, 2006, review of *Banjo Granny,* p. 1121.
Publishers Weekly, October 30, 2006, review of *Banjo Granny,* p. 60.
School Library Journal, December, 2006, Tamara E. Richman, review of *Banjo Granny,* p. 95.

ONLINE

Houghton Mifflin Web site, http://www.houghtonmifflin books.com/ (October 27, 2008), "Sarah Martin Busse."*

C

CARRICK, Paul 1972-

Personal

Born May 2, 1972, in Martha's Vineyard, MA; son of Donald (an illustrator) and Carol (a writer) Carrick. *Education:* Rhode Island School of Design, B.F.A., 1994. *Hobbies and other interests:* Motorcycling, wargaming, hiking.

Addresses

Home and office—P.O. Box 15281, Boston, MA 02215. *E-mail*—paul@nightserpent.com.

Career

Illustrator. Contributor of illustrations to game companies, including Wizards of the Coast, Chaosium, Five Rings, Alderac, Precedence, Z-Man Games, Mind Ventures, XID Creative, Green Knight, Atlas Games, and Eclipse Studios. Illustrator for role-playing and card games, including Dungeons and Dragons, Call of Cthulu, Legend of the Five Rings (card game), and Wheel of Time (card game).

Writings

SELF-ILLUSTRATED

Watch out for Wolfgang!, Charlesbridge (Watertown, MA), 2009.

ILLUSTRATOR

Carol Carrick, *Mothers Are like That,* Clarion (New York, NY), 2000.

(With Bruce Shillinglaw) Kathleen Weidner Zoehfeld, *Dinosaur Parents, Dinosaur Young: Uncovering the Mystery of Dinosaur Families,* Clarion (New York, NY), 2001.

Carol Carrick, *The Polar Bears Are Hungry,* Clarion (New York, NY), 2002.

Anastasia Suen, *Wired,* Charlesbridge (Watertown, MA), 2007.

Sidelights

Paul Carrick grew up on Martha's Vineyard, Massachusetts, in a creative family. His mother, Carol Carrick, has written more than fifty books, many of them illustrated by her husband, Donald Carrick, and some featuring a young boy named Paul. Because Martha's Vineyard was primarily a summer resort while Carrick was growing up, most of the year there was little going on and Carrick developed an interest in art and role-playing games. While attending the Rhode Island School of Design, he struggled to get his professors to appreciate his work in the fantasy art genre. "It took the full four years to earn the respect from some of the teachers," he recalled on his home page. "Some felt this type of art in no way could be sophisticated." After completing his degree, Carrick traveled to GenCon, one of the largest conventions for fantasy role-playing games in the United States, where he made contacts with several publishers. Beginning in 1993, he became an illustrator for such well-known role-playing games as Dungeons and Dragons and Call of Cthulu, as well as creating art for collectable card games.

In addition to illustrating texts by various authors, Carrick has also tried his hand at writing. He is the author and illustrator for *Watch out for Wolfgang!* After the death of his father, Carrick and his mother teamed up on Carrick's first illustrated picture book, *Mothers Are like That.* Featuring "shadowy acrylic paintings," as GraceAnne A. DeCandido described them in *Booklist,* the books shows mothers of all sizes and species caring for their young. Carrick's illustrations "brim with child-appealing, close-up portraits," in the opinion of *Horn Book* critic Martha V. Parravano, and *School Library Journal* reviewer Marian Drabkin cited Carrick's use of "soft colors and gentle shadows." A *Publishers Weekly*

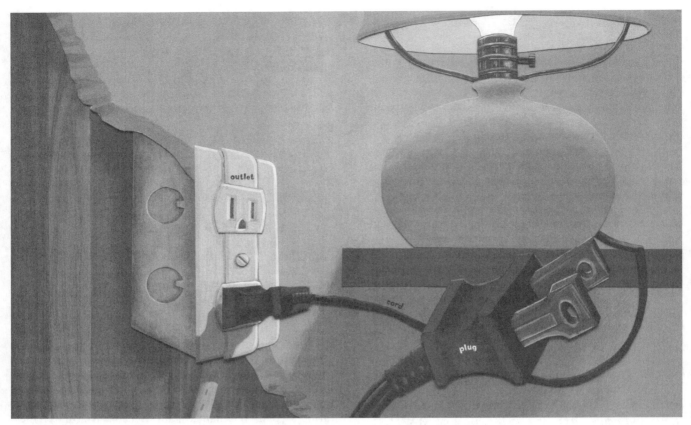

Carrick's realistic paintings help illustrate the basic electrical concepts addressed in Anastasia Suen's picture book **Wired.** (Illustration copyright © 2007 by Paul Carrick. All rights reserved. Used by permission of Charlesbridge Publishing, Inc.)

critic concluded of *Mothers Are like That* that the book marks the illustrator's "promising picture book debut with luminous, realistic acrylic art."

The mother-son team collaborates again on *The Polar Bears Are Hungry.* In what Carol L. MacKay called "breathtaking scenes" in her *School Library Journal* review, Carrick employs an interesting technique, "outlin-[ing] his subjects in luminous electric blue" to emphasize the distinctive lighting of the Arctic environment. While a *Kirkus Reviews* contributor found some of Carrick's human characters to be "stiff," the reviewer concluded that the illustrations "capture the bears and seals perfectly." As Connie Fletcher wrote in *Booklist,* in *The Polar Bears Are Hungry* "acrylic paints portray the vibrant colors of the Arctic."

In addition to working with his mother, Carrick has also worked with other authors on creating books for young readers. Both *Dinosaur Parents, Dinosaur Young: Uncovering the Mystery of Dinosaur Families* and *Wired* feature science topics, the former focusing on paleontology and the latter introducing electrical concepts. In *Horn Book* commented on Carrick's illustrations for *Dinosaur Parents, Dinosaur Young,* describing them as "soft-focus artistic renditions of live dinosaurs." In *Wired,* featuring a text by Anastasia Suen, the artist's "acrylic mixed-media illustrations are informative, with clear labels to identify specific components," according to Steven Engelfried in *School Library Journal.*

Biographical and Critical Sources

PERIODICALS

Booklist, March 15, 2000, GraceAnne A. DeCandido, review of *Mothers Are like That,* p. 1386; April 15, 2001, Gillian Engberg, review of *Dinosaur Parents, Dinosaur Young: Uncovering the Mystery of Dinosaur Families,* p. 1549; October 15, 2002, Connie Fletcher, review of *The Polar Bears Are Hungry,* p. 410; August, 2007, Gillian Engberg, review of *Wired,* p. 72.

Horn Book, March, 2000, Martha V. Parravano, review of *Mothers Are like That,* p. 181; May, 2001, review of *Dinosaur Parents, Dinosaur Young,* p. 353.

Kirkus Reviews, August 15, 2002, review of *The Polar Bears Are Hungry,* p. 1220.

Publishers Weekly, March 6, 2000, review of *Mothers Are like That,* p. 109.

School Library Journal, May, 2000, Marian Drabkin, review of *Mothers Are like That,* p. 132; July, 2001, Carolyn Angus, review of *Dinosaur Parents, Dinosaur Young,* p. 134; November, 2002, Carol L. MacKay, review of *The Polar Bears Are Hungry,* p. 142; July, 2007, Steven Engelfried, review of *Wired,* p. 95.

Science Books & Films, May, 2003, review of *The Polar Bears Are Hungry,* p. 101.

ONLINE

Paul Carrick Home Page, http://www.nightserpent.com
    (October 27, 2008).*

*   *   *

CASTALDI, Elicia

Personal

Born November 9, in Providence, RI. *Education:* Rhode
Island School of Design, B.F.A., 2001.

Addresses

Office—146 Duane St., No. 3B, New York, NY 10013.

Career

Children's illustrator and freelance Web site designer.
Providence Monthly, illustrator, 2001-03; freelance
graphic designer; Macy's East, New York, NY, art director, 2004—.

Member

Society of Children's Book Writers and Illustrators.

Awards, Honors

National Parent Publications Gold Award, New York
Public Library 100 Titles for Reading and Sharing des-
ignation, and Cybil Award nomination, all 2007, and
Texas Lonestar listee, 2008-09, all for *Middle School Is
Worse than Meatloaf.*

Illustrator

Pamela Duncan Edwards, *Miss Polly Has a Dolly,* Putnam
    (New York, NY), 2003.
Jennifer L. Holm, *Middle School Is Worse than Meatloaf:
    A Year Told through Stuff,* Atheneum (New York, NY),
    2007.

Sidelights

Elicia Castaldi grew up in Rhode Island, near the Rhode
Island School of Design (RISD), and she was inspired
by the students she saw on campus who were following
their dreams to become artists. In 1997, Castaldi was
accepted into RISD, and since graduating she has established her career as an illustrator of children's books
while also serving as the art director of a prestigious urban department store.

In her first illustration project, the picture book *Miss
Polly Has a Dolly,* by Pamela Duncan Edwards, Castaldi
combines several elements. "Paint, collage, and computer graphics create simple figures and lots of patterns," explained Jane Marino in a review of the book
for *School Library Journal.* In *Publishers Weekly* a
critic commented that, in her debut, "Castaldi . . . creates loose collages of paper scraps, photos and crayony
lines."

Castaldi's signature collages feature prominently in
*Middle School Is Worse than Meatloaf: A Year Told
through Stuff.* Written by Newbery Honor-winning author Jennifer L. Holm, the novel combines prose with
patchwork images featuring bits and pieces of seventh-
grader Ginny's life: hair-dye boxes, drug-store receipts,
candy wrappers, report cards, newspaper clippings, and
the like. These images tell parts of Holm's story, such
as the day Ginny's disastrous dye job was repaired at a
local salon, and the tragedy of her dwindling bank
account. Noting the prominence of the artwork in the
storytelling, *School Library Journal* critic Diana Pierce
categorized *Middle School Is Worse than Meatloaf* as
"not quite a graphic novel but not a traditional narrative
either." Readers "enjoy piecing together the plot through
the bits and pieces of 'stuff' depicted in Castaldi's collages," wrote a *Kirkus Reviews* writer, while a *Publishers Weekly* reviewer concluded that the book's "punchy
visuals and the sharp, funny details reel in the audience
and don't let go."

Biographical and Critical Sources

PERIODICALS

Booklist, October 15, 2007, Suzanne Harold, review of
    *Middle School Is Worse than Meatloaf: A Year Told
    through Stuff,* p. 48.
Bulletin of the Center for Children's Books, October, 2007,
    Karen Coats, review of *Middle School Is Worse than
    Meatloaf,* p. 89.
Kirkus Reviews, July 1, 2007, review of *Middle School Is
    Worse than Meatloaf.*
Publishers Weekly, December 8, 2003, review of *Miss
    Polly Has a Dolly,* p. 60; July 30, 2007, review of
    Middle School Is Worse than Meatloaf, p. 82.
School Library Journal, November, 2003, Jane Marino, re-
    view of *Mis Polly Has a Dolly,* p. 91; September,
    2007, Diana Pierce, review of *Middle School Is Worse
    than Meatloaf,* p. 198.

ONLINE

Elicia Castaldi Home Page, http://www.eliciacastaldi.com
    (October 27, 2008).*

*   *   *

COCCA-LEFFLER, Maryann 1958-

Personal

Born July 25, 1958, in Everett, MA; daughter of Theodore F. (an engineer) and Rose (a homemaker) Cocca;
married Eric M. Leffler (in equipment rental), April 5,
1981; children: Janine, Kristin. *Education:* Massachusetts College of Art, B.F.A., 1980.

Maryann Cocca-Leffler (Photo by Kristin Leffler. Reproduced by permission.)

Addresses

Home—Amherst, NH. *E-mail*—MCLeffler@aol.com.

Career

Children's book illustrator and author.

Member

Society of Children's Book Writers and Illustrators.

Awards, Honors

Science Writing Award, American Institute of Physics, 1987, for *Splash! All about Baths;* Pick of the Lists citation, American Booksellers Association (ABA), for *Missing: One Stuffed Rabbit, Wanda's Roses, Mr. Tanen's Ties,* and *Bus Route to Boston;* Parents' Choice Approved Book designation, for *Bus Route to Boston;* Children's Book Award, Florida Reading Association, 2001, Hoosier Young Book Award, 2003, and Pick of the Lists citation, ABA, all for *Mr. Tanen's Ties;* Cooperative Children's Book Center Choice selection, 2008, for *Jack's Talent.*

Writings

SELF-ILLUSTRATED

Wednesday Is Spaghetti Day, Scholastic (New York, NY), 1990.

Grandma and Me (board book), Random House (New York, NY), 1990.

Ice Cold Birthday (easy reader), Grosset & Dunlap (New York, NY), 1992.

Count the Days till Christmas, Scholastic (New York, NY), 1993.

What a Pest! (easy reader), Grosset & Dunlap (New York, NY), 1994.

Clams All Year, Boyds Mills Press (Honesdale, PA), 1996.

Lots of Hearts, Grosset & Dunlap (New York, NY), 1996.

Silly Willy, Grosset & Dunlap (New York, NY), 1996.

Mommy Hugs, Little Simon (New York, NY), 1997.

Daddy Hugs, Little Simon (New York, NY), 1997.

Missing: One Stuffed Rabbit, Albert Whitman (Morton Grove, IL), 1998.

Princess for a Day, Grosset & Dunlap (New York, NY), 1998.

Mr. Tanen's Ties, Albert Whitman (Morton Grove, IL), 1999.

Jungle Halloween, Albert Whitman (Morton Grove, IL), 2000.

Bus Route to Boston, Boyds Mills Press (Honesdale, PA), 2000.

Edgar Degas: Paintings That Dance, Grosset & Dunlap (New York, NY), 2001.

Bravery Soup, Albert Whitman (Morton Grove, IL), 2002.

Mr. Tanen's Tie Trouble, Albert Whitman (Morton Grove, IL), 2003.

Calling All Cats, Grosset & Dunlap (New York, NY), 2004.

Dog Wash Day, Grosset & Dunlap (New York, NY), 2004.

Mr. Tanen's Ties Rule!, Albert Whitman (Morton Grove, IL), 2005.

Spotlight on Stacey, Kane Press (New York, NY), 2007.

Jack's Talent, Farrar, Straus & Giroux (New York, NY), 2007.

Princess K.I.M. and the Lie That Grew, Albert Whitman (Morton Grove, IL), 2009.

My Dance Recital, Random House (New York, NY), 2009.

Easter Bunny in Training, HarperCollins (New York, NY), 2009.

ILLUSTRATOR

Eileen Spinelli, *Thanksgiving at the Tappletons,* Addison Wesley (Reading, MA), 1982, re-illustrated edition, HarperCollins (New York, NY), 1992.

Susan Alton Schmeltz, *Oh So Silly!,* Parents Magazine Press (New York, NY), 1983.

Rita Goldan Gelman and Susan Kovacs Buxbaum, *Splash! All about Baths,* Little, Brown (Boston, MA), 1987.

Stephen Krensky, *Big Time Bears,* Little, Brown (Boston, MA), 1989.

Ruth Young, *A Trip to Mars,* Orchard Books (New York, NY), 1990.

Wendy Cheyette Lewison, *MUD,* Random House (New York, NY), 1990.

Marcia Leonard, *Alphabet Bandits,* Troll (Mahwah, NJ), 1990.

My ABC's at Home (board book), Grosset & Dunlap (New York, NY), 1990.

Marcia Leonard, *The Kitten Twins,* Troll (Mahwah, NJ), 1990.

These Are Baby's Things, Random House (New York, NY), 1990.

Hey Diddle Diddle (nursery rhymes), Grosset & Dunlap (New York, NY), 1991.

John Schindel, *Something's Fishy,* Simon & Schuster (New York, NY), 1993.

The Elves and the Shoemaker, Grosset & Dunlap (New York, NY), 1993.

Pat Brisson, *Wanda's Roses,* Boyd's Mills Press (Honesdale, PA), 1994.

Wendy Cheyette Lewison, *Hello Snow!,* Grosset & Dunlap (New York, NY), 1994.

Eve Bunting, *I Don't Want to Go to Camp,* Boyds Mills Press (Honesdale, PA), 1996.

Eve Bunting, *My Backpack,* Boyds Mills Press (Honesdale, PA), 1997.

Michelle Poploff, *Tea Party for Two,* Delacorte Press (New York, NY), 1997.

Diane Cocca-Spofford, *The Good-Bye Game,* Infinity Plus One (Ridgewood, NJ), 1998.

Barbara Juster Esbensen, *Jumping Day,* Boyds Mills Press (Honesdale, PA), 1999.

Wendy Cheyette Lewison, *The Big Snowball,* Grosset & Dunlap (New York, NY), 2000.

Diane Cocca-Spofford, *Do You Love Me?,* Infinity Plus One (Ridgewood, NJ), 2001.

Judy Donnelly, *The Pilgrims and Me,* Grosset & Dunlap (New York, NY), 2002.

Michelle Knudsen, *Carl the Complainer,* Kane Press (New York, NY), 2005.

Gloria Koster, *The Peanut-free Café,* Albert Whitman (Morton Grove, IL), 2006.

Alice Mead, *Isabella's Above-ground Pool,* Kane Press (New York, NY), 2006.

Sidelights

Author and illustrator Maryann Cocca-Leffler is the creator of many self-illustrated titles, including *Mr. Tanen's Ties* and *Jack's Talent,* and the illustrator of more than twenty others, such as Gloria Koster's *The Peanut-free Café.* Known for the bright colors and cheerful presentation of her artwork and her simple, clear texts, which are appropriate for beginning readers, Cocca-Leffler once told *SATA:* "As long as I can remember, I've always wanted to be an artist. I used to draw and paint on anything; paper bags, rocks, sea-shells, and even a mural on my parent's garage door (my parents still regret the day I painted over it!)."

Born in 1958, in Everett, Massachusetts, the author grew up in an Italian family where, as she noted on her home page, "dinnertime was always a major feast. Many days you could find my mother, Rose, in the kitchen, rolling meatballs or my father, Ted, in his garden picking tomatoes." The second oldest of five children, Cocca-Leffler liked to play school, listen to the music of the Beatles, and draw and paint. She determined early on that she wanted to be an artist when she grew up. "I remember back in fourth grade, my teacher, Sis-

ter Isabel Thomas, saw promise in me as an artist and gave me my very first set of pastels," the author told *SATA.* "I still have them!"

Cocca-Leffler's everyday experiences also inspired her career as a children's author. For example, she learned early on that it is not good to tell a little lie, because lies grow. In second grade she told her classmates that her father owned the Coca-Cola Company. (He didn't.) That teeny tiny lie was the inspiration for her picture book *Princess K.I.M. and the Lie That Grew.*

"In high school, my Uncle Dan and I took sculpting classes at night," the future author also recalled to *SATA.* "He and my entire family were always encouraging. I always did well in school, but art class was my favorite. When it came time to decide on a college, I submitted my portfolio to Massachusetts College of Art. My parents were a bit worried; they couldn't believe anyone could make a living as an artist. I remember them saying, 'You need something to fall back on.' They suggested I try a liberal arts college. I wanted and needed intense art training, therefore I went on to study at Massachusetts College, majoring in illustration. During my junior year, my style began to take shape. It did not fit into the editorial role. While other illustration majors found it easy to depict 'the Iran-hostage-crisis,' I found it difficult. I remember a classmate saying, 'Maryann, you can never draw anything that looks MEAN!' Children book illustration, on the other hand, seemed to be a perfect fit for my style."

Cleaning out a corner of her parents' cellar, she turned it into a space for her first studio. She painted a bright

Illustration from Cocca-Leffler's 2009 picture book **Princess K.I.M and The Lie That Grew.** (Albert Whitman, 2009. Illustration copyright © 2009 by Maryann Cocca-Leffler. Courtesy of Maryann Cocca-Leffler.)

mural on the oil tank in the process, one of several she created as a young painter. For four years she used this dark cellar studio, all the while dreaming of becoming a children's book illustrator. "After graduation, I lined up several freelance elementary textbook jobs, one on an elementary math book for Houghton Mifflin," Cocca-Leffler further explained. "I drew a million little objects, but it was a start. Fearing that I would never make any real money as an illustrator, my father, with good intentions, got me a job, three days a week, drawing aircraft and missiles for a defense contractor. I lasted three months."

Finally Cocca-Leffler decided to freelance full-time. "I took many jobs just for the money, including drawing toilet plumbing supplies. But at the same time I continued to illustrate children's textbooks. I was determined to find work using my own style of illustration instead of styling my illustration to fit a job. I made the rounds with my portfolio to Boston-area publishers. In 1981 I got an offer to illustrate my first children's book, *Thanksgiving at the Tappletons.*" Written by Eileen Spinelli, this picture book deals with calamity in the preparation of Thanksgiving dinner at the Tappleton house. However, despite their difficulties, the family realizes that they do indeed have something to be thankful for. Reviewing the revised 1992 edition of *Thanksgiving at the Tappletons* in *Booklist*, Ilene Cooper found that the "art captures the slapstick fun" of Spinelli's text. Cocca-Leffler's artwork for this book set her off on her new career, but at first progress was slow.

"1981 was also the year I got married," the illustrator recalled. "When we returned from our honeymoon, my husband, Eric, played our phone number in the state lottery. We won $3,500! With the money we printed eight full-color greeting cards which I designed and started our own greeting card company, Marcel & Co. I worked in the greeting card business for the next five years, accumulating 100 of my own designs and selling them through sales representatives around the country. It was tough competing with the big guys, so we sold our line to a company in Arizona. My years illustrating greeting cards helped me establish my style and aided in the development of my characters. With these skills and the use of my greeting cards as a promotional tool, I was able to re-enter the children's book field. I have been illustrating and writing children's book ever since."

While creating artwork for other authors, Cocca-Leffler also turned her hand to her own self-illustrated title. "*Wednesday Is Spaghetti Day* was the first book I both wrote and illustrated. I got the idea when I was cat-sitting my cousin Laura's two cats. One day, after coming home to a mess, I said, 'I wonder what these cats do when you leave them home alone?' That's when the idea was born. Six years and seven publishers later, *Wednesday Is Spaghetti Day* was finally published." In Cocca-Leffler's debut picture book, Catrina the cat cannot wait until the Tremonte family leaves, for she has invited all her feline friends over for an Italian feast. When the guests arrive, Catrina tosses her cat food out and proceeds to put together a real Italian banquet. "I grew up in a close Italian family where there was always plenty of love, togetherness, and FOOD!" the author told *SATA*. "The recipe the cats use in *Wednesday Is Spaghetti Day* is my Mom's."

For *Grandma and Me*, Cocca-Leffler took inspiration not from her own childhood, but from that of her children. "*Grandma and Me* is based on my daughter Janine, who spent every Tuesday with her Nana Rose, so I could spend time in my studio. Ever since they were babies, I have enjoyed sharing books with my daughters." Cocca-Leffler's family has also inspired other original picture books "The two sisters in *Ice Cold Birthday* and its sequel *What a Pest!* are sometimes my two daughters and sometimes my sister and I. The idea for the ice cream-cookie cake in *Ice Cold Birthday* came from a hastily made cake we made for my sister when we forgot her birthday. And like in *What a Pest!*, I actually did get the chicken pox right before I was to perform on stage."

Clams All Year is based on one summer a young Cocca-Leffler and her family spent in Hull, Massachusetts. One night a big storm brought in lots of clams: so many, in fact, that the family was able to eat clams all year. Kathy Piehl, writing in *School Library Journal*, commended the book's artwork, which, she said, captures "the love and exuberance of an extended family." A contributor for *Publishers Weekly* similarly concluded that Cocca-Leffler's "simply told tale of a close-knit family has a timeless, understated warmth."

As her children grew, they provided ideas for more self-illustrated titles, including *Missing: One Stuffed Rabbit* and *Jungle Halloween*. An experience her daughter Janine had in the first grade brought about *Missing*. In her class, one of the students got to take the prized Coco home each night and write about the events in a diary. In the fictional Janine's case, this visit is cut short when the rabbit is lost in a mall, and when she later learns that the toy has been given as part of a toy distribution to a hospital, the students agree that the wheelchair-bound girl who gets Coco should keep the stuffed animal. "There is plenty to look at here—and sharp eyes will spot where and when Coco gets lost," wrote Cooper. DeAnn Tabuchi also lauded the "bold, colorful" artwork in a *School Library Journal* review of *Missing*, calling it "appealing, as is the totally satisfying conclusion."

Cocca-Leffler's daughter Kristin's fourth birthday party is depicted in *Princess for a Day*, while a jungle mural the author painted on her bedroom wall prompted *Jungle Halloween*. In the latter picture book, rhyming verses relate the tale of jungle animals who get all dressed up for a Halloween party. In *School Library Journal* Linda M. Kenton commented that Cocca-Leffler's book stays

Cocca-Leffler introduces readers to a fun-loving teacher at work in her colorful picture book **Mr. Tanen's Ties Rule!** (Albert Whitman & Company, 2005. Illustration copyright © 2005 by Maryann Cocca-Leffler. Reproduced by permission.)

away from traditional Halloween motifs which "can easily frighten preschoolers," and went on to call *Jungle Halloween* a "surefire showstopper for storytimes."

Mr. Tanen's Ties "is based on the REAL Mr. Tanen, who is the principal of my daughters' former elementary school," Cocca-Leffler noted on her home page. In the book, the beloved principal of Lynnhurst School is very well known for wearing brightly colored and unusual ties to announce various events. However, Mr. Tanen's boss, Mr. Apple, is not so approving; He orders Tanen to get rid of this neckwear and don a more-sensible, plain blue tie. When Mr. Tanen takes some time off, Mr. Apple substitutes for him, and the students manage to give the dour man some zany neckwear of his own, with miraculous results. This award-winning title was praised by a critic in *Kirkus Reviews* for making the world of adults "a lot less formidable, and a lot more eccentric." In *Booklist* Cooper lauded Cocca-Leffler's "fresh and upbeat" book, calling its artwork "just as bright as Mr. Tanen's ties."

In a sequel, *Mr. Tanen's Tie Trouble,* the principal helps rescue his school from financial difficulties by offering to sell his collection of almost 1,000 wacky neckties. The townspeople show up in force at the auction, which earns enough money to pay for a new playground, and Mr. Tanen receives a wonderful surprise at the ribbon-

cutting ceremony. A contributor in *Kirkus Reviews* praised Cocca-Leffler's "snappy and smiling watercolor-and-chalk illustrations," and *School Library Journal* critic Kristin de Lacoste similarly noted that the "bright and vivid watercolor illustrations perfectly portray the details of the cheerful neckwear in this upbeat story." Students and teachers at Lynnhurst School switch roles for a day, just as a federal official pays a surprise visit, in *Mr. Tanen's Ties Rule!* "Gaily colored neckties flutter through a set of splashy watercolor school scenes," noted a contributor in *Kirkus Reviews.*

A young girl is the fictional author of a school report on a French impressionist painter in *Edgar Degas: Paintings That Dance,* part of the "Smart about Art" series. The book, like others in the series, uses the school report format to tell the events of the artist's life, and it also employs reproductions as well as child-like cartoons to illustrate the "report." In *Booklist* Gillian Engberg wrote of *Edgar Degas* that the book serves up a "successful blend of fact and humor that makes sophisticated concepts completely accessible and even entertaining," while a *Publishers Weekly* critic cited the "clear, accessible format" of the series.

Cocca-Leffler reverts once again to her early childhood experiences for *Bus Route to Boston.* "I grew up on a bus route," she noted on her home page. "As a young girl, I remember frequent Saturday bus trips, which traveled down our street, through crowded neighborhoods, over the bridge, then all the way to Boston. My mother, sister, and I went bargain hunting in Filene's Basement, enjoyed ice cream at Bailey's, shopped for vegetables at Haymarket, and ventured into the North End for pizza and cannoli. Through my story and paintings I have shared these warm childhood memories." In the book, a day on the bus extends from the first meeting with Bill the driver to stops at all of the special places from Cocca-Leffler's memory, ending with a homecoming in late afternoon. Cooper praised the book as a "warm, loving memoir [that] will have plenty of resonance for today's children," and further commented that the "oversize, nicely crowded acrylic artwork . . . is lots of fun." Marianne Saccardi, reviewing the title for *School Library Journal,* similarly called attention to the "simple and unadorned" language and humorous art, dubbing *Bus Route to Boston* a "charming slice of life in a time past."

In *Bravery Soup* a young raccoon named Carlin is frightened by everything, even his own shadow. Carlin wants to sip some of Big Bear's Bravery Soup and become like this fearless animal. First, however, the raccoon must make a dangerous journey through the Forbidden Forest and up Skulk Mountain to the lair of a terrible monster in order to acquire a vital ingredient for the soup. Along the way, Carlin discovers that he already possesses bravery inside himself. Calling the work "a satisfying example of how facing fears helps to conquer them," *Booklist* critic Connie Fletcher noted that

Cocca-Leffler's use of "bright acrylics and humorous details" keep children from being too frightened by scary elements in the story. A reviewer for *Publishers Weekly* also felt that the illustrations "convey suspense as well as the warm friendship between the animal friends."

Cocca-Leffler developed the idea for *Jack's Talent* after visiting a local elementary school. In the work, a youngster finds it difficult to identify his special skill while introducing himself to his new classmates, until his teacher notices his gift for memorization. "Cocca-Leffler's joyful paintings show the children engaged in their favorite activities," Susan Dove Lempke commented in *Horn Book*. "The artwork is cheerful," wrote Susan E. Murray in *School Library Journal*, "and the brief, repetitive text reads aloud smoothly."

In addition to her own books, Cocca-Leffler has also illustrated numerous titles by other authors. Koster's *The Peanut-free Café* centers on young Simon, who enjoys the same treat every day for lunch: a bagel smeared with peanut butter. When Grant, a new student with se-

vere food allergies, arrives at Simon's school, the principal opens a "peanut-free" zone in the cafeteria. When Simon notices how often Grant sits alone, he comes up with some clever ideas to make Grant's table a gathering place for other children. According to *School Library Journal*, reviewer Debbie Stewart Hoskins, "Cocca-Leffler's humorous and exuberant illustrations make the book fun." In *Isabella's Above-ground Pool*, a chapter book by Alice Mead, third-grader Isabella Speedwalker-Juarez faces a difficult adjustment to a new living situation, including the loss of her cherished swimming pool. A critic in *Kirkus Reviews* applauded the "lively cartoon-style drawings" by Cocca-Leffler.

"I haven't changed much since I was a kid . . . except I got older!" Cocca-Leffler noted on her home page. "I still think like an eight year old, which really helps when you write for kids." The author/illustrator concluded to *SATA:* "To be able to express these ideas and images through my books and at the same time experience the shared joy of illustrating is the best job in the world."

A young girl learns to appreciate American history in Cocca-Leffler's self-illustrated beginning reader Spotlight on Stacey.

Biographical and Critical Sources

PERIODICALS

Booklist, October 1, 1992, Ilene Cooper, review of *Thanksgiving at the Tappletons,* p. 338; June 1, 1996, Susan Dove Lempke, review of *Clams All Year,* p. 1730; March 15, 1998, Ilene Cooper, review of *Missing: One Stuffed Rabbit,* p. 1246; May 15, 1999, Ilene Cooper, review of *Mr. Tanen's Ties,* p. 1702; February 1, 2000, Ilene Cooper, review of *Bus Route to Boston,* p. 1028; September 1, 2000, Hazel Rochman, review of *Jungle Halloween,* p. 131; November 15, 2001, Gillian Engberg, review of *Edgar Degas: Paintings That Dance,* p. 572; April 15, 2002, Connie Fletcher, review of *Bravery Soup,* p. 1406; June 1, 2003, Kathy Broderick, review of *Mr. Tanen's Tie Trouble,* p. 1783; February 1, 2006, Ilene Cooper, review of *The Peanut-free Café,* p. 55; April 1, 2006, Kay Weisman, review of *Isabella's Above-ground Pool,* p. 49.

Horn Book, September-October, 2007, Susan Dove Lempke, review of *Jack's Talent,* p. 558.

Kirkus Reviews, March 15, 1999, review of *Mr. Tanen's Ties,* p. 449; February 15, 2002, review of *Bravery Soup,* p. 252; February 1, 2003, review of *Mr. Tanen's Ties Rules!,* p. 227; February 15, 2005, review of *Mr. Tanen's Tie Trouble,* p. 226; February 15, 2006, review of *The Peanut-free Café,* p. 185; April 1, 2006, review of *Isabella's Above-ground Pool,* p. 352; July 1, 2007, review of *Jack's Talent.*

Publishers Weekly, November 5, 1982, review of *Thanksgiving at the Tappletons;* May 27, 1996, review of *Clams All Year,* p. 78; May 12, 1997, review of *My Backpack,* p. 76; February 21, 2000, review of *Bus Route to Boston,* p. 87; September 25, 2000, review of *Jungle Halloween,* p. 62; November 19, 2001, review of *Edgar Degas,* p. 70; March 1, 2002, review of *Bravery Soup,* p. 70; August 13, 2007, review of *Jack's Talent,* p. 66.

School Library Journal, March, 1990, Laura Culberg, review of *Wednesday Is Spaghetti Day,* p. 189; July, 1996, Kathy Piehl, review of *Clams All Year,* pp. 57-58; February, 1998, Jan Shepherd Ross, review of *Tea Party for Two,* p. 90; May, 1998, DeAnn Tabuchi, review of *Missing,* p. 113; March, 1999, Shelley Woods, review of *Mr. Tanen's Ties,* pp. 171-172; April, 1999, Linda Ludke, review of *Jumping Day,* pp. 92-93; April, 2000, Marianne Saccardi, review of *Bus Route to Boston,* p. 94; September, 2000, Linda M. Kenton, review of *Jungle Halloween,* p. 186; November, 2001, Susan Lissim, review of *Edgar Degas,* p. 143; March, 2002, Maryann H. Owen, review of *Bravery Soup,* p. 173; May, 2003, Kristin de Lacoste, review of *Mr. Tanen's Tie Trouble,* p. 110; May, 2005, Mary Hazelton, review of *Mr. Tanen's Ties Rule!,* p. 79; May, 2006, Jennifer Cogan, review of *Isabella's Above-ground Pool,* p. 95; September, 2006, Debbie Stewart Hoskins, review of *The Peanut-free Café,* p. 176; June, 2007, Gina Powell, review of *Spotlight on Stacey,* p. 94; November, 2007, Susan E. Murray, review of *Jack's Talent,* p. 87.

ONLINE

Boyds Mills Press Web site, http://www.boydsmillspress. com/ (April 9, 2002), "Maryann Cocca-Leffler."

Maryann Cocca-Leffler Web log, http://www.marethings. blogspot.com/ (September 30, 2008).

Maryann Cocca-Leffler Home Page, http://www.maryann coccaleffler.com (September 30, 2008).

*   *   *

COHN, Diana

Personal

Female. *Education:* Columbia University, M.Ed.

Addresses

E-mail—diana@dreamcarver.org.

Career

Author and educator. The Bee Works (environmental organization), cofounder, with Stephen L. Buchmann.

Member

National Writers Union.

Awards, Honors

Smithsonian magazine Notable Books for Children designation, 2002, for *Dream Carver;* Jane Addams Honor Book designation, Skipping Stones Award, and Best of Beyond Difference Award, all for *Sí, se puede!/ Yes, We Can!;* (with Stephen L. Buchmann and Paul Mirocha) Paterson Prize for Books for Young People honor, 2008, for *The Bee Tree.*

Writings

Dream Carver, illustrated by Amy Cordova, Chronicle (San Francisco, CA), 2002.

Sí, se puede!/Yes, We Can!: Janitor Strike in L.A., illustrated by Francisco Delgado, Cinco Puntos (El Paso, TX), 2002.

Mr. Goethe's Garden, illustrated by Paul Mirocha, Bell Pond (Great Barrington, MA), 2003.

(With Stephen L. Buchmann) *The Bee Tree,* illustrated by Paul Mirocha, Cinco Puntos (El Paso, TX), 2007.

Sidelights

Author and educator Diana Cohn writes picture books with themes that encourage readers to believe in themselves and stand up for what is right. Her first book, *Dream Carver,* was inspired by real-life wood-carver Manuel Jimenez. In the story, Mateo, a young wood-carver, follows his dream and creates life-size wooden animals painted in brilliant colors that are strikingly different from the traditional miniature figurines he has been taught to make. Although his father disapproves, Mateo is rewarded when his animals are well loved at a festival, and others recognize the value of his art. *Dream Carver* "shows how imagination can become a compelling force for change," wrote Ann Welton in *School Library Journal.* Coop Renner, writing for the same periodical, maintained that *Dream Carver* "opens a new way of seeing," and a *Publishers Weekly* critic concluded that "Cohn captures the boy's pursuit with straightforward eloquence" in her English/Spanish text. In *Booklist* Julie Cummins concluded that Cohn's text and the colorful illustrations by Amy Cordova "do justice to the vibrant Mexican art form."

With *Sí, se puede!/ Yes, We Can!,* Cohn expanded into a fully bilingual book, telling the story of the workers' strike in Los Angeles that took place during the 1980s. Told from the point of view of Carlito, whose mother is one of the janitors on strike, the story offers an understanding of why the workers needed to go on strike and shows how Carlito grows to support his mother in her efforts to gain fair pay. Cohn "does an admirable job of explaining . . . why the strike is necessary," wrote Maria Otero-Boisvert in *School Library Journal,* and in

Diana Cohn joins scientist Stephen L. Buchmann to tell a fascinating story in **The Bee Tree,** *a picture book featuring art by Paul Mirocha.* (Cinco Puntos Press, www.cincopuntos.com, 2007. Illustration copyright © 2007 by Paul Mirocha. Reproduced by permission.)

Booklist Hazel Rochman deemed Cohn's text for *Sí, se puede!* "political and passionate."

As a hobbyist beekeeper, Cohn became interested in the honey-hunting tradition of the indigenous people of Malaysia, and she teams up with entomologist Stephen L. Buchmann to describe both the process and the myth behind it in *The Bee Tree.* Cohn met Buchmann while she was working on a radio documentary about North America's pollination crisis. Together, the scientist and writer co-founded an education organization, The Bee Works, to help people become better informed about pollination ecology. *The Bee Tree* also educates readers on the subject as Buchmann and Cohn supplement their story about a young boy learning the honey-collecting traditions with facts and photographs about Malaysia's rainforest. "Although the story can stand alone, this additional information adds significantly to the book's effectiveness," wrote Kathy Piehl in *School Library Journal.*

Biographical and Critical Sources

PERIODICALS

Booklist, June 1, 2002, Julie Cummins, review of *Dream Carver,* p. 1721; October 1, 2002, Hazel Rochman, review of *Sí, se puede!/ Yes, We Can!: Janitor Strike in L.A.,* p. 334.
Bulletin of the Center for Children's Books, October, 2002, review of *Dream Carver,* p. 53.
Kirkus Reviews, June 1, 2002, review of *Dream Carver,* p. 802.
Publishers Weekly, April 29, 2002, review of *Dream Carver,* p. 70; September 9, 2002, review of *Sí, se puede!,* p. 71.
School Library Journal, July, 2002, Ann Welton, review of *Dream Carver,* p. 86; August, 2002, Maria Otero-Boisvert, review of *Sí, se puede!,* p. S61; November, 2002, Ann Welton, review of *Sí, se puede!,* p. 152; July, 2005, Coop Renner, review of *Dream Carver,* p. 43, and review of *Sí, se puede!,* p. 44; July, 2007, Kathy Piehl, review of *The Bee Tree,* p. 67.
Tribune Books (Chicago, IL), July 21, 2002, review of *Dream Carver,* p. 5.

ONLINE

Cinco Puntos Press Web site, http://www.cincopuntos.com/ (October 27, 2008), "Diana Cohn."
Diana Cohn Home Page, http://www.dreamcarver.org (October 27, 2008).*

*   *   *

COLLINS, Yvonne

Personal

Born in Canada; married. *Education:* University of Toronto, B.A. (criminology).

Addresses

Home—Canada.

Career

Writer and member of film crews. Worked as television production assistant, 1981-83, and on camera crews for film and television, beginning 1994.

Awards, Honors

Woody Award, Panavision Canada, 2003.

Writings

YOUNG-ADULT NOVELS

(With Sandy Rideout) *Introducing Vivien Leigh Reid: Daughter of the Diva,* St. Martin's Press (New York, NY), 2005.

(With Sandy Rideout) *Now Starring Vivien Leigh Reid: Diva in Training,* St. Martin's Press (New York, NY), 2006.

(With Sandy Rideout) *The Black Sheep,* Hyperion (New York, NY), 2007.

(With Sandy Rideout) *The New and Improved Vivien Leigh Reid: Diva in Control,* St. Martin's Press (New York, NY), 2007.

(With Sandy Rideout) *Girl v. Boy,* Hyperion (New York, NY), 2008.

NONFICTION

(With Sandy Rideout) *Totally Me: The Teenage Girl's Survival Guide,* Adams Media Corporation (Holbrook, MA), 2000.

ADULT NOVELS

(With Sandy Rideout) *Speechless,* Red Dress Ink (Don Mills, Ontario, Canada), 2004.

(With Sandy Rideout) *What I Really Want to Do Is Direct,* Red Dress Ink (Don Mills, Ontario, Canada), 2005.

Sidelights

It took Yvette Collins a while to figure out what she wanted to do as a career. She earned her B.A. from the University of Toronto in criminology and hoped to go into law enforcement. "Fortunately for the citizens of Toronto, I flunked the psychological profile," the Canadian writer admitted on the home page she shares with writing partner and friend Sandy Rideout. Collins also worked at a restaurant, where she met her future husband, before establishing a career as a camera crew member for television and feature films. In addition to writing with Rideout, Collins has worked on such well-known films as *Titanic, Blues Brothers 2000,* and *Chicago.*

The teen novel series by Yvonne Collins and Sally Rideout includes **The New And Improved Vivien Leigh Reid,** *featuring artwork by Wai.* (St. Martin's Press, 2007. Cover art by Wai. Reproduced by permission.)

Though Collins and Rideout met as teens while volunteering together at their local public library, it was not until Collins' niece asked them to put some of their sage wisdom on paper that they became coauthors. Their first book, *Totally Me: The Teenage Girl's Survival Guide,* shares their time-tested advice regarding the common travails of teen girls.

In their first novel for teens, Collins and Rideout drew on Collins's experience in the film industry. *Introducing Vivian Leigh Reid: Daughter of the Diva* introduces fifteen-year-old Leigh, who is the daughter of a movie star. In the book, her father ships her off to Ireland to stay with her actress mother, a woman who she barely knows. When Leigh arrives, she is given a bit part in the film her mom is starring in. The opportunity gives the estranged mother and daughter a chance to bond, despite jealousies and a very close living space, and the experience leaves them with matching tattoos and quality memories. "The story is witty, unpredictable, and well written," wrote Amanda MacGregor in her *Kliatt* review of *Introducing Vivian Leigh Reid.* Cindy Welch, writing in *Booklist,* called Leigh "a likable, spunky American teen."

Leigh's adventures in film continue in *Now Starring Vivien Leigh Reid: Diva in Training.* Bitten by the acting bug, Leigh decides to spend the summer of her sixteenth year in Los Angeles, taking an acting course and staying with her mom. After landing the role of a British snob in a soap-opera, the teen has trouble separating her character's bad attitude from her own behavior. Despite her mother's diva tendencies, the movie star offers Leigh the advice she needs to keep the role from getting the best of her. "This volume is pop-culture fun with a moral," wrote Tracy Karbel in *School Library Journal.* In *The New and Improved Vivien Leigh Reid* Leigh's mom becomes engaged to a film producer who offers the teen a role on his television show. Determined to prove that she can be an actress without a bad attitude, she jumps at the chance, landing a part that casts her as a humanoid warthog and means she must perform stunts in an awkward costume. "Leigh is a likeable, funny, and realistic heroine," wrote Amanda MacGregor in her *Kliatt* review of the budding actress's third book-length adventure.

Another area of the television industry is the setting for *The Black Sheep,* the name of both the book and the reality television program that fifteen-year-old Kendra Bishop tries out for in order to get away from her boring, uptight family. Tired of New York, Kendra is delighted to switch places with Maya, daughter of California hippies and sister to a dreamboat would-be marine biologist. With her every move recorded on film by a producer who wants to keep the drama high, Kendra develops a crush on Maya's brother Mitch, but also develops a deep concern for the sea otters her surrogate parents are fighting to save. "Kendra's bright and breezy first-person narration moves things along at a rapid clip," wrote a contributor to *Publishers Weekly,* and a *Kirkus Reviews* critic called Kendra "an admirable character who discovers inner strength."

Biographical and Critical Sources

PERIODICALS

Booklist, March 1, 2004, Kristine Huntley, review of *Speechless,* p. 1144; June 1, 2005, Cindy Welch, review of *Introducing Vivien Leigh Reid: Daughter of the Diva,* p. 1781; December 15, 2005, Kristine Huntley, review of *What I Really Want to Do Is Direct,* p. 29; May 15, 2007, Ilene Cooper, review of *The Black Sheep,* p. 39.
Kirkus Reviews, May 1, 2007, review of *The Black Sheep.*
Kliatt, July, 2005, Amanda MacGregor, review of *Introducing Vivien Leigh Reid,* p. 19; May, 2007, Amanda MacGregor, review of *The New and Improved Vivien Leigh Reid: Diva in Control,* p. 22.
Publishers Weekly, May 28, 2007, review of *The Black Sheep,* p. 64.
School Library Journal, September, 2005, Suzanne Gordon, review of *Introducing Vivien Leigh Reid,* p. 202; January, 2006, Tracy Karbel, review of *Now Starring Vivien Leigh Reid: Diva in Training,* p. 129; March, 2007, Laurie Slagenwhite, review of *The New and Improved Vivien Leigh Reid,* p. 206; September, 2007, Jeffrey Hastings, review of *The Black Sheep,* p. 194.
Voice of Youth Advocates, April, 2006, Lucy Schall, review of *Now Starring Vivien Leigh Reid,* p. 40.

ONLINE

Yvonne Collins and Sandy Rideout Home Page, http://www.collinsrideout.com (October 27, 2008).*

*   *   *

CROGGON, Alison 1962-

Personal

Born 1962, in South Africa; married Daniel Keene (a playwright); children: three, including Josh.

Addresses

Home—Melbourne, Victoria, Australia. *E-mail*—ajcroggon@aapt.net.au; ajcroggon@bigpond.com.

Career

Writer, poet, playwright, editor, and critic. Poetry editor for *Overland Extra,* 1992, *Modern Writing,* 1992-94, and *Voices,* 1996; founding editor of literary arts journal *Masthead.* Previously worked as a journalist for *Herald,* Melbourne, Victoria, Australia. Board member for Keene/Taylor Theatre Project, 1997-2001; member of artistic counsel for Malthouse Theatre, Melbourne, 2005-06; 2000 Australia Council writer-in-residence at Cambridge University, Cambridge England.

Awards, Honors

Anne Elder and Dame Mary Gilmore prizes, both 1991, both for *This Is the Stone;* Highly Commended designation, Vogel/Australian National Literary Award, 1995, for *Navigatio;* Pushcart Prize nomination, 2003, for *Attempts at Being;* Aurealis Award shortlist, for *The Gift;* grants and fellowships from Australia Council, Victorian Ministry for the Arts, and Victorian Council for the Arts.

Writings

(Author of text) *The Burrow: Opera in Prologue and Five Scenes,* introductory note by Elliot Gyger, Pellinor (Sydney, New South Wales, Australia), 1994.
(Author of text, with Daniel Keene and Jacinta le Plastrier) *Skinless Kiss of Angels* (audio CD), score by Michael Smetanin, ABC Classics, 1995.
Navigatio (novella), Black Pepper (North Fitzroy, Victoria, Australia), 1996.

Lenz (play; based on the novella by Georg Buchner), produced in Melbourne, Victoria, Australia, 1996.

(Author of lyrics) *Confidentially Yours* (musical), produced in Australia, 1998.

(Author of libretto) *Gauguin,* music by Michael Smetanin, produced at Melbourne International Festival of the Arts (Melbourne, Victoria, Australia), 2000.

Blue (play), produced in Canberra, Australia Capital Territory, Australia), 2001.

POETRY

This Is the Stone (published with *Pharaohs Returning* by Fiona Perry), Penguin Books (New York, NY), 1991.

The Blue Gate, Black Pepper (North Fitzroy, Victoria, Australia), 1997.

Mnemosyne, Wild Honey (County Wicklow, Ireland), 2002.

Attempts at Being, Salt (Applecross, WA), 2002.

The Common Flesh: New and Selected Poems, Arc (Todmorden, England), 2003.

November Burning, Vagabond Press (Newton, New South Wales, Australia), 2004.

Ash, Cusp Books (Los Angeles, CA), 2006.

Also author of *Monologues for an Apocalypse,* aired on ABC Radio National in Australia, 2001. Contributor of poetry to numerous anthologies, chapbooks, and periodicals.

Author's works have also been published in England and Germany.

"PELLINOR" YOUNG-ADULT FANTASY NOVEL SERIES

The Gift, Penguin Books (Camberwell, Victoria, Australia), 2002, published as *The Naming,* Candlewick Press (Cambridge, MA), 2005.

The Riddle, Penguin Books (Camberwell, Victoria, Australia), 2004, Candlewick Press (Cambridge, MA), 2006.

The Crow, Penguin Books (Camberwell, Victoria, Australia), 2006.

The Singing, Penguin Books (Camberwell, Victoria, Australia), 2008, Candlewick Press (New York, NY), 2009.

Adaptations

Poems have been adapted for music.

Sidelights

Alison Croggon is a prolific Australian writer whose work includes poetry, plays, opera libretti, and fantasy fiction. Croggon's interest in fantasy began as a child when she read *The Lord of the Rings* by J.R.R. Tolkien. Despite her interest in this genre, Croggon turned to writing poetry and plays and did not begin writing fantasy until 1999 when her son Josh was old enough to also read Tolkien's classic trilogy.

The first book in Croggon's projected "Pellinor" quartet was published in Australia as *The Gift* and in the United States as *The Naming.* The story, told in the form of a found document, focuses on sixteen-year-old slave Maerad. When she encounters a mysterious stranger named Bard Cadvan, the man offers to help her escape from the small mountain village where she is held. As the story progresses, Maerad discovers her true heritage and learns that she has magical powers, which she eventually uses to help her newfound friends, including her long-lost brother.

Critics generally praised Croggon's first foray into fantasy. Carolyn Phelan, writing in *Booklist,* noted that in *The Naming* the author "makes good use of imagery in her writing." Other critics also extolled *The Naming,* including Leslie Farmer who wrote in *Kliatt:* "This fantasy is a solid winner. The characters are well developed, and the plot twists keep the reader engaged." In addition, the author's ability to create a fantasy realm that nevertheless seems realistic was widely noted by reviewers. For example, Beth L. Meister, writing in *School Library Journal,* commented that Croggon "has created a world that is both authentic and exotic, welcoming and frightening," and a *Kirkus Reviews* contributor referred to *The Naming* as "a lush, vivid epic."

In *The Riddle,* a sequel to *The Naming,* Maerad has discovered that she is a bard. Now she is pursuing the mystery of the Treesong even as she deals with the fact that her ultimate destiny is to be the Chosen One. She is aided in her search by her original rescuer, Bard Cadvan, until he is lost in an avalanche. The story then follows Maerad as she travels on her own, confronting her weaknesses and powers as she battles against time and the takeover of the kingdom. In *Kliatt* Farmer noted that "fantasy readers will probably enjoy this saga." Other critics also noted the book's appeal to lovers of fantasy, Cristi Voth writing in *School Library Journal* that *The Riddle* is "an engrossing world that fantasy aficionados will be eager to revisit." A *Kirkus Reviews* contributor noted that the author's "world is rich and passionate, brimming with archetypal motifs but freshly splendorous in its own right." As with the first book, reviewers of *The Riddle* commented on the author's indebtedness to Tolkien and *The Lord of the Rings,* with *Booklist* reviewer Carolyn Phelan writing that Croggon's "respect for Tolkien's trilogy shows clearly in the book's conception, structure, and . . . backstory notes."

Biographical and Critical Sources

PERIODICALS

Booklist, May 1, 2005, Carolyn Phelan, review of *The Naming,* p. 1579; November 1, 2006, Carolyn Phelan, review of *The Riddle,* p. 41.

Bookseller, January 16, 2004, Claudia Mody, review of *The Gift,* p. 37.

Kirkus Reviews, June 1, 2005, review of *The Naming,* p. 634; August 15, 2006, review of *The Riddle,* p. 838.

Kliatt, July, 2005, Lesley Farmer, review of *The Naming,* p. 10; September, 2006, Lesley Farmer, review of *The Riddle,* p. 8.

School Library Journal, October, 2005, Beth L. Meister, review of *The Naming,* p. 157; January, 2007, Cristi Voth, review of *The Riddle,* p. 126.

ONLINE

Alison Croggon Home Page, http://www.alisoncroggon. com (October 28, 2008).

Walker Books Web site, http:// www.walkerbooks.co.uk/ (October 28, 2008), "Alison Croggon."*

*   *   *

CURREY, Anna

Personal

Born in Norfolk, England; married; children: Elinor, Pamela. *Hobbies and other interests:* Sculpture, printmaking,

Addresses

Home—England.

Career

Illustrator and author of children's books.

Writings

SELF-ILLUSTRATED

Tickling Tigers, Barron's Educational (Hauppauge, NY), 1996.

Barnaby's Surprise, Piccadilly Press (London, England), 1997.

Albertine, Hodder Children's (London, England), 1997.

Truffle's Christmas, Orchard Books (New York, NY), 2000.

Truffle Goes to Town, David Bennett (St. Albans, England), 2002.

Jasper's Bath, Oxford University Press (Oxford, England), 2004.

ILLUSTRATOR

Diane Wilmer, *Mr Pepino's Cabbage,* Collins (London, England), 1989.

Toby Forward, *Storm Magic,* Simon & Schuster (London, England), 1991.

Kaye Umanksy, *Sophie and Abigail,* Gollancz (London, England), 1995, Good Books (Intercourse, PA), 2004.

Kaye Umanksy, *Sophie in Charge,* Gollancz (London, England), 1995, Good Books (Intercourse, PA), 2005.

Kaye Umanksy, *Sophie and the Mother's Day Card,* Gollancz (London, England), 1995, Good Books (Intercourse, PA), 2005.

Kaye Umanksy, *Sophie and the Wonderful Picture,* Gollancz (London, England), 1995, Good Books (Intercourse, PA), 2004.

Vivian French, *Squeaky Cleaners in a Hole!,* Hodder Children's (London, England), 1996.

Vivian French, *Squeaky Cleaners in a Tip!,* Hodder Children's (London, England), 1996.

Vivian French, *Squeaky Cleaners in a Stew!,* Hodder Children's (London, England), 1996.

Vivian French, *Squeaky Cleaners in a Muddle!,* Hodder Children's (London, England), 1996.

Maurice Jones, *Welcome Home, Little Bear,* Oxford University Press (Oxford, England), 1997, Barron's (Hauppauge, NY), 1998.

Alison Green, editor, *Macmillan Treasury of Nursery Rhymes and Poems,* foreword by Roger McGough, Macmillan Children's (London, England), 1998.

Rose Impey, *TJ's Sunflower Race,* Hodder Children's (London, England), 1999.

Rose Impey, *TJ's Accident,* Hodder Children's (London, England), 1999.

Rose Impey, *TJ and the Baby Bird,* Hodder Children's (London, England), 1999.

Rose Impey, *TJ and the Great Snail Show,* Hodder Children's (London, England), 1999.

I Want Another Little Brother: Poems about Families, notes by Pie Corbett, Macmillan Children's (London, England), 1999, Puffin (New York, NY), 2001.

Pop Goes the Weasel: Nonsense Rhymes, Macmillan Children's (London, England), 1999.

If You Should Meet a Crocodile: Poems about Wild Animals, Macmillan Children's (London, England), 1999.

One, Two, Buckle My Shoe: Action and Counting Poems, Macmillan Children's (London, England), 1999.

Scharlotte Rich, *Who Made the Wild Woods?,* WaterBrook (Colorado Springs, CO), 1999.

Mary Hoffman, reteller, *Macmillan Treasury of Nursery Stories,* Macmillan Children's (London, England), 2000.

Cock a Doodle Do!: Farmyard Poems, Macmillan Children's (London, England), 2000.

Mary Hoffman, reteller, *The Gingerbread Man and Other Stories,* Macmillan Children's (London, England), 2001.

Mary Hoffman, reteller, *Puss in Boots and Other Stories,* Macmillan Children's (London, England), 2001.

Miriam Moss, *I Forgot to Say I Love You,* Macmillan Children's (London, England), 2003, published as *Don't Forget I Love You,* Dial (New York, NY), 2004.

Julia Donaldson, *One Ted Falls out of Bed,* Macmillan Children's (London, England), 2004, Holt (New York, NY), 2006.

Julia Donaldson, *Rosie's Hat,* Macmillan Children's (London, England), 2005.

Donna Jo Napoli, *The Wishing Club: A Story about Fractions,* Holt (New York, NY), 2007.

Donna Jo Napoli and Richard Tchen, *Corkscrew Counts: A Story about Multiplication,* Holt (New York, NY), 2008.

Miriam Moss, *Bedtime, Billy Bear!,* Macmillan Children's (London, England), 2007, published as *A Babysitter for Billy Bear,* Dial (New York, NY), 2008.

Sidelights

Born in Norfolk, England and raised in Ireland, Anna Currey spent much of her childhood drawing the animals she found around her home. As an adult, she exercises her native artistic talent by illustrating children's books for writers such as Mary Hoffman, Julia Donaldson, Rose Impey, Kaye Umansky, and Donna Jo Napoli. In *Booklist* Hazel Rochman commented of the artist's work for Napoli's *The Wishing Club: A Story about Fractions* that "Currey's soft-toned ink-and-watercolor illustrations show the complex number patterns in small diagrams." Reviewing the same title, a *Kirkus Reviews* critic praised the artist for her ability to "capture the wonder and puzzlement in the children's faces as they ponder their wishing star."

Currey's collaborations with Donaldson include *One Ted Falls out of Bed,* a counting book in which the objects being counted were described in *Kirkus Reviews* as "large and easy for young listeners to spot and count." Marge Loch-Wouters commented of the same work in *School Library Journal* that "the toys in the airy illustrations that sweep across the pages are packed with personality."

Currey joins Miriam Moss to produce the picture books *Don't Forget I Love You* and *A Babysitter for Billy Bear.* A critic for *Publishers Weekly* noted that Currey's images for the first-named title depict "a timeless, idealized world, but includes enough familiar details to make the story feel contemporary." Similarly, a contributor to *Kirkus Reviews* described Currey's illustrations for *A Babysitter for Billy Bear* as "instantly recognizable to young readers; homey kitchen scenes and the wild disarray of Billy's bedroom are familiar landmarks."

Umansky is a popular author in her native England, and Currey has illustrated several of her humorous picture books featuring a friendly character named Sophie. The artist's illustrations for *Sophie and the Wonderful Picture* were described by Ken Marantz in *School Arts* as "light-hearted," while *Sophie and the Mother's Day Card* features what a *Kirkus Reviews* critic described as "soft-focus watercolor-and-ink illustrations [that] are an excellent match to the tone and setting of the text."

Biographical and Critical Sources

PERIODICALS

Booklist, October 15, 1996, Ilene Cooper, review of *Tickling Tigers,* p. 432; September 15, 2000, Kathy Broderick, review of *Truffle's Christmas,* p. 247; January 1, 2005, Terry Glover, review of *Don't Forget I Love You,* p. 878; June 1, 2006, Kathy Broderick, review of *One Ted Falls out of Bed,* p. 80; June 1, 2007, Hazel Rochman, review of *The Wishing Club: A Story about Fractions,* p. 87.

Canadian Review of Materials, September 17, 1999, review of *The Macmillan Treasury of Nursery Rhymes and Poems.*

Horn Book, July-August, 2006, Kitty Flynn, review of *One Ted Falls out of Bed,* p. 424.

Kirkus Reviews, December 15, 2003, review of *Don't Forget I Love You,* p. 1453; May 15, 2005, review of *Sophie and the Mother's Day Card,* p. 360; May 15, 2006, review of *One Ted Falls out of Bed,* p. 516; June 15, 2007, review of *The Wishing Club.*

New Statesman, December 4, 1998, review of *The Macmillan Treasury of Nursery Rhymes and Poems,* p. 62.

Publishers Weekly, February 22, 1999, review of *Who Made the Wild Woods?,* p. 85; September 25, 2000, Elizabeth Devereaux, review of *Truffle's Christmas,* p. 68; December 15, 2003, review of *Don't Forget I Love You,* p. 46; May 22, 2006, review of *One Ted Falls out of Bed,* p. 50.

School Arts, October, 2004, Ken Marantz, review of *Sophie and the Wonderful Picture,* p. 66.

School Library Journal, October, 2000, review of *Truffle's Christmas,* p. 58; February, 2004, Marianne Saccardi, review of *Don't Forget I Love You,* p. 120; June, 2006, Marge Loch-Wouters, review of *One Ted Falls out of Bed,* p. 110; September, 2007, Mary Jean Smith, review of *The Wishing Club,* p. 172.

Times Educational Supplement, November 20, 1998, review of *The Macmillan Treasury of Nursery Rhymes and Poems,* p. 11.

ONLINE

Pan Macmillan Web site, http://www.panmacmillan.com/ (October 27, 2008), profile of Currey.*

D

DILLON, Diane 1933-

Personal

Born March 13, 1933, in Glendale, CA; daughter of Adelbert Paul (a teacher) and Phyllis (a pianist) Sorber; married Leo Dillon (an artist and illustrator), March 17, 1957; children: Lionel ("Lee"). *Education:* Attended Los Angeles City College, 1951-52, and Skidmore College, 1952-53; attended American Institute of Graphic Arts, 1955; Parsons School of Design, degree, 1956; attended School of Visual Arts, 1957.

Addresses

Home—Brooklyn, NY.

Career

Artist and illustrator. Dave Fris Advertising Agency, Albany, NY, staff artist, 1956-57; freelance artist and illustrator, 1957—; School of Visual Arts, instructor, 1971-74. *Exhibitions:* Gallery on the Green, Boston, MA; Metropolitan Museum, New York, NY; Boulder Center for the Visual Arts, Boulder, CO; Butler Institute of American Art, Youngstown, OH; Delaware Art Museum, Wilmington; Bratislava Book Show, Bratislava, Slovakia; American Institute of Graphic Arts, New York, NY; Art Directors Club of New York; Brooklyn Public Library, Brooklyn, NY; New York Historical Society; Earthlight Gallery, Boston; The Pentagon, Washington, DC; Delaware Museum, Washington, DC; Society of Illustrators, NY; and National Center for Children's Illustrated Literature, Abilene, TX. Artist of stained-glass ceiling in Eagle Gallery, New York, NY.

Member

Society of Illustrators (president, 1987-89), Graphic Artists Guild (president, 1981-83).

Awards, Honors

All with husband, Leo Dillon: Children's Spring Book Festival Honor Book designation, *New York Herald Tribune,* 1963, for *Hakon of Rogen's Saga;* certificates of

Diane and Leo Dillon (Reproduced by permission of Leo Dillon.)

merit, Society of Illustrators, 1968-77; Children's Book of the Year designation, Child Study Association, 1968, for *Dark Venture,* 1971, for *The Untold Tale,* 1973, for *Behind the Back of the Mountain,* 1974, for *Burning Star* and *Songs and Stories from Uganda,* 1975, for *The Hundred Penny Box, Why Mosquitoes Buzz in People's Ears,* and *Song of the Boat,* 1976, for *Ashanti to Zulu,* and 1986, for *Brother to the Wind;* Hugo Award, International Science Fiction Association, 1971; Outstanding Book of the Year citation, *New York Times,* 1975, for *Why Mosquitoes Buzz in People's Ears* and *The Hundred Penny Box,* and 1990, for *The Tale of the Mandarin Ducks;* Newbery Honor Book designation, 1996, for *The Hundred Penny Box;* Caldecott Medal, American Library Association (ALA), 1976, for *Why Mosquitoes Buzz in People's Ears,* and 1977, for *Ashanti to Zulu;* Best Illustrated Children's Book designation, *New York Times,* 1976, for *Ashanti to Zulu,* and 1985, for *The People Could Fly;* Illustration Honor, *Boston Globe/ Horn Book* Awards, 1976, for *Song of the Boat,* and

1977, for *Ashanti to Zulu;* Hamilton King Award, Society of Illustrators, 1977, for *Ashanti to Zulu;* Art Books for Children citation, Brooklyn Museum/Brooklyn Public Library, 1977, for *Why Mosquitoes Buzz in People's Ears;* Highly Commended designation, Hans Christian Andersen Medal, International Board on Books for Young People (IBBY), 1978; Lewis Carroll Shelf Award, 1978, for *Who's in Rabbit's House?;* Balrog Award, 1982, for lifetime contribution to sci-fi/fantasy art; honor list for illustration, IBBY, and honorable mention, Coretta Scott King Award, ALA, both 1986, both for *The People Could Fly;* Coretta Scott King Award for illustration, 1991, for *Aïda,* and 1996, for *Her Stories; Boston Globe/Horn Book* Award for illustration, 1991, for *The Tale of the Mandarin Ducks;* Chesley Award, 1997; inducted into Society of Illustrators Hall of Fame, 1997; Best Books designation, *Publishers Weekly* and *School Library Journal,* both 1998, both for *To Every Thing There Is a Season;* Virginia Hamilton Literary Award for body of work, 2002; Coretta Scott King Honor Book designation, 2005, for *The People Could Fly,* and 2008, for *Jazz on a Saturday Night;* Knickerbocker Award for body of work, New York Library Association, 2006; honorary D.F.A., Montserrat School of Art, 2006; Life Achievement Award, World Fantasy Convention, 2008.

Writings

SELF-ILLUSTRATED; WITH HUSBAND, LEO DILLON

Rap a Tap Tap: Here's Bojangles—Think of That!, Blue Sky Press (New York, NY), 2002.
Jazz on a Saturday Night, Blue Sky Press (New York, NY), 2007.
Mother Goose: Numbers on the Loose, Harcourt (Orlando, FL), 2007.

ILLUSTRATOR; WITH LEO DILLON

Erik C. Haugaard, *Hakon of Rogen's Saga,* Houghton (Boston, MA), 1963.
Erik C. Haugaard, *A Slave's Tale,* Houghton (Boston, MA), 1965.
Basil Davidson and the editors of Time-Life, *African Kingdoms,* Time-Life Books (New York, NY), 1966.
Sorche Nic Leodhas (pseudonym of Leclair G. Alger), *Claymore and Kilt: Tales of Scottish Kings and Castles,* Holt (New York, NY), 1967.
F.M. Pilkington, *Shamrock and Spear: Tales and Legends from Ireland,* Holt (New York, NY), 1968.
Erik C. Haugaard, *The Rider and His Horse,* Houghton (Boston, MA), 1968.
Audrey W. Beyer, *Dark Venture,* Knopf (New York, NY), 1968.
Frederick Laing, *Why Heimdall Blew His Horn: Tale of the Norse Gods,* Silver Burdett, 1969.
John Bierhorst and Henry R. Schoolcraft, editors, *The Ring in the Prairie: A Shawnee Legend,* Dial (New York, NY), 1970.

Alta Jablow, *Gassire's Lute: A West African Epic,* Dutton (New York, NY), 1971.
Alma Murray and Robert Thomas, editors, *The Search,* Scholastic (New York, NY), 1971.
Erik C. Haugaard, *The Untold Tale,* Houghton (Boston, MA), 1971.
Verna Aardema, *Behind the Back of the Mountain: Black Folktales from Southern Africa,* Dial (New York, NY), 1973.
Eth Clifford (pseudonym of Ethel C. Rosenberg), *Burning Star,* Houghton (Boston, MA), 1974.
W. Moses Serwadda, *Songs and Stories from Uganda,* Crowell, 1974.
Jan Carew, *The Third Gift,* Little, Brown (Boston, MA), 1974.
Natalie Belting, *Whirlwind Is a Ghost Dancing,* Dutton (New York, NY), 1974.
Lorenz Graham, *Song of the Boat,* Crowell, 1975.
Harlan Ellison, editor, *Dangerous Visions,* New American Library (New York, NY), 1975.
Sharon Bell Mathis, *The Hundred Penny Box,* Viking (New York, NY), 1975, reprinted, Puffin (New York, NY), 2006.
Verna Aardema, reteller, *Why Mosquitoes Buzz in People's Ears: A West African Tale,* Dial (New York, NY), 1975.
Margaret W. Musgrove, *Ashanti to Zulu: African Traditions,* Dial (New York, NY), 1976.
Verna Aardema, reteller, *Who's in Rabbit's House?: A Masai Tale,* Dial (New York, NY), 1977.
Eloise Greenfield, *Honey, I Love: And Other Love Poems,* Crowell, 1978.
Frederick Laing, *Tales from Scandinavia,* Silver Burdett, 1979.
P.L. Travers, *Two Pairs of Shoes,* Viking (New York, NY), 1980.
Jan Carew, *Children of the Sun,* Little, Brown (Boston, MA), 1980.
Dorothy S. Strickland, editor, *Listen Children: An Anthology of Black Literature,* Bantam (New York, NY), 1982.
Mildred Pitts Walter, *Brother to the Wind,* Lothrop, 1985.
Virginia Hamilton, reteller, *The People Could Fly: American Black Folktales,* Knopf (New York, NY), 1985, adapted as *The People Could Fly: The Picture Book,* Knopf (New York, NY), 2004.
Michael Patrick Hearn, *The Porcelain Cat,* Little, Brown (Boston, MA), 1987, reprinted, Simon & Schuster (New York, NY), 2004.
Barbara A. Brenner, *The Color Wizard: Level 1,* Bantam (New York, NY), 1989.
Alice Bach and J. Cheryl Exum, *Moses' Ark: Stories from the Bible,* Delacorte (New York, NY), 1989.
Leontyne Price, editor, *Aida: A Picture Book for All Ages,* Harcourt (New York, NY), 1990.
Katherine Paterson, *The Tale of the Mandarin Ducks,* Dutton (New York, NY), 1990.
Alice Bach and J. Cheryl Exum, *Miriam's Well: Stories about Women in the Bible,* Delacorte (New York, NY), 1991.
Claire Martin, *The Race of the Golden Apples,* Dial (New York, NY), 1991.

Nancy Willard, *Pish, Posh, Said Hieronymus Bosch,* Harcourt (New York, NY), 1991.

Nancy White Carlstrom, *Northern Lullaby,* Putnam (New York, NY), 1992.

Nancy Willard, *The Sorcerer's Apprentice,* Scholastic (New York, NY), 1993.

Virginia Hamilton, *Many Thousand Gone: African Americans from Slavery to Freedom,* Knopf (New York, NY), 1993.

Ray Bradbury, *Switch on the Night,* Knopf (New York, NY), 1993.

N.N. Charles, *What Am I?: Looking through Shapes at Apples and Grapes,* Scholastic (New York, NY), 1994.

Virginia Hamilton, *Her Stories: African-American Folktales, Fairy Tales, and True Tales,* Scholastic (New York, NY), 1995.

Howard Norman, *The Girl Who Dreamed Only Geese, and Other Tales of the Far North,* Harcourt Brace (New York, NY), 1997.

To Every Thing There Is a Season: Verses from Ecclesiastes, Blue Sky Press (New York, NY), 1998.

Shirley Rousseau Murphy, *Wind Child,* HarperCollins (New York, NY), 1999.

Virginia Hamilton, *The Girl Who Spun Gold,* Blue Sky Press (New York, NY), 2000.

Jules Verne, *20,000 Leagues under the Sea,* translated by Anthony Bonner, HarperCollins (New York, NY), 2000.

Sylvia Louise Engdahl, *Enchantress from the Stars,* foreword by Lois Lowry, Walker (New York, NY), 2001.

Margaret Wise Brown, *Two Little Trains,* HarperCollins (New York, NY), 2001.

Khephra Burns, *Mansa Musa: The Lion of Mali,* Harcourt (San Diego, CA), 2001.

John Herman, *One Winter's Night,* Philomel (New York, NY), 2003.

Howard Norman, *Between Heaven and Earth: Bird Tales from around the World,* Harcourt (Orlando, FL), 2004.

Margaret Wise Brown, *Where Have You Been?,* new edition, HarperCollins (New York, NY), 2004.

Ellen Jackson, *Earth Mother,* Walker & Company (New York, NY), 2005.

Rob D. Walker, *Mama Says,* Blue Sky Press (New York, NY), 2008.

Mem Fox, *The Night Goblin,* Harcourt (Orlando, FL), 2009.

Marjorie Kinnan Rawlings, *The Secret River,* Atheneum Books for Young Readers (New York, NY), 2009.

Contributor to books, including Mitsumasa Anno, compiler, *All in a Day,* Dowanya (Japan), 1986; *Once upon a Time: Celebrating the Magic of Children's Books in Honor of the Twentieth Anniversary of Reading Is Fundamental,* Putnam, 1986; and *On the Wings of Peace: Writers and Illustrators Speak out for Peace, in Memory of Hiroshima and Nagasaki,* Houghton Mifflin (Boston, MA), 1995. Contributor of illustrations to periodicals, including *Ladies' Home Journal, Saturday Evening Post,* and *Washington Post.*

Work included in the Kerlan Collection, University of Minnesota.

Adaptations

Why Mosquitoes Buzz in People's Ears was adapted as a filmstrip with audiocassette and as a motion picture, Weston Woods, 1977; *Ashanti to Zulu* was adapted as a filmstrip with audiocassette, Weston Woods, 1977; *Brother to the Wind* was adapted as a filmstrip with audiocassette, Weston Woods, 1988; *The People Could Fly* was released on audiocassette, Knopf, 1988; *The Tale of the Mandarin Ducks* was produced on video cassette by Weston Woods, 1998; *Rap a Tap Tap* was adapted as an audiobook by Live Oak Media, 2005.

Sidelights

Husband and wife Leo and Diane Dillon are a prolific and acclaimed team of American illustrators and artists. They are noted for producing imaginative, bold drawings and illustrations which range from the highly realistic to the abstract. Since the 1960s, the Dillons have gained renown for their collaborative book illustrations, which stretch across genres such as science fiction, medieval writings, literary classics, and folk tales. They are best known, however, for their contributions to children's picture books and are the only illustrators to receive consecutive Caldecott medals, the highest illustration achievement in children's literature. Unique in that they always work in collaboration, the Dillons describe their creative output as emanating from a "third artist." As they once related to *SATA:* "After a work is finished, not even we can be certain who did what. The third artist is a combination of the two of us and is different than either of us individually."

Though the Dillons work together as illustrators, they bring to their art very different personal backgrounds and experience. Leo Dillon was born in 1933, in the East New York section of Brooklyn, the son of immigrant parents from Trinidad. Both of his parents—his father owned a small trucking business and his mother was a dressmaker—encouraged him in his drawing. Family friend Ralph Volman soon became Leo's "mentor—a painter, a draftsman, a writer, a world traveler," as the artist once recalled. "It was Ralph Volman who took me to Greenwich Village for the first time to see the annual sidewalk art show. . . . Volman gave me a drawing board. He came to our house every Sunday and would show me his pen-and-ink drawings, a very tight 'English style.' He also spent a good deal of time with my drawings, giving me criticism and encouragement."

Captivated by the work of the Old Masters and showing promise as an artist, Leo later attended New York City's High School of Industrial Design, where he trained for a commercial art career. There he was particularly influenced by one teacher, Benjamin Clements, who "realized that I could do more than illustrate Coke bottles, and pushed me to expand my mind," as Leo once told *SATA.* After graduation he enlisted in the U.S. Navy, in order to eventually attend college on the GI Bill. "For the three years I spent in the service, I drew lots of por-

Virginia Hamilton's **The People Could Fly** *has become a classic on the strength of Diane and Leo Dillon's stylized art.* (Illustration copyright © 1985 by Leo and Diane Dillon. Used by permission of Alfred A. Knopf Children's Books, a division of Random House, Inc.)

traits on 'commission' from guys who wanted pictures of their girlfriends," he related. "I painted in the ship's hold, and mixed my pigments from nautical paint." After completing his service, Dillon enrolled at the prestigious Parsons School of Design, where he would meet his future wife and working partner.

Born the same year as her husband, Diane Dillon grew up in Los Angeles, where her schoolteacher and inventor father possessed a working knowledge of drafting that helped guide her early interest in drawing. She was also encouraged by her mother, a concert pianist and organist. "As a child I drew all the time," she once told *SATA,* "and my parents encouraged me, particularly my father, who had artistic talent. He would look carefully at what I'd done and then offer corrections, telling me which side the shadow should fall on, for example. He was away for a year during the war from 1943 to 1944, and he sent me a set of pastels in a wood box, which meant a lot. It was not only permission to do what I wanted to do, but the *tools* I needed to do it with." As a young girl, Diane was also influenced by the fashion illustrations of the famous Dorothy Hood, whose drawings appeared in the newspapers. "Hood was way ahead of her time," Diane said. "Her drawing style was very modern. I loved the look of her line, so *different* from anything else being done then. The fact that those wonderful figures were drawn by a woman was an inspiration for me."

Although Diane demonstrated artistic talent throughout high school, she did not receive serious art training un-

til college, when she attended Los Angeles City College and studied advertising art. After a year she contracted tuberculosis and was forced to withdraw, recuperating for a year in a sanitarium where she spent most of her time reading, drawing, and knitting. After her recovery, Diane attended Skidmore College in Saratoga Springs, New York, transferring to Parsons in her junior year.

At Parsons, Diane and Leo became instant competitors, yet also discovered an immediate and mutual admiration for each other's work. "I walked into a classroom and saw a student painting of various pieces of fabric and a sewing machine," Diane once related. "It was very realistic—the subtle shadows of the pins in the cloth and the way the folds were done gave it an extraordinary three-dimensional quality. I was immediately overcome by two feelings: 'I'm in over my head,' and 'Here is a challenge I *must* meet.' The painting was Leo's, and to this day, his work sets a standard for me." In *Horn Book* Leo recalled a similar experience on first encountering Diane's work. "One day I noticed a painting hanging on the wall at a student exhibition. It was a painting of a chair . . . and I knew it had to be by a new student because nobody in our class at the time could paint like that. . . . This artist knew perspective, which is one of the most difficult things a beginner has to learn. . . . This artist was a whole lot better than I. I figured I'd better find out who he was. *He* was Diane."

"We spent a lot of time and energy trying to prove ourselves to each other," Leo recalled to *SATA.* "In the midst of all this, born of the mutual recognition of our respective strengths, we fell in love. We tried to keep our relationship a secret because in those days interracial couples were not easily accepted. We knew of couples like us who had been beaten up walking down the street." After graduation, Diane went to work for an advertising firm in Albany, New York, but returned the following year to be with Leo. They were married in 1957, and Leo went to work as an art director for West Park Publications in New York. Diane stayed home, "determined to be the model 1950s housewife, and that didn't include drawing or painting," she wrote in *Horn Book*. The two soon started collaborating professionally, however. Leo "casually began bringing work home, encouraging me to work with him on design problems, easing me back into art," Diane told *Horn Book*. "That was the beginning of our working together as one artist."

Beginning in the late 1950s, the Dillons worked as freelance artists under the name Studio 2. "Because we wanted to work in a variety of styles, we thought it better not to use our names," Diane explained. "We figured, rightly, that we would have more variety if clients thought we were a studio full of artists." By the early 1960s, they began attracting kudos for their drawings and illustrations for textbooks, book jackets, album covers, and prints, their subjects ranging from African folk tales and Scandinavian mythology to science fiction and fantasy, medieval literature, and Shakespeare. They also had the opportunity to experiment in their style through their collaboration with Harlan Ellison, a Chicago-based magazine editor who assigned the Dillons illustration assignments for texts by Nat Hentoff and Ben Hecht, as well as their groundbreaking cover illustration for *Gentleman Junkie and Other Stories of the Hung-Up Generation*.

Still constantly experimenting, the Dillons employ such unusual elements as embroidery, plastic, and leading into their art, creating a stained-glass effect. Many of their drawings have the appearance of woodcuts, an effect the Dillons achieve through an innovative use of the frisket—a type of cut stencil. "Because we both work on every piece of art, we favor techniques that give us a lot of control," the couple explained. "We don't leave ourselves open to 'accident.' We need a technique so sure that a line begun by one of us can be completed by the other with no visual hint of interruption. We are constantly experimenting with various types of media. This is exhilarating, but there are times when it's extremely frustrating, trying to overcome technical problems. That period of not knowing what is wrong can be excruciating. But over the years we've come to accept that trial and error is part of the process. Technique is to the graphic artist what words are to the writer."

The Dillons won their first Caldecott Medal for their first picture-book assignment: Verna Aardema's 1976 text for *Why Mosquitoes Buzz in People's Ears: A West African Tale*. "We were delighted that this book was perfect for reading aloud," the couple once commented to *SATA*. "It is an illustrator's job to go beyond the text, to illustrate what is between the lines, not just to repeat the words. *Why Mosquitoes Buzz in People's Ears* is a repetitive tale in which the events are interpreted by different animals, each with a distinct point of view. We found ourselves concentrating on the play between the animals." The Dillons expand upon the original story by accenting several of the minor animal characters; in one case, they introduce a new character, a little red bird. "We began to think of her as the observer or reader and added her to the other spreads," they explained in their Caldecott Medal acceptance speech, reprinted in *Horn Book*. "Thus on each page you will find her watching, witnessing the events as they unfold. On the last page, when the story is over, she flies away. For us she is like the storyteller, gathering information, then passing it on to the next generation." Commenting on the Dillons' achievement, *Horn Book* reviewer Phyllis J. Fogelman praised "their talent as artists who collaborate so completely," and cited "their amazing ability to capture so sensitively such warmth, humor, and feeling in art so stylized as that for *Why Mosquitoes Buzz in People's Ears*."

The Dillons' work for Margaret Musgrove's *Ashanti to Zulu: African Traditions* garnered them a second Calde-

The Dillons contribute their stylized artwork to the pages of Virginia Hamilton's woman-centered folktale collection **Her Stories.** (Illustration copyright © 1995 by Leo and Diane Dillon. Reproduced by permission of Scholastic, Inc.)

The Dillons' focus on African-American themes enriches their artwork for Wade and Cheryl Willis Hudson's inspiring picture book **In Praise of Our Fathers and Our Mothers.** (Just Us Books, Inc. 1997. Illustration copyright © 1997 by George Ford. Used by permission of George Ford.)

cott medal in 1977. An alphabet book, *Ashanti to Zulu* describes different traditions among the diverse cultures of Africa, focusing on such aspects as dwellings, clothing, hairstyles, and family life. "We wanted our illustrations . . . to be something other artists could look to as source material," the Dillons once explained to *SATA*. "We strove for realism, for we wanted to be absolutely accurate with the details as well as have the elegance one normally associates with fairy tales." While the Dillons accurately depict the differences among African cultures, they also impart universal aspects. "We began to appreciate the grandeur in ordinary living, in what actually exists," they stated in the Caldecott Medal acceptance speech for this work. "It is the intelligence in a person's eyes or the nuances of body language—things shared by all people—that make for real beauty. We strove to be accurate with the factual details but especially wanted to stress the things we all have in common—a smile, a touch, our humanity. We took artistic license with particular situations so that they reflected the tenderness that exists among all people."

As their career has progressed, the Dillons have continued to collaborate with distinguished authors to produce outstanding illustrated books for children. Reviewing the couple's work for Michael Patrick Hearn's sorcerer's apprentice tale, *The Porcelain Cat,* Patricia MacLachlan wrote in the *New York Times Book Review* that the "Dillons' extraordinary pictures add great depth

and meaning" to Hearn's story. In *School Library Journal* Patricia Dooley dubbed the collaboration between the Dillons and Hearn "a 'smashing' success."

The Dillons' most acclaimed collaborations have been with eminent children's author Virginia Hamilton. The first of these highly praised books, *The People Could Fly: American Black Folktales,* retells two dozen tales that originated in black slave communities within America; the book has more-recently been adapted as a picture book for younger children. A companion volume, *Many Thousand Gone: African Americans from Slavery to Freedom,* relates the history of slavery in the United States and profiles the lives of familiar figures such as Frederick Douglass and Harriet Tubman as well as lesser-known figures remembered only by their first name. *School Library Journal* contributor Lyn Miller-Lachmann praised the Dillons' "refreshingly original" illustrations for *Many Thousand Gone,* noting that the "text and visuals combine to create a powerful and moving whole." The Dillons' third collaboration with Hamilton, *Her Stories: African-American Folktales, Fairy Tales, and True Tales,* is a unique collection of tales centered around black American females that earned both author and illustrators Coretta Scott King awards, while *The Girl Who Spun Gold* retells the Rumplestiltskin story in a West Indian setting. "The Dillons' glowingly detailed acrylic illustrations extend the horror, comedy, rhythm, and spirit of the tales," wrote Hazel Rochman in a *Booklist* review of *Her Stories*, and the critic dubbed *The Girl Who Spun Gold* a "stirring picture book" brought to life in "exquisite illustrations" "in the style of Gustav Klimt's patterned compositions."

Other award-winning books illustrated by the Dillons include Katherine Paterson's picture book *The Tale of the Mandarin Ducks,* for which they received the *Boston Globe/Horn Book* Award, and Nancy Willard's *Pish, Posh, Said Hieronymus Bosch* and *The Sorcerer's Apprentice.* About the last, Nancy Vasilakis wrote in *Horn Book:* "The whole enterprise is a masterful and creative meeting of the minds between author and illustrators." Another acclaimed collaboration is Nancy White Carlstrom's *Northern Lullaby,* which features a young Native-American narrator saying goodnight to the world around her as she drifts off to sleep. Cooper, writing in *Booklist,* called *Northern Lullaby* "a felicitous collaboration" and asserted that the "Dillons' art here is as fine as any work they've done before." In their art for Ellen Jackson's *Earth Mother,* a porquois story set in Africa, the couple contributes "watercolor-and-colored-pencil illustrations [that are] filled with geometric patterns, are magical; [and are] . . . soft and elegant and as artfully composed as an art nouveau poster," according to *Booklist* critic Karin Snelson.

Turning to traditional fare, the Dillons' art brings to life a beloved Bible verse in *To Every Thing There Is a Season: Verses from Ecclesiastes,* while popular nursery rhymes are captured in what a *Kirkus Reviews* critic

Sharon Bell Mathis's award-winning **The Hundred Penny Box** *is among the Dillons' many acclaimed picture-book projects.* (Illustration copyright © 1975 by Leo and Diane Dillon. All rights reserved. Used by permission of Viking Penguin, an imprint of Penguin Putnam Books for Young Readers, a division of Penguin Putnam, Inc.)

dubbed "gorgeously rendered illustrations" in *Mother Goose: Numbers on the Loose.* Called by *Bulletin of the Center for Children's Books* reviewer Janice M. Del Negro "a visual extravaganza," the art in *To Every Thing There Is a Season* draws from cultures and artistic styles ranging from ancient to modern. For example, the illustration paired with the line "A time to kill, and a time to heal," reflects a style inspired by seventh-century Mexican Mixtec culture. Although Del Negro found the book somewhat "overproduced" due to the contrast between the Dillons' sophisticated illustrations and the simple verse, *School Library Journal* critic Patricia Pearl Dole appreciated *To Every Thing There Is a Season* for its "ecumenical, artistic, and cultural experience" and its "intrinsic plea for worldwide understanding."

In addition to their work with noted writers, the Dillons have also created original self-illustrated stories. *Rap a Tap Tap: Here's Bojangles—Think of That!* profiles the life of Bill Robinson, who gained fame for his tap dancing in the early twentieth century. Featuring what Cooper described as "a bouncy text, and eye-catching art," the Dillons' picture book also depicts the energetic Mr. Bojangles as "practically dancing off the edge of the page" in collage illustrations featuring a colorful city background. Another musical offering, *Jazz on a Saturday Night,* allows young readers to enjoy a concert by be-bop greats John Coltrane, Charlie Parker, Thelonious Monk, Miles Davis, Max Roach, Stanley Clarke, and

Ella Fitzgerald. A "rhythmic tribute to traditional jazz," according to *School Library Journal* reviewer Joyce Adams Burner, *Jazz on a Saturday Night* is enriched by artwork "rendered in deep matte tones with a suggestion of collage, [that] switch between stage and audience, with swirling background patterns portraying the flow of music." Praising the Dillons for introducing jazz to a new generation, a *Publishers Weekly* critic described *Rap a Tap Tap* as a colorful ticket to "what might be termed the king of all jam sessions."

Biographical and Critical Sources

BOOKS

The Art of Leo and Diane Dillon, edited by Byron Preiss, Ballantine (New York, NY), 1981.
Children's Literature Review, Volume 44, Gale (Detroit, MI), 1997, pp. 17-49.
Newbery and Caldecott Medalists and Honor Book Winners, compiled by Jim Roginski, Libraries Unlimited, 1982.

PERIODICALS

Booklist, June 15, 1992, Ilene Cooper, review of *Northern Lullaby,* p. 1834; December 1, 1992, Hazel Rochman, review of *Many Thousand Gone: African Americans from Slavery to Freedom,* p. 665; November 1, 1993, Hazel Rochman, review of *The Sorcerer's Apprentice,* p. 529; November 15, 1994, Carolyn Phelan, review of *What Am I? Looking through Shapes at Apples and Grapes,* p. 605; November 1, 1995, Hazel Rochman, review of *Her Stories: African-American Folktales, Fairy Tales, and True Tales,* p. 470; September 15, 1997, Karen Morgan, review of *The Girl Who Dreamed Only Geese, and Other Stories of the Far North,* p. 233; October 1, 1998, Ilene Cooper, review of *To Everything There Is a Season: Verses from Ecclesiastes,* p. 344; August, 2000, Hazel Rochman, review of *The Girl Who Spun Gold,* p. 2134; April 15, 2001, Carolyn Phelan, review of *Two Little Trains,* p. 1550; December 1, 2001, Gillian Engberg, review of *Mansa Musa: The Lion of Mali,* p. 642; October 15, 2002, Ilene Cooper, review of *Rap a Tap Tap: Here's Bojangles—Think of That!,* p. 406; September 14, 2003, Julie Cummins, review of *One Winter's Night,* p. 245; May 1, 2004, Carolyn Phelan, review of *Where Have You Been?,* p. 156; August, 2005, Karin Snelson, review of *Earth Mother,* p. 2023; September 1, 2007, John Peters, review of *Mother Goose: Numbers on the Loose,* p. 122; September 15, 2007, Bill Ott, review of *Jazz on a Saturday Night,* p. 62.
Bulletin of the Center for Children's Books, November, 1998, Janice M. Del Negro, review of *To Every Thing There Is a Season,* p. 89; December, 2002, review of *Rap a Tap Tap,* p. 151.
Horn Book, August, 1976, Phyllis J. Fogelman, "Leo and Diane Dillon," pp. 378-383, and Diane and Leo Dillon, "Caldecott Award Acceptance"; August, 1977, Di-

ane and Leo Dillon, "Caldecott Award Acceptance," Leo Dillon, "Diane Dillon," pp. 422-423, and Diane Dillon, "Leo Dillon," pp. 423-425; September-October, 1993, Hanna B. Zeiger, review of *Many Thousands Gone,* p. 621; March-April, 1994, Nancy Vasilakis, review of *The Sorcerer's Apprentice,* p. 193; January-February, 1996, Maria B. Salvadore, review of *Her Stories,* pp. 81-82; September-October, 1998, Roger Sutton, review of *To Every Thing There Is a Season,* pp. 619-620; November-December, 2001, Anita L. Burkam, review of *Mansa Musa,* p. 733; September-October, 2007, Robin Smith, review of *Jazz on a Saturday Night,* p. 559; November-December, 2007, Joanna Rudge Long, review of *Mother Goose,* p. 691.

Kirkus Reviews, September 15, 1998, review of *To Every Thing There Is a Season,* p. 1383; May 1, 2002, review of *The Sorcerer's Apprentice,* p. 655; August 1, 2002, review of *Rap a Tap Tap,* p. 1126; September 1, 2007, reviews of *Jazz on a Saturday Night* and *Mother Goose.*

New York Times Book Review, November 8, 1987, Patricia MacLachlan, review of *The Porcelain Cat,* p. 50; November 15, 1998, Valerie Sayers, review of *To Every Thing There Is a Season,* p. 55.

Publishers Weekly, June 28, 1991, review of *The Race of the Golden Apples,* p. 101; August 8, 1994, review of *What Am I Looking For?* p. 428; November 13, 1995, review of *The Tale of the Mandarin Ducks,* p. 60; July 27, 1998, review of *To Everything There Is a Season,* p. 76; July 31, 2000, review of *The Girl Who Spun Gold,* p. 95; October 22, 2001, review of *Mansa Musa,* p. 74; August 12, 2002, review of *Rap a Tap Tap,* p.

The Dillons playfully marshal a host of animals into new configurations in **Mother Goose: Numbers on the Loose.** (Illustration copyright © 2007 by Leo Dillon and Diane Dillon. Reproduced by permission of Houghton Mifflin Harcourt Publishing Company.)

299; August 6, 2007, review of *Jazz on a Saturday Night,* p. 187; October 8, 2007, review of *Mother Goose,* p. 51.

School Library Journal, November, 1987, Patricia Dooley, review of *The Porcelain Cat,* p. 90; October, 1990, Kay Vandergrift, review of *The Tale of the Mandarin Ducks,* p. 111; January, 1992, Patricia Dooley, review of *Miriam's Well: Stories about Women in the Bible,* p. 118; May, 1993, Lyn Miller-Lachmann, review of *Many Thousand Gone,* p. 116; January, 1994, Patricia Dooley, review of *The Sorcerer's Apprentice,* pp. 116-117; September, 1998, Patricia Pearl Dole, review of *To Every Thing There Is a Season,* p. 198; September, 2000, Carol Ann Wilson, review of *The Girl Who Spun Gold,* p. 217; September, 2002, Wendy Lukehart, review of *Rap a Tap Tap,* p. 189; June, 2004, Sophie R. Brookover, review of *Where Have You Been?,* p. 103; September, 2007, Joyce Adams Burner, review of *Jazz on a Saturday Night,* p. 162.

ONLINE

Embracing the Child Web site, http://www.embracingthechild.org/ (October 20, 2008), "Leo and Diane Dillon."

Locus Online, http://www.locusmag.com/ (April 1, 2000), interview with Leo and Diane Dillon.

Teaching Books Web site, http://www.teachingbooks.net/ (September 2, 2005), interview with Leo and Diane Dillon.*

* * *

DILLON, Leo 1933-

Personal

Born March 2, 1933, in Brooklyn, NY; son of Lionel J. (owner of a truck business) and Marie (a dressmaker) Dillon; married Diane Sorber (an artist and illustrator), March 17, 1957; children: Lionel ("Lee"). *Education:* Attended Parsons School of Design, 1953, 1956; also attended School of Visual Arts, 1958.

Addresses

Home—Brooklyn, NY.

Career

Artist and illustrator. Dave Fris Advertising Agency, Albany, NY, staff artist, 1956-57; freelance artist and illustrator, 1957—; instructor, School of Visual Arts, 1971-74. *Exhibitions:* Gallery on the Green, Boston, MA; Metropolitan Museum, New York, NY; Boulder Center for the Visual Arts, Boulder, CO; Butler Institute of American Art, Youngstown, OH; Delaware Art Museum, Wilmington; Bratislava Book Show, Bratislava, Slovakia; American Institute of Graphic Arts, New York, NY; Art Directors Club of New York; Brooklyn Public Library, Brooklyn, NY; New York Historical Society; Earthlight Gallery, Boston; The Pentagon, Washington, DC; Delaware Museum, Washington, DC; Society of Illustrators, NY. Artist of stained-glass ceiling in Eagle Gallery, New York, NY.

Member

Society of Illustrators, Graphic Artists Guild.

Awards, Honors

All with wife, Diane Dillon: Children's Spring Book Festival Honor Book designation, *New York Herald Tribune,* 1963, for *Hakon of Rogen's Saga;* certificates of merit, Society of Illustrators, 1968-77; Children's Book of the Year designation, Child Study Association, 1968, for *Dark Venture,* 1971, for *The Untold Tale,* 1973, for *Behind the Back of the Mountain,* 1974, for *Burning Star* and *Songs and Stories from Uganda,* 1975, for *The Hundred Penny Box, Why Mosquitoes Buzz in People's Ears,* and *Song of the Boat,* 1976, for *Ashanti to Zulu,* and 1986, for *Brother to the Wind;* Hugo Award, International Science Fiction Association, 1971; Outstanding Book of the Year citation, *New York Times,* 1975, for *Why Mosquitoes Buzz in People's Ears* and *The Hundred Penny Box,* and 1990, for *The Tale of the Mandarin Ducks;* Newbery Honor Book designation, 1996, for *The Hundred Penny Box;* Caldecott Medal, American Library Association (ALA), 1976, for *Why Mosquitoes Buzz in People's Ears,* and 1977, for *Ashanti to Zulu;* Best Illustrated Children's Book designation, *New York Times,* 1976, for *Ashanti to Zulu,* and 1985, for *The People Could Fly;* Illustration Honor, *Boston Globe/ Horn Book* Awards, 1976, for *Song of the Boat,* and 1977, for *Ashanti to Zulu;* Hamilton King Award, Society of Illustrators, 1977, for *Ashanti to Zulu;* Art Books for Children citation, Brooklyn Museum/Brooklyn Public Library, 1977, for *Why Mosquitoes Buzz in People's Ears;* Highly Commended designation, Hans Christian Andersen Medal, International Board on Books for Young People (IBBY), 1978; Lewis Carroll Shelf Award, 1978, for *Who's in Rabbit's House?;* Balrog Award, 1982, for lifetime contribution to sci-fi/fantasy art; honor list for illustration, IBBY, and honorable mention, Coretta Scott King Award, ALA, both 1986, both for *The People Could Fly;* Coretta Scott King Award for illustration, 1991, for *Aïda,* and 1996, for *Her Stories; Boston Globe/Horn Book* Award for illustration, 1991, for *The Tale of the Mandarin Ducks;* Chesley Award, 1997; inducted into Society of Illustrators Hall of Fame, 1997; Best Books designation, *Publishers Weekly* and *School Library Journal,* both 1998, both for *To Every Thing There Is a Season;* Virginia Hamilton Literary Award for body of work, 2002; Coretta Scott King Honor Book designation, 2005, for *The People Could Fly,* and 2008, for *Jazz on a Saturday Night;* Knickerbocker Award for body of work, New York Library Association, 2006; honorary D.F.A., Montserrat School of Art, 2006; Life Achievement Award, World Fantasy Convention, 2008.

Writings

SELF-ILLUSTRATED; WITH WIFE DIANE DILLON

Rap a Tap Tap: Here's Bojangles—Think of That!, Blue Sky Press (New York, NY), 2002.

Jazz on a Saturday Night, Blue Sky Press (New York, NY), 2007.

Mother Goose: Numbers on the Loose, Harcourt (Orlando, FL), 2007.

ILLUSTRATOR; WITH DIANE DILLON

Erik C. Haugaard, *Hakon of Rogen's Saga,* Houghton (Boston, MA), 1963.

Erik C. Haugaard, *A Slave's Tale,* Houghton (Boston, MA), 1965.

Basil Davidson and the editors of Time-Life, *African Kingdoms,* Time-Life Books (New York, NY), 1966.

Sorche Nic Leodhas (pseudonym of Leclair G. Alger), *Claymore and Kilt: Tales of Scottish Kings and Castles,* Holt (New York, NY), 1967.

F.M. Pilkington, *Shamrock and Spear: Tales and Legends from Ireland,* Holt (New York, NY), 1968.

Erik C. Haugaard, *The Rider and His Horse,* Houghton (Boston, MA), 1968.

Audrey W. Beyer, *Dark Venture,* Knopf (New York, NY), 1968.

Frederick Laing, *Why Heimdall Blew His Horn: Tale of the Norse Gods,* Silver Burdett, 1969.

John Bierhorst and Henry R. Schoolcraft, editors, *The Ring in the Prairie: A Shawnee Legend,* Dial (New York, NY), 1970.

Alta Jablow, *Gassire's Lute: A West African Epic,* Dutton (New York, NY), 1971.

Alma Murray and Robert Thomas, editors, *The Search,* Scholastic (New York, NY), 1971.

Erik C. Haugaard, *The Untold Tale,* Houghton (Boston, MA), 1971.

Verna Aardema, *Behind the Back of the Mountain: Black Folktales from Southern Africa,* Dial (New York, NY), 1973.

Eth Clifford (pseudonym of Ethel C. Rosenberg), *Burning Star,* Houghton (Boston, MA), 1974.

W. Moses Serwadda, *Songs and Stories from Uganda,* Crowell, 1974.

Jan Carew, *The Third Gift,* Little, Brown (Boston, MA), 1974.

Natalie Belting, *Whirlwind Is a Ghost Dancing,* Dutton (New York, NY), 1974.

Lorenz Graham, *Song of the Boat,* Crowell, 1975.

Harlan Ellison, editor, *Dangerous Visions,* New American Library (New York, NY), 1975.

Sharon Bell Mathis, *The Hundred Penny Box,* Viking (New York, NY), 1975, reprinted, Puffin (New York, NY), 2006.

Verna Aardema, reteller, *Why Mosquitoes Buzz in People's Ears: A West African Tale,* Dial (New York, NY), 1975.

Margaret W. Musgrove, *Ashanti to Zulu: African Traditions,* Dial (New York, NY), 1976.

Verna Aardema, reteller, *Who's in Rabbit's House?: A Masai Tale,* Dial (New York, NY), 1977.

Eloise Greenfield, *Honey, I Love: And Other Love Poems,* Crowell, 1978.

Frederick Laing, *Tales from Scandinavia,* Silver Burdett, 1979.

P.L. Travers, *Two Pairs of Shoes,* Viking (New York, NY), 1980.

Jan Carew, *Children of the Sun,* Little, Brown (Boston, MA), 1980.

Dorothy S. Strickland, editor, *Listen Children: An Anthology of Black Literature,* Bantam (New York, NY), 1982.

Mildred Pitts Walter, *Brother to the Wind,* Lothrop, 1985.

Virginia Hamilton, reteller, *The People Could Fly: American Black Folktales,* Knopf (New York, NY), 1985, adapted as *The People Could Fly: The Picture Book,* Knopf (New York, NY), 2004.

Michael Patrick Hearn, *The Porcelain Cat,* Little, Brown (Boston, MA), 1987, reprinted, Simon & Schuster (New York, NY), 2004.

Barbara A. Brenner, *The Color Wizard: Level 1,* Bantam (New York, NY), 1989.

Alice Bach and J. Cheryl Exum, *Moses' Ark: Stories from the Bible,* Delacorte (New York, NY), 1989.

Leontyne Price, editor, *Aida: A Picture Book for All Ages,* Harcourt (New York, NY), 1990.

Katherine Paterson, *The Tale of the Mandarin Ducks,* Dutton (New York, NY), 1990.

Alice Bach and J. Cheryl Exum, *Miriam's Well: Stories about Women in the Bible,* Delacorte (New York, NY), 1991.

Claire Martin, *The Race of the Golden Apples,* Dial (New York, NY), 1991.

Nancy Willard, *Pish, Posh, Said Hieronymus Bosch,* Harcourt (New York, NY), 1991.

Nancy White Carlstrom, *Northern Lullaby,* Putnam (New York, NY), 1992.

Nancy Willard, (edited by Leo D. Dillon) *The Sorcerer's Apprentice,* Scholastic (New York, NY), 1993.

Virginia Hamilton, *Many Thousand Gone: African Americans from Slavery to Freedom,* Knopf (New York, NY), 1993.

Ray Bradbury, *Switch on the Night,* Knopf (New York, NY), 1993.

N.N. Charles, *What Am I?: Looking through Shapes at Apples and Grapes,* Scholastic (New York, NY), 1994.

Virginia Hamilton, *Her Stories: African-American Folktales, Fairy Tales, and True Tales,* Scholastic (New York, NY), 1995.

Howard Norman, *The Girl Who Dreamed Only Geese, and Other Tales of the Far North,* Harcourt Brace (New York, NY), 1997.

To Every Thing There Is a Season: Verses from Ecclesiastes, Blue Sky Press (New York, NY), 1998.

Shirley Rousseau Murphy, *Wind Child,* HarperCollins (New York, NY), 1999.

Virginia Hamilton, *The Girl Who Spun Gold,* Blue Sky Press (New York, NY), 2000.

Jules Verne, *20,000 Leagues under the Sea,* translated by Anthony Bonner, HarperCollins (New York, NY), 2000.

Sylvia Louise Engdahl, *Enchantress from the Stars,* foreword by Lois Lowry, Walker (New York, NY), 2001.

Margaret Wise Brown, *Two Little Trains,* HarperCollins (New York, NY), 2001.

Khephra Burns, *Mansa Musa: The Lion of Mali,* Harcourt (San Diego, CA), 2001.

John Herman, *One Winter's Night,* Philomel (New York, NY), 2003.

Howard Norman, *Between Heaven and Earth: Bird Tales from around the World,* Harcourt (Orlando, FL), 2004.

Margaret Wise Brown, *Where Have You Been?,* new edition, HarperCollins (New York, NY), 2004.

Ellen Jackson, *Earth Mother,* Walker & Company (New York, NY), 2005.

Rob D. Walker, *Mama Says,* Blue Sky Press (New York, NY), 2008.

Mem Fox, *The Night Goblin,* Harcourt (Orlando, FL), 2009.

Marjorie Kinnan Rawlings, *The Secret River,* Atheneum Books for Young Readers (New York, NY), 2009.

Contributor to books, including Mitsumasa Anno, compiler, *All in a Day,* Dowanya (Japan), 1986; *Once upon a Time: Celebrating the Magic of Children's Books in Honor of the Twentieth Anniversary of Reading Is Fundamental,* Putnam, 1986; and *On the Wings of Peace: Writers and Illustrators Speak out for Peace, in Memory of Hiroshima and Nagasaki,* Houghton Mifflin (Boston, MA), 1995. Contributor of illustrations to periodicals, including *Ladies' Home Journal, Saturday Evening Post,* and *Washington Post.*

Work included in the Kerlan Collection, University of Minnesota.

Adaptations

Why Mosquitoes Buzz in People's Ears was adapted as a filmstrip with audiocassette and as a motion picture, Weston Woods, 1977; *Ashanti to Zulu* was adapted as a filmstrip with audiocassette, Weston Woods, 1977; *Brother to the Wind* was adapted as a filmstrip with audiocassette, Weston Woods, 1988; *The People Could Fly* was released on audiocassette, Knopf, 1988; *The Tale of the Mandarin Ducks* was produced on video cassette by Weston Woods, 1998; *Rap a Tap Tap* was adapted for audiobook by Live Oak Media, 2005.

Sidelights

For Sidelights essay on Leo Dillon, please see entry on Diane Dillon, elsewhere in this volume.

Biographical and Critical Sources

BOOKS

The Art of Leo and Diane Dillon, edited by Byron Preiss, Ballantine (New York, NY), 1981.

Children's Literature Review, Volume 44, Gale (Detroit, MI), 1997, pp. 17-49.

Newbery and Caldecott Medalists and Honor Book Winners, compiled by Jim Roginski, Libraries Unlimited, 1982.

PERIODICALS

Booklist, June 15, 1992, Ilene Cooper, review of *Northern Lullaby,* p. 1834; December 1, 1992, Hazel Rochman, review of *Many Thousand Gone: African Americans from Slavery to Freedom,* p. 665; November 1, 1993, Hazel Rochman, review of *The Sorcerer's Apprentice,* p. 529; November 15, 1994, Carolyn Phelan, review of *What Am I? Looking through Shapes at Apples and Grapes,* p. 605; November 1, 1995, Hazel Rochman, review of *Her Stories: African-American Folktales, Fairy Tales, and True Tales,* p. 470; September 15, 1997, Karen Morgan, review of *The Girl Who Dreamed Only Geese, and Other Stories of the Far North,* p. 233; October 1, 1998, Ilene Cooper, review of *To Everything There Is a Season: Verses from Ecclesiastes,* p. 344; August, 2000, Hazel Rochman, review of *The Girl Who Spun Gold,* p. 2134; April 15, 2001, Carolyn Phelan, review of *Two Little Trains,* p. 1550; December 1, 2001, Gillian Engberg, review of *Mansa Musa: The Lion of Mali,* p. 642; October 15, 2002, Ilene Cooper, review of *Rap a Tap Tap: Here's Bojangles—Think of That!,* p. 406; September 14, 2003, Julie Cummins, review of *One Winter's Night,* p. 245; May 1, 2004, Carolyn Phelan, review of *Where Have You Been?,* p. 156; August, 2005, Karin Snelson, review of *Earth Mother,* p. 2023; September 1, 2007, John Peters, review of *Mother Goose: Numbers on the Loose,* p. 122; September 15, 2007, Bill Ott, review of *Jazz on a Saturday Night,* p. 62.

Bulletin of the Center for Children's Books, November, 1998, Janice M. Del Negro, review of *To Every Thing There Is a Season,* p. 89; December, 2002, review of *Rap a Tap Tap,* p. 151.

Horn Book, August, 1976, Phyllis J. Fogelman, "Leo and Diane Dillon," pp. 378-383, and Diane and Leo Dillon, "Caldecott Award Acceptance"; August, 1977, Diane and Leo Dillon, "Caldecott Award Acceptance," Leo Dillon, "Diane Dillon," pp. 422-423, and Diane Dillon, "Leo Dillon," pp. 423-425; September-October, 1993, Hanna B. Zeiger, review of *Many Thousands Gone,* p. 621; March-April, 1994, Nancy Vasilakis, review of *The Sorcerer's Apprentice,* p. 193; January-February, 1996, Maria B. Salvadore, review of *Her Stories,* pp. 81-82; September-October, 1998, Roger Sutton, review of *To Every Thing There Is a Season,* pp. 619-620; November-December, 2001, Anita L. Burkam, review of *Mansa Musa,* p. 733; September-October, 2007, Robin Smith, review of *Jazz on a Saturday Night,* p. 559; November-December, 2007, Joanna Rudge Long, review of *Mother Goose,* p. 691.

Kirkus Reviews, September 15, 1998, review of *To Every Thing There Is a Season,* p. 1383; May 1, 2002, review of *The Sorcerer's Apprentice,* p. 655; August 1, 2002, review of *Rap a Tap Tap,* p. 1126; September 1, 2007, reviews of *Jazz on a Saturday Night* and *Mother Goose.*

New York Times Book Review, November 8, 1987, Patricia MacLachlan, review of *The Porcelain Cat,* p. 50; November 15, 1998, Valerie Sayers, review of *To Every Thing There Is a Season,* p. 55.

Publishers Weekly, June 28, 1991, review of *The Race of the Golden Apples,* p. 101; August 8, 1994, review of

What Am I Looking For? p. 428; November 13, 1995, review of *The Tale of the Mandarin Ducks,* p. 60; July 27, 1998, review of *To Everything There Is a Season,* p. 76; July 31, 2000, review of *The Girl Who Spun Gold,* p. 95; October 22, 2001, review of *Mansa Musa,* p. 74; August 12, 2002, review of *Rap a Tap Tap,* p. 299; August 6, 2007, review of *Jazz on a Saturday Night,* p. 187; October 8, 2007, review of *Mother Goose,* p. 51.

School Library Journal, November, 1987, Patricia Dooley, review of *The Porcelain Cat,* p. 90; October, 1990, Kay Vandergrift, review of *The Tale of the Mandarin Ducks,* p. 111; January, 1992, Patricia Dooley, review of *Miriam's Well: Stories about Women in the Bible,* p. 118; May, 1993, Lyn Miller-Lachmann, review of *Many Thousand Gone,* p. 116; January, 1994, Patricia Dooley, review of *The Sorcerer's Apprentice,* pp. 116-117; September, 1998, Patricia Pearl Dole, review of *To Every Thing There Is a Season,* p. 198; September, 2000, Carol Ann Wilson, review of *The Girl Who Spun Gold,* p. 217; September, 2002, Wendy Lukehart, review of *Rap a Tap Tap,* p. 189; June, 2004, Sophie R. Brookover, review of *Where Have You Been?,* p. 103; September, 2007, Joyce Adams Burner, review of *Jazz on a Saturday Night,* p. 162.

ONLINE

Embracing the Child Web site, http://www.embracingthechild.org/ (October 20, 2008), "Leo and Diane Dillon."

Locus Online, http://www.locusmag.com/ (April 1, 2000), interview with Leo and Diane Dillon.

Teaching Books Web site, http://www.teachingbooks.net/ (September 2, 2005), interview with Leo and Diane Dillon.*

* * *

DORMAN, Brandon

Personal

Married. *Education:* Brigham Young University-Idaho, B.F.A.

Addresses

Home—Enumclaw, WA. *Agent*—Lou Representatives, Peter Lott, 501 5th Ave., Ste. 1708, New York, NY 10017. *E-mail*—bdillustration@gmail.com.

Career

Illustrator.

Illustrator

Jon Berkeley, *The Palace of Laughter,* HarperCollins (New York, NY), 2006.

Melvin Berger and Gilda Berger, *Can You Fly High, Wright Brothers?: A Book about Airplanes,* Scholastic (New York, NY), 2006.

Rebecca Gundersen Thornley, *I Know He Is There: A Lift-a-Flap Book about Faith,* Deseret (Salt Lake City, UT), 2006.

Melvin Berger and Gilda Berger, *What Makes the Light Bright, Mr. Edison?,* Scholastic (New York, NY), 2006.

Dean Lorey, *Nightmare Academy,* HarperCollins (New York, NY), 2007.

Melvin Berger and Gilda Berger, *Did It Take Creativity to Find Relativity, Albert Einstein?,* Scholastic (New York, NY), 2007.

Melvin Berger and Gilda Berger, *Did You Invent the Phone Alone, Alexander Graham Bell?,* Scholastic (New York, NY), 2007.

Jon Berkeley, *The Tiger's Egg* (sequel to *The Palace of Laughter*), HarperCollins (New York, NY), 2007.

Caralyn Buehner, *In the Garden,* Deseret (New York, NY), 2007.

N.E. Bode (pseudonym of Julianna Baggott), *The Slippery Map,* HarperCollins (New York, NY), 2007.

Jack Prelutsky, *The Wizard,* Greenwillow (New York, NY), 2007.

Jack Prelutsky, *Be Glad Your Nose Is on Your Face, and Other Poems: Some of the Best of Jack Prelutsky,* Greenwillow (New York, NY), 2008.

Jon Berkeley, *Between the Light* (sequel to *The Tiger's Egg*), HarperCollins (New York, NY), 2008.

Marjorie Dennis Murray, *Halloween Night,* Greenwillow (New York, NY), 2008.

Sidelights

Brandon Dorman, an illustrator based in the Pacific Northwest, creates art for a wide variety of children's books, including novels by Jon Berkeley and Dean Lorey, popular nonfiction by Melvin and Gilda Berger, and verses by noted poet Jack Prelutsky. Many of the books featuring Dorman's art are fantasies, such as *The Palace of Laughter* and *The Tiger's Egg,* two novels in Berkeley's "Wednesday Tales" series. A supernatural mystery, *The Tiger's Eye* follows orphaned Miles Wednesday in his search for his missing father. Christi Voth Esterle wrote in a *School Library Journal* review of this work that *The Tiger's Egg* contains "a lot of exciting scenes, and the pen-and-ink illustrations enliven the action." In a review of Lorey's *Nightmare Academy* for *School Library Journal,* Sharon Senser McKeller noted that Dorman's "four full-page, intricate black-and-white pencil drawings illustrate the tensest action in the novel, adding some spooky charm."

Dorman's drawings for Prelutsky's poems have also gathered praise, *School Library Journal* reviewer Lee Bock wrote of *The Wizard* that "the digitally created spreads are spectacular." In *Kirkus Reviews* a contributor commented of the same book that Dorman's "elaborately detailed digital paintings give a properly eerie setting" to Prelutsky's verse, and in *Booklist* Randall Enos described *The Wizard* as "sumptuous."

Biographical and Critical Sources

PERIODICALS

Booklist, September 1, 2007, Randall Enos, review of *The Wizard,* p. 130.

Bulletin of the Center for Children's Books, November, 2006, Karen Coats, review of *The Palace of Laughter,* p. 114; October, 2007, April Spisak, review of *Nightmare Academy,* p. 97.

Kirkus Reviews, August 15, 2007, review of *The Slippery Map*; July 15, 2007, review of *Nightmare Academy*; July 5, 2007, review of *The Wizard.*

Publishers Weekly, August 21, 2006, review of *The Palace of Laughter,* p. 68; July 9, 2007, review of *The Wizard,* p. 53; September 24, 2007, review of *The Slippery Map,* p. 71.

School Library Journal, August, 2006, Christi Voth, review of *The Palace of Laughter,* p. 114; July, 2007, Lee Bock, Review of *The Wizard,* p. 84; December, 2007, Christy Voth Esterle, review of *The Tiger's Egg,* p. 119; December, 2007, Kim Dare, review of *The Slippery Map,* p. 120; December 2007, Sharon Senser McKellar, review of *Nightmare Academy,* p. 135.

Voice of Youth Advocates, August, 2007, Sarah Coffer and Kate Rose, review of *Nightmare Academy,* p. 258.

ONLINE

Brandon Dorman Home Page, http://www.brandondorman.com (October 27, 2008).

HarperCollins Web site, http://www.harpercollins.com/ (October 27, 2008), profile of Dorman.*

*   *   *

DORROS, Alex 1991-

Personal

Born 1991; son of Arthur Dorros (a writer). *Hobbies and other interests:* Photography.

Addresses

Home—Seattle, WA. *E-mail*—alex.dorros@garfield messenger.com.

Career

Student and writer.

Writings

(With father, Arthur Dorros) *Número uno,* illustrated by Susan Guevara, Abrams (New York, NY), 2007.

Alex Dorros teams up with his father, writer Arthur Dorros, to create the picture book Número uno, *featuring artwork by Susan Guevara.* (Abrams

Sidelights

High school student Alex Dorros came up with an idea for a book in sixth grade while completing a class assignment to write a fable. For many students, the idea was forgotten after the assignment was completed, but Dorros had another plan: he collaborated with his father, writer Arthur Dorros, and turned his fable into a picture-book text. The result, *Número uno,* was published in 2007, when Dorros *fille* was only sixteen years old.

Living in a family that speaks both Spanish and English, Dorros and his father incorporate both languages into their tale, which depicts two friends who, while working together to construct a bridge, argue about which of them is "número uno." Hercules Hernandez is the builder, and his friend Socrates Rivera is the architect; the former is extremely strong while the latter is super-intelligent. As the work continues, the pair bickers about whether strength or smarts are more important. Dorros found that, at times, the writing process echoed the story, as he and his father occasionally bickered about the text. "Working on a book with your dad is definitely not the easiest of tasks," the young writer acknowledged on his home page.

In *Número uno,* the two squabbling friends create so much trouble trying to build a bridge that a young boy devises a competition, sending the men away from the village and into the mountains so that the villagers can decide who is number one. Of course, both brains and strength are needed to complete the bridge, a moral that the wise young boy supplies when the architect and builder return. Noting the dialogue inserted into the illustrations by Susan Guevara, Linda M. Kenton wrote in her *School Library Journal* review that in *Número uno* "funny details abound." In *Horn Book* Roger Sutton commented that the simple Spanish-language dialogue "punctuates the story-hour-ready text with verve," and Abby Nolan commented in *Booklist* that the "short bursts of dialogue, all in Spanish and readily understood through context, will make this fun to read aloud."

Biographical and Critical Sources

PERIODICALS

Booklist, May 15, 2007, Abby Nolan, review of *Número uno,* p. 52.
Horn Book, July-August, 2007, Roger Sutton, review of *Número uno,* p. 377.
School Library Journal, August, 2007, Linda M. Kenton, review of *Número uno,* p. 78.

ONLINE

Arthur Dorros Home Page, http://arthurdorros.com (October 27, 2008).
Alex Dorros Home Page, http://www.alexdorros.com (October 27, 2008).*

*   *   *

DRUITT, Tobias
See PURKISS, Diane

E-F

ENRIGHT, Dominique

Personal

Born in England; daughter of D.J. Enright (a poet, writer, and critic) and Madeline Harders; children: three children.

Addresses

Home—England.

Career

Writer and editor. Buchan & Enright (publishing house), cofounder.

Writings

Winston Churchill: The Greatest Briton, Michael O'Mara (London, England), 2003.

The Little Book of Facts UK, Michael O'Mara (London, England), 2004.

How to Be the Best at Everything, illustrated by Niki Catlow, Buster Books (London, England), 2004, expanded with Guy Macdonald as *The Boys' Book: How to Be the Best at Everything,* 2006, Scholastic (New York, NY), 2007.

Children's Miscellany, Volume 2, illustrated by Niki Catlow, Buster Books (London, England), 2005, published as *Children's Miscellany Too: More Useless Information That's Essential to Know,* Chronicle Books (San Francisco, CA), 2006.

In Other Words: The Meanings and Memoirs of Euphemisms, Michael O'Mara (London, England), 2005.

Children's Miscellany, Volume 3, illustrated by Niki Catlow, Buster Books (London, England), 2006.

EDITOR

Witty, Wicked, and Wise, Michael O'Mara (London, England), 2000, published as *Wicked Wit of Women,* 2003.

The Wicked Wit of Winston Churchill, Michael O'Mara (London, England), 2001.

Cover of Dominique Enright's fact-filled primer The Boys' Book: How to Be the Best at Everything. (Cover art by Getty Images. Illustration copyright © Buster Books 2004, 2005, 2006. Reproduced by permission.)

The Wicked Wit of Jane Austen, Michael O'Mara (London, England), 2002.

The Wicked Wit of Noel Coward, Michael O'Mara (London, England), 2002.

Kipling: If and Other Poems, Michael O'Mara (London, England), 2003.

Keats: Ode to a Nightingale and Other Poems, Michael O'Mara (London, England), 2003.

Burns: A Red, Red Rose and Other Poems, Michael O'Mara (London, England), 2003.

The Wicked Wit of William Shakespeare: 427 Quotes, Excerpts, and Passages, Gramercy (New York, NY), 2007.

Author's work has been translated into Spanish.

Sidelights

Writer and editor Dominique Enright is the daughter of D.J. Enright, a noted British poet and critic. She began her career in publishing not as a writer, but as an editor, and was the co-founder of the Buchan & Enright publishing house. In the late 1990s, Enright became primarily a freelance writer and editor, compiling several books of witticisms by famous British writers and speakers. Her first edited work, *Witty, Wicked, and Wise,* features quotes and barbs from female political figures from Queen Elizabeth I to Catherine the Great, as well as women writers such as Dorothy Parker and Jane Austen, and features nearly 600 quotes. In other edited works she collects quotes taken from several pithy Brits: one volume each for former British Prime Minister Winston Churchill and writers Austen, Noel Coward, and William Shakespeare.

In addition to editing collections of quips, Enright has compiled several collections of poetry and has authored a biography of Churchill and a history of common phrases and idioms in the English language. In addition, her *The Little Books of Facts UK* collects a number of quick statistics about the United Kingdom that are useful for the trivia obsessed.

Enright's first book geared for young readers was published in England and subsequently adapted for U.S. audiences with the help of Guy Macdonald. *The Boys' Book: How to Be the Best at Everything,* together with its companion volume, *The Girls' Book: How to Be the Best at Everything,* were described as "jokier and more kid friendly" than similar how-to books, according to Roger Sutton in *Horn Book.* The titles offer tips on topics ranging from fighting off crocodiles to ripping phone books in half or surviving a zombie attack. The how-to instructions range from "benign . . . to outrageous . . . to outrageously exaggerated," wrote Baran Elaine Black in her *School Library Journal* review of *The Boys' Book,* and a *Kirkus Reviews* contributor deemed Enright's volume "worth picking up for all those lads . . . eager to learn" the various offbeat skills offered.

Biographical and Critical Sources

PERIODICALS

Horn Book, September-October, 2007, Roger Sutton, review of *The Boys' Book: How to Be the Best at Everything,* p. 596.
Kirkus Reviews, July 15, 2007, review of *The Boys' Book.*
School Library Journal, September, 2007, Elaine Baran Black, review of *The Boys' Book,* p. 216.*

*   *   *

FELIN, M. Sindy

Personal

Daughter of Haitian immigrants. *Education:* Wesleyan University, B.A., 1994.

Addresses

Home—Suburban Washington, DC.

Career

Writer.

Awards, Honors

National Book Award in Young People's Literature finalist, 2007, for *Touching Snow.*

Writings

Touching Snow, Atheneum Books for Young Readers (New York, NY), 2007.

Sidelights

M. Sindy Felin's debut novel, *Touching Snow,* was one of five finalists for the 2007 National Book Award in the young people's literature category. Touching on themes of abuse and revenge, the novel tells the story of a Haitian-American girl who wants to transcend her culture's tradition of male dominance. The novel's title refers to the way Haitians describe moving to America: they will "touch snow."

Karina Lamond, the conflicted heroine of *Touching Snow,* lives in constant fear of her stepfather, a man who sees no dividing line between punishment and battery. When Karina's father beats the girl's sister into unconsciousness, the family finds itself at a difficult crossroads: Either they cover up the crime, or some members will be deported to Haiti because they are illegal immigrants. The solution Karina finally discovers is scarring but perhaps inevitable. According to a *Publish-*

ers Weekly reviewer, *Touching Snow* "carries a strong message about the complexities of abuse and why victims are not always willing to take a stand."

Felin is herself the daughter of Haitian immigrants, and critics have noted that *Touching Snow* is "richly textured with Haitian folklore and superstition," according to a *Kirkus Reviews* contributor. The novel stems not from the author's personal experiences, but from her observations of the disparity between American and Haitian forms of punishment. Although the book's subject matter is grim, according to *Horn Book* critic Claire E. Gross, Felin's "remarkably nuanced characters give this challenging read just enough humanity to make it bearable." In *Kliatt* Claire Rosser compared *Touching Snow* to Alice Walker's novel *The Color Purple,* suggesting that it similarly confronts mature themes of violence and sexuality. According to Rosser, in Felin's novel readers encounter "amazingly resilient heroines, [together] with an original authentic voice telling the story of survival."

Biographical and Critical Sources

PERIODICALS

Booklist, May 15, 2007, Francisca Goldsmith, review of *Touching Snow,* p. 43.
Bulletin of the Center for Children's Books, September, 2007, Karen Coats, review of *Touching Snow,* p. 19.
Horn Book, July-August, 2007, Claire E. Gross, review of *Touching Snow,* p. 394.
Kirkus Reviews, May 15, 2007, review of *Touching Snow.*
Kliatt, May, 2007, Claire Rosser, review of *Touching Snow,* p. 10.
Publishers Weekly, June 4, 2007, review of *Touching Snow,* p. 52.
School Library Journal, September, 2007, Carolyn Lehman, review of *Touching Snow,* p. 195.
Voice of Youth Advocates, April, 2007, C.J. Bott, review of *Touching Snow,* p. 46.

ONLINE

National Book Award Web site, http://www.nationalbook.org/ (November 11, 2008), Rita Williams-Garcia, "M. Sindy Felin."
Simon & Schuster Web site, http://www.simonsays.com/ (November 11, 2008), "M. Sindy Felin Shares the Emotionally Charged and Utterly Gripping Back Story of Her Novel *Touching Snow.**

*   *   *

FRIEND, Catherine 1957-

Personal

Born March 15, 1957; partner's name Melissa. *Education:* B.A. (Spanish and economics); M.A. (economics). *Hobbies and other interests:* Playing the piano, painting.

Addresses

Home—P.O. Box 21, Zumbrota, MN 55992. *E-mail*—Catherine@catherinefriend.com.

Career

Writer and farmer. Former teacher of writing, Institute of Children's Literature. Worked variously as a freelance editor, bookstore employee, cheese packer, and assembly-line worker.

Awards, Honors

McKnight artist fellowship, and Loft Award for Children's Literature, Loft Literary Center, both 2007, both for *Barn Boot Blues;* Golden Crown literary award, and *Lambda* Literary Award finalist, both 2007, both for *Hit by a Farm: How I Learned to Stop Worrying and Love the Barn;* Goldie Award, 2008, for *The Spanish Pearl* and *The Crown of Valencia.*

Writings

My Head Is Full of Colors, illustrated by Kiki, Hyperion Books for Children (New York, NY), 1994.
The Sawfin Stickleback: A Very Fishy Story, illustrated by Dan Yaccarino, Hyperion Books for Children (New York, NY), 1994.
The Perfect Nest, illustrated by John Manders, Candlewick Press (Cambridge, MA), 2007.

EASY READERS

Funny Ruby, illustrated by Rachel Merriman, Candlewick Press (Cambridge, MA), 2000.
Silly Ruby, illustrated by Rachel Merriman, Candlewick Press (Cambridge, MA), 2000.
Eddie the Raccoon, illustrated by Wong Herbert Yee, Candlewick Press (Cambridge, MA), 2004.

FOR ADULTS

Hit by a Farm: How I Learned to Stop Worrying and Love the Barn, Marlowe & Company (New York, NY), 2006.
The Spanish Pearl, Bold Strokes Books, 2007.
The Crown of Valencia, Bold Strokes Books, 2007.
A Pirate's Heart, Bold Strokes Books, 2008.
The Compassionate Carnivore; or, How to Keep Animals Happy, Save Old Macdonald's Farm, Reduce Your Hoofprint, and Still Eat Meat, Da Capo Press (Cambridge, MA), 2008.

Sidelights

Catherine Friend enjoys a busy but rewarding life as a writer who also runs a farm in Minnesota with her partner of more than twenty-five years. Writing for both

Featuring colorful artwork by Wong Herbert Yee, Catherine Friend's **Eddie the Raccoon** *follows its young hero in and out of trouble.* (Illustration copyright © 2000 by Wong Herbert Yee. Reproduced by permission of the publisher, Candlewick Press, Inc., Somerville. MA.)

children and adults, her published books range from basic easy readers to humorous adult titles about farming and animal husbandry. Her best-known children's book, *The Perfect Nest,* was inspired by Friend's interaction with the farmyard fowl with which she and her partner share their rural home.

In *The Perfect Nest,* a hungry cat named Jack builds a soft and enticing nest in which he hopes a hen will lay an egg the cat can use in an omelet. Jack is delighted when the nest attracts not only a hen, but also a goose and a duck, each of which lays an egg. Jack's troubles begin when he chases away the bird parents too late; far too mature for use in an omelet, the eggs are ready to hatch. "With its big pages and energetic telling, this will make a great story-time book," wrote Susan Dove Lempke in *Horn Book,* while *School Library Journal* contributor Catherine Callegari dubbed *The Perfect Nest* a "highly comical yet heartwarming tale" that is "laugh-out-loud funny." A correspondent for *Kirkus Reviews* praised the illustrations by John Manders and concluded that Friend's picture book provides "perfect free-feathered fun."

In *Hit by a Farm: How I Learned to Stop Worrying and Love the Barn* Friend takes a humorous but unsenti-

mental look at the difficulties of farm work and how time-consuming it can be. Noting that the author's "simple life" theme might even attract teen readers, *Booklist* critic Nancy Bent added that *Hit by a Farm* "will charm all who yearn for more rural roots" and provide food for thought for those readers "with romantic notions of living off the land."

Biographical and Critical Sources

BOOKS

Friend, Catherine, *Hit by a Farm: How I Learned to Stop Worrying and Love the Barn,* Marlowe & Company (New York, NY), 2006.

PERIODICALS

Booklist, March 15, 1994, Ilene Cooper, review of *My Head Is Full of Colors,* p. 1372; July, 2004, Stephanie Zvirin, review of *Eddie the Raccoon,* p. 1850; April 15, 2006, Nancy Bent, review of *Hit by a Farm,* p. 14.

Horn Book, March-April, 2007, Susan Dove Lempke, review of *The Perfect Nest,* p. 180.

Kirkus Reviews, January 15, 2007, review of *The Perfect Nest,* p. 72.

Publishers Weekly, April 25, 1994, review of *My Head Is Full of Colors,* p. 77; October 3, 1994, review of *The Sawfin Stickleback: A Very Fishy Story,* p. 68.

School Library Journal, June, 1994, Kate McClelland, review of *My Head Is Full of Colors,* p. 99; December, 1994, Kathy Piehl, review of *The Sawfin Stickleback,* p. 74; February, 2001, Adele Greenlee, review of *Funny Ruby,* p. 100; January, 2005, Marilyn Taniguchi, review of *Eddie the Raccoon,* p. 92; March, 2007, Catherine Callegari, review of *The Perfect Nest,* p. 160.

ONLINE

Bold Strokes Books Web site, http://www.boldstrokesbooks. com/ (November 11, 2008), "Catherine Friend."

Catherine Friend Home Page, http://www.catherinefriend. com (November 11, 2008).*

*   *   *

FROST, Helen 1949-
(Helen Marie Frost)

Personal

Born March 4, 1949, in Brookings, SD; married Chad Thompson, 1983; children: Lloyd (stepson), Glen. *Education:* Syracuse University, B.A.; Indiana University, M.A., 1994. *Hobbies and other interests:* Hiking, cross-country skiing, raising and releasing monarch butterflies, genealogy.

Addresses

Home—Fort Wayne, IN. *E-mail*—info@helenfrost.net.

Career

Educator and author. Kilquhanity House School (boarding school), Scotland, teacher, 1976-78; elementary school teacher/principal in Telida, AK, 1981-84, then Ketchikan, AK; Indiana University/Purdue University at Fort Wayne, instructor. Fort Wayne Dance Collective, member of interdisciplinary artistic team, 1995-2006.

Awards, Honors

Robert H. Winner Memorial Award, Poetry Society of America, 1992; Mary Carolyn Davies Award, Poetry Society of America, 1993; Women Poets Series Competition winner, Ampersand Press, 1993; Michael Printz Honor Book designation, American Library Association, 2004, for *Keesha's House;* Lee Bennett Hopkins Poetry Award Honor designation, 2007, for *The Braid;* several other awards and honors.

Helen Frost (Photo courtesy of James D. Gabbard)

Writings

JUVENILE FICTION; NOVELS IN POEMS

Keesha's House (young-adult novel), Farrar, Straus (New York, NY), 2003.

Spinning through the Universe: A Novel in Poems from Room 214 (middle-grade novel), Farrar, Straus (New York, NY), 2004.

The Braid (young-adult novel), Farrar, Straus (New York, NY), 2006.

Diamond Willow (middle-grade novel), Farrar, Straus (New York, NY), 2008.

JUVENILE NONFICTION

Monarch and Milkweed, illustrated by Leonid Gore, Atheneum (New York, NY), 2008.

"BIRDS" SERIES; JUVENILE NONFICTION

Bird Eggs, Pebble Books (Mankato, MN), 1999.
Bird Nests, Pebble Books (Mankato, MN), 1999.
Baby Birds, Pebble Books (Mankato, MN), 1999.
Bird Families, Pebble Books (Mankato, MN), 1999.

"BUTTERFLIES" SERIES; JUVENILE NONFICTION

Butterfly Eggs, Pebble Books (Mankato, MN), 1999.
Caterpillars, Pebble Books (Mankato, MN), 1999.
Butterfly Colors, Pebble Books (Mankato, MN), 1999.
Monarch Butterflies, Pebble Books (Mankato, MN), 1999.

"DENTAL HEALTH" SERIES; JUVENILE NONFICTION

Your Teeth, Pebble Books (Mankato, MN), 1999.
Going to the Dentist, Pebble Books (Mankato, MN), 1999.
Food for Healthy Teeth, Pebble Books (Mankato, MN), 1999.
Brushing Well, Pebble Books (Mankato, MN), 1999.

"FOOD GUIDE PYRAMID" SERIES; JUVENILE NONFICTION

The Fruit Group, Pebble Books (Mankato, MN), 2000.
Eating Right, Pebble Books (Mankato, MN), 2000.
The Vegetable Group, Pebble Books (Mankato, MN), 2000.
The Dairy Group, Pebble Books (Mankato, MN), 2000.
Fats, Oils, and Sweets, Pebble Books (Mankato, MN), 2000.
Drinking Water, Pebble Books (Mankato, MN), 2000.
The Grain Group, Pebble Books (Mankato, MN), 2000.
The Meat and Protein Group, Pebble Books (Mankato, MN), 2000.

"WATER" SERIES; JUVENILE NONFICTION

Keeping Water Clean, Pebble Books (Mankato, MN), 2000.
The Water Cycle, Pebble Books (Mankato, MN), 2000.
Water as a Solid, Pebble Books (Mankato, MN), 2000.
Water as a Liquid, Pebble Books (Mankato, MN), 2000.
Water as a Gas, Pebble Books (Mankato, MN), 2000.
We Need Water, Pebble Books (Mankato, MN), 2000.

Books in series have been translated into Spanish.

"NATIONAL HOLIDAYS" SERIES; JUVENILE NONFICTION

Memorial Day, Pebble Books (Mankato, MN), 2000.
Independence Day, Pebble Books (Mankato, MN), 2000.
Martin Luther King, Jr., Day, Pebble Books (Mankato, MN), 2000.
Presidents' Day, Pebble Books (Mankato, MN), 2000.

"SENSES" SERIES; JUVENILE NONFICTION

Your Senses, Pebble Books (Mankato, MN), 2000.
Smelling, Pebble Books (Mankato, MN), 2000.
Touching, Pebble Books (Mankato, MN), 2000.
Tasting, Pebble Books (Mankato, MN), 2000.
Seeing, Pebble Books (Mankato, MN), 2000.
Hearing, Pebble Books (Mankato, MN), 2000.

"EMOTIONS" SERIES; JUVENILE NONFICTION

Feeling Sad, Pebble Books (Mankato, MN), 2001.
Feeling Angry, Pebble Books (Mankato, MN), 2001.
Feeling Scared, Pebble Books (Mankato, MN), 2001.
Feeling Happy, Pebble Books (Mankato, MN), 2001.

"HUMAN BODY SYSTEMS" SERIES; JUVENILE NONFICTION

The Circulatory System, Pebble Books (Mankato, MN), 2001.
The Respiratory System, Pebble Books (Mankato, MN), 2001.
The Nervous System, Pebble Books (Mankato, MN), 2001.
The Muscular System, Pebble Books (Mankato, MN), 2001.
The Skeletal System, Pebble Books (Mankato, MN), 2001.
The Digestive System, Pebble Books (Mankato, MN), 2001.

"LOOKING AT SIMPLE MACHINES" SERIES; JUVENILE NONFICTION

What Are Inclined Planes?, Pebble Books (Mankato, MN), 2001.
What Are Levers?, Pebble Books (Mankato, MN), 2001.
What Are Screws?, Pebble Books (Mankato, MN), 2001.
What Are Wedges?, Pebble Books (Mankato, MN), 2001.
What Are Wheels and Axles?, Pebble Books (Mankato, MN), 2001.
What Are Pulleys?, Pebble Books (Mankato, MN), 2001.

"ALL ABOUT PETS" SERIES; JUVENILE NONFICTION

Cats, Pebble Books (Mankato, MN), 2001.
Fish, Pebble Books (Mankato, MN), 2001.
Hamsters, Pebble Books (Mankato, MN), 2001.
Dogs, Pebble Books (Mankato, MN), 2001.
Rabbits, Pebble Books (Mankato, MN), 2001.
Birds, Pebble Books (Mankato, MN), 2001.

"INSECTS" SERIES; JUVENILE NONFICTION

Praying Mantises, Pebble Books (Mankato, MN), 2001.
Walkingsticks, Pebble Books (Mankato, MN), 2001.
Water Bugs, Capstone Press (Mankato, MN), 2001.
Moths, Capstone Press (Mankato, MN), 2001.
Wasps, Capstone Press (Mankato, MN), 2001.
Cicadas, Capstone Press (Mankato, MN), 2001.

"OUR WORLD" SERIES; JUVENILE NONFICTION

A Look at China, Pebble Books (Mankato, MN), 2002.
A Look at France, Pebble Books (Mankato, MN), 2002.
A Look at Kenya, Pebble Books (Mankato, MN), 2002.
A Look at Russia, Pebble Books (Mankato, MN), 2002.
A Look at Japan, Pebble Books (Mankato, MN), 2002.
A Look at Canada, Pebble Books (Mankato, MN), 2002.
A Look at Australia, Pebble Books (Mankato, MN), 2002.

A Look at Mexico, Pebble Books (Mankato, MN), 2002.
A Look at Egypt, Pebble Books (Mankato, MN), 2003.
A Look at Cuba, Pebble Books (Mankato, MN), 2003.
A Look at Germany, Pebble Books (Mankato, MN), 2003.
A Look at Vietnam, Pebble Books (Mankato, MN), 2003.

"RAIN FOREST ANIMALS" SERIES; JUVENILE NONFICTION

Jaguars, Pebble Books (Mankato, MN), 2002.
Boa Constrictors, Pebble Books (Mankato, MN), 2002.
Gorillas, Capstone Press (Mankato, MN), 2002.
Tree Frogs, Pebble Books (Mankato, MN), 2002.
Tarantulas, Pebble Books (Mankato, MN), 2002.
Parrots, Capstone Press (Mankato, MN), 2002.
Lemurs, Pebble Books (Mankato, MN), 2003.
Chimpanzees, Pebble Books (Mankato, MN), 2003.
Leaf-Cutting Ants, Pebble Books (Mankato, MN), 2003.
Tigers, Pebble Books (Mankato, MN), 2003.

"COMING TO AMERICA" SERIES; JUVENILE NONFICTION

German Immigrants, 1820-1920, Blue Earth Books (Mankato, MN), 2002.
Russian Immigrants, 1860-1949, Blue Earth Books (Mankato, MN), 2003.

"FAMOUS AMERICANS" SERIES; JUVENILE NONFICTION

John F. Kennedy, Pebble Books (Mankato, MN), 2003.
Sojourner Truth, Pebble Books (Mankato, MN), 2003.
Betsy Ross, Pebble Books (Mankato, MN), 2003.
Thurgood Marshall, Pebble Books (Mankato, MN), 2003.

"LET'S MEET" SERIES; JUVENILE NONFICTION

Let's Meet Jackie Robinson, Chelsea Clubhouse Books (Philadelphia, PA), 2004.
Let's Meet Booker T. Washington, Chelsea Clubhouse (Philadelphia, PA), 2004.
Let's Meet Ida B. Wells-Barnett, Chelsea Clubhouse Books (Philadelphia, PA), 2004.

"WEATHER" SERIES; JUVENILE NONFICTION

Ice, Capstone Press (Mankato, MN), 2004.
Fog, Capstone Press (Mankato, MN), 2004.
Snow, Capstone Press (Mankato, MN), 2004.
Wind, Capstone Press (Mankato, MN), 2004.

"DINOSAURS AND PREHISTORIC ANIMALS" SERIES; JUVENILE NONFICTION

Woolly Mammoth, Capstone Press (Mankato, MN), 2004.
Tyrannosaurus Rex, Capstone Press (Mankato, MN), 2004.
Triceratops, Capstone Press (Mankato, MN), 2004.
Sabertooth Cat, Capstone Press (Mankato, MN), 2004.
Allosaurus, Capstone Press (Mankato, MN), 2004.
Stegosaurus, Capstone Press (Mankato, MN), 2004.

Books in series have been translated into Spanish.

"HELPERS IN OUR COMMUNITY" SERIES; JUVENILE NONFICTION

We Need Auto Mechanics, Capstone Press (Mankato, MN), 2004.
We Need Plumbers, Capstone Press (Mankato, MN), 2004.
We Need School Bus Drivers, Pebble Books (Mankato, MN), 2004.
We Need Pharmacists, Capstone Press (Mankato, MN), 2005.

"POLAR ANIMALS" SERIES; JUVENILE NONFICTION

Snowy Owls, Pebble Books (Mankato, MN), 2007.
Puffins, Pebble Books (Mankato, MN), 2007.
Caribou, Pebble Books (Mankato, MN), 2007.
Arctic Hares, Pebble Books (Mankato, MN), 2007.

FOR ADULTS

(Editor) *Season of Dead Water* (poetry and prose anthology), Breitenbush Books (Portland, OR), 1990.
Skin of a Fish, Bones of a Bird: Poems, Ampersand Press (Bristol, RI), 1993.
(Editor) *Why Darkness Seems So Light: Young People Speak Out about Violence* (also see below), Pecan Grove Press, 1998.
(With Harvey Cocks) *Why Darkness Seems So Light* (play; based on Frost's book of the same title), Pioneer Drama, 1999.
When I Whistle, Nobody Listens: Helping Young People Write about Difficult Issues, Heinemann (Portsmouth, NH), 2001.

Sidelights

In addition to her work as a teacher—she has taught students in Scotland, Vermont, and Alaska, as well as Indiana and, as a poet-in-residence, throughout the United States—Helen Frost is a poet and playwright as well as a prolific author of fiction and nonfiction for young readers. Frost's fictional works include the Michael J. Printz young-adult honor book *Keesha's House* as well as middle-grade novels such as *Diamond Willow* and the historical novel *The Braid.* Drawing on her experiences as a classroom teacher, Frost's numerous nonfiction contributions to informative series for elementary-grade students reflect her varied interests in science and history. In addition to writing for young people, Frost is also the author of *When I Whisper, Nobody Listens: Helping Young People Write about Difficult Issues,* a book that *Journal of Adolescent and Adult Literacy* contributor M.P. Cavanaugh explained is designed to "prepare teachers to work with students on sensitive issues and to provide nonviolent solutions to some of their problems."

Keesha's House, a novel-in-poems for older readers, focuses on seven inner-city teens whose lives are in turmoil until they find refuge in a home owned by a caring adult named Joe. Dubbed "Keesha's House" in honor of the first person to be welcomed there, Joe's home becomes a haven for pregnant teen Stephie; Katie, who is escaping her stepfather's sexual molestation; gay teen Harris, whose parents do not accept his sexual orientation; unhappy foster-child Dontay; Carmen, who is battling an addiction to alcohol; high-school basketball star Jason, who struggles between college and his responsibility as the father of Stephie's baby; and Keesha herself, whose father becomes violent with his children after their mother dies. Praised as a "moving" work containing "dramatic monologues that are personal, poetic, and immediate" by *Booklist* contributor Hazel Rochman, *Keesha's House* features sonnet and sestina verse forms that reflect contemporary speech, making the book easy going for those unfamiliar with poetry. In *Publishers Weekly* a reviewer found the work "thoughtfully composed and ultimately touching," while Michele Winship wrote in *Kliatt* that the poems in *Keesha's House* "weave together stories that depict the harsh reality of teenage life."

A book that "brings to life the voices and spirit of a fifth-grade classroom," according to a *Publishers Weekly* contributor, *Spinning through the Universe: A Novel in Poems from Room 214* contains verses that reflect the dreams, worries, enthusiasms, and day-to-day lives of Mrs. Williams's fifth-grade class. Each of the twenty-six students composes a poem in a different poetic form, waxing poetic on subjects ranging from a lost bicycle to the death of a parent. Characterized by the *Publishers Weekly* critic as "brief, deceptively casual poetic monologues," these poems are followed by a concluding chapter about reading and writing poetry. Poetic forms described by Frost include haiku, blank verse, sonnets, sestinas, rondelets, and other less-familiar forms. In fact, an entire section devoted to acrostics prompted *School Library Journal* contributor Lee Bock to note that "readers will enjoy decoding them to reveal an additional thought about each character." Bock dubbed *Spinning through the Universe* a "boon for poetry classes," while in *Kirkus Reviews* a critic wrote that Frost's use of "original imagery and understated, natural voices make these poems sensitive and insightful."

Frost moves from the present to the past in *The Braid*, transporting readers across the Atlantic to Scotland and back through time to the mid-nineteenth century. In Frost's evocative narrative poems, teenaged sisters Jeannie and Sarah speak of life on the remote island of Barra, in the Scottish Hebrides. When their family is forced from the lands they have occupied for years as part of the landholder's efforts to free up grazing pasture for sheep, Jeannie accompanies her parents on the arduous sea voyage to eastern Canada. Unwilling to leave her homeland, Sarah hides so that she can remain in Scotland and care for her elderly grandmother. The historic backdrop of the novel—the Highland Clearances—are not familiar to many North American readers, explained Janis Flint-Ferguson in her *Kliatt* review, and Frost's novel "gives voice to the tragic circum-

stances that populated Nova Scotia, Canada." In twin strands of poetry, the two sisters relate their sadness over the miles that separate them and describe the harsh and often tragic circumstances they encounter as a result of their choice. In these tales Frost interweaves "themes of home, shelter, and heritage, as well as the yearning for family wherever one lives," according to Rochman in *Booklist*. Paralleling the action in her tale, Frost employs a braid-like structure to her narrative: as the sisters alternate their stories, the last word of each line in one sister's poem becomes the first word in each line of the other sister's poem. Despite being so highly crafted, Frost's text reads with "such delicacy that few readers will note [the novel's] formal structure," asserted *Horn Book* reviewer Joanna Rudge Long, the critic adding that *The Braid* is "compellingly poignant" and its teen characters "courageous and well realized."

While Frost has become well known for her novels-in-poems for older readers, she has also written numerous series of early-reader nonfiction: short books presenting basic facts and information in a minimal text well-illustrated with photographs, maps, diagrams, and other artwork. With approximately twenty sentences per book, volumes such as *A Look at France* in the "Our World" series, and *What Are Levers?* in the "Looking at Simple Machines" series, were written to appeal to beginning scholars and use a simple vocabulary to convey rudimentary information. More detail is provided in Frost's contributions to the "Coming to America" series, designed for older readers. Praising the author's research in *German Immigrants, 1820-1920* as "solid," *Booklist* reviewer Rochman added that the book serves young readers of German and Scandinavian ancestry as "a good place to start researching family history."

With her varied experiences as a teacher of at-risk students, Frost encourages teachers and librarians to recognize the value of both reading and writing poetry to young adults. "I bet half the teenagers I know have notebooks . . . ," she explained to *School Library Journal* contributor Rick Margolis. "When I meet a group of 10 kids, I can almost guarantee that one of them is going to say, 'I'm a poet,' and bring in reams of poems the next week. And if I ask, 'How many of you like to write poetry?' at least half of them will say they do."

Biographical and Critical Sources

PERIODICALS

Booklist, October 15, 2001, Hazel Rochman, review of *German Immigrants, 1820-1920*, p. 406; March 1, 2003, Hazel Rochman, review of *Keesha's House*, p. 1192; April 1, 2004, Hazel Rochman, review of *Spinning through the Universe: A Novel in Poems from Room 214*, p. 1363; June 1, 2006, Hazel Rochman, review of *The Braid*, p. 74; January 1, 2008, Carolyn Phelan, review of *Monarch and Milkweed*, p. 79.

Bulletin of the Center for Children's Books, December, 2006, Deborah Stevenson, review of *The Braid,* p. 170.

Horn Book, November-December, 2006, Joanna Rudge Long, review of *The Braid,* p. 709; July-August, 2008, Deirdre F. Baker, review of *Diamond Willow,* p. 444.

Journal of Adolescent & Adult Literacy, November, 2002, M.P. Cavanaugh, review of *When I Whisper, Nobody Listens: Helping Young People Write about Difficult Issues,* p. 275.

Kirkus Reviews, March 1, 2004, review of *Spinning through the Universe,* p. 221; October 1, 2006, review of *The Braid,* p. 1014; February 1, 2008, review of *Monarch and Milkweed;* June 15, 2008, review of *Diamond Willow.*

Kliatt, March, 2003, Michele Winship, review of *Keesha's House,* p. 10; November, 2006, Janis Flint-Ferguson, review of *The Braid,* p. 10.

Publishers Weekly, May 25, 1990, Penny Kaganoff, review of *Season of Dead Water,* p. 54; April 21, 2003, review of *Keesha's House,* p. 63; April 5, 2004, review of *Spinning through the Universe,* p. 63; October 16, 2006, review of *The Braid,* p. 55.

School Library Journal, August, 2000, Pamela K. Bombay, review of *Martin Luther King, Jr., Day,* p. 169; October, 2000, Carolyn Jenks, review of *Drinking Water,* p. 147; January, 2001, Judith Constantinides, review of *Feeling Angry,* p. 117; April, 2001, Dona J. Helmer, review of *The Circulatory System,* p. 130; August, 2001, Blair Christolon, review of *What Are Levers?,* p. 168; September, 2001, Karey Wehner, review of *Moths,* p. 214; December, 2001, Elizabeth Talbot, review of *A Look at Russia,* p. 121; June, 2002, Ann W. Moore, review of *A Look at France,* p. 120; October, 2002, Linda Ludke, review of *A Look at Canada,* p. 144; October, 2003, Jennifer Ralston, review of *Keesha's House,* p. 99; November, 2003, Michele Shaw, review of *Betsy Ross,* p. 125; April, 2004, Lee Bock, review of *Spinning through the Universe,* p. 154; April, 2004, review of *Keesha's House,* p. 64; October, 2006, Rick Margolis, "A Gentle Frost," interview, p. 38, and Jill Heritage Maza, review of *The Braid,* p. 154; January, 2008, Heidi Estrin, review of *Monarch and Milkweed,* p. 104; June, 2008, Marilyn Taniguchi, review of *Diamond Willow,* p. 140.

ONLINE

Helen Frost Home Page, http:// www.helenfrost.net (October 27, 2008).

<hr />

Autobiography Feature

<hr />

Helen Frost

H elen Frost contributed the following autobiographical essay to *SATA:*

1. Brookings, South Dakota—1949-56

In the 100 years before I was born, my ancestors traveled from Scotland, Denmark, Norway, and England to Prince Edward Island, Georgia, Minnesota, Michigan, Wisconsin, South Carolina, Virginia, Florida, North Dakota, and South Dakota. In those same 100 years, the place I was born changed from being the home of the Lakota Sioux and magnificent herds of buffalo, to being claimed and settled by immigrants from far-off places. Like all children, I was born not knowing any of this. I am still learning what it means.

I was born in Brookings, South Dakota, on March 4, 1949—in the middle of a century, in the middle of a continent, and, as it would turn out, in the middle of a large family. I was the fifth daughter of Reuben ("Jack") and Jean Frost, in a family that would eventually include ten children. I remember learning to walk, standing on wobbly legs as my parents and older sisters stood in a circle around me with outstretched arms, asking, "Whose girl are you?" Later, as the circle expanded, I became one of the people reaching out to a younger sister or brother, encouraging their first steps.

My memories of those early years are happy. My older sisters taught me to ride a tricycle, climb trees, make doll clothes. They stuck up for me if one of the neighbor kids was mean; they pushed me on the tire swing Dad hung from the apple tree; they wrapped me in a blanket and held me close as we sang around a campfire at the end of a picnic at Oakwood Park; they read to me; showed me how to write, draw, and roller skate.

I know we must have argued, because one of my grandmother's expressions was "quit your scrapping" (or, as I remember it, "kwitcherscrappin," twin to my father's "kwitcherbellyachin"), but we all knew we were secure, loved, and listened to.

Although my aunts, uncles, grandmothers, and cousins didn't live in Brookings, we got together frequently, and they were important to me. When I was three, my cousin was hospitalized with polio and all the grownups were preoccupied with that. Listening to their conversation, I looked up and asked my uncle, "How is Ruth

"In a picnic basket in the house in Brookings, South Dakota, 1949. Photo by Helen Caroline Frost (my aunt; she is no longer living)." (Reprinted with permission of Helen Frost.)

Mary?" I still remember him kneeling down and answering my question with honesty and clarity, though he was also careful, I realize now, not to frighten me.

One other very early memory, or maybe it is a family story told so often I feel I can remember it: When I was two, our family was sitting in the front row of the balcony at church and I threw my snow pants over the railing. My fast-thinking, quick-acting father reached out and caught them by the strap on one finger, much to the suppressed amusement of everyone sitting behind us and the good luck of those in the pews below.

When I ask my mother, now ninety years old, for her memories of me as a young child, she recalls, "You were always interested in everything. You wanted to try everything. Jack and I enjoyed watching you grow up and become able to do all those things you'd been trying to do."

I was especially interested in the natural world. I loved being outdoors: I caught tadpoles and watched them grow into frogs; I watched ants go in and out of their anthills; I caught fireflies in jars on summer evenings. I teased my sister by dangling spiders in front of her face (I said I was a happy child; I didn't say I was a perfect angel).

Monarch butterflies were magical to me, as they still are today, though at that time I collected them, rather than protecting them as I do now. My father made me a butterfly net; my mother showed me how to capture butterflies and put alcohol on a piece of Kleenex tucked into the jar lid so they would die quickly with a minimum of damage to their wings.

My father made me a mounting board, and found special straight pins for me to use in mounting butterflies and other insects. When I was three, my parents took me to the entomology lab at South Dakota State College: drawers and cases full of beetles, butterflies, dragonflies and walkingsticks. I learned the word "entomologist," and started telling people I was going to be one when I grew up.

Maybe that was how I began to be a poet, by savoring that intricate word, "entomologist," equally with the insects I so loved, fascinated both by the things of the world and the discovery that they had names: snapping turtle, campanile, Skinner's Butte, cistern, ugly mutt. I

"During the brief time that I was the youngest: Learning to eat ice cream cones, 1950. Clockwise from left: Kathy, Margaret, Mary, Helen, Barbie" (Reprinted with permission of Helen Frost.)

was also interested in abstract words that carried weight and power—"enemy" is one I remember thinking about, and "sin," and "wicked."

My father told us stories. He used our names for his characters, animal or human, hero or villain, and we made a game of staying at the edges of the room so as not to be "caught" listening, and thus having a ferocious monster or nasty old pirate named after us. Once the character was named, though, we'd come in close to hear the story, climbing into Dad's lap or hanging on the back and arms of his chair. Later I learned that his storytelling was also an expression of love for my mother—that he was "keeping us out of her hair" while she got dinner ready or soothed a fussy baby. He invented his stories as he went along, sometimes pausing and letting us fill in the details: the joyful education of the imagination.

The line between imagination and real life remained hazy for me for quite a while. Summer evenings after supper, someone might say "Let's go for a ride." We would all pile into the station wagon and drive out into the countryside, just for the fun of it. I must have dreamed that I played on the clouds with my sisters, bouncing and sliding around on them, because I remember thinking, when I got a little older, maybe six or seven, "We haven't played on the clouds for a long time." And then, at some point, I realized we never really could have done that.

Even before I could write, I liked to pretend I could, scribbling what looked to me like grownup handwriting, and reading what I thought I had written. Someone gave us a big box of "shiny paper" and my mother kept it on a high shelf in the hall closet. It seemed to be an infinite supply, always there for the asking, like Ritz crackers and water. "Mom," we'd say, running in from playing outdoors, "can I have a drink and a cracker?" Or, on a rainy day, "Can I have some shiny paper?"

We had a shoebox full of broken crayons, with their papers peeling off, a metal pencil sharpener half-buried in the mix of shavings at the bottom of the box. I remember the smell of that box and the smell of crayons melting on a hot radiator. Once, when my parents and older sisters went to Niagara Falls, I stayed with my grandmother for a week, and she bought me a box of sixteen new crayons—a whole box, all to myself—and made me an apron with sixteen little pockets to put them in.

In Brookings, from an early age, we were free to roam the neighborhood. At noon every day, the local power plant blew a whistle. Our mother, and the neighbor kids' mothers, sent us out to play with the instructions to "come home at the twelve-o'clock whistle."

I don't want to stop writing about my early childhood: The dead turtle I dug out of the mud when I was five (my father helped me extract the turtle so I could keep the shell); the fistfuls of dandelions we'd bring to my mother (she would stop whatever she was doing to put them in a jar of water); the porch off our second-floor bedroom that my sisters would dare me to climb out on, and then down the trellis to the great waiting night ("you'll be a daredevil if you do it"); our neighbor "Crazy Jim" who once dragged a dog down the street by its ears; ribbon candy at Christmas; ghost costumes for Halloween; the IXL store owned by Judy Billings' uncle, who gave us free popsicles on hot summer days; a broken collar bone; a deep cut on my knee; mumps and measles; Grandma Viney staying with us each time a new baby was born; weeding the vegetable garden; climbing the apple trees; my sister biting a neighbor girl; Dad learning to fly small airplanes and flying over our house ("waggle your wings at us," we'd beg before he left); X-ray machines in the shoe store. This list could go on for pages.

But I have a whole life ahead of me. It's time to go to school.

There was a tradition in Brookings each spring, a day called "Visiting Day," where every kindergartner could bring a four year old to school for one day. We would talk about it and plan it out years in advance: "My big sister can bring your sister, and then she can bring me, and then I'll bring your little brother." By the time Leslie Billings brought me to Visiting Day, I was very excited about starting school. My mother had promised that I could get a library card on my first day of school, and going to Visiting Day with Leslie meant that day was right around the corner.

On the way home from the first day of kindergarten, I proudly stopped at the Brookings Public Library, up the steps of the red-brick building on the corner, through the door, to the left, down the stairs, to the children's section in the basement. The librarian, Miss Ruby Jarman, already knew that I was a "Frost girl" and that I loved insects; from that very first day I got my library card, she began to suggest books she thought I'd like, and she was usually right. A card in the back of each book had the signatures of each person who had checked out the book, and stamps of all the dates on which the book had been due—like a simple book review system, if I saw names of people I knew and admired, perhaps children a few years older than I was, I wanted to read the same book they had read.

I loved kindergarten—finger-painting on big sheets of paper, playing with a giant set of dominoes (so big we had to hold one domino in both hands), circle games ("Farmer in the Dell," "Skip to My Lou," "Go in and out the Window"), rest time (I remember lying on a towel in a patch of sunlight, the teacher leaning down to tuck a strand of hair behind my ear), and story time (*Millions of Cats, The Story of Ping, Make Way for Ducklings*).

One day I broke down in tears of frustration—the teacher couldn't see what was so hard about what she had asked of us; all the other children were happily completing the project, while I sniffled and complained that I'd never get it done. When my mother came to pick me up, the teacher expressed surprised concern about my behavior.

"What were they supposed to do?" my mother asked.

"Just a simple task—draw a picture of your family."

My mother laughed and explained why I may have found that daunting—our family by that time numbered nine people.

At home, I loved to go down in the basement and be with my father in his workshop. He built a dresser, a picnic box, benches for our kitchen table, a rocking horse, a toy stove—his work was solid, precisely measured, not decoratively elegant, but full of functional detail that will last for generations. His motto was "If something is worth doing, it is worth doing right." If we were in the workshop when Dad got hungry (or maybe when he thought we were), he had a bowl of walnuts and pecans that he would crack open with a hammer and share with us. Sometimes he peeled oranges and gave us each a section.

2. Eugene, Oregon, and Back to Brookings—1956-60

The summer after I was in first grade, we moved from South Dakota to Eugene, Oregon, for one school year so that my father, at the age of fifty-three, could complete his Ph.D. in Physical Education. (His undergraduate degree was in Classics, but he had been, as well as a teacher, a basketball and baseball coach, an umpire, a referee, and an athletic director.) My parents sold our big house at 202 Fifth Street and managed to get all the accumulated belongings of nine people pared down to what would fit into a station wagon and a box-like trailer we called "The Monster." It seemed to us that our parents were ruthless as they threw our treasures into an old cistern in the backyard and then put the cover back on the cistern and sealed it up—"No you can't keep your rock collection. You can choose one doll and one other toy. Here is a drawstring bag for your clothes."

At least it was a chance to get rid of the "Coach, That's My Dad!" T-shirts that I hated—someone at a coaching conference gave a bunch of them to Dad and we wore them because they were free; I hated people "reading me" when I wore one. (I still don't like to wear clothes that say things on them.)

We gave up a lot of our treasures during that move. The attic in *Keesha's House*—the turtle shell, my favorite Lennon Sisters paper dolls—is, in part, based on the memory of what we left behind in the attic of that house. We were supposed to get it all back when we returned, but for some reason, we never did. I wonder if some other child living in the house in the years since then explored the attic and found my butterfly net.

"My mother taking up the hem of a dress I inherited from my cousin, 1954" (Reprinted with permission of Helen Frost.)

We took two weeks to drive to Oregon, camping along the way—we saw the Badlands, the Black Hills, Yellowstone Park; we went over a pass in the Rocky Mountains with "The Monster" swaying dangerously behind us. It was on that trip that I got the nickname "R.K."

for "Reckless Kid." I loved walking away from our campsites to go exploring. I wanted to put my hand into the geysers and hot springs at Yellowstone to see if they were really hot. At a rest area in Yellowstone, a family of black bears seemed friendly enough that I held out a lifesaver on my hand. I was excited when one of the bear cubs approached to accept my gift. "Whose child is that?!" roared the park ranger, and my parents had to acknowledge that I was theirs.

The year in Oregon was a big adventure. I discovered the Pacific Ocean, Agate Beach, and Crater Lake. Perhaps more important, I learned that I could move to a new place, learn my way around, and make new friends. We lived near Julian's Bakery, where they sold day-old bread, "five loaves for a dollar," and I loved to be entrusted with a dollar to walk down the street and bring home those five loaves. Years later, when I was in Eugene as an adult, I came out of my hotel and smelled a deeply familiar smell—it was Julian's Bakery, and from the aroma of baking bread, I had a complete mental map of the neighborhood—I went for a walk and found the place our house had been, and knew the way to my friend Terry's house and the way to Condon Elementary School, where I attended second grade.

In October of that year, my brother Dick was born. Until that time, I had been reticent about participating in "Show and Tell" at school, but when I whispered the news to my teacher, she said to the class, "I think Helen has some news to share with us this morning."

I reluctantly got up and said, "We have seven girls and we finally got a boy." The whole class gasped in appreciation, and I was hooked—after that, I had something to say almost every day, and I have rarely been nervous about public speaking since.

That year, I discovered that I could read chapter books, and I wrote my first poems. The poems were nothing remarkable, mostly playing around with little rhymes like "chalk, walk, talk," but I valued them enough to illustrate them, copy them out into a handmade book (construction paper tied with yarn), titled, "*My Poem Book,* by Helen Frost" and give the book to my sister Barbie for Christmas. A year later, I found the poems embarrassing, which I see now as a good thing; I was learning to see the difference between "what I used to write" and "what I can do now," and to wonder if I could write something better.

I also enjoyed writing letters to my grandmothers. Initially, of course, my mother made me do it, but then it became something I liked to do. Some of those letters have been returned to me, saved first by my grandmothers, then by my parents, for forty or fifty years. My grandfathers both died before my parents were married, and my grandmothers both lived with other single women relatives. I once shortened the salutation of a letter to my mother's mother, whose first name was Viney, writing "Dear Viney Family" to save the trouble of spelling out "Dear Grandma Viney, Auntie, and Aunt Margaret."

We returned to Brookings after our year in Oregon, and lived in a new house in a different neighborhood. I

made friends with a new group of neighbor kids, and walked to school with them in third, fourth, and fifth grades.

It is fifth grade that stands out in my memory. Many of the poems in *Spinning through the Universe* have their seeds in the events of that year. There was a girl everyone made fun of; a girl who was kind to her; constantly shifting boundaries of friendship and belonging; boys and girls just beginning to express interest in one another. We loved to ride our bikes around town, and when someone's cat had kittens, everyone else begged their parents to let them keep one.

I walked to and from school that year with a group of friends: Kristin, Tink, and Ann, and sometimes one or two others. There was an alley on the way home with a huge bell, and we dared each other to ring the bell as we ran past. A group of boys we called "the chasers" ran after us—I don't recall that they ever caught us, and I don't think we, or they, would have known what to do if they did. But running from the chasers and ringing "Nellie Bell" felt dangerous and thrilling.

We sometimes stopped at a candy store on the way home. I didn't get an allowance, which was a problem for me: when other kids bought candy, should I accept some when they shared, even though I never had money to buy and share myself? I bristled at the comment of one of the girls, "It's okay if you don't buy candy, Helen. We understand that you have so many kids in your family that your parents can't afford it." We weren't poor, and I knew that—we had enough of everything we needed—but I didn't ask for "extras." I think now that my parents would have given me money if I had explained the problem, but I never told them. Once, I told my older sister Margaret, who gave me some of her babysitting money so I could buy candy. I recall that now as one of many examples of having "enough" in my life—enough food, enough love, enough rest and outdoor fun, and enough understanding and kindness, from many sources.

3. Wilbraham, Massachusetts—1960-67

At the end of fifth grade we moved again when my father accepted a job at Springfield College, in Springfield, Massachusetts. We were leaving a lot behind, not just for a year this time, but "for good" (an interesting expression). My grandmothers, aunts, uncles, and cousins all lived in the Midwest—no more summers together at Lake Kabekona in northern Minnesota, or weekend trips to visit relatives. No more evening drives through the South Dakota cornfields; it would be years until I lived near cornfields again, as an adult in Indiana—the chirping of crickets, the flash of fireflies always bring back these memories of my childhood.

I was also leaving behind the sense of neighborhood that children develop when they play outdoors, back and forth from one house to another. I drew on memories of this experience of community when I was writing *The Braid*; I knew how it felt to leave everything behind and imagined how it must have been in 1840, when there were no telephones, airplanes, or e-mail, and letters took a long time, even if people could read and write, which the characters in *The Braid* could not.

We moved to a house in Wilbraham, a suburb of Springfield, and I began sixth grade in another new school. An old cemetery near our house had headstones marking the lives of people who had lived up to two hundred years before. I loved walking there, imagining the stories between the dates. "1877-1881" it might say, beneath a carved lamb or a cherubic angel, and I would wonder how the child had died, think about her parents and siblings, see if their graves were nearby. Many New England houses had dates affixed to their front doors; it seemed that history had been going on longer in Massachusetts than it had in South Dakota. Not true,

of course, but I was essentially oblivious to all the history in both places that had occurred before the recent arrival of my own ancestors.

Until I was sixteen, I was also somewhat oblivious to the existence of nonwhite and non-Christian Americans. Our family had a few friends from other countries, but in my suburban schools, there were no minority students. This was an impoverishment in my growing-up years. I read newspapers, and saw television reports about the civil rights movement—the Montgomery bus boycott, the March on Washington, the Birmingham church bombing—and I was incensed at the injustice of segregation and racism, but it seemed far away. I thought of segregation as something that happened in the south; I was not very deeply aware that I, along with everyone I knew, was a victim of "de facto segregation." Segregation "in fact," if not by law, kept me apart from many people who might have been my friends.

MARY   MARGARET   HELEN   DOROTHY   KATHRYN
     JEAN   NANCY   BARBARA   JACK
          HERBERT   RICHARD   KAREN

"Family Christmas card, 1960. I'm in the middle of the back row" (Reprinted with permission of Helen Frost.)

Junior high was a time of self-definition in so many ways. I wasn't always clear about who I was or who I wanted to be. I'd been a Girl Scout in Brookings, and joined again when we moved to Wilbraham—but when one of the "popular kids" in seventh grade told me that being a Girl Scout was not cool, and nobody would like me if I was one, I dropped out. I was grateful to her for sharing this information with me—if someone was willing to tell me how to be cool, I was willing to listen. Okay, I was clueless: I must have worn my Girl Scout uniform to school—how else would she have known? But still, it annoys me that some people believe they can take it upon themselves to define what is okay and what is not okay for other people.

Better than "cool" were the substantive friendships I formed with girls my age, doing interesting things together outside of school. I joined a "Stamp Club," a group of five girls who met at Cindy Wales' house on Friday evenings. We'd spread our stamp collections across her dining room table, trading and comparing stamps and noting details about geography, history, foreign languages. Glassine envelopes, tweezers, books with pictures of all the stamps from different countries—what a sweet memory: five thirteen-year-old girls peering through magnifying glasses to discern watermarks and the dates of postmarks. I lost touch with those girls when they all went to a private high school, but years later, Cindy and I met again, and the friendship we had shared in junior high was easy to rekindle.

I went to Minnechaug Regional High School, where I took college prep classes and participated in lots of extracurricular activities: vocal music, drama, synchronized swimming, yearbook, school newspaper. (Many of these things that are scheduled as classes in most high schools today were after-school activities that met once or twice a week, so it was possible to do several of them at once.) Working on the school literary magazine was my first experience of a shared community of writers, an experience I have found or created everywhere I have lived since then.

During the summers of high school and college, I worked at summer camps—two summers at Camp Frederick Edwards (or "Freddy Eddy"), two summers at Camp Calumet Lutheran, two summers at day camps in Springfield (one for emotionally disturbed children), and one at an overnight camp in the Berkshires for wealthy children from New York City.

Freddy Eddy was a camp for children who were growing up in poverty. In my work there, beginning the summer I was sixteen, I came to realize that not everyone had, as I did, two parents, a safe and comfortable home, the expectation of going to college, enough to eat—enough of everything, actually. I began to recognize the sheer luck of it all. I saw how poverty can make it difficult for people to become, in the words I gave to Keesha at the end of *Keesha's House,* "who they are meant to be."

*"**Working on the high school literary magazine—my first writers group—1965**" (Reprinted with permission of Helen Frost.)*

I still remember those children's names—they were only three years younger than I was, so they are as old as my husband, and we would be peers now, but in my mind they are still: Eileen, screaming about Ringo Starr one day, and the next day running away from camp, walking miles down the road before we found her; brave Sylvia going out into the dark night on a camping trip to prove that there was nobody hiding behind a nearby tree, and running back screaming, "There IS someone there!" causing pandemonium in the tent where eight thirteen-year-old girls and their sixteen-year-old counselor had been telling ghost stories; Deb who didn't like me; Kathy who did; Louise sneaking out to see the boys. And the boys themselves—Eddie, who made me a jewelry box out of popsicle sticks, is the one I remember best.

I became friends with the other teenagers on the camp staff. It was good for me to know another group of people my age, people who didn't know me as my "school self." I was completely taken by surprise when a boy liked me, and I liked him too, though my first forays into romance were not exactly handled with self-assured aplomb. I suspect this is true for most people—there's a lot to learn about that aspect of social life and it's not easy to learn it. Fun and exciting, but not easy.

Two of the boy counselors I knew at Camp Freddy Eddy died before the end of high school. Jimmy, whose beautiful sister Chris was also my friend, shot himself a few months before graduation. He was handsome and popular and friendly; I have no idea what went wrong. Chuck died when he walked across a freeway—whether it was suicide or an accident no one could be sure. I thought about Chuck when I was writing Harris's poems in *Keesha's House*; in fact, when I planned that book, I thought Harris would commit suicide, and I intended to have blank pages in the rest of the book wherever Harris would have told his story. It would have been a way to express what I felt about the deaths of several friends in high school, the indelible absence of their voices for the rest of our lives. But when I brought my memories of Chuck from the 1960s into the 1990s, the aspect of him that was tormented about (perhaps) being gay took a different path. Where Chuck never knew how to respond to that kind of meanness, and had no allies or support structure, Harris found ways to protect himself. There was no way Harris would have killed himself; I was glad to discover that about him.

At home during my teen years, I was very much a "middle child"—my older sisters were in college, coming home only occasionally (sometimes with boyfriends they eventually married, or didn't marry); I'd often babysit the "three little kids" at home, and babysit for other people when I was not needed at home.

When I was a junior in high school, my grandmother died, and my parents left me in charge of the five younger children (ages six to fourteen) for a week while they drove from Massachusetts to Minnesota and back for the funeral. It seems like a lot of responsibility for someone so young—they hadn't had time to leave us with many groceries or any precooked meals—but I don't remember being overwhelmed by it. My mother told me later that the younger children were my chaperones as much as I was their babysitter—how much trouble can a teenager get into with a bunch of little kids watching her every move?

4. College, Syracuse University—1967-71

I went to Syracuse University because they had a good journalism school, but before I ever took a journalism course, I met the poets—the professors (Philip Booth, W.D. Snodgrass), the graduate students (Bob Foster, Don Mager, Barb Feldman), and the undergraduates (Denise O'Meara, Ingrid Thompson, Bob Ward). Again, I found my community among creative writers, and that community expanded and became central in my college life. I never did take a journalism class.

I didn't major in creative writing either—there was no such major for undergraduates. When I was looking for a way to fulfill a math requirement as painlessly as possible, I came across a course called "Mathematics for Elementary Teachers" taught by Robert Davis. "Wow, it counts as a requirement," I thought, and I enrolled. Bob Davis not only taught me to love math, he got me excited about teaching, which I had previously rejected as a potential career on the basis of a statement my father had made: "Teaching is a good career for a woman . . . ;" he said; "you can do it wherever your husband is."

If he had put that another way, "Teaching is a flexible job; teachers have the freedom to travel and see the world," I might have been interested. But in the late 1960s, enough feminist rhetoric had found its way to my ears that I had no intention of planning my life around this mythical husband I might meet someday.

Certainly, I did not accept the idea that a woman (or "a good wife") would automatically follow her husband wherever his career led them both.

But then there was this class—mathematics as a way of discerning pattern (hey, wasn't that also what poetry was doing?), math as a way of engaging children (what if I'd had teachers who taught math this way?), and, in 1968, the first ideas about how to use computers in schools. There was a (!) computer on campus available to students, and Dr. Davis expected us to make use of it. He arranged for children from local schools to come to the campus for tutoring sessions, and encouraged us to show them how to use computers.

I loved teaching. I became an elementary education major, and Bob Davis added my name to his extensive file of people he put in touch with one another. He told us about schools in England where they used an "integrated day" curriculum—a project-based model where learning was not broken down into subjects, but students learned integrally, naturally, organically. When I was ready to do my student teaching, he helped me arrange to do it at such a school.

Those years I was a college student, 1967-1971, were years of great cultural change. It was an interesting time to be a young adult, breaking out of adolescence into adulthood at the same time the world was breaking open, or so it seemed to us. I became outspoken in my feminism, in my advocacy for children's rights and for changes in schools, in my support of civil rights and my opposition to the war in Vietnam. Although some of my most strident positions have since been tempered with deeper thought and life experience, they formed a solid platform from which to make the decisions that launched me into my adult life.

I was also a little goofy (some might say more than a little). I once strung popcorn from one earring to the other, like a necklace, and wore that to a Buffy St. Marie concert. (I met a lot of hungry people that evening.) I found outlandish clothes at thrift stores—an oversize black wool coat with elaborate braiding on the shoulders, a blue knit dress with the initials IHG embroidered on it (I delighted in making up different responses when people asked me what that stood for), and perhaps my greatest joy, a pair of white roller skates—picture me roller-skating to classes in my long black coat. Or, in jeans and a flannel shirt, skinny enough that I was often asked if I was a boy or a girl, which I thought was great—I loved being "ambiguous," just as I loved asymmetry—I'd cut my hair long on one side and short on the other, or wear two different shoes. My roommate was an art major, and she inspired me to join her in creating "food art" such as scarves stained with coffee, ketchup, grape juice, and blueberries, which we gave to friends as Christmas gifts.

Strobe lights, incense, black light posters, Sergeant Pepper's Lonely Hearts Club Band, Jimi Hendrix, Janis Joplin, Bob Dylan, The Rolling Stones—all that was in the culture around me, and I enjoyed it (or, as we would have said, "I dug it"), but it was at the periphery of my college experience, not central to it.

And what was central? Children and poetry.

Three or four times a week, I walked from the Syracuse University campus, to a housing project about a mile away to work at Wilson Park, an after-school recreation center where I taught arts and crafts in a little room in the basement. The first year, 1967, the entire staff was white, while all the children were black. Three years later, all of my supervisors and fellow staff members were black.

I learned that the color named "flesh" in a crayon box was not the color of everyone's flesh; that a band-aid did not blend with the color of everyone's skin. One afternoon, a boy came in waving a Sears catalogue. He passed it around, showing everyone one page: "Look at the color of this girl." It was the first time any of us had seen a black model in any mainstream publication.

I was working at Wilson Park in April, 1968, when Martin Luther King, Jr., was assassinated. The days that followed were challenging. A boy named Michael, usually cheerful and sunny, greeted me on my first day back at work after the assassination with a hard glare: "The white people killed Martin Luther King," he said.

"But Michael," I protested, "I didn't kill him."

"White people did," he answered. I began to think more deeply about what that meant, what responsibility I did bear for the stubborn persistence of inequality in my country. When I linked arms with others to sing "We Shall Overcome," it was with a sense of determination, and whatever optimism I could muster, but I saw the mountain, and knew that the climb was steep.

In the fall of 1970, we had an African culture night at Wilson Park with African cooking and music. My supervisor ordered a sewing machine and yards and yards of beautiful African cloth and I helped all the children, and many of the staff, make dashikis. They were beautiful, all together on the stage, children and adults singing and dancing together.

It was the first of many times in my life when I have stepped outside of the cultural milieu of my family background and found acceptance and richness among people who could easily have dismissed me as "other," but chose not to do so.

5. Travel, Young-Adult Years—1970-80

When it came time to do my student teaching, I traveled across the Atlantic for the first time and found my way to Julian's Primary School, in Streatham, England (just outside London), the school that Bob Davis had told me about where teachers were using the "Integrated Day" approach. The whole semester was a great adventure. I stayed in a bed-and-breakfast at first, and learned to drink tea; then I moved into a "flat" of my own, using all my thrift-store experience to furnish it.

I loved the school—children learned to read by reading, they learned math and science by using math in their science projects, and they learned to write by writing about math and science and history, as well as by writing stories and poems. One teacher started the year with blank walls and encouraged the students to put up their art work, math graphs, stories, history reports and science project posters. When the walls were filled, the students put up new work on top of the old work, so by the time I arrived in January, the work was several layers deep, and the classroom had a well-established culture. It was a joyful, active place, with lots of simultaneous conversations and activities.

I had applied for a number of teaching jobs before I left for England, and in April, an assistant superintendent called me from Hingham, Massachusetts, to offer me a job. He was impressed that I was doing my student teaching in England; he seemed to like the progressive philosophy of the school, and in that brief transatlantic job interview, we established that I would be a sixth-grade teacher, working cooperatively with two other teachers. I didn't discover until I showed up to begin teaching, full of idealistic enthusiasm, that neither the other two sixth-grade teachers nor the principal understood or shared my ideas about teaching.

I believed that children could be disciplined without rewards and punishment and that such self-discipline formed an essential groundwork for true learning. I believed that children and adults deserved respect—that respect should be a given, not something to be earned. I believed that learning should come from within and grow outward as each child discovers how to make a contribution to the world. I knew that it was my job to like, and perhaps even love, every child in my classroom.

I found that the school, like many schools, was structured around assumptions that were in direct opposition to those beliefs, and I was not yet strong enough to stand up against the pressure to conform ("Miss Frost might not punish you," said another teacher to one of my students who had committed the crime of bouncing a ball while he was lining up to go in from recess, "but I will.") I could neither change my beliefs in order to be effective as a teacher within that system, nor gain the experience I needed quickly enough to implement them. I taught sixth grade until Columbus Day, when, under some pressure from administrators, I resigned. It was a frightening and discouraging experience, a feeling that I did not belong in a world I had hoped to be a part of. It helps me understand children who do not feel that they belong in the school system, or young people like some of the characters in *Keesha's House* who face rejection and other obstacles as they try to find their place in the world.

Although *Spinning through the Universe* drew on that experience, as well as subsequent, more successful, teaching, Mrs. Williams, the teacher in Room 214, is

Telida, Alaska, on the Kuskokwim River, 1983. (Photograph by Gretchen McManus Liuzzi. Reprinted with permission of the photographer.)

not based on myself as a teacher. Perhaps she is a version of the teacher I tried, and try, to be. The room number represents Valentines Day; it is a room of love.

After I left Hingham, I moved several times and had a number of different jobs, some part time and some full time—working at the Boston College Library, teaching in a preschool playgroup, working for the U.S. Census Bureau, substitute teaching, making stuffed animals and selling them at craft fairs.

Eventually, I came to rest in Burlington, Vermont, where I was offered a delightful job as a teacher at the Starksboro Meeting House Preschool and Kindergarten, a parent cooperative run by like-minded people who appreciated my vision and love of children. The parents of the children became my friends and I found support as I grew more confident in my teaching. I often stayed in the home of Pebble and Turner Brooks on a piece of beautiful Vermont farmland known as "The Peaceable Kingdom," where I met Posie (Edith Thacher) and Clem Hurd, and saw them at work on their books, many of which were dedicated to the children I taught in the preschool.

It was a part-time job, so I had time to continue writing poetry. Again, I found a community of writers in Burlington. We held open readings at an old firehouse on Main Street once a month. None of us had much money, so we shared books and got together to talk about them: *Paterson,* by William Carlos Williams; Pablo Neruda's *Twenty Love Songs* and *A Song of Despair.* I read Denise Levertov, Adrienne Rich, Elizabeth Bishop, Muriel Rukeyser, and began to see that I was included in a rich tradition of women poets. My first published poem since high school appeared in an anthology created by the Firehouse Poets Mimeo Cooperative.

I lived in Vermont for two years, and then applied to Kilquhanity House School, a progressive boarding school in Scotland that I had heard about while I was doing my student teaching. I was hired as a housemother and a teacher at "Killy," as the school was known, and I taught there for two and a half years. The school, begun in the 1930s by John and Morag Aitkenhead, who had worked with A.S. Neill at Summerhill, was based on democratic principles; we had a council meeting each week where every child and adult had a vote on any issue that anyone at the school wanted to bring to the meeting. Neill's book, *Summerhill,* had helped shape my sense of what teaching could be, and I learned a lot by working with others to put my ideas into practice. Many of the characters in my books are drawn more precisely because of children and teens I knew and loved at Killy.

It was while I was working at Killy that I spent the summer of 1977 on the Isle of Barra in the Outer Hebrides (Western Isles) of Scotland. I set off with a backpack, taking a train to Oban and a ferry to Castlebay, stopping briefly at Lochboisdale. I pitched my tent on a beautiful piece of land where I could see the ferries come and go, and watch seals and otters at play. A middle-aged couple with a little black dog walked by my tent every day, sometimes bringing me scones or gingerbread—I realize now that they were keeping an eye on me; people who live on a small island would be aware of a young woman camping by herself for six weeks. After I got to know them a bit, they told me that they guessed I was a teacher.

For a few weeks that summer, I was joined by my friend, Collette, another Kilquhanity teacher. In talking with a man who owned the uninhabited island of Mingulay at that time, she received an invitation for the two of us to spend a week camping there, which we enthusiastically accepted. Mingulay is a beautiful island, with a sandy beach laced with tiny seashells on one side, and on the other side, the roar of the wild sea crashing against 750-foot cliffs, home to a puffin colony and raucous with gannets, cormorants, and gulls.

In 1977, the houses in the abandoned village were still more or less intact, and as I looked inside them, I won-dered about the history of the people who had lived there. Twenty-five years later, when I began to write *The Braid,* the sights, sounds, smells, and weather of the island all came back to me, accompanied by a mix of nostalgia, curiosity, and mystery.

6. Alaska and a Few Side Trips—1979-91

By December, 1978, my brothers and sisters were all adults, living all over the United States and other parts of the world. We had a family reunion that year, and I came home from Scotland just in time to be present for it. All but four of us were married by then, and five of my sisters had children, ranging in age from a few months to eight years. More children for me to know and love—eventually, I would have twenty-two nieces and nephews, in addition to my own children—but I'm getting ahead of myself.

After my father retired in 1974, my parents moved to Colorado, where they lived in a home with a beautiful view of the Sangre de Cristos Mountains. The winter and spring of 1979, they were living in Texas for a few months, and my brother and I stayed in their house while they were gone. I spent those months writing and thinking about what I might do next. I applied for summer jobs in Alaska, and was hired as the breakfast host-

"Attention to the natural world: a tide pool on the Massachusetts coast, mid-1970s." (Photograph by Gretchen McManus Liuzzi. Reprinted with permission of the photographer.)

"With Chad Thompson near McKinley Park, Alaska, spring, 1983" (Photograph by Gretchen McManus Liuzzi. Reprinted with permission of the photographer.)

ess at McKinley National Park (now called Denali National Park). I worked at the park for two summers—I hiked up mountains, waded through glacial rivers, had a few too-close encounters with grizzly bears, picked blueberries, watched the northern lights, made many new friends, and decided that I wanted to live in Alaska.

I spent one winter in Fairbanks, teaching at a preschool and taking classes in order to get my Alaska teaching certificate. I chose courses in cross-cultural education, which were helpful the following year when I began teaching at a one-teacher school in Telida, an Athabascan community of about twenty-five people, located on the Swift Fork of the Kuskokwim River, in the shadow of Mount McKinley. That first year, I had five students, one in each grade from kindergarten to grade four.

There were no roads into Telida—people came and went by boat in the summer, by snowmobile or dog-sled in the winter, and by small plane whenever the weather allowed. There was a regularly scheduled mail plane once a week; when it came in, most people in Telida went down to the landing strip to see who or what it was bringing. On the day the mail plane brought me, the new teacher, everyone was welcoming and helpful, carrying everything I brought with me to the log house that was to be my home for the next three years ("What you got all them junks for?" Johnny asked, referring to all the things I had packed, knowing there was no store in Telida).

The children wondered, I learned later, where my own family was, and why I was joining theirs—how would a single woman fit into this community, where all the children were cousins, and "Big Grandma" was either a grandmother or great-grandmother to all the children I taught. "Small Grandma," a generation older than "Big Grandma," was the widow of Carl Seseui, who was five years old when an army expedition was lost near Telida. Carl saw the unusual tracks of horses and army boots and asked his father what kind of animal made them. This led to the rescue of the army expedition; people in Telida clothed them, fed them for two months, and led them to safety.

I loved teaching those beautiful children, and of course I learned more than I taught. In the gentlest possible way, without ever making me feel ignorant, the children and adults taught me to read bird and animal tracks in the snow (spruce hen, ptarmigan, marten, moose, bear, lynx, otter, arctic fox), to recognize where a moose had bedded down for the night, to treat animals respectfully so that they might want to give themselves to us for our food, where to find blueberries and cranberries, what beavers eat and how they store food for the winter, how to sew moose hide with three-cornered needles, where the old village used to be, and why the people who lived there moved downriver to the present location.

I also learned how difficult it can be to live in a culture different from your own: where I had learned that "making eye contact" was a sign of respect, in Telida, people did not to look into another person's eyes; I had to learn not to ask direct questions, and to pause longer than I was accustomed to before replying after someone else had spoken. The children learned from their parents and grandparents without asking questions or showing off what they had learned, and I tried to adapt my teaching style to fit those ways of learning. I found that my basic philosophy of teaching fit well in Telida— with great respect for the individuality of each child, I created an environment where learning could happen. Sometimes that was on camping trips, where we fished and hunted and learned the stories of the places we pitched our tents; sometimes it was in the classroom where we explored mathematical patterns, wrote stories, and read great books together.

Some of the books I read with the Telida children: *The Carrot Seed, The Yearling, Abel's Island, The Secret Garden, Charlotte's Web.* (Joey, ten years old, gasped at the realization that "That spider's going to have babies, and then those babies will have babies, and then those babies will have babies—that pig will ALWAYS have a friend!") I learned to be sensitive to racism in children's books. I saw how easily children recognized when a book was written by someone who did not know or care that they existed, or who perpetuated insulting stereotypes about them.

One couple in Telida lived seventeen miles upriver; one weekend I set off on cross-country skis with their daughter Agnes, and we skied all the way to their house. Although the town of Old Fork in *Diamond Willow* is a fictional town, that trip helped me imagine Willow's dog-mushing trip to her grandparents' house and the welcome she received when she arrived.

Although I was very happy in Telida, some of my friends were concerned that I would never meet a husband there. But my closest friend, Gretchen, who had known me since we were roommates at Syracuse, reassured me with the wise words, "When you move closer to something you love, everything you love comes closer to you." I loved teaching, I loved Alaska, I loved the children whose school days were entrusted to me, and sure enough, at the beginning of my second year in Telida, I met someone else I would come to love.

There were nine schools in the Iditarod Area School District, which covered an area about the size of the state of Ohio. On the same weekend that I went into McGrath for a meeting of the nine principal-teachers, Chad Thompson, a linguist, came from Fairbanks to McGrath to lead a workshop for Athabascan language teachers. A friend invited me to stay at her house, apologizing for the fact that another person, this linguist, was also staying there. She later told us that she hadn't been sure we would like each other.

As it turned out, we did—very much. As we walked into town that first morning, several people stopped to offer us a ride—"No, we're enjoying the walk," we

both said, as if we were strolling along a palm-lined island beach somewhere, rather than a gravel road in McGrath on a late-October morning, twenty-below-plus windchill.

We exchanged a few letters, and after we met again at the annual Bilingual Education conference in Anchorage in February, I started looking forward to Friday evenings, when *The Dukes of Hazzard* came on TV and everyone in Telida gathered at the school to watch it on the one television in town. That meant that the one telephone was free, and for that half hour, private.

When Chad came to visit me in May, we decided to get married—it says something about him that he wanted to marry me even after a canoe trip which ended with me accidentally tipping him into the frigid Kuskokwim River (chunks of ice were still floating on it). He won the hearts of my Telida family that weekend, and when he met my parents a few months later, they were as convinced as everyone else that this was a good match. I had signed a contract for a third year of teaching in Telida, and I honored that, but we got married that summer anyway, with Chad's five-year-old son, Lloyd, as our ring-bearer.

The following spring, as soon as school was out, I flew into Fairbanks to join Chad in his—now "our"— apartment. Lloyd joined us a few weeks later, and the following January, Glen was born. It was a very sudden change, from being single in a small cabin in Telida, to having a husband and two children in Fairbanks. I was ready for the new pleasures and responsibilities of family life, and I had a wonderful new family.

We bought a house on the edge of town, and split a big pile of wood for the woodstove. We often saw moose tracks in our driveway. One day when I was holding Glen and watching Lloyd practice his soccer moves, I looked up and saw a moose run behind the house, through the woodpile, and on down the dog-mushing

"July 23, 1983: Lloyd was the ring-bearer in our wedding. We are looking at our friendship rings, made for us by Chad's mother" (Photograph by Gretchen McManus Liuzzi. Reprinted with permission of the photographer.)

"Lloyd and Glen, Fairbanks, Alaska, 1986. This is where the moose ran through our yard the previous summer" (Reprinted with permission of Helen Frost.)

trail behind our house. A few minutes earlier, Lloyd had been playing right in the place the moose ran through.

The first few years of my life with young children allowed me a more flexible schedule than I'd had while I was teaching. I could usually carve out an hour or two each day for my writing while Glen was napping and Lloyd was in school. This was when I wrote most of the poems that became the book *Skin of a Fish, Bones of a Bird*. Once again, I met other writers in Fairbanks who encouraged me to keep writing and to begin sending things out for publication.

I rejected the standard advice to start out by sending poems to places that were "easy to get into" and instead, on the premise that "if I like what you publish, maybe you'll like what I write." I sent my work to the journals and literary magazines I most admired. Of course some of these poems came flying back to me, but a number of them were accepted, and soon I started thinking about putting together a book manuscript. It took about eight years from the time I started sending poems out until *Skin of a Fish, Bones of a Bird* won a contest and was accepted, in a magical phone call from editor Martha Christina, for publication by Ampersand Press.

During those eight years, we moved four times: In 1986 we moved to Eugene, Oregon, where Chad got his Ph.D. in linguistics. While we lived in Eugene, my father died, after a thirteen-month illness. Glen was four that year, and I took him with me on a Greyhound bus to go to the funeral. After some conversation and time to mull things over, Glen declared, "Now Grandpa can see the dinosaurs."

A few months after my father died, we moved to Arcata, California, where Chad worked on a dictionary of the Hupa language. We were invited to attend the sacred White Deerskin Dance, and several other very moving ceremonies and celebrations.

When the Exxon Valdez oil spill happened, I grieved for the people and animals of Prince William Sound, imagining such a catastrophe happening to my friends in Telida—the water, land and animals poisoned; the life of the community disrupted by media attention and disconnected money. I spent most of that year gathering writers' responses to the oil spill and editing the anthology *Season of Dead Water*, which was published by Breitenbush, a small press in Oregon.

In 1990, we moved back to Alaska, to Ketchikan, where I taught at White Cliff Elementary School. Glen was in kindergarten by then, at the same school where I taught fifth grade. My memories of that class were a source of warmth and love when I created the classroom in *Spinning through the Universe*.

Ketchikan is a beautiful place, and we could happily have settled there for a lifetime—bald eagles soaring over the fjords and islands, majestic totems, good people. But teaching full time left me no time for writing, and it was difficult for Chad to find work as a linguist. When he was offered a university teaching job in Fort Wayne, Indiana, we got out our atlas one more time, and planned our trip across western Canada, down through North Dakota, and across the Midwest to our new home.

7. Fort Wayne, Indiana—1991-Present

When we came to Fort Wayne, Glen was in first grade and Lloyd was starting high school. I had written several stories for children, but hadn't found a publisher for them. In the sixteen years we have lived here, the children have grown up (Lloyd is married now, and has brought two delightful children into our family); Chad has taught linguistics to thousands of college students; and I have gradually become a full-time writer, writing mostly for children and young adults.

The first few years we lived in Fort Wayne, I found a number of ways to combine teaching and writing: I taught composition at several colleges, taught poetry in schools throughout the state, and kept up with my own writing. For a few years, I wrote nonfiction books, mostly for early readers, on topics assigned to me by editors of educational publishing houses. I had experience in teaching reading, in writing for children, and in research, and the assignments drew on all those skills. I learned a lot about topics I might not otherwise have explored.

In my creative writing, I wrote for both children and adults, but for a long time—I'm not sure why—I wrote poetry for adults and prose for children. It wasn't until I started working on *Keesha's House* and *Spinning through the Universe* that my stories for young people began to find their form in poetry.

I began work on those two books simultaneously. In a notebook divided into sections for "adults," "children," and "young adults," it's interesting to see how several different books got their starts. Some ideas migrated from one section to another, notably a poem in the adult section which eventually became the picture book *Monarch and Milkweed.*

The poems that became *Keesha's House* were deeply influenced by my work with young people in Fort Wayne, particularly by two projects which began as a community response to high rates of youth violence. In 1995, I began working with Lisa Tsetse of the Fort Wayne Dance Collective, as part of a program designed to bring artists together with young people who might be at risk for involvement in violence. Lisa and I, along with several other artists, went into juvenile detention centers, group homes, schools, and other places where we found young people who had often been hurt, and who had sometimes hurt others. Working with art, respect, and honesty, we came to know many complex and interesting young people. Each year, I typed and

edited an anthology of their poems, and the poems were included as part of a public performance, along with dancing and masks and giant puppets and drumming and singing. Our work was often painful, but it was deeply transforming for us, and, we hoped and witnessed, for the young people.

In 1998, I worked with the Fort Wayne YWCA and the Fort Wayne Youtheatre to write and produce a play based on young people's experience of violence in our community. I was invited to six high schools—urban, rural, and suburban—where I helped 240 students write stories, poems, and scripts; then I worked with Harvey Cocks to craft the stories into a play, *Why Darkness Seems So Light.* The play was published by Pioneer Drama, and has been produced in many communities. Pecan Grove Press published a selection of the students' stories in an anthology of the same title.

Teachers often asked me what I did to help students feel safe enough to write about such sensitive issues, and, realizing how much I had to say about that, I wrote a book for teachers, *When I Whisper, Nobody Listens: Helping Young People Write about Difficult Issues,* which was published by Heinemann in September, 2001.

Chad, Lloyd, Glen, Helen: Fort Wayne, Indiana, 1992. (Reprinted with permission of Helen Frost.)

"Looking at the cliffs of Mingulay, 2004" (Photograph by John Pendrey. Reprinted with permission of the photographer.)

I continued working on *Keesha's House,* partly as a way of creating a refuge for teens who did not feel safe in their homes, or loved by their community. I wanted to say, "I see you. I respect you. You're important." I was receiving difficult stories from so many young people, and I often saw them for a few weeks and then never knew what happened to them. Writing *Keesha's House* was one way I could imagine them in safety, and using the formal structures of poetry helped me express the emotional depth of the characters' voices.

When I held the finished manuscript in my hands, I felt like I do when one of my children amazes me by doing something gracious or intelligent. It had something to do with me, but it also felt like it had a life of its own. I thought carefully about how to find the right publisher. I loved many books published by Farrar, Straus & Giroux—adult poetry books as well as books for young readers—and I called a friend, Doreen Rappaport, who lives in New York City and knows a lot about children's publishing. We had met at a writers retreat about ten years earlier, and she had been helpful to me on many occasions. I told her that I had completed a book written in sestinas and sonnets, and wanted to send it to FSG. I asked which editor she felt would be most receptive to such a book.

"Frances Foster," she said, "she's a wonderful editor and is open to all sorts of writing." I looked up Frances's other books, and realized that she was publishing many authors I loved. Then I spent four hours composing a cover letter in which I tried to convince her that she might love my book too. Three months later, in October, 2000, she called to say that she did. "Riveting," I wrote in quotes on the notepad I kept by the phone, and "a modest advance."

People often ask me "How do you get a book published?" The only answer I can give from my own experience is, "Work hard for thirty years and then get

lucky." I knew the day I received that phone call that I was very lucky, and I am still learning how lucky I am. Frances continues to work with me on each new book— first she encouraged me to finish *Spinning through the Universe,* and then she enthusiastically approved what might have seemed like a dramatic change of course when I proposed the work of historical fiction that would become *The Braid.*

Sometimes one bit of luck, especially hard-earned good luck, draws other good fortune in its wake. *Keesha's House,* skillfully edited and beautifully designed, held the attention of the Printz committee, which honored it in 2004. At the American Library Association meeting in Orlando that year, Frances introduced me to many people in the world of children's books, and we had an entire afternoon to discuss what I thought was an almost-finished manuscript of *The Braid.* When she gently remarked, "I think you are close to finding your voice and your form," I realized it was not as near-finished as I'd hoped. I went home and worked with my idea of braiding the poems together until I was convinced it could work as I imagined it might. Frances was also convinced, enough to offer me a contract before the book was finished, the first time I had had that luxury.

And then I really got down to work. (Along with the contract, came a deadline!) I'd never worked so intensely on anything—after a morning's work, I was always ravenously hungry! It was exhilarating to discover the seemingly infinite flexibility and power of language. I was, in some ways, outside the story, almost like a slow and careful reader, and at the same time, right at the center as the story revealed itself to me. Sometimes Chad would come home and find me in some other place—Mingulay or Cape Breton, he might have wondered—and he'd ask "What happened to Jeannie today?" But it wasn't so much *what* had happened to my characters as it was the experience of going so deeply into poetry that dazzled me.

We had taken two family vacations to Nova Scotia, and I had explored Cape Breton with my story in mind, but I needed to spend more time on Barra and Mingulay. I applied for a grant from the Indiana Arts Commission, which I received, allowing me to go to Scotland in September, 2004. My memories from the summer I spent there twenty-seven years earlier were quite clear, and I met people who helped me go deeper into my research, so that when I returned home, the final stretch of writing went quickly and smoothly.

Again, when the book came out, in fall, 2006, it was well received by readers, both teen and adult, by reviewers, and by award committees. Equally important to me, my friends and family and people I met on my trip to Barra wrote to tell me they loved the book.

"Our family in Colorado, 2005: Penny (Lloyd's wife), Jordan, Lloyd, Chad, Cameron, Glen, Helen. Cameron and Jordan are Lloyd's stepchildren"
(Reprinted with permission of Helen Frost.)

Many of my nieces and nephews are adults now, some with children of their own, so there is a whole new generation of readers coming along. At my mother's ninetieth birthday party, with thirty-one of us in attendance (about half of our family now), I watched two-year-old Naima and three-year-old Christine sit down at a little table and "pretend write" as I once did on that shiny paper in Brookings, more than fifty years ago—perhaps there is a new generation of writers coming along, too.

I had two books published in 2008: *Diamond Willow,* a contemporary story set in interior Alaska, is related to *The Braid* in a way that I will leave for perceptive readers to discern. And *Monarch and Milkweed* may be an entomologist's way of telling the story of my life: a story of being held close, then opening up and riding away on the wind, finding the nourishment you need to make your way home—not "back home" but always "forward home."

When I celebrated my fifty-eight birthday, I thought: it took me the first fifty years of my life to gather the skills and experiences I need to do what I most love, and now I'm doing it. I'm like an eight year old with a new bike—or maybe an eighteen year old on roller skates—looking out at all the adventure opening out in front of me.

*　　*　　*

FROST, Helen Marie
See FROST, Helen

G-H

GONYEA, Mark

Personal

Born in New York, NY. *Education:* Joe Kubert School of Cartooning and Graphic Art, graduate.

Addresses

Home—VT. *E-mail*—mark@mroblivious.com.

Career

Author and illustrator; freelance graphic artist, 1996—. *Heavy Metal* (magazine), designer, 1995-96; Vermont Teddy Bear Company, graphic artist, 1998-2000, assistant art director, 2002-04, art director, 2004, art director of subsidiary SendAMERICA, 2000-02.

Writings

A Book about Design: Complicated Doesn't Make It Good, Holt (New York, NY), 2005.
Another Book about Design: Complicated Doesn't Make It Bad, Holt (New York, NY), 2007.

Sidelights

A graduate of the Joe Kubert School of Cartooning and Graphic Art, Mark Gonyea worked as a magazine designer in New York City before moving to Vermont and working for many years designing and directing art and branding projects for the Vermont Teddy Bear Company. Gonyea used this real-world experience as a graphic designer to write two books teaching the concepts of art and design to young readers: *A Book about Design: Complicated Doesn't Make It Good* and *Another Book about Design: Complicated Doesn't Make It Bad.*

In *A Book about Design* Gonyea uses spare prose to introduce basic concepts about viewers' perception of size, shape, and color. The design of his book is also spare, demonstrating the simplicity the book's text discusses. The author's "minimalist approach to text and composition makes this book an effective advertisement for his message about the beauty of uncluttered design," wrote Wendy Lukehart in a *School Library Journal* review of *A Book of Design.* While a *Publishers Weekly* critic pointed out that some design basics, such as the color wheel, are never mentioned, Rebecca Martin concluded in *School Arts* that the book will be useful to students because Gonyea's text is "always tinged with a sense of humor." A *Kirkus Reviews* contributor predicted of *A Book about Design* that readers "will delight in this energetic treatment" of a creative subject.

To create the counterpoint of the recommendations made in his first text, Gonyea defends complexity in *Another Book about Design.* Again using a concise text, the author discusses concepts of patterns—such as foreground and background and positive versus negative space—exploring how and why some complicated designs are appealing and effective. Gonyea's "interactive sequel . . . will leave kids eager to play with the concepts," wrote Gillian Engberg in *Booklist.* Robin L. Gibson, writing in *School Library Journal,* called *Another Book about Design* a "lively volume" that is "just as successful" as *A Book about Design.*

Biographical and Critical Sources

PERIODICALS

Booklist, May 1, 2005, Jennifer Mattson, review of *A Book about Design: Complicated Doesn't Make It Good,* p. 1581; July 1, 2007, Gillian Engberg, review of *Another Book about Design: Complicated Doesn't Make It Bad,* p. 52.
Bulletin of the Center for Children's Books, October, 2007, review of *Another Book about Design,* p. 86.
Tribune Books (Chicago, IL), July 28, 2007, Mary Harris Russell, review of *Another Book about Design,* p. 7.

Kirkus Reviews, May 15, 2005, review of *A Book about Design,* p. 588.

Publishers Weekly, June 27, 2005, review of *A Book about Design,* p. 62; August 13, 2007, "Worth a Thousand Words," p. 69.

School Library Journal, July, 2005, Wendy Lukehart, review of *A Book about Design,* p. 89; September, 2007, Robin L. Gibson, review of *Another Book about Design,* p. 182.

ONLINE

Mark Gonyea Home Page, http://www.mroblivious.com (October 26, 2008).

Macmillan Web site, http://us.macmillan.com/ (October 26, 2008), "Mark Gonyea."*

* * *

GRACE, N.B.
See HARPER, Suzanne

* * *

HALE, Marian

Personal

Married.

Addresses

Home—Rockport, TX.

Career

Writer.

Writings

YOUNG-ADULT NOVELS

The Truth about Sparrows, Henry Holt (New York, NY), 2004.

Dark Water Rising, Henry Holt (New York, NY), 2006.

Adaptations

The Truth about Sparrows was adapted for audio by Listening Library, 2005.

Sidelights

In her first novel for young adults, *The Truth about Sparrows,* Marian Hale tells the Depression-era story of twelve-year-old Sadie Wynne and her family as they flee drought in Missouri and head off to Texas to start a new life. Sadie is devastated to leave her old life and friends behind and struggles with her family to survive during their journey, working in cotton fields and washing in animal troughs along the way. When the family finally arrives in a small fishing village on the Gulf of Mexico, Sadie's crippled father has trouble finding work, and the girl discovers that her difficulties are far from over. Her family is forced to live in a shantytown in a house made of cardboard boxes. Furthermore, Sadie does not hear from her best friend in Missouri and finds herself the brunt of derisions aimed at her from a snobbish local girl. Eventually, however, the preteen learns to focus on the positive rather than the negative aspects of her life.

Critics generally praised *The Truth about Sparrows.* "Sadie emerges as an endearing, complex character who rages against her displacement," wrote Gillian Engberg in *Booklist,* while *Horn Book* reviewer Betty Carter deemed the girl "triumphant and memorable, as is her entire family." A *Kirkus Reviews* contributor called *The Truth about Sparrows* a "beautifully realized work, memorable for its Gulf Coast setting and the luminous voice" of its young narrator. Cindy Darling Codell, writing in *School Library Journal,* noted that, "rich with social history, this first novel is informative, enjoyable, and evocative."

Hale's next novel, *Dark Water Rising,* features seventeen-year-old Seth, a discontented teenager in the year 1900 who has just moved to Galveston, Texas, with his family. Annoyed with having to constantly watch his little sister, Seth is also discouraged because he hopes to be a carpenter while his parents want him to attend college. Seth nevertheless comes to think that Galveston is a fun place, and his life improves daily, until a devastating storm hits the city on September 8, 1900. The historic Galveston flood that resulted killed more than 8,000 people and destroyed 3,600 homes and businesses. In Hale's fictional chronicle, Seth seeks to discover whether or not the other members of his family and his newfound girlfriend have survived the horrendous carnage. The book includes historic photographs of the storm's effects.

Among the many positive reviews of *Dark Water Rising* was one by Janet Hilbun, who wrote in *School Library Journal* that "fact and fiction are blended effortlessly together in an exciting read that leaves readers with a sense of hope." In a review for *Booklist,* Francisca Goldsmith called *Dark Water Rising* a "fine example of historical fiction [that] has something for almost everyone." Also commenting on the novel's historical accuracy, Janis Flint-Ferguson wrote in *Kliatt:* "This novel recreates the first of the 20th century storms and gives readers a realistic look at an earlier time period and how folks recovered from their own storm of the century." A *Kirkus Reviews* contributor called *Dark Water Rising* "exciting, tear jerking, and life affirming."

Biographical and Critical Sources

PERIODICALS

Booklist, October 1, 2004, Gillian Engberg, review of *The Truth about Sparrows*, p. 326; November 15, 2004, Hazel Rochman, review of *The Truth about Sparrows*, p. 599; January 1, 2005, review of *The Truth about Sparrows*, p. 773; October 15, 2006, Francisca Goldsmith, review of *Dark Water Rising*, p. 46.

Horn Book, September-October, 2004, Betty Carter, review of *The Truth about Sparrows*, p. 585.

Kirkus Reviews, July 15, 2004, review of *The Truth about Sparrows*, p. 685; August 1, 2006, review of *Dark Water Rising*, p. 787.

Kliatt, September, 2006, Janis Flint-Ferguson, review of *Dark Water Rising*, p. 12.

Publishers Weekly, November 1, 2004, review of *The Truth about Sparrows*, p. 63.

Reading Teacher, November, 2005, Sharon Olson, review of *The Truth about Sparrows*, p. 277.

School Library Journal, October, 2004, Cindy Darling Codell, review of *The Truth about Sparrows*, p. 166; August, 2005, Blair Christolon, review of *Dark Water Rising*, p. 50; October, 2006, Janet Hilbun, review of *Dark Water Rising*, p. 156.

Stone Soup, May-June, 2006, Julia Worcester, review of *The Truth about Sparrows*, p. 40.

ONLINE

Cynsations Blog, http://cynthialeitichsmith.blogspot.com/ (September 11, 2004), Cynthia Leitich Smith review of *The Truth about Sparrows*.*

* * *

HARPER, Suzanne
(N.B. Grace)

Personal

Born in OH. *Education:* University of Texas, Austin, B.A.; University of Southern California, M.A.

Addresses

Home—New York, NY.

Career

Editor and writer. Whittle Communications, member of editorial staff; Disney Adventures, member of staff, beginning 1990, became managing editor, then executive editor, editor-in-chief, beginning 1997; Simon & Schuster Children's Publishing, New York, NY, senior vice president, 2004-05.

Writings

Lightning: Sheets, Streaks, Beads, and Balls, Franklin Watts (New York, NY), 1997.

Clouds: From Mare's Tails to Thunderheads, Franklin Watts (New York, NY), 1997.

(With Brian Boitano) *Boitano's Edge: Inside the Real World of Figure Skating*, Simon & Schuster (New York, NY), 1997.

Goofy and Gross Body Tricks, Golden Books (New York, NY), 1997.

Jungle Cubs: Rain, Rain, Go Away!, Golden Books (New York, NY), 1998.

Annabelle's Wish, Golden Books (New York, NY), 1999.

Hands On!: 33 More Things Every Girl Should Know: Skills for Living Your Life from 33 Extraordinary Women, Crown (New York, NY), 2001.

(Reteller) *Goldilocks and the Three Bears*, Little, Brown Kids (New York, NY), 2006.

(Reteller) *The Three Little Pigs*, Little, Brown Kids (New York, NY), 2006.

(With John Christian Orndorff) *Terrorists, Tornadoes, and Tsunamis: How to Prepare for Life's Danger Zones*, Harry Abrams (New York, NY), 2007.

The Secret Life of Sparrow Delaney (novel), Greenwillow (New York, NY), 2007.

The Juliet Club (novel), Greenwillow (New York, NY), 2008.

Rock the Waves (based on *Hannah Montana* television series), Disney Press (New York, NY), 2008.

Also author of plays, including *The Belief Factor, The Worthy Matron of Eastern Star,* and *Shady Grove.*

DISNEY TIE-INS; UNDER PSEUDONYM N.B. GRACE

High School Musical: The Junior Novel, Disney Press (New York, NY), 2006.

Far-out Phil, Disney Press (New York, NY), 2006.

Double Trouble (based on television series *The Suite Life of Zack and Cody*), Disney Press (New York, NY), 2006.

Broadway Dreams (based on *High School Musical*), Disney Press (New York, NY), 2007.

Disney High School Musical 2: The Junior Novel, Disney Press (New York, NY), 2007.

Disney's High School Musical: Stories from East High: Crunch Time (also see below), Disney Press (New York, NY), 2007.

High School Musical: All Access, Disney Press (New York, NY), 2007.

High School Musical Original Junior Novel No. 1, Disney Press (New York, NY), 2007.

(With Alice Alfonsi and Catherine Hapka) *High School Musical: Stories from East High* (includes *Crunch Time*), Spotlight (Edina, MN), 2008.

Bonjour, Wildcats (based on *High School Musical*), Disney Press (New York, NY), 2009.

UNDER PSEUDONYM N.B. GRACE

UFO Mysteries, Childs World (Chanhassen, MN), 2007.

Women in Space, Childs World (Chanhassen, MN), 2007.

(Editor) Joseph Périgot, *Dealing with Dad*, illustrated by Christian Quennehen, translated by Gita Daneshjoo, Amulet (New York, NY), 2007.

Mummies Unwrapped!: The Science of Mummy-making,
  Franklin Watts (New York, NY), 2008.
(Editor) Marie-José Auderset, *Walking Tall: How to Build
  Confidence and Be the Best You Can Be,* illustrated by
  Gaëtan de Séguin, Amulet (New York, NY), 2008.
UFOs: What Scientists Say May Shock You!, Franklin
  Watts (New York, NY), 2008.

Sidelights

Born in Ohio, editor and author Suzanne Harper grew
up in Texas before earning her M.A. in California and
eventually settling in New York City. Harper began her
career with books as an editor at Whittle Communications before landing a position on the *Disney Adventures* magazine. Her relationship with entertainment giant Disney has continued over the years, and she has
written many novels and adaptations of Disney television programs, publishing them under her own name as
well as under her pen name, N.B. Grace.

Harper's novels *Lightning: Sheets, Streaks, Beads, and
Balls* and *Clouds: From Mare's Tails to Thunderheads*
were written on assignment for the library market. Then
came *Boitano's Edge: Inside the Real World of Figure
Skating,* which she coauthored with Olympic gold med-
alist Brian Boitano. In *Booklist* Kay Weisman predicted
that the "fascinating, behind-the-scenes details" the coauthors reveal about one of the most widely viewed
televised sports will keep readers turning pages. As a
Publishers Weekly critic concluded of *Boitano's Edge:*
"Young skaters are sure to give this title a top score of
6.0."

Another of Harper's nonfiction titles, *Hands On!: 33
More Things Every Girl Should Know: Skills for Living
Your Life from 33 Extraordinary Women* features anec-
dotes and tales from such contributors as Lois Lowry,
Sara Moulton, Norma Fox Mazer, and Naomi Shihab
Nye. A *Publishers Weekly* reviewer characterized the
work as "an easy book to dip in and out of," and Judith
M. Garner wrote in *Book Report* that *Hands On!* is
"packed with good information on topics students need
to read." In addition to her nonfiction titles, Harper has
also produced adaptations of *Goldilocks and the Three
Bears* and *The Three Little Pigs.*

The original young-adult novel *The Secret Life of Sparrow Delaney* marked a departure for Harper. In the
novel, Sparrow Delaney is the seventh daughter of a
psychic, and everyone expects great things from her.
Tricking everyone in her family into believing she has
no real supernatural powers, Sparrow finds it particularly hard to keep her secret when the ghost of a handsome boy named Luke demands that she become his
conduit to the living. As she gets to know both Luke
and his still-living brother, Jack, Sparrow wonders if
being a psychic might be her destiny after all. "The intriguing premise is developed into a well-plotted story,"
wrote Ilene Cooper in *Booklist.* "With its masterful
charm and superbly creative storyline, the only possible

fault with this book is that Harper has not already written two or three sequels to it," Cara Chancellor stated
in *Kliatt.* Marie C. Hansen commented in *School Library Journal* on Harper's research into Spiritism and
the New York-area setting for the novel, complimenting
the author for "creating an accurate atmosphere." As a
Publishers Weekly contributor concluded of *The Secret
Life of Sparrow Delaney:* "For all of the imagination
the author displays in inventing a spirit world, she
shows equal skill in probing the nuances of tender emotions, too."

In completing her second teen novel, *The Juliet Club,*
Harper studied the plays of English dramatist William
Shakespeare, practiced stage fencing, and visited Ve-
rona, Italy, twice, the first time as she was preparing to
write the book and the second time after her draft was
written. The second visit allowed her to add details to
the story that might have been absent otherwise. "There
are parts of the book that come directly from that trip,"
Harper explained on the *Slayground Blog.*

Biographical and Critical Sources

PERIODICALS

Booklist, February 15, 1998, Kay Weisman, review of
  *Boitano's Edge: Inside the Real World of Figure Skat-
  ing,* p. 1001; February 1, 2001, Gillian Engberg, review of *Hands On!: 33 More Things Every Girl
  Should Know: Skills for Living Your Life from 33 Extraordinary Women,* p. 1044; April 15, 2007, Ed Sullivan, review of *Terrorists, Tornadoes, and Tsunamis:
  How to Prepare for Life's Danger Zones,* p. 36; July
  1, 2007, Ilene Cooper, review of *The Secret Life of
  Sparrow Delaney,* p. 52.
Book Report, September-October, 2001, Judith M. Garner,
  review of *Hands On!,* p. 72.
Bulletin of the Center for Children's Books, September,
  2007, Cindy Welch, review of *The Secret Life of Spar-
  row Delaney,* p. 30.
Kirkus Reviews, June 15, 2007, review of *The Secret Life
  of Sparrow Delaney.*
Kliatt, July, 2007, Cara Chancellor, review of *The Secret
  Life of Sparrow Delaney,* p. 16.
Publishers Weekly, December 8, 1997, review of *Boitano's
  Edge,* p. 73; July 30, 2007, review of *The Secret Life
  of Sparrow Delaney,* p. 85.
School Library Journal, April, 1998, Frances Feiher, re-
  view of *Boitano's Edge,* p. 141; March, 2001, Katie
  O'Dell, review of *Hands On!,* p. 267; December,
  2006, Blair Christolon, review of *Goldilocks and the
  Three Bears,* p. 122; November, 2007, Marie C.
  Hansen, review of *The Secret Life of Sparrow Delaney,*
  p. 124; May, 2007, Jeffrey A. French, review of *Terrorists, Tornadoes, and Tsunamis,* p. 160.
Voice of Youth Advocates, April, 2007, Steven Kral, review
  of *Terrorists, Tornadoes, and Tsunamis,* p. 81.

ONLINE

Harper Collins Web site, http://www.harpercollins.com/ (October 26, 2008), "Suzanne Harper."

Simon Says Web site, http://www.simonsays.com/ (June 21, 2004), "Suzanne Harper."

Slayground Blog, http://www.slayground.net/bildungs roman/ (May 18, 2008), interview with Harper.

Suzanne Harper Home Page, http://www.suzanneharper. com (October 26, 2008).*

* * *

HOLTZMAN, Jerome 1926-2008

OBITUARY NOTICE—

See index for *SATA* sketch: Born July 12, 1926, in Chicago, IL; died of a stroke, July 19, 2008, in Evanston, IL. Sportswriter, sports historian, columnist, editor, and author. Upon his retirement from the *Chicago Tribune,* Holtzman was honored by baseball commissioner Bud Selig as the official historian of baseball. Unofficially he had held the title for decades. Anchored in Chicago, Holtzman observed the development of the game throughout his career, as a baseball reporter for the *Chicago Sun-Times* and its predecessor company from 1957 until 1981, when he moved to the *Chicago Tribune* as a baseball columnist. He followed the sport for nearly thirty years with his hometown teams, the Cubs and the White Sox, but his knowledge of the sport was encyclopedic and, according to sources, his reporting was both fair and reliable. He had respect for the players—all of them. It was Holtzman who developed the "save rule," which statisticians could use to determine and acknowledge the value of relief pitchers as well as the headliners who started the games. In 1969 the save rule was adopted formally as the first major enhancement of baseball statistics in almost fifty years. Holtzman was also a member of the Baseball Hall of Fame Veterans Committee, which recognizes Hall of Fame nominees who had been neglected or overlooked by the larger voting membership of the Baseball Writers Association of America. Holtzman retired from the Chicago *Tribune* around 1998; by then he had also achieved national recognition as a longtime columnist for the *Sporting News* and author of the annual season summary of the *Official Baseball Guide.* He had several books to his credit as well. Holtzman was the author of *The Commissioners: Baseball's Midlife Crisis* (1998) and *Baseball, Chicago Style: A Tale of Two Teams, One City* (2001). He acknowledged his respect for other sportswriters in the edited collection *No Cheering in the Press Box* (1974), an oral history of baseball in the words of his colleagues from Paul Gallico to Red Smith. He recognized the contributions of mainstream authors in *Fielder's Choice: An Anthology of Baseball Fiction* (1979), a collection of stories by many professional writers, from James Thurber and Ring Lardner to Bernard Malamud

and Chaim Potok. His own writings were collected in *Jerome Holtzman on Baseball* (2005). Holtzman was not inducted into the writers' section of the Baseball Hall of Fame until 1989, but he had been known as "the dean" of baseball writers for years.

OBITUARIES AND OTHER SOURCES:

PERIODICALS

Chicago Tribune, July 22, 2008, sec. 1, pp. 1, 11.
Los Angeles Times, July 22, 2008, p. B8.
New York Times, July 22, 2008, p. C12.

* * *

HORVATH, Polly 1957-

Personal

Born January 30, 1957, in Kalamazoo, MI; daughter of John Anthony (a teacher) and Betty Ann (a writer) Horvath; married Arnold Keller (a professor); children: Emily Willa, Rebecca Avery. *Education:* Attended Canadian College of Dance and Martha Graham School of Contemporary Dance.

Addresses

Home—Metchosin, British Columbia, Canada. *Agent*—Amy Berkower, Writers House, 21 W. 26th St., New York, NY 10010. *E-mail*—ph@pollyhorvath.com.

Career

Writer. Former ballet teacher.

Awards, Honors

Notable Book selection, American Library Association (ALA), *Boston Globe/Horn Book* Honor Book designation, and National Book Award finalist, all for *The Trolls; Boston Globe/Horn Book* Honor Book designation, 2001, and Newbery Medal Honor Book designation, ALA, White Raven Award, and Book of the Year for Children Award nomination, Canadian Library Association (CLA), all 2002, all for *Everything on a Waffle;* National Book Award for Young People's Literature, Best Books for Young Adults selection, ALA, and Young-Adult Book of the Year, CLA, all 2004, all for *The Canning Season;* Young-Adult Book of the Year shortlist, CLA, 2007, and Sheila A. Egoff Children's Literature Prize, both for *The Corps of the Bare-boned Plane.*

Writings

An Occasional Cow, illustrated by Gioia Fiammenghi, Farrar, Straus & Giroux (New York, NY), 1989.

No More Cornflakes, Farrar, Straus & Giroux (New York, NY), 1990.

The Happy Yellow Car, Farrar, Straus & Giroux (New York, NY), 1994.

When the Circus Came to Town, Farrar, Straus & Giroux (New York, NY), 1996.

The Trolls, Farrar, Straus & Giroux (New York, NY), 1999.

Everything on a Waffle, Farrar, Straus & Giroux (New York, NY), 2001.

The Canning Season, Farrar, Straus & Giroux (New York, NY), 2003.

The Pepins and Their Problems, illustrated by Marylin Hafner, Farrar, Straus & Giroux (New York, NY), 2004.

The Vacation, Groundwood Books (Toronto, Ontario, Canada), 2005.

The Corps of the Bare-boned Plane, Farrar, Straus & Giroux (New York, NY), 2007.

My One Hundred Adventures, Schwartz & Wade Books (New York, NY), 2008.

M Is for Mountie: An RCMP Alphabet, illustrated by Lorna Bennett, Sleeping Bear Press, (Chelsea, MI), 2008.

Adaptations

Everything on a Waffle and *The Trolls* were adapted for audiocassette and produced by Listening Library.

Sidelights

Children's author Polly Horvath's novels for middle-grade readers and young adults rely on ridiculous situations and slapstick action to achieve the humorous effect that has so delighted critics. Her protagonists are often precociously bright and outspoken young girls who provide a perspective on those around them that has been praised for challenging and enlightening young readers. Employing sophisticated wordplay, Horvath relies on exaggeration and the contrast between a high-flown narrative and ridiculous incidents to create the whimsical perspective that makes novels such as *Everything on a Waffle, The Pepins and Their Problems,* and *The Vacation* so popular.

Born in 1957, Horvath developed an early interest in telling stories. "I was eight when I started writing," she remarked on the *Scholastic* Web site. "I did all kinds of writing—novels, poetry, funny stories," she added, noting that in high school she was encouraged by an English teacher, who read all of her works, and a German teacher who provided her with an office in the school library. "I did have an agent for a while when I was in my teens," she recalled. "I didn't publish anything but it gave me a huge amount of experience writing and sending out manuscripts." Horvath later studied at the Canadian College of Dance in Toronto and the Martha Graham School of Contemporary Dance in New York City, but also continued to write, supporting herself by teaching ballet classes. Her first published work, the middle-grade novel *An Occasional Cow,* took seven years to complete.

In *An Occasional Cow,* ten-year-old Imogene is unwillingly sent to stay with cousins in Iowa for the summer and she expects to be bored by the unsophisticated country folk and their ideas of entertainment. She meets her cousin Josephine there and has several fights with the girl before the two become friends. According to David Gale in *School Library Journal,* "part of the fun" in *An Occasional Cow* is "the overblown and sophisticated vocabulary of the precocious protagonists."

Another well-spoken pre-teen takes center stage in *No More Cornflakes.* In this work, lonely ten-year-old Hortense is trying to deal with the overwhelming changes occurring in her family, starting with her mother's pregnancy. The novel's "characters are less eccentric and more believable" than those in *An Occasional Cow,* commented Nancy Vasilakis in a *Horn Book* of Horvath's second book. "Hortense is the Midwest's answer to Anastasia Krupnik—witty, sophisticated, and literate," concluded Deborah Stevenson in a review of *No More Cornflakes* for the *Bulletin of the Center for Children's Books.*

The Happy Yellow Car is "an outrageously funny family story," wrote Virginia Golodetz in *School Library Journal.* Horvath's novel, set during the Great Depression of the 1930s, begins as Betty Grunt's father comes home with a fancy yellow car. It is soon discovered that Mr. Grunt has paid for the shiny new automobile with the money Betty's mother had saved to pay for Betty's college education. This blow is quickly forgotten, however, when Betty is elected Pork Fry Queen and begins a frantic search for the dollar necessary to pay for her flowers. The novel's "shenanigans [are] made more comical for sophisticated readers by Horvath's satirically flowery narrative," commented a critic in *Kirkus Reviews.* A *Publishers Weekly* contributor also emphasized the novel's humor, remarking that while the ending of *The Happy Yellow Car* is abrupt, Horvath compensates for this with her "fresh humor and razor-sharp dialogue."

Fifth-grade friends-in-arms Ivy and Alfred are the dual stars of *When the Circus Came to Town,* as they work to take the bite out of a town-wide snub after a family of circus performers moves in next door. The two youngsters fight the efforts of the stuffy church casserole committee, the members of whom wish to prevent the new family from attending the next town-wide bake-off. At the event, a "pie-throwing brouhaha . . . comes to an unexpectedly melodramatic climax," according to Margaret A. Bush in her positive review of Horvath's novel in *Horn Book.* Praising *When the Circus Came to Town* as a "rollicking ode to silliness," a *Publishers Weekly* contributor added that Horvath "remains a master of the middlegrade comedy." Noting the serious subtext—a condemnation of intolerance—underlying the "wacky, offbeat novel," *Booklist* reviewer Stephanie Zvirin also praised the novel for "prompting discussion of a serious subject."

The Trolls, a National Book Award finalist, centers on three siblings—Melissa, Amanda, and Pee Wee Anderson—who fall under the care of their loquacious Aunt Sally while their parents vacation in Paris. During her stay, Sally regales the children with uproarious family tales, but when she notices that Pee Wee is being mistreated by his older sisters, she discloses a shameful episode from her own past that involved the children's father. "Horvath, a master storyteller herself, skillfully parallels the two generations as she conveys the unthinking cruelty older siblings often bestow upon younger ones," noted Horn Book reviewer Christine Heppermann.

A Newbery Medal honor book, Everything on a Waffle takes place in Horvath's home province of British Columbia, Canada, where eleven-year-old Primrose Squarp worries at the prolonged absence-at-sea of both her fisherman parents. Eventually, Primrose is farmed out to a succession of temporary parents, including a distant uncle and a crotchety old woman, before winding up in a foster home. Throughout her journey, the young girl maintains a troupe of loyal friends, including her uncle and the owner of a restaurant where everything is served on a waffle. Horvath, who marks Primrose's journey with recipes at the end of each chapter, "doesn't offer an easily encapsulated plot but instead sees Primrose through her time of troubles as she bounces off people and events like a pinball," explained Bulletin of the Center for Children's Books contributor Deborah Stevenson. Calling Everything on a Waffle a "perceptive, barbed tale," a Kirkus Reviews contributor noted that the plucky protagonist "is a serious, sturdy soul, able to hold her own against [the story's] . . . quirky . . . supporting cast." "Subtlety and slapstick is a challenging combination," added Horn Book contributor Sarah Ellis; in Everything on a Waffle "Horvath pulls it off beautifully."

The Canning Season also concerns a displaced adolescent. The only child of an emotionally detached mother, thirteen-year-old Ratchet Clark is sent to the Maine woods to live with her eccentric, elderly great aunts, Tilly and Penpen. During the long summer, Ratchet finds companionship with another abandoned teen, Harper, who arrives unexpectedly in Glen Rosa. The Canning Season won the National Book Award for Young People's Literature and received strong reviews. "Horvath's descriptive powers are singular . . ., her uncensored Mad Hatter wit simply delicious, her storytelling skills consummate," noted a Publishers Weekly contributor of the award-winning novel.

In The Pepins and Their Problems, a work that drew comparisons to Helen Cresswell's "Bagthorpe" series, a dim-witted family attempts to solve a series of seemingly never-ending problems. Using her "psychic" powers, Horvath takes suggestions from her readers for assisting the Pepins, who are cursed with a cow that gives lemonade and an invasion of toads. "Horvath's mock serious commentary sets just the right tone," observed

Steven Engelfried in School Library Journal, and a reviewer in Publishers Weekly stated that the "brazenly funny developments keep the conceit and the comedy energetic all the way to the finish line."

The relationship between a twelve-year-old boy and a pair of quirky relatives takes center stage in The Vacation, "another delightfully offbeat yarn," remarked School Library Journal critic Connie Tyrrell Burns. When his parents abruptly leave to become missionaries in Africa, young Henry is left in the care of his bickering spinster aunts, Magnolia and Pigg, who promptly embark on an aimless cross-country road trip during which Henry comes to a number of "life-altering conclusions about surviving in an unpredictable world," according to a Publishers Weekly reviewer. Horvath "has a unique style, intermingling the grotesque and the absurd with the poignant," noted Kliatt critic Janis Flint-Ferguson. "This novel is no exception."

Another award-winning title, The Corps of the Bare-boned Plane, centers on orphaned cousins Meline and Joceyln, who are sent to a remote island off British Columbia to live with their scholarly Uncle Marten. As the girls deal with the loss of their parents, they learn that the island was once used as a military base and attempt to construct an airplane from scavenged parts. They also form an unusual bond with their reclusive uncle and his assistants: Mrs. Mendelbaum, a Holocaust survivor, and Humdinger, an enigmatic butler. Writing in Horn Book, Vicky Smith called The Corps of the Bare-boned Plane "a remarkable examination of the extremes of emotional distress," and Burns observed that the "novel's message lies in the importance of connectedness and the conviction that love comes at the cost of tremendous loss and grieving."

In a Publishers Weekly interview with Kit Alderdice, Horvath stated that the most gratifying aspect of her critical success is "being able to write without having to do something else like teach or find another way to support myself. It's just a huge luxury to me, to have whole days [to write in]. I never take that for granted. Because I'm probably never going to be a popular writer in the sense of selling millions of books, getting critical attention and awards has just boosted the books enough that I can write full time, which has been wonderful."

Biographical and Critical Sources

PERIODICALS

Book, May-June, 2002, review of Everything on a Waffle, p. 29.
Booklist, November 15, 1996, Stephanie Zvirin, review of When the Circus Came to Town, p. 588; March 1, 1999, Carolyn Phelan, review of The Trolls, p. 1206; April 1, 2003, Ilene Cooper, review of The Canning Season, p. 1387; August, 2004, Kay Weisman, review

of *The Pepins and Their Problems,* p. 1934; June 1, 2005, Ilene Cooper, review of *The Vacation,* p. 1810; June 1, 2007, Jennifer Mattson, review of *The Corps of the Bare-boned Plane,* p. 55.

Bulletin of the Center for Children's Books, May, 1989, Betsey Hearne, review of *An Occasional Cow,* p. 225: October, 1990, Deborah Stevenson, review of *No More Cornflakes,* p. 31; November, 1994, Deborah Stevenson, review of *The Happy Yellow Car,* p. 89; February, 1999, Deborah Stevenson, review of *The Trolls,* p. 193; March, 2001, Deborah Stevenson, review of *Everything on a Waffle,* p. 263.

Horn Book, January-February, 1991, Nancy Vasilakis, review of *No More Cornflakes,* p. 69; January, 1997, Margaret A. Bush, review of *When the Circus Came to Town,* p. 57; July, 1999, Christine Heppermann, review of *The Trolls,* p. 466; May, 2001, Sarah Ellis, review of *Everything on a Waffle,* p. 326; January-February, 2002, Cathryn M. Mercier, review of *Everything on a Waffle,* p. 40; September-October, Joanna Rudge Long, review of *The Pepins and Their Problems,* p. 586; July-August, 2005, Vicky Smith, review of *The Vacation,* p. 469; September-October, 2007, Vicky Smith, review of *The Corps of the Bare-boned Plane,* p. 579.

Kirkus Reviews, April 1, 1989, review of *An Occasional Cow,* p. 547; September 15, 1994, review of *The Happy Yellow Car,* p. 1274; February 15, 2001, review of *Everything on a Waffle,* p. 259; December 1, 2003, review of *The Canning Season,* p. 1403; July 15, 2004, review of *The Pepins and Their Problems,* p. 687; July 15, 2005, review of *The Vacation,* p. 791; July 15, 2007, review of *The Corps of the Bare-boned Plane.*

Kliatt, July, 2005, Janis Flint-Ferguson, review of *The Vacation,* p. 11; July, 2007, Paula Rohrlick, review of *The Corps of the Bare-boned Plane,* p. 16.

Maclean's, February 4, 2002, "The Perils of Primrose," p. 62.

Publishers Weekly, July 25, 1994, review of *The Happy Yellow Car,* p. 56; September 16, 1996, review of *When the Circus Came to Town,* p. 84; February 8, 1999, review of *The Trolls,* p. 214; April 9, 2001, review of *Everything on a Waffle,* p. 75; June 9, 2003, review of *The Canning Season,* p. 53; June 28, 2004, review of *The Pepins and Their Problems,* p. 50; June 27, 2005, review of *The Vacation,* p. 64; August 27, 2007, review of *The Corps of the Bare-boned Plane,* p. 91; August 21, 2008, Kit Alderdice, interview with Horvath.

Resource Links, October, 2003, Heather Empey, review of *The Canning Season,* p. 35; February, 2006, Linda Irvine, review of *The Vacation,* p. 23; February, 2008, Eva Wilson, review of *The Corps of the Bare-boned Plane,* p. 30.

School Library Journal, June, 1989, David Gale, review of *An Occasional Cow,* p. 106; September, 1994, Virginia Golodetz, review of *The Happy Yellow Car,* pp. 216, 218; December, 1996, Carrie A. Guarria, review of *When the Circus Came to Town,* p. 122; April, 1999, Christy Norris Blanchette, review of *The Trolls,* pp. 97, 99; April, 2001, Steven Engelfried, review of *Everything on a Waffle,* p. 144; August, 2004, Steven Engelfried, review of *The Pepins and Their Problems,* p. 124; August, 2005, Connie Tyrrell Burns, review of *The Vacation,* p. 129; September, 2007, Connie Tyrrell Burns, review of *The Corps of the Bare-boned Plane,* p. 198.

Voice of Youth Advocates, December, 1994, Becky Kornman, review of *The Happy Yellow Car,* p. 274.

ONLINE

Macmillan Web site, http://us.macmillan.com/ (September 30, 2008), "Polly Horvath."

Polly Horvath Home Page, http://www.pollyhorvath.com (September 30, 2008).

Scholastic Web site, http://www2.scholastic.com/ (September 30, 2008), "Polly Horvath."*

J-K

JANOVITZ, Marilyn

Personal

Female. *Education:* Attended School of Visual Arts (New York, NY) and Philadelphia College of Art.

Addresses

E-mail—mjanovitz@earthlink.net.

Career

Writer and illustrator. Has worked as a textile designer.

Writings

SELF-ILLUSTRATED

(Adapter) *Baa Baa, Black Sheep,* Hyperion (New York, NY), 1991.

(Adapter) *Hickory Dickory Dock,* Hyperion (New York, NY), 1991.

(Adapter) *Hey Diddle Diddle,* Hyperion (New York, NY), 1992.

(Adapter) *Pat-a-Cake,* Hyperion (New York, NY), 1992.

Is It Time?, North-South (New York, NY), 1994.

Look Out, Bird!, North-South (New York, NY), 1994.

Can I Help?, North-South (New York, NY), 1996.

Bowl Patrol!, North-South (New York, NY), 1996.

What Could Be Keeping Santa?, North-South (New York, NY), 1997.

Little Fox, North-South (New York, NY), 1999.

Good Morning, Little Fox, North-South (New York, NY), 2001.

(Adapter) *Three Little Kittens,* North-South (New York, NY), 2002.

We Love Christmas, Night Sky (New York, NY), 2003.

Maybe, My Baby, North-South (New York, NY), 2003.

A, B, See!, Chronicle (San Francisco, CA), 2005.

We Love School, North-South (New York, NY), 2007.

Author's work has been translated into Spanish.

ILLUSTRATOR

Margaret Driscoll Timmons, *The Ugly Duckling,* Silver Burdett (Morristown, NJ), 1990.

Robert M. McClung, *America's First Elephant,* Morrow Junior (New York, NY), 1991.

Miriam Schlein, *Just like Me,* Hyperion (New York, NY), 1993.

Ann E. Burg, *Pirate Pickle and the White Balloon,* Children's Press (New York, NY), 2007.

Contributor of illustrations to periodicals, including *CIO, New York Times, Wall Street Journal, Presstime, Ms., Macworld, Forbes,* and *Chief Executive.*

Sidelights

In addition to having her work published in several major periodicals, Marilyn Janovitz has contributed art to picture books since the early 1990s. In 1991 Janovitz also produced the first of her many original self-illustrated titles, and her illustrations have appeared alongside retellings or adaptations of traditional children's stories.

One of Janovitz's early books, *Look Out, Bird!,* features an original rhyming story that follows a chain reaction that begins with a snail slipping, causing a bird to take flight and frighten a frog, the chain of catastrophes eventually returning to the snail. Annie Ayres commented on the "rollicking rhythm [and] abundant alliteration" of Janovitz's text in her *Booklist* review, while a *Publishers Weekly* contributor noted that the author/illustrator's "bold palette contrasts handsomely with her stark white backgrounds." Another simple story, *What Could Be Keeping Santa?,* is designed to appeal to the same early audience, showing the reindeer waiting for Santa and wondering why the jolly man is not yet ready to deliver presents. "The story is light and ephemeral," wrote Ilene Cooper in *Booklist,* while a *Publishers Weekly* contributor praised the book's "cheery pastel watercolor and colored-pencil art."

Little Fox, a young fox loves his mother's chair, finding it just right for cuddling, but sadly, the chair breaks. As Janovitz's story continues, Little Fox and his parents find a replacement. As Shelle Rosenfeld commented in *Booklist,* the author/illustrator's "airy, pastel pencil-and-watercolor illustrations [are] sparked with intricate textures and detail." In a sequel, *Good Morning, Little Fox,* Little Fox and his father face a scary new breakfast food: porridge. Mother Fox leaves the pair on their own while she runs errands, and when they become too hungry to wait for her to make them something different when she returns, Father Fox and son try the porridge and love it. "This sweet story will strike a chord

with youngsters," wrote Marlene Gawron in her *School Library Journal* review, and in *Booklist* Gillian Engberg concluded that Janovitz's "images of lounging and rowdy housecleaning emphasize the bond between Little Fox and his dad."

Along with creating original tales, Janovitz retells traditional nursery rhymes in *Baa Baa, Black Sheep* and *Three Little Kittens.* Discussing the latter, *Booklist* critic Helen Rosenberg cited Janovitz's "delightful, brightly colored illustrations." A *Publishers Weekly* contributor noted that, while faithful to the original rhyme, the author/illustrator "reveal[s] a humorous back story

The soft-edged, gentle art of Marilyn Janovitz is a perfect fit for Miriam Schlein's picture book **Just like Me.** (Illustration copyright © 1993 by Marilyn Janovitz. All rights reserved. Reprinted by permission of Hyperion Books for Children.)

through full-bleed illustrations." In *School Library Journal*, Bina Williams wrote of *Three Little Kittens* that "the illustrations are bright and cheery with adorably mischievous felines."

In the alphabet book *A, B, See!*, Janovitz creates four-panel images in which each letter converts to an animal that begins its name with that letter. The book also features lift-the-flap elements that encourage readers to guess at the hidden pictures. The format of *A, B, See!* provides "an enticing invitation to play," wrote a *Kirkus Reviews* contributor. The "colorful creatures will have great appeal to youngsters," according to Maura Bresnahan in *School Library Journal.*

Janovitz offers encouragement to kindergartners in *We Love School!*, a book that describes the fun of a kindergarten classroom. "This simple book will be a big hit," predicted Teresa Pfeifer in her *School Library Journal* review. In *Booklist*, Carolyn Phelan deemed the picture book "well designed to calm young children's jitters," and a *Kirkus Reviews* contributor called Janovitz's art for the book "visually sweet and wholesome."

Biographical and Critical Sources

PERIODICALS

Booklist, July, 1994, Annie Ayres, review of *Look Out, Bird!*, p. 1954; October 15, 1996, Hazel Rochman, review of *Bowl Patrol!*, p. 435; May 1, 1996, Carolyn Phelan, review of *Can I Help?*, p. 1512; October 1, 1997, Ilene Cooper, review of *What Could Be Keeping Santa?*, p. 336; December 1, 1999, Shelle Rosenfeld, review of *Little Fox*, p. 712; May 1, 2001, Gillian Engberg, review of *Good Morning, Little Fox*, p. 1690; October 1, 2002, Helen Rosenberg, review of *Three Little Kittens*, p. 328; August, 2007, Carolyn Phelan, review of *We Love School!*, p. 83.

Childhood Education, fall, 2001, Sherry Mowrey, review of *Good Morning, Little Fox*, p. 50.

Kirkus Reviews, February 1, 2003, review of *Maybe, My Baby*, p. 232; June 1, 2005, review of *A, B, See!*, p. 638; June 15, 2007, review of *We Love School.*

Publishers Weekly, April 25, 1994, review of *Look Out, Bird!*, p. 76; October 6, 1997, review of *What Could Be Keeping Santa?*, p. 54; June 17, 2002, review of *Three Little Kittens*, p. 63; September 22, 2003, review of *We Love Christmas!*, p. 69.

School Library Journal, June, 2001, Marlene Gawron, review of *Good Morning, Little Fox*, p. 120; August, 2002, Bina Williams, review of *Three Little Kittens*, p. 158; July, 2005, Maura Bresnahan, review of *A, B, See!*, p. 90; December, 2007, Teresa Pfeifer, review of *We Love School!*, p. 92.

ONLINE

Marilyn Janovitz Home Page, http://www.marilynjanovitz. com (October 26, 2008).

North South Web site, http://www.northsouth.com/ (October 26, 2008), "Marilyn Janovitz."*

*   *   *

JOHNSTON, Mark

Personal

Born in NY; married.

Addresses

Home—Greenville, SC.

Career

Writer. Greenville Technical College, Greenville, SC, former instructor in English. *Military service:* U.S. Army, served as private.

Writings

(With Robyn Freedman Spizman) *Secret Agent*, Atheneum Books for Young Readers (New York, NY), 2005.
(With Robyn Freedman Spizman) *The Secret Agents Strike Back*, Atheneum Books for Young Readers (New York, NY), 2008.

Sidelights

Mark Johnston spent many years attempting to get his work published, and he achieved success when he teamed up with fellow writer and journalist Robyn Freedman Spizman. Johnston and Spizman's books for middle-grade readers, *Secret Agent* and *The Secret Agents Strike Back*, feature an adventurous hero named Kyle Parker, who becomes a self-styled undercover literary agent when he decides to help get his father's manuscript published. In the "Secret Agent" books, Kyle teams up with friend Lucinda in order to navigate the tricky corridors of high-profile New York City publishing.

Although Kyle and Lucinda are high-school students, Johnston and Spizman's intended audience is slightly younger. In *Kliatt*, Claire Rosser called *Secret Agent* "an amusing, offbeat story . . . light and funny too, with appeal to the middle school group." A *Kirkus Reviews* contributor wrote that the central characters undertake "their clandestine caper with humor and suspense," while *Booklist* writer Todd Morning described the book as "a quirky tale about resourceful young people." In *School Library Journal*, Mary R. Hofmann praised *Secret Agent* as "a strangely compelling adventure in which readers root for Kyle's success."

Kyle and Lucinda continue their adventures in *The Secret Agents Strike Back*, and as they embark on a new set of adventures the teens begin to realize that an element of romance has taken root in their friendship.

Biographical and Critical Sources

PERIODICALS

Booklist, April 15, 2005, Todd Morning, review of *Secret Agent,* p. 1457.
Bulletin of the Center for Children's Books, September, 2005, Karen Coats, review of *Secret Agent,* p. 46.
Kirkus Reviews, April 1, 2005, review of *Secret Agent,* p. 426.
Kliatt, May, 2005, Claire Rosser, review of *Secret Agent,* p. 18.
School Library Journal, March, 2005, Mary R. Hofmann, review of *Secret Agent,* p. 218.
Voice of Youth Advocates, August, 2005, Kevin Beach, review of *Secret Agent,* p. 226.

ONLINE

Mindy Friddle Web Site, http://www.mindyfriddle.com/ (November 10, 2008), interview with Johnston.
Simon & Schuster Web site, http://www.simonsays.com/ (November 10, 2008), "Mark Johnston."*

* * *

KIDD, Richard 1952-2008

OBITUARY NOTICE—

See index for *SATA* sketch: Born June 22, 1952, in Newcastle upon Tyne, England; died by drowning, July 19, 2008, in the Philippines. Artist, painter, educator, and children's author. Kidd began his career as an award-winning artist. His first award was an Abbey painting scholarship for the British School at Rome that he received in 1974, when he was not long out of his teens. Kidd's landscape art reflected his love for the outdoor world at its most rugged and challenging. He painted the mountainous terrain of the Scottish highlands and the remote splendor of the islands of the North Sea, writing that a sense of place and immediacy—even urgency—was a critical element of his best work. At its peak, Kidd's art was exhibited throughout the world, including shows in San Francisco and New York City in the 1980s. He also exhibited regularly at the Biscuit Factory in his hometown, and he taught painting classes at British universities. It was parenthood, perhaps, that led Kidd toward the written word. When his own daughters were quite small, he published *Almost Famous Daisy!* (1996), part children's story, part art primer for the very young, winning criticism for his meandering text but praise for his beautiful illustrations. He persisted. *Monsieur Thermidor: A Fantastic Fishy Tale* (1997) and *Lobsters in Love: A Whirlpool Romance* (2001), both illustrated by his wife, Lindsey, follow the adventures of a lobster who owns a restaurant that serves his secret seaweed soup, until he needs to share the confidential recipe to save his life, first from a rival chef and later from a fisherman. Kidd's later books were mysteries for older readers. These include *Giant Goldfish Robbery* (1999), the story of a boy's quest to save his neighbor's valuable giant koi carp. Another, *Deadly Famous* (2001), is about a boy who suspects that a local artists' disappearance is part of a plot to increase the value of his artwork. Kidd wrote nearly a dozen children's books, but it may be his artistic journey through the wild places that will linger longest in the memory of his admirers and critics.

OBITUARIES AND OTHER SOURCES:

PERIODICALS

Times (London, England), July 26, 2008, p. 67.

* * *

KONIGSBURG, E.L. 1930-
(Elaine Lobl Konigsburg)

Personal

Born February 10, 1930, in New York, NY; daughter of Adolph (a businessman) and Beulah Lobl; married David Konigsburg (a psychologist), July 6, 1952; children: Paul, Laurie, Ross. *Education:* Carnegie Mellon University, B.S., 1952; graduate study, University of Pittsburgh, 1952-54. *Religion:* Jewish.

Addresses

Home—Vedra, FL.

Career

Writer. Shenango Valley Provision Co., Sharon, PA, bookkeeper, 1947-48; Bartram School, Jacksonville, FL, science teacher, 1954-55, 1960-62.

Awards, Honors

Honor Book designation, *Book Week,* Children's Spring Book Fair, 1967, and Newbery Honor Book designation, American Library Association (ALA), 1968, both for *Jennifer, Hecate, Macbeth, William McKinley, and Me, Elizabeth;* Newbery Medal, ALA, and Lewis Carroll Shelf Award, both 1968, and William Allen White Award, 1970, all for *From the Mixed-up Files of Mrs. Basil E. Frankweiler;* Carnegie Mellon Merit Award, 1971; Notable Children's Book designation, ALA, and National Book Award finalist, both 1974, both for *A Proud Taste for Scarlet and Miniver;* Notable Children's Book designation, ALA, and American Book Award nomination, both 1980, both for *Throwing Shadows;* Children's Books of the Year designation, Child Study Association of America, for *Jennifer, Hecate,*

E.L. Konigsburg (Reproduced by permission.)

Macbeth, William McKinley, and Me, Elizabeth, About the B'nai Bagels, A Proud Taste for Scarlet and Miniver, and *Journey to an 800 Number*; Notable Children's Book designation, ALA, Parents' Choice Award for Literature, and Notable Children's Trade Book for the Language Arts designation, National Council of Teachers of English, all 1987, all for *Up from Jericho Tel;* Special Recognition Award, Cultural Council of Greater Jacksonville, FL, 1997; Newbery Medal, 1997, for *The View from Saturday;* Best Books for Young Adults selections, ALA, for *The Second Mrs. Giaconda* and *Father's Arcane Daughter.*

Writings

FOR CHILDREN; SELF-ILLUSTRATED

Jennifer, Hecate, Macbeth, William McKinley, and Me, Elizabeth, Atheneum (New York, NY), 1967, published as *Jennifer, Hecate, MacBeth, and Me,* Macmillan (London, England), 1968, reprinted, Aladdin (New York, NY), 2007.

From the Mixed-up Files of Mrs. Basil E. Frankweiler, Atheneum (New York, NY), 1967, thirty-fifth anniversary edition, with new afterword by Konigsburg, 2002.

About the B'nai Bagels, Atheneum (New York, NY), 1969.

(George), Atheneum (New York, NY), 1970, published as *Benjamin Dickenson Carr and His (George),* Penguin (Harmondsworth, England), 1974.

A Proud Taste for Scarlet and Miniver, Atheneum (New York, NY), 1973.

The Dragon in the Ghetto Caper, Atheneum (New York, NY), 1974.

Samuel Todd's Book of Great Colors, Atheneum (New York, NY), 1990.

Samuel Todd's Book of Great Inventions, Atheneum (New York, NY), 1991.

Amy Elizabeth Explores Bloomingdale's, Atheneum (New York, NY), 1992.

FOR CHILDREN

Altogether, One at a Time (short stories), illustrated by Gail E. Haley, Mercer Meyer, Gary Parker, and Laurel Schindelman, Atheneum (New York, NY), 1971, second edition, Macmillan (New York, NY), 1989.

The Second Mrs. Giaconda, illustrated with museum plates, Atheneum (New York, NY), 1975, reprinted, Simon & Schuster (New York, NY), 2005.

Father's Arcane Daughter, Atheneum (New York, NY), 1976, published as *My Father's Daughter,* Aladdin (New York, NY), 2008.

Throwing Shadows (short stories), Atheneum (New York, NY), 1979, reprinted, Aladdin (New York, NY), 2007.

Journey to an 800 Number, Atheneum (New York, NY), 1982, published as *Journey by First Class Camel,* Hamish Hamilton (London, England), 1983.

Up from Jericho Tel, Atheneum (New York, NY), 1986.

T-Backs, T-Shirts, COAT, and Suit, Atheneum (New York, NY), 1993.

The View from Saturday, Atheneum (New York, NY), 1996.

Silent to the Bone, Atheneum (New York, NY), 2000.

The Outcasts of 19 Schuyler Place, Atheneum (New York, NY), 2004.

The Mysterious Edge of the Heroic World, Atheneum (New York, NY), 2007.

FOR ADULTS; NONFICTION

The Mask beneath the Face: Reading about and with, Writing about and for Children, Library of Congress, 1990.

TalkTalk: A Children's Book Author Speaks to Grown-Ups, Atheneum (New York, NY), 1995.

OTHER

Also author of promotional pamphlets for Atheneum and contributor to Braille anthology, *Expectations 1980,* Braille Institute, 1980.

Author's manuscripts and original art are held in collections at University of Pittsburgh, Pennsylvania.

Adaptations

From the Mixed-up Files of Mrs. Basil E. Frankweiler was adapted as an audio recording, Miller-Brody/Random House, 1969; a motion picture starring Ingrid Bergman, Cinema 5, 1973, released as *The Hideaways,*

Bing Crosby Productions, 1974; and made into a television movie starring Lauren Bacall, 1995. *Jennifer, Hecate, Macbeth, William McKinley, and Me, Elizabeth* was adapted as the television movie *Jennifer and Me,* NBC-TV, 1973, and as a cassette, Listening Library, 1986. *The Second Mrs. Giaconda* was adapted as a play produced in Jacksonville, FL, 1976. *Father's Arcane Daughter* was adapted for television as *Caroline?,* Hallmark Hall of Fame, 1990. Many of Konigsburg's books have been adapted as audiobooks, including *About the B'nai Bagels, From the Mixed-up Files of Mrs. Basil E. Frankweiler, The Outcasts of 19 Schuyler Place,* and *The Mysterious Edge of the Heroic World. From the Mixed-up Files of Mrs. Basil E. Frankweiler* was adapted as a Braille edition.

Sidelights

Known for her witty and often self-illustrated works for young people, E.L. Konigsburg has carved out a unique niche, whether writing out of personal experience or verging far afield to focus on the medieval world and the Renaissance. An impressive figure in children's literature, Konigsburg is also the only author to have had two books on the Newbery list simultaneously: When *From the Mixed-up Files of Mrs. Basil E. Frankweiler* won the 1968 Newbery Medal, *Jennifer, Hecate, Macbeth, William McKinley, and Me, Elizabeth* was a runner-up for the same award. She has also won a second coveted Newbery medal, capturing the 1997 award for her novel *The View from Saturday.*

Konigsburg did not set her sights on writing as a career until later in life. Born in New York City in 1930, she was the middle of three daughters. She grew up in small towns in Pennsylvania, not only absorbing books such as *The Secret Garden* and *Mary Poppins,* but also much unabashed "trash along the lines of *True Confessions,*" as she once reported in *Saturday Review.* "I have no objection to trash. I've read a lot of it and firmly believe it helped me hone my taste." Konigsburg also mentioned that as a child she did much of her reading in the bathroom because "it was the only room in our house that had a lock on the door." She also drew often as a child and was a good student in school, graduating as valedictorian of her class. Yet for a young person growing up in the small mill towns of Pennsylvania as Konigsburg did, college was not necessarily the next step. There were advantages to such an upbringing, however. As Konigsburg has commented, "Growing up in a small town gives you two things: a sense of place and a feeling of self-consciousness—self-consciousness about one's education and exposure, both of which tend to be limited. On the other hand, limited possibilities also mean creating your own options. A small town allows you to grow in your own direction, without a bombardment of outside stimulation."

And that is precisely what Konigsburg did: she grew in her own way and decided to head for college. Completely ignorant of such things as scholarships, she de-

vised a plan whereby she would alternate working for a year with a year of school. The first year out of high school she took a bookkeeping job at a local meat plant and there met David Konigsburg, the man who would become her husband. The following year, Konigsburg enrolled in Carnegie Mellon University in Pittsburgh, choosing to major in chemistry. She survived not a few laboratory accidents on the way to eventually earning her degree. Early in her college career, however, a helpful instructor directed Konigsburg to scholarships and work-study assistance, so that she was able to continue her studies without break. Konigsburg noted that college was "a crucial 'opening up'" period. "I worked hard and did well. However, the artistic side of me was essentially dormant." She graduated with honors, married David Konigsburg, and embarked on graduate study at the University of Pittsburgh. Meanwhile, her husband was also studying, preparing himself for a career in industrial psychology. When her husband won a post in Jacksonville, Florida, Konigsburg picked up and moved with him, working for several years as a science teacher

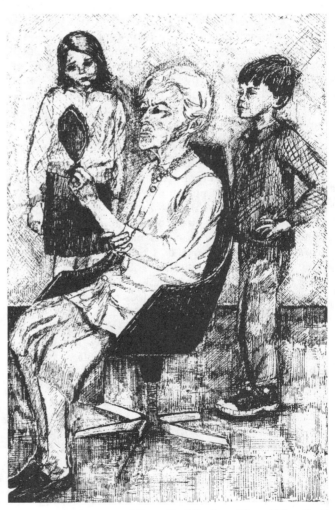

Konigsburg's classic novel **From the Mixed-up Files of Mrs. Basil Frankweiler** *is brought to life in the author's unique pen-and-ink art.*

in an all-girls school. The teaching experience opened up a new world for her, giving her insight into the lives of these young girls whom she expected to be terribly spoiled. She also quickly learned that economic ease did nothing to ease inner problems.

Konigsburg left teaching in 1955 after the birth of her first child, Paul. A year later a daughter, Laurie, was born, and in 1959 a third child, Ross. Konigsburg became a full-time mom, taking some time out, however, to pursue painting. She returned to teaching in the early 1960s, until her husband's work required a move to New York. When all three children were finally in school, Konigsburg began writing, employing themes and events close to her family life in her books. She also used her children as her first audience, reading them her morning's work when they came home for lunch. Laughter would encourage her to continue in the same vein; glum faces prompted revision and rewrites. Konigsburg once commented that she had noticed that her kids were growing up very differently from the way she did, but that their growing up "was related to this middle-class kind of child I had seen when I had taught at the private girls' school. I recognized that I wanted to write something that reflected their kind of growing up, something that addressed the problems that come about even though you don't have to worry if you wear out your shoes whether your parents can buy you a new pair, something that tackles the basic problems of who am I? What makes me the same as everyone else? What makes me different?"

Such questions led Konigsburg to her first two books. *Jennifer, Hecate, Macbeth, William McKinley, and Me, Elizabeth,* was based on her daughter's experience making friends in their new home in Port Chester, New York, while *From the Mixed-up Files of Mrs. Basil E. Frankweiler* was inspired by the finicky manner in which her kids behaved on a picnic. Konigsburg also illustrated both these books, as she has many of her titles, using her children as models. The first novel tells the story of Elizabeth, who is new in town, and her attempts at finding friendship. It does not help that she is small for her age, and Cynthia, the cool kid in school, is quick to dismiss her. But then Elizabeth meets Jennifer, another classic outsider who styles herself as a witch. Elizabeth soon becomes her apprentice, and suddenly life is full of adventures. Jennifer is a source of mystery for Elizabeth: she never lets the new girl know where or how she lives, and this is just fine for Elizabeth, who is smitten by Jennifer to the point of declaring that even if she "discovered that Jennifer lived in an ordinary house and did ordinary things, I would know it was a disguise."

Critical reception for *Jennifer, Hecate, Macbeth, William McKinley, and Me, Elizabeth* was quite positive. *Booklist* contributor Ruth P. Bull called it "a fresh, lively story, skillfully expressed," and a contributor for *Publishers Weekly* warned against allowing a too-cute title scare readers away from "one of the freshest, funniest books of the season." This same reviewer went on presciently to say that the reader will have "the smug pleasure" of saying in later years—when the author would surely make a name for herself—that he or she had read Konigsburg when she was just beginning. Writing in *Horn Book,* Ruth Hill Viguers also praised the book, noting that *Jennifer, Hecate, Macbeth, William McKinley, and Me, Elizabeth* "is full of humor and of situations completely in tune with the imaginations of ten-year-old girls."

From the Mixed-up Files of Mrs. Basil E. Frankweiler had its genesis in a family picnic in Yellowstone Park. While Konigsburg's children were complaining about the insects and warm milk and general lack of civilization, Konigsburg realized that if they should ever run away from home, they would surely carry with them all the stuffy suburban ways that were so inbred in them. This started her thinking of a pair of children who run away from home to the Metropolitan Museum of Art, a safe sort of imitation of faraway places. Claudia, tired of being taken for granted at home, plans to run away and takes her younger brother Jamie—the one with a sense for finances—with her on this safe adventure. Together they elude guards at the Met, sleep on royal beds, bathe in the cafeteria pool, and loiter on the fringes of school lecture tours during the day. Their arrival at the museum coincides with the showing of a recent museum acquisition, a marble angel believed to have been sculpted by Michelangelo. Soon they are under the spell of the angel and want to know the identity of the carver, which brings them to the statue's former owner, Mrs. Frankweiler. The story is narrated in the form of a letter from Mrs. Frankweiler to her lawyer, and it is she who confronts Claudia with the truth about herself. "Returning with a secret is what she really wants," says Mrs. Frankweiler. "Claudia doesn't want adventure. She likes baths and feeling comfortable too much for that kind of thing. Secrets are the kind of adventure she needs. Secrets are safe, and they do much to make you different. On the inside, where it counts."

In *Booklist* Bull called *From the Mixed-up Files of Mrs. Basil E. Frankweiler* "fresh and crisply written" with "uncommonly real and likable characters," praising the humor and dialogue as well. Viguers, writing in *Horn Book,* noted that although the novel violates every rule of writing for children, it remains "one of the most original stories of many years." A *Kirkus Reviews* critic commented that whereas Konigsburg's first novel was a "dilly," her second book is "just as fast and fresh and funny, but less spoofing, more penetrating." Plaudits continued from Alice Fleming, who noted in the *New York Times Book Review* that Konigsburg "is a lively, amusing and painlessly educational storyteller." *Washington Post Book World* reviewer Polly Goodwin echoed this view, dubbing *From the Mixed-up Files of Mrs. Basil E. Frankweiler* "an exceptional story, notable for superlative writing, fresh humor, an original theme, clear-eyed understanding of children, and two young protagonists whom readers will find funny, real and unforgettable."

In Konigsburg's acceptance speech for her first Newbery, she talked about her overriding feeling of owing kids a good story. "[I try to] let the telling be like fudge-ripple ice cream. You keep licking the vanilla, but every now and then you come to something richer and deeper and with a stronger flavor." Her books all explore this richer and deeper territory, while employing humor in large doses. However, instant success is a hard act to follow, and her third book, *About the B'nai Bagels,* a Little League baseball story with a Jewish Mother twist, was not as well received as the first two. In a further suburban tale, *(George),* Ben is a twelve year old with an inner voice he calls George who acts as a sort of higher intelligence and conscience for the boy. When Ben, who is a bright student, is placed in a high-school chemistry class, George starts acting out, causing a crisis of identity.

A fascination for medieval times led Konigsburg to write *A Proud Taste for Scarlet and Miniver,* an historical fantasy—told from the participants' points of view in heaven—about the life of Eleanor of Aquitaine. Though some critics found the book to be too modern for the subject, in the *Bulletin of the Center for Children's Books* Zena Sutherland called it "one of the most fresh, imaginative, and deft biographies to come along in a long, long time." Paul Heins, writing in *Horn Book,* also noted that Konigsburg's drawings "are skillfully as well as appropriately modeled upon medieval manuscript illuminations and add their share of joy to the book." Following in this historical vein is *The Second Mrs. Giaconda,* the story of Leonardo da Vinci's middle years. Konigsburg posits a solution to the riddle of the Mona Lisa and serves up a "unique bit of creative historical interpretation" with a glimpse of Renaissance culture she has "artfully and authentically illumined," according to Shirley M. Wilton in *School Library Journal.*

Another more experimental novel—in theme rather than period—is *Father's Arcane Daughter,* a mystery that has also been published as *My Father's Daughter.* The novel focuses on the return of Caroline, a young woman who had been kidnapped and presumed dead seventeen years earlier. The story focuses on the effects of Caroline's reappearance on her father, his new wife, and their young children in a "haunting, marvelously developed plot," according to a reviewer in *Publishers Weekly.*

Konigsburg returns to more familiar ground with *The Dragon in the Ghetto Caper* and *Throwing Shadows,* the latter a short-story collection that was nominated for an American Book award. Both *Journey to an 800 Number* and *Amy Elizabeth Explores Bloomingdale's* are considered to be vintage Konigsburg, the second recounting the story of a girl and her grandmother as they attempt to find the time to see Bloomingdale's department store. A reviewer for *Publishers Weekly* called *Amy Elizabeth Explores Bloomingdale's* a "vivid portrait of a distraction-filled city—and of a most affectionate relationship."

Up from Jericho Tel relates the encounter between the ghost of a dead actress and two children, who are turned invisible and sent out with a group of street performers to search for a missing necklace. "A witty, fast-paced story," is how a reviewer in *Publishers Weekly* characterized the novel. A contributor to the *Bulletin of the Center for Children's Books,* reviewing *Up from Jericho Tel,* provided a summation of Konigsburg's distinctive gift to children's literature: "Whether she is writing a realistic or a fanciful story, Konigsburg always provides fresh ideas, tart wit and humor, and memorable characters."

With *T-Backs, T-Shirts, COAT, and Suit,* Konigsburg again pairs a quirky title with an engaging story. Here young Chloe spends the summer in Florida with her stepfather's sister. While she helps the woman run a meals-on-wheels van, the girl becomes involved in a local controversy over T-back swimming suits. Rachel Axelrod, reviewing the book in *Voice of Youth Advocates,* concluded that with *T-Backs, T-Shirts, COAT, and Suit* Konigsburg "has produced another winner!"

The View from Saturday tells the story of four members of a championship quiz bowl team and the paraplegic teacher who coaches them. A series of first-person narratives from the students displays links between their lives in a story that is "glowing with humor and dusted with magic," according to a critic in *Publishers Weekly.* Julie Cummins concluded in *School Library Journal* that "brilliant writing melds with crystalline characterizations in this sparkling story that is a jewel in the author's crown of outstanding work." Konigsburg won the 1997 Newbery Medal for this novel, her second in three decades of writing. Commenting on the connection between *The View from Saturday* and Konigsburg's previous medal winner, *The Mixed-up Files of Mrs. Basil E. Frankweiler,* the author's daughter, Laurie Konigsburg Todd, noted in *Horn Book:* "Although the inspiration for these Newbery books was as disparate as the three decades which separate their publication, their theme is the same. In fact, every one of E.L. Konigsburg's . . . novels are about children who seek, find, and ultimately enjoy who they are. Despite this common denominator, [her] writing is the antithesis of the formula book. Her characters are one-of-a-kind."

More one-of-a-kind characters are introduced in *Silent to the Bone,* the story of a thirteen year old who is wrongly accused of injuring his baby sister. Branwell, shocked by such an accusation, loses the power of speech, and it is left to his friend Connor to reach out to him and discover the truth about what really happened. Accused by the English au pair of dropping and shaking his infant half-sister, Branwell cannot defend himself and is confined at a juvenile center. Employing handwritten flash cards, Connor is able to piece together the events leading up to the 911 call which opens the book. By the end of this journey of discovery, not only is the real villain revealed, but both Bran and Connor come to grips with larger truths in their

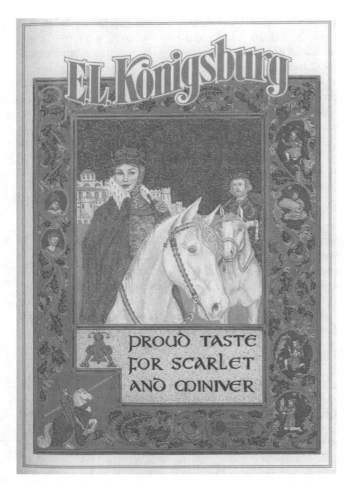

The cover of Konigsburg's historical novel **A Proud Taste for Scarlet and Miniver** *features the author's original art.* (Copyright © 1973 by E.L. Konigsburg. Used by permission of Dell Publishing, a division of Random House, Inc.)

own lives, including the dynamics of stepfamilies. "No one is better than Konigsburg at plumbing the hearts and minds of smart, savvy kids," commented *Horn Book* critic Peter D. Sieruta, who called *Silent to the Bone* an "edgy, thought-provoking novel . . . written with Konigsburg's characteristic wit and perspicuity." In *Booklist* Hazel Rochman pleaded for a second reading of the book, not simply for clues to the identity of the real perpetrator, but for "the wit, and insight, the farce, and the gentleness of the telling." Reviewing *Silent to the Bone, New York Times Book Review* contributor Roger Sutton commented that Konigsburg "is one of our brainiest writers for young people, not only in the considerable cerebral powers she brings to her books but in the intellectual demands she makes on her characters."

Margaret Rose Kane, Connor's half sister in *Silent to the Bone,* recalls her twelfth summer in *The Outcasts of 19 Schuyler Place.* In this story the girl's parents have gone to Peru for the summer, and Margaret's abhorrence of summer camp generates complaints from her cabin mates until she is rescued by her two elderly uncles. When the uncles rescue her from camp and take her to their urban home, she quickly joins in a crusade to save the massive sculptures the uncles have constructed in their garden and which now are under siege by annoyed neighbors armed with city ordinances. Calling *The Outcasts of 19 Schuyler Place* "intelligently structured, humorously told, and richly observant," *Booklist* critic Jennifer Mattson also praised Konigsburg's unconventional and determined young heroine. For Cindy Darling Codell, writing in *School Library Journal,* the true stars of the novel are Margaret's Hungarian-Jewish uncles, "crotchety with age, but full of love and life and a sure understanding of what it means to be an individual American." In *Kirkus Reviews* a reviewer also had praise for the book, writing that in *The Outcasts of 19 Schuyler Place* Konigsburg "passionately confront[s] . . . readers with the critical importance of history, art, beauty, community, love, and, above all, the necessity to invest oneself in meaningful action."

Drawing on characters and themes from both *The Outcasts of 19 Schuyler Place* and *From the Mixed-up Files of Mrs. Basil E. Frankweiler, The Mysterious Edge of the Heroic World* investigates the origins of a provocative "degenerate" Modigliani drawing that dates to Nazi Germany. The work of art is discovered by preteens William and Amedeo as they help elderly Jewish neighbor and opera diva Mrs. Zender catalogue her possessions in preparation for moving into a Florida retirement home. Through the help of Amedeo's museum-curator godfather, the drawing becomes a key to the treatment of homosexuals and other undesirables during the Holocaust, as well as revealing the drama within the Zender family. Dubbing Konigsburg "a master of characterization," *School Library Journal* contributor Renee Steinberg described *The Mysterious Edge of the Heroic World* "an appealing tale of friendship, loyalty, and mystery," while Cooper wrote that the author "writes with a singular intelligence that permeates every page" of her novel. "Quirky, wandering, sometimes unbelievable," *The Mysterious Edge of the Heroic World* "nevertheless takes firm root in the reader's mind, training their eye to watch for stories that need discovering," concluded a *Kirkus Reviews* writer.

For those who have met them through the pages of Konigsburg's novels, characters such as Jennifer, Elizabeth, Claudia, Bran, Margaret, and Amedeo have become not only best friends to readers, but also telegraphic symbols of complex emotions and adolescent conditions. "The strong demands Konigsburg makes of her characters and the fine moral intelligence she gives them imply much respect for children, a respect she has continued to express in all of her books," asserted Perry Nodelman in his essay on the beloved author for the *Dictionary of Literary Biography.* A writer who takes her craft seriously yet who manages to avoid heavy-handed thematic writing, Konigsburg views children's books as "the primary vehicle for keeping alive the means of linear learning," as she herself explains in her book *TalkTalk: A Children's Book Author Speaks to Grown-Ups.* Children's books "are the key to the accumulated wisdom, wit, gossip, truth, myth, history, philosophy, and recipes for salting potatoes during the past 6,000 years of civilization," she adds. "Children's books are the Rosetta Stone to the hearts and minds of writers from Moses to Mao. And that is the last measure in the growth of children's literature as I've witnessed it—a growing necessity."

Biographical and Critical Sources

BOOKS

Children's Literature Review, Volume 1, Gale (Detroit, MI), 1976.

Dictionary of Literary Biography, Volume 52: *American Writers for Children from 1960, Fiction,* Gale (Detroit, MI), 1986.

Hanks, Dorrel Thomas, *E.L. Konigsburg,* Twayne, 1992.

Konigsburg, E.L., *From the Mixed-up Files of Mrs. Basil E. Frankweiler,* Atheneum (New York, NY), 1967.

Konigsburg, E.L., *Jennifer, Hecate, Macbeth, William McKinley, and Me, Elizabeth,* Atheneum (New York, NY), 1967.

Konigsburg, E.L., *TalkTalk: A Children's Book Author Speaks to Grown-Ups,* Atheneum (New York, NY), 1995.

Twentieth-Century Children's Writers, fourth edition, St. James Press (Detroit, MI), 1995.

PERIODICALS

Booklist, June 1, 1967, Ruth P. Bull, review of *Jennifer, Hecate, Macbeth, William McKinley, and Me, Elizabeth,* p. 1048; October 1, 1967, Ruth P. Bull, review of *From the Mixed-up Files of Mrs. Basil E. Frankweiler,* p. 199; August, 2000, Hazel Rochman, review of *Silent to the Bone,* p. 2135; December 15, 2003, Jennifer Mattson, review of *The Outcasts of 19 Schuyler Place,* p. 749; September 15, 2001, Ilene Cooper, review of *The Mysterious Edge of the Heroic World,* p. 65.

Bulletin of the Center for Children's Books, September, 1973, Zena Sutherland, review of *A Proud Taste for Scarlet and Miniver,* pp. 10-11; March, 1982, review of *Journey to an 800 Number,* p. 133; March, 1986, review of *Up from Jericho Tel,* p. 131; May, 1990, review of *Samuel Todd's Book of Great Colors,* p. 216; September, 1992, review of *Amy Elizabeth Explores Bloomingdales,* p. 16; November, 1996, review of *The View from Saturday,* p. 103; June, 2004, review of *The Outcasts of 19 Schuyler Place,* p. 448.

Horn Book, March-April, 1967, Ruth Hill Viguers, review of *Jennifer, Hecate, Macbeth, William McKinley, and Me, Elizabeth,* pp. 206-207; September-October, 1967, Ruth Hill Viguers, review of *From the Mixed-up Files of Mrs. Basil E. Frankweiler,* p. 595; July-August, 1968, E.L. Konigsburg, "Newbery Award Acceptance," pp. 391-395; September-October, 1973, Paul Heins, review of *A Proud Taste for Scarlet and Mini-*

ver, pp. 466-467; May-June, 1982, review of *Journey to an 800 Number,* pp. 289-290; May-June, 1986, Ethel R. Tweitchell, review of *Up from Jericho Tel,* p. 327; January-February, 1997, Roger Sutton, review of *The View from Saturday,* p. 60; July-August, 1997, Laurie Konigsburg Todd, "E.L. Konigsburg," pp. 415-417; November-December, 2000, Peter D. Sieruta, review of *Silent to the Bone,* p. 756; March-April, 2004, Peter D. Sieruta, review of *The Outcasts of 19 Schuyler Place,* p. 184.

Kirkus Reviews, July 1, 1967, review of *From the Mixed-up Files of Mrs. Basil E. Frankweiler,* p. 740; December 15, 2003, review of *The Outcasts of 19 Schuyler Place,* p. 1451; August 15, 2007, review of *The Mysterious Edge of the Heroic World.*

New York Times Book Review, November 5, 1967, Alice Fleming, review of *From the Mixed-up Files of Mrs. Basil E. Frankweiler,* p. 44; November 19, 2000, Roger Sutton, "In the Blink of an Eye," p. 54.

Publishers Weekly, April 10, 1967, review of *Jennifer, Hecate, Macbeth, William McKinley, and Me, Elizabeth,* p. 80; July 19, 1976, review of *Father's Arcane Daughter,* p. 13; April 25, 1986, review of *Up from Jericho Tell,* p. 80; July 22, 1996, review of *The View from Saturday,* p. 242; September 6, 1999, review of *Samuel Todd's Book of Great Colors,* p. 106; September 13, 1999, review of *Amy Elizabeth Explores Bloomingdale's,* p. 86; April 12, 2004, review of *The Outcasts of 19 Schuyler Place,* p. 25; July 30, 2007, review of *The Mysterious Edge of the Heroic World,* p. 82.

Saturday Review, November 9, 1968, E.L. Konigsburg, "A Book Is a Private Thing," pp. 45-46.

School Library Journal, September, 1975, Shirley M. Wilton, review of *The Second Mrs. Giaconda,* p. 121; May, 1986, Roth S. Vose, review of *Up from Jericho Tel,* p. 93; March, 1990, Susan Hepler, review of *Samuel Todd's Book of Great Colors,* p. 208; October, 1991, Starr LaTronica, review of *Samuel Todd's Book of Great Inventions,* p. 98; September, 1992, Judith Gloyer, review of *Amy Elizabeth Explores Bloomingdales,* p. 206; October, 1993, Nancy Menaldi-Scanlan, review of *T-Backs, T-Shirts, COAT, and Suit,* p. 124; September, 1996, Julie Cummins, review of *The View from Saturday,* p. 204; January, 2004, Cindy Darling Codell, review of *The Outcasts of 19 Schuyler Place,* p. 130; September, 2007, Renee Steinberg, review of *The Mysterious Edge of the Heroic World,* p. 202.

Voice of Youth Advocates, December, 1993, Rachel Axelrod, review of *T-Backs, T-Shirts, COAT, and Suit,* p. 254.

Washington Post Book World, November 5, 1967, Polly Goodwin, review of *From the Mixed-up Files of Mrs. Basil E. Frankweiler,* p. 22.

ONLINE

Houghton Mifflin Reading Web site, http://www.eduplace.com/ (October 20, 2008), "E.L. Konigsburg."

Simon & Schuster Web site, http://www.simonsays.com/ (October 20, 2008), "E.L. Konigsburg."

OTHER

Good Conversation!: A Talk with E.L. Konigsburg (video), Tim Podell Productions, 1995.*

* * *

KONIGSBURG, Elaine Lobl
See KONIGSBURG, E.L.

* * *

KRINITZ, Esther Nisenthal 1927-2001

Personal

Born 1927, in Mniszek, Poland; immigrated to United States, 1949, naturalized citizen; died March, 2001; married Max Krinitz, November, 1946; children: Bernice Steinhardt, Helene McQuade. *Religion:* Jewish.

Career

Worked as a seamstress and dressmaker; textile artist. *Exhibitions:* Work has been exhibited at American Visionary Art Museum, Baltimore, MD; Lisa Watson Children's Museum, Miami, FL; Guilford College, Greensborough, NC; Juda L. Magnes Museum, Berkeley, CA; and Arnot Art Museum, Elmira, NY.

Writings

(With daughter, Bernice Steinhardt) *Memories of Survival,* Hyperion (New York, NY), 2005.

Sidelights

Esther Nisenthal Krinitz was fifteen years old when the Nazis rounded up the Jewish citizens of Mniszek, Poland, where she lived, and sent them to concentration camps. Esther persuaded her sister Mania to run away with her, and for the rest of World War II the sisters pretended to be Roman Catholics as they worked at a farm in rural Poland. When the Russians liberated the country and Krinitz discovered that the rest of her family had been exterminated, she moved to Germany, where she met her husband, Max Krinitz. In 1949, the Krinitz's immigrated to the United States and made a new home. Beginning in 1977, Krinitz channeled her talent as a seamstress and began to re-create her life in thirty-six textile collages, incorporating embroidery, crochet, knitting, and appliqué techniques, along with hand-embroidered captions explaining the action in each panel. These highly detailed artworks follow Krinitz from her farming childhood and depict the traumatic events that characterized her war years and beyond, to her life in America.

Four years after Krinitz's death in 2001, her daughter, Bernice Steinhardt, published a collaborative memoir that includes the art Krinitz created to document her life. The book, *Memories of Survival,* joins a body of work from those who managed to elude the Holocaust. Because Krinitz was a teenager when the Holocaust began, her memoir is appropriate for children and young adults. As coauthor, Steinhardt fills in the details her mother recounted to her over the years. As Hazel Rochman noted in *Booklist,* "the telling is quiet . . . with depth and color that will make readers look closely." A *Publishers Weekly* reviewer commented of *Memories of Survival* that Krinitz's textile images "stand as one woman's testimony to hope, endurance, and the unquenchable passion to bear witness," and *Horn Book* critic Robin Smith concluded that Krinitz's handiworks "move the heartbreaking tale forward and leave the reader stunned."

Biographical and Critical Sources

BOOKS

(With Bernice Steinhardt) *Memories of Survival,* Hyperion (New York, NY), 2005.

Esther Nisenthal Krinitz presents an evocative, handiwork history in **Memories of Survival,** *a picture book coauthored with daughter Bernice Steinhardt.* (Copyright © 2005 by Esther Nisenthal and Bernice Steinhardt. All rights reserved. Reprinted by permission of Hyperion Books for Children.)

PERIODICALS

Booklist, October 15, 2005, Hazel Rochman, review of *Memories of Survival,* p. 47.

Bulletin of the Center for Children's Books, March, 2006, April Spisak, review of *Memories of Survival,* p. 317.

Horn Book, November-December, 2005, Robin Smith, review of *Memories of Survival,* p. 737.

Kirkus Reviews, October 1, 2005, review of *Memories of Survival,* p. 1082.

Publishers Weekly, October 10, 2005, review of *Memories of Survival,* p. 61.

School Library Journal, November, 2005, Rachel Kamin, review of *Memories of Survival,* p. 165.

ONLINE

Art & Remembrance Web site, http://www.artandremem brance.org/ (November 10, 2008), "Esther Nisenthal Krititz."

Hyperion Books for Children Web site, http://www. hyperionbooksforchildren.com/ (November 10, 2008), "Esther Nisenthal Krititz."

OTHER

Interview with Esther Nisenthal Krinitz (documentary film), directed by Lawrence Kasdan, Art and Remembrance, 1998.*

L

LEE TAE-JUN 1904-1956(?)

Personal
Born 1904, in Korea; died c. 1956.

Career
Writer.

Awards, Honors
Korean Children's Book of the Year award, and Baek-sang Publishing Award (Korea), both for *Waiting for Mama.*

Writings

Waiting for Mama (bilingual English-Hangeul; originally published in a Korean newspaper, 1938), 1948, with illustrations by Kim Dong-Seong, afterword by Andreas Schirmer, translated by Eun Hee Chun, North-South Books (New York, NY), 2007.

Author's work also published in German.

Biographical and Critical Sources

PERIODICALS

Kirkus Reviews, July 15, 2007, review of *Waiting for Mama.*

School Library Journal, September, 2007, Mary Hazelton, review of *Waiting for Mama,* p. 168.*

*   *   *

LE GUIN, Ursula K. 1929-

Personal
Surname pronounced "Luh-*Gwin*"; born October 21, 1929, in Berkeley, CA; daughter of Alfred L. (an anthropologist) and Theodora Covel Brown (a writer)

Ursula K. Le Guin (Copyright © by Marian Wood Kolisch. Reproduced by permission.)

Kroeber; married Charles Alfred Le Guin (an historian), December 22, 1953; children: Elisabeth, Caroline, Theodore. *Education:* Radcliffe College, A.B., 1951; Columbia University, A.M., 1952.

Addresses
Office—P.O. Box 10541, Portland, OR 97296-0541. *Agent*—Virginia Kidd, P.O. Box 278, Milford, PA 18337.

Career
Writer. Emory University, Atlanta, GA, former department secretary; part-time instructor in French at Mercer

University, Macon, GA, 1954-55, and University of Idaho, Moscow, 1956. Visiting lecturer and writer-in-residence at various locations, including Portland State University, University of California—San Diego, University of Reading (England), Kenyon College, Tulane University, and First Australian workshop in Speculative Fiction. Creative consultant for Public Broadcasting Service, for television production of *The Lathe of Heaven,* 1979.

Member

Women's International League for Peace and Freedom, Authors League of America, Writers Guild, PEN, Science Fiction Research Association, Science Fiction Writers Association, Science Fiction Poetry Association, Writers Guild West, Phi Beta Kappa.

Awards, Honors

National Fulbright fellowship, 1953; *Boston Globe/ Horn Book* Award, 1968; Nebula Award nomination for best novelette, Science Fiction Writers of America (now Science Fiction and Fantasy Writers of America), 1969, for "Nine Lives"; Nebula Award, and Hugo Award, International Science Fiction Association, both for best novel, both 1970, for *The Left Hand of Darkness;* Nebula Award nomination, 1971, and Hugo Award nomination, and *Locus* Award, both 1973, all for *The Lathe of Heaven;* Newbery Silver Medal Award, and National Book Award finalist for Children's Literature, both 1972, both for *The Tombs of Atuan;* Nebula Award nomination for best novella, 1972, and Hugo Award, 1973, both for *The Word for World Is Forest;* National Book Award for Children's Books, 1973, for *The Farthest Shore;* Hugo Award for best short story, 1974, for "The Ones Who Walk Away from Omelas"; American Library Association Best Young-Adult Books citation, 1974, and Hugo Award, Nebula Award, Jupiter Award for best novel, and Jules Verne Award, all 1975, all for *The Dispossessed;* Nebula Award, and Jupiter Award for best short story, both 1975, both for "The Day before the Revolution"; Nebula Award nomination for best novelette, 1975, for "The New Atlantis"; Nebula Award nomination for best novelette, and Jupiter Award, both 1976, both for "The Diary of the Rose"; Prix Lectures-Jeunesse, 1978, for *Very Far Away from Anywhere Else;* Gandalf Award (Grand Master of Fantasy), 1979; Nebula Award nomination for best novelette, 1979, for "The Pathways of Desire"; *Locus* Award, 1984, for *The Compass Rose;* American Book Award nomination, 1985, and Janet Heidinger Kafka Prize for Fiction, University of Rochester English Department and Writer's Workshop, 1986, both for *Always Coming Home;* Nebula Award nomination for best novelette, 1988, for *Buffalo Gals, Won't You Come Out Tonight,* and 1990, for "The Shobies' Story"; Hugo Award for best novelette, 1988, and World Fantasy Award for best novella, World Fantasy Convention, 1988, both for *Buffalo Gals, Won't You Come Out Tonight;* Nebula Award for best novel, 1991, for *Tehanu;* Nebula Award nomi-

nation for best novelette, 1994, and James Tiptree, Jr., Award, 1995, both for "The Matter of Seggri"; Nebula Award nomination for best novella, 1994, and Sturgeon Award, both for "Forgiveness Day"; Nebula Award for best novelette, 1996, for "Solitude"; Life Achievement Award, World Fantasy Convention, 1995; James Tiptree, Jr., Award, 1997, for "Mountain Ways"; Mythopoeic Fantasy Award finalist, World Fantasy Award in novel category, and Nebula Award nomination, all 2002, all for *The Other Wind;* Nebula Award Grand Master, 2002; PEN/Malamud Award for short fiction, 2002; Hugo Award nomination in best novelette category, and *Locus* Award, both 2003, both for "The Wild Girls"; Margaret A. Edwards Award for lifetime achievement, Young Adult Library Services Association, 2004; named May Hill Arbuthnot lecturer, Association for Library Service to Children, 2004. Honorary degrees include: D.Litt., Bucknell University, 1978, and Lawrence University, 1979; D.H.L., Lewis and Clark College, 1983, and Occidental College, 1985.

Writings

FOR CHILDREN

Solomon Leviathan's Nine Hundred Thirty-first Trip around the World (originally published in *Puffin's Pleasures*; also see below), illustrated by Alicia Austin, Puffin Books (London, England), 1976, Cheap Street (New Castle, VA), 1983.

Leese Webster, illustrated by James Brunsman, Atheneum (New York, NY), 1979.

Adventures in Kroy, Cheap Street (New Castle, VA), 1982.

The Adventures of Cobbler's Rune, illustrated by Alicia Austin, Cheap Street (New Castle, VA), 1983.

A Visit from Dr. Katz (picture book), illustrated by Ann Barrow, Atheneum (New York, NY), 1988.

Fire and Stone, illustrated by Laura Marshell, Atheneum (New York, NY), 1989.

Fish Soup (picture book), illustrated by Patrick Wynne, Atheneum (New York, NY), 1992.

A Ride on the Red Mare's Back (picture book), illustrated by Julie Downing, Orchard Books (New York, NY), 1992.

Tom Mouse, illustrated by Julie Downing, Roaring Brook Press (Brookfield, CT), 2002.

"EARTHSEA" NOVEL SERIES

A Wizard of Earthsea (also see below), illustrated by Ruth Robbins, Houghton (Boston, MA), 1968, reprinted, Bantam (New York, NY), 2004.

The Tombs of Atuan (also see below), illustrated by Gall Garraty, Atheneum (New York, NY), 1970.

The Farthest Shore (also see below), illustrated by Gall Garraty, Atheneum (New York, NY), 1972.

Earthsea (includes *A Wizard of Earthsea, The Tombs of Atuan,* and *The Farthest Shore*), Gollancz (London, England), 1977, published as *The Earthsea Trilogy,* Penguin (London, England), 1979.

Tehanu, Atheneum (New York, NY), 1990.
Tales from Earthsea, Harcourt (New York, NY), 2001.
The Other Wind, Harcourt (New York, NY), 2001.

"CATWINGS" SERIES

Catwings, illustrated by S.D. Schindler, Orchard Books (New York, NY), 1988.
Catwings Return, illustrated by S.D. Schindler, Orchard Books (New York, NY), 1989.
Wonderful Alexander and the Catwings, illustrated by S.D. Schindler, Orchard Books (New York, NY), 1994.
Jane on Her Own: A Catwings Tale, illustrated by S.D. Schindler, Orchard Books (New York, NY), 1999.

NOVELS

Rocannon's World (bound with *The Kar-Chee Reign* by Avram Davidson; also see below), Ace Books (New York, NY), 1966.
Planet of Exile (bound with *Mankind under the Lease* by Thomas M. Disch; also see below), Ace Books (New York, NY), 1966.
City of Illusions (also see below), Ace Books (New York, NY), 1967.
The Left Hand of Darkness, Ace Books (New York, NY), 1969, with new afterword and appendixes by author, Walker & Co. (New York, NY), 1994.
The Lathe of Heaven, Scribner (New York, NY), 1971, reprinted, Perennial Classics (New York, NY), 2003.
The Dispossessed: An Ambiguous Utopia, Harper (New York, NY), 1974, reprinted, Perennial Classics (New York, NY), 2003.
Very Far Away from Anywhere Else, Atheneum (New York, NY), 1976, published as *A Very Long Way from Anywhere Else,* Gollancz (London, England), 1976, reprinted under original title, Harcourt (Orlando, FL), 2004.
Three Hainish Novels (includes *Rocannon's World, Planet of Exile,* and *City of Illusions*; also see below), Doubleday (New York, NY), 1978.
Malafrena, Putnam (New York, NY), 1979.
The Beginning Place, Harper (New York, NY), 1980, published as *Threshold,* Gollancz (London, England), 1980.
The Eye of the Heron, and Other Stories (includes novella originally published in collection *Millennial Women*; also see below), Harper (New York, NY), 1983.
The Visionary (bound with *Wonders Hidden,* by Scott R. Sanders), McGraw (New York, NY), 1984.
Always Coming Home (includes audio cassette), music by Todd Barton, illustrated by Margaret Chodos, Harper (New York, NY), 1985, published without cassette, Bantam (New York, NY), 1987.
Worlds of Exile and Illusion (includes *Rocannon's World, Planet of Exile,* and *City of Illusions*), Orb (New York, NY), 1996.
The Telling, Harcourt (New York, NY), 2000.
Lavinia, Harcourt (Orlando, FL), 2008.

"ANNALS OF THE WESTERN SHORE" NOVEL SERIES

Gifts, Harcourt (Orlando, FL), 2004.
Voices, Harcourt (Orlando, FL), 2006.
Powers, Harcourt (Orlando, FL), 2007.

POETRY

Wild Angels, Capra (Santa Barbara, CA), 1974.
(With mother, Theodora K. Quinn) *Tillai and Tylissos,* Red Bull, 1979.
Torrey Pines Reserve (broadsheet), Lord John (Northridge, CA), 1980.
Hard Words and Other Poems, Harper (New York, NY), 1981.
(With Henk Pander) *In the Red Zone,* Lord John (Northridge, CA), 1983.
Wild Oats and Fireweed, Harper (New York, NY), 1988.
Blue Moon over Thurman Street, photographs by Roger Dorband, NewSage Press (Portland, OR), 1993.
Buffalo Gals, Won't You Come Out Tonight, illustrated by Susan Seddon Boulet, Pomegranate Artbooks (San Francisco, CA), 1994.
Going Out with Peacocks, and Other Poems, HarperPerennial (New York, NY), 1994.
(With Diana Bellessi) *The Twins, The Dream: Two Voices/ Las gemelas, el sueño: dos voces,* Arte Público (Houston, TX), 1997.
Sixty Odd: New Poems, Shambhala (Boston, MA), 1999.
Incredible Good Fortune: New Poems, Shambhala (Boston, MA), 2006.

SHORT STORIES

The Wind's Twelve Quarters, Harper (New York, NY), 1975, reprinted, Perennial (New York, NY), 2004.
Orsinian Tales, Harper (New York, NY), 1976, reprinted, Perennial (New York, NY), 2004.
The Water Is Wide, Pendragon Press (Portland, OR), 1976.
The Compass Rose, Harper (New York, NY), 1982, reprinted, Perennial (New York, NY), 2005.
Buffalo Gals and Other Animal Presences (and poems), Capra (Santa Barbara, CA), 1987.
Searoad: Chronicles of Klatsand, HarperCollins (New York, NY), 1991.
The Ones Who Walk away from Omelas, Creative Education (Mankato, MN), 1993.
A Fisherman of the Inland Sea: Science-Fiction Stories, HarperPrism (New York, NY), 1994.
Four Ways to Forgiveness, HarperPrism (New York, NY), 1995.
Unlocking the Air: And Other Stories, HarperCollins (New York, NY), 1996.
The Birthday of the World, and Other Stories, HarperCollins (New York, NY), 2002.
Changing Planes, illustrated by Eric Beddows, Harcourt (Orlando, FL), 2003.

EDITOR

Nebula Award Stories 11, Gollancz (London, England), 1976, Harper (New York, NY), 1977.

(With Virginia Kidd) *Interfaces: An Anthology of Speculative Fiction,* Ace Books (New York, NY), 1980.

(With Virginia Kidd) *Edges: Thirteen New Tales from the Borderlands of the Imagination,* Pocket Books (New York, NY), 1980.

(With Brian Attebery) *The Norton Book of Science Fiction: North American Science Fiction, 1960-1990,* Norton (New York, NY), 1993.

H.G. Wells, *Selected Stories,* Modern Library (New York, NY), 2004.

TRANSLATOR

(With J.P. Seaton) *Lao Tzu: Tao The Ching: A Book about the Way and the Power of the Way,* Shambhala (Boston, MA), 1997.

Gabriela Mistral, *Selected Poems,* University of New Mexico Press (Albuquerque, NM), 2003.

Angelica Gorodischer, *Kalpa Imperial: The Greatest Empire That Never Was,* Small Beer Press (Northampton, MA), 2003.

OTHER

From Elfland to Poughkeepsie (lecture), Pendragon Press (Portland, OR), 1973.

Dreams Must Explain Themselves (critical essays), Algol Press (New York, NY), 1975.

The Word for World Is Forest (novella; originally published in *Again, Dangerous Visions*; also see below), Berkley (New York, NY), 1976.

The Language of the Night: Essays on Fantasy and Science Fiction, edited by Susan Wood, Putnam (New York, NY), 1978, revised edition, edited by Le Guin, Women's Press (London, England), 1989.

King Dog: A Screenplay (bound with *Dostoevsky: A Screenplay,* by Raymond Carver and Tess Gallagher), Capra (Santa Barbara, CA), 1985.

(With Todd Barton) *Music and Poetry of the Kesh* (cassette), Valley Productions, 1985.

(With David Bedford) *Rigel Nine: An Audio Opera,* Charisma, 1985.

Dancing at the Edge of the World: Thoughts on Words, Women, Places (essays), Grove (New York, NY), 1989.

The Way of the Waters Going: Images of the Northern California Coastal Range, photographs by Ernest Waugh and Alan Nicolson, Harper (New York, NY), 1989.

Myth and Archetype in Science Fiction, Pulphouse, 1991.

Talk about Writing, Pulphouse, 1991.

Earthsea Revisioned (lecture), Children's Literature New England (Cambridge, MA), 1993.

(Author of text) *Uses of Music in Uttermost Parts* (music sound recording), music by Elinor Armer, Koch International (Port Washington, NY), 1995.

Steering the Craft: Exercises and Discussions on Story Writing for the Lone Navigator; or, The Mutinous Crew, Eighth Mountain Press (Portland, OR), 1998.

The Wave in the Mind: Talks and Essays on the Writer, the Reader, and the Imagination, Shambhala (Boston, MA), 2004.

Contributor to anthologies, including *Orbit 5,* 1969; *Orbit 6,* 1970; *Best SF: 1969,* 1970; *World's Best Science Fiction,* 1970; *Those Who Can,* 1970; *Nebula Award Stories 5,* 1970; *Quark Number 1,* 1970; *The Dead Astronaut,* 1971; *New Dimensions I,* 1972; *Clarion II,* 1972; *Again, Dangerous Visions,* Volume 1, 1972; *The Best from Playboy,* number 7, 1973; *New Dimensions III,* 1973; *Clarion III,* 1973; *Universe 5,* 1974; *The Best from Galaxy,* Volume 2, 1974, Volume 3, 1975; *Dream Trips,* 1974; *Orbit 14,* 1974; *Epoch,* 1975; *Nebula Award Stories 10,* 1975; *The New Atlantis and Other Novellas of Science Fiction,* 1975; *The Thorny Paradise,* 1975; *Bitches and Sad Ladies,* 1975; *More Women of Wonder,* 1976; *The Best Science Fiction of the Year Number 5,* 1976; *Science Fiction at Large,* 1976, 1977; *Future Power,* 1976; *Puffin's Pleasure,* 1976; *Best Science-Fiction Stories of the Year,* 1977; *Psy Fi One,* 1977; *The Norton Anthology of Short Fiction,* 1978; *The Altered I: An Encounter with Science Fiction,* 1978; *Millennial Women,* 1978; *Cassandra Rising,* 1978; and *Dark Imaginings,* 1978. Author of postcard short story, *Post Card Partnership,* 1975, and *Sword & Sorcery Annual,* 1975.

Contributor of short stories, novellas, essays, and reviews to periodicals, including *Science Fiction Studies, Antaeus, Parabola, New Republic, Redbook, Playgirl, Playboy, New Yorker, Yale Review,* and *Omni.* Recorded audioversions of books, including *The Ones Who Walk Away from Omelas and Other Stories* and *The Lathe of Heaven,* Alternate World, 1976; *Gwilan's Harp and Intracom,* Caedmon, 1977; and *The Left Hand of Darkness,* Warner Audio.

Adaptations

The Lathe of Heaven was adapted by Diane English and Roger Swaybill into a film directed by Fred Barzyk and David R. Loxton and televised by Public Broadcasting Service, 1979. A new version, with screenplay by Alan Sharp and direction by Philip Haas, was produced by A&E Television Networks. The "Earthsea" books were adapted by Gavin Scott into a mini-series epic, produced by Hallmark Entertainment for Sci Fi Channel, 2004. *The Tombs of Atuan* was adapted as a filmstrip with record or audiocassette by Newbery Award Records, 1980; "The Ones Who Walk away from Omelas" was produced as a musical drama at Portland Civic Theatre, 1981. *A Wizard of Earthsea, The Tombs of Atuan, The Farthest Shore,* and *The Beginning Place* were made into sound recordings, 1992.

Sidelights

Whether she writes within the genres of children's books, young-adult realism and fantasy, or adult science fiction, Ursula K. Le Guin is considered by many to be one of the most creative writers of her generation. She is best known for her fantasy fiction, particularly the acclaimed "Earthsea" books, but her science-fiction novels have also won Le Guin a wide following. According to Brian Attebery, writing in the *Dictionary of Literary Biography,* "Le Guin's fiction is extraordinarily risky: it is full of hypotheses about morality, love, society, and ways of enriching life expressed in the symbolic language found in myth, dream, or poetry."

Le Guin was born in 1929, to Theodora and Alfred Kroeber. Her father was a professor of anthropology at the University of California and her mother was a writer. Le Guin once recalled that their summer house was "an old, tumble-down ranch in the Napa Valley . . . [and] a gathering place for scientists, writers, students, and California Indians. Even though I didn't pay much attention, I heard a lot of interesting, grown-up conversation." She also grew up hearing a variety of Native American tales from her father and reading a great deal of mythology; she particularly liked Norse myths.

Le Guin has three older brothers, but she views her upbringing as totally nonsexist because her parents expected the same of all their children. Her home was also nonreligious. As she once related, "There was no religious practice of any kind. There was also no feeling that any religion was better than another or worse; they just weren't part of our life. They were something other people did." Eventually, Le Guin developed a strong respect for Taoism, the Eastern religion of acceptance and change. The impact of the Taoist *I Ching* has influenced many of her books, and she published a translation of it, *Lao Tzu: Tao The Ching: A Book about the Way and the Power of the Way,* in 1997.

In addition to the *I Ching,* Le Guin's writing is informed by her feminism and her progressive views about social relationships. Although her early works focus mostly on male heroes, she eventually began portraying women in central, action-oriented roles. Her acclaimed novel *The Left Hand of Darkness* is set in a world where people have no fixed gender, but become male or female when they desire sexual activity. Other works find Le Guin dealing with issues of race—in *The Lathe of Heaven* she includes a romance between a white man and a black woman—and sexual preference. These aspects of her writing helped revolutionize science fiction, a genre characterized by *Book* writer Ellen Emry Heltzel as "a white, male enclave reflecting its original base of readers." In Heltzel's view, Le Guin "is sensitive to issues of race, class and gender and is among a generation of writers who have elevated the role of human feeling in the formerly hard-wired SF field."

As children, Le Guin and one of her brothers enjoyed *Amazing Stories,* a short-story magazine. She made her first short story submission to the magazine at age twelve, but the story was rejected. "It was all right with me," she once said. "It was junk. At least I had a real rejection slip to show for it." While Le Guin always thought of herself as a writer, after completing her bachelor's degree at Radcliffe, she decided to follow her fa-

ther's advice and find a marketable career. She studied Romance languages with the intent of teaching and earned her master's degree from Columbia University. She was pursuing a doctorate in French and Italian renaissance literature when she met Charles Le Guin while traveling to France via the *Queen Mary* on a Fulbright fellowship. "We had a shipboard romance and, as the French have developed bureaucracy into a way of life, spent our first six months trying to marry," Le Guin recalled. After returning to the States, the couple moved to Atlanta, Georgia, where her husband taught at Emory University and Le Guin worked as a secretary and wrote. She spent the next several years balancing a part-time job, her writing, and her family, which came to include three children: Elisabeth, Caroline, and Theodore. The Le Guins eventually settled in Portland, Oregon.

During the 1950s, Le Guin wrote five novels, four of which were set in the imaginary country of Orsinia, but she was unable to find a publisher willing to take a risk on her unusual style. She finally turned to the science fiction/fantasy genre in order to get into print, and her first sale was a time-travel fantasy published in *Fantastic Stories and Imagination* magazine. For Le Guin, developing a science-fiction style took time, and she called her first published novels "fairy tales in space suits." Part of her "Hainish Cycle," these books branch off from a central idea: that humanity came from the planet Hain, which colonized several other planets and eventually became separated by a galactic war. The "Hainish Cycle" includes *Rocannon's World, Planet of Exile, City of Illusions, The Left Hand of Darkness, The Dispossessed: An Ambiguous Utopia, The Word for World Is Forest,* and *The Telling,* as well as several short stories.

In the late 1960s, editor Herman Schein of Parnassus Press asked Le Guin to write a novel for eleven to seventeen year olds. The result was the fantasy *A Wizard of Earthsea,* which follows the adventures of the apprentice sorcerer Ged. Critics praised the novel both for its story and the complexity of Le Guin's created world, which consists of a chain of islands. Many reviewers compared Earthsea to J.R.R. Tolkien's Middle Earth and C.S. Lewis's Narnia. Reviewing the book for *Horn Book,* Eleanor Cameron wrote: "To me, it is as if Ursula Le Guin herself has lived on the Archipelago, minutely observing and noting down the habits and idiosyncrasies of the culture from island to island. . . . Nothing has escaped the notice of her imagination's seeking eye."

Le Guin followed *A Wizard of Earthsea* with *The Tombs of Atuan,* a darker novel set in the same world. Here the young priestess Tenar, Le Guin's her first major female character, discovers Ged wandering through sacred places forbidden to anyone but the priestesses and their eunuchs. Tenar's life changes through this meeting; Le Guin once described the story as "a feminine coming of age." *The Farthest Shore* finds Ged a mature wizard who now journeys with a young prince to the westernmost end of the world to discover why Earthsea is losing its magic. There, Ged meets his ultimate challenge. *The Farthest Shore* won the National Book Award for Children's Literature, and in *Dictionary of Literary Biography,* Andrew Gordon called it "a novel of epic scope."

Tehanu deals less with the magic of wizards than the importance of everyday life. In the novel, Tenar, now a farmer's widow, discovers a little girl who has been raped by her father and his friends and left to die. She adopts the child and is then joined by Ged, who arrives drained of power and strength. The three form an unlikely family as they battle an unexpected threat to Tenar's island home. "*Tehanu* is a book of great depth and subtlety . . . confronting and altering the bedrock values of the old high fantasy on which the first Earthsea books were based," observed Jill Paton Walsh in *Twentieth-Century Young Adult Writers.* "It rejects the male-gendered tales of heroism, and in their place builds on women's experiences as the benchmarks of virtue, courage, love. The damaged child is at the centre of the book, and the triumph over evil is hers." Describing *Tehanu* as "deceptively short, and written in a deceptively simple style," Robin McKinley asserted in a *New York Times Book Review* appraisal of the novel that, rather than extending her young-adult fantasy series, Le Guin's novel tells a sophisticated story that acknowledges "the necessary and life-giving contributions of female magic—sometimes disguised as domesticity."

Le Guin returns to the world of Earthsea with *Tales from Earthsea,* a short-story collection that includes a tale describing the origins of the magic school at which Ged studied, plus four other stories and a background essay on Earthsea. The collection "not only stands alone but also serves as an introduction to new readers," commented Jackie Cassada in her *Library Journal* review. Chris Barsanti praised Le Guin's tales in *Book,* describing the contents of *Tales from Earthsea* as "delightfully crafted mini epics."

In the closing volume of the "Earthsea" saga, *The Other Wind,* a sorcerer's longing for his deceased wife begins to erode the barrier between the living and the dead and also causes other disruptions in Earthsea. *The Other Wind* "will leave its readers wanting yet another," maintained Estes in a *Booklist* review of the much-anticipated series installment. A *Publishers Weekly* reviewer noted that, while in *Tehanu* "Le Guin rethought the traditional connection between gender and magic," in *The Other Wind* "she reconsiders the relationship between magic and something even more basic: life and death itself."

Salon.com contributor Faith L. Justice noted of the "Earthsea" novels that, while they appear to be "coming-of-age stories, . . . Le Guin's artful storytelling and complex underlying themes elevate the works beyond mundane fantasy and the young-adult audience

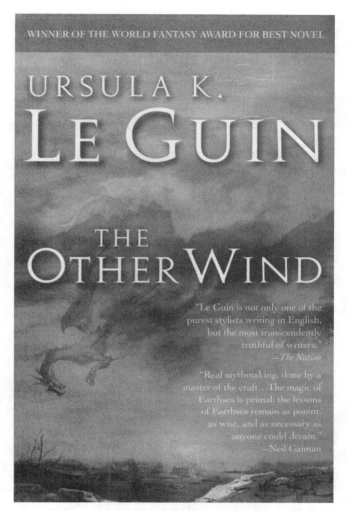

Cover of Ursula K. Le Guin's award-winning fantasy novel **The Other Wind,** *featuring artwork by Cliff Nielsen.* (Illustration by Cliff Nielsen. Reproduced by permission of Ace Books, a division of Penguin Putnam, Inc.)

for which they are intended." As the series progresses, the characters learn "the need for balance—light/dark, male/female, action/inaction," Justice commented.

With her "Annals of the Western Shore"—*Gifts, Voices,* and *Powers*—Le Guin returns to the fantasy genre, creating what she described as "book-centered books" in an interview with Dennis Pilon for *Canadian Dimensions.* "How do the spoken and the written word interact? What is the importance of a library? . . . Now, on the verge of the material written word being hugely augmented and partly replaced by the more ephemeral electronic word, it seemed a good time to look back at what writing is, what the book has meant," Le Guin mused.

In *Gifts* readers follow the narrative of sixteen-year-old Orrec. The son of the master of Caspromant, a region of the Uplands, Orrec has inherited the ability to kill with one glance, and for this reason he chooses to wear a blindfold. When he and friend Gry befriend a runaway named Emmon, he explains that each of the five Upland families have unique talents such as his. Although Orrec believes that these gifts, when allowed to remain pure, sustain a balance among the families, he gradually begins to question this assumption. Calling *Gifts* a "provocative" work of fiction, a *Publishers Weekly* concluded that Le Guin's story "may well prompt teens to examine their own talents" and question "whether they simply accept those 'gifts' assigned to them by other or whether the 'gifts' are their true passions." In *Kirkus Reviews* a contributor hailed the novel as "a gripping tale about personal motivation, the consequences of choice and the corruption of power," while in *Booklist* Jennifer Mattson praised *Gifts* as "rich in the earthy magic and intelligent plot twists that made the 'Earthsea' novels classics."

Readers of the "Annals of the Western Shore" follow Orrec and Gry into *Voices,* and here they have traveled, as adults, to a conquered city where they meet seventeen-year-old Memer. Living with fear and hunger, Memer is given hope and insight by her new friends and ultimately comes to terms with her occupiers and her future by listening to Orrec's inspiring stories. In *Powers,* a slave named Gavir is raised alongside the children of a privileged medieval ruling family. Wise and possessed of a view into the future, he begins to question the traditions he has been taught to accept and

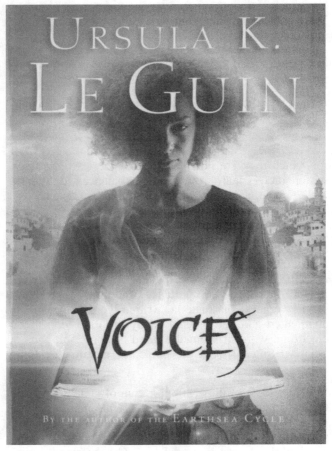

Voices, *the second book in Le Guin's young-adult fantasy trilogy the "Annals of the Western Shore."* (Illustration copyright © 2006 by Larry Rostant. Reproduced by permission of Houghton Mifflin Harcourt Publishing Company.)

adhere to when he confronts personal tragedy and the potential for evil among his fellow humans. Revealed in a prose that "flows as unstintingly as ever," *Voices* contains "themes of revenge, family legacies, personal mortality, and a humanistic magic redolent more of earthy mysteries than flashy sorcery," according to *School Library Journal* critic Matthew L. Moffett. Comparing Gavir to the hero of Voltaire's *Candide,* Claire Rosser noted in her *Kliatt* review of *Powers* that Le Guin's story inspires readers to consider "what freedom means in a person's life and in a society." Calling *Powers* "the series' best installment," Mattson added that, "told with shimmering lyricism, [Le Guin's] . . . coming-of-age saga will leave readers . . . transformed by the power of words." In *Horn Book* Joanna Rudge Long wrote that the novel "explores a rich complexity of hypothetical cultures that elicit new insights into our own."

Le Guin turns from fantasy to reality in *Very Far Away from Anywhere Else,* which describes the deepening relationship between two extremely talented but lonely, nonconformist teens. The relationship between Owen and Natalie is jeopardized when Owen makes sexual advances toward Natalie. *The Beginning Place,* written a few years later, mixes fantasy and reality in the story of two young adults who, at different times, discover a strange world on the borders of their dull suburb. In *Lavinia,* she turns to the past and casts a light on a minor character in Virgil's Aeneid: the second wife of Aeneas. The daughter of the king and queen of Latinum, Lavinia is given in marriage to Aeneas when he arrives from Troy. Her hand had formerly been promised to the king of a neighboring land, and with Lavinia's marriage jealousy provokes that king to war. Le Guin's refashioning of history in *Lavinia* is "as unique and strange as any fantasy," observed a *Publishers Weekly,* and in *Booklist* Margaret Flanagan deemed the novel "a winning combination of history and mythology" that will be "compulsively readable."

In addition to her novels, poems, and stories for older teens and adult readers, Le Guin has also produced children's storybooks and picture books. In *Leese Webster* she relates the story of a talented spider, while *A Visit from Dr. Katz* is a picture book showing how a sick little girl is amused by two kittens. The plot of *Fire and Stone* revolves around a dragon who eats stones instead of people, while in *Fish Soup* two adults have differing visions of the perfect child and each see their fantasies become reality.

Popular with young children, *Catwings* and its follow-up picture books *Catwings Return, Wonderful Alexander and the Catwings,* and *Jane on Her Own: A Catwings Tale,* feature the adventures of several winged cats. In *Catwings* four flying cats—Harriet, James, Thelma, and Roger—escape city dangers to live in the country, where they are adopted by two children. In the *New York Times Book Review,* Crescent Dragonwagon wrote that Le Guin's "dialogue, humor, skill as a storyteller, and emo-

Cover of Le Guin's beloved picture book **Catwings,** *a story about flying cats featuring artwork by S.D. Schindler.* (Illustration copyright © 1988 by S.D. Schindler. Reproduced by permission of Orchard Books, an imprint of Scholastic, Inc.)

tional veracity combine near-flawlessly in a story that is both contemporary and timeless." The cats' "collective winged adventures, their looking after one another, and the understated charm of Ms. Le Guin's writing keeps us captivated," the critic added. In *Jane on Her Own* Jane travels to the city in search of new experiences, and when she is trapped by a man who wants to exploit the flying cat by putting her on television, Jane must find a way to escape. In *Booklist* Carolyn Phelan and Jack Helbig praised Le Guin's "consistently catlike point of view" in a story dealing with "loneliness, belonging, and freedom."

A Ride on the Red Mare's Back looks at the issue of responsibility. In it, a young girl learns that her little brother has been taken by trolls, and she goes out alone to rescue him, taking only a toy red horse, a warm scarf, knitting needles and yarn, and a bit of bread. Once the girl locates the boy in the trolls' castle, she finds that her brother has changed: he now wants to become a troll. "The boy's desire is an old one," Michael Dirda explained in a review for the *Washington Post Book World:* "Is it better to be a happy pig or an un-

happy Socrates? Most of us don't get the chance to be quite either." Dirda concluded that *A Ride on the Red Mare's Back* "is indisputably suspenseful, thought-provoking, and beautifully illustrated."

Another picture book by Le Guin, *Tom Mouse* introduces readers to a mouse who wants to see the world. Bewhiskered Tom leaves his mouse family to travel across the country by train, and when a businesswoman takes up residence in the sleeping car Tom occupies, he hides from her. Gradually, however, the tiny young mouse realizes that his presence has been discovered and that the woman sees him as a friend. *Tom Mouse* was described as a "celebration of the open road and the kindness of strangers" by a contributor to *Kirkus Reviews,* and in *Horn Book* Susan P. Bloom concluded that Le Guin's "tale of comradeship between two otherwise lonely globetrotters has an inviting freshness in its quiet telling."

Throughout her career, critics have praised the variety, force, and depth of intelligence Le Guin brings to all her writing. "Hers is certainly one of the most powerful talents ever exercised in writing for the young," Walsh remarked. For Le Guin, young imaginations need to be nourished, and stories with elements of fantasy play an important part in creative development. "I believe that all the best faculties of a mature human being exist in the child," she told Gordon, "and that if these faculties are encouraged in youth they will act well and wisely in the adult."

Admitting that she began writing for younger readers "with great trepidation," Le Guin told *School Library Journal* interviewer Francisca Goldsmith that she finds young-adult audiences "to be the most wonderful readers and responders." She also addressed her responsibility to younger readers. "The words that I work in are the words of the story," Le Guin explained to Goldsmith. "I'm not a philosopher. I'm not a moralist. . . . My responsibility is to my art and to the people who perceive it, the readers. That's an aesthetic responsibility and if it's aesthetically right, then it will probably also be morally right. I'm saying what Keats said. I'm saying 'Truth is beauty and beauty is truth.' That's a very rash statement. But it goes so deep in me that I just can't get around it."

Biographical and Critical Sources

BOOKS

Children's Literature Review, Gale (Detroit, MI), Volume 3, 1978, Volume 28, 1992.
Contemporary Literary Criticism, Gale (Detroit, MI), Volume 8, 1978, Volume 13, 1980, Volume 22, 1982, Volume 45, 1987, Volume 71, 1992.
Contemporary Novelists, 6th edition, St. James Press (Detroit, MI), 1996.

Dictionary of Literary Biography, Gale (Detroit, MI), Volume 8: *Twentieth-Century American Science Fiction Writers, Part 1*, 1981, pp. 263-280, Volume 52: *American Writers for Children since 1960: Fiction*, 1986, pp. 233-241.

Haviland, Virginia, editor, *The Openhearted Audience: Ten Authors Talk about Writing for Children*, Library of Congress (Washington, DC), 1980.

Kroeber, Theodora, *Alfred Kroeber: A Personal Configuration*, University of California Press (Berkeley, CA), 1970.

Reginald, Robert, and George Edgar Slusser, editors, *Zephyr and Boreas: Winds of Change in the Fiction of Ursula K. Le Guin*, Borgo Press (San Bernardino, CA), 1996.

St. James Guide to Science-Fiction Writers, St. James Press (Detroit, MI), 1996.

Silvey, Anita, editor, *Children's Books and Their Creators*, Houghton (Boston, MA), 1995.

Slusser, George Edgar, *Between Two Worlds: The Literary Dilemma of Ursula K. Le Guin*, Borgo Press (San Bernardino, CA), 1995.

PERIODICALS

Book, September-October, 2000, Ellen Emry Heltzel, "Portland Trailblazer: Ursula K. Le Guin"; May, 2001, Chris Barsanti, review of *Tales from Earthsea*, p. 71.

Booklist, February 1, 1999, Carolyn Phelan and Jack Helbig, review of *Jane on Her Own: A Catwings Tale*, p. 974; March 1, 2001, Sally Estes, review of *Tales from Earthsea*, p. 1233; June 1, 2001, Sally Estes, review of *The Other Wind*, p. 1798; April 15, 2003, Sally Estes, review of *Changing Planes*, p. 1428; February 1, 2004, Donna Seaman, review of *The Wave in the Mind: Talks and Essays on the Reader, and the Imagination*, p. 942; August, 2004, Jennifer Mattson, review of *Gifts*, p. 1924; August 1, 2006, Jennifer Mattson, review of *Voices*, p. 75; October 1, 2007, Jennifer Mattson, review of *Powers*, p. 57; March 15, 2008, Margaret Flanagan, review of *Lavinia*, p. 28.

Canadian Dimension, September-October, 2007, Dennis Pilon, interview with Le Guin, p. 39.

Horn Book, April, 1971, Eleanor Cameron, "High Fantasy: A Wizard of Earthsea," pp. 129-138; November-December, 1988, Ann A. Flowers, review of *Catwings*, p. 781; May-June, 2002, Susan P. Bloom, review of *Tom Mouse*, p. 316; September-October, 2006, Joanna Rudge Long, review of *Voices*, p. 590; September-October, 2007, Joanna Rudge Long, review of *Powers*, p. 580.

Kirkus Reviews, July 1, 2001, review of *The Other Wind*, p. 904; February 15, 2002, review of *Tom Mouse*, p. 260; May 1, 2003, review of *Changing Planes*, p. 633; March 1, 2006, review of *Gifts*, p. 12; August 15, 2007, review of *Powers*; February 15, 2008, review of *Lavinia*.

Kliatt, January, 2002, Bette D. Ammon, review of *Wizard of Earthsea*, p. 49; July, 2002, Bette D. Ammon, review of *Tales from Earthsea*, p. 31; March, 2003, Janet Julian, review of *The Other Wind*, p. 36; Septem-

ber, 2004, Paula Rohrlick, review of *Gifts*, p. 13; September, 2007, Claire Rosser, review of *Powers*, p. 14.

Library Journal, May 15, 2001, Jackie Cassada, review of *Tales from Earthsea*, p. 166; July, 2001, Jackie Cassada, review of *The Other Wind*, p. 130; September 15, 2003, review of *Kalpa Imperial: The Greatest Empire That Never Was*, p. 91; March 1, 2008, Winda Wilda Williams, review of *Lavinia*, p. 74.

Mythlore, spring-summer, 2008, Melanie A. Rawls, "Witches, Wives, and Dragons: The Evolution of the Women in Ursula K. Le Guin's 'Earthsea'," p. 129.

New York Times Book Review, November 13, 1988, Crescent Dragonwagon, review of *Catwings;* May 20, 1990, Robin McKinley, review of *Tehanu*, p. 38; October 15, 1995, Gerald Jonas, review of *Four Ways to Forgiveness*.

Publishers Weekly, January 19, 1990, review of *Tehanu*, p. 110; August 10, 1992, review of *A Ride on the Red Mare's Back*, p. 70; October 5, 1992, review of *Fish Soup*, p. 71; September 25, 1995, Sara Jameson, "Ursula K. Le Guin: A Galaxy of Books and Laurels," p. 32; August 7, 2000, review of *The Telling*, p. 79; March 5, 2001, review of *Tales from Earthsea*, p. 66; August 13, 2001, review of *The Other Wind*, p. 290; July 19, 2004, review of *Gifts*, p. 163; December 24, 2007, review of *Lavinia*, p. 24.

School Library Journal, August, 1989, review of *Catwings Return*, p. 124; April, 1990, Ruth S. Vose, review of *Tehanu*, p. 142; September, 1992, Kay E. Vandergrift, review of *A Ride on the Red Mare's Back*, p. 207; April, 1999, Anne Conner, review of *Jane on Her Own*, p. 101; May, 2002, Kathie Meizner, review of *Tom Mouse*, p. 120; June, 2004, Francisca Goldsmith, interview with Le Guin, p. 52; September, 2004, Bruce Anne Shook, review of *Gifts*, p. 210; August, 2006, Beth Wright, review of *Voices*, p. 123; September, 2007, Margaret A. Chang, review of *Powers*, p. 202; May, 2008, Matthew L. Moffett, review of *Lavinia*, p. 161.

Washington Post Book World, August 9, 1992, Michael Dirda, review of *A Ride on the Red Mare's Back*, p. 11.

ONLINE

Salon.com, http://www.salon.com/ (January 23, 2001), Faith L. Justice, "Ursula K. Le Guin."

Ursula K. Le Guin Home Page, http://www.ursulakleguin.com (October 25, 2008).*

*   *   *

LOEHR, Patrick 1968(?)-

Personal

Born c. 1968.

Addresses

Home—Denver, CO. *E-mail*—patloehr@hotmail.com.

Career

Artist, illustrator, and educator. Metropolitan State College, Denver, CO, instructor in illustration. *Exhibitions:* Artwork has been exhibited internationally.

Writings

SELF-ILLUSTRATED

Mucumber McGee and the Half-eaten Hot Dog, Katherine Tegan Books (New York, NY), 2008.
Mucumber McGee and the Lunch Lady's Liver, Katherine Tegan Books (New York, NY), 2008.

Biographical and Critical Sources

PERIODICALS

Kirkus Reviews, June 15, 2007, review of *Mucumber McGee and the Half-eaten Hot Dog;* September 15, 2008, review of *Mucumber McGee and the Lunch Lady's Liver.*
School Library Journal, September, 2007, Julie Roach, review of *Mucumber McGee and the Half-eaten Hot Dog,* p. 170.

ONLINE

Patrick Loehr Home Page, http://www.patrickloehr.com (October 10, 2008).*

M

MacDONALD, Margaret Read 1940-

Personal
Born January 21, 1940, in Seymour, IN; daughter of Murray Ernest (a carpenter and builder) and Mildred (a homemaker; maiden name, Amick) Read; married James Bruce MacDonald (an auditor), August 20, 1965; children: Jennifer Skye, Julie Liana. *Education:* Indiana University, A.B., 1962, Ph.D., 1979; University of Washington, M.L.S., 1964; University of Hawaii, M.Ed. Ec., 1969.

Addresses
Home—Kirkland, WA. *E-mail*—mrm@margaretread macdonald.com.

Career
Librarian, storyteller, and writer. King County Library System, Seattle, WA, children's librarian, 1964-65; Hawaii State Library, Honolulu, bookmobile librarian, 1966-68; Mountain Valley Library System, Sacramento, CA, children's consultant, 1969-70; Montgomery County Library System, White Oak, MO, children's librarian, 1970-72; University of Washington, Seattle, visiting lecturer in librarianship, 1975-79; King County Library System, Seattle, children's librarian, 1979-2002. Professional storyteller, including international performances in Japan, Borneo, China, Indonesia, Hong Kong, Malaysia, Philippines, Singapore, Thailand, Brazil, Argentina, Cuba, Austria, Czech Republic, France, Germany, Hungary, Luxembourg, Poland, Republic of Georgia, Australia, and New Zealand, 1992—. Washington State Folklife Council, member of board of directors, 1986-90, president, 1989-90; Youth Theatre Northwest, member of board of directors, 1988-91, president, 1989-90.

Member
International Board on Books for Young People, National Storytelling Association (member of board of directors, 1992-95), American Folklore Society (president of Children's Folklore Section, 1993-94), American Library Association, Association for Library Service to Children, Society of Children's Book Writers and Illustrators, Children's Literature Association, Washington Library Media Association, Washington Library Association.

Awards, Honors
RTSD Outstanding Reference Source, American Library Association, 1982, for *The Storyteller's Sourcebook;* Notable Children's Trade Book in the Field of Social Studies, National Council for the Social Studies/ Children's Book Council (NCSS/CBC), 1992, for *Peace Tales; Storytelling World* Award, 1995, for story "The Lion's Whisker," 1996, for *The Old Woman Who Lived in a Vinegar Bottle,* 2007, for *The Great Smelly, Slobbery, Small-toothed Dog; Storytelling World* Storytelling Information Award, 1995, for *The Storyteller's Start-up Book;* Fulbright scholar, Mahasarakham University, Thailand, 1995-97; Talking Leaves Award, National Storytelling Network, 2001, for body of work; Outstanding Author and Storyteller Award, Washington Organization for Reading Development, 2001-02; Aesop Accolade, and Parents' Choice Award, both for *Mabela the Clever;* Parents' Choice Award, 2001, for *Fat Cat;* Tennessee Volunteer State Award, for *Pickin' Peas;* Aesop Award, 2005, for *From the Winds of Manquito.*

Writings

FOR CHILDREN

The Skit Book: 101 Skits from Kids, illustrated by Marie-Louise Scull, Linnet Books (Hamden, CT), 1989.
Peace Tales: World Folktales to Talk About, illustrated by Zobra Anasazi, Linnet Books (Hamden, CT), 1992.
Tom Thumb, illustrated by Joanne Caroselli, Oryx, 1993.
(Editor) Supaporn Vathanaprida, *Thai Tales: Folktales of Thailand,* illustrated by Boonsong Rohitasuke, Libraries Unlimited (Englewood, CO), 1994.

The Old Woman Who Lived in a Vinegar Bottle: A British Fairy Tale, illustrated by Nancy Dunaway Fowlkes, August House (Little Rock, AR), 1995.

Tuck-Me-in Tales: Bedtime Stories from around the World, illustrated by Yvonne LeBrun Davis, August House (Little Rock, AR), 1996.

(With Winifred Jaeger) *The Round Book,* illustrated by Yvonne LeBrun Davis, Linnet Books (Hamden, CT), 1997, published as *The Round Book: Rounds Kids Love to Sing,* illustrated by Yvonne LeBrun Davis, Linnet Books (North Haven, CT), 1999.

Slop! A Welsh Folktale, illustrated by Yvonne LeBrun Davis, Fulcrum (Golden, CO), 1997.

(Reteller) *Pickin' Peas,* illustrated by Pat Cummings, HarperCollins (New York, NY), 1998.

(Reteller, with Supaporn Vathananprida) *The Girl Who Wore Too Much: A Folktale from Thailand,* illustrated by Yvonne LeBrun Davis, August House (Little Rock, AR), 1998.

Earth Care: World Folktales to Talk About, Linnet Books (North Haven, CT), 1999.

Shake-It-up Tales!: Stories to Sing, Dance, Drum, and Act Out, August House (Little Rock, AR), 2000.

(Reteller) *Fat Cat: A Danish Folktale,* illustrated by Julie Paschkis, August House (Little Rock, AR), 2001.

(Reteller) *Mabela the Clever,* illustrated by Tim Coffey, Albert Whitman (Morton Grove, IL), 2001.

(Editor) Murti Bunanta, *Indonesian Folktales,* illustrated by G.M. Sudarta, Libraries Unlimited (Westport, CT), 2003.

Three-Minute Tales: Stories from around the World to Tell or Read When Time Is Short, August House (Little Rock, AR), 2003.

(Editor) Elvia Pérez Nápoles, *From the Winds of Manguito/Desde los vientos de Manguito: Cuban Folktales in English and Spanish,* translated by Paul Martín, illustrated by Victor Hernández Mora, Libraries Unlimited (Westport, CT), 2004.

A Hen, a Chick, and a String Guitar, illustrated by Sophie Fatus, Barefoot Books (Cambridge, MA), 2005.

(Reteller) *The Squeaky Door,* illustrated by Mary Newell DePalma, HarperCollins (New York, NY), 2006.

(Reteller) *Tunjur! Tunjur! Tunjur!: A Palestinian Arab Folktale,* collected by Ibrahim Muhawi and Sharif Kanaana, illustrated by Alik Arzoumanian, Marshall Cavendish (New York, NY), 2006.

(Reteller) *Conejito!: A Folktale from Panama,* illustrated by Geraldo Valerio, August House (Little Rock, AK), 2006.

(Reteller) *Go to Sleep, Gecko!: A Balinese Folktale,* illustrated by Geraldo Valerio, August House (Little Rock, AK), 2006.

The Teeny Weeny Bop!, illustrated by Diane Greenseid, Albert Whitman (Morton Grove, IL), 2006.

(Editor) Livia de Almeida and Ana María Portella, *Folktales of Brazil,* Libraries Unlimited, 2006.

The Old Woman and Her Pig: An Appalachian Folktale, illustrated by John Kanzler, HarperCollins (New York, NY), 2007.

The Little Rooster's Diamond Button, illustrated by Will Terry, Albert Whitman (Morton Grove, IL), 2007.

Five-Minute Tales, August House (Little Rock, AK), 2007.

The Great Smelly, Slobbery, Small-tooth Dog: A Folktale from Great Britain, illustrated by Julie Paschkis, August House (Little Rock, AK), 2007.

Bat's Big Game, illustrated by Eugenia Nobati, Albert Whitman (Morton Grove, IL), 2008.

(Editor) Wajuppa Tossa and Kongdeuane Nettavong, *Lao Folktales,* Libraries Unlimited, 2008.

FOR ADULTS

The Storyteller's Sourcebook: A Subject, Title, and Motif Index to Folklore Collections for Children, Thomson Gale (Detroit, MI), 1982.

Twenty Tellable Tales: Audience Participation Folktales for the Beginning Storyteller, H.W. Wilson (Bronx, NY), 1986, revised edition, American Library Association, 2005.

Booksharing: 101 Programs to Use with Preschoolers, illustrations by Julie Liana MacDonald, Shoe String Press (North Haven, CT), 1988.

When the Lights Go Out: Twenty Scary Tales to Tell, illustrated by Roxane Murphy Smith, H.W. Wilson (Bronx, NY), 1988.

Scipio, Indiana: Threads from the Past, Ye Galleon (Fairfield, WV), 1988.

Look Back and See: Twenty Lively Tales for Gentle Tellers, illustrations by R.M. Smith, H.W. Wilson (Bronx, NY), 1991.

(Editor) *The Folklore of World Holidays,* Thomson Gale (Detroit, MI), 1992.

The Storyteller's Start-up Book: Finding, Learning, Performing, and Using Folktales, Including Twelve Tellable Tales, August House (Little Rock, AR), 1993.

Celebrate the World: Twenty Tellable Folktales for Multicultural Festivals, illustrations by R.M. Smith, H.W. Wilson (Bronx, NY), 1994.

Bookplay: 101 Creative Themes to Share with Young Children, illustrations by Julia L. MacDonald, Library Professional Publications (North Haven, CT), 1995.

Ghost Stories from the Pacific Northwest, August House (Little Rock, AR), 1995.

The Parent's Guide to Storytelling: How to Make up New Stories and Retell Old Favorites, illustrations by Mark T. Smith, HarperCollins (New York, NY), 1995, second edition, August House (Little Rock, AR), 2001.

Scipio Storytelling: Talk in a Southern Indiana Community, University Press of America (Lanham, MD), 1996.

(Editor) *Traditional Storytelling Today: An International Sourcebook,* Fitzroy Dearborn (Chicago, IL), 1999.

(With Brian W. Sturm) *The Storyteller's Sourcebook: A Subject, Title, and Motif Index to Folklore Collections for Children, 1983-1999,* Thomson Gale (Detroit, MI), 2001.

Ten Traditional Tellers, University of Illinois Press (Carbondale, IL), 2006.

Tell the World: Telling across Language Barriers, Libraries Unlimited, 2007.

Contributor to books, including *Once upon a Folktale: Capturing the Folklore Process with Children,* edited by Gloria T. Blatt, Teachers College Press (New York,

NY), 1993; and *The Storyteller's Guide: Storytellers Share Advice,* by Bill Mooney and David Holt, August House (Little Rock, AR), 1996.

Author's works have been translated into Chinese, Finish, French, Swedish, Norwegian, Thai, Bahasa Indonesian, Spanish, Japanese, and Korean.

Adaptations

Peace Tales was adapted as a videotape titled *Folktales of Peace,* Mennonite Central Committee, which received a CINE Golden Eagle Award from the Council on International Nontheatrical Events, 1996; *Tuck-Me-in Tales* was adapted for audiocassette, with music by Richard Scholtz, August House, 1997; *Fat Cat* was adapted for audiocassette as *Fat Cat and Friends,* music by Richard Scholtz, August House, 2002; many other works by MacDonald have been adapted to audio and video format.

Sidelights

A children's librarian and professional storyteller, Margaret Read MacDonald is best known for her books associated with folk tales and the art of storytelling. "People through the ages have told folk tales to each other," she once noted to *SATA,* "and a lot of folk tales talk about things we need to listen to. . . . I am always looking for folk tales that say important things in an interesting way." While some of MacDonald's works focus on individual tales, such as her picture books, others collect tales that center on a particular theme or country. In many cases the author adds detailed notes for beginning storytellers on how to tell the folktale to an audience. Appreciated for her thorough research and vast knowledge of folklore, MacDonald is also credited for her "gift of making stories easy to tell without sacrificing quality," noted *School Library Journal* reviewer Donna L. Scanlon. Cris Riedel, also writing in *School Library Journal,* echoed Scanlon's praise for the author, dubbing MacDonald the "grande dame of storytelling."

Among MacDonald's notable picture-book tales are *The Old Woman Who Lived in a Vinegar Bottle: A British Fairy Tale, Tunjur! Tunjur! Tunjur!: A Palestinian Folktale,* and *Little Rooster's Diamond Button,* the last an adaptation of a Hungarian story. A British version of "The Fisherman and His Wife," *The Old Woman Who Lived in a Vinegar Bottle* finds an elderly woman discontent while living in a vinegar bottle. When a kind fairy provides her better living quarters, the old woman turns greedy and soon demands more and more. In *Booklist* Susan Dove Lempke enjoyed MacDonald's version of the story, which "is so rhythmic and conversational even a first-time storyteller will be successful." Similarly, a *Kirkus Reviews* critic appreciated MacDonald's "rapid, comic style."

Featuring illustrations by Alik Arzoumanian, *Tunjur! Tunjur! Tunjur!* describes a heartfelt wish that carries with it unforeseen consequences. In this case, a lonely woman longs for a child, but when her prayers are answered by a cooking pot come alive, the woman must deal with the roly-poly creature's immoral behavior. MacDonald's "smooth pacing anchors the story," wrote a *Publishers Weekly* critic, the reviewer adding that Arzoumanian's Arab-inspired mosaic art "will draw readers into the action" conjured up by MacDonald's "fluid prose." Will Terry's "eye-popping, comic illustrations [for *Little Rooster's Diamond Button*] make this fresh version of an old folktale into a rollicking romp," wrote Connie Fletcher, praising another of MacDonald's retellings in *Booklist.* Studded with colorful Spanish expressions and brought to life in Geraldo Valerio's colorful art, *Conejito: A Folktale from Panama* continues the author's exploration of culture, sharing what a *Publishers Weekly* critic deemed a "giddy-kick-up-your-heels" story that provides children and adults alike with "a wealth of audience participation opportunities."

In MacDonald's *Pickin' Peas,* a little girl has to outsmart a clever rabbit in order to keep her peas from being eaten right out of the garden. "Fans of Brer Rabbit stories will have a very good time with this classic tale," assured Shelle Rosenfeld in her *Booklist* review of the story. *The Great Smelly, Slobbery, Small-tooth Dog,* a variant on "Beauty and the Beast," is "a joyous gift to storytellers and youngsters alike," according to *School Library Journal* critic Mary Jean Smith, the critic praising the entertaining tale of a girl who is forced by her father to be repayment for the man's debt to a large, scruffy dog. In *Mabela the Clever* MacDonald focuses her story on a small mouse who must rescue her village from a clever cat that, while claiming to want peace, is actually angling for a quick bite to eat. The picture book "is engineered for storytime success," according to Catherine T. Quattlebaum, reviewing *Mabela the Clever* for *School Library Journal,* and a *Horn Book* critic concluded that MacDonald "shapes the tale with humor and familiar story conventions."

Another story featuring a feline, *Fat Cat,* was adapted from a Danish tale of a greedy cat who gets his just desserts. Helen Rosenberg, reviewing *Fat Cat* for *Booklist,* considered the work "a surefire hit for reading aloud." *School Library Journal* reviewer Kathleen Simonetta commented on MacDonald's use of "short, rhythmic sentences and repeated refrains" that encourage audience members to chime in, while Sunnie Grant, reviewing the title for *Kliatt,* predicted that *Fat Cat* is "sure to become a family favorite."

Peace Tales: World Folktales to Talk About, Earth Care: World Folktales to Talk About, Thai Tales: Folktales of Thailand, and *Three-Minute Tales: Stories from around the World to Tell or Read When Time Is Short* are examples of MacDonald's folktale collections organized by theme or country. In *Peace Tales* the author's focus is on conflict and resolution, whether on a small scale or a large one, while in *Earth Care* MacDonald focuses on environmentalism and taking care of the planet. Featuring stories from thirty countries, *Earth Care* "is an

Alik Arzoumanian contributes stylized artwork to Margaret Read MacDonald's exotic picture book Tunjur! Tunjur! Tunjur! (Marshall Cavendish Corporation, 2006. Illustration copyright © by Alik Arzoumanian. Reproduced by permission.)

invaluable resource for both environmental studies and consciousness-raising," according to *Booklist* critic John Peters. Riedel, writing in *School Library Journal,* termed the book "a grand collection," and a reviewer for *E* commented of *Earth Care* that "families will also love reading the tales aloud."

When the Lights Go Out: Twenty Scary Tales to Tell contains stories "that will absorb and chill primary and preschool audiences," according to *Booklist* reviewer Barbara Elleman. To aid beginning storytellers in this work, MacDonald includes a detailed list of sources, background information section on tale origins and vari-

ants, and tips on how to tell the story to an audience. *School Library Journal* reviewer Patricia Manning noted that, although not everyone can be transformed into an excellent storyteller, MacDonald's book "may help them find confidence to get started." Other books designed for novice storytellers include *Twenty Tellable Tales: Audience Participation Folktales for the Beginning Storyteller* and *The Storyteller's Start-up Book: Finding, Learning, Performing, and Using Folktales, Including Twelve Tellable Tales.*

Shake-It-up Tales!: Stories to Sing, Dance, Drum, and Act Out presents twenty stories designed to encourage audience participating during the telling. The entries are divided into categories determined by whether they are best accompanied with music, best designed to be acted out, or designed to encourage impromptu audience participation. Jennifer M. Parker, reviewing the book for *School Library Journal,* called *Shake-It-up Tales!,* "overall, a great resource." For storytellers with an international bent but only a few minutes to spare, MacDonald's *Three-Minute Tales* and *Five-Minute Tales* include dozens of stories that can be told quickly. *Three-Minute Tales* "supplies full measures of chuckles and grins, tears, chills, wisdom, and entertainment," commented a *Kirkus Reviews* contributor, while Hazel Rochman commented in *Booklist* that the tales are "easy to tell, easy to teach children and adults, and easy to remember." In *School Library Journal* Marlyn K. Beebe recommended *Three-Minute Tales* to "professional and parenting collections," while Dan Keding wrote in *Sing Out!* that for professionals, "this is the book that will come through in a pinch."

MacDonald once told *SATA:* "When I was in third grade my mother took me to the public library for the first time. We didn't have school libraries in those days, so you can imagine my excitement when I climbed those steep stone steps . . . pushed open that huge wooden door . . . and entered a room full of books all around!

I could take a pile home every week to read! After that Momma and I walked downtown once a week and each got a new load of books to carry home.

"Soon my head was full of imaginings and I got myself a notebook and started to write poems and plays of my own. My friends and I could make papier-maché puppets and act out the plays I wrote. Later, when I was in college, I found out that I could just keep on reading books and putting on puppet shows and telling stories as a career! What fun! I got to have a great time every day of my whole life!

"After a while, I wanted to share some of the fantastic folk tales I had discovered with other readers. So I started putting some of them into books. At first I wrote several collections of folk tales. Teachers and librarians loved reading and telling these to kids. But then I thought it would be fun for some of these stories to be made into picture books so that kids and parents could share them too.

"I work really hard to write these folktale picture books in such a way that the reader will read them out loud the way I would want to tell them if I were there to tell the story. This means trying to find language that sounds the way folks talk. To make sure I have got the words right, I read them aloud to many groups of kids. When

Featuring two unusual friends, MacDonald's original folktale **Go to Sleep, Gecko!** *is brought to life in Geraldo Valerio's art.* (August House Publishers, Inc., 2006. Illustration copyright © 2006 by Geraldo Valerio. All rights reserved. Reproduced by permission.)

I visit schools to talk about books, I am always trying out new stories to see how the listeners like them. I get a lot of really useful ideas from the children I meet. Sometimes a class comes up with just the right solution for a picture book problem I am stuck on.

"When I think I have the book almost perfect, I give it to my son-in-law, Tom, to read out loud. I think he is a typical father. If it sounds right when he reads it out loud, it is okay. If he stumbles over the words . . . I have to go back and work on it some more. Having a friend read your story out loud is a really good way to edit.

"Another thing that excited me when I was young was the idea of travel. I used to pore over the *National Geographic* magazines and think of all the places there were to go in the world. Now I get to visit those places. I am invited to come and tell stories to children in many countries. And I teach their teachers fun folk tales to share with the students. Sometimes the teachers teach me great stories to share . . . like an amazing story of a scary rolling head that my friend in Sabah on the island of Borneo told!

"Mainly, I use folk tales because they are such fun to share. I hope readers will tell my stories out loud and pass them on to somebody else. These are 'folk' literature. I didn't make them up. I just heard them somewhere and shaped them so they would be fun to speak. I have put them in a book for the moment. But the story really wants to get out and into your head. It wants you to tell it! Folk tales belong to everybody. So please take one and pass it on!"

Biographical and Critical Sources

PERIODICALS

American Libraries, January, 2005, "Once upon a Time," p. 86.

Booklist, October 1, 1988, Barbara Elleman, review of *When the Lights Go Out: Twenty Scary Tales to Tell,* p. 331; October 1, 1995, Susan Dove Lempke, review of *The Old Woman Who Lived in a Vinegar Bottle: A British Fairy Tale,* p. 323; October 1, 1996, Julie Corsaro, review of *Tuck-Me-in Tales: Bedtime Stories from around the World,* p. 355; November 1, 1997, Karen Morgan, review of *Slop!: A Welsh Folktale,* p. 477; July, 1998, Shelle Rosenfeld, review of *Pickin' Peas,* p. 1887; September 1, 1999, Carolyn Phelan, review of *The Round Book: Rounds Kids Love to Sing,* p. 129; January 1, 2000, John Peters, review of *Earth Care,* p. 897; July, 2001, review of *Mabela the Clever,* p. 2014; November 15, 2001, Helen Rosenberg, review of *Fat Cat,* p. 577; September 15, 2005, Hazel Rochman, review of *Three-Minute Tales: Stories from around the World to Tell or Read When Time Is Short,* p. 183; December 1, 2005, Stephanie Zvirin, review

of *The Squeaky Door,* p. 54; March 1, 2006, Gillian Engberg, review of *Tunjur! Tunjur! Tunjur!: A Palestinian Folktale,* p. 96; March 15, 2006, GraceAnne A. DeCandido, review of *Conejito: A Folktale from Panama,* p. 51; May 15, 2006, John Stewig, review of *The Teeny Weeny Bop!,* p. 51; February 15, 2007, Connie Fletcher, review of *Little Rooster's Diamond Button,* p. 81; November 1, 2007, Gillian Engberg, review of *The Great Smelly, Slobbery, Small-tooth Dog,* p. 47; June 1, 2008, Shelle Rosenfeld, review of *Bat's Big Game,* p. 86.

Bulletin of the Center for Children's Books, September, 1998, review of *Pickin' Peas,* p. 22; September, 1999, review of *The Round Book,* p. 37; February, 2000, review of *Earth Care,* p. 230; September, 2000, review of *Shake-It-up Tales,* p. 44; November, 2001, review of *Fat Cat,* p. 109; May, 2005, review of *A Hen, a Chick, and a String Guitar,* p. 393; March, 2006, Elizabeth Bush, review of *The Squeaky Door,* p. 319; July-August, 2006, Maggie Hommel, review of *Conejito,* p. 508; December, 2006, Hope Morrison, review of *Go to Sleep, Gecko!: A Balinese Folktale,* p. 179; April, 2007, Hope Morrison, review of *The Old Woman and Her Pig: An Appalachian Folktale,* p. 336; May, 2007, Hope Morrison, review of *Little Rooster's Diamond Button,* p. 375.

Choice, January, 2000, J. Gregg, review of *Traditional Storytelling Today,* p. 914.

E, September, 2000, review of *Earth Care,* p. 61.

Horn Book, September, 2001, Mary A. Burns, review of *Mabela the Clever,* p. 603.

Kirkus Reviews, September 1, 1995, review of *The Old Woman Who Lived in a Vinegar Bottle,* p. 1283; September 1, 2001, review of *Fat Cat,* p. 1296; September 1, 2004, review of *Three-Minute Tales,* p. 870; April 15, 2005, review of *A Hen, a Chick, and a String Guitar,* p. 477; December 15, 2005, review of *The Squeaky Door,* p. 1325; February 1, 2006, review of *The Teeny Weeny Bop!,* p. 134; March 1, 2006, review of *Conejito,* p. 236; October 1, 2006, review of *Go to Sleep, Gecko!,* p. 1019; January 15, 2007, review of *Little Rooster's Diamond Button,* p. 76; September 15, 2007, review of *The Great Smelly, Slobbery, Small-tooth Dog;* February 15, 2008, review of *Bat's Big Game.*

Kliatt, May, 2003, Sunnie Grant, review of *Fat Cat,* p. 46; January, 2005, Ann Hart, review of *Three-Minute Tales,* p. 28.

Library Journal, August, 1992, John W. Eldridge, review of *The Storyteller's Sourcebook,* p. 1451; July, 1993, Patricia Dooley, review of *The Storyteller's Start-up Book: Finding, Learning, Performing, and Using Folktales,* p. 81.

Publishers Weekly, June 22, 1992, review of *Peace Tales: World Folktales to Talk About,* p. 63; June 8, 1998, review of *Pickin' Peas,* p. 59; December 20, 1999, review of *Telling Tales,* p. 82; May 14, 2001, review of *Mabela the Clever,* p. 81; January 16, 2006, review of *The Squeaky Door,* p. 63; January 30, 2006, review of

MacDonald teams up with artist Eugenia Nobati to tell a sports story of a different sort in **Bat's Big Game.** (Albert Whitman, 2008. Illustration copyright © 2008 by Eugenia Nobati. Reproduced by permission.)

Tunjur! Tunjur! Tunjur!, p. 68; May 15, 2006, review of *Conejito,* p. 71; February 12, 2007, review of *Little Rooster's Diamond Button,* p. 85.

Reference & Research Book News, November, 1999, review of *Traditional Storytelling Today,* p. 9; November, 2001, review of *The Storyteller's Sourcebook,* p. 63; February, 2004, review of *Indonesian Folktales,* p. 72.

School Librarian, winter, 1999, review of *Traditional Storytelling Today,* p. 222.

School Library Journal, August, 1989, Patricia Manning, review of *When the Lights Go Out,* p. 88; June, 1990, Meryl Silverstein, review of *The Skit Book: 101 Skits from Kids,* pp. 132-133; October, 1992, Mollie Bynum, review of *Peace Tales,* p. 132; January, 1996, Donna L. Scanlon, review of *The Old Woman Who Lived in a Vinegar Bottle,* pp. 102-103; November, 1996, Susan Garland, review of *Tuck-Me-in Tales,* p. 99; July, 1998, Margaret A. Chang, review of *The Girl Who Wore Too Much,* p. 89; October, 1998, Tana

Elias, review of *Pickin' Peas,* p. 107; July, 1999, Mollie Bynum, review of *The Round Book,* p. 110; April, 2000, Cris Riedel, review of *Earth Care,* p. 152; October, 2000, Jennifer M. Parker, review of *Shake-It-up Tales,* p. 198; June, 2001, Catherine T. Quattlebaum, review of *Mabela the Clever,* p. 139; January, 2002, Kathleen Simonetta, review of *Fat Cat,* p. 120; October, 2004, Marlyn K. Beebe, review of *Three-Minute Tales,* p. 202; May, 2005, Kathleen Whalin, review of *A Hen, a Chick, and a String Guitar,* p. 111; January, 2006, Elaine Lesh Morgan, review of *The Squeaky Door,* p. 108; April, 2006, Miriam Lang Budin, reviews of *Tunjur! Tunjur! Tunjur!,* p. 128, and Lee Bock, review of *Conejito,* p. 129; August, 2006, Martha Simpson, review of *The Teeny Weeny Bop!,* p. 93; October, 2006, Wendy Woodfill, review of *Go to Sleep, Gecko!,* p. 138; October, 2006, Barbara Auerbach, review of *Mabela the Clever,* p. 65; February, 2007, Martha Simpson, review of *The Old Woman and Her Pig,* p. 110; March, 2007, Donna Cardon, review of *Little Rooster's Diamond Button,* p. 198; December, 2007, Mary Jean Smith, review of *The Great Smelly, Slobbery, Small-tooth Dog,* p. 112; June, 2008, Donna Cardon, review of *Bat's Big Game,* p. 127.

Science Books & Films, July, 2000, review of *Earth Care,* p. 173.

Sing Out!, spring, 2005, Dan Keding, review of *Three Minute Tales* and *Indonesian Folktales,* pp. 108-109.

Teacher Librarian, December, 2001, review of *Parent's Guide to Storytelling,* p. 39.

Tribune Books (Chicago, IL), June 24, 2001, review of *Mabela the Clever,* p. 5.

Voice of Youth Advocates, December, 2000, review of *Shake-It-up Tales,* p. 378.

Wilson Library Bulletin, June, 1993, Frances Bradburn, review of *Peace Tales,* p. 102.

ONLINE

Margaret Read MacDonald Home Page, http://www.margaretreadmacdonald.com (October 21, 2008).

MACK, Jeff

Personal

Born in Syracuse, NY. *Education:* Attended college in Oswego, NY, and Florence, Italy; studied painting and creative writing. *Hobbies and other interests:* Travel, reading, gourmet food, listening to music, hiking, watching movies, playing trumpet and musical saw.

Addresses

Home—Easthampton, MA. *E-mail*—jeff@jeffmack.com.

Career

Writer, illustrator, and mural painter. Has also worked as poster artist and faux finisher of walls and furniture.

Writings

(Self-illustrated) *Hush Little Polar Bear,* Roaring Brook Press (New York, NY), 2008.

In his colorful art, Jeff Mack introduces readers to the floppy-eared stars of Linda Westberg Peters' picture book **We're Rabbits!** (Illustration copyright © 2004 by Jeffrey M. Mack. Reproduced by permission of Houghton Mifflin Harcourt Publishing Company.)

A group of farmyard friends anticipates the arrival of a new neighbor in Mack's artwork for Eve Bunting's story **Hurry! Hurry!** (Illustration copyright © 2007 by Jeffrey M. Mack. Reproduced by permission of Houghton Mifflin Harcourt Publishing Company.)

ILLUSTRATOR

Dawn Bentley, *The Icky Sticky Chameleon,* Piggy Toes Press (Santa Monica, CA), 2001.

Linda Ashman, *Rub-a-dub Sub,* Harcourt Books (San Diego, CA), 2003.

Lisa Westberg Peters, *We're Rabbits!,* Harcourt Books (Orlando, FL), 2004.

Linda Ashman, *Starry Safari,* Harcourt Books (Orlando, FL), 2005.

Eve Bunting, *Hurry! Hurry!,* Harcourt Books (Orlando, FL), 2007.

Kathryn Osebold Galbraith, *Boo, Bunny!,* Harcourt Books (Orlando, FL), 2008.

ILLUSTRATOR; "BUNNICULA AND FRIENDS" SERIES

James Howe, *Hot Fudge,* Atheneum Books for Young Readers (New York, NY), 2004.

James Howe, *The Vampire Bunny,* adapted by Heather Henson, Atheneum Books for Young Readers (New York, NY), 2004.

James Howe, *Scared Silly,* Atheneum Books for Young Readers (New York, NY), 2005.

James Howe, *Rabbit Cadabra,* Atheneum Books for Young Readers (New York, NY), 2006.

James Howe, *The Fright before Christmas,* Atheneum Books for Young Readers (New York, NY), 2006.

James Howe, *Creepy Crawly Birthday,* Atheneum Books for Young Readers (New York, NY), 2007.

Sidelights

As a child, Jeff Mack practiced for his eventual career as an illustrator by making up stories about his brothers and sisters getting eaten by monsters. "I can't even tell you how many monsters I drew back then," he recalled on his home page. "Eleventy hundred billion, perhaps." Mack never lost his interest in art, and after studying painting in both the United States and abroad, he has achieved his goal by bringing to life the picture-book stories of several writers in addition to creating the original self-illustrated book *Hush Little Polar Bear,* which a *Kirkus Reviews* writer described as a 'sweet metaliterary journey" in which Mack's story of a young girl's nighttime journey with a stuffed toy is brought to life in his "genial, soft-edged" acrylic illustrations.

Mack's whimsical, cartoonish creatures are featured in books such as *Rub-a-dub Sub* and *Starry Safari,* both with a text by Linda Ashman. His more realistic acrylic paintings bring to life Lisa Westberg Peters' text for *We're Rabbits!,* in which a trio of hungry wild bunnies cajole fresh produce from a frustrated gardener. In her *School Library Journal* review of *Starry Safari,* Maryann H. Owen maintained that Mack's "richly colored pictures and constant action" effectively depict Ashman's "rip-roaring, exciting excursion." In *Publishers Weekly* a critic noted that *Rub-a-dub Sub* benefits from Mack's "neon-bright colors and intricate textures," both of which "heighten the [undersea] setting's exotic beauty." Mack's art also appears in Eve Bunting's picture book *Hurry! Hurry!,* which is set in a busy farmyard. In her *Booklist* review of *Hurry! Hurry!,* Gillian Engberg concluded that "Mack's high-spirited pictures . . . really tell the story."

In his ongoing collaboration with popular children's author James Howe, Mack has contributed art to Howe's bestselling "Bunnicula" series. Howe's books about the voracious Bunnicula are aimed at third-to fifth-grade readers, but in the "Bunnicula and Friends" books the collaborators introduce the character to beginning readers. "Bunnicula and friends have never been more adorable," noted a *Kirkus Reviews* correspondent in a piece on *The Vampire Bunny.* Karen Stuppi, writing in *School Library Journal,* concluded that Mack's illustrations for *The Vampire Bunny* "enhance the text through humorous and emotive depictions of the characters."

Biographical and Critical Sources

PERIODICALS

Booklist, June 1, 2003, John Peters, review of *Rub-a-dub Sub,* p. 1782; March 15, 2004, Terry Glover, review of *We're Rabbits!,* p. 1310; August, 2005, Julie Cummins, review of *Starry Safari,* p. 2033; February 1, 2007, Gillian Engberg, review of *Hurry! Hurry!,* p. 46.

Bulletin of the Center for Children's Books, July-August, 2007, Hope Morrison, review of *Hurry! Hurry!,* p. 454.

Horn Book, March-April, 2007, Lauren Adams, review of *Hurry! Hurry!,* p. 178.

Kirkus Reviews, May 1, 2003, review of *Rub-a-dub Sub,* p. 673; January 1, 2004, review of *We're Rabbits!,* p. 40; January 15, 2004, review of *The Vampire Bunny,* p. 84; June 1, 2005, review of *Starry Safari,* p. 632; February 1, 2007, review of *Hurry! Hurry!,* p. 121; October 15, 2008, review of *Hush Little Polar Bear.*

Publishers Weekly, April 7, 2003, review of *Rub-a-dub Sub,* p. 64; November 10, 2008, review of *Hush Little Polar Bear.*

School Library Journal, July, 2003, Linda M. Kenton, review of *Rub-a-dub Sub,* p. 86; June, 2004, Karen Stuppi, review of *The Vampire Bunny,* p. 110; July, 2005, Maryann H. Owen, review of *Starry Safari,* p. 64; June, 2006, Susan Hepler, review of *Rabbit-Cadabra!,* p. 119; March, 2007, Maryann H. Owen, review of *Hurry! Hurry!,* p. 152.

ONLINE

Harcourt Books Web site, http://www.harcourtbooks.com/ (November 7, 2008), interview with Lisa Westberg Peters and Mack.

Jeff Mack Home Page, http://www.jeffmack.com (November 7, 2008), author biography.

Simon & Schuster Web site, http://www.simonsays.com/ (November 7, 2008), "Jeff Mack."

MATAS, Carol 1949-

Personal

Born November 14, 1949, in Winnipeg, Manitoba, Canada; daughter of Roy Joseph (a judge) and Ruth Gloria Matas; married Per K. Brask (a professor of theater), February 19, 1977; children: Rebecca Ellen, Aaron Samuel. *Education:* University of Western Ontario, B.A. (English), 1969; graduate, Actor's Lab (London, England), 1972. *Religion:* Jewish.

Addresses

Home—Canada. *Agent*—Transatlantic Literary Agency, Inc., 72 Glengowan Rd, Toronto, Ontario M4N 1G4, Canada. *E-mail*—carol@carolmatas.com.

Career

Writer and actor. University of Winnipeg, Manitoba, Canada, instructor of creative writing in Continuing Education Division. Bemidji State University, Bemidji, MN, visiting professor; Manitoba Arts Council, artist-in-the-schools; Centennial Library, Winnipeg, writer-in-residence.

Member

International PEN, Writers' Union of Canada, Society of Children's Book Writers and Illustrators, Canadian Society of Children's Authors, Illustrators, and Performers, Children's Book Centre, Manitoba Writers Guild.

Awards, Honors

Geoffrey Bilson Award for Historical Fiction for Young Readers, 1988, Sydney Taylor Awards Honor Book designation, Association of Jewish Libraries, and *New York Times Book Review* Notable Book designation, both 1989, Notable Children's Trade Book in the Field of Social Studies, National Council for the Social Studies (NCSS)/Children's Book Council (CBC), 1990, Young Adults' Choice, International Reading Association, 1991, and Canadian Children's Book Centre (CCBC) Our Choice designation, all for *Lisa's War;* Mr. Christie's Honour Book designation, 1989, CCBC Our Choice designation, and Young Adult Canadian Book Award runner up, both 1990, Woodward Park Award, and Notable Children's Trade Book in the Field of Social Studies, NCSS/CBC, both 1991, all for *Code Name Kris;* Notable Book designation, Canadian Library Association (CLA), 1992, for *The Race;* Governor General's Literary Award nomination, Silver Birch Award, Ruth Schwartz Award nomination, and Mr. Christie's Honor Book designation, all 1993, Notable Children's Trade Book in the Field of Social Studies designation, NCSS/CBC, Books for the Teen Age selection, New York Public Library, both 1994, and Manitoba Young Reader's Choice Award, 1996, all for *Daniel's Story;* Sydney Taylor Award, and CLA Notable Book designation, both 1993, and Notable Children's Trade Book in

Carol Matas (Photograph by Billie Nodelman. Reproduced by permission.)

the Field of Social Studies designation, NCSS/CBC, and Books for the Teen Age designation, New York Public Library, both 1994, all for *Sworn Enemies;* CCBC Our Choice designation, 1993, and Governor General's Literary Award nomination, and Books for the Teen Age designation, New York Public Library, both 1994, all for *The Burning Time;* Manitoba Book of the Year nomination, and CCBC Outstanding Book of the Year designation, both 1995, and Manitoba Young Readers Choice Award nomination, 1997, all for *The Primrose Path;* Best Books for Young Adults and Quick Picks for Young Adults designations, American Library Association (ALA), Best Book of the Year nomination, and Best Book of the Year for Children nomination, both McNally Robinson Book Award, Ruth Schwartz Award nomination, Jewish Book Award, and Mr. Christie Honour Book designation, all 1996, Books for the Teen Age designation, New York Public Library, Notable Children's Trade Book designation, NCSS/CBC, South Carolina Junior Book Award nomination, 1997, and Utah Young-Adult Book Award nomination, 1998, all for *After the War;* Notable Children's Trade Book in the Field of Social Studies designation, NCSS/CBC, Books for the Teen Age designation, New York Public Library, and Rachel Bessin/Isaac Frichwasser Memorial Award for Y.A. Fiction, all 1998, all for *The Garden;* Notable Children's Trade Book in the Field of Social Studies designation, NCSS/CBC, and Geoffrey Bilson Award nomination, both 1999, both for *Greater than Angels;* McNally Robinson Book of the Year Award for Young People nomination, Book for the Teen

Age designation, New York Public Library, CCBC Our Choice designation, and Geoffrey Bilson Award nomination, all 2000, all for *In My Enemy's House;* Manitoba Book for Young Readers Award nomination, 2001, Margaret McWilliams Award, Manitoba Historical Society, and Hackmatack Children's Choice Award nomination, all for *Rebecca;* Hackmatack Award finalist, 2006, for *Rosie in Los Angeles;* McNally Robinson Book for Young Readers Award finalist, Margaret McWilliams Award, Manitoba Historical Society, Geoffrey Bilson Award finalist, and CBC Our Choice Merit honor, all 2006, and Frances and Samuel Stein Memorial Prize in Youth Literature, 2007, all for *Turned Away;* CBC Our Choice selection, for *Past Crimes;* Sydney Taylor Notable Book for Older Readers designation, 2007, for *The Whirlwind.*

Writings

FICTION

The D.N.A. Dimension, Gage Publishing (Toronto, Ontario, Canada), 1982.

The Fusion Factor, Fifth House (Saskatoon, Saskatchewan, Canada), 1986, published as *It's up to Us,* Stoddard (Toronto, Ontario, Canada), 1991.

Zanu, Fifth House (Saskatoon, Saskatchewan, Canada), 1986.

Me, Myself, and I, Fifth House (Saskatoon, Saskatchewan, Canada), 1987.

Lisa (also see below), Lester & Orpen Dennys (Toronto, Ontario, Canada), 1987, published as *Lisa's War,* Scribner (New York, NY), 1989.

Jesper, Lester & Orpen Dennys (Toronto, Ontario, Canada), 1989, published as *Code Name Kris,* Scribner (New York, NY), 1990, reprinted under original title, Scholastic Canada (Toronto, Ontario, Canada), 2005.

Adventure in Legoland, Scholastic (New York, NY), 1991.

The Race, HarperCollins (New York, NY), 1991.

(Adaptor, with husband Per Brask), *Lisa* (play; based on Matas' novel), produced by Prairie Theater Exchange, 1991.

Sworn Enemies, Bantam (New York, NY), 1993.

Safari Adventure in Legoland, Scholastic (New York, NY), 1993.

The Escape, produced in Winnipeg, Manitoba, Canada, 1993.

Daniel's Story, Scholastic (New York, NY), 1993.

The Lost Locket, Scholastic (New York, NY), 1994.

The Burning Time, Bantam (New York, NY), 1994.

(With Perry Nodelman) *Of Two Minds,* Bain & Cox (Winnipeg, Manitoba, Canada), 1994, Simon & Schuster (New York, NY), 1995.

The Primrose Path, Bain & Cox (Winnipeg, Manitoba, Canada), 1995.

After the War, Simon & Schuster (New York, NY), 1996.

(With Perry Nodelman) *More Minds,* Simon & Schuster (New York, NY), 1996.

The Freak, Key Porter (Toronto, Ontario, Canada), 1997.

The Garden, Simon & Schuster (New York, NY), 1997.

Greater than Angels, Simon & Schuster (New York, NY), 1998.

(With Perry Nodelman) *Out of Their Minds,* Simon & Schuster (New York, NY), 1998.

Telling, Key Porter (Toronto, Ontario, Canada), 1998.

In My Enemy's House, Simon & Schuster (New York, NY), 1999.

(With Perry Nodelman) *A Meeting of Minds,* Simon & Schuster (New York, NY), 1999.

Cloning Miranda, Scholastic Canada (Toronto, Ontario, Canada), 1999.

Rebecca, Scholastic Canada (Toronto, Ontario, Canada), 2000.

The War Within: A Novel of the Civil War, Simon & Schuster (New York, NY), 2001.

Dear Canada, Scholastic Canada (Toronto, Ontario, Canada), 2001.

Sparks Fly Upward, Clarion (New York, NY), 2002.

Ben, Simon & Schuster (New York, NY), 2002.

The Second Clone, Scholastic Canada (Toronto, Ontario, Canada), 2002.

Footsteps in the Snow: The Red River Diary of Isobel Scott, Scholastic Canada (Toronto, Ontario, Canada), 2002.

Turned Away: The World War II Diary of Devorah Bernstein, Scholastic Canada (Markham, Ontario, Canada), 2005.

The Dark Clone, Scholastic Canada (Markham, Ontario, Canada), 2005.

Past Crimes, Key Porter Books (Toronto, Ontario, Canada), 2006.

The Whirlwind, Orca, 2007.

Visions, Key Porter Books (Toronto, Ontario, Canada), 2007.

(With Perry Nodelman) *The Proof That Ghosts Exist,* Key Porter Books (Toronto, Ontario, Canada), 2008.

Far, Key Porter Books (Toronto, Ontario, Canada), 2008.

Adaptor (with Brask) of stage play *Jesper,* based on Matas' novel.

Author's work has been translated into Danish, French, Swedish, Spanish, Turkish, Japanese, German, Taiwanese, Russian, Bulgarian, Indonesian, and Dutch.

"ROSIE TRILOGY"; MIDDLE-GRADE NOVELS

Rosie in New York City: Gotcha!, illustrated by Angelo Rinaldi, Aladdin (New York, NY), 2003.

Rosie in Chicago: Play Ball!, Aladdin (New York, NY), 2003.

Rosie in Los Angeles: Action!, Aladdin (New York, NY), 2004.

Adaptations

Sworn Enemies was adapted as a staged reading, New York, NY, 1994; *Telling* was adapted as a radio play, broadcast by CBC Manitoba, 1994.

Sidelights

A Canadian author who pens historical novels and other fiction for young readers, Carol Matas is known for writing hard-hitting stories that thrust adolescent protagonists into life-and-death situations while confronting readers with the vagaries and complexities of life. In such award-winning novels as *Lisa's War, Code Name Kris, Daniel's Story, The Whirlwind,* and *After the War,* she casts the events of World War II not simply as an historical backdrop, but as a central agent in stories of heroism and despair. Employing starkly realistic and highly adventurous narratives, Matas not only entertains but hopes to provoke her readers into seeing the world anew. In a review of *Turned Away: The World War II Diary of Devorah Bernstein,* which Matas contributes to the popular "Dear Canada" series of middle-grade historical novels, *Resource Links* contributor Suzanne Finkelstein, praised the author's "well-written, extensively researched and detailed" story about the Canadian government's controversial efforts to prevent war-

Cover of Carol Matas's historic novel **The Burning Time,** *a study of witch hunts in sixteenth-century France.* (Bantam Doubleday Dell, 1996. Used by permission of Dell Publishing, a division of Random House, Inc.)

time German-Jewish immigration as "immensely teachable" and useful for sparking discussions. As the author noted in an interview for *Canadian Children's Literature* the World War II era "offers an incredible wealth of dramatic stories as well as an opportunity to explore issues and to put my characters in life or death situations where moral dilemmas have to be faced."

Interestingly, given her prolific career, Matas had no intention of pursuing a career as a writer; in fact, her early ambitions led her to the theater. As a young woman, she trained at Actor's Lab in London, then returned to her native Winnipeg to pursue a career in drama. Then, during her first pregnancy she left the theater and channeled her creative energy into writing a fantasy novel titled *Carstan and Kasper.* While caring for her young daughter, Matas continued to write and gradually honed her focus on writing for children. Her second completed manuscript, *Fusion Factor,* found a publisher after a score of rejections, and by this time Matas had already written and placed another book, *The D.N.A. Dimension.* By the mid-1980s four of her books were in print, among them the related novels *Zanu* and *Me, Myself and I,* both which feature a twelve-year-old protagonist named after Matas's daughter Rebecca.

Matas's early novels, as well as 2005's *The Dark Clone,* feature science-fiction themes that incorporate nuclear destruction, genetic engineering, and eco-catastrophe. In *The Dark Clone* high achiever Miranda is shocked when a videotape surfaces showing her identical twin destroying public property, and the teen's search for answers leads her to a cloning program designed to provide humans with spare parts for medical procedures. In *The Fusion Factor,* a girl named Rebecca travels into the future to an underground city populated by genetically impaired survivors of a nuclear holocaust who are kidnapping healthy children from the past for breeding purposes. In *Zanu* Rebecca is transported to a seemingly perfect future world, only to discover the rot beneath the surface. Zanu is a corporate world, completely controlled by big business; those who do not conform are banished to a wilderness destroyed by industrial pollution. In both of these books, the future appears bleak and the preteen's only hope is to return to her own time and find a way to change the future she has encountered. Sandra Odegard, reviewing both books in *Canadian Children's Literature,* commented that "Matas suggests that challenging the established power structure of any society calls upon physical, as well as moral, courage." Mary Ainslie Smith, in *Books in Canada,* offered a similar estimation of both *The Fusion Factor* and *Zanu,* asserting that the author's "spunky and ultimately optimistic" heroine "wants to believe that one person can make . . . a difference," and "her determination to work for a better world should get some healthy ideas stirring in the minds of the readers of these two books."

First published in Canada under the title *Lisa, Lisa's War* was inspired by the stories of Matas's husband's father and grandfather, who participated in the Danish underground during World War II. When a friend gave her a book about how the Danish people managed to save most of the Jews of their country, she recognized another angle for her story. "I never sat down and said, 'I want to write historical fiction,'" she once commented. "Rather I found a story, from the past, which I simply had to tell." Lisa is a Jewish teenager growing up in Copenhagen during the Nazi occupation, and after joining the resistance at age twelve, she becoming involved in exploits ranging from the distribution of leaflets, to blowing up bridges and helping Jews avoid Nazi capture. Despite her fears that the resistance is becoming almost as violent and uncompromising as the Nazi movement it is fighting, Lisa is ultimately forced to kill a German in order to save many others. Although the book describes "many violent acts," Welwyn Wilton Katz added in *Books in Canada* that *Lisa's War* "is made less dark by the characters' desire to move beyond them." In a *Voice of Youth Advocates* review, Marian Rafal concluded that the "great escape to Sweden by over 6,000 Jews is a gripping tale of adventure and courage," and *Canadian Literature* critic J.R. Wytenbroek commented that the book "combines personal emotion with historical fact in just the right proportions to produce a first hand look into what it must have been like to be a Jew in occupied Europe during those dark years." In *Horn Book* Mary M. Burns, noted the graphic nature of the novel, concluding that *Lisa's War* "is not an adventure story with war as a backdrop but an account of events that irrevocably changed the lives of human beings." In *Publishers Weekly* a commentator deemed the work "an unsettling, important novel."

A sequel to *Lisa's War*—and published in Canada under the title *Jesper*—*Code Name Kris* narrates the adventures of Jesper, an adolescent friend of Lisa and her older brother, as he battles the Nazis after Lisa and her family have escaped to neutral Sweden. Captured as a resister, Jesper chronicles the events leading up to his arrest as he awaits execution. His exploits with the resistance become bolder still as he is forced to grow up and grow old in the ways of the world, and the uncertainty of life is brought home to Jesper when he discovers that a man he once idolized has become a Nazi collaborator. Writing in *Quill & Quire,* Frieda Wishinsky noted that in *Code Name Kris* Matas "has seamlessly woven in actual events and places in Copenhagen to describe a time when young people grew up quickly in a world ripped apart by war." A *Five Owls* reviewer noted that the narrative of this sequel "moves quickly and is full of action," and Graham Caie commented in *Canadian Children's Literature* that Matas's careful research and thorough detail "give this historical novel greater credibility and depth."

Used in classrooms throughout North America, *Daniel's Story* was commissioned by the United States' Holocaust Memorial Museum and serves as a complement to an exhibit about children during the Holocaust. Told in

Matas turns to World War II in her historical novel **Daniel's Story,** *featuring artwork by Paul Henry.* (Illustration copyright © 1993 by Paul Henry. Reproduced by permission of Scholastic, Inc.)

flashbacks from the point of view of a survivor, *Daniel's Story* details the life of its young narrator from age six to eighteen. Daniel's happy childhood is shattered when he and his family are deported from Frankfurt to the Lodz ghetto and subsequently to the concentration camps Auschwitz, Bergen-Belsen, and Buchenwald. Finally, in 1945, the boy is liberated, although most of those around him have died. Reflecting the view of some reviewers, Betsy Hearne wrote in the *Bulletin of the Center for Children's Books* that *Daniel's Story* "never seems to take on a fictional life of its own but remains almost a descriptive explanation of Jewish suffering at the hands of the Nazis." In contrast, however, Kenneth Oppel acknowledged in *Quill & Quire* that Matas's young hero is "apparently a composite of real children who endured the Holocaust," and although he "does assume allegorical status in the novel, . . . the human voice of a child is always there." In *Canadian Review of Materials* Anne Louise Mahoney described Daniel as "a likeable character, strong and committed to seeing truth and justice win out in the end," and Oppel concluded that *Daniel's Story* "is a book all children should read."

Matas extends the story of war and its dislocation in *After the War,* a chronicle of the adventures of a fifteen-year-old survivor of the camps. In the novel, Ruth Mendleberg joins a Zionist group and tries to reach a new homeland in Palestine. As Matas once noted, *After the War* "raises questions about the meaning of life when everything has been lost; and [is] a story that has not yet been told for young people." Interwoven with the action of a perilous journey across the European continent by a group of young death-camp survivors are flashbacks of Ruth's wartime life: the roundups and massacres she wishes to forget. Robyn Nicoline Ryan, in *School Library Journal,* called *After the War* "a thought-provoking novel that offers great insight into the current problems in the Middle East." Betsy Hearne commented in the *Bulletin of the Center for Children's Books* that "Matas' recreation of life on the run acquires some authentic urgency," and a *Booklist* reviewer noted that the novel crafts historical incidents "into a tightly edited drama."

The Garden continues the story of survivors in Palestine as they now fight a new enemy resident in the Arab nations surrounding them. *Greater than Angels* returns to war-torn Europe with the story of young Anna Hirsch, who is deported with her family from Germany to France. She is eventually sent to the village of Le Chambon, where she joins the townsfolk in resisting the Nazis and planning a daring escape to Switzerland. A *Publishers Weekly* reviewer praised the novel as a solidly researched and vivid account of the heroism of the Le Chambon villagers, who came to the aid of the approximately 2,500 Jews who sought refuge there. *In My Enemy's House* recounts the story of Marisa, a Jewish girl whose blonde hair and blue eyes permit her to pass as Polish. When Marisa moves to Germany, she is able to find work and to see Nazi hatred from the inside.

For fourteen-year-old Ben Friedman, the protagonist of *The Whirlwind,* the search for safety from the Nazis leads him to America. However, when the Japanese bomb Pearl Harbor, fear again invades Ben's life, as his Seattle classmates channel their anger over the loss of American lives to the German Jews of living in their community. In *The Whirlwind* "Matas places vital, universal truths about life within a historical context, adhering to reality without being overly graphic," according to *Kliatt* contributor Marissa Elliott, the critic praising the novel as "a poignant look at what it means to come of age in a world of uncertainty."

In addition to her wartime novels, Matas has written of other historical periods, sometimes placing her protagonists in the modern world. *The Race* uses contemporary Canadian politics as a backdrop to the coming-of-age story of Ali Green, a fourteen-year-old youth delegate at a Liberal leadership convention as well as the daughter of the front-running candidate. "Ali is a truly likable character," noted *Quill & Quire* contributor Anne Louise Mahoney, adding: "Her first-person narrative is full of humour and teenage angst, and brings a fresh perspective to politics and life in general." In another favorable review of *The Race, Canadian Review of Materials* contributor Gordon Heasley described the book as "an engaging young adult narrative that artfully combines the stories of a questioning adolescent and the elaborate political process of a leadership race."

In *Past Crimes* a young woman and her family are seemingly threatened by something outside reality. Ros works at a family-planning clinic when every aspect of her life is terrorized. Her husband has been shot, and her home has burned down. Now living with her parents, she is haunted by strange dreams that become more fearful when a doctor who performs abortions at the clinic is shot and killed. As her dreams reveal themselves to be inspired by the Spanish Inquisition, Ros takes a course in Jewish studies, hoping to make sense of the tangible fears that by now include the kidnapping of her young son. A multifaceted story, *Past Crimes* posits jealousy and reincarnation as possible sources, treating readers to what *Booklist* contributor Hazel Rochman described as a "contemporary mystery-thriller that revolves around love and betrayal."

In *The Burning Time* Matas focuses on the witch trials that took place in sixteenth-century France. Rose is aged fifteen when her mother, a healer and midwife, is accused of being a witch by jealous neighbors and spurned suitors. Soon Rose is also accused and must flee to save herself. Although Hazel Rochman, writing in *Booklist,* felt that "the political message overwhelms the novel," she concluded that "it's the history that's compelling here, the facts that are left out of the traditional textbooks, the role played by those strong women outsiders who threatened the male hierarchy." A reviewer for *Voice of Youth Advocates* commented of *The Burning Time* that "this gripping story of survival with its aspects of horror and witches will make it much more popular than most other young adult historical fiction."

Another historical novel based in Jewish history, *Sworn Enemies* deals with the kidnaping and forced conversion of Jewish youths for the Czarist army in nineteenth-century Russia. Here sixteen-year-old Aaron is betrayed by a fellow Jew, Zev, and rousted into the Czar's army. Ironically, Zev is also caught, and the two will again confront one another as they each attempt to escape. A *Kirkus Reviews* critic called *Sworn Enemies* a "harrowing, thought-provoking, skillfully written novel about a past whose vile legacy persists." Writing in the *New York Times Book Review,* Roger Sutton asserted that "Matas is a good storyteller, and her novel will tell young readers about a less than familiar aspect of Jewish history." Also noting the author's facility with the format of historical fiction, Sutton commented that she "makes the time-travel jump easily . . . , and if the questions she poses sometimes seem equally easy, then she may help her readers to ask the same questions in their own lives."

Matas presents an uncommon perspective on the war between the states in *The War Within: A Novel of the Civil War.* Here readers are introduced to the U.S. Civil War years through the consciousness of thirteen-year-old Hannah Green, the daughter of a Jewish merchant living in Mississippi. After Union General Ulysses S. Grant occupies the area and orders all Jews to leave, Hannah and her family move north to Illinois, where the girl faces deep questions about bigotry, racism, and her own values as she experiences both the sting of anti-Semitism and the shame of her own racist attitudes. In *Booklist* Carolyn Phelan appreciated the novel for addressing complex issues but suggested that there are "perhaps too many" themes for a novel of its scope. Still, Phelan added, readers of *The War Within* will appreciate the book's "riptide of action" and its "appealing cast of strong, vivid characters," as well as its "decidedly different slant" on the Civil War experience. In *Kliatt* Deborah Kaplan cited Matas's use of period documents, writing that in its focus on "a little-known part

Cover of **Of Two Minds,** *an imaginative fantasy novel coauthored by Matas and Perry Nodelman.* (Illustration © 1998 by Scholastic, Inc. Reproduced by permission.)

of American history," the novel's "focus on the development of personal conscience is inspiring."

Geared for younger readers, Matas's chapter book *The Lost Locket* finds eight-year-old Roz searching for a stolen family heirloom in a "delightful and suspenseful book," according to *Canadian Literature* critic Wytenbroek. Her "Rosie" series, which include *Rosie in New York City: Gotcha!*, *Rosie in Chicago: Play Ball!*, and *Rosie in Los Angeles: Action!*, a young Russian-Jewish immigrant travels to several U.S. cities as her father pursues his career during the early 1900s. Describing *Rosie in Chicago,* which finds the twelve year old disguising herself as a young man to help out her uncle Abe's shorthanded baseball team, Susan Shaver wrote in *School Library Journal* that Matas treats younger readers to "a fun book full of drama, excitement, suspense, and life lessons." Collaborating with Perry Nodelman, Matas has also written the fantasy novels *Of Two Minds* and *More Minds,* which focus on the kingdom of Gepeth and the extraordinary mental powers of Princess Lenora. In a review for *Books in Canada,* Pat Barclay described *Of Two Minds* as "an allegory about democracy vs. dictatorship and what happens when a people gives too much power to its leader."

Based on Matas's family history, *Sparks Fly Upward* introduces twelve-year-old Rebecca Bernstein, who lives with her extended family in rural Saskatchewan until a fire forces a move to Winnipeg. When her father has trouble finding work in the new city and sends Rebecca to live with a Christian foster family, the girl confronts anti-Semitism but also finds a best friend in the family's daughter, Sophie. A scuffle within the foster family eventually prompts Mr. Bernstein to forbid the friendship, forcing Rebecca to discover for herself the value of friendship and loyalty. In *School Library Journal* Kathleen Isaacs enjoyed the story's unusual setting, writing that *Sparks Fly Upward* "should appeal to middle-grade readers, especially girls."

"For me," Matas related in an interview with coauthor Nodelman in *Canadian Children's Literature,* "the greatest pleasure is to read a book that is compelling *and* substantive. . . . But I'm not trying to preach a message—quite the opposite. I'm trying to open a question, a dialogue, give my reader food for thought." "My first goal in writing is to tell a good story," she once observed. "I had such pleasure from the experience of reading when I was a child that if I could give that experience to the young people reading my books that would be enough. (In Hebrew there is a word, *Dayenu,* which means 'it would have been enough.') But I'm afraid my ambitions don't stop there. I also want to challenge my readers and make them think. I suppose that is why I love to write for young people, whose minds are still open, who have not yet decided everything yet. And finally, I like to write about topics that have not been written about before because I think that makes the reading experience even more exciting for the reader." Indeed, posing difficult questions is at the

heart of Matas's fiction. As she concluded in her interview for *Canadian Children's Literature,* "the world is a complex place and . . . what I'm trying to do is present this world, in all its complexities, to my readers. And hope they are both challenged *and* entertained."

Biographical and Critical Sources

BOOKS

Children's Literature Review, Volume 52, Gale (Detroit, MI), 1999.
St. James Guide to Young Adults Writers, 2nd edition, St. James Press (Detroit, MI), 1999.

PERIODICALS

Booklist, September 1, 1994, Hazel Rochman, review of *The Burning Time,* p. 35; April 1, 1996, review of *After the War,* p. 1361; April 1, 2001, Carolyn Phelan, review of *The War Within: A Novel of the Civil War,* p. 1484; April 1, 2002, Hazel Rochman, review of *Sparks Fly Upward,* p. 1328; May 15, 2003, John Peters, review of *Rosie in New York City: Gotcha!,* p. 1666; March 1, 2007, Hazel Rochman, review of *The Whirlwind,* p. 74; August, 2007, Hazel Rochman, review of *Past Crimes,* p. 64.
Books in Canada, March, 1987, Mary Ainslie Smith, "Back to the Future," p. 37; April, 1988, Welwyn Wilton Katz, review of *Lisa,* p. 36; December, 1994, Pat Barclay, review of *Of Two Minds,* p. 57; May, 2002, *Footsteps in the Snow: The Red River Diary of Isobel Scott,* p. 43.
Bulletin of the Center for Children's Books, May, 1993, Betsy Hearne, review of *Daniel's Story,* p. 289; April, 1996, Betsy Hearne, review of *After the War,* pp. 271-272; July, 2002, review of *Sparks Fly Upward,* p. 409; July-August, 2007, Hope Morrison, review of *The Whirlwind,* p. 477.
Canadian Literature, spring, 1996, J.R. Wytenbroek, reviews of *Lisa, The Lost Locket,* and *Sworn Enemies,* p. 108.
Canadian Review of Materials, May, 1992, Gordon Heasley, review of *The Race,* p. 168; September, 1993, Anne Louise Mahoney, review of *Daniel's Story,* p. 153.
Five Owls, January-February, 1991, review of *Code Name Kris,* p. 61; September 6, 2002, review of *Footsteps in the Snow;* September 19, 2003, review of *Rosie in New York City.*
Horn Book, May-June, 1989, Mary M. Burns, review of *Lisa's War,* pp. 377-378.
Kirkus Reviews, January 1, 1993, review of *Sworn Enemies,* p. 66.
Kliatt, November, 2002, Deborah Kaplan, review of *The War Within,* p. 20; July, 2007, Marissa Elliott, review of *The Whirlwind,* p. 26; September, 2007, Amanda MacGregor, review of *Past Crimes,* p. 24.
New York Times Book Review, April 11, 1993, Roger Sutton, review of *Sworn Enemies,* p. 30.

Publishers Weekly, February 10, 1989, review of *Lisa's War,* p. 73; April 27, 1998, review of *Greater than Angels,* p. 68; June 23, 2003, review of *Rosie in New York City,* p. 67.

Quill & Quire, October, 1989, Frieda Wishinsky, review of *Jesper,* p. 14; October, 1991, Anne Louise Mahoney, review of *The Race,* p. 35; February, 1993, Kenneth Oppel, review of *Daniel's Story,* p. 35.

Resource Links, February, 2004, Jill McClay, review of *Rosie in New York City,* p. 19; June, 2005, Anne Hatcher, review of *Rosie in Los Angeles: Action!,* p. 34; February, 2003, Jill McClay, review of *Footsteps in the Snow,* p. 13; April, 2004, Mavis Holder, review of *Rosie in Chicago: Play Ball!,* p. 23; October, 2005, Gail Lennon, review of *The Dark Clone,* p. 35; February, 2006, Suzanne Finkelstein, review of *Turned Away: The World War II Diary of Devorah Bernstein,* p. 26, and Joanne de Groot, review of *Jesper,* p. 49; February, 2007, Margaret Mackey, review of *Past Crimes,* p. 39; April, 2007, Margaret Mackey, review of *The Whirlwind,* p. 45; December, 2007, Frances Stanford, review of *The Burning Time,* p. 40.

School Library Journal, May, 1996, Robyn Nicoline Ryan, review of *After the War,* p. 135; March, 1999, Cyrisse Jaffee, review of *In My Enemy's House,* p. 212; June, 2001, Crystal Faris, review of *The War Within,* p. 152; March, 2002, Kathleen Isaacs, review of *Sparks Fly Upward,* p. 234; August, 2003, Sharon R. Pearce, review of *Rosie in New York City,* p. 163; February, 2004, Susan Shaver, review of *Rosie in Chicago,* p. 149; March, 2004, Terrie Dorio, review of *Rosie in Los Angeles,* p. 218; May, 2007, Donna Rosenblum, review of *The Whirlwind,* p. 138.

Voice of Youth Advocates, June, 1989, Marian Rafal, review of *Lisa's War,* p. 104; October, 1994, review of *The Burning Time,* p. 210.

ONLINE

Carol Matas Home Page, http://www.carolmatas.com (October 13, 2008).

*   *   *

MATTHEWS, Elizabeth 1978-

Personal

Born 1978; children: Gabe. *Education:* Rhode Island School of Design, degree.

Addresses

Home—Cumberland, RI.

Career

Writer and illustrator. Designer of greeting cards.

Writings

SELF-ILLUSTRATED

Precious Treasure: The Story of Patrick, foreword by Kimberly Hahn, Emmaus Road (Steubenville, OH), 2002.

Different like Coco, Candlewick (Cambridge, MA), 2007.

Sidelights

Elizabeth Matthews got her start as an illustrator by designing greeting cards. She attended the Rhode Island School of Design, a school well known for producing picture-book talent, and with *Different like Coco,* she proved that the school's reputation is well founded. In her engaging illustrated biography for young children, Matthews introduces famous early twentieth-century French fashion designer Coco Chanel and her rags-to-riches story.

Gabrielle "Coco" Chanel was born and, left parentless at age twelve, she learned to sew at an orphanage. Because she was unable to afford the expensive clothing of society ladies, Coco designed a whole new line of fashion, getting rid of corsets and full skirts and instead tailoring her clothing to women with thin builds. "Matthews' writing style is right on the mark, as breezy and appealing as Coco herself," wrote Ilene Cooper in *Booklist.* Lauren Adams, writing for *Horn Book,* commented that the author/illustrator's "amusing pen-and-ink drawings capture Coco's bearing and style," and Kathleen Whalin recommended *Different like Coco* to *School Library Journal* readers on the strength of Matthews' "elegant pen-and-ink and watercolor cartoons." A *Kirkus Reviews* contributor predicted that "young readers will love the sweep and detail of the images."

Noting that Chanel's story is more complicated than the "necessarily simplified version" presented in Matthews'

Elizabeth Matthews captures the optimism of talented French fashion designer Coco Chanel in her self-illustrated picture book **Different like Coco.** (Copyright © 2007 by Elizabeth Matthews. Reproduced by permission of the publisher, Candlewick Press, Inc., Somerville, MA.)

biography, *New York Times Book Review* contributor Krystyna Poray Goddu felt that, "While appealing, *Different like Coco* is misleading in its lighthearted portrayal of a figure who was every bit as sharp, arrogant and lonely as she was defiant and glamorous." According to the critic, Matthews focuses on a simple moral of embracing differences rather than explaining the dramatic impact Chanel made on women's fashion. A *Publishers Weekly* critic felt, however, that while Matthews "saves some of the juiciest tidbits" for the timeline that appends her story, *Different like Coco* provides young readers with a "snapshot of European history through one extraordinary woman's life."

Biographical and Critical Sources

PERIODICALS

Booklist, March 1, 2007, Ilene Cooper, review of *Different like Coco,* p. 83.

Horn Book, March-April, 2007, Lauren Adams, review of *Different like Coco,* p. 214.

Kirkus Reviews, January 15, 2007, review of *Different like Coco,* p. 77.

New York Times Book Review, June 3, 2007, Krystyna Poray Goddu, review of *Different like Coco,* p. 35.

People, December 24, 2007, review of *Different like Coco,* p. 55.

Publishers Weekly, March 12, 2007, review of *Different like Coco,* p. 57.

School Library Journal, March, 2007, Kathleen Whalin, review of *Different like Coco,* p. 180.

ONLINE

One Minute Book Reviews Web site, http://oneminute bookreviews.wordpress.com/ (October 21, 2007), Janice Harayda, review of *Different like Coco.**

*   *   *

McKIMMIE, Chris

Personal

Born in Perth, Western Australia, Australia.

Addresses

Home—Paddington, Queensland, Australia. *E-mail*—cmckimmie@optusnet.com.au.

Career

Writer, illustrator, educator, graphic designer, and artist. Queensland College of Art at Griffith University, Queensland, Australia, founder of illustration program. Staff designer for Australian Broadcast Corporation, Austra-

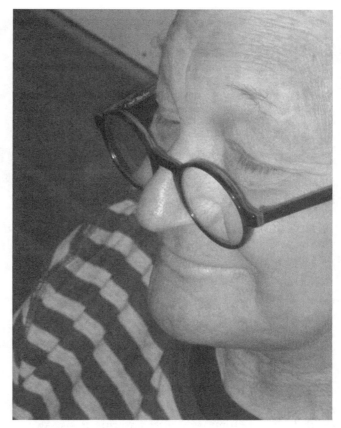

Chris McKimmie (Photo courtesy of Chris McKimmie.)

lian National Parks and Wildlife Service, and University of Western Australia Press. Production designer for films, including *Stations* (short) and *Australian Dream.* *Exhibitions:* Work exhibited in galleries, including at Gallery 482, Brisbane, Queensland, Australia.

Writings

SELF-ILLUSTRATED

Brian Banana Duck Sunshine Yellow, Allen & Unwin (East Melbourne, Victoria, Australia), 2006.

Maisie Moo and Invisible Lucy, Allen & Unwin (East Melbourne, Victoria, Australia), 2007.

Special Kev, Allen & Unwin (East Melbourne, Victoria, Australia), 2008.

Also author of self-illustrated books *One Rainy Day, The Shape I'm In, One Day, The Painted Bird, Two Friends,* and *Apple to Zoo.* Contributor of illustrations to periodicals, including *Graphis Annual.*

Biographical and Critical Sources

ONLINE

Allen & Unwin Web site, http://www.allenandunwin.com/ (October 10, 2008), "Chris McKimmie."

Chris McKimmie Home Page, http://www.chrismckimmie.com (October 10, 2008).

Preschool Entertainment Web site, http://www.preschool entertainment.com/ (October 10, 2008), Magdalena Ball, interview with McKimmie.

*   *   *

McNEAL, Laura

Personal

Born in Tempe, AZ; married Tom McNeal (a writer), 1993; children: two. *Education:* Brigham Young University, B.A.; Syracuse University, M.A. (fiction writing).

Addresses

Home—Fallbrook, CA.

Career

Has taught middle-school and high-school English in Salt Lake City, UT; former journalist and writer.

Awards, Honors

(With husband, Tom McNeal) California Book Award for juvenile literature, 1999, for *Crooked;* PEN award, 2003, for *Zipped.*

Writings

WITH HUSBAND, TOM MCNEAL

The Dog Who Lost His Bob (juvenile fiction), illustrated by John Sandford, Albert Whitman (Morton Grove, IL), 1996.

Crooked (young-adult novel), Alfred A. Knopf (New York, NY), 1999.

Zipped (young-adult novel), Alfred A. Knopf (New York, NY), 2003.

Crushed (young-adult novel), Alfred A. Knopf (New York, NY), 2006.

The Decoding of Lana Morris (young-adult novel), Alfred A. Knopf (New York, NY), 2007.

OTHER

Short stories included in anthology *The Bigger the Better, the Tighter the Sweater.* Contributor to periodicals, including *San Diego Reader.*

Sidelights

For Sidelights, see entry on husband, Tom McNeal, elsewhere in this volume.

Biographical and Critical Sources

PERIODICALS

Booklist, September 1, 1996, Stephanie Zvirin, review of *The Dog Who Lost His Bob,* p. 144; October 15, 1999, Debbie Carton, review of *Crooked,* p. 429; January 1, 2006, Jennifer Mattson, review of *Crushed,* p. 84; April 1, 2007, Jennifer Hubert, review of *The Decoding of Lana Morris,* p. 41.

Bulletin of the Center for Children's Books, February, 2006, Deborah Stevenson, review of *Crushed,* p. 275; July-August, 2007, Deborah Stevenson, review of *The Decoding of Lana Morris,* p. 478.

Horn Book, November, 1999, Lauren Adams, review of *Crooked,* p. 743; January 1, 2006, Jennifer Mattson, review of *Crushed,* p. 84.

Kirkus Reviews, February 15, 2003, review of *Zipped,* p. 312; December 15, 2005, review of *Crushed,* p. 1325; April 15, 2007, review of *The Decoding of Lana Morris.*

Kliatt, January, 2005, Claire Rosser, review of *Zipped,* p. 15; January, 2006, Claire Rosser, review of *Crushed,* p. 10; May, 2007, Myrna Marler, review of *The Decoding of Lana Morris,* p. 16.

Publishers Weekly, January 17, 2000, review of *Crooked,* p. 57; February 10, 2003, review of *Zipped,* p. 188; February 6, 2006, review of *Crushed,* p. 71; May 7, 2007, review of *The Decoding of Lana Morris,* p. 61.

School Library Journal, February, 2003, Miranda Doyle, review of *Zipped,* p. 142; January, 2006, Karen Hoth, review of *Crushed,* p. 138; June, 2007, Geri Diorio, review of *The Decoding of Lana Morris,* p. 154.

Voice of Youth Advocates, February, 2006, Lois Parker-Hennion, review of *Crushed,* p. 488; August, 2007, Marla K. Unruh, review of *The Decoding of Lana Morris,* p. 260.

ONLINE

Tom and Laura McNeal Home Page, http://mcnealbooks.com (October 20, 2008).

San Diego Reader, http://www.sdreader.com/ (January 26, 2006), Laura McNeal, "A Conversation with the Author."*

*   *   *

McNEAL, Tom

Personal

Born in Santa Ana, CA; married Laura Rhoton (a writer), 1993; children: two. *Education:* University of California, Berkeley, B.A. (English); University of California, Irvine, M.F.A. (creative writing).

Addresses

Home—Fallbrook, CA.

Career

Writer. Former teacher; Stanford University, Stanford, CA, former Jones lecturer in creative writing.

Awards, Honors

Wallace Stegner fellow, Stanford University; California Book Award for fiction and James H. Michener Award for fiction, both for *Goodnight Nebraska;* with wife, Laura McNeal: California Book Award for juvenile literature, 1999, for *Crooked;* PEN award, 2003, for *Zipped.*

Writings

Goodnight, Nebraska (novel), Random House (New York, NY), 1998.

Work represented in anthologies, including *The Best American Short Stories, O. Henry Prize Stories,* and *Pushcart Prize Stories.* Contributor of short stories to periodicals, including *Atlantic Monthly, Playboy, Zoetrope,* and *Redbook.*

WITH WIFE, LAURA MCNEAL

The Dog Who Lost His Bob (juvenile fiction), illustrated by John Sandford, Albert Whitman (Morton Grove, IL), 1996.
Crooked (young-adult novel), Alfred A. Knopf (New York, NY), 1999.
Zipped (young-adult novel), Alfred A. Knopf (New York, NY), 2003.
Crushed (young-adult novel), Alfred A. Knopf (New York, NY), 2006.
The Decoding of Lana Morris (young-adult novel), Alfred A. Knopf (New York, NY), 2007.

Adaptations

McNeal's short story "What Happened to Tully" was adapted by Hilary Birmingham as the award-winning independent film *Tully.*

Sidelights

The author of the award-winning novel *Goodnight, Nebraska,* Tom McNeal is best known to teen readers through the books he coauthors with his wife, Laura McNeal. In their novel *Crooked,* the title of which is a reference to the protagonist's nose, Clara Wilson loses her best friend and her mother, who walks out and leaves her with her father. Clara becomes friends with Amos MacKenzie, whose own father is ill and whose mother has found religion. Amos intervenes when hoodlums Charles and Eddie Tripp attempt an act of vandalism and is beaten by them with a baseball bat, thereby becoming a hero. Clara becomes infatuated with the dangerous Eddie, who competes with Amos for her

affection. *Horn Book* reviewer Lauren Adams wrote of Clara and Amos: "The strands of their stories are cleverly intertwined in this well-plotted and engaging novel." "The book's strength lies in the interactions between Clara and Amos and their relationships with their respective families," observed a *Publishers Weekly* contributor.

Set in the same town as *Crooked, Zipped* introduces Mick Nichols, a teen whose mom left him and his father years earlier. Mike has a wonderful relationship with his young stepmother, Nora, until he discovers e-mails indicating that she is having an affair. Mick cares for classmate Lisa, who is romantically interested in a Mormon missionary, and he also has a friendship with a somewhat older female college student. When Mick learns the identity of Nora's lover, he attempts to punish the young man through an act of vandalism, but he eventually learns that the adults in his life, as well as his peers, are experiencing complex problems of their own. The title of the McNeals' story refers to the way in which all the elements of the story are connected. *School Library Journal* critic Miranda Doyle wrote of *Crooked:* "Mick's father and stepmother are fully fleshed out characters, not stereotypes." "Themes of good and evil and the gray zone in between, of betrayal, of forgiveness, of love, of tolerance, abound," added Claire Rosser appreciatively in *Kliatt.*

Praised by a *Publishers Weekly* critic as "engaging and complex," *Crushed* finds Audrey Reed transferring from her exclusive private school to Jemison High. Here the pampered teen begins a romance with Wickham Hill, a smooth-talking and confident classmate who convinces Audrey to help him cheat on a test. Clyde Mumsford is a shy boy who also likes Audrey and whose mother is dying at home. Other adults in this story suffer setbacks, as well, including Audrey's father, whose failing business leads to their losing the family home. One character whose identity is not revealed until the end of the story is the editor of a gossip newspaper that reveals the secrets of the characters, including the indiscretion of a teacher. The story addresses the issues of cliques, bullying, and betrayal. Rosser noted in another *Kliatt* review that *Crushed* is similar to previous young-adult books by the McNeals in that "the adults are characters the reader gets to know and care about as well." "Readers will sympathize with these individuals, some of whom mature, and some of whom do not," attested Karen Hoth in a *School Library Journal* of the novel.

In a break from their usual fare, the McNeals inject an element of fantasy into *The Decoding of Lana Morris.* Placed into the foster system as a consequence of her mother's drug addiction, sixteen-year-old Lana moves to small-town Nebraska to live with the Winters, a childless couple. The Winters have opened their home to other foster children, and Lana is distressed to finds herself sharing a home with several special-needs children. Although she soon builds friendships with her fellow fosters, her foster mother shows herself to be

ZIPPED

Laura and Tom McNeal

Cover of Zipped, *a young-adult novel by the husband-and-wife writing team of Tom and Laura McNeal.* (Illustration copyright © 2003 by Laura and Tom McNeal. Used by permission of Alfred A. Knopf, an imprint of Random House Children's Books, a division of Random House, Inc.)

cold and unlovable, and Lana longs to escape. When a friend takes her to a quirky thrift store in town, she buys an old drawing kit, and when she uses it she realizes that everything she draws on the old paper actually happens—but not always in expected ways. Realizing that there can be unforeseen consequences to wishes, the lonely teen must now reexamine her desires and her motivations, in the light of this new power. While noting that the novel attempts to address a large number of issues, a *Kirkus Reviews* writer concluded that the Mc-Neals' "writing is lovely and the characters are real people who elicit genuine feelings from readers." "If the reader can suspend disbelief," *The Decoding of Lana Morris* "is a good story about finding [one's] self and the essential sweetness of life among the dross that surrounds it," concluded Myrna Marler in *Kliatt.* Citing the "distinct and thoughtfully crafted voices" in *The Decoding of Lana Morris, Voice of Youth Advocates* reviewer Marla K. Unruh added that the McNeals' story "reveal[s] zany teen humor, adolescent longings, adult treachery, and youthful belief that wrongs should be righted."

Tom McNeal's solo novel, *Goodnight, Nebraska* is set in a town very much like one the author himself lived in as a boy. The protagonist, Randall Hunsacker, is a young man who leaves his past behind in Salt Lake City when he settles in Goodnight. There the powerful football player and mechanic meets and marries Marcy Lockhardt and attempts to mend his life. *Booklist* contributor Ted Leventhal felt that the end result—of Randall's isolation and ignorance—is portrayed by McNeal much as it is in Truman Capote's *In Cold Blood,* but added that "McNeal's mythical small town remains warmly compelling" and the "storytelling is magnificent."

Biographical and Critical Sources

PERIODICALS

Booklist, September 1, 1996, Stephanie Zvirin, review of *The Dog Who Lost His Bob,* p. 144; February 1, 1998, Ted Leventhal, review of *Goodnight, Nebraska,* p. 899; October 15, 1999, Debbie Carton, review of *Crooked,* p. 429; January 1, 2006, Jennifer Mattson, review of *Crushed,* p. 84; April 1, 2007, Jennifer Hubert, review of *The Decoding of Lana Morris,* p. 41.

Bulletin of the Center for Children's Books, February, 2006, Deborah Stevenson, review of *Crushed,* p. 275; July-August, 2007, Deborah Stevenson, review of *The Decoding of Lana Morris,* p. 478.

Horn Book, November, 1999, Lauren Adams, review of *Crooked,* p. 743.

Kirkus Reviews, February 15, 2003, review of *Zipped,* p. 312; December 15, 2005, review of *Crushed,* p. 1325; April 15, 2007, review of *The Decoding of Lana Morris.*

Kliatt, January, 2005, Claire Rosser, review of *Zipped,* p. 15; January, 2006, Claire Rosser, review of *Crushed,* p. 10; May, 2007, Myrna Marler, review of *The Decoding of Lana Morris,* p. 16.

Library Journal, January, 1998, Charles Michaud, review of *Goodnight, Nebraska,* p. 143.

Publishers Weekly, January 5, 1998, review of *Goodnight, Nebraska,* p. 58; January 17, 2000, review of *Crooked,* p. 57; February 10, 2003, review of *Zipped,* p. 188; February 6, 2006, review of *Crushed,* p. 71; May 7, 2007, review of *The Decoding of Lana Morris,* p. 61.

School Library Journal, February, 2003, Miranda Doyle, review of *Zipped,* p. 142; January, 2006, Karen Hoth, review of *Crushed,* p. 138; June, 2007, Geri Diorio, review of *The Decoding of Lana Morris,* p. 154.

Voice of Youth Advocates, February, 2006, Lois Parker-Hennion, review of *Crushed,* p. 488; August, 2007, Marla K. Unruh, review of *The Decoding of Lana Morris,* p. 260.

ONLINE

Tom and Laura McNeal Home Page, http://mcnealbooks. com (October 20, 2008).

Nebraska Center for Writers Web site, http://mockingbird. creighton.edu/ (July 3, 2006), brief biography of McNeal.*

*   *   *

MECHLING, Lauren 1978(?)-

Personal

Born c. 1978, in New York, NY.

Addresses

Home—Brooklyn, NY. *E-mail*—authors@socialclimber books.com.

Career

Writer.

Writings

YOUNG-ADULT NOVELS

(With Laura Moser) *The Rise and Fall of a 10th-Grade Social Climber,* Houghton Mifflin Books (Boston, MA), 2005.
(With Laura Moser) *All Q, No A: More Tales of a 10th-Grade Social Climber,* Houghton Mifflin Books (Boston, MA), 2006.
(With Laura Moser) *Foreign Exposure: The Social Climber Abroad,* Houghton Mifflin Books (Boston, MA), 2007.
Dream Girl, Delacorte Press (New York, NY), 2008.

Contributor to periodicals, including *Seventeen, Jane, New York Times,* and the *Wall Street Journal.*

Sidelights

Lauren Mechling and Laura Moser are coauthors of a trio of young-adult novels that focus on Mimi Schulman, a high-school sophomore attempting to navigate the tricky terrain of her posh, new, private school. Although *The Rise and Fall of a 10th-Grade Social Climber, All Q, No A: More Tales of a 10th-Grade Social Climber,* and *Foreign Exposure: The Social Climber Abroad* form a series, they can be read as stand-alone titles, as each one features a distinct, self-contained plot.

Moser and Mechling, friends since college, conceived Mimi's adventures when they compared their own high-school years: Mechling attended an expensive private school in Manhattan while Moser grew up in Houston before relocating to the East Coast. In addition to working with her friend on the "Social Climber" books, Mechling is also the author of the young-adult novel *Dream Girls,* a mystery novel in which a teen clairvoy-

ant overlooks her unusual gift while attempting to navigate romance and the social order at her new private school. In *Publishers Weekly* a reviewer praised *Dream Girl* for its "lively awareness of girl-on-girl dynamics," while Myrna Marler concluded in *Kliatt* that, with its "odd assortment of quirky but likable characters," Mechling's novel is "fast-paced and good escape reading."

The Rise and Fall of a 10th-Grade Social Climber starts with Mimi's move from Houston to Manhattan to live with her newly divorced father. There the teen joins another Houston replant, Sam, at the exclusive Baldwin High. Joining Baldwin's top girl clique, the Coolies, now becomes Mimi's goal. However, her decision demands reconsideration when she realizes that the Coolies have deep-seated problems that they mask by drinking and using drugs. A budding journalist, Mimi keeps a diary of the group's parties, and eventually the diary falls into the wrong hands. In *All Q, No A,* Mimi hopes for a better avenue for her writing talents by agreeing to interview one of the school's wealthy patrons. Her interview subject dodges her questions, however, and

Cover of Lauren Mechling and Laura Moser's humorous teen novel **The Rise and Fall of a 10th-Grade Social Climber.** (Cover photography by PBNJ/Corbis. Copyright © 2005 by Lauren Mechling and Laura Moser. All rights reserved. Reprinted by permission of Houghton Mifflin Harcourt Publishing Company.)

when she investigates the story Mimi unearths unflattering information that brings her into conflict with school administrators and results in her expulsion from Baldwin High. Summer vacation finally arrives in *Foreign Exposure,* wherein Mimi's troubles continue. Sent to visit her mother in Berlin, the girl is forced into a horrific baby-sitting job, but not for long. On her own initiative, she joins a school friend in London and nets an internship at a celebrity tabloid, with unforeseen consequences.

According to several reviewers, Moser and Mechling's "Social Climber" series offers a frank portrait of teen life within the economically privileged class. Commenting on *The Rise and Fall of a 10th-Grade Social Climber* in *Booklist,* Debbie Carton judged that he details about parties, clothing, and fashion trends make the story "an irresistible read" about modern teen which the coauthors have "captured to perfection." In her *Kliatt* review of *All Q, No A,* Amanda MacGregor noted that "Mimi grows as a character and feels much more genuine and appealing." According to *School Library Journal* contributor Heather E. Miller, in the second series installment "friendships and self-worth are the center of attention." "Mimi brings unexpected depth to the story," MacGregor added, noting that the teen narrator "continues to explore who she is and what she wants."

Biographical and Critical Sources

PERIODICALS

Booklist, April 15, 2005, Debbie Carton, review of *The Rise and Fall of a 10th-Grade Social Climber,* p. 1449.

Kirkus Reviews, May 1, 2005, review of *The Rise and Fall of a 10th-Grade Social Climber,* p. 543; June 1, 2008, review of *Dream Girl.*

Kliatt, November, 2006, Amanda MacGregor, review of *All Q, No A: More Tales of a 10th-Grade Social Climber,* p. 22; July, 2007, review of *Foreign Exposure: The Social Climber Abroad,* p. 27; July, 2008, Myrna Marler, review of *Dream Girl,* p. 19.

New York Time Book Review, September 14, 2008, review of *Dream Girl,* p. 17.

Publishers Weekly, July 21, 2008, review of *Dream Girl,* p. 161.

School Library Journal, June, 2005, Jennifer Feigelman, review of *The Rise and Fall of a 10th-Grade Social Climber,* p. 166; September, 2006, Heather E. Miller, review of *All Q, No A,* p. 212; June, 2007, Rhona Campbell, review of *Foreign Exposure,* p. 154.

Voice of Youth Advocates, June, 2005, Lynn Evarts, review of *The Rise and Fall of a 10th-Grade Social Climber,* p. 134.

ONLINE

Boston.com, http://www.boston.com/ (June 11, 2006), Kate Bolick, interview with Laura Moser and Lauren Mechling.

Houghton Mifflin Books Web site, http://www.houghton mifflinbooks.com/ (November 5, 2008), "Lauren Mechling."

Social Climber Books Web site, http://www.socialclimber books.com/ (November 5, 2008).*

* * *

MENG, Cece

Personal

Married; children: two children.

Addresses

Home—Santa Cruz, CA. *E-mail*—bookclub4kids@aol. com.

Career

Writer and consultant to small businesses.

Awards, Honors

NAPPA Honor Book designation, 2008, for *The Wonderful Thing about Hiccups.*

Writings

PICTURE BOOKS

The Wonderful Thing about Hiccups, illustrated by Janet Pedersen, Clarion (New York, NY), 2007.

Tough Chicks, illustrated by Melissa Suber, Clarion (New York, NY), 2009.

Biographical and Critical Sources

PERIODICALS

Kirkus Reviews, May 1, 2007, review of *The Wonderful Thing about Hiccups.*

School Library Journal, November, 2007, Linda M. Kenton, review of *The Wonderful Thing about Hiccups,* p. 96.

ONLINE

Cece Meng Home Page, http://www.cecemeng.com (October 10, 2008).*

* * *

MICHAELS, Rune

Personal

Born in Iceland; married. *Education:* Studied psychology at University of Iceland and University of Copenhagen.

Addresses

Home—Reykjavik, Iceland. *E-mail*—rune@rune michaels.com.

Career

Writer.

Writings

Genesis Alpha, Atheneum Books for Young Readers (New York, NY), 2007.
The Reminder, Atheneum Books for Young Readers (New York, NY), 2008.

Sidelights

With *Genesis Alpha,* Icelandic writer Rune Michaels treats readers to a murder mystery with deep philosophical underpinnings. Josh and Max are brothers, but their bond is deeper than that shared by most siblings. Josh was conceived and born specifically to provide the stem cells that could cure Max's terminal cancer. Max survives, and even after he moves away the brothers continue to be close, communicating via the computer game Genesis Alpha. When Max is arrested and accused of a brutal murder of a young woman, Josh tries to piece together what his older brother might have done, and this search leads him to a troubling question: If Josh had never been born and Max had note been cured, would the murdered girl still be alive? Josh also asks himself what role the online game played in the sequence of events in the real world, especially after he discovers that Max met his victim through her interaction in the game.

According to *Kliatt* contributor Michele Winship, *Genesis Alpha* "takes risks by addressing several challenging themes and issues of morality." Some reviewers cited Michaels' ability to address issues related to the power of modern technology in her tightly plotted whodunit. Although *School Library Journal* critic Anthony C. Doyle found the story to be "unbelievable in several places," a *Kirkus Reviews* contributor dubbed *Genesis Alpha* a "fascinating and realistic page-turner" that is "virtually impossible to put down." In *Booklist,* Francis Bradburn called *Genesis Alpha* a "fascinating, troubling thriller."

In her second novel, *The Reminder,* Michaels tells a more conventional story about a teenaged orphan named Daisy—or "Daze"—as the girl's life veers into the paranormal. When she begins hearing her dead mother's voice, Daze is compelled to act on the late woman's behalf, even as she struggles with her own doubts about the supernatural and how her grief might be affecting her subconscious.

Biographical and Critical Sources

PERIODICALS

Booklist, May 1, 2007, Frances Bradburn, review of *Genesis Alpha,* p. 44.
Bulletin of the Center for Children's Books, September, 2007, April Spisak, review of *Genesis Alpha,* p. 41.
Kirkus Reviews, May 1, 2007, review of *Genesis Alpha.*
Kliatt, May, 2007, Michele Winship, review of *Genesis Alpha,* p. 16.
School Library Journal, July, 2007, Anthony C. Doyle, review of *Genesis Alpha,* p. 106.
Voice of Youth Advocates, June, 2007, Michele Winship, review of *Genesis Alpha,* p. 165.

ONLINE

Rune Michaels Home Page, http://www.runemichaels.com (November 7, 2008).
Simon & Schuster Web site, http://www.simonsays.com/ (November 7, 2008), "Rune Michaels."*

*　　*　　*

MOSER, Laura 1978(?)-

Personal

Born c. 1978, in Houston, TX. *Education:* Attended Amherst College.

Addresses

Home—Brooklyn, NY. *E-mail*—authors@socialclimber books.com.

Career

Writer.

Writings

YOUNG-ADULT NOVELS

(With Lauren Mechling) *The Rise and Fall of a 10th-Grade Social Climber,* Houghton Mifflin Books (Boston, MA), 2005.
(With Lauren Mechling) *All Q, No A: More Tales of a 10th-Grade Social Climber,* Houghton Mifflin Books (Boston, MA), 2006.
(With Lauren Mechling) *Foreign Exposure: The Social Climber Abroad,* Houghton Mifflin Books (Boston, MA), 2007.

Also author of a biography of film star Bette Davis. Contributor to periodicals, including *Newsday, Slate,* and London *Guardian.*

Sidelights

For Sidelights essay, see entry on Lauren Mechling, elsewhere in this volume.

Biographical and Critical Sources

PERIODICALS

Booklist, April 15, 2005, Debbie Carton, review of *The Rise and Fall of a 10th-Grade Social Climber,* p. 1449.

Kirkus Reviews, May 1, 2005, review of *The Rise and Fall of a 10th-Grade Social Climber,* p. 543.

Kliatt, November, 2006, Amanda MacGregor, review of *All Q, No A: More Tales of a 10th-Grade Social Climber,* p. 22; July, 2007, review of *Foreign Exposure: The Social Climber Abroad,* p. 27.

School Library Journal, June, 2005, Jennifer Feigelman, review of *The Rise and Fall of a 10th-Grade Social Climber,* p. 166; September, 2006, Heather E. Miller, review of *All Q, No A,* p. 212; June, 2007, Rhona Campbell, review of *Foreign Exposure,* p. 154.

Voice of Youth Advocates, June, 2005, Lynn Evarts, review of *The Rise and Fall of a 10th-Grade Social Climber,* p. 134.

ONLINE

Boston.com, http://www.boston.com/ (June 11, 2006), Kate Bolick, interview with Moser and Lauren Mechling.

Houghton Mifflin Books Web site, http://www.houghton mifflinbooks.com/ (November 5, 2008), "Laura Moser."

Social Climber Books Web site, http://www.socialclimber books.com/ (November 5, 2008).*

*   *   *

MOSZ, Gosia 1972-

Personal

Born 1972, in Poland.

Addresses

Home—Poland; London, England. *Agent*—Jane Feder, 305 E. 24th St., New York, NY 10010. *E-mail*—gosia@ mosz.com.

Career

Illustrator and graphic designer.

Awards, Honors

Notable Children's Book of Jewish Content designation, Association of Jewish Libraries, for *Hanukkah Moon.*

Illustrator

Anna Lewkowska, *Sen o kranie Parakwarii* (title means "The Dream of Paraquaria"), Nasza Ksiegarnia (Warsaw, Poland), 2004.

Lewis Carroll, *Alice's Adventures in Wonderland and through the Looking Glass,* Polish translation by Antoni Marianowicz and Hanna Baltyn, [Poland], 2005.

Joanna Kulmowa, *Niefruwak Ptechotny* (title means "Walker No-Fly"), Nasza Ksiegarnia (Warsaw, Poland), 2005.

Danuta Parlak, *Tajemnicze notesy Tywonki,* Drudzień (Etop, Poland), 2006.

Deborah da Costa, *Hanukkah Moon,* Kar-Ben Publishing (Minneapolis, MN), 2007.

Illustrations included in books by educational publishers, including *Little Red Riding Hood,* for Harcourt School Publishing, and *How the Milky Way Came to Be,* for Macmillan.

Biographical and Critical Sources

PERIODICALS

Booklist, September 15, 2007, Kay Weisman, review of *Hanukkah Moon,* p. 67.

Bulletin of the Center for Children's Books, October, 2007, Elizabeth Bush, review of *Hanukkah Moon,* p. 80.

Publishers Weekly, October 29, 2007, review of *Hanukkah Moon,* p. 56.

ONLINE

Gosia Mosz Home Page, http://www.mosz.com (October 10, 2008).*

N-P

NEWGARDEN, Mark 1959-

Personal

Born August 1, 1959; partner of Megan Montague Cash (an author and illustrator). *Education:* School of Visual Arts (New York, NY), B.F.A., 1982.

Addresses

Office—Laffpix, Inc., 18 Havemeyer St., Brooklyn, NY 11211. *E-mail*—mark@laffpix.com.

Career

Illustrator, cartoonist, and visual artist. Topps Co., creator of "Garbage Pail Kids" and numerous bubble-gum card series 1984-91; novelty and toy designer; freelance creative consultant; writer and director of animated online films; creator of programming for Nickelodeon, Cartoon Network, and others. Instructor at School of Visual Arts and Parsons School of Art, New York, NY. *Exhibitions:* Work exhibited at Smithsonian Institute, Washington, DC; Cooper-Hewitt Museum, New York, NY; Brooklyn Museum, Brooklyn, NY; Museum of Television and Radio, New York, NY; and Institute of Contemporary Arts, London, England.

Awards, Honors

Named among Faces to Watch, *Entertainment Weekly,* 1992; *Print* magazine Interaction 2001 and Interaction 2002 honors; ASIFA-East award, 2001; Art Director's Club of New York award, 2001; Bronze award, *ID* magazine Interactive Media Awards, 2001; Silver award, Broadcast Design Award International 2001; First Place Gold Medal, Society of Illustrators' Original Art show, 2007, and WAPB Award for illustration, 2008, both for *Bob-Wow Bugs a Bug.*

Writings

"BOW-WOW" SERIES; PICTURE BOOKS

(With Megan Cash) *Bow-Wow Bugs a Bug,* Harcourt (Orlando, FL), 2007.

(With Megan Cash) *Bow-Wow Nabs by Number,* Harcourt (Orlando, FL), 2007.
(With Megan Cash) *Bow-Wow Gets Lunch,* Harcourt (Orlando, FL), 2007.
(With Megan Cash) *Bow-Wow Hears Things,* Harcourt (Orlando, FL), 2008.
(With Megan Cash) *Bow-Wow Attracts Opposites,* Harcourt (Orlando, FL), 2008.
(With Megan Cash) *Bow-Wow Twelve Months Running,* Harcourt (Orlando, FL), 2009.
(With Megan Cash) *Bow-Wow's Colorful Life,* Harcourt (Orlando, FL), 2009.

OTHER

(With PictureBox, Inc.) *Cheap Laffs: The Art of the Novelty Item,* photographs by Michael Smelling, Harry Abrams (New York, NY), 2004.
We All Die Alone (collected comics and stories), Fantagraphics (Seattle, WA), 2006.

Author of weekly comic strip "Mark Newgarden," syndicated 1988-91. Contributor of drawings and comics to numerous periodicals, including *New York Times, Village Voice, Rolling Stone, Esquire, Nickelodeon, McSweeny's,* and *Raw.*

Biographical and Critical Sources

BOOKS

Dooley, Michael, and Steve Heller, *The Education of a Comics Artist,* Allworth Press, 2005.
Brunetti, Ivan, *An Anthology of Graphic Fiction,* Yale University Press (New Haven, CT), 2006.

PERIODICALS

Blab, summer, 1989, Monte Beauchamp, "Garbage, Gum, and Lawsuits" (interview), p. 117.

Booklist, December 15, 2005, Ray Olson, review of *We All Die Alone,* p. 12.

Comics Journal, August, 1993, "Confessions of a Post-Modern Nancy Boy" (interview), p. 74.

Creem, May, 1992, Bill Forman, "Sticker Shock," p. 28.

Entertainment Weekly, January 31. 1992, "Faces to Watch," p. 34.

Horn Book, July-August, 2007, Christine M. Heppermann, review of *Bow-Wow Bugs a Bug,* p. 383.

International Design, January-February, 2006, "The I.D. Forty: Who Deserves More Attention?"

Kirkus Reviews, May 1, 2007, review of *Bow-Wow Bugs a Bug.*

New York Times, March 19, 2006, Mark Dery, "A Cartoonist in Despair? Now That's Funny."

Publishers Weekly, June 11, 2007, review of *Bow-Wow Bugs a Bug,* p. 58; December 19, 2005, review of *We All Die Alone,* p. 47.

School Library Journal, July, 2007, Rachel Kamin, review of *Bow-Wow Bugs a Bug,* p. 82.

ONLINE

Bow-Wow Books Web site, http://www.bow-wowbooks. com/ (October 10, 2008).

Mark Newgarden Home Page, http://www.laffpix.com (October 10, 2008).

*   *   *

NOYES, Deborah 1965-
(Deborah Noyes Wayshak)

Personal

Born September 13, 1965, in Carmel, CA; daughter of Peter (in the military and a police officer) and Valerie (in the service industry and a homemaker) Noyes; married Courtney Wayshak (a teacher); children: Clyde, Michaela. *Ethnicity:* "British Isles, mainly." *Education:* University of Massachusetts, B.A. (English), 1987; Vermont College, M.F.A. (writing), 1993. *Politics:* Democrat. *Religion:* "Raised Catholic." *Hobbies and other interests:* Black-and-white photography and printmaking, nature and hiking, traveling.

Addresses

Home—Somerville, MA. *Agent*—Jill Grinberg, Jill Grinberg Literary Management, 244 5th Ave., 11th Fl., New York, NY 10001. *E-mail*—deborahnoyes@gmail.com.

Career

Franklin Park Zoo, Boston, MA, zookeeper, 1990; *Boston Review,* Boston, managing editor, 1991-92; freelance writer, 1992—; Candlewick Press, Cambridge, MA, copywriter, 1997-2000, editor, 2000—. Western New England College, Woburn, MA, adjunct lecturer, 1994-2002; Emerson College, Boston, adjunct lecturer, 2003—.

Member

Society of Children's Book Writers and Illustrators.

Awards, Honors

Best Book for Young Adults selection, American Library Association (ALA), Books for the Teen Age selection, New York Public Library, and Best Book for Children and Teens selection, Chicago Public Library, all for *Gothic!;* Notable Social Studies Trade Book, National Council for the Social Studies/Children's Book Council, for *Hana in the Time of the Tulips;* Best Book for Young Adults selection, ALA, Books for the Teen Age selection, New York Public Library, and Henry Bergh Children's Book Award, American Society for the Prevention of Cruelty to Animals, 2006, all for *One Kingdom;* Best Book for Young Adults selection, ALA, for *The Restless Dead;* Best Children's Book of the Year selection, Bank Street College of Education, 2008, for *Red Butterfly;* honored among Boston Public Library's Literary Lights for Children, 2007.

Writings

FICTION

It's Vladimir!, illustrated by Christopher Mills, Marshall Cavendish (Tarrytown, NY), 2001.

(Editor) *Gothic! Ten Original Dark Tales,* Candlewick Press (Cambridge, MA), 2004.

Hana in the Time of the Tulips, illustrated by Bagram Ibatoulline, Candlewick Press (Cambridge, MA), 2004.

Angel and Apostle, Unbridled Books (Denver, CO), 2005.

When I Met the Wolf Girls, illustrated by August Hall, Houghton Mifflin (Boston, MA), 2007.

Red Butterfly: How a Princess Smuggled the Secret of Silk out of China, illustrated by Sophie Blackall, Candlewick Press (Cambridge, MA), 2007.

(Editor) *The Restless Dead: Ten Original Stories of the Supernatural,* Candlewick Press (Cambridge, MA), 2007.

The Ghosts of Kerfol, illustrated by Sophie Blackall, Candlewick Press (Cambridge, MA), 2008.

Prudence and Moxie, illustrated by AnnaLaura Cantone, Houghton Mifflin (Boston, MA), 2008.

OTHER

(And photographer) *One Kingdom: Our Lives with Animals,* Houghton Mifflin (Boston, MA), 2006.

Encyclopedia of the End: Mysterious Death in Fact, Fancy, Folklore, and More, Houghton Mifflin (Boston, MA), 2008.

(Photographer) Avis Harley, *African Acrostics,* Candlewick Press (Cambridge, MA), 2009.

Contributor of short stories and reviews to periodicals, including *Seventeen, Threepenny Review, Bloomsbury Review, San Francisco Chronicle, Stories, Chicago Tribune, Cicada,* and *Boston Sunday Globe.*

Sidelights

Deborah Noyes, a writer, editor, and photographer, is the author of such award-winning titles as _Hana in the Time of the Tulips_ and _One Kingdom: Our Lives with Animals._ She has also edited a pair of highly acclaimed anthologies, _Gothic! Ten Original Dark Tales_ and _The Restless Dead: Ten Original Stories of the Supernatural._ "I like strong texture and atmosphere in a story, and I'm drawn to history," Noyes commented on the _Candlewick Press_ Web site. "The past plays on my imagination in a way the present and future don't. I also love fairy tales and fabulist tales; folklore, myths, and legends; odd natural history minutiae; and moody, intense supernatural stuff."

Noyes' first picture book, _It's Vladimir!,_ focuses on an impatient young vampire who desperately wants to earn his bat wings. Vladimir's constant tantrums drive his family members from their castle, however, and he must turn to a host of forest creatures for support and advice. According to _Booklist_ reviewer Marta Segal, "the [story's] moral is balanced by winning humor and the idea

Cover of Deborah Noyes' story anthology **Gothic! Ten Original Dark Tales,** _featuring photography by Pia Schachter._ (Cover photograph copyright © 2006 by Pia Schachter. Reproduced by permission of the publisher, Candlewick Press, Inc., Somerville, MA.)

of wishes coming true." Set in seventeenth-century Holland and illustrated by Bagram Ibatoulline, Noyes' _Hana in the Time of the Tulips_ concerns a young girl whose father ignores her after he becomes caught up in the period's tulip craze. Here Noyes "tells an unusual story with appealing rhythm and rich, fanciful language," noted Gillian Engberg in a _Booklist_ review of the picture book.

Based on actual events, _When I Met the Wolf Girls_ describes the story of two feral children, Amala and Kamala, who are brought to live in an Indian orphanage by a missionary who hopes to civilize them. Examining themes of colonialism and religion, _When I Met the Wolf Girls_ also explores "the notion of taming the wild, which permeates the story and infuses it with a sense of sadness," as Marianne Saccardi commented in _School Library Journal._ In the lushly illustrated _Red Butterfly: How a Princess Smuggled the Secret of Silk out of China,_ Noyes and illustrator Sophie Blackall offer a picture-book take on an ancient legend. As she prepares to leave her homeland to marry the ruler of Khotan, the emperor's daughter hides silkworms and mulberry seeds in her hair, hoping to retain pieces of her past life. "Noyes' graceful text includes allusions to nature and the shifting seasons in a style reminiscent of traditional Chinese poetry," Engberg stated.

Turning to older readers, Noyes has also penned _Angel and Apostle,_ an adult historical novel of interest to teens, and _The Ghosts of Kerfol,_ a collection of stories. The former reimagines Nathaniel Hawthorne's _The Scarlet Letter_ from the perspective of Pearl, Hester Prynne's daughter, and the story follows the impish sprite into adulthood. The author "tackles passion and Puritanism in a riveting historical tale with timeless overtones," wrote _Library Journal_ reviewer Beth E. Andersen in a review of _Angel and Apostle. The Ghosts of Kerfol,_ which contains five ghostly tales inspired by an Edith Wharton story, was praised as "beautiful and genuinely frightening," by a contributor in _Kirkus Reviews._

In _Gothic!_ Noyes collects ten stories by such acclaimed young-adult authors as Joan Aiken, Neil Gaiman, and M.T. Anderson. A companion volume, _The Restless Dead,_ includes tales by Annette Curtis Klause, Kelly Link, and Holly Black. "As both a reader and an editor, I'm drawn to the place where popular/genre and literary intersect, and these writers, great stylists and masters of the weird, really delivered," Noyes stated in an online _Cynsations_ interview with Cynthia Leitich Smith. "For me, anthologies are an excuse to invite a bunch of writers I admire out to play."

One Kingdom, a nonfiction work illustrated with photographs by Noyes, examines the relationships between animals and humans in myth, history, and science. A former zookeeper, Noyes raises a number of questions about society's treatment of animals, including the eth-

Noyes recounts the fascinating journey of the secret for spinning silk thread in her picture book Red Butterfly, *featuring artwork by Sophie Blackall.*
(Illustration copyright © 2007 by Sophie Blackall. Reproduced by permission of the publisher, Candlewick Press, Inc., Somerville, MA.)

ics of captivity. In the words of *Horn Book* critic Betty Carter, the author "inserts herself into the narrative as she becomes a partner in a freewheeling inquiry with the reader."

Noyes once remarked to *SATA:* "The poet Marianne Moore argued that good poetry should present 'imaginary gardens with real toads in them.' This pretty much sums up my ideas about writing for kids. I love the interplay of the real and the fantastic, the way these worlds, for many of us, are constantly overlapping.

"I'm an avid student of the *craft* of writing, the particulars of language and imagery, and I try to think like a poet when I can, with my senses. But I'm always drawn back to the universal, too—the stuff of history, myth, and legend—the storyteller's toolbox. I love supernatural tales and fairy tales and never tire of watching them transmogrify, of listening as new voices reinvent them. Many of the projects I'm working on retell old tales or try to view history—whether seventeenth-century Holland, imperial China, or the American landscapes of the U.S. Civil War and the Great Depression—through a new or unusual lens. I also think a lot about character. Most of my stories, even the fanciful ones, are (for better or worse) less about *what* happens than about whom

it happens to and why. Even my photos strive, however simply, for a raw emotional connection of some kind, though their subject is more often animal than human.

"Apart from family and friends, reading and writing have been the great gifts of my life. I'm so grateful for the chance to help pass those gifts along to kids."

Biographical and Critical Sources

PERIODICALS

Booklist, October 15, 2001, Marta Segal, review of *It's Vladimir!,* p. 401; October 15, 2004, Jennifer Mattson, review of *Gothic! Ten Original Dark Tales,* p. 404; November 1, 2004, Gillian Engberg, review of *Hana in the Time of the Tulips,* p. 498; October 15, 2004, Kristine Huntley, review of *Angel and Apostle,* p. 31; October 15, 2006, Ed Sullivan, review of *One Kingdom: Our Lives with Animals,* p. 38; March 15, 2007, Hazel Rochman, review of *When I Met the Wolf Girls,* p. 47; May 15, 2007, Debbie Carton, review of *The Restless Dead: Ten Original Stories of the Supernatural,* p. 54; November 15, 2007, Gillian Engberg, review of *Red Butterfly: How a Princess Smuggled the Secret of Silk out of China,* p. 50.

Horn Book, November-December, 2004, Lauren Adams, review of *Gothic!,* p. 714; September-October, 2006, Betty Carter, review of *One Kingdom,* p. 609; May-June, 2007, Elissa Gershowitz, review of *When I Met the Wolf Girls,* p. 270.

Kirkus Reviews, September 1, 2004, review of *Gothic!,* p. 871; September 15, 2004, review of *Hana in the Time of the Tulips,* p. 197; April 15, 2007, review of *When I Met the Wolf Girls;* August 1, 2007, review of *The Restless Dead;* October 1, 2007, review of *Red Butterfly;* July 15, 2008, review of *The Ghosts of Kerfol.*

Kliatt, January, 2007, Joseph DeMarco, review of *Gothic!,* p. 28.

Library Journal, October 15, 2005, Beth E. Andersen, review of *Angel and Apostle,* p. 47.

Publishers Weekly, November 22, 2004, review of *Hana in the Time of the Tulips,* p. 60; August 22, 2005, review of *Angel and Apostle,* p. 36; November 19, 2007, review of *Red Butterfly,* p. 56; July 21, 2008, review of *The Ghosts of Kerfol,* p. 161.

School Library Journal, October, 2001, Patti Gonzales, review of *It's Vladimir!,* p. 127; October, 2004, Kathy Krasniewicz, review of *Hana in the Time of Tulips,* p. 126; November, 2006, Janet S. Thompson, review of *One Kingdom,* p. 163; June, 2007, Marianne Saccardi, review of *When I Met the Wolf Girls,* p. 156; September, 2007, Anthony C. Doyle, review of *The Restless Dead,* p. 204; December, 2007, Margaret Bush, review of *Red Butterfly,* p. 140.

ONLINE

Candlewick Press Web site, http://www.candlewick.com/ (September 30, 2008), "Deborah Noyes."

Cynsations Web log, http://cynthialeitichsmith.blogspot. com/ (October 4, 2006), Cynthia Leitich Smith, interview with Noyes.

Deborah Noyes Home Page, http://www.deborahnoyes. com (September 30, 2008).

Deborah Noyes Web log, http://hauntedplaylist.blogspot. com/ (September 30, 2008).

*   *   *

PIXLEY, Marcella

Personal

Education: Vassar College, B.A., 1992.

Addresses

Home—Westford, MA.

Career

Teacher and writer. Eighth-grade language arts teacher.

Writings

Freak, Farrar, Straus & Giroux (New York, NY), 2007.

Contributor of poetry to periodicals, including *Prairie Schooner.*

Sidelights

Marcella Pixley's debut novel *Freak* deals with issues familiar to many middle-school students: bullying, crushes, the search for uniqueness, sibling rivalry, and family miscommunication. In the novel, Pixley grapples with each of these issues from the perspective of central character Miriam Fisher. Awkward and unpopular, Miriam happily spends her days reading the *Oxford English Dictionary* and writing journal entries and poetry. Unfortunately, events conspire to undermine the preteen's comfortable routine. The school bullies single Miriam out for abuse, and her older sister—usually reliable as a friend and confidante—deserts her when she is accepted into the popular crowd at the high school. Then Miriam's parents agree to take in high-school senior Artie while his parents travel abroad. When the shy Miriam develops a crush on Artie, she must then watch in dismay as her sister becomes romantically involved with their new housemate. Pushed to her limit, Miriam responds with extreme measures, all of which are documented in her diary.

A *Publishers Weekly* correspondent called *Freak* "a disturbing tale that taps into the harsh reality of what it means to be a middle-school outcast." In the novel, Pixley's far-from-perfect protagonist is realistically portrayed, her endearing traits offset by fits of temper and intellectual snobbery, making *Freaks* "a powerful look at middle school angst and transformation," according to *School Library Journal* critic Nora G. Murphy. In *Booklist* Debbie Carton remarked that Miriam's conflicts "are especially riveting and believable," and a *Kirkus Reviews* critic praised Pixley's novel as "an expertly—and lovingly—narrated story."

Biographical and Critical Sources

PERIODICALS

Booklist, September 15, 2007, Debbie Carton, review of *Freak,* p. 62.

Bulletin of the Center for Children's Books, October, 2007, Deborah Stevenson, review of *Freak,* p. 105.

Kirkus Reviews, September 1, 2007, review of *Freak.*

Kliatt, September, 2007, Claire Rosser, review of *Freak,* p. 17.

Publishers Weekly, November 5, 2007, review of *Freak,* p. 65.

School Library Journal, November, 2007, Nora G. Murphy, review of *Freak,* p. 134.

Voice of Youth Advocates, August, 2007, C.J. Bott, review of *Freak,* p. 248.

ONLINE

Macmillan Publishing Web site, http://www.us.macmillan. com/ (October 31, 2008), "Marcella Pixley."*

PURKISS, Diane 1961-
(Tobias Druitt, a joint pseudonym)

Personal

Born June 30, 1961, in Sydney, New South Wales, Australia; immigrated to England; married; children: Michael Dowling. *Education:* University of Queensland, B.A. (first-class honours); Merton College Oxford, D.Phil.

Addresses

Office—Department of English, Keble College Oxford, Oxford OX1 3PG, England. *E-mail*—diane.purkiss@keble.ox.ac.uk.

Career

Educator and author. University of East Anglia, lecturer in English, 1991-93; University of Reading, lecturer in English, 1992-98; Exeter University, Exeter, England, professor of professor of English, 1998-2000; Keble College Oxford, Oxford, England, fellow and tutor, 2000—.

Writings

FOR CHILDREN

(With son Michael Dowling, under joint pseudonym Tobias Druitt) *Corydon and the Island of Monsters,* Simon & Schuster (New York, NY), 2005.

(With Michael Dowling, under joint pseudonym Tobias Druitt) *Corydon and the Fall of Atlantis,* Simon & Schuster (New York, NY), 2006.

(With Michael Dowling, under joint pseudonym Tobias Druitt) *Corydon and the Siege of Troy,* Simon & Schuster (London, England), 2007.

OTHER

(Editor, with Clare Brant, and contributor) *Women, Texts, and Histories: 1575-1760,* Routledge (New York, NY), 1992.

(Editor) *Renaissance Women: The Plays of Elizabeth Cary: The Poems of Aemilia Lanyer,* Pickering & Chatto (Brookfield, VT), 1994.

The Witch in History: Early Modern and Twentieth-Century Representations, Routledge (New York, NY), 1996.

At the Bottom of the Garden: A Dark History of Fairies, Hobgoblins, and Other Troublesome Things, New York University Press (New York, NY), 2000, published as *Troublesome Things: A History of Fairies and Fairy Stories,* Penguin (London, England), 2000, published as *Fairies and Fairy Stories: A History,* Tempus, 2007.

Literature, Gender, and Politics during the English Civil War, Cambridge University Press (New York, NY), 2005.

The English Civil War: A People's History, HarperCollins (London, England), 2006, published as *The English Civil War: Papists, Gentlewomen, Soldiers, and Witch-finders in the Birth of Modern Britain,* Basic Books (Boulder, CO), 2006.

A History of Food in England, HarperCollins (London, England), 2008.

The Dissolution of the English Monasteries, HarperCollins (London, England), 2010.

Contributor to anthologies, including *Feminist Companion to Mythology,* Pandora (London, England), 1992; *Women/Writing/History,* Batsford (London, England), 1992; *Rethinking Sexual Harassment,* Sage (London, England), 1994; *Representing Dido,* Faber & Faber (London, England), 1998; *The English Civil Wars in the Literary Imagination,* University of Missouri Press (Columbia, MO), 1999; *Languages of Witchcraft,* 2000; *The Double Voice,* Macmillan (London, England), 2000; *Medea in Performance,* Oxford University Press (Oxford, England), 2000; *Attending to Women in Early Modern England,* University of Delaware Press, 2002; *History and Theory,* 2003; *Shakespeare and Popular Culture,* 2003; *Early Girls,* Ashgate (New York, NY), 2008; and *Shakespeare and Oral Culture,* Ashgate, 2008. Contributor to periodicals, including *Baetyl, Cardozo Law Review, Journal of Medieval and Early Modern Studies, Representations of the Self in Early Modern Britain, Tulsa Studies in Women's Literature,* and *Women and Writing.*

Sidelights

Diane Purkiss is a fellow and tutor of English at Keble College, Oxford, and her research areas include the writings of John Milton, Renaissance drama, the English Civil War, and the supernatural in the early modern period. In addition to her academic work, which includes several books and numerous scholarly essays, Purkiss is one half of the pseudonymous Tobias Druitt, author of the "Corydon" fantasy novels. The other half of Tobias Druitt is Michael Dowling, Purkiss's son, who was eight years old when the first "Corydon" novel, *Corydon and the Island of Monsters,* was being written.

Based on characters from Greek mythology, *Corydon and the Island of Monsters* introduces readers to a young shepherd who is an outcast from his village because of a birth defect that has left him with a goat's hoof instead of one of his feet. Captured by pirates, Corydon is caged as a monster and exhibited as part of a traveling freak show. Together with Medusa, Lamia, Minotaur, Sphinx, and the Gorgon sisters, Corydon works to fulfill his destiny—to battle Perseus, Zeus, and a disjointed army of Greek heroes who are intent upon destroying all monsters—and learns the identity of his father along the way. "With all the elements of a true adventure story," *Corydon and the Island of Monsters* "will have wide appeal," predicted a *Publishers Weekly* critic, and in *Booklist* Krista Hutley noted that the "fascinating, well-rounded" characters" make reading *Corydon and the Island of Monsters* "a treat for readers who enjoy viewing old stories from new vantage points." Purkiss's "witty, profoundly sapient take" on ancient myths "will leave readers impatient for the sequels," concluded a *Kirkus Reviews* contributor in discussing the first "Corydon" novel.

Using the Druitt pen name, Purkiss and Dowling continue the adventures of their goat-footed young hero in *Corydon and the Fall of Atlantis* and *Corydon and the Siege of Troy*. In the former, Corydon and his monstrous friends travel to the ill-fated Atlantis to rescue Minotaur, only to find that intrigue is rife in that culturally advanced city. When Troy is attacked by Akhilleus and his band of Olympian superheroes, Trojan prince Sikandar begs Corydon for help in *Corydon and the Siege of Troy*. According to a *Kirkus Reviews* writer, *Corydon and the Fall of Atlantis* features "ingeniously twisted mythology, punctuated by exciting, Odyssey-like encounters" set in the ancient world.

"Anyone who has ever thought that fairies are 'tiresome little wingy thingies who are always good' will be swiftly disabused of that notion," wrote a *Publishers Weekly* critic in a review of *At the Bottom of the Garden: A Dark History of Fairies, Hobgoblins, and Other Troublesome Things*. This scholarly work by Purkiss has since been republished as *Fairies and Fairy Stories: A History*. Backing up her history with scholarly research, Purkiss shows that fairies were once regarded with fear and dread: they were frightening beings from another world who could steal or kill children, abduct young men, cause illness or blindness, or rape human women. In the seventeenth century, their reputation shifted: people now regarded fairies as bringers of luck or wealth to those they favored. In the nineteenth and early twentieth century, they were seen as pure, child-like beings that represented innocence and light. In the London *Sunday Times*, Lucy Hughes-Hallett called *At the Bottom of the Garden* "both splendidly scholarly and breezily accessible," and "a monstrous, magnificent fairy ride." In the *Times*, Michele Roberts praised it as "an elegantly written and witty book," and Sara Maitland wrote in the *Spectator* that Purkiss's work is "both illuminating and enormous fun."

In *The Witch in History: Early Modern and Twentieth-Century Representations* Purkiss examines how witches have been regarded during different periods in history. Presenting records of witchcraft trials, she shows how some women used fantasies of witchcraft to feel more empowered in their daily lives. She also studies witches as depicted in the works of William Shakespeare, Ben Jonson, and others, and shows how these writers not only drew upon popular images of witches, but also re-shaped these images. According to *Booklist* critic Gilbert Taylor, Purkiss "effectively evokes an impressionis-

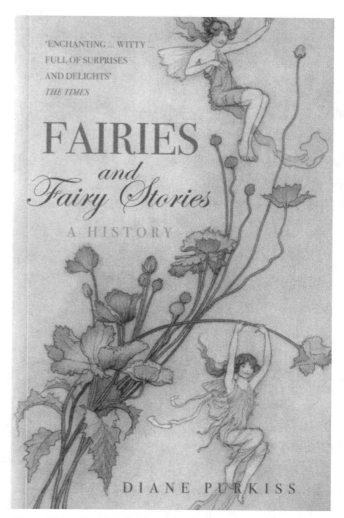

Cover of Diane Purkiss's **Fairies and Fairy Stories: A History,** *a newly titled edition of her study of earthly magic that features cover art by Warwick Goble.* (Tempus, 2000. Illustration by Warwick Goble/Mary Evans Picture Library. Copyright © Mary Evans Picture Library. Reproduced by permission.)

tic experience of living through tumultuous times" in *The English Civil War: Papists, Gentlewomen, Soldiers, and Witchfinders in the Birth of Modern Britain*, a work that draws on its author's broad expertise as an historian. In *Library Journal* Susanne Markgren also praised the book, dubbing it "a rich history [of a] . . . turbulent period" that contains "more detail, drama, and intrigue than many works of fiction."

Biographical and Critical Sources

PERIODICALS

Ariel, July, 1998, Wendy Schissel, review of *The Witch in History: Early Modern and Twentieth-Century Representations*, p. 198.

Booklist, February 1, 2006, Krista Hutley, review of *Corydon and the Island of Monsters*, p. 44; July 1, 2006, Gilbert Taylor, review of *The English Civil War: Papists, Gentlewomen, Soldiers, and Witchfinders in the Birth of Modern Britain*, p. 26.

Bulletin of the Center of Children's Books, March, 2006, Karen Coats, review of *Corydon and the Island of Monsters,* p. 309.

Contemporary Review, spring, 1997, Chris Arthur, review of *The Witch in History,* p. 158; summer, 2007, review of *The English Civil War,* p. 258.

Eighteenth-Century Life, May, 1998, Michael Hunter, "Witchcraft and the Decline of Belief," p. 139.

Journal of Women's History, winter, 1999, Heather Lee Miller, review of *The Witch in History,* p. 232.

Kirkus Reviews, January 1, 2006, review of *Corydon and the Island of Monsters,* p. 39; December 15, 2006, review of *Corydon and the Fall of Atlantis,* p. 1266.

Library Journal, June 15, 2006, Susanne Markgren, review of *The English Civil War,* p. 84.

New York Review of Books, October 23, 1997, Alison Lurie, review of *The Witch in History,* p. 48.

Notes and Queries, September, 1993, Isobel Grundy, review of *Women, Texts, and Histories: 1575-1760,* p. 366.

Publishers Weekly, February 5, 2001, review of *At the Bottom of the Garden: A Dark History of Fairies, Hobgoblins, and Other Troublesome Things,* p. 78; February 1, 2006, review of *Corydon and the Island of Monsters,* p. 90; May 15, 2006, review of *The English Civil War,* p. 63.

Renaissance Quarterly, summer, 1998, Brian P. Levack, review of *The Witch in History,* p. 655; fall, 2006, James Loxley, review of *Literature, Gender, and Politics during the English Civil War,* p. 982.

Review of English Studies, February, 1995, Jacqueline Pearson, review of *Women, Texts, and Histories,* p. 89.

School Librarian, spring, 2006, Alison Hurst, review of *Corydon and the Siege of Troy,* p. 36.

School Library Journal, March, 2006, Patricia D. Lothrop, review of *Corydon and the Island of Monsters,* p. 220; March, 2007, Beth Wright, review of *Corydon and the Fall of Atlantis,* p. 202.

Sixteenth Century Journal, spring, 1994, Robert C. Evans, review of *Women, Texts, and Histories,* p. 210; winter, 1997, Kathryn A. Edwards, review of *The Witch in History,* p. 1433.

Spectator, January 6, 2001, Sara Maitland, review of *Troublesome Things,* p. 25.

Sunday Telegraph (London, England), December 17, 2000, Lucy Hughes-Hallett, "Fairies Could Be Dangerously, Seductively Beautiful, or Repulsively, Hairily Naked," p. 38; December 24, 2000, Richard Davenport-Hines, "The Tooth Fairy Had Fangs," p. 15.

Times (London, England), November 29, 2000, Michele Roberts, "Enchanting Visions of Fairyland," p. 14; January 20, 2001, "Fairies Don't Just Live at the Bottom of the Garden," p. 12.

Times Literary Supplement, June 22, 2001, Andrew Wawn, "Farewell Rewards and Fairies," p. 36.

Tribune Books (Chicago, IL), February 18, 2007, Mary Harris Russell, review of *Corydon and the Fall of Atlantis,* p. 7.

Voice of Youth Advocates, April, 2006, Tracy Piombo, review of *Corydon and the Island of Monsters,* p. 58; April, 2007, Stacey Hayman, review of *Corydon and the Fall of Atlantis,* p. 64.

ONLINE

Keble College Oxford Web site, http://www.keble.ox.ac.uk/academics/ (October 13, 2008), "Dr. Diane Purkiss."

Tobias Druitt Web site, http://www.tobiasdruitt.co.uk/ (October 15, 2006).*

R

RAMIREZ, Orlando L. 1972-

Personal

Born May 26, 1972, in Carolina, Puerto Rico. *Education:* Ringling School of Art and Design, B.F.A. (illustration and design).

Addresses

Office—Pinwheel Media, Stuart, FL 34997. *E-mail*—orlydesigns1@aol.com.

Career

Illustrator and multimedia designer. Hallmark Cards, greeting-card artist, 1994-2000; America Online, art director and senior designer, 2000-05.

Illustrator

Cheech Marin, *Cheech, the School Bus Driver,* HarperCollins (New York, NY), 2007.
Cheech Marin, *Captain Cheech,* HarperCollins (New York, NY), 2008.
Cheech Marin, *Cheech and the Spooky Ghost Bus,* Harper-Collins (New York, NY), 2009.

Biographical and Critical Sources

PERIODICALS

Kirkus Reviews, June 15, 2007, review of *Cheech, the School Bus Driver.*
Publishers Weekly, June 18, 2007, review of *Cheech, the School Bus Driver,* p. 53.
School Library Journal, August, 2007, Linda M. Kenton, review of *Cheech, the School Bus Driver,* p. 86; July, 2008, Wendy Lukehart, review of *Captain Cheech,* p. 78.

ONLINE

Orlando L. Ramirez Home Page, http://www.orlando ramirez.com (October 10, 2008).*

RIDEOUT, Sandy

Personal

Education: University of Toronto, B.A. (English). *Hobbies and other interests:* Running.

Addresses

Home—Toronto, Ontario, Canada.

Career

Writer and corporate communications officer.

Writings

YOUNG-ADULT NOVELS

(With Yvonne Collins) *Introducing Vivien Leigh Reid: Daughter of the Diva,* St. Martin's Press (New York, NY), 2005.
(With Yvonne Collins) *Now Starring Vivien Leigh Reid: Diva in Training,* St. Martin's Press (New York, NY), 2006.
(With Yvonne Collins) *The New and Improved Vivien Leigh Reid: Diva in Control,* St. Martin's Press (New York, NY), 2007.
(With Yvonne Collins) *The Black Sheep,* Hyperion Press (New York, NY), 2007.
(With Yvonne Collins) *Girl v. Boy,* Hyperion Press (New York, NY), 2008.

NONFICTION

(With Yvonne Collins) *Totally Me: The Teenage Girl's Survival Guide,* Adams Media Corporation (Holbrook, MA), 2000.

ADULT NOVELS

(With Yvonne Collins) *Speechless,* Red Dress Ink Press (Don Mills, Ontario, Canada), 2004.

(With Yvonne Collins) *What I Really Want to Do Is Direct,* Red Dress Ink Press (Don Mills, Ontario, Canada), 2005.

Sidelights

Sandy Rideout and Yvonne Collins work as a team on writing projects, most of which are novels for young adults. The two women met during their teen years while working at a public library, and they became fast friends. Their best-known joint project, the "Vivien Leigh Reid" novel series, introduces an aspiring teen diva who works in the entertainment industry. Another novel, *The Black Sheep,* also revolves around a reality television program, and both these projects draw upon Collins' experiences as a television and film-camera operator. Rideout, an English major, contributes her talents to the collaboration in the form of "fresh energy and interesting characters," to quote Cindy Welch in a *Booklist* review of series opener *Introducing Vivien Leigh Reid: Daughter of the Diva.*

Vivien Leigh Reid is the daughter of a B-list actress who is struggling to stay in the limelight, and in *Introducing Vivien Leigh Reid* the girl reluctantly joins her mother on location in rural Ireland. Once there, Vivien also lands a role in the film in which her mother is starring. This mother-daughter bonding opportunity does not proceed smoothly, however, when both compete for the attention of the film's handsome leading man. In *Now Starring Vivien Leigh Reid: Diva in Training,* Vivien's ego runs amok when she spends the summer in Los Angeles and earns a role on a soap opera. Her outsized behavior deflates in *The New and Improved Vivien Leigh Reid: Diva in Control* when the role she lands in a science-fiction television series is an ugly, half-human warthog. Vivian "is a likeable, funny, and realistic heroine," wrote Amanda MacGregor in her *Kliatt* review of *The New and Improved Vivien Leigh Reid.* According to Tracy Karbel in her *School Library Journal* review of *Now Starring Vivien Leigh Reid,* Rideout and Collins' novel is "pop-culture fun with a moral," and Vivien's "extreme diva behavior . . . makes for a juicy read." Reviewing *Introducing Vivian Leigh Reed,* MacGregor described the collaborative novel as "witty, unpredictable, and well written," adding that the coauthors' "unique setting and likeable characters will keep readers interested."

Rideout and Collins re-visit the world of television in *The Black Sheep.* Here fifteen-year-old Kendra is dissatisfied with her privileged but stressful life living with over-achieving Manhattan banker parents. When the teen enters a contest and finds herself on a reality T.V. show, she has the chance to trade places with the daughter of easygoing hippie parents in California. Once on the West Coast, Kendra joins this large family and promptly becomes attracted to one of the siblings, a budding wildlife biologist trying to save endangered sea otters. However, the young woman's attempts to embrace otter rescue—and otherwise truly experience an alternate lifestyle—are stymied again and again by a pushy television crew that documents her every move and twists her words to their own ends. As Ilene Cooper wrote in *Booklist,* Rideout and Collins "have the reality-show shenanigans down pat," and Cooper dubbed *The Black Sheep* "au courant" fiction. A *Publishers Weekly* reviewer also viewed the novel positively, describing *The Black Sheep* as a "cheery fish-out-of-water romance" that contains "heartfelt reflections on family and fame."

Biographical and Critical Sources

PERIODICALS

Booklist, June 1, 2005, Cindy Welch, review of *Introducing Vivien Leigh Reid: Daughter of the Diva,* p. 1781; May 15, 2007, Ilene Cooper, review of *The Black Sheep,* p. 39.

Kliatt, July, 2005, Amanda MacGregor, review of *Introducing Vivien Leigh Reid,* p. 19; May, 2007, Amanda MacGregor, review of *The New and Improved Vivien Leigh Reid: Diva in Control,* p. 22.

Publishers Weekly, May 28, 2007, review of *The Black Sheep,* p. 64.

School Library Journal, September, 2005, Suzanne Gordon, review of *Introducing Vivien Leigh Reid,* p. 202; January, 2006, Tracy Karbel, review of *Now Starring Vivien Leigh Reid: Diva in Training,* p. 129; March, 2007, Laurie Slagenwhite, review of *The New and Improved Vivien Leigh Reid,* p. 206; September, 2007, Jeffrey Hastings, review of *The Black Sheep,* p. 194.

Voice of Youth Advocates, April, 2006, Lucy Schall, review of *Now Starring Vivien Leigh Reid,* p. 40; August, 2007, Beth Karpas, review of *The Black Sheep,* p. 237.

ONLINE

Yvonne Collins and Sandy Rideout Home Page, http://www.collinsrideout.com (November 4, 2008).*

* * *

ROBB, Don 1937-

Personal

Born November 24, 1937; married. *Education:* Ohio University in Athens, B.A. *Hobbies and other interests:* Reading, cooking.

Addresses

Home—Andover, MA. *Office*—Charlesbridge Publishing, 85 Main St., Watertown, MA 02472.

Career

Editor and writer. Charlesbridge Publishing, Watertown, MA, staff member, 1981—; writer. Former foreign-language teacher in Toledo, OH, and Hackensack, NJ;

Holt, Rinehart & Winston Publishers, New York, NY, former foreign-language consultant; Houghton Mifflin (publisher), Boston, MA, former vice president.

Writings

Hail to the Chief: The American Presidency, illustrated by Alan Witschonke, Charlesbridge Publishing (Watertown, MA), 2000.

This Is America: The American Spirit in Places and People, illustrated by Christine Joy Pratt, Charlesbridge Publishing (Watertown, MA), 2005.

Ox, House, Stick: The History of Our Alphabet, illustrated by Anne Smith, Charlesbridge Publishing (Watertown, MA), 2007.

Sidelights

Don Robb worked for more than twenty years in the publishing industry before he began writing his own books for children. He is affiliated with Massachusetts-based Charlesbridge Publishing as both an author and a member of the company's staff. Robb's books include the nonfiction titles *Hail to the Chief: The American Presidency, This Is America: The American Spirit in Places and People,* and *Ox, House, Stick: The History of Our Alphabet.*

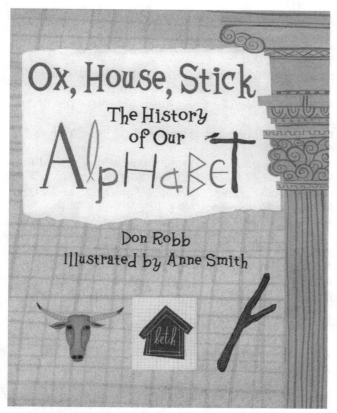

Don Robb reveals the history of the English alphabet in Ox, House, Stick, *a picture book featuring artwork by Anne Smith.* (Illustration copyright © 2007 by Anne Smith. All rights reserved. Used with permission by Charlesbridge Publishing, Inc.)

Hail to the Chief, featuring artwork by Alan Witschonke, is an elementary-grade picture book useful for teaching youngsters about America's best-known presidents. *This Is America,* illustrated by Christine Joy Pratt, explores famous people and places that have made the United States the country it is today. In her *School Library Journal* review of *This Is America,* Susan Lissim dubbed Robb's book "an appealing way to explore U.S. history and democracy."

With its intriguing title, *Ox, House, Stick* introduces elementary-grade readers to the history of the modern alphabet, beginning with the earliest pictograms and following the evolution forward in time to the Roman letters used today. Robb explains both why and how writing began and evolved over time, including the changing shape of letters and the need for punctuation. "This quality work fills a significant gap in children's information literature," concluded Jayne Damron in a review of the book for *School Library Journal.* In *Horn Book,* Joanna Rudge Long described *Ox, House, Stick* as "an excellent first resource" that is "skillfully organized to . . . inspire interest," while in *Booklist* Gillian Engberg deemed it "a fascinating look at the Roman alphabet." In a review of Robb's book for *Kirkus Reviews,* a contributor praised *Ox, House, Stick* as a "pleasingly informative offering."

Biographical and Critical Sources

PERIODICALS

Booklist, August, 2007, Gillian Engberg, review of *Ox, House, Stick: The History of Our Alphabet,* p. 72.

Horn Book, November-December, 2007, Joanna Rudge Long, review of *Ox, House, Stick,* p. 698.

Kirkus Reviews, June 15, 2007, review of *Ox, House, Stick.*

School Library Journal, March, 2001, Margaret C. Howell, review of *Hail to the Chief: The American Presidency,* p. 242; May, 2005, Susan Lissim, review of *This Is America: The American Spirit in Places and People,* p. 114; August, 2007, Jayne Damron, review of *Ox, House, Stick,* p. 138.

ONLINE

Charlesbridge Publishing Web site, http://www.charlesbridge.com/ (November 4, 2008), "Don Robb."*

*   *   *

ROCKWELL, Anne F. 1934-

Personal

Born February 8, 1934, in Memphis, TN; daughter of Emerson (an advertising executive) and Sabina Foote; married Harlow Rockwell (a writer and artist), March

16, 1955 (died 1988); children: Hannah, Elizabeth, Oliver Penn. *Education:* Attended Sculpture Center and Pratt Graphic Arts Center. *Politics:* "Liberal Democrat." *Religion:* Episcopalian.

Addresses

Home—Old Greenwich, CT.

Career

Author and illustrator. Silver Burdett Publishers, Morristown, NJ, member of production department, 1952; Young & Rubicam (advertising agency), art-buying secretary, 1953; Goldwater Memorial Hospital, New York, NY, assistant recreation leader, 1954-56.

Member

Authors Guild, Authors League of America.

Awards, Honors

Boys Club Junior Book Award certificate, 1968, for *The Minstrel and the Mountain;* American Institute of Graphic Arts selection for children's book show, 1971-72, for *The Toolbox,* 1973-74, for *Head-to-Toe Games (and How to Play Them), The Awful Mess,* and *Paul and Arthur and the Little Explorer;* Children's Book Showcase selection, 1973, for *Toad,* and 1975, for *Befana; No More Work* and *Poor Goose* named among children's books of the year, Child Study Association, 1976; Notable Books for Children citation, *Smithsonian* magazine, 1996, for *The Storm;* Society of School Librarians International Book Awards honor designation, 1999, for *Our Earth;* Best Children's Books of the Year citation, Bank Street College of Education, 2000, for *Our Stars,* 2002, for *Morgan Plays Soccer; New York Times* Best Illustrated Children's Book of the Year designation, 2000, Notable Books for Children citation, American Library Association (ALA), Not Just for Children Any More citation, Children's Book Council, Coretta Scott King Award Honor Book designation, and *Storytelling World* Award honor designation, all 2001, and Amelia Bloomer listee, ALA, 2002, all for *Only Passing Through;* Best Children's Books of the Year citation, Bank Street College of Education, and Top Ten Religious Books for Youth designation, ALA, both 2002, both for *The Prince Who Ran Away.*

Writings

SELF-ILLUSTRATED PICTURE BOOKS

Paul and Arthur Search for the Egg, Doubleday (New York, NY), 1964.

Gypsy Girl's Best Shoes, Parents Magazine Press (New York, NY), 1966.

Sally's Caterpillar, illustrated by husband, Harlow Rockwell, Parents Magazine Press (New York, NY), 1966.

Filippo's Dome: Brunelleschi and the Cathedral of Florence, Atheneum (New York, NY), 1967.

The Stolen Necklace: A Picture Story from India, World (Cleveland, OH), 1968.

Glass, Stones, and Crown: The Abbe Suger and the Building of St. Denis, Atheneum (New York, NY), 1968.

The Good Llama: A Picture Story from Peru, World (Cleveland, OH), 1968.

Temple on a Hill: The Building of the Parthenon, Atheneum (New York, NY), 1968.

The Wonderful Eggs of Furicchia: A Picture Story from Italy, World (Cleveland, OH), 1968.

(Compiler) *Savez-vous planter les choux?, and Other French Songs,* World (Cleveland, OH), 1968.

When the Drum Sang: An African Folktale, Parents Magazine Press (New York, NY), 1970.

(Adapter) *The Monkey's Whiskers: A Brazilian Folktale,* Parents Magazine Press (New York, NY), 1971.

El toro pinto, and Other Songs in Spanish, Macmillan (New York, NY), 1971.

Paintbrush and Peacepipe: The Story of George Catlin, Atheneum (New York, NY), 1971.

Tuhurahura and the Whale, Parents Magazine Press (New York, NY), 1971.

What Bobolino Knew, McCall (New York, NY), 1971.

The Dancing Stars: An Iroquois Legend, Crowell (New York, NY), 1972.

Paul and Arthur and the Little Explorer, Parents Magazine Press (New York, NY), 1972.

The Awful Mess, Parents Magazine Press (New York, NY), 1973.

The Boy Who Drew Sheep, Atheneum (New York, NY), 1973.

Games (and How to Play Them), Crowell (New York, NY), 1973.

(Reteller) *The Wolf Who Had a Wonderful Dream: A French Folktale,* Crowell (New York, NY), 1973.

Befana: A Christmas Story, Atheneum (New York, NY), 1974.

Gift for a Gift, Parents Magazine Press (New York, NY), 1974.

The Gollywhopper Egg, Macmillan (New York, NY), 1974.

The Story Snail, Macmillan (New York, NY), 1974.

(Reteller) *The Three Bears and Fifteen Other Stories,* Crowell (New York, NY), 1975.

Big Boss, Macmillan (New York, NY), 1975.

(Reteller) *Poor Goose: A French Folktale,* Crowell (New York, NY), 1976.

No More Work, Greenwillow (New York, NY), 1976.

I Like the Library, Dutton (New York, NY), 1977.

A Bear, a Bobcat, and Three Ghosts, Macmillan (New York, NY), 1977.

Albert B. Cub and Zebra: An Alphabet Storybook, Crowell (New York, NY), 1977.

Willy Runs Away, Dutton (New York, NY), 1978.

Timothy Todd's Good Things Are Gone, Macmillan (New York, NY), 1978.

Gogo's Pay Day, Doubleday (New York, NY), 1978.

Gogo's Car Breaks Down, illustrated by Harlow Rockwell, Doubleday (New York, NY), 1978.

Buster and the Bogeyman, Four Winds (New York, NY), 1978.

(Reteller) *The Old Woman and Her Pig and Ten Other Stories,* Crowell (New York, NY), 1979.

The Girl with a Donkey Tail, Dutton (New York, NY), 1979.

The Bump in the Night, Greenwillow (New York, NY), 1979.

Walking Shoes, Doubleday (New York, NY), 1980.

Honk Honk!, Dutton (New York, NY), 1980.

Henry the Cat and the Big Sneeze, Greenwillow (New York, NY), 1980.

Gray Goose and Gander and Other Mother Goose Rhymes, Crowell (New York, NY), 1980.

When We Grow Up, Dutton (New York, NY), 1981.

Thump Thump Thump!, Dutton (New York, NY), 1981.

Boats, Dutton (New York, NY), 1982.

(Reteller) Hans Christian Andersen, *The Emperor's New Clothes,* Crowell (New York, NY), 1982.

Big Bad Goat, Dutton (New York, NY), 1982.

The Mother Goose Cookie-Candy Book, Random House (New York, NY), 1983.

Cars, Dutton (New York, NY), 1984.

Trucks, Dutton (New York, NY), 1984.

In Our House, Crowell (New York, NY), 1985.

Planes, Dutton (New York, NY), 1985.

First Comes Spring, Crowell (New York, NY), 1985.

The Three Sillies and Ten Other Stories to Read Aloud, Harper (New York, NY), 1986.

Big Wheels, Dutton (New York, NY), 1986, reprinted, Walker (New York, NY), 2003.

Fire Engines, Dutton (New York, NY), 1986.

Things That Go, Dutton (New York, NY), 1986.

At Night, Crowell (New York, NY), 1986.

At the Playground, Crowell (New York, NY), 1986.

In the Morning, Crowell (New York, NY), 1986.

In the Rain, Crowell (New York, NY), 1986.

Come to Town, Crowell (New York, NY), 1987.

Bear Child's Book of Hours, Crowell (New York, NY), 1987.

Bikes, Dutton (New York, NY), 1987.

Handy Hank Will Fix It, Holt (New York, NY), 1988.

Hugo at the Window, Macmillan (New York, NY), 1988.

Things to Play With, Macmillan (New York, NY), 1988.

Puss in Boots and Other Stories, Macmillan (New York, NY), 1988.

Trains, Dutton (New York, NY), 1988.

On Our Vacation, Dutton (New York, NY), 1989.

Bear Child's Book of Special Days, Dutton (New York, NY), 1989.

Willy Can Count, Arcade (New York, NY), 1989.

Hugo at the Park, Macmillan (New York, NY), 1990.

When Hugo Went to School, Macmillan (New York, NY), 1990.

Root-a-Toot-Toot, Macmillan (New York, NY), 1991.

What We Like, Macmillan (New York, NY), 1992.

Mr. Panda's Painting, Macmillan (New York, NY), 1993.

The Robber Baby: Stories from the Greek Myths, Greenwillow (New York, NY), 1994.

The Way to Captain Yankee's, Macmillan (New York, NY), 1994.

Ducklings and Pollywogs, Macmillan (New York, NY), 1994.

(With David Brion) *Space Vehicles,* Dutton (New York, NY), 1994.

No! No! No!, Macmillan (New York, NY), 1995.

(Reteller) *The Acorn Tree and Other Folktales,* Greenwillow (New York, NY), 1995.

The One-eyed Giant and Other Monsters from the Greek Myths, Greenwillow (New York, NY), 1996.

Romulus and Remus, Simon & Schuster (New York, NY), 1997.

Our Earth, Harcourt Brace (San Diego, CA), 1998.

Our Stars, Harcourt Brace (San Diego, CA), 1999.

Bumblebee, Bumblebee, Do You Know Me?: A Garden Guessing Game, HarperCollins (New York, NY), 1999.

Long Ago Yesterday, Greenwillow (New York, NY), 1999.

The Boy Who Wouldn't Obey: A Mayan Legend, Greenwillow (New York, NY), 2000.

Only Passing Through: The Story of Sojourner Truth, Knopf (New York, NY), 2000.

Welcome to Kindergarten, Walker (New York, NY), 2001.

Seba the Scribe: A Story of Ancient Egypt, HarperCollins (New York, NY), 2003.

At the Firehouse, HarperCollins (New York, NY), 2003.

At the Train Station, HarperCollins (New York, NY), 2005.

Here Comes the Night, Henry Holt (New York, NY), 2006.

Big Wheels, Walker & Company (New York, NY), 2006.

My Preschool, Henry Holt (New York, NY), 2008.

WITH HUSBAND, HARLOW ROCKWELL; SELF-ILLUSTRATED

Olly's Polliwogs, Doubleday (New York, NY), 1970.

Molly's Woodland Garden, Doubleday (New York, NY), 1971.

The Toolbox, Macmillan (New York, NY), 1971, reprinted, Walker (New York, NY), 2004.

Machines, Macmillan (New York, NY), 1972.

Thruway, Macmillan (New York, NY), 1972.

Toad, Doubleday (New York, NY), 1972.

Head to Toe, Doubleday (New York, NY), 1973.

Blackout, Macmillan (New York, NY), 1979.

The Supermarket, Macmillan (New York, NY), 1979.

Out to Sea, Macmillan (New York, NY), 1980.

My Barber, Macmillan (New York, NY), 1981.

Happy Birthday to Me, Macmillan (New York, NY), 1981.

I Play in My Room, Macmillan (New York, NY), 1981.

Can I Help?, Macmillan (New York, NY), 1982.

How My Garden Grew, Macmillan (New York, NY), 1982.

I Love My Pets, Macmillan (New York, NY), 1982.

Sick in Bed, Macmillan (New York, NY), 1982.

The Night We Slept Outside, Macmillan (New York, NY), 1983.

My Back Yard, Macmillan (New York, NY), 1984.

Our Garage Sale, Greenwillow (New York, NY), 1984.

When I Go Visiting, Macmillan (New York, NY), 1984.

Nice and Clean, Macmillan (New York, NY), 1984.

My Baby-Sitter, Macmillan (New York, NY), 1985.

The Emergency Room, Macmillan (New York, NY), 1985, published as *Going to Casualty,* Hamish Hamilton (London, England), 1987.

At the Beach, Macmillan (New York, NY), 1987.

The First Snowfall, Macmillan (New York, NY), 1987.

PICTURE BOOKS

Up a Tall Tree, illustrated by Jim Arnosky, Doubleday (New York, NY), 1981.

My Spring Robin, illustrated by Harlow Rockwell and daughter Lizzy Rockwell, Macmillan (New York, NY), 1989.

Apples and Pumpkins, illustrated by Lizzy Rockwell, Macmillan (New York, NY), 1989, reprinted, Aladdin (New York, NY), 2005.

Our Yard Is Full of Birds, illustrated by Lizzy Rockwell, Macmillan (New York, NY), 1992.

Pots and Pans, illustrated by Lizzy Rockwell, Macmillan (New York, NY), 1993.

The Storm, illustrated by Robert Sauber, Hyperion (New York, NY), 1994.

Sweet Potato Pie, illustrated by Carolyn Croll, Random House (New York, NY), 1996.

I Fly, illustrated by Annette Cable, Crown (New York, NY), 1997.

Once upon a Time This Morning, illustrated by Suçie Stevenson, Greenwillow (New York, NY), 1997.

Show and Tell Day, illustrated by Lizzy Rockwell, HarperCollins (New York, NY), 1997.

Halloween Day, illustrated by Lizzy Rockwell, HarperCollins (New York, NY), 1997.

One Bean, illustrated by Megan Halsey, Walker (New York, NY), 1998.

Pumpkin Day, Pumpkin Night, illustrated by Megan Halsey, Walker (New York, NY), 1999.

Ferryboat Ride!, illustrated by Maggie Smith, Crown (New York, NY), 1999.

Thanksgiving Day, illustrated by Lizzy Rockwell, HarperCollins (New York, NY), 1999.

Valentine's Day, illustrated by Lizzy Rockwell, HarperCollins (New York, NY), 1999.

Career Day, illustrated by Lizzy Rockwell, HarperCollins (New York, NY), 2000.

What Good Are Alligators?, illustrated by Lizzy Rockwell, HarperCollins (New York, NY), 2000.

Valentine's Day, illustrated by Lizzy Rockwell, HarperCollins (New York, NY), 2001.

The Prince Who Ran Away: The Story of Gautama Buddha, illustrated by Fahimeh Amiri, Knopf (New York, NY), 2001.

Morgan Plays Soccer ("Good Sports" series), illustrated by Paul Meisel, HarperCollins (New York, NY), 2001.

Growing like Me, illustrated by Holly Keller, Silver Whistle (San Diego, CA), 2001.

Bugs Are Insects, illustrated by Steve Jenkins, HarperCollins (New York, NY), 2001.

They Called Her Molly Pitcher, illustrated by Cynthia von Buhler, Knopf (New York, NY), 2002.

My Pet Hamster, illustrated by Bernice Lum, HarperCollins (New York, NY), 2002.

Becoming Butterflies, illustrated by Megan Halsey, Walker (New York, NY), 2002.

100 School Days, illustrated by Lizzy Rockwell, HarperCollins (New York, NY), 2002.

Katie Catz Makes a Splash ("Good Sports" series), illustrated by Paul Meisel, HarperCollins (New York, NY), 2003.

Two Blue Jays, illustrated by Megan Halsey, Walker (New York, NY), 2003.

Four Seasons Make a Year, illustrated by Megan Halsey, Walker (New York, NY), 2004.

Chip and the Karate Kick ("Good Sports" series), illustrated by Paul Meisel, HarperCollins (New York, NY), 2004.

Big George, illustrated by Matthew Trueman, Silver Whistle (San Diego, CA), 2004.

Mother's Day, illustrated by Lizzy Rockwell, HarperCollins (New York, NY), 2004.

Father's Day, illustrated by Lizzy Rockwell, HarperCollins (New York, NY), 2005.

Little Shark, illustrated by Megan Halsey, Walker (New York, NY), 2005.

Honey in a Hive, illustrated by S.D. Schindler, HarperCollins (New York, NY), 2005.

Good Morning, Digger, illustrated by Melanie Hope Greenberg, Viking (New York, NY), 2005.

Brendan and Belinda and the Slam Dunk! ("Good Sports" series), illustrated by Paul Meisel, HarperCollins (New York, NY), 2005.

Father's Day, illustrated by Lizzy Rockwell, HarperCollins (New York, NY), 2005.

Why Are the Ice Caps Melting?: The Dangers of Global Warming, illustrated by Paul Meisel, HarperCollins (New York, NY), 2006.

Who Lives in an Alligator Hole?, illustrated by Lizzy Rockwell, HarperCollins (New York, NY), 2006.

Backyard Bear, illustrated by Megan Halsey, Walker & Company (New York, NY), 2006.

Presidents' Day, illustrated by Lizzy Rockwell, HarperCollins (New York, NY), 2008.

Clouds, illustrated by Frané Lessac, HarperCollins (New York, NY), 2008.

What's So Bad about Gasoline?: Fossil Fuels and What They Do, illustrated by Paul Meisel, HarperCollins (New York, NY), 2009.

Big George: How a Shy Boy Became President Washington, illustrated by Matt Phelan, Silver Whistle (San Diego, CA), 2009.

ILLUSTRATOR

Marjorie Hopkins, *The Three Visitors,* Parents Magazine Press (New York, NY), 1967.

Jane Yolen, *The Minstrel and the Mountain: A Tale of Peace,* World (Cleveland, OH), 1967.

Lillian Bason, *Eric and the Little Canal Boat,* Parents Magazine Press (New York, NY), 1967.

Marjorie Hopkins, *The* Glass Valentine, Parents Magazine Press (New York, NY), 1968.

Paul Showers, *What Happens to a Hamburger?,* Crowell (New York, NY), 1970.

Kathryn Hitte, *Mexacali Soup,* Parents Magazine Press (New York, NY), 1970.

Joseph Jacobs, *Munacher and Manacher: An Irish Story,* Crowell (New York, NY), 1970.

Anne Petry, *Legends of the Saints,* Crowell (New York, NY), 1970.

Joseph Jacobs, *Master of All Masters,* Grosset (New York, NY), 1972.

Marjorie Hopkins, *A Gift for Tolum*, Parents Magazine Press (New York, NY), 1972.

Walter Dean Myers, *The Dancers*, Parents Magazine Press (New York, NY), 1972.

Barbara Brenner, *Cunningham's Rooster*, Parents Magazine Press (New York, NY), 1975.

Barbara Williams, *Never Hit a Porcupine*, Dutton (New York, NY), 1977.

Gerda Mantinband, *Bing Bong Band and Fiddle Dee Dee*, Doubleday (New York, NY), 1979.

Clyde Robert Bulla, *The Stubborn Old Woman*, Crowell (New York, NY), 1980.

Patricia Plante and David Bergman, retellers, *The Turtle and the Two Ducks and Ten Other Animal Fables Freely Retold from La Fontaine*, Crowell (New York, NY), 1980.

Steven Kroll, *Toot! Toot!*, Holiday House (New York, NY), 1983.

Adaptations

The Stolen Necklace: A Picture Story from India was adapted as a film by Paramount/Oxford, 1971; *The Toolbox* and *Machines* were adapted as filmstrips, Threshold Filmstrips, 1974.

Sidelights

In a career spanning more than three decades, prolific author-illustrator Anne F. Rockwell has created more than one hundred titles of her own, collaborated with husband Harlow Rockwell and daughter Lizzy Rockwell on dozens of volumes and amassed illustrator credits on nearly twenty picture books by other authors. Rockwell has also gradually decreased the age of her target audience. Initially producing works for middle graders, she has increasingly turned to picture books and board books for preschool and beginning readers, writing in genres from myths and folktales to simple science to feel-good animal picture books. All of Rockwell's works maintain "a simplicity within diversity . . . which both satisfies and stimulates young readers," according to Christine Doyle Stott in the *St. James Guide to Children's Writers*.

Rockwell was born in Memphis, Tennessee, and spent time in the Midwest and Southwest while growing up. Although she attended both the Sculpture Center and Pratt Graphic Arts Center, she relied mainly on self-teaching to learn her trade. She worked at an advertising agency before marrying fellow artist Harlow Rockwell. After the couple had their first child, Rockwell realized that she wanted to produce children's books to share the joy of reading she had first experienced as a youngster.

Rockwell's books for middle-grade audience include biographical and historical works such as *Filippo's Dome; Brunelleschi and the Cathedral of Florence, Glass, Stones, and Crown: The Abbe Suger and the Building of St. Denis, Temple on a Hill: The Building of the Parthenon,* and *Paintbrush and Peacepipe: The*

Story of George Catlin. In the first of these, "a simple, pleasing account," according to Ruth P. Bull in *Booklist*, Rockwell tells the story of Filippo Brunelleschi and the building of the Cathedral of Florence. She does the same for the Gothic gem of St. Denis in Paris with *Glass, Stones, and Crown,* mingling the biography of the church's founder with the story of the building's architecture. *Glass, Stones, and Crown* "is a book as interesting for its historical material as for its architectural focus," declared a reviewer for the *Bulletin of the Center for Children's Books*. The Parthenon is placed in an historical context in *Temple on a Hill,* and George Catlin, a famous painter of Native Americans, comes under Rockwell's biographical lens in *Paintbrush and Peacepipe,* called a "superior and pertinent biography" by a *Publishers Weekly* critic.

In a trio of early self-illustrated books—*The Dancing Stars: An Iroquois Legend, The Good Llama: A Picture Story from Peru,* and *The Stolen Necklace: A Picture Story from India*—Rockwell introduces readers to folktales from different cultures. In the late 1970s, however, the author/illustrator moved her focus to informative works for children just learning to read. In works such as *I Like the Library, Walking Shoes,* and *When We Grow Up,* she pairs a simple text with detailed, attention-grabbing pictures.

Rockwell's books have earned critical praise for their straightforward presentations of everyday objects and occurrences. Her nonfiction books explaining various types of transportation—which include *Boats, Cars, Planes, Trucks, Trains,* and *Bikes*—feature lively watercolor illustrations depicting animals operating each vehicle along with an easy-to-understand text. Reviewing *Boats,* a *Publishers Weekly* contributor wrote that "'Neatness counts' is the maxim Rockwell seems to have taken to heart, but her fastidious standards don't inhibit the artist from infusing the pictures in her many books with animation, appealing creatures and lovely colors." In *Horn Book,* Ann A. Flowers called *Boats* "an outstanding example of an informational picture book."

In her self-illustrated *Willy Can Count,* Rockwell presents a counting game played by mother and son during a walk. In her illustrations, she provides plenty of objects to count, prompting Joanna G. Jones to remark in *School Library Journal* that *Willy Can Count* is "bound to become a favorite." Another addition to her line of informational books, *Our Stars,* deals with stars, planets, meteors, comets, and moons, while *Ferryboat Ride!* introduces nautical concepts such as "bow" and "stern" in its story of a young girl and her family on their trip to a summer vacation spot. A *Publishers Weekly* critic concluded of *Ferryboat Ride!* that readers "will want to set sail themselves after experiencing this ferryboat ride."

Rockwell tackles the difficult concepts of slavery in *Only Passing Through,* a biography of nineteenth-century abolitionist and former slave Sojourner Truth. Praising the author's ability, Mickey commented in *Christian Parenting Today* that "telling the truth about slavery without overwhelming young readers takes a master's touch," something, the critic implied, that Rockwell demonstrates. *Only Passing Through* "clearly shows Sojourner's courage," commented a *School Library Journal* reviewer.

Another famous American woman, Molly Hays, is the subject of *They Called Her Molly Pitcher.* Hays followed her husband to the battlefield during the Revolutionary War, providing water to colonial soldiers, taking over the firing of her husband's cannon when he fell wounded, and, after the war, being awarded the rank of sergeant by General George Washington. Rockwell's biography, featuring illustrations by Cynthia von Buhler, is "a pleasure to read," according to a *Kirkus Reviews* contributor, while a *Publishers Weekly* critic deemed *They Called Her Molly Pitcher* a "stirring picture book

biography." Susan P. Bloom wrote in *Horn Book* that the story is "long but lively," and *School Library Journal* reviewer Anne Chapman concluded that Rockwell's "language is inviting, the story, exciting."

In addition to her informational titles, Rockwell's solo picture-book efforts for young readers fall into three main categories: easy readers, stories about animals, and folktales and legends. In the first category—by far the largest—Rockwell employs simple, often repetitive language with bright, bold pictures to capture the attention of preschoolers and beginning readers. Typical of such easy readers are *The Gollywhopper Egg, The Story Snail, No! No! No!, Bumblebee, Bumblebee, Do You Know Me?,* and *Here Comes the Night.* Working in collaboration with illustrator Megan Halsey, she has also produced *Pumpkin Day, Pumpkin Night, Becoming Butterflies,* and *Backyard Bear,* while *Good Morning, Digger* is a team effort produced by Rockwell and artist Melanie Hope Greenberg.

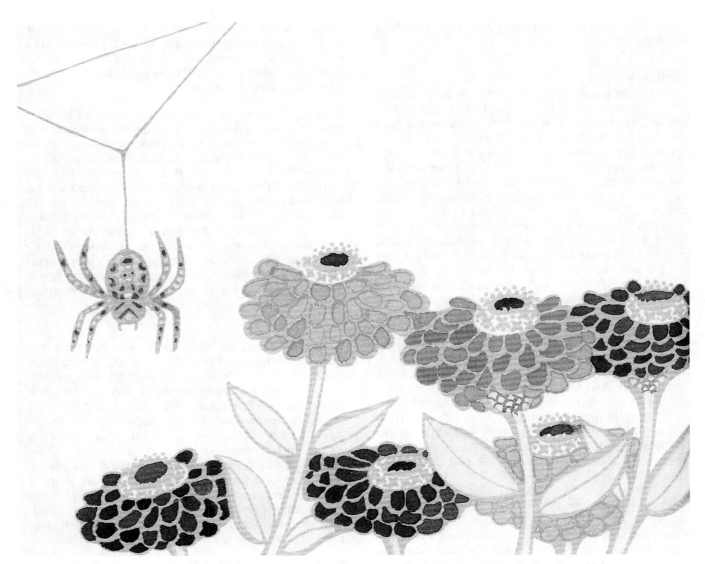

Anne F. Rockwell takes readers out into the garden in her self-illustrated picture book Bumblebee, Bumblebee, Do You Know Me? (Copyright © 1999 by Anne Rockwell. Used by permission of HarperCollins Publishers. In the United Kingdom by Dystel & Goderich Literary Management Agency.)

The tale of a magical snail who teaches young John a hundred stories with which to amaze his friends, *The Story Snail* is "fun for the beginning reader," according to *Horn Book* contributor Virginia Haviland. Another little boy is at the center of *No! No! No!,* and this cantankerous and out-of-sorts lad is having such a bad day that only a soothing bedtime story can put him to rights. In *Booklist* Hazel Rochman concluded of *No! No! No!* that "kids will laugh at the common misfortune; they'll sympathize with the irritation and draw comfort from the ending when things begin to change." Rockwell tells a story that would soothe even the hero of *No! No! No!* in *Here Comes the Night,* a self-illustrated story about the close of a family's day that a *Kirkus Reviews* writer deemed "a wonderful edition to the venerable sleepy-time tradition." In *Bumblebee, Bumblebee, Do You Know Me?* Rockwell presents young readers with "a graceful primer on the inhabitants of the backyard garden," according to a *Publishers Weekly* writer.

The search for a perfect Halloween decoration is the focus of *Pumpkin Day, Pumpkin Night,* a joint creation of Rockwell and Halsey. In *Becoming Butterflies,* another collaboration, author and artist give a lesson in how caterpillars grow into butterflies. A *Kirkus Reviews* contributor recommended *Becoming Butterflies* as "good to go to for general background reading," while *School Library Journal* critic Ellen Heath noted that Rockwell's "text makes clear the science of metamorphosis, and leavens the story with the humor of the children's comments." Also enlivened by Halsey's art, Rockwell's story for *Backyard Bear* follows a young bear cub as it strays into a human neighborhood in search of good things to eat, creating quite a stir in the process. Calling the book's ink-drawn illustrations "lovely," *School Library Journal* critic Andrea Tarr added that *Backyard Bear* features a "text [that] is simple and straightforward enough for beginning readers," while a *Kirkus Reviews* writer judged the book "a good springboard to further research and discussions."

Halsey and Rockwell also team up on *Two Blue Jays.* Set in the classroom that served as the backdrop of *Becoming Butterflies,* the book finds students excited to discover blue jays nesting outside their classroom window. A *Kirkus Reviews* critic called *Two Blue Jays* "a clear, concise explanation of a natural event," while a *Publishers Weekly* contributor noted that author and illustrator "share an abundance of bird information in an organic, personal way."

Bugs Are Insects, My Pet Hamster, Growing like Me, and *Clouds* are informational books for very young readers. In the first, an entry into the "Let's-Read-and-Find-out-Science" series, Rockwell illuminates the differences between bugs, beetles, spiders, and insects. Her "spare, carefully written text makes the distinction between insects and bugs quite clear," noted Shelley Townsend-Hudson in her *Booklist* review, while *School Library Journal* reviewer Lisa Gangemi Kropp considered *Bugs Are Insects* to be a "well-written and infor-

mative book." A reviewer for *Horn Book* noted of the same volume that Rockwell gets the lessons across "without ever talking down to her audience," while in *Kirkus Reviews* a critic judged *Clouds* to be "a good weather resources" for beginning readers with substantial vocabularies.

My Pet Hamster, another "Let's-Read-and-Find-out-Science" title, features a young girl discussing how to care for her pet. *Growing like Me* follows a toddler through his day as he points out how everything grows and changes to his little brother. Rochman praised the author's use of "simple, rhythmic words," while a *Publishers Weekly* critic considered *Growing like Me* "an amiable introduction to natural growth." Featuring what *Booklist* critic Kay Weisman deemed "realistic" illustrations by S.D. Schindler, *Honey in a Hive* continues Rockwell's "Let's Read-and-Find-out Science" entries in its exploration of the life of honey bees and life in a honey-bee hive.

Geared for young boys, *Good Morning, Little Digger* shares a boy's front-row seat at his bedroom window as the empty lot next door is excavated and developed into a community center. With its onomatopoeic text, which features machine sounds, the book is "tailor-made for fans of construction," according to a *Publishers Weekly* contributor, while in *School Library Journal* Laurel L. Takovakis deemed Rockwell's "sunny" story "fun for storytime or for one-on-one sharing." Another boy-friendly picture book, *At the Firehouse* takes place on Visitor's Day at a small firehouse, as a young boy meets the fire captain and his loyal Dalmatian pup. "Rockwell has a good sense of what intrigues young children," wrote *Booklist* contributor Carolyn Phelan in a review of *At the Firehouse.*

For readers beginning their first years of school, Rockwell penned *Welcome to Kindergarten,* which Judith Constantinides described as "a quiet, reassuring look at kindergarten routines." Another factual book gives young readers a tour of the fire department with *At the Firehouse,* which a *Kirkus Reviews* contributor considered to be "Rockwell at her best: lively, informative, and tuned to the sorts of details that fascinate younger children." Lisa Dennis, writing in *School Library Journal,* deemed *At the Firehouse* "a perfect introduction to the popular topic."

Animals are a favorite Rockwell motif in many of her picture books. A bear child is featured in *First Comes Spring,* "a good choice for sharing with groups and a popular choice for story hours," according to *Horn Book* contributor Elizabeth S. Watson. An entire bear family heads off to a busy day in *Come to Town,* a book that Nancy A. Gifford, writing in *School Library Journal,* predicted "should be extremely popular with preschool children and should be useful for nursery schools." Another sort of bear altogether is at the center of *Mr. Panda's Painting.* When the panda in question, a painter, runs out of paint, he heads off to the art store to buy some more, purchasing an entire rainbow of color. Stephanie Zvirin noted in *Booklist* that "Rockwell's crisp, simple shades, outlined in thick black lines, have much child appeal."

Myths and folktales are another constant motif for Rockwell, and she has collected them from around the world. *The Wolf Who Had a Wonderful Dream* is a French folktale, set in Normandy, while *What Bobolino Knew* is a Sicilian legend, and *Befana* is a European Christmas tale. More recent additions to the list include the Greek myths collected in both *The Robber Baby* and *The One-eyed Giant and Other Monsters from the Greek Myths.* Reviewing the former title in *Booklist,* Carolyn Phelan noted that "Rockwell has written a dependable source of Greek myths in a format suitable for the early elementary grades."

The Acorn Tree and Other Folktales features Rockwell's retellings from Aesop, among others. *The Prince Who Ran Away* combines a biography and folktales as Rockwell tells stories from the life of Siddhartha, the man who became known as Buddha. While the stories are simplified so that young readers can understand the religious concepts involved, on the whole a *Kirkus Reviews* contributor found that "Rockwell's version is accessible." A *Publishers Weekly* reviewer commented that the author's "accomplished prose . . . blends fac-

tual information with fanciful miracle tales," and Coop Renner of *School Library Journal* noted that the book seems to "present Buddhism as Buddha might have seen it." Still, "children will probably still need to share this with an adult," cautioned Gillian Engberg, writing for *Booklist.*

In 2001, Rockwell teamed up with Paul Meisel to create the "Good Sports" series, which begins with *Morgan Plays Soccer.* Morgan, a young bear, moves into a new neighborhood, and his monkey neighbor, Nina Jane, talks him into playing on the soccer team. Though he has trouble remembering not to catch the ball, he begins to develop confidence and is especially pleased when the coach places him as the goalie, where he can catch all he wants. "Rockwell spotlights a common childhood scenario," noted a reviewer for *Publishers Weekly.* Blair Christolon, writing for *School Library Journal,* considered the book "an appealing addition for that ever-popular soccer season." Lauren Peterson wrote in *Booklist,* "What comes across best, perhaps, is the importance of finding one's special talent and the value of patience and practice.

Rockwell and Meisel continue their "Good Sports" series with *Katie Catz Makes a Splash, Chip and the Karate Kick,* and *Brendan and Belinda and the Slam Dunk!* In *Katie Catz Makes a Splash* Katie the cat is reluctant to learn to swim, but her mother thinks it is an important skill, so Katie goes off to the pool to face her fears. A rabbit martial artist signs up for karate lessons in *Chip and the Karate Kick,* which finds Chip frustrated that his sensei will not let him advance until he learns that martial arts is more than just kicking and punching. In *Brendan and Belinda and the Slam Dunk!* pig twins Brendan and Belinda play basketball with every youth league around, thanks to their basketball-crazy father. A *Publishers Weekly* contributor noticed of *Katie Catz Makes a Splash* that Rockwell focuses "on the rewards of courage and hard work," while readers of *Chip and the Karate Kick* will "benefit from [Rockwell's] . . . understated study in developing a better attitude," according to a *Kirkus Reviews* contributor.

In another productive collaboration, Rockwell wrote and illustrated numerous books with her husband, Harlow Rockwell, until his death in 1988. Their book *Toad* presents "a congenial and informative look at the life cycle" of that popular amphibian, according to a *Publishers Weekly* contributor, while *Out to Sea* describes an unintended maritime adventure involving a brother and sister. Another work, *The Emergency Room,* describes a protagonist's trip to the hospital after spraining his ankle. P. Susan Gerrity, writing in the *New York Times Book Review,* remarked that *The Emergency Room* "provides excellent background information" and will reassure children afraid of visiting the hospital. The same demystification process is undertaken in *My Barber,* in which "clean lines, spacious composition, solid blocks of color, and plenty of white space" are all combined, according to a *Bulletin of the Center for Chil-*

Rockwell's popular animal friends are the stars of **Morgan Plays Soccer,** *an easy-reader featuring artwork by Paul Meisel.* (Illustration copyright © 2001 by Paul Meisel. All rights reserved. Used by permission of HarperCollins Publishers.)

***Rockwell and illustrator daughter Lizzy Rockwell team up on several picture books, including* 100 School Days.** (Illustration copyright © 2002 by Anne Rockwell. Used by permission of HarperCollins Publishers.)

dren's Books contributor, to take the mystery out of a trip to the barber. The husband and wife team continued their "My World" series with *How My Garden Grew* and *Sick in Bed,* both of which "are alive with realism and color," noted Peggy Forehand in *School Library Journal.*

Rockwell has continued the tradition of family collaboration, working with her illustrator daughter Lizzy Rockwell on several titles. Their *Apples and Pumpkins* is a "charming seasonal picture book with an easy-to-read text," according to Roseanne Cerny in *School Li-*

brary Journal, while *Our Yard Is Full of Birds* is "an appealing backyard bird book" appropriate for "the very young," according to Phelan. Mother and daughter have also teamed up for a series on holidays of the year. A *Kirkus Reviews* critic noted that *Halloween Day* contains a "simple" text and "sweet watercolor illustrations," making the book age-appropriate for the very young. Piper L. Nyman, reviewing *Valentine's Day* for *School Library Journal,* praised the "simple and accessible text" found in the book. Celebrating the hundredth day of school as a holiday of its own, the Rockwells produced *100 School Days,* in which students study counting. *School Library Journal* contributor Lisa Gangemi praised that Lizzy Rockwell's "realistically rendered illustrations are drenched in color." Carolyn Phelan, writing in *Booklist,* assured, "Teachers will be happy to add this to . . . stories about the one hundredth day of school." *Mother's Day* "adds to a winning streak of classroom books," according to Connie Fletcher in *Booklist,* the critic concluding that "This winsome, instructive book . . . can be read anytime."

Praising Rockwell's body of work, a *Kirkus Reviews* writer described the prolific writer/illustrator as "a well-loved author known for her simple books for the very young." Rockwell herself concurs with at least the second part of this description. As she wrote in the *St. James Guide to Children's Writers,* "My books are for the youngest of children. I loved, and still love, young children's picture books. I feel fortunate to have retained a sense of how young children see the world which enables me to do books for them. . . . I see that they are visually very alert and that illustrations can communicate where words are still difficult. In pictures they *see* everything."

Biographical and Critical Sources

BOOKS

Authors of Books for Young People, 3rd edition, Scarecrow (Metuchen, NJ), 1990.

Silvey, Anita, editor, *Children's Books and Their Creators,* Houghton (Boston, MA), 1995.

St. James Guide to Children's Writers, 5th edition, edited by Sara Pendergast and Tom Pendergast, St. James Press (Detroit, MI), 1999.

Something about the Author Autobiography Series, Volume 19, Gale (Detroit, MI), 1995.

PERIODICALS

Booklist, June 1, 1967, Ruth P. Bull, review of *Filippo's Dome: Brunelleschi and the Cathedral of Florence,* p. 1148; January 15, 1992, Carolyn Phelan, review of *Our Yard Is Full of Birds,* p. 946; October 15, 1992, Ilene Cooper, review of *What We Like,* p. 436; November 1, 1993, Stephanie Zvirin, review of *Mr. Panda's Painting,* p. 532; June 1 and 15, 1994, Carolyn Phelan, review of *The Robber Baby: Stories from the Greek Myths,* p. 1832; December 15, 1994, Mary Harris Veeder, review of *Ducklings and Pollywogs,* p. 760; May, 1995, Hazel Rochman, review of *No! No! No!,* p. 1580; October 1, 1995, Janice Del Negro, review of *The Acorn Tree and Other Folktales,* pp. 324-325; May 1, 2001, Hazel Rochman, review of *Growing like Me,* p. 1284, Shelley Townsend-Hudson, review of *Bugs Are Insects,* p. 1687; August, 2001, Lauren Peterson, review of *Morgan Plays Soccer,* p. 2132; December 15, 2001, Gillian Engberg, review of

The Prince Who Ran Away: The Story of Gautama Buddha, p. 731; February 15, 2002, Patricia Austin, review of *Only Passing Through,* p. 1038; March 15, 2002, Shelle Rosenfeld, review of *Becoming Butterflies,* p. 1261; April 15, 2002, Carolyn Phelan, review of *They Called Her Molly Pitcher,* p. 1400; September 15, 2001, Carolyn Phelan, review of *100 School Days,* p. 242; March 15, 2002, Shelle Rosenfeld, review of *Becoming Butterflies,* p. 1261; April 15, 2002, Carolyn Phelan, review of *They Called Her Molly Pitcher,* p. 1400; May 1, 2003, Gillian Engberg, review of *Two Blue Jays,* p. 1606; November 15, 2003, Carolyn Phelan, review of *At the Firehouse,* p. 603; February 15, 2004, Carolyn Phelan, review of *Four Seasons Make a Year,* p. 1061, Connie Fletcher, review of *Mother's Day,* p. 1064; May 1, 2004, Jennifer Mattson, review of *Chip and the Karate Kick,* p. 1564; April 1, 2005, Anne Rockwell, review of *Honey in a Hive,* p. 1362; December 1, 2006, Carolyn Phelan, review of *Why Are the Ice Caps Melting?: The Dangers of Global Warming,* p. 50.

Bulletin of the Center for Children's Books, March, 1969, review of *Glass, Stones, and Crown,* p. 117; May, 1981, review of *My Barber,* p. 179; March, 1992, review of *Our Yard Is Full of Birds,* p. 191; March, 1993, review of *Pots and Pans,* p. 224; April, 1996, review of *The One-eyed Giant and Other Monsters from the Greek Myths,* p. 278; June, 2002, review of *They Called Her Molly Pitcher,* p. 381; July-August, 2005, review of *Little Shark,* p. 309; December, 2006, Elizabeth Bush, review of *Why Are the Ice Caps Melting?,* p. 187.

Christian Parenting Today, March, 2001, Mickey, review of *Only Passing Through: The Story of Sojourner Truth,* p. 62.

Horn Book, October, 1979, Virginia Haviland, review of *The Story Snail,* pp. 133-134; October, 1982, Ann A. Flowers, review of *Boats,* pp. 512-513; July-August, 1985, Elizabeth S. Watson, review of *First Comes Spring,* p. 442; November, 1987, p. 731; November-December, 1989, Carolyn K. Jenks, review of *Apples and Pumpkins,* p. 764; September, 2001, review of *Bugs Are Insects,* p. 614; May-June, 2002, Susan P. Bloom, review of *They Called Her Molly Pitcher,* p. 349.

Instructor, November-December, 2002, Judy Freeman, review of *They Called Her Molly Pitcher,* p. 57.

Kirkus Reviews, June 1, 1994, review of *The Robber Baby,* p. 781; June 15, 1997, review of *Halloween Day,* p. 956; October 15, 2001, review of *The Prince Who Ran Away,* p. 1491; January 15, 2002, review of *Becoming Butterflies,* p. 107; April 1, 2002, review of *They Called Her Molly Pitcher,* p. 498; June 15, 2002, review of *100 School Days,* p. 887; February 15, 2003, review of *Two Blue Jays,* p. 316; August 1, 2003, review of *At the Firehouse,* p. 1023; February 1, 2004, review of *Four Seasons Make a Year,* p. 138; May 1, 2004, review of *Chip and the Karate Kick,* p. 447; April 15, 2005, review of *Good Morning, Digger,* p. 480; April 15, 2006, review of *Here Comes the Night,* p. 414; September 15, 2006, review of *Backyard Bear,* p. 965; October 15, 2006, review of *Why Are the Ice*

Caps Melting?, p. 1079; November 1, 2006, review of *Who Lives in an Alligator Hole?,* p. 1124; June 15, 2007, review of *Brendan and Belinda and the Slam Dunk!;* June 15, 2008, review of *My Preschool;* October 15, 2008, review of *Clouds.*

New York Times Book Review, April 21, 1985, Susan P. Gerrity, review of *The Emergency Room,* p. 18; September 14, 2008, review of *Clouds,* p. 17.

Publishers Weekly, November 15, 1971, review of *Paintbrush and Peacepipe,* p. 72; June 26, 1972, review of *Toad,* p. 63; January 14, 1974, review of *The Gollywhopper Egg,* pp. 94-95; October 15, 1982, review of *Boats,* p. 65; January 11, 1999, review of *Bumblebee, Bumblebee, Do You Know Me?* p. 70; May 17, 1999, review of *Ferryboat Ride!,* p. 79; March 12, 2001, *Growing like Me,* p. 88; July 16, 2001, review of *Morgan Plays Soccer,* p. 179; November 19, 2001, review of *The Prince Who Ran Away,* p. 67; April 29, 2002, review of *They Called Her Molly Pitcher,* p. 71; March 3, 2003, review of *Two Blue Jays,* p. 75; May 5, 2003, review of *Katie Catz Makes a Splash,* p. 220; October 27, 2003, review of *At the Firehouse,* p. 72; April 25, 2005, review of *Good Morning, Digger,* p. 55.

School Library Journal, May, 1982, Peggy Forehand, review of *How My Garden Grew* and *Sick in Bed,* p. 56; November, 1987, Nancy A. Gifford, review of *Come to Town,* p. 96; August, 1989, review of *On Our Vacation,* p. 131; November, 1989, Roseanne Cerny, review of *Apples and Pumpkins,* pp. 91-92; January, 1990, Joanna G. Jones, review of *Willy Can Count,* p. 89; February, 1993, Judith Constantinides, review of *What We Like,* p. 78; January, 1995, Christine A. Moesch, review of *Ducklings and Pollywogs,* p. 92; July, 1995, Beth Irish, review of *No! No! No!,* p. 68; October, 1995, Harriett Fargnoli, review of *The Acorn Tree and Other Folktales,* pp. 128-129; February, 1999, Dina Sherman, review of *Bumblebee, Bumblebee, Do You Know Me?: A Garden Guessing Game,* p. 88; May, 1999, Elaine Fort Weischedel, review of *Our Stars,* p. 112; June, 1999, Ginny Gustin, review of *Ferryboat Ride!,* p. 106; March, 2001, Judith Constantinides, review of *Welcome to Kindergarten,* p. 133; April, 2001, Piper L. Nyman, review of *Valentine's Day,* p. 121, and Judith Constantinides, review of *Growing like Me,* p. 134; August, 2001, Blair Christolon, review of *Morgan Plays Soccer,* p. 158; October, 2001, Lisa Gangemi Krapp, review of *Bugs Are Insects,* p. 146; December, 2001, Coop Renner, review of *The Prince Who Ran Away,* p. 128; March, 2002, review of *Only Passing Through,* p. 90, and Ellen Heath, review of *Becoming Butterflies,* p. 220; June, 2002, Anne Chapman, review of *They Called Her Molly Pitcher,* p. 124; September, 2002, Lisa Gangemi, review of *100 School Days,* p. 205; May, 2003, Susan Scheps, review of *Two Blue Jays,* p. 128; December, 2003, Lisa Dennis, review of *At the Firehouse,* p. 124; March, 2004, Andrea Tarr, review of *Mother's Day,* p. 180; June, 2004, Gay Lynn Van Vleck, review of *Chip and the Karate Kick,* p. 118; July, 2004, Lisa G. Kropp, review of *100 School Days,* p. 44; June, 2005, Karey Wehner, review of *Good Morning, Digger,* p. 126; October, 2006, Andrea Tarr, review of *Backyard Bear,* p. 124; January, 2008, Grace Oliff, review of *Presidents' Day,* p. 97; April, 2008, G. Alyssa Parkinson, review of *My Preschool,* p. 120.

ONLINE

Anne Rockwell Home Page, http://www.annerockwell.com (October 10, 2008).

Children's Literature Web site, http://www.childrenslit.com/ (July 18, 2005).*

S

SALTZBERG, Barney 1955-

Personal

Born April 30, 1955, in Los Angeles, CA; son of Irving and Ruth Saltzberg; married 1985; wife's name Susan; children: two children. *Education:* Sonoma State College, degree, 1977.

Addresses

Home—Los Angeles, CA. *E-mail*—info@barney saltzberg.com.

Career

Artist, illustrator, author, and singer-songwriter. Performer at concerts for children; songwriter and producer of recordings adapted from Public Broadcasting System (PBS) children's television series *Arthur.* Founder, Crazy Hair Day Literacy Campaign (reading initiative).

Member

Society of Children's Book Writers and Illustrators.

Awards, Honors

Oppenheim Toy Portfolio award, 1998, for *The Flying Garbanzos;* California Young Reader Medal finalist, 1999, for *Mrs. Morgan's Lawns;* Parents' Choice Award, 2000, and California Young Reader Medal nomination, 2003, both for *The Soccer Mom from Outer Space.*

Writings

SELF-ILLUSTRATED

Utter Nonsense, McGraw-Hill (New York, NY), 1980.
It Must Have Been the Wind, Harper & Row (New York, NY), 1982.

Barney Saltzberg (Photograph by Linda Vanoff. Reproduced by permission of Barney Saltzberg.)

What to Say to Clara, Atheneum (New York, NY), 1984.
The Yawn, Atheneum (New York, NY), 1985.
Cromwell, Atheneum (New York, NY), 1986.
Hi Bird, Bye Bird, Barron's (New York, NY), 1990.
What Would You Do with a Bone?, Barron's (New York, NY), 1990.

Mrs. Morgan's Lawn, Hyperion (New York, NY), 1993.

This Is a Great Place for a Hot Dog Stand, Hyperion (New York, NY), 1994.

Where, Oh, Where's My Underwear?, Hyperion (New York, NY), 1994.

Show and Tell, Hyperion (New York, NY), 1994.

Phoebe and the Spelling Bee, Hyperion (New York, NY), 1996.

Backyard Cowboy, paper engineering by Renée Jablow, Hyperion (New York, NY), 1996.

(With Laura Numeroff) *Two for Stew,* illustrated by Salvatore Murdocca, Simon & Schuster (New York, NY), 1996.

The Flying Garbanzos, Crown (New York, NY), 1998.

Animal Kisses, Harcourt (San Diego, CA), 2000.

The Soccer Mom from Outer Space, Crown (New York, NY), 2000.

Baby Animal Kisses, Harcourt (New York, NY), 2000.

The Problem with Pumpkins: A Hip and Hop Story, Harcourt (San Diego, CA), 2001.

Hip, Hip, Hooray Day!: A Hip and Hop Story, Harcourt (San Diego, CA), 2002.

Peekaboo Kisses, Harcourt (San Diego, CA), 2002.

Crazy Hair Day, Candlewick Press (Cambridge, MA), 2003.

Noisy Kisses: A Touch and Feel Book, Harcourt (San Diego, CA), 2004.

I Love Cats, Candlewick Press (Cambridge, MA), 2005.

I Love Dogs, Candlewick Press (Cambridge, MA), 2005.

Cornelius P. Mud, Are You Ready for Bed?, Candlewick Press (Cambridge, MA), 2005.

Star of the Week, Candlewick Press (Cambridge, MA), 2006.

Goodnight Kisses, Harcourt (New York, NY), 2006.

Hi, Bunny. Bye, Bunny, Harcourt (New York, NY), 2007.

Hi, Blueberry!, Harcourt (San Diego, CA), 2007.

Cornelius P. Mud, Are You Ready for School?, Candlewick Press (Cambridge, MA), 2007.

Stanley and the Class Pet, Candlewick Press (Cambridge, MA), 2008.

Peekaboo, Blueberry!, Harcourt (Orlando, FL), 2008.

ILLUSTRATOR

Lisa Rojany, *Jake and Jenny on the Farm* (interactive book), Price Stern Sloan (Los Angeles, CA), 1990.

Wendy Boyd-Smith, *There's No Barking at the Table Cookbook,* Lip Smackers, Inc., 1991.

Lisa Rojany, *Jake and Jenny on the Town* (interactive book), Price Stern Sloan (Los Angeles, CA), 1993.

Lisa A. Marsoli and Stacie Strong, *Bow, Wow, and You on the Farm,* Child's Play of England, 1996.

Judy Sierra, *There's a Zoo in Room 22,* Harcourt (San Diego, CA), 2000.

Amy Ehrlich, *Kazam's Magic,* Candlewick Press (Cambridge, MA), 2001.

Amy Ehrlich, *Bravo, Kazam!,* Candlewick Press (Cambridge, MA), 2002.

Stuart J. Murphy, *Slugger's Carwash,* HarperCollins (New York, NY), 2002.

How Many Elephants? (lift-the-flap book), Candlewick Press (Cambridge, MA), 2004.

Adaptations

Many of Saltzberg's books have been adapted as audiobooks, including *Crazy Hair Day,* produced by Inkless Music as a benefit for Concern Foundation for Cancer Research, 2007.

Sidelights

Barney Saltzberg is an author and illustrator of children's books whose books include *The Flying Garbanzos, The Soccer Mom from Outer Space, Crazy Hair Day,* and several books featuring an unlikely porcine hero named Cornelius P. Mud. In addition to writing, Saltzberg also composes songs, often performing concerts for children in schools, libraries, and hospitals across the United States. Discussing the beginning of his writing career on his home page, the versatile author/artist explained that although he dreamt of being a musician early on in his life, a career in children's books did not become a possibility until he took a printmaking class while studying art at Sonoma State College in California. The assignment he completed for this class resulted in one of his first children's books, *It Must Have Been the Wind.*

Like *It Must Have Been the Wind,* many of Saltzberg's books for children feature original stories and art. In *What to Say to Clara,* for example, he pairs his text with black-and-white cartoons that bring to life the simple story of a shy boy named Otis and his attempts to gather enough courage to speak to a classmate. "Droll" and "firmly etched" drawings accompany the text of this "larky" story, noted a reviewer in *Publishers Weekly.* He features another simple narrative in *The Yawn,* a wordless book in which a young boy begins his day with a huge yawn, passing it on to a dog, who passes it on again, fueling a chain reaction that even affects the Man in the Moon. In a review for *School Library Journal,* Deb Andrews praised the simple illustrations in *The Yawn,* adding that Saltzberg's work will "spark discussion among young children."

A classic picture-book villain, the crabby and unpleasant neighbor, is the star of *Mrs. Morgan's Lawn.* In Saltzberg's story, a boy dreads asking Mrs. Morgan to return his ball after it lands in her yard and imagines various other alternative methods to retrieve the toy. "The boy's forthright narration rings true," reflected by the author's humorous and "naïve . . . illustrations," observed Elizabeth Bush in her *Booklist* review of *Mrs. Morgan's Lawn.* Saltzberg also focuses on everyday activities and realistic actions in books such as *Where, Oh Where Is My Underwear?, Show and Tell,* and *Backyard Cowboy.*

The author/illustrator shares a more involved story in *This Is a Great Place for a Hot Dog Stand,* a tale highlighting "individual enterprise and ingenuity" according to Jane Marino in *School Library Journal.* The book tells of hopes and dreams, as Izzy, a factory worker, quits his job to begin a business selling hot dogs. In

A young boy's creative zeal backfires in Saltzberg's humorous self-illustrated picture book Crazy Hair Day. (Copyright © 2003 by Barney Saltzberg. Reproduced by permission of the publisher, Candlewick Press, Inc., Somerville, MA.)

Phoebe and the Spelling Bee, Saltzberg returns to a familiar theme: dealing with fear and unpleasant tasks. Writing in *Booklist,* Stephanie Zvirin remarked that although the spelling list Phoebe is confronted with would be a bit complicated for the book's intended audience, readers "will readily recognize themselves in Phoebe's . . . attempts to avoid . . . something new and scary." A reviewer for *Publishers Weekly* praised Saltzberg for providing children with a new tactic to learning words.

A family of circus acrobats take center-stage in *The Flying Garbanzos,* in which the five-member Garbanzo family—including a two-year-old baby named Beanie— fly and perform acrobatic tricks even when they are not on stage. Saltzberg's whimsical picture book is "sure to be a hit," according to *School Library Journal* critic Virginia Golodetz, while in *Publishers Weekly* a reviewer remarked that "fast action and shouted dialogue ensure that the pages turn in a hurry."

Outrageous behavior of another sort is the focus of *The Soccer Mom from Outer Space,* an exaggerated look at an overly enthusiastic mother. Lena's mom's excitement in the days leading up to her daughter's first soccer game prompts Dad to recount the story of his own mother and her antics during his own childhood sports career. Reviewing the picture book for *School Library Journal,* Blair Christolon noted that while children will certainly relate to the story, *The Soccer Mom from Outer Space* is also a "particularly good choice for coaches to use for a meeting with new soccer parents."

A less-involved set of parents provides the humor in Saltzberg's picture books featuring a rambunctious young pig. In *Cornelius P. Mud, Are You Ready for Bed?* the young pig is queried regarding his daily night-time ritual: putting away toys, using the bathroom, etcetera. Although the book's text shows the piglet answering in the affirmative, Saltzberg's illustrations tell a quite different story. In *Horn Book* Kitty Flynn noted that the "simple text" in the book features a "twist on a familiar storyline and the bold dynamic pictures are . . . attention grabbers." A similar story plays out in *Cornelius P. Mud, Are You Ready for School?* as Cornelius answers his mother's questions while getting ready to leave for school. "The cheerful colors and Cornelius's lively antics make his world the happy-go-lucky kind of place that children enjoy visiting," according to *Booklist* critic Randall Enos.

Inspired by a young cancer patient's worries about returning to school following chemotherapy, *Crazy Hair Day* introduces a young hamster named Stanley Birdbaum as he prepares for school. This is no ordinary day, however; as Stanley tells his mom, it is Crazy Hair Day, and the two have fun fluffing, spiking, and coloring the hamster's fur. When Stanley arrives at school, however, he is mortified to learn that it is actually school picture day. After hiding in the bathroom for a while, the hamster emerges and finds that all his classmates have followed his lead, making the day Crazy Hair Picture Day. "Saltzberg conveys the pleasing goofiness of special days at school," noted a *Kirkus Reviews* contributor in a review of *Crazy Hair Day,* while in *Booklist* Jennifer Mattson concluded that "the authenticity of Stanley's situation is likely to put readers in the mood to share their most embarrassing moments." In *School Library Journal,* Jody McCoy dubbed *Crazy Hair Day* a "delightful tale of confusion and compassion."

Stanley returns in *Star of the Week,* as the young hamster is selected to share his favorite things with the class. When Stanley's favorite foods and favorite toy do not elicit enthusiasm, he feels a tad rejected, but on the third day his chalkboard art wins raves. In his ink-and-acrylic art, Saltzberg "creates Stanley's world with warmth and keen attention to detail," according to *Booklist* critic Carolyn Phelan, and in *School Library Journal* Kathy Piehl concluded that *Star of the Week* "perfectly captures the stage fright that almost everyone has experienced."

Biographical and Critical Sources

BOOKS

Ward, Martha E., and others, *Authors of Books for Young People,* Scarecrow Press (Metuchen, NJ), 1990.

PERIODICALS

Booklist, December 1, 1993, Elizabeth Bush, review of *Mrs. Morgan's Lawn,* p. 701; October 1, 1997, Stephanie Zvirin, review of *Phoebe and the Spelling Bee,* p. 339; September 15, 2001, Ilene Cooper, review of *The Problem with Pumpkins: A Hip and Hop Story,* p. 236; November 1, 2003, Jennifer Mattson, review of *Crazy Hair Day,* p. 506; May 1, 2005, Ilene Cooper, review of *Cornelius P. Mud, Are You Ready for Bed?,* p. 1593; February 1, 2006, Carolyn Phelan, review of *Star of the Week,* p. 57; June 1, 2007, Randall Enos, review of *Cornelius P. Mud, Are You Ready for School?,* p. 80.

Bulletin of the Center for Children's Books, December, 2003, Karen Coats, review of *Crazy Hair Day,* p. 164; September, 2005, Timnah Card, review of *Cornelius P. Mud, Are You Ready for Bed?,* p. 41.

Horn Book, May-June, 2005, Kitty Flynn, review of *Cornelius P. Mud, Are You Ready for Bed?,* p. 314.

Kirkus Reviews, February 15, 2002, review of *Hip, Hip, Hooray Day!,* p. 264; July 15, 2003, review of *Crazy Hair Day,* p. 967; April 1, 2005, review of *Cornelius P. Mud, Are You Ready for Bed?,* p. 424; January 15, 2006, review of *Star of the Week,* p. 89; June 15, 2007, review of *Cornelius P. Mud, Are You Ready for School?;* May 15, 2008, review of *Stanley and the Class Pet.*

Publishers Weekly, December 21, 1984, review of *What to Say to Clara,* p. 88; November 8, 1993, review of *Mrs. Morgan's Lawn,* p. 75; October 13, 1997, review of *Phoebe and the Spelling Bee,* p. 74; September 7, 1998, review of *The Flying Garbanzos,* p. 93; September 24, 2001, review of *The Problem with Pumpkins,* p. 43; July 1, 2002, review of *Peekaboo Kisses,* p. 81; August 18, 2003, review of *Crazy Hair Day,* p. 78.

School Library Journal, August, 1982, review of *It Must Have Been the Wind,* p. 105; December, 1984, review of *What to Say to Clara,* p. 76; December, 1985, Deb Andrews, review of *The Yawn,* p. 82; April, 1986, Ronald Van de Voorde, review of *Cromwell,* p. 79; May, 1995, Jane Marino, review of *This Is a Great Place for a Hot Dog Stand,* p. 94; September, 1998, Virginia Golodetz, review of *The Flying Garbanzos,* p. 181; August, 2000, Blair Christolon, review of *The Soccer Mom from Outer Space,* p. 164; April, 2002, Roxanne Burg, review of *Hip, Hip, Horray Day!,* p. 122; December, 2003, Jody McCoy, review of *Crazy Hair Day,* p. 125; March, 2005, Kelley Rae Unger, review of *Cornelius P. Mud, Are You Ready for Bed?,* p. 186; August, 2004, Andrea Tarr, reviews of *I Love Cats* and *I Love Dogs,* p. 105; February, 2006, Kathy Piehl, review of *Star of the Week,* p. 109.

Tribune Books (Chicago, IL), September 7, 2003, review of *Crazy Hair Day,* p. 51; February 26, 2006, Mary Harris Russell, review of *Star of the Week,* p. 7.

ONLINE

Barney Saltzberg Home Page, http://www.barneysaltzberg. com (October 26, 2008).*

*   *   *

SAVAGE, Stephen 1965-

Personal
Born February 14, 1965.

Addresses
E-mail—Stephen.Savage@earthlink.net.

Career
Author and illustrator of children's books.

Illustrator
Lauren Thompson, *Polar Bear Night,* Scholastic Press (New York, NY), 2004.

Sidelights
Stephen Savage is an illustrator and graphic artist. Lauren Thompson's *Polar Bear Night,* a bedtime story, is the first picture book to benefit from Savage's distinctive graphic art. The story follows a polar bear cub as she ventures out from her warm den on a winter's night, driven by the feeling that something special is about to happen. The bear cub passes other drowsy Arctic animals as she forges on, ultimately climbing to the top of a snowdrift in time to witness a shower of falling stars. In *Publishers Weekly* a critic described Savage's linocut images for *Polar Bear Night* as "striking compositions" in which "the darkness is quietly beautiful." A *Kirkus Reviews* critic also viewed Savage's work favorably, writing that the book "sparkles just like ice crystals on a moonlit night." In her *New York Times Book Review* appraisal of *Polar Bear Night,* Janet Zarem wrote: "Perhaps the biggest challenge for a bedtime story is to teach children that darkness can be a friend," and *Polar Bear Night* "meets that challenge. . . . The stylized simplicity of Savage's illustrations reflects both the solace of night and the fellowship of nature."

Biographical and Critical Sources

PERIODICALS

Booklist, November 15, 2004, Jennifer Mattson, review of *Polar Bear Night,* p. 585.

Horn Book, November-December, 2004, Lauren Adams, review of *Polar Bear Night,* p. 703.
Kirkus Reviews, October 15, 2004, review of *Polar Bear Night,* p. 1014.
New York Times Book Review, November 14, 2004, Janet Zarem, "A Bear Cub's Arctic Lullaby," p. 30.
Publishers Weekly, November 22, 2004, review of *Polar Bear Night,* p. 59.
School Library Journal, November, 2004, Jane Marino, review of *Polar Bear Night,* p. 118.

ONLINE

Stephen Savage Home Page, http://www.stephensavage. net/ (October 29, 2008).*

*   *   *

SCHERER, Jeffrey

Personal
Married Winnie Yu; children: Sammy, Annie. *Education:* Attended Joe Kubert School of Cartoon Design; School of Visual Arts (New York, NY), B.F.A. (illustration). *Hobbies and other interests:* Bird watching.

Addresses
Home—Voorheesville, NY. *E-mail*—jeffreys@jeffrey scherer.com.

Career
Illustrator and graphic artist. *Times Union,* Albany, NY, graphic artist, 1989—.

Awards, Honors
Several awards for newspaper design.

Writings

SELF-ILLUSTRATED

One Snowy Day, Scholastic (New York, NY), 1996.

ILLUSTRATOR

James Preller, *Wake Me in Spring,* Scholastic (New York, NY), 1994.
Grace Maccarone, *"What Is That?" Said the Cat,* Scholastic (New York, NY), 1995.
Mary Serfozo, *The Big Bug Dug,* Scholastic (New York, NY), 2001.
Elizabeth Bennett, *A New Friend,* Scholastic (New York, NY), 2002.

Dana Meachen Rau, *Pet Your Pet,* Compass Point Books (Minneapolis, MN), 2002.
The Ants Go Marching, Scholastic (New York, NY), 2002.
Elizabeth Bennett, *The Big Sleepover,* Scholastic (New York, NY), 2003.
Elizabeth Bennett, *The Big Bunch: The Beach Mystery,* Scholastic (New York, NY), 2003.
Elizabeth Bennett, *The New Bug,* Scholastic (New York, NY), 2003.
Melissa Stewart, *Down to Earth,* Compass Point Books (Minneapolis, MN), 2004.
Mary Serfozo, *Whooo's There?,* Random House (New York, NY), 2007.

Contributor of illustration to periodicals, including *Wild Animal Baby* and *Your Big Backyard.* Illustrator of on-line comic "Finest Amphibians," written by Mike Virtanen.

Biographical and Critical Sources

PERIODICALS

Booklist, February 1, 1998, Ilene Cooper, review of *One Snowy Day,* p. 928.
Kirkus Reviews, June 15, 2007, review of *Whooo's There?*
School Library Journal, August, 2007, Kirsten Cutler, review of *Whooo's There?,* p. 92.

ONLINE

Jeffrey Scherer Home Page, http://www.jeffreyscherer.com (October 13, 2008).*

*   *   *

SCHORR, Melissa 1972-
   (Melissa Robin Schorr)

Personal

Born 1972, in NY; daughter of Arthur (a finance manager) and Thelma (a music teacher) Schorr; married Gary Matthew Cohen, September 29, 2002; children: Alexa. *Education:* Northwestern University, Medill School of Journalism, B.A., 1994.

Addresses

Home—Boston, MA. *E-mail*—melissa@melissaschorr.com.

Career

Writer, journalist, and novelist. Former member of editorial staff, *Gentleman's Quarterly* and *Working Woman;* reporter for *People,* staff reporter for *Oakland Tribune* and *Las Vegas Sun;* health writer for *ABCNews.com.*

Awards, Honors

Knight Science Journalism fellowship, Massachusetts Institute of Technology, 2000; first-place award for feature writing, Nevada Press Association.

Writings

Goy Crazy (novel), Hyperion (New York, NY), 2006.

Contributor to magazines, Web sites, and periodicals, including *Glamour, Allure, Self, Marie Clare, Bride's, In Talk, Esquire, San Francisco, National Geographic Traveler, Wired, Chicago Tribune, Wall Street Journal, San Jose Mercury News, Lifetimetv.com, WebMD,* and *Reuters Health.* Former columnist, *Las Vegas Sun.*

Sidelights

Melissa Schorr is a journalist whose debut novel, *Goy Crazy,* is based in part on an article she did for *Gentleman's Quarterly* magazine. In the article, titled "The Joys of Goys," the Jewish Schorr takes a humorous look at her experiences dating non-Jewish men. With *Goy Crazy,* she tells the story of Jewish teenager Rachel Lowenstein, a sophomore at Riverdale High School in the Bronx. A "good girl" who considers her life boring, Rachel keenly feels all the pressures from her peer group to do things her parents would not recommend. Finally, she decides that she needs to liven up her days with a little misbehavior. Prime among her newfound goals is dating a gorgeous blond gentile boy, the Catholic Luke Christiansen. Knowing that her parents would disapprove, Rachel accounts for her time with Luke by telling them that she is dating Jewish neighbor and childhood friend Howard Goldstein. At first, the rush of teenage love and the thrill of rebellion is exciting, but as time goes by Rachel begins to feel guilty about deceiving her parents and acting against her Jewish heritage. Soon, she begins to reconsider her personal values and her religious faith, finding her connection to both very strong. While dating Luke may have been a fun way to try out a little teenage rebellion, Howard Goldstein, she realizes, has much to recommend him.

A *Kirkus Reviews* critic noted that *Goy Crazy* is "droll and sharp with scenes that are comical, troubling, and poignantly sincere." *Booklist* reviewer Stephanie Zvirin observed that "Schorr does a lot right: dialogue is wry and funny, and Rachel, smart and sensitive." "This humorous depiction of first love offers a witty first-person narrative and situations to which all readers can relate," remarked a *Publishers Weekly* reviewer. The *Kirkus Reviews* contributor concluded of *Goy Crazy* that Schorr's novel is "well-written chick-lit with a Jewish slant."

Biographical and Critical Sources

PERIODICALS

Booklist, October 1, 2006, Stephanie Zvirin, review of *Goy Crazy,* p. 62.

Dallas Morning News, November 4, 2006, Harriet P. Gross, review of *Goy Crazy.*

Kirkus Reviews, August 15, 2006, review of *Goy Crazy,* p. 851.

Publishers Weekly, October 23, 2006, review of *Goy Crazy,* p. 52.

ONLINE

Author's Den Web site, http://www.authorsden.com/ (March 28, 2007), biography of Melissa Schorr.

Goy Crazy Web site, http://goycrazy.com/ (March 28, 2007).

Melissa Schorr Home Page, http://www.melissaschorr.com (October 28, 2008).*

*   *   *

SCHORR, Melissa Robin
See SCHORR, Melissa

*   *   *

SCOTT, Elizabeth

Personal

Born in VA; daughter of high school teachers; married. *Education:* College degree.

Addresses

Home—P.O. Box 638, Manassas Park, VA 20113. *E-mail*—elizabeth@elizabethwrites.com.

Career

Writer. Has worked as an editor, an office manager, and in sales.

Writings

Bloom, Simon Pulse (New York, NY), 2007.
Perfect You, Simon Pulse (New York, NY), 2008.
Stealing Heaven, HarperCollins (New York, NY), 2008.
Living Dead Girl, Simon Pulse (New York, NY), 2008.
Something, Maybe, Simon Pulse (New York, NY), 2009.
Love You, Hate You, Miss You, HarperCollins (New York, NY), 2009.

Sidelights

Within only a few years of having her first novel published, Elizabeth Scott has established herself as an author of honest and unvarnished stories about young women struggling to manage schoolwork, romantic relationships, friendships, family life, and self-image. In

novels such as *Bloom, Perfect You,* and *Stealing Heaven,* Scott creates female characters with recognizable personality traits, not all of them admirable.

Lauren, the protagonist of Scott's debut novel *Bloom,* cannot quite understand why she has won the heart of the most popular boy in her school, especially since they seem to have nothing in common. When an old friend named Evan arrives in town, Lauren finds herself in a love triangle as she tries to figure out what qualities she values most in a relationship. Even as she deceives her boyfriend in order to spend time with Evan, Lauren wonders why her old friend's more-dangerous lifestyle appeals to her. Reviewing *Bloom* for *Kliatt,* Amanda MacGregor called Lauren "a refreshingly complex character . . . trying to figure out how to be herself." According to *School Library Journal* contributor Sarah Krygier, the conflict Scott introduces in her novel "rings true," creating "enough drama to keep readers interested."

Perfect You explores the life of Kate, a character for whom everything seems to be falling apart. While Kate's best friend ditches her, her clueless father blissfully sells vitamins at the local mall. Meanwhile, Kate's grandmother keeps trying to run the teen's life, and her complicated relationship with her boyfriend is becoming mostly physical. In *School Library Journal* Natasha Forrester wrote that in *Perfect You* Scott "does a good job portraying a teen who is simultaneously self-centered and sympathetic."

Biographical and Critical Sources

PERIODICALS

Bulletin of the Center for Children's Books, July-August, 2007, Deborah Stevenson, review of *Bloom,* p. 484.

Kliatt, May, 2007, Amanda MacGregor, review of *Bloom,* p. 28.

School Library Journal, June, 2007, Sarah Krygier, review of *Bloom,* p. 160; April, 2008, Natasha Forrester, review of *Perfect You,* p. 148.

Voice of Youth Advocates, June, 2007, Angelica Delgado, review of *Bloom,* p. 152.

ONLINE

Elizabeth Scott Home Page, http://www.elizabethwrites.com (October 28, 2008).

*   *   *

SERFOZO, Mary 1925-

Personal

Surname accented on second syllable; born February 21, 1925, in Seattle, WA; daughter of Patrick (an engineer) and Olive Cannon; married John Serfozo, August

8, 1953; children: Stephen, David. *Education:* University of Washington, B.A. *Politics:* "Independent." *Religion:* Roman Catholic. *Hobbies and other interests:* Travel, swimming, reading, becoming computer literate.

Addresses

Home—Paso Robles, CA.

Career

Freelance author and copywriter. Has worked variously as an assistant editor of *Mademoiselle* magazine, a copywriter for a California advertising agency, and in publicity for Elizabeth Arden in New York City, Pan American Airways, and the Hawaiian sugar industry in Honolulu.

Awards, Honors

American Bookseller Pick of the Lists, and Children's Choice Certificate of Excellence, for *Who Said Red?; Parenting* magazine Reading Magic Award, for *Who Wants One?*

Writings

Welcome, Roberto!/Bienvenido, Roberto!, photographs by husband, John Serfozo, Follett, 1969.

Who Said Red?, illustrated by Keiko Narahashi, Margaret K. McElderry Books (New York, NY), 1988.

Who Wants One?, illustrated by Keiko Narahashi, Margaret K. McElderry Books (New York, NY), 1989.

Rain Talk, illustrated by Keiko Narahashi, Margaret K. McElderry Books (New York, NY), 1990.

Dirty Kurt, illustrated by Nancy Poydar, Margaret K. McElderry Books (New York, NY), 1992.

Benjamin Bigfoot, illustrated by Jos. A. Smith, Margaret K. McElderry Books (New York, NY), 1993.

Joe Joe, illustrated by Nina S. Montezinos, Margaret K. McElderry Books (New York, NY), 1993.

What's What?: A Guessing Game, illustrated by Keiko Narahashi, Margaret K. McElderry Books (New York, NY), 1996.

There's a Square: A Book about Shapes, illustrated by David Carter, Scholastic (New York, NY), 1996.

A Head Is for Hats, illustrated by Katy Bratun, Scholastic (New York, NY), 1999.

Plumply, Dumply Pumpkin, illustrated by Valeria Petrone, Margaret K. McElderry Books (New York, NY), 2001.

The Big Bug Dug, illustrated by Jeffrey Scherer, Scholastic (New York, NY), 2001.

Whooo's There?, illustrated by Jeffrey Scherer, Random House (New York, NY), 2007.

Also author of bilingual classroom packages.

Sidelights

Mary Serfozo was inspired to write her first published children's book, *Who Said Red?,* when she observed a group of children listening to her local librarian sing and play the guitar. When it came time for the children to sing their line in every chorus, they "joined in so joyously," Serfozo told Diane Roback in *Publishers Weekly,* "I thought it would be fun in a read-aloud book to have a line that kids would know was coming up." Since writing *Who Said Red?,* Serfozo has created a number of concept books for younger children, her simple texts enhanced by illustrators such as Keiko Narahashi, Valeria Petrone, Jos. A. Smith, Nancy Poydar, and Jeffrey Scherer. A collaboration with Scherer, *Whooo's There?,* was praised as a "tranquil and engaging bedtime sojourn . . . just right for one-on-one sharing" by a *Kirkus Reviews* writer, and in her *School Library Journal* review of *Plumply, Dumply Pumpkin* Piper L. Nyman asserted that Petrone's "large, vibrant illustrations are a perfect match" for Serfozo's "engaging read-aloud."

Featuring illustrations by acclaimed artist Narahashi, *Who Said Red?* is a colorful tale of a young boy and his teasing older sister. Karen Leggett, writing in the *New York Times Book Review,* called the book "ripe . . . with possibilities for playing, learning, reading and laughing," while Emily Arnold McCully deemed Narahashi's simple, spare illustrations "cozy, full of energy and detail and [with] . . . room for the imagination to roam."

The brother-and-sister team featured in *Who Said Red?* are once again brought to life via Narahashi's art in *Who Wants One?* Here the imaginative older sister pulls an array of increasingly silly items out of a magic box and offers them to her younger brother one after another. The little boy refuses each numbered offering in turn with a firm, insisting that he only wants one. Finally, the boy's sister presents him with one: one precious puppy, that is. In her review for *School Library Journal,* Luann Toth called *Who Wants One?* a "magical presentation of the numbers from one to ten and back again." "This jaunty and original counting book is a standout," a *Publishers Weekly* critic similarly concluded.

Another collaboration between Serfozo and Narahashi, *What's What?: A Guessing Game,* posits simple questions followed by a three-line poem that illustrates basic concepts while leading to a surprise ending. In *Publishers Weekly,* a critic cited the book's "simple text" and "appealing watercolors," while Hazel Rochman concluded in *Booklist* that the "story, ideas, design, and illustrations [in *What's What?*] work beautifully together." In *Rain Talk* author and illustrator move from poetry to prose to relay a simple story about a girl's walk in the rain with her dog. Noting Serfozo's engaging use of onomatopoeia, another *Publishers Weekly* critic also cited Narahashi's "bright appealing watercolors."

Several of Serfozo's books revolve around the start of school. The main character in *Dirty Kurt* cannot seem to keep himself clean. No matter what he does, he is a "magnet for filth," as reviewer Laura Culberg noted in

School Library Journal. When his mother expresses concern that the kids in his new school will think he is a "dirt ball with feet," Kurt solves the problem by going out to play bundled up in his raincoat. "Kids, just like dirt, will be drawn to Kurt," stated Culberg.

The problem for the main character in *Benjamin Bigfoot* is that he wants to wear his father's big shoes to school. When Ben's mother takes him to meet the new teacher before school starts, he discovers that the big shoes are not exactly comfortable for climbing, sliding, or bike riding. *A Head Is for Hats* also focuses on a young boy discovering the ways of the world, and this time Serfozo's story helps readers find uses for feet, heads, hands, and more. Susan Hepler praised *Benjamin Bigfoot* in *School Library Journal,* observing that the simple story "shows a five-year-old working through a situation on his own with the support of sympathetic adults." *A Head Is for Hats* treats children to what *Booklist* critic Carolyn Phelan described as "simple, satisfying fare for reading aloud" or for budding readers.

Serfozo began telling stories in the third grade, winning ten dollars in a Christmas Seal essay contest. "I didn't get around to picture books until I was about ready to retire," she once explained to *SATA.* "I was writing advertising copy for the first time in a wordy career, and finding it quite illuminating. As with picture books, much of what I did involved choosing the right few words to go in a limited space and combine with art to make an impact. My boss was not impressed to learn of the parallel I saw between his target market and the average five-year-old, but it certainly exists. My picture book texts have been described as 'spare,' and I recognize this as a reflection of the discipline imposed by the column inch.

"I write picture books because I feel right at home with preschoolers who love the sound of words—like to roll them on their tongues and repeat them endlessly. I like rhymes and rhythms and exaggeration and humor. And I'm delighted to see my ideas come alive through the insight of an illustrator. I've been writing my entire life, and most of the time it has been rewarding. None of it has been this much fun."

Biographical and Critical Sources

PERIODICALS

Booklist, February 1, 1992, Hazel Rochman, review of *Dirty Kurt,* p. 1042; October 1, 1996, Hazel Rochman, review of *What's What?: A Guessing Game,* p. 351; October 1, 2000, Carolyn Phelan, review of *A Head Is for Hats,* p. 352; September 1, 2001, Shelle Rosenfeld, review of *Plumply, Dumply Pumpkin,* p. 122.

Bulletin of the Center for Children's Books, October, 1996, review of *What's What?,* p. 75.

Kirkus Reviews, July 1, 2001, review of *Plumply, Dumply Pumpkin,* p. 947; June 15, 2007, review of *Whooo's There?*

New York Times Book Review, November 13, 1988, Karen Leggett, review of *Who Said Red?,* p. 63; May 19, 1991, Emily Arnold McCully, review of *Who Said Red?*

Publishers Weekly, September 9, 1988, review of *Who Said Red?,* p. 130; July 14, 1989, review of *Who Wants One?,* p. 75; July 28, 1989, Diane Roback, "Coming Attractions," p. 136; July 27, 1990, review of *Rain Talk,* p. 232; January 18, 1993, review of *Benjamin Bigfoot,* p. 471; January 15, 1996, review of *There's a Square: A Book about Shapes,* p. 461; September 2, 1996, review of *What's What?,* p. 130; September 24, 2001, review of *Plumply, Dumply Pumpkin,* p. 42.

School Library Journal, January, 1989, Nancy Menaldi-Scanlan, review of *Who Said Red?,* p. 66; December, 1989, Luann Toth, review of *Who Wants One?,* p. 96; March, 1992, Laura Culberg, review of *Dirty Kurt,* p. 224; August, 1993, Susan Hepler, review of *Benjamin Bigfoot,* p. 151; January, 1994, Marianne Saccardi, review of *Joe Joe,* p. 98; September, 2001, Piper L. Nyman, review of *Plumply, Dumply Pumpkin,* p. 206; August, 2007, Kirsten Cutler, review of *Whooo's There?,* p. 92.*

*   *   *

SINGER, Nicky 1956-

Personal

Born 1956, in Chalfont-St.-Peter, Buckinghamshire, England; married; children: two sons, one daughter.

Addresses

Home—England.

Career

Writer. Performing Arts Labs (writer's workshop), cofounder and codirector; British Broadcasting Corporation, London, England, presenter of *Labours of Eve* (television documentary series), 1995; Asylum Wall (writers' group developing interactive media), member. Member of South East Arts Board.

Awards, Honors

Blue Peter Book of the Year designation, 2002, for *Feather Boy;* British Book Trust Teenage Prize shortlist, 2003, for *Doll.*

Writings

What She Wanted, Orion Press (London, England), 1996.

My Mother's Daughter, Orion Press (London, England), 1998.

(With Jackie Singer) *The Little Book of the Millennium,* Headline Press (London, England), 1999.

(With Kim Pickin) *The Tiny Book of Time: Creating Time for the Things That Matter,* Headline Press (London, England), 1999.

YOUNG-ADULT NOVELS

Feather Boy, Delacorte Press (New York, NY), 2001.
Doll, CollinsFlamingo (London, England), 2003.
The Innocent's Story, Oxford University Press (Oxford, England), 2005, Holiday House (New York, NY), 2007.
Gem X, Oxford University Press (Oxford, England), 2006, Holiday House (New York, NY), 2008.

Adaptations

Feather Boy was adapted as an audiobook.

Sidelights

British author Nicky Singer tackles themes involving religion, the supernatural, and scientific progress in her fiction for young adults. Her novel *Feather Boy* won England's Blue Peter Book of the Year award in 2002, and the following year *Doll* was shortlisted for the British Book Trust Teenage Prize. These and other novels by Singer feature young teenagers in desperate—and sometimes life-threatening—situations who must cultivate both courage and understanding as they navigate difficult emotional terrain.

Feather Boy introduces readers to gangly and self-conscious narrator Robert. Bullied and lonely, Robert accepts an assignment to interview an elderly resident of a local nursing home. The resident, Edith Sorrel, presses the boy to uncover the secrets of her past and to construct a wider and more spiritual world view. According to Roger Leslie in *Booklist, Feather Boy* relates "a compelling story about courage, death, and self-forgiveness," while *Bookseller* critic Sheila Wood deemed Singer's fiction debut a "fascinating, emotional and captivating book that deserves wide recognition."

The Innocent's Story begins with an act of violence, as thirteen-year-old Cassina becomes the victim of a terrorist bomb. While her body has been killed, Cassina's spirit lingers but must inhabit moist territory—the minds of others. Cassina wanders from the brains of her devastated family members into the thoughts of the terrorist bomber himself. Here the disparate views on life, death, and religion cause Cassina to ponder philosophies she never quite understood in life. Singer's "original paranormal story raises compelling moral issues," noted a contributor to *Kirkus Reviews,* and *Booklist* correspondent Hazel Rochman concluded that the novel "humanizes the demon stereotypes" of religiously motivated terrorists. In *Publishers Weekly,* a reviewer characterized *The Innocent's Story* as "compassionate in its approach to a host of topical and difficult issues."

Cover of Nicky Singer's **The Innocent's Story,** *an evocative story with a haunting theme.* (Holiday House, 2005. Jacket photography by Kamil Vojnar/Getty Images. Reproduced by permission.)

Biographical and Critical Sources

PERIODICALS

Booklist, May 1, 2002, Roger Leslie, review of *Feather Boy,* p. 1519; May 15, 2007, Hazel Rochman, review of *The Innocent's Story,* p. 54.

Book Report, November-December, 2002, Judith Beavers, review of *Feather Boy,* p. 49.

Bookseller, October 12, 2001, Sheila Wood, review of *Feather Boy,* p. 41.

Horn Book, November-December, 2002, Kristi Beavin, review of *Feather Boy,* p. 790.

Kirkus Reviews, April 1, 2002, review of *Feather Boy,* p. 499; May 15, 2007, review of *The Innocent's Story;* February 15, 2008, review of *Gem X.*

Kliatt, May, 2004, Myrna Dee Marler, review of *Feather Boy,* p. 24.

Publishers Weekly, February 25, 2002, review of *Feather Boy,* p. 67; June 25, 2007, review of *The Innocent's Story,* p. 61.

School Library Journal, April, 2002, Alison Follos, review of *Feather Boy,* p. 158; September, 2007, Riva Pollard, review of *The Innocent's Story,* p. 208.

Times Educational Supplement, March 14, 2003, review of *Doll,* p. 26.

ONLINE

HarperCollins Web site, http://www.harpercollins.com/ (October 27, 2008), "Nicky Singer."

Oxford University Press Web site, http://www.oup.com/ (October 27, 2008), "Nicky Singer."*

*   *   *

SPIZMAN, Robyn Freedman 1953-

Personal

Born January 28, 1953, in Atlanta, GA; daughter of Jack and Phyllis (a community volunteer) Freedman; married Willy Spizman (a corporate executive in public relations), July 20, 1975; children: Justin, Ali. *Ethnicity:* "Caucasian." *Education:* Georgia State University, B.A.; also attended University of Texas at Austin.

Addresses

Home—Atlanta, GA. *E-mail*—spizagency@aol.com.

Career

Writer and consumer advocate. Former art teacher; WXIA-TV, Atlanta, GA, presenter of television series *Been There Bought That* for over twenty-five years; guest on national television programs. Make-a-Wish Foundation, member of national advisory council.

Writings

MIDDLE-GRADE NOVELS

(With Mark Johnston) *Secret Agent,* Atheneum Books (New York, NY), 2005.

(With Mark Johnston) *The Secret Agents Strike Back,* Atheneum Books (New York, NY), 2007.

FOR GENERAL READERS

Good Apple and Bulletin Board Bonanza, McGraw-Hill (New York, NY), 1981.

Personalizing with Paint, Plaid Enterprises (Norcross, GA), 1983.

All Aboard with Bulletin Boards, Good Apple (Carthage, IL), 1983.

Bulletin Boards: Monthly Calendars of Learning Fun, Good Apple (Carthage, IL), 1984.

Bulletin Boards: Ideas for Science and Health, Good Apple (Carthage, IL), 1984.

Bulletin Boards: Letters, Borders, and Background Materials, McGraw-Hill (New York, NY), 1984.

Bulletin Boards to Promote Good Study Skills and Positive Self-Concepts, Good Apple (Carthage, IL), 1984.

Bulletin Boards: For Social Studies and Current Events, Good Apple (Carthage, IL), 1984.

Bulletin Boards: For the Whole School to Enjoy, McGraw-Hill (New York, NY), 1984.

Bulletin Boards: For Reading, Spelling, and Language Skills, Good Apple (Carthage, IL), 1984.

(With Evelyn Pesiri) *Bulletin Boards: Seasonal Ideas and Activities,* Good Apple (Carthage, IL), 1984.

Bulletin Boards: Ideas for Holidays and Special Days, Good Apple (Carthage, IL), 1984.

Bulletin Boards: To Reinforce Basic Math Skills, Good Apple (Carthage, IL), 1984.

Bulletin Boards: For Students to Make and Use, McGraw-Hill (New York, NY), 1985.

Lollipop Grapes and Clothespin Critters: Quick On-the-Spot Remedies for Restless Children 2-10, Addison-Wesley (Reading, MA), 1985.

(With Stephen W. Garber and Marianne Daniels Garber) *Good Behavior: Over 1,200 Sensible Solutions to Your Child's Problems from Birth to Age Twelve,* Villard Books (New York, NY), 1987.

Bulletin Boards Plus, Good Apple (Carthage, IL), 1989.

(With Stephen W. Garber and Marianne Daniels Garber) *If Your Child Is Hyperactive, Inattentive, Impulsive, Distractible: Helping the ADD (Attention Deficit Disorder) Hyperactive Child,* Villard Books (New York, NY), 1990, published as *If Your Child Is Hyperactive, Inattentive, Impulsive, Distractible: Helping the ADD/Hyperactive Child,* 1995.

What on Earth Can You Do with Kids?, Good Apple (Carthage, IL), 1991.

Water Intermediate, Good Apple (Carthage, IL), 1992.

(With Marianne Daniels Garber) *Air (Primary),* Good Apple (Carthage, IL), 1992.

Land (Intermediate), Good Apple (Carthage, IL), 1992.

The Good Apple Big Book of Bulletin Boards, Good Apple (Carthage, IL), 1993.

(With Stephen W. Garber and Marianne Daniels Garber) *Monsters under the Bed and Other Childhood Fears: Helping Your Child Overcome Anxieties, Fears, and Phobias,* Villard Books (New York, NY), 1993.

(With Marianne Daniels Garber and Janet Ambrust) *At-Home Activities for Math and Science: Hundreds of Activities to Increase Children's Love of Learning,* Good Apple (Carthage, IL), 1994.

(With Marianne Daniels Garber and Janet Ambrust) *At-Home Activities for Reading, Language Arts, and Social Studies: Hundreds of Activities to Increase Children's Love of Learning,* Good Apple (Carthage, IL), 1994.

(With Marianne Daniels Garber and Corbin Hillam) *Helping Kids Get Organized: Activities That Teach Time Management, Clutter Cleaning, Project Planning, and More,* Good Apple (Carthage, IL), 1994.

(With Tracey Green) *The Bad Day Book,* Longstreet Press (Atlanta, GA), 1994.

The Thank You Book: Hundreds of Clever, Meaningful, and Purposeful Ways to Say Thank You, Longstreet Press (Atlanta, GA), 1994, updated edition, 1997.

(With Stephen W. Garber and Marianne Daniels Garber) *Good Behavior Made Easy Handbook,* Family Life Productions, 1995.

(With H. Jackson Brown, Jr.) *A Hero in Every Heart: Champions from All Walks of Life Share Powerful Messages to Inspire the Hero in Each of Us,* Thomas Nelson (Nashville, TN), 1996.

(With H. Jackson Brown, Jr.) *A Hero in Every Heart: Messages to Motivate and Inspire the Best in You,* Thomas Nelson (Nashville, TN), 1996.

(With Marianne Daniels Garber) *Beyond Ritalin: Facts about Medication and Other Strategies for Helping Children, Adolescents, and Adults with Attention Deficit Disorders,* Villard Books (New York, NY), 1996.

When Words Matter Most: Thoughtful Deeds and Kind Words for Every Occasion, Crown Publishers (New York, NY), 1996.

Kids on Board: Fun Things to Do While Commuting or Road Tripping with Children, Fairview Press (Minneapolis, MN), 1997.

Kitchen 101: Essential Information for Organizing Your Kitchen and Pantry, Ballantine Books (New York, NY), 1998.

Getting Organized: Wonderful Solutions for Making the Most of Your Living Space, Ballantine Books (New York, NY), 1998.

Supermarket Secrets, Ballantine Books (New York, NY), 1998.

Free and Fabulous, Ballantine Books (New York, NY), 1998.

Quick Tips for Busy People, Ballantine Books (New York, NY), 1998.

Meals in Minutes, Ballantine Books (New York, NY), 1998.

The Perfect Present: The Ultimate Gift Guide for Every Occasion, Crown Publishers (New York, NY), 1998.

Bet You Didn't Know: Smart Answers for Every Aspect of Your Life, Ballantine Books (New York, NY), 2000.

(With Ken Leebow) *300 Incredible Things to Learn on the Internet,* 300Incredible.com (Marietta, GA), 2000.

(With Ken Leebow) *300 Incredible Things for Women on the Internet,* 300Incredible.com (Marietta, GA), 2000.

(With H. Jackson Brown) *Life's Little Instruction Book for Incurable Romantics: A Pulse-quickening Collection for and about People in Love,* Rutledge Hill Press (Nashville, TN), 2001.

(With Michael Popkin) *Getting Through to Your Kids: Talking to Children about Sex, Drugs and Alcohol, Safety, Violence, Death, Smoking, Self-Esteem, and Other Critical Issues,* Perigee (New York, NY), 2002.

(With Tory Johnson and Lindsey Pollack) *Women for Hire: The Ultimate Guide to Getting a Job,* Perigee (New York, NY), 2002.

The Giftionary: An A-Z Reference Guide for Solving Your Gift-giving Dilemmas . . . Forever!, St. Martin's Griffin (New York, NY), 2003.

(With Tory Johnson) *Women for Hire's Get-Ahead Guide to Career Success,* Perigee (New York, NY), 2004.

Make It Memorable: An A-Z Guide to Making Any Event, Gift, or Occasion . . . Dazzling!, St. Martin's Griffin (New York, NY), 2004.

(With Tory Johnson) *Take This Book to Work: How to Ask for (and Get) Money, Fulfillment, and Advancement,* St. Martin's Press (New York, NY), 2006.

(With Stuart Gustafson) *Questions to Bring You Closer to Dad: 100-plus Conversation Starters for Fathers and Children of Any Age,* Adams Media (New York, NY), 2007.

(With Tory Johnson) *Will Work from Home: Earn the Cash—Without the Commute,* Berkley Books (New York, NY), 2008.

(With Rick Frishman) *Where's Your Wow?: Sixteen Ways to Make Your Competitors Wish They Were You,* McGraw-Hill (New York, NY), 2008.

(With Stuart Gustafson) *Questions to Bring You Closer to Grandma and Grandpa: 100-plus Conversation Starters for Grandparents of Any Age,* Adams Media (New York, NY), 2008.

(With Stuart Gustafson) *Questions to Bring You Closer to Mom: 100-plus Conversation Starters for Mothers and Children of Any Age,* Adams Media (New York, NY), 2008.

Also contributor to 21-volume "Crafts for Children" series, 1992-97. Author (with Diane Pfifer) of *Dear Daughter: With Love from My Kitchen.*

"AUTHOR 101" SERIES

(With Rick Frishman and Mark Steisel) *Bestselling Book Publicity: The Insider's Guide to Promoting Your Book—and Yourself,* Adams Publishing Group (Avon, MA), 2006.

(With Rick Frishman and Mark Steisel) *Bestselling Secrets from Top Agents: The Insider's Guide to What Agents and Publishers Really Want,* Adams Media (Avon, MA), 2006.

(With Rick Frishman and Mark Steisel) *Bestselling Book Proposals: The Insider's Guide to Selling Your Work,* Adams Media (Avon, MA), 2006.

(With Rick Frishman and Mark Steisel) *Bestselling Nonfiction: The Insider's Guide to Making Reality Sell,* Adams Media (Avon, MA), 2006.

Sidelights

A former art teacher, Robyn Freedman Spizman became a writer and television consumer advocate almost simultaneously. When she wrote her first book about a painting craft, Spizman appeared on a local television program to promote it and that appearance led to a job as the program's "Super Shopper." Among the many nonfiction titles she has written since are the "Author 101" writer's guides, which are coauthored with Rick Frishman and Mark Steisel. Spizman also teams up with Mark Johnston to enter the children's-book market with the middle-grade novels *Secret Agent* and *The Secret Agent Strikes Back.* Praising the "Author 101" installment *Bestselling Secrets from Top Agents: The Insider's Guide to What Agents and Publishers Really Want,* Chuck Leddy described the book in *Writer* as a "terrific introduction" to its subject that "lives up to its title."

Spizman once commented about writing her first work of fiction. "Having reported on books, gifts, and topics that relate to children," she explained, "my goal has al-

Robyn Freedman Spizman and Mark Johnston team up on the young-adult novel Secret Agent, *featuring artwork by Benjamin Wachenje.* (Aladdin, an imprint of Simon & Schuster Children's Publishing Division, 2006. Illustration copyright © 2006 by Benjamin Wachenje. Reproduced by permission.)

ways been to write a children's book series. I imagined a character named Kyle Parker, whose dream was to help sell his father's book. His dad was a struggling writer and his mom wanted his father to get a real job. Kyle thought if only he could sell his dad's book, he'd get his parents back together, since they had separated. To that end, Kyle enlists the kids in the neighborhood to become secret agents, and Kyle poses as an actual literary agent, breaking into the book world in New York City."

In *Secret Agent,* Spizman and Johnston bring Kyle Parker to life in the pages of a story that finds the high-school freshman infiltrating the New York City publishing world with the help of his friends, and stirring up publicity about his father's book and its "mystery author" in the process. In *Booklist,* Todd Morning praised Spizman and Johnston's fiction debut for containing "resourceful young people and an amusing and elaborate sting operation at its core." According to *School Library Journal* contributor Mary R. Hofmann, *Secret Agent* serves up "a strangely compelling adventure in which readers root for Kyle's success." Calling Kyle "ingenious," Claire Rosser wrote in *Kliatt* that *Secret*

Agent is "light and funny," as well as "easy to read but [also] demanding some sophistication on the part of the reader."

Kyle's adventures continue in *The Secret Agents Strike Back* as he and good friend Lucinda Wilson attempt to help Lucinda's professor mom put to rest a mystery from her past that could compromise the woman's academic career. Praising the novel as "fast paced" and a good choice for reluctant readers, Donna Atmur added in *School Library Journal* that *The Secret Agents Strike Back* "is a lighthearted adventure filled with quirky characters."

"I love book writing . . . ," Spizman also commented. "It is my sincere hope that my works touch readers in the same way that each of them has inspired or entertained me. I feel very fortunate to be a writer and wake up every day bringing books to life, sharing the works of other authors and enjoying every second of it! I look forward to spreading my knowledge and experience."

Biographical and Critical Sources

PERIODICALS

Booklist, April 15, 2005, Todd Morning, review of *Secret Agent,* p. 1457; August 1, 2008, Barbara Jacobs, review of *Will Work from Home: Earn the Cash—Without the Commute,* p. 18.

Bulletin of the Center for Children's Books, September, 2005, Karen Coats, review of *Secret Agent,* p. 46.

Kirkus Reviews, April 1, 2005, review of *Secret Agent,* p. 426; April 15, 2007, review of *The Secret Agents Strike Back.*

Kliatt, May, 2005, review of *Secret Agent,* p. 18.

Publishers Weekly, August 21, 2006, review of *Take This Book to Work: How to Ask for (and Get) Money, Fulfillment, and Advancement,* p. 59.

School Library Journal, March, 2005, Mary R. Hofmann, review of *Secret Agent,* p. 218; June, 2007, Donna Atmur, review of *The Secret Agents Strike Back,* p. 161.

Voice of Youth Advocates, August, 2005, Kevin Beach, review of *Secret Agent,* p. 226.

Women's Wear Daily, October 5, 2005, Caperton Gillett, "Luck Be a Lady: A Trio of Successful Atlanta Businesswomen Gather to Discuss Their Trip to the Top," p. 81.

Writer, April, 2006, Chuck Leddy, review of *Bestselling Book Proposals: The Insider's Guide to Selling Your Work,* p. 47, and *Bestselling Secrets from Top Agents,* p. 52.

ONLINE

Robyn Freedman Spizman Home Page, http://www.robynspizman.com (October 10, 2008).

STEVENSON, Suçie 1956-

Personal

Born Susan Stevenson, 1956, in Greenwich, CT; daughter of James (a journalist, playwright, novelist, cartoonist, and children's book author) and Jane (an artist) Stevenson.

Addresses

Home—Cape Cod, MA. *Agent*—Liza Pulitzer-Voges, Kirchoff/Wohlberg, Inc., 866 United Nations Plaza, Ste. 525, New York, NY 10017.

Career

Illustrator and author of children's books. Has also worked as a manual laborer, shellfisher, housepainter, mason's helper, theater technician, set painter, mural painter, and flower-delivery-truck driver.

Awards, Honors

Parent's Choice Award, 1994, for *Baby-O,* written by Nancy White Carlstrom. All with author Cynthia Rylant: Garden State Children's Book Award, 1990, for *Henry and Mudge in Puddle Trouble,* 1992, for *Henry and Mudge Get the Cold Shivers,* 1993, for *Henry and Mudge and the Happy Cat,* 1994, for *Henry and Mudge and the Bedtime Thumps,* 1995, for *Henry and Mudge and the Long Weekend,* 1996, for *Henry and Mudge and the Wild Wind,* and 1997, for *Henry and Mudge and the Careful Cousin; Parenting* magazine Reading Magic Award, 1992, for *Henry and Mudge and the Long Weekend,* and 1994, for *Henry and Mudge and the Careful Cousin;* 100 Titles for Reading and Sharing designation, New York Public Library, 1994, for *Henry and Mudge and the Careful Cousin;* Garden State Children's Book Award in easy-to-read category, New Jersey Library Association, 2000, for *Henry and Mudge in the Family Trees;* Theodor Seuss Geisel Award, Association for Library Service to Children, 2006, for *Henry and Mudge and the Great Grandpas.*

Writings

SELF-ILLUSTRATED CHILDREN'S BOOKS

Do I Have to Take Violet?, Dodd, Mead (New York, NY), 1987.

I Forgot, Orchard Books (New York, NY), 1988.

Christmas Eve, Dodd, Mead (New York, NY), 1988.

Jessica the Blue Streak, Orchard Books (New York, NY), 1989.

(Reteller) *The Princess and the Pea,* Doubleday (New York, NY), 1992.

(Reteller) *The Twelve Dancing Princesses,* Yearling (New York, NY), 1995.

(Reteller) Hans Christian Andersen, *The Emperor's New Clothes,* Delacorte (New York, NY), 1997.

ILLUSTRATOR

Cynthia Rylant, *Birthday Presents,* Orchard Books (New York, NY), 1987.

David A. Adler, *I Know I'm a Witch,* Holt (New York, NY), 1988.

Niki Yektai, *Crazy Clothes,* Bradbury Press (New York, NY), 1988.

Barbara Ann Porte, *Ruthann and Her Pig,* Orchard Books (New York, NY), 1989.

Frieda Wishinsky, *Oonga Boonga,* Little, Brown (Boston, MA), 1990.

Elvira Woodruff, *Tubtime,* Holiday House (New York, NY), 1990.

Nancy White Carlstrom, *Baby-O,* Little, Brown (Boston, MA), 1992.

Joyce Champion, *Emily and Alice,* Harcourt (New York, NY), 1993.

Joyce Champion, *Emily and Alice Again,* Gulliver Books (San Diego, CA), 1995.

Mary Small, *A Pony Named Shawney,* Mondo Publishing (Greenvale, NY), 1996.

Anne Rockwell, *Once upon a Time This Morning,* Greenwillow (New York, NY), 1997.

Joyce Champion, *Emily and Alice, Best Friends* Harcourt (New York, NY), 2001.

Cynthia Rylant, *Puppy Mudge Wants to Play,* Simon & Schuster (New York, NY), 2005.

Cynthia Rylant, *Puppy Mudge Finds a Friend,* Simon & Schuster (New York, NY), 2005.

ILLUSTRATOR; "HENRY AND MUDGE" CHILDREN'S BOOKS; ALL WRITTEN BY CYNTHIA RYLANT

Henry and Mudge: The First Book of Their Adventures, Bradbury Press (New York, NY), 1987.

Henry and Mudge in Puddle Trouble: The Second Book of Their Adventures, Bradbury Press (New York, NY), 1987.

Henry and Mudge in the Green Time: The Third Book of Their Adventures, Bradbury Press (New York, NY), 1987.

Henry and Mudge under the Yellow Moon: The Fourth Book of Their Adventures, Bradbury Press (New York, NY), 1988.

Henry and Mudge in the Sparkle Days: The Fifth Book of Their Adventures, Bradbury Press (New York, NY), 1988.

Henry and Mudge and the Forever Sea: The Sixth Book of Their Adventures, Bradbury Press (New York, NY), 1989.

Henry and Mudge Get the Cold Shivers: The Seventh Book of Their Adventures, Bradbury Press (New York, NY), 1989.

Henry and Mudge and the Happy Cat: The Eighth Book of Their Adventures, Bradbury Press (New York, NY), 1990.

Henry and Mudge and the Bedtime Thumps: The Ninth Book of Their Adventures, Bradbury Press (New York, NY), 1991.

Henry and Mudge Take the Big Test: The Tenth Book of Their Adventures, Bradbury Press (New York, NY), 1991.

Henry and Mudge and the Long Weekend: The Eleventh Book of Their Adventures, Bradbury Press (New York, NY), 1992.

Henry and Mudge and the Wild Wind: The Twelfth Book of Their Adventures, Bradbury Press (New York, NY), 1993.

Henry and Mudge and the Careful Cousin: The Thirteenth Book of Their Adventures, Bradbury Press (New York, NY), 1994.

Henry and Mudge and the Best Day of All: The Fourteenth Book of Their Adventures, Bradbury Press (New York, NY), 1994.

Henry and Mudge in the Family Trees: The Fifteenth Book of Their Adventures, Simon & Schuster (New York, NY), 1997.

Henry and Mudge and the Sneaky Crackers: The Sixteenth Book of Their Adventures, Simon & Schuster (New York, NY), 1998.

Henry and Mudge and the Starry Night: The Seventeenth Book of Their Adventures, Simon & Schuster (New York, NY), 1998.

Henry and Mudge and Annie's Good Move: The Eighteenth Book of Their Adventures, Simon & Schuster (New York, NY), 1998.

Henry and Mudge and the Snowman Plan: The Nineteenth Book of Their Adventures, Simon & Schuster (New York, NY), 1999.

Henry and Mudge and Annie's Perfect Pet: The Twentieth Book of Their Adventures, Simon & Schuster (New York, NY), 2000.

Henry and Mudge and a Very Merry Christmas: The Twenty-fifth Book of Their Adventures, Simon & Schuster (New York, NY), 2004.

Henry and Mudge and the Great Grandpas: The Twenty-sixth Book of Their Adventures, Simon & Schuster (New York, NY), 2005.

Henry and Mudge and the Big Sleepover: The Twenty-eighth Book of Their Adventures, Simon & Schuster (New York, NY), 2006.

Some of the "Henry and Mudge" books have been translated into Spanish.

ILLUSTRATOR; "ANNIE AND SNOWBALL" CHILDREN'S BOOKS

Cynthia Rylant, *Annie and Snowball and the Dress-up Birthday: The First Book of Their Adventures,* Simon & Schuster (New York, NY), 2007.

Cynthia Rylant, *Annie and Snowball and the Prettiest House: The Second Book of Their Adventures,* Simon & Schuster (New York, NY), 2007.

Cynthia Rylant, *Annie and Snowball and the Teacup Club: The Third Book of Their Adventures,* Simon & Schuster (New York, NY), 2008.

Cynthia Rylant, *Annie and Snowball and the Pink Surprise: The Fourth Book of Their Adventures,* Simon & Schuster (New York, NY), 2008.

Cynthia Rylant, *Annie and Snowball and the Cozy Nest: The Fifth Book of Their Adventures,* Simon & Schuster (New York, NY), 2009.

OTHER

Also contributor of articles to magazines, including *New Yorker.*

Sidelights

The daughter of famous cartoonist, illustrator, and author James Stevenson, Suçie Stevenson has gained a large measure of fame herself as the illustrator of Cynthia Rylant's popular "Henry and Mudge" and "Annie and Snowball" beginning readers. A gifted writer as well as artist, Stevenson has also received critical praise for her original picture books, such as *Do I Have to Take Violet?, I Forgot, Christmas Eve,* and *Jessica's*

Suçie Stevenson's work on Cynthia Rylant's "Henry and Mudge" books includes art for **Henry and Mudge and the Big Sleepover.** (Illustration copyright © 2006 by Suçie Stevenson. Reprinted with the permission of Simon & Schuster Books for Young Readers, an imprint of Simon & Schuster Children's Publishing Division.)

Blue Streak. As Stephanie Zvirin asserted in a *Booklist* review, "Stevenson's exuberant art adds a great touch of comedy" to Rylant's series installment *Henry and Mudge and Annie's Good Move The Eighteenth Book of Their Adventures,* while the whimsical and energetic pen-and-ink and watercolor illustrations she contributes to *Henry and Mudge and the Snowman Plan: The Nineteenth Book of Their Adventures* "lend a gentle and simple touch" to Rylant's "gentle adventure," according to *School Library Journal* critic Selene S. Vasquez.

Despite growing up in the home of a celebrity author and artist, Stevenson was not certain she would ever follow in her father's footsteps. Although she enjoyed drawing, she once recalled in a *Publishers Weekly* interview with Diane Roback, "I didn't have any faith that I was any good." So, instead of pursuing more creative endeavors, Stevenson tried a number of odd jobs, including shellfisher, mason's helper, and truck driver. Eventually, however, she determined to put her artistic skills to use. She found her first success publishing articles in the *New Yorker* magazine, and later tried her hand at illustrating children's books. Submitting two works for publication to a variety of publishers, she was told that she had talent as an illustrator, but not as a children's author. Nevertheless, Stevenson soon published several of her own picture books in addition to illustrating the texts of other children's writers.

Stevenson found an agent, then gained the support of publisher Richard Jackson at Orchard Books. This led to her well-known collaboration with Rylant on the "Henry and Mudge" series, which has expanded into dozens of books as well as a spin-off series featuring Henry's neighbor Annie and her pet bunny Snowball. Stevenson's father, who was best known for his *New Yorker* cartoons, also had an important influence on her artistry. "What I aim for is a really loose style—simple, cartoony. I try to make things look the way they feel to me instead of how they actually look," she said in *Publishers Weekly.* This style has served as the perfect complement to Rylant's stories, which have earned both author and illustrator the first-annual Theodore Seuss Geisel Award, among others.

In her first original picture book, *Do I Have to Take Violet?,* Stevenson addresses a scenario that is very familiar to most siblings: an older sister, in this case a bunny named Elly, is forced by her mother to take her little sister, Violet, on a bike ride. Elly teases Violet with stories of monsters, and Violet tries to trick her sister, but the two eventually decide to get along. *School Library Journal* contributor Luann Toth wrote that the tale is "nicely done and certainly enhanced by Stevenson's . . . paintings." Elly and Violet appear again in *Christmas Eve,* squabbling while trying to prepare a holiday gift for their parents. Diane Roback, writing in *Publishers Weekly,* praised Stevenson for making the childish rivalry in both books "uncanny and real," and called *Christmas Eve* "funny and dear."

Stevenson's simple cartoon art adds a new dimension to her holiday-themed story in **Christmas Eve.**

Stevenson creates another endearing character in Arthur Peter Platypus, Jr., the star of *I Forgot.* Arthur's problem is that he cannot seem to remember anything. For example, he wears the wrong hat when it rains and forgets to take his lunch box to school. Then, one day, while pondering his troubles, he realizes that he remembers important things, such as his address and his mother's birthday, which is that very day. He takes balloons, banners, and flowers to his mother as a gift, and Arthur is happy to conclude that at least he remembers the most important things in life. Stevenson adds interest to the story by having Arthur try various methods to improve his memory, and her colorful art "captures the little platypus' movements and moods," according to a *Booklist* critic. Comparing *I Forgot* to Robert Kraus's *Leo the Late Bloomer, School Library Journal* contributor Pamela Miller Ness called Stevenson's story "a little book with a big, comforting message."

Stevenson's self-illustrated books include retellings of traditional fairy tales. In her adaptations *The Princess and the Pea, The Twelve Dancing Princesses,* and *The Emperor's New Clothes,* the main characters are animals. For example, in retelling Hans Christian Andersen's *The Princess and the Pea,* Stevenson casts bunnies in key roles, and she takes further liberties by setting her version of the well-known tale on a tropical island instead of in Europe. A *Publishers Weekly* critic dubbed *The Princess and the Pea* "accessible and entertaining," appreciating Stevenson's humor. The author/illustrator offers another humorous tale, this time with an all-dog cast, in her interpretation of *The Twelve Dancing Princesses.* Calling this work "an entertaining interpretation" of the story first collected by the Brothers Grimm, *Booklist* critic Carolyn Phelan added that Stevenson's version of *The Twelve Dancing Princesses* features a "conversational text [that] is both upbeat and downhome."

Biographical and Critical Sources

PERIODICALS

Booklist, February 15, 1988, review of *I Forgot,* p. 1003; July, 1993, Stephanie Zvirin, review of *Henry and Mudge and the Wild Wind: The Twelfth Book of Their Adventures,* pp. 1980-1981; January 1, 1996, Carolyn Phelan, review of *The Twelve Dancing Princesses,* p. 850; April 1, 1997, Hazel Rochman, review of *Once upon a Time This Morning,* p. 1339; August, 1997, Carolyn Phelan, review of *Henry and Mudge in the Family Trees: The Fifteenth Book of Their Adventures,* p. 1910; February 1, 1998, Stephanie Zvirin, review of *Henry and Mudge and the Sneaky Crackers: The Sixteenth Book of Their Adventures,* p. 928; May 1, 1998, Hazel Rochman, review of *Henry and Mudge and the Starry Night: The Seventeenth Book of Their Adventures,* p. 1526; July, 1998, Stephanie Zvirin, review of *Henry and Mudge and Annie's Perfect Pet: The Twentieth Book of Their Adventures,* p. 716; October 1, 1999, Shelle Rosenfeld, review of *Henry and Mudge and the Snowman Plan: The Nineteenth Book of Their Adventures,* p. 366; May 15, 2005, Hazel Rochman, review of *Puppy Mudge Wants to Play,* p. 1667.

Bulletin of the Center for Children's Books, May, 1988, review of *I Forgot,* p. 189; April, 1997, review of *Once upon a Time This Morning,* p. 293; March, 1998, review of *Henry and Mudge and the Sneaky Crackers,* p. 258; May 1, 2005, Hazel Rochman, review of *Henry and Mudge and the Great Grandpas: The Twenty-sixth Book of Their Adventures,* p. 1587; August, 2005, Melinda Piehler, review of *Henry and Mudge and the Great Grandpas,* p. 105; August 1, 2006, Carolyn Phelan, review of *Henry and Mudge and the Big Sleepover: The Twenty-eighth Book of Their Adventures,* p. 93; July-August, 2007, Hope Morrison, review of *Annie and Snowball and the Dress-up Birthday: The First Book of Their Adventures,* p. 484.

Horn Book, November-December, 1987, Elizabeth S. Watson, review of *Henry and Mudge under the Yellow Moon: The Fourth Book of Their Adventures,* p. 735; May-June, 1988, Margaret A. Bush, review of *I Forgot,* p. 347; July-August, 1988, Elizabeth S. Watson, review of *Crazy Clothes,* pp. 487-488; November-December, 1989, Elizabeth S. Watson, review of *Henry and Mudge Get the Cold Shivers: The Seventh Book of Their Adventures,* p. 795; May-June, 1990, Edith R. Twichell, review of *Oonga Boonga,* p. 356; November-December, 1991, Hanna B. Zeiger, review of *Henry and Mudge Take the Big Test: The Tenth Book of Their Adventures,* p. 759; July-August, 1992, Mary M. Burns, review of *Henry and Mudge and the Long Weekend: The Eleventh Book of Their Adventures,* p.

449; March-April, 1994, Ellen Fader, review of *Henry and Mudge and the Careful Cousin: The Thirteenth Book of Their Adventures,* pp. 195-196; July, 1998, Stephanie Zvirin, review of *Henry and Mudge and Annie's Good Move: The Eighteenth Book of Their Adventures,* p. 1891.

Publishers Weekly, December 25, 1987, Diane Roback, "Flying Starts," p. 36; December 23, 1988, review of *Christmas Eve,* p. 81; January 13, 1989, review of *Jessica the Blue Streak,* p. 88; July 28, 1989, review of *Ruthann and Her Pig,* p. 222; August 3, 1992, review of *The Princess and the Pea,* p. 71; January 6, 1997, review of *Once upon a Time This Morning,* p. 72.

School Library Journal, June-July, 1987, Luann Toth, review of *Do I Have to Take Violet?,* pp. 90-91; March, 1988, Pamela Miller Ness, review of *I Forgot,* p. 177; July, 1989, Maria B. Salvadore, review of *Henry and Mudge and the Forever Sea: The Sixth Book of Their Adventures,* p. 76; May, 1990, Ellen Fader, review of *Oonga Boonga,* p. 93; April, 1992, Gale W. Sherman, review of *Henry and Mudge and the Long Weekend,* p. 100; May, 1995, Claudia Cooper, review of *Emily and Alice Again,* p. 94; March, 1996, Jan Shepherd Ross, review of *The Twelve Dancing Princesses,* p. 193; January, 1997, review of *Henry and Mudge and the Happy Cat,* p. 37; March, 1997, Dina Sherman, review of *Once upon a Time This Morning,* p. 164; October, 1997, Dina Sherman, review of *Henry and Mudge in the Family Trees,* p. 109; March, 1998, Lisa Radmer, review of *Henry and Mudge and the Bedtime Thumps,* p. 157; April, 1998, Suzanne Hawley, review of *Henry and Mudge and the Starry Night,* p. 108; August, 1998, Nancy A. Gifford, review of *Henry and Mudge and the Sneaky Crackers,* p. 145; October, 1998, Gale W. Sherman, review of *Henry and Mudge and Annie's Good Move,* p. 113; March, 2000, Selene S. Vasquez, review of *Henry and Mudge and the Snowman Plan,* p. 212; April, 2000, Diane Janoff, review of *Henry and Mudge and Annie's Perfect Pet,* p. 113; July, 2006, Elaine Lesh Morgan, review of *Henry and Mudge and the Big Sleepover,* p. 87; April, 2007, Laura Scott, review of *Annie and Snowball and the Dress-up Birthday,* p. 115; November, 2007, Erika Qualls, review of *Annie and Snowball and the Prettiest House: The Second Book of Their Adventures,* p. 100.*

* * *

STINE, Jovial Bob
See STINE, R.L.

* * *

STINE, R.L. 1943-
(Eric Affabee, Zachary Blue, Jovial Bob Stine, Robert Lawrence Stine)

Personal

Born October 8, 1943 in Columbus, OH; son of Lewis (a shipping manager) and Anne Stine; married Jane

R.L. Stine (Photograph by Richard Hutchings. Reproduced by permission of R.L. Stine.)

Waldhorn (owner/managing director of Parachute Press), June 22, 1969; children: Matthew Daniel. *Education:* Ohio State University, B.A. 1965; graduate study at New York University, 1966-67. *Religion:* Jewish. *Hobbies and other interests:* Swimming, watching old movie classics from the 1930s and 1940s, reading (especially P.G. Wodehouse novels).

Addresses

Home—New York, NY. *Office*—c/o Parachute Press, 156 5th Ave., New York, NY 10010.

Career

Author of books for children and adults. Social studies teacher at a junior high school, Columbus, OH, 1965-66; freelance journalist, 1966-68; Scholastic, Inc., New York, NY, assistant editor of *Junior Scholastic* magazine, 1968-71, editor of *Search* magazine, 1972-75, editor/creator of *Bananas* magazine, 1975-84, and *Maniac* magazine, 1984-85; *Eureeka's Castle,* Nickelodeon cable television network, head writer, 1986-87.

Member

Writers Guild of America, Mystery Writers of America.

Awards, Honors

Children's Choice awards, American Library Association; Lifetime Achievement Award, Ohioanna Library Association; *Guinness World Records* listing for best-selling children's series in history, 2000, for "Goosebumps" series; three-time winner of Nickelodeon Kid's Choice Award.

Writings

YOUNG-ADULT FICTION

Blind Date, Scholastic (New York, NY), 1986.
Twisted, Scholastic (New York, NY), 1987.
Broken Date ("Crosswinds" series), Simon & Schuster (New York, NY), 1988.
The Baby-Sitter, Scholastic (New York, NY), 1989.
Phone Calls, Archway (New York, NY), 1990.
How I Broke up with Ernie, Archway (New York, NY), 1990.
Curtains, Archway (New York, NY), 1990.
The Boyfriend, Scholastic (New York, NY), 1990.
Beach Party, Scholastic (New York, NY), 1990.
Snowman, Scholastic (New York, NY), 1991.
The Girlfriend, Scholastic (New York, NY), 1991.
Baby-Sitter II, Scholastic (New York, NY), 1991.
Beach House, Scholastic (New York, NY), 1992.
Hit and Run, Scholastic (New York, NY), 1992.
Hitchhiker, Scholastic (New York, NY), 1993.
Baby-Sitter III, Scholastic (New York, NY), 1993.
The Dead Girl Friend, Scholastic (New York, NY), 1993.
Halloween Night, Scholastic (New York, NY), 1993.
Call Waiting, Scholastic (New York, NY), 1994.
Halloween Night 2, Scholastic (New York, NY), 1994.
Dangerous Girls, HarperCollins (New York, NY), 2003.
Dangerous Girls: The Taste of Night, HarperCollins (New York, NY), 2004.

Contributor of short fiction to anthologies, including *Halloween Howls,* MediaFusion, 2003.

YOUNG-ADULT NOVELS; "FEAR STREET" SERIES

The New Girl, Archway (New York, NY), 1989, reprinted, Simon Pulse (New York, NY), 2006.
The Surprise Party, Archway (New York, NY), 1990.
The Overnight, Archway (New York, NY), 1990.
Missing, Archway (New York, NY), 1990.
The Wrong Number, Archway (New York, NY), 1990.
The Sleepwalker, Archway (New York, NY), 1990.
Haunted, Archway (New York, NY), 1990.
Halloween Party, Archway (New York, NY), 1990, reprinted, Simon Pulse (New York, NY), 2006.
The Stepsister, Archway (New York, NY), 1990, new edition, Simon Pulse (New York, NY), 2005.
Ski Weekend, Archway (New York, NY), 1991.
The Fire Game, Archway (New York, NY), 1991.
Lights Out, Archway (New York, NY), 1991.
The Secret Bedroom, Archway (New York, NY), 1991.
The Knife, Archway (New York, NY), 1992.
Prom Queen, Archway (New York, NY), 1992.
First Date, Archway (New York, NY), 1992.
The Best Friend, Archway (New York, NY), 1992.

The Cheater, Archway (New York, NY), 1993.
Sunburn, Archway (New York, NY), 1993.
The New Boy, Archway (New York, NY), 1994.
The Dare, Archway (New York, NY), 1994.
Bad Dreams, Archway (New York, NY), 1994.
Double Date, Archway (New York, NY), 1994.
The Thrill Club, Archway (New York, NY), 1994.
One Evil Summer, Archway (New York, NY), 1994.
The Mind Reader, Archway (New York, NY), 1994.
Wrong Number 2, Archway (New York, NY), 1995.
Truth or Dare, Archway (New York, NY), 1995.
Dead End, Archway (New York, NY), 1995.
Final Grade, Archway (New York, NY), 1995.
Switched, Archway (New York, NY), 1995.
College Weekend, Archway (New York, NY), 1995.
The Stepsister 2, Archway (New York, NY), 1995.
What Holly Heard, Pocket Books (New York, NY), 1996.
The Face, Pocket Books (New York, NY), 1996.
Secret Admirer, Pocket Books (New York, NY), 1996.
The Perfect Date, Pocket Books (New York, NY), 1996.
The Confession, Pocket Books (New York, NY), 1996.
The Boy Next Door, Simon & Schuster (New York, NY), 1996.
Night Games, Pocket Books (New York, NY), 1996.
Runaway, Archway (New York, NY), 1997.
Killer's Kiss, Archway (New York, NY), 1997, new edition, Simon Pulse (New York, NY), 2005.
All-Night Party, Archway (New York, NY), 1997, new edition, Simon Pulse (New York, NY), 2005.
The Rich Girl, Archway (New York, NY), 1997, new edition, Simon Pulse (New York, NY), 2005.
Cat, Archway (New York, NY), 1997.
Fear Hall: The Beginning, Archway (New York, NY), 1997.
Fear Hall: The Conclusion, Archway (New York, NY), 1997.
Who Killed the Homecoming Queen?, Archway (New York, NY), 1998.
Into the Dark, Archway (New York, NY), 1998.
Best Friend 2, Archway (New York, NY), 1998.
Trapped, Archway (New York, NY), 1998.

YOUNG-ADULT NOVELS; "FEAR STREET SUPER CHILLER" SERIES

Party Summer, Archway (New York, NY), 1991.
Silent Night, Archway (New York, NY), 1992.
The Goodnight Kiss, Archway (New York, NY), 1992.
Broken Hearts, Archway (New York, NY), 1993.
Silent Night 2, Archway (New York, NY), 1993.
The Dead Lifeguard, Archway (New York, NY), 1994.
Bad Moonlight, Archway (New York, NY), 1995.
The New Year's Party, Archway (New York, NY), 1995.
Goodnight Kiss 2, Archway (New York, NY), 1996.
Silent Night 3, Archway (New York, NY), 1996.
High Tide, Archway (New York, NY), 1997.

YOUNG-ADULT NOVELS; "FEAR STREET CHEERLEADERS" SERIES

The First Evil, Archway (New York, NY), 1992.
The Second Evil, Archway (New York, NY), 1992.
The Third Evil, Archway (New York, NY), 1992.

The New Evil, Archway (New York, NY), 1994.
The Evil Lives, Archway (New York, NY), 1997.

YOUNG-ADULT NOVELS; "FEAR STREET SAGA" SERIES

The Betrayal, Archway (New York, NY), 1993.
The Secret, Archway (New York, NY), 1993.
The Burning, Archway (New York, NY), 1993.
A New Fear, Pocket Books (New York, NY), 1996.
House of Whispers, Simon & Schuster (New York, NY), 1996.
Forbidden Secrets, Simon & Schuster (New York, NY), 1996.
The Sign of Fear, Simon & Schuster (New York, NY), 1996.
The Hidden Evil, Archway (New York, NY), 1997.
Daughters of Silence, Archway (New York, NY), 1997.
Children of Fear, Archway (New York, NY), 1997.
Dance of Death, Simon & Schuster (New York, NY), 1997.
Heart of the Hunter, Simon & Schuster (New York, NY), 1997.
Awakening Evil, Simon & Schuster (New York, NY), 1998.
Circle of Fear, Simon & Schuster (New York, NY), 1998.
Chamber of Fear, Simon & Schuster (New York, NY), 1998.
Faces of Terror, Simon & Schuster (New York, NY), 1998.
One Last Kiss, Simon & Schuster (New York, NY), 1998.
Door of Death, Simon & Schuster (New York, NY), 1998.

YOUNG-ADULT NOVELS; "99 FEAR STREET TRILOGY"

The First Horror, Archway (New York, NY), 1994.
The Second Horror, Archway (New York, NY), 1994.
The Third Horror, Archway (New York, NY), 1994.

YOUNG-ADULT NOVELS; "CATALUNA CHRONICLES"

The Evil Moon, Archway (New York, NY), 1995.
The Dark Secret, Archway (New York, NY), 1995.
The Deadly Fire, Archway (New York, NY), 1995.

YOUNG-ADULT NOVELS; "GHOSTS OF FEAR STREET" SERIES

Hide and Shriek, Pocket Books (New York, NY), 1996.
Who's Been Sleeping in My Grave?, Pocket Books (New York, NY), 1996.
The Attack of the Aqua Apes, Pocket Books (New York, NY), 1996.
Nightmare in 3-D, Pocket Books (New York, NY), 1996.
Stay Away from the Treehouse, Pocket Books (New York, NY), 1996.
The Eye of the Fortuneteller, Pocket Books (New York, NY), 1996.
Fright Knight, Pocket Books (New York, NY), 1996.
The Ooze, Pocket Books (New York, NY), 1996.
Revenge of the Shadow People, Pocket Books (New York, NY), 1996.
The Bugman Lives!, Pocket Books (New York, NY), 1996.

The Boy Who Ate Fear Street, Pocket Books (New York, NY), 1996.

Night of the Werecat, Pocket Books (New York, NY), 1996.

How to Be a Vampire, Pocket Books (New York, NY), 1996.

Body Switchers from Outer Space, Pocket Books (New York, NY), 1996.

Fright Christmas, Pocket Books (New York, NY), 1996.

Don't Ever Get Sick at Granny's, Pocket Books (New York, NY), 1997.

House of a Thousand Screams, Pocket Books (New York, NY), 1997.

Camp Fear Ghouls, Pocket Books (New York, NY), 1997.

Three Evil Wishes, Pocket Books (New York, NY), 1997.

Spell of the Screaming Jokers, Pocket Books (New York, NY), 1997.

The Creature from Club Lagoona, Pocket Books (New York, NY), 1997.

Field of Screams, Pocket Books (New York, NY), 1997.

Why I'm Not Afraid of Ghosts, Pocket Books (New York, NY), 1997.

Monster Dog, Pocket Books (New York, NY), 1997.

Halloween Bugs Me!, Pocket Books (New York, NY), 1997.

Go to Your Tomb—Right Now!, Pocket Books (New York, NY), 1997.

Parents from the Thirteenth Dimension, Pocket Books (New York, NY), 1997.

Hide and Shriek 2, Pocket Books (New York, NY), 1998.

Tale of the Blue Monkey, Pocket Books (New York, NY), 1998.

I Was a Sixth-Grade Zombie, Pocket Books (New York, NY), 1998.

Escape of the He-Beast, Pocket Books (New York, NY), 1998.

Caution: Aliens at Work, Pocket Books (New York, NY), 1998.

Attack of the Vampire Worms, Pocket Books (New York, NY), 1998.

Horror Hotel: The Vampire Checks In, Pocket Books (New York, NY), 1998.

Horror Hotel: Ghost in the Guest Room, Pocket Books (New York, NY), 1998.

The Funhouse of Dr. Freek, Pocket Books (New York, NY), 1998.

YOUNG-ADULT NOVELS; "FEAR STREET SENIORS" SERIES

Let's Party, Golden Books (New York, NY), 1998.

In Too Deep, Golden Books (New York, NY), 1998.

The Thirst, Golden Books (New York, NY), 1998.

No Answer, Golden Books (New York, NY), 1998.

Last Chance, Golden Books (New York, NY), 1999.

The Gift, Golden Books (New York, NY), 1999.

Fight Team Fight, Golden Books (New York, NY), 1999.

Sweetheart Evil Heart, Golden Books (New York, NY), 1999.

Spring Break, Golden Books (New York, NY), 1999.

Wicked, Golden Books (New York, NY), 1999.

Prom Date, Golden Books (New York, NY), 1999.

Graduation Day, Golden Books (New York, NY), 1999.

YOUNG-ADULT NOVELS; "FEAR STREET NIGHTS" SERIES

Moonlight Games, Simon Pulse (New York, NY), 2005.

Midnight Games, Simon Pulse (New York, NY), 2005.

Darkest Dawn, Simon Pulse (New York, NY), 2005.

MIDDLE-GRADE FICTION; "GOOSEBUMPS" SERIES

Welcome to Dead House, Scholastic (New York, NY), 1992.

Stay out of the Basement, Scholastic (New York, NY), 1992.

Monster Blood, Scholastic (New York, NY), 1992.

Say Cheese and Die, Scholastic (New York, NY), 1992.

The Curse of the Mummy's Tomb, Scholastic (New York, NY), 1993.

Let's Get Invisible, Scholastic (New York, NY), 1993.

Night of the Living Dummy, Scholastic (New York, NY), 1993.

The Girl Who Cried Monster, Scholastic (New York, NY), 1993.

Welcome to Camp Nightmare, Scholastic (New York, NY), 1993.

The Ghost Next Door, Scholastic (New York, NY), 1993.

The Haunted Mask, Scholastic (New York, NY), 1993.

Be Careful What You Wish For, Scholastic (New York, NY), 1993.

Piano Lessons Can Be Murder, Scholastic (New York, NY), 1993.

The Werewolf of Fever Swamp, Scholastic (New York, NY), 1993.

You Can't Scare Me, Scholastic (New York, NY), 1993.

One Day at Horrorland, Scholastic (New York, NY), 1994.

Why I'm Afraid of Bees, Scholastic (New York, NY), 1994.

Monster Blood 2, Scholastic (New York, NY), 1994.

Deep Trouble, Scholastic (New York, NY), 1994.

The Scarecrow Walks at Midnight, Scholastic (New York, NY), 1994.

Go Eat Worms!, Scholastic (New York, NY), 1994.

Ghost Beach, Scholastic (New York, NY), 1994.

Return of the Mummy, Scholastic (New York, NY), 1994.

Phantom of the Auditorium, Scholastic (New York, NY), 1994.

Attack of the Mutant, Scholastic (New York, NY), 1994.

My Hairiest Adventure, Scholastic (New York, NY), 1994.

A Night in Terror Tower, Scholastic (New York, NY), 1995.

The Cuckoo Clock of Doom, Scholastic (New York, NY), 1995.

Monster Blood 3, Scholastic (New York, NY), 1995.

It Came from beneath the Sink, Scholastic (New York, NY), 1995.

Night of the Living Dummy 2, Scholastic (New York, NY), 1995.

The Barking Ghost, Scholastic (New York, NY), 1995.

The Horror at Camp Jellyjam, Scholastic (New York, NY), 1995.

Revenge of the Lawn Gnomes, Scholastic (New York, NY), 1995.

A Shocker on Shock Street, Scholastic (New York, NY), 1995.

The Haunted Mask 2, Scholastic (New York, NY), 1995.

The Headless Ghost, Scholastic (New York, NY), 1995.

The Abominable Snowman of Pasadena, Scholastic (New York, NY), 1995.

How I Got My Shrunken Head, Scholastic (New York, NY), 1996.

Night of the Living Dummy 3, Scholastic (New York, NY), 1996.

Bad Hare Day, Scholastic (New York, NY), 1996.

Egg Monsters from Mars, Scholastic (New York, NY), 1996.

The Beast from the East, Scholastic (New York, NY), 1996.

Say Cheese and Die—Again!, Scholastic (New York, NY), 1996.

Ghost Camp, Scholastic (New York, NY), 1996.

How to Kill a Monster, Scholastic (New York, NY), 1996.

Legend of the Lost Legend, Scholastic (New York, NY), 1996.

Attack of the Jack O'Lanterns, Scholastic (New York, NY), 1996.

Vampire Breath, Scholastic (New York, NY), 1996.

Calling All Creeps!, Scholastic (New York, NY), 1996.

Beware the Snowman, Scholastic (New York, NY), 1997.

How I Learned to Fly, Scholastic (New York, NY), 1997.

Chicken, Chicken, Scholastic (New York, NY), 1997.

Don't Go to Sleep!, Scholastic (New York, NY), 1997.

The Blob That Ate Everyone, Scholastic (New York, NY), 1997.

The Curse of Camp Cold Lake, Scholastic (New York, NY), 1997.

My Best Friend Is Invisible, Scholastic (New York, NY), 1997.

Deep Trouble 2, Scholastic (New York, NY), 1997.

The Haunted School, Scholastic (New York, NY), 1997.

Werewolf Skin, Scholastic (New York, NY), 1997.

I Live in Your Basement!, Scholastic (New York, NY), 1997.

Monster Blood 4, Scholastic (New York, NY), 1997.

MIDDLE-GRADE FICTION; "GIVE YOURSELF GOOSEBUMPS" SERIES

Escape from the Carnival of Horrors, Scholastic (New York, NY), 1995.

Tick Tock, You're Dead!, Scholastic (New York, NY), 1995.

Trapped in Bat Wing Hall, Scholastic (New York, NY), 1995.

The Deadly Experiments of Dr. Eeek, Scholastic (New York, NY), 1996.

Night in Werewolf Woods, Scholastic (New York, NY), 1996.

Beware of the Purple Peanut Butter, Scholastic (New York, NY), 1996.

Under the Magician's Spell, Scholastic (New York, NY), 1996.

The Curse of the Creeping Coffins, Scholastic (New York, NY), 1996.

The Knight in Screaming Armor, Scholastic (New York, NY), 1996.

Diary of a Mad Mummy, Scholastic (New York, NY), 1996.

Deep in the Jungle of Doom, Scholastic (New York, NY), 1996.

Welcome to the Wicked Wax Museum, Scholastic (New York, NY), 1996.

Scream of the Evil Genie, Scholastic (New York, NY), 1997.

The Creepy Creations of Professor Shock, Scholastic (New York, NY), 1997.

Please Don't Feed the Vampire, Scholastic (New York, NY), 1997.

Secret Agent Grandma, Scholastic (New York, NY), 1997.

Little Comic Shop of Horrors, Scholastic (New York, NY), 1997.

Attack of the Beastly Babysitter, Scholastic (New York, NY), 1997.

Escape from Camp Run for Your Life, Scholastic (New York, NY), 1997.

Toy Terror: Batteries Included, Scholastic (New York, NY), 1997.

The Twisted Tale of Tiki Island, Scholastic (New York, NY), 1997.

Return to the Carnival of Horrors, Scholastic (New York, NY), 1998.

Zapped in Space, Scholastic (New York, NY), 1998.

Lost in Stinkeye Swamp, Scholastic (New York, NY), 1998.

Shop till You Drop . . . Dead, Scholastic (New York, NY), 1998.

Alone in Snake-bit Canyon, Scholastic (New York, NY), 1998.

Checkout Time at the Dead-End Hotel, Scholastic (New York, NY), 1998.

Night of a Thousand Claws, Scholastic (New York, NY), 1998.

Invaders from the Big Screen, Scholastic (New York, NY), 1998.

You're Plant Food!, Scholastic (New York, NY), 1998.

The Werewolf of Twisted Tree Lodge, Scholastic (New York, NY), 1998.

It's Only a Nightmare!, Scholastic (New York, NY), 1998.

It Came from the Internet, Scholastic (New York, NY), 1999.

Elevator to Nowhere, Scholastic (New York, NY), 1999.

Hocus-Pocus Horror, Scholastic (New York, NY), 1999.

Ship of Ghouls, Scholastic (New York, NY), 1999.

Escape from Horror House, Scholastic (New York, NY), 1999.

Into the Twister of Terror, Scholastic (New York, NY), 1999.

Scary Birthday to You!, Scholastic (New York, NY), 1999.

Zombie School, Scholastic (New York, NY), 1999.

Danger Time, Scholastic (New York, NY), 2000.

All-Day Nightmare, Scholastic (New York, NY), 2000.

MIDDLE-GRADE FICTION; "GIVE YOURSELF GOOSEBUMPS SPECIAL EDITION" SERIES

Into the Jaws of Doom, Scholastic (New York, NY), 1998.

Return to Terror Tower, Scholastic (New York, NY), 1998.

Trapped in the Circus of Fear, Scholastic (New York, NY), 1998.

One Night in Payne House, Scholastic (New York, NY), 1998.

Weekend at Poison Lake, Scholastic (New York, NY), 1998.

The Curse of the Cave Creatures, Scholastic (New York, NY), 1999.

Revenge of the Body Squeezers, Scholastic (New York, NY), 1999.

Trick or . . . Trapped, Scholastic (New York, NY), 1999.

MIDDLE-GRADE FICTION; "GOOSEBUMPS 2000" SERIES

Cry of the Cat, Scholastic (New York, NY), 1998.

Bride of the Living Dummy, Scholastic (New York, NY), 1998.

Creature Teacher, Scholastic (New York, NY), 1998.

Invasion of the Body Squeezers, Scholastic (New York, NY), 1998.

Invasion of the Body Squeezers 2, Scholastic (New York, NY), 1998.

I Am Your Evil Twin, Scholastic (New York, NY), 1998.

Revenge R Us, Scholastic (New York, NY), 1998.

Fright Camp, Scholastic (New York, NY), 1998.

Are You Terrified Yet?, Scholastic (New York, NY), 1998.

Headless Halloween, Scholastic (New York, NY), 1999.

Attack of the Graveyard Ghouls, Scholastic (New York, NY), 1999.

Brain Juice, Scholastic (New York, NY), 1999.

Return to Horrorland, Scholastic (New York, NY), 1999.

Jekyll and Heidi, Scholastic (New York, NY), 1999.

Scream School, Scholastic (New York, NY), 1999.

The Mummy Walks, Scholastic (New York, NY), 1999.

The Werewolf in the Living Room, Scholastic (New York, NY), 1999.

Horror of the Black Ring, Scholastic (New York, NY), 1999.

Return to Ghost Camp, Scholastic (New York, NY), 1999.

Be Afraid—Be Very Afraid!, Scholastic (New York, NY), 1999.

The Haunted Car!, Scholastic (New York, NY), 1999.

Full Moon Fever, Scholastic (New York, NY), 1999.

Slappy's Nightmare, Scholastic (New York, NY), 1999.

Earth Geeks Must Go!, Scholastic (New York, NY), 1999.

Ghost in the Mirror, Scholastic (New York, NY), 2000.

Thirty Tales to Give You Goosebumps, Scholastic (New York, NY), 2004.

Also author of *Tales to Give You Goosebumps* and *More Tales to Give You Goosebumps.*

MIDDLE-GRADE FICTION; "GOOSEBUMPS HORRORLAND" SERIES

Revenge of the Living Dummy, Scholastic (New York, NY), 2008.

Dr. Maniac vs. Robby Schwartz, Scholastic (New York, NY), 2008.

My Friends Call Me Monster, Scholastic (New York, NY), 2009.

Who's Your Mummy?, Scholastic (New York, NY), 2009.

Say Cheese . . . and Die Screaming!, Scholastic (New York, NY), 2009.

MIDDLE-GRADE FICTION; "NIGHTMARE ROOM" SERIES

Don't Forget Me!, Avon (New York, NY), 2000.

Locker 13, Avon (New York, NY), 2000.

My Name Is Evil, Avon (New York, NY), 2000.

Liar, Liar, HarperCollins (New York, NY), 2000.

Dear Diary, I'm Dead, HarperCollins (New York, NY), 2000.

They Call Me Creature, HarperCollins (New York, NY), 2001.

The Howler, Avon (New York, NY), 2001.

Shadow Girl, Avon (New York, NY), 2001.

Camp Nowhere, HarperCollins (New York, NY), 2001.

Full Moon Halloween, Avon (New York, NY), 2001.

Scare School, Avon (New York, NY), 2001.

Visitors, Avon (New York, NY), 2001.

The Nightmare Room: The Nightmare Begins! (omnibus), Avon (New York, NY), 2005.

The Nightmare Room: The Nightmare Continues! (omnibus), Avon (New York, NY), 2005.

MIDDLE-GRADE FICTION; "NIGHTMARE ROOM THRILOGY"

Fear Games, Avon (New York, NY), 2001.

What Scares You Most?, Avon (New York, NY), 2001.

No Survivors, Avon (New York, NY), 2001.

FOR CHILDREN

The Time Raider, illustrated by David Febland, Scholastic (New York, NY), 1982.

The Golden Sword of Dragonwalk, illustrated by David Febland, Scholastic (New York, NY), 1983.

Horrors of the Haunted Museum, Scholastic (New York, NY), 1984.

Instant Millionaire, illustrated by Jowill Woodman, Scholastic (New York, NY), 1984.

Through the Forest of Twisted Dreams, Avon (New York, NY), 1984.

The Badlands of Hark, illustrated by Bob Roper, Scholastic (New York, NY), 1985.

The Invaders of Hark, Scholastic (New York, NY), 1985.

Demons of the Deep, illustrated by Fred Carrillo, Golden Books (New York, NY), 1985.

Challenge of the Wolf Knight ("Wizards, Warriors, and You" series), Avon (New York, NY), 1985.

James Bond in Win, Place, or Die, Ballantine (New York, NY), 1985.

Conquest of the Time Master, Avon (New York, NY), 1985.

Cavern of the Phantoms, Avon (New York, NY), 1986.

Mystery of the Imposter, Avon (New York, NY), 1986.

Golden Girl and the Vanishing Unicorn ("Golden Girl" series), Ballantine (New York, NY), 1986.

The Beast, Minstrel (New York, NY), 1994.

I Saw You That Night!, Scholastic (New York, NY), 1994.

The Beast 2, Minstrel (New York, NY), 1995.

Scream Jennifer Scream, Golden Books (New York, NY), 1998.

When Good Ghouls Go Bad, Avon (New York, NY), 2001.

FOR CHILDREN; "INDIANA JONES" SERIES

Indiana Jones and the Curse of Horror Island, Ballantine (New York, NY), 1984.

Indiana Jones and the Giants of the Silver Tower, Ballantine (New York, NY), 1984.

Indiana Jones and the Cult of the Mummy's Crypt, Ballantine (New York, NY), 1985.

Indiana Jones and the Ape Slaves of Howling Island, Ballantine (New York, NY), 1987.

FOR CHILDREN; "G.I. JOE" SERIES

Operation: Deadly Decoy, Ballantine (New York, NY), 1986.

Operation: Mindbender, Ballantine (New York, NY), 1986.

Serpentor and the Mummy Warrior, Ballantine (New York, NY), 1987.

Jungle Raid, Ballantine (New York, NY), 1988.

Siege of Serpentor, Ballantine (New York, NY), 1988.

FOR CHILDREN; UNDER NAME JOVIAL BOB STINE

The Absurdly Silly Encyclopedia and Flyswatter, illustrated by Bob Taylor, Scholastic (New York, NY), 1978.

How to Be Funny: An Extremely Silly Guidebook, illustrated by Carol Nicklaus, Dutton (New York, NY), 1978.

The Complete Book of Nerds, illustrated by Sam Viviano, Scholastic (New York, NY), 1979.

The Dynamite Do-It-Yourself Pen Pal Kit, illustrated by Jared Lee, Scholastic (New York, NY), 1980.

Dynamite's Funny Book of the Sad Facts of Life, illustrated by Jared Lee, Scholastic (New York, NY), 1980.

Going Out! Going Steady! Going Bananas!, photographs by Dan Nelken, Scholastic (New York, NY), 1980.

The Pig's Book of World Records, illustrated by Peter Lippman, Random House (New York, NY), 1980.

(With wife, Jane Stine) *The Sick of Being Sick Book,* edited by Ann Durrell, illustrated by Carol Nicklaus, Dutton (New York, NY), 1980.

Bananas Looks at TV, Scholastic (New York, NY), 1981.

The Beast Handbook, illustrated by Bob Taylor, Scholastic (New York, NY), 1981.

(With Jane Stine) *The Cool Kids' Guide to Summer Camp,* illustrated by Jerry Zimmerman, Scholastic (New York, NY), 1981.

Gnasty Gnomes, illustrated by Peter Lippman, Random House (New York, NY), 1981.

Don't Stand in the Soup, illustrated by Carol Nicklaus, Bantam (New York, NY), 1982.

(With Jane Stine) *Bored with Being Bored!: How to Beat the Boredom Blahs,* illustrated by Jerry Zimmerman, Four Winds (New York, NY), 1982.

Blips!: The First Book of Video Game Funnies, illustrated by Bryan Hendrix, Scholastic (New York, NY), 1983.

(With Jane Stine) *Everything You Need to Survive: Brothers and Sisters,* illustrated by Sal Murdocca, Random House (New York, NY), 1983.

(With Jane Stine) *Everything You Need to Survive: First Dates,* illustrated by Sal Murdocca, Random House (New York, NY), 1983.

(With Jane Stine) *Everything You Need to Survive: Homework,* illustrated by Sal Murdocca, Random House (New York, NY), 1983.

(With Jane Stine) *Everything You Need to Survive: Money Problems,* illustrated by Sal Murdocca, Random House (New York, NY), 1983.

Jovial Bob's Computer Joke Book, Scholastic (New York, NY), 1985.

Miami Mice, illustrated by Eric Gurney, Scholastic (New York, NY), 1986.

One Hundred and One Silly Monster Jokes, Scholastic (New York, NY), 1986.

The Doggone Dog Joke Book, Parachute Press, 1986.

Pork & Beans: Play Date, illustrated by Jose Aruego and Ariane Dewey, Scholastic (New York, NY), 1989.

Ghostbusters II Storybook, Scholastic (New York, NY), 1989.

One Hundred and One Vacation Jokes, illustrated by Rick Majica, Scholastic (New York, NY), 1990.

The Amazing Adventures of Me, Myself and I, Bantam (New York, NY), 1991.

FOR CHILDREN; "MOSTLY GHOSTLY" SERIES

Have You Met My Ghoulfriend?, Delacorte (New York, NY), 2004.

Who Let the Ghosts Out?, Delacorte (New York, NY), 2004.

Freaks and Shrieks, Delacorte (New York, NY), 2005.

Ghouls Gone Wild, Delacorte (New York, NY), 2005.

Let's Get This Party Haunted!, Delacorte (New York, NY), 2005.

Little Camp of Horrors, Delacorte (New York, NY), 2005.

One Night in Doom House, Delacorte (New York, NY), 2005.

Don't Close Your Eyes!, Delacorte (New York, NY), 2006.

FOR CHILDREN; "ROTTEN SCHOOL" SERIES

The Big Blueberry Barf-off!, illustrated by Trip Park, HarperCollins (New York, NY), 2005.

The Great Smelling Bee, illustrated by Trip Park, HarperCollins (New York, NY), 2005.

The Good, the Bad, and the Very Slimy, illustrated by Trip Park, HarperCollins (New York, NY), 2005.

Lose, Team, Lose!, illustrated by Trip Park, HarperCollins (New York, NY), 2005.

Shake, Rattle, and Hurl!, illustrated by Trip Park, HarperCollins (New York, NY), 2006.

The Heinie Prize, illustrated by Trip Park, HarperCollins (New York, NY), 2006.

Dudes, the School Bus Is Haunted!, illustrated by Trip Park, HarperCollins (New York, NY), 2006.

The Teacher from Heck, illustrated by Trip Park, HarperCollins (New York, NY), 2006.

Party Poopers, illustrated by Trip Park, HarperCollins (New York, NY), 2006.

The Rottenest Angel, illustrated by Trip Park, HarperCollins (New York, NY), 2007.

Punk'd and Skunked, illustrated by Trip Park, HarperCollins (New York, NY), 2007.

Battle of the Dum-Diddys, illustrated by Trip Park, HarperCollins (New York, NY), 2007.

Got Cake?, illustrated by Trip Park, HarperCollins (New York, NY), 2007.

Night of the Creepy Things Poopers, illustrated by Trip Park, HarperCollins (New York, NY), 2007.

Calling All Birdbrains, illustrated by Trip Park, HarperCollins (New York, NY), 2007.

Dumb Clucks, illustrated by Trip Park, HarperCollins (New York, NY), 2008.

OTHER

Superstitious (adult horror), Warner Books (New York, NY), 1995.

It Came from Ohio: My Life as a Writer, (autobiography), Scholastic (New York, NY), 1997.

Nightmare Hour (short stories), HarperCollins (New York, NY), 1999.

The Haunting Hour: Chill in the Dead of the Night (short stories), HarperCollins (New York, NY), 2001.

Beware! R.L. Stine Picks His Favorite Scary Stories, HarperCollins (New York, NY), 2002.

Also author of several "Twistaplot" books for Scholastic and "You Choose the Storyline" books for Ballantine and Avon.

Adaptations

The "Goosebumps" series was produced as a live-action television series for the Fox Television Network beginning 1995; *When Good Ghouls Go Bad* was adapted for video by Fox, 2001; *The Nightmare Room* series was adapted for a television show by Kids WB network, 2001. The graphic novels *Scary Summer, Goosebumps: Creepy Creatures,* and *Terror Trips,* published by Graphix, c. 2006, are based on Stine's work. The "Goosebumps" books were adapted as a feature film franchise by Columbia Pictures, beginning 2009.

Sidelights

With hundreds of millions of books in print—bearing such titles as *The Howler, When Good Ghouls Go Bad,* and *Twister*—R.L. Stine is the world's undisputed top-selling children's author. While criticized by some, the many novels in Stine's phenomenally popular "Fear Street," "Goosebumps," and "Nightmare Room" series have made avid bookworms out of even the most reluctant young readers. His "Fear Street" series illustrates the captivating quality of Stine's literary stew: likeable and realistic teen characters, a seemingly normal small-town setting, and a horrific threat that results in at least one untimely and ickily gruesome end.

Pursuing his writing career full speed, the prolific Stine has been known to write up to two dozen horror novels a year, both as installments in his ongoing series and as

R.L. Stine's "Goosebumps" series attracts readers through exciting plots and cover art on the order of Tim Jacobus' work for **Curse of the Mummy's Tomb.** (Illustration copyright © 1993 by Scholastic, Inc. Reproduced by permission.)

standalone volumes such as *Dangerous Girls,* which a *Publishers Weekly* critic dubbed "a fast and breezy vampire tale punctuated with a few nasty shocks." Surprising, in view of his consistent focus on the bloody, ghoulish, and unearthly, Stine never exactly planned to write horror novels. In fact, For many years, he wrote under the name "Jovial Bob Stine," and his specialty was humorous books that made younger kids laugh.

Stine began his career in children's publishing at New York City-based Scholastic, Inc., where he created the magazines *Bananas* and *Maniac.* His focus on humor eventually prompted Ellen Rudin, an editor at New York City's Dutton publishing, to ask Stine to consider writing a humorous book for younger readers. Stine had not thought seriously about writing a book, but he readily agreed to work up an idea anyway, and the result was *How to Be Funny: An Extremely Silly Guidebook,* which was published in 1978 under the Jovial Bob Stine pseudonym. Many more funny books followed during the late 1970s and well into the 1980s, some coauthored by Stine's wife, Jane, who at that time was the editor of *Dynamite,* another children's magazine published by Scholastic.

During the 1980s, Stine began producing his "Twista-plot" books for Scholastic, along with "You Choose the Storyline" books for both Ballantine and Avon. These series books, which could feature as many as thirty endings and numerous plot twists, proved to be great training for Stine's future work as a novelist. Because of the many titles he produced, he sometimes published these books using the pseudonyms Eric Affabee and Zachary Blue.

When Scholastic began having financial trouble in the mid-1980s, Stine was let go in a company-wide reorganization. Far from a personal disaster, however, Stine's job loss proved to be a blessing because it allowed him the time to write books. Jean Feiwel, editorial director of Scholastic Books, had suggested that the author try his hand at a horror novel, and Stine's novel *Blind Date* was the result. Published in 1986, *Blind Date* features a teenaged boy with a memory lapse, the mysterious teenaged girl who wants to date him, and plenty of twists and turns in the plot.

Like other horror novels Stine has written, *Blind Date* had a title long before it had characters or a storyline; in fact, Feiwel suggested the title and Stine built his

The Ooze, *an installment in Stine's mega-popular "Fear Street" saga, features horror-fan-friendly art by Mark Garro.* (Copyright © 1996 by Parachute Press, Inc. Reprinted by permission of Aladdin Paperbacks, an imprint of Simon & Schuster Children's Publishing Division.)

story around it. "If I can get a title first, then I start getting ideas for it," the author later commented. "Like *The Baby-Sitter.* You start to think, what's scary about being a baby-sitter? Or *The Stepsister . . .* what would be scary about getting a new stepsister? Usually the title will lead me to ideas about what the book should be."

With the success of *Blind Date* and the two other novels that followed, *Twisted* and *The Baby-Sitter,* it occurred to Stine and wife Jane that a series of novels released on a regular basis might sell well. By this time, Jane had also left Scholastic to open her own book packaging company, Parachute Press. Jane suggested to her husband that he come up with a concept for a series that she could market through Parachute Press. "When the words 'Fear Street' sort of magically appeared [while brainstorming], I wrote them down, and then came up with the concept," Stine later recalled.

The voluminous "Fear Street" series, which includes such spin-off series as "Fear Street Cheerleaders," "Fear Street Saga," "Cataluna Chronicles," and "Ghost of Fear Street," is a collection of novels connected primarily by their setting. The main characters usually reside on Fear Street, a place "where your worst nightmares live," according to the cover copy on early titles. All the series' characters attend Shadyside High, a school where the death rate must be horrific, since nearly every book features at least one murder. As Paul Gray noted in *Time,* Stine's "Fear Street" novels subscribe to "a fairly consistent set of formulas." The teenage heroes or heroines are normal (although not always nice) kids who suddenly find their lives fraught with danger. Sometimes the menace comes from supernatural forces, as in the "Fear Street Cheerleaders" series. The first book of this spin-off introduces Bobbi and Corky Corcoran, sisters who join the cheerleading squad at their new school, Shadyside High. After Bobbi dies in a bizarre accident, Corky realizes that there may have been some truth to her sister's ravings about the strange things she had seen and experienced just before her death. Investigating Bobbi's demise, Corky discovers the "evil," a century-old force that has risen from the grave. Although Corky seemingly outwits the evil by the end of the book, it returns to terrorize the cheerleading squad through several more volumes, until Corky is finally able to permanently destroy it.

Sometimes the villains in the "Fear Street" novels are mere mortals with murderous tendencies, as in *Silent Night* and *Broken Hearts,* part of the "Fear Street Super Chillers" series. *Silent Night* introduces Reva Dalby, a beautiful but aloof rich girl who finds herself on the receiving end of some cruel practical jokes. When two people are murdered, it appears that Reva may be the killer's next target. *Broken Hearts* features another entirely human killer. This time the murderer announces his intentions by sending future victims valentines with nasty messages inside. Whatever the source of the menace, Stine's self-reliant teen protagonists do not turn to

Stine shifts the horror/humor mix toward humor in his "Goosebumps Horrorland" series, which includes **Creep from the Deep.** (Cover art by Brandon Dorman copyright © 2008 by Scholastic, Inc. Reproduced by permission of Scholastic, Inc.)

parents, teachers, or other adults for salvation; instead, they consult their friends and do their best to find their own way out of their horrific predicaments. Sometimes, like Bobbi in *The First Evil* and Josie in *Broken Hearts,* they never find a way out, but simply die trying.

Other important components of the "Fear Street" formula are an emphasis on plot over character, and a hair-raising pace. One way Stine keeps his stories moving is to end every chapter with a cliff hanger, a feature teen readers find particularly appealing. It does not seem to matter that the suspense instantly subsides when the reader turns the page, such as when the "hideous, bloated head of a corpse" in Corky's bed turns out to be a Halloween mask, or when the man who tries to accost Reva in a dimly lit department store turns out to be a mannequin she has brushed against. As Stine once commented, his fans "like the fact that there is some kind of jolt at the end of every chapter. They know that if they read to the end of the chapter they're going to have some kind of funny surprise, something scary, something that's going to happen . . . and force them to keep reading."

With the 1992 publication of *Welcome to Dead House,* Stine inaugurated his popular "Goosebumps," and le-

gions of middle-grade fans were quickly hooked. Eventually reaching over 300 million copies in print, the "Goosebumps" books have remained in print and are discovered by thousands of new fans each year. As with his "Fear Street" series, Stine has also created spin-off series in the "Goosebumps" sequence, such as "Goosebumps HorrorLand" and "Give Yourself Goosebumps." Previewing *Revenge of the Living Dummy,* the first volume of Stine's ongoing "Goosebumps HorrorLand" saga, a *Publishers Weekly* critic cited such compelling story elements as a shrunken head and a demonic ventriloquist's dummy as ingredients in a "deliciously chilling" story. In addition to novels, the popular "Goosebumps" books have been adapted as graphic novels as well as a feature film.

Stine's "Nightmare Room" series, while continuing his focus on the ghastly and gruesome, is aimed at the slightly younger eight-to twelve-year-olds market. As he told Andrea Sachs in *Time,* the "Nightmare Room" books are "more like a fun house" than the "roller coaster ride" the "Goosebumps" books offer. According to Sachs, "Nightmare Room" installments such as *Don't Forget Me!* and *Locker 13* "read like slightly more sophisticated installments of 'Goosebumps,'" and pair "dialogue attuned to the speech of the young" with Stine's signature storylines: "teenagers being frightened witless in a context assuring readers that nothing truly dangerous will occur."

Other series for younger readers include Stine's "Mostly Ghostly" books, in which eleven-year-old amateur magician Max Doyle stars in such novels as *Who Let the Ghosts Out?* and *Have You Met My Ghoulfriend?* As their titles suggest, the "Mostly Ghostly" books find Stine returning to his roots as a humorist; in *School Library Journal* Molly S. Kinney wrote of the middle-grade series that "the mood is much more lighthearted and the pacing is slower with fewer terrifying events." Weighing in even more heavily on the humor scale, Stine's "Rotten School" books "will suit those who fine merriment in bodily functions run amok," according to *School Library Journal* critic Gay Lynn Van Vleck. With cartoon artwork by Trip Park that is designed to appeal to an intended upper-elementary-grade readership, the "Rotten School" series includes such installments as *The Great Smelling Bee, The Good, the Bad, and the Very Slimy,* and *The Big Blueberry Barf-off!*

While Stine's legions of fans have no quibbles with the formulaic nature of his twisted tales, critics have sometimes been less generous. In a review of *Twisted,* for example, a *Publishers Weekly* reviewer wrote that, "for shock value, this book adds up to a lot of cheap tricks." Another *Publishers Weekly* critic noted of *Ski Weekend* that Stine's "contrived plot barely manages to hold together a series of bland cliffhangers." In reviewing *The Second Evil* for *Voice of Youth Advocates,* Caroline S. McKinney declared that "these formula stories are very predictable and require very little thought on the part of the reader."

Despite the reviews of some curmudgeonly critics, other reviewers have acknowledged Stine's talent for hooking readers and keeping them entertained, a talent many recognize as particularly valuable to teens who are increasingly seduced by more visual media. Alice Cronin, writing a review of "Fear Street" installment *The Sleepwalker* for *School Library Journal,* stated that "Stine writes a good story. Teens will love the action." Appraising *Curtains,* a *Publishers Weekly* columnist noted that although "the book . . . will never be mistaken for serious literature, it is sure to engross Stine's considerable following." In *Voice of Youth Advocates,* Sylvia C. Mitchell declared of *Silent Night:* "If all series books were this good, I'd begin to drop my . . . prejudices against them."

Stine is the first to admit that the merit of his work lies in its entertainment value, and he sees nothing wrong with that. "I believe that kids as well as adults are entitled to books of no socially redeeming value," he once noted. Although his books may be frightening, the scares are "safe scares," as he told Gray. "You're home in your room and reading. The books are not half as scary as the real world." In fact, the horror in Stine's books intentionally retains an element of the unreal. "I wouldn't do child abuse, or AIDS, or suicide, or anything that could really touch someone's life like that," he explained. "The books are supposed to be just entertainment, that's all they are."

While the horror may be unreal, the human characters in the "Fear Street," "Goosebumps," and "Mostly Ghostly" books are realistic and usually likeable. Stine works hard at making his young characters talk like real kids, dress like real kids, and have the concerns of real kids. Even when they are wrestling with an unseen evil or tracking down a mysterious killer, they still care about whether or not they have a date for Saturday night. Fortunately, son Matt has provided the author with plenty of firsthand experience regarding modern teens. Stine does his homework, too, reading teen magazines, watching music videos, and mining teen-focused internet sites. One thing Stine does not do, however, is incorporate the latest teen slang. "I don't have them saying things like 'gnarly,' and other stuff people accuse me of putting in," the writer once remarked. "I'd like these books to be read five years from now, and that kind of slang really dates them fast. Besides," he added, "most kids talk normal."

Stine is often asked for advice on becoming successful as a writer, and he advises budding authors not to do what he first did: sending his work to publishers, hoping to make a sale. Instead, he counsels teen writers to read, read, and then read some more. That way "you pick up all these different styles, almost by osmosis," he said, "and you'll be a better writer for it."

Aspiring writers might also want to take a tip from Stine's method of crafting his horror stories. He always begins with a chapter-by-chapter outline that details the action. Even though he admits that creating an outline is "an arduous process," doing so "helps me see whether or not the books make sense. I always start with the ending—that's the first thing I know. Then I can go back and figure out how to fool the reader, how to keep them from guessing the ending. By the time I sit down to write the book, I really know everything that's going to happen. I can just have fun and write it."

Biographical and Critical Sources

BOOKS

Children's Literature Review, Volume 37, Gale (Detroit, MI), 1996, pp. 101-123.
Guinness World Records 2000: Millennium Edition, Mint (New York, NY), 2000.
Jones, Patrick, *What's So Scary about R.L. Stine?,* Scarecrow Press (Metuchen, NJ), 1998.
Roginski, Jim, *Behind the Covers,* Libraries Unlimited, 1985, pp. 206-213.
St. James Guide to Young Adult Writers, 2nd edition, St. James Press (Detroit, MI), 1999.

PERIODICALS

Booklist, October 15, 1999, Candace Smith, review of *Nightmare Hour,* p. 446; January 1, 2002, Frances Bradburn, review of *The Haunting Hour: Chill in the Dead of the Night,* p. 859; September 1, 2004, Cindy Welch, review of *The Taste of Night,* p. 109.
Bulletin of the Center for Children's Books, November, 2001, review of *The Haunting Hour,* p. 117; October, 2002, review of *Beware! R.L. Stine Picks His Favorite Scary Stories,* p. 80.
Horn Book, July-August, 1997, Elizabeth S. Watson, review of *It Came from Ohio!: My Life as a Writer,* p. 478.
New York Times, March 25, 2008, Brian Stelter, "'Goosebumps' Rises from the Literary Grave," p. E1.
Publishers Weekly, July 10, 1987, review of *Twisted,* p. 87; September 28, 1990, review of *Curtains,* p. 104; December 7, 1990, review of *Ski Weekend,* p. 830; August 30, 1999, review of *Nightmare Hour,* p. 85; September 25, 2000, review of *Don't Forget Me!,* p. 118; August 4, 2003, review of *Dangerous Girls,* p. 80; August 30, 2004, review of *Who Let the Ghosts Out?,* p. 55; March 10, 2008, review of *Revenge of the Living Dummy,* p. 81.
School Library Journal, September, 1990, Alice Cronin, review of *The Sleepwalker;* July, 1997, Melissa Hudak, review of *It Came from Ohio!,* p. 112; December, 1999, Molly S. Kinney, review of *Nightmare Hour,* p. 142; April, 2001, Elaine Baran Black, review of *Don't Forget Me!,* p. 149; October, 2002, Molly S. Kinney, review of *Beware!,* p. 174; August, 2003, Kimberly L. Paone, review of *Dangerous Girls,* p. 166; August, 2004, Sharon Rawlins, review of *The Taste of Night,* p. 129; October, 2004, Molly S. Kin-

ney, review of *Have You Met My Ghoulfriend?,* p. 178; September, 2005, Gay Lynn Van Vleck, review of *The Great Smelling Bee,* p. 187.

Time, August 2, 1992, Paul Gray, "Carnage: An Open Book," p. 54; August 28, 2000, Andrea Sachs, "Another Stab at Chills," pp. 56-57.

Voice of Youth Advocates, April, 1992, Sylvia C. Mitchell, review of *Silent Night,* pp. 36-37; February, 1993, Caroline S. McKinney, review of *The Second Evil,* p. 360; June, 1993, review of *Broken Hearts,* p. 105; August, 1993, review of *The Cheater,* p. 158; February, 1994, reviews of *Sunburn, The Dare,* and *The Betrayal,* p. 41.

ONLINE

Nightmare Room Web site, http://www.thenighmareroom. com/ (October 20, 2008).
R.L. Stine Home Page, http://www.rlsine.com (October 20, 2008).
Scholastic Web site, http://www.scholastic.com/ (October 20, 2008), official "Goosebumps" site.*

*   *   *

STINE, Robert Lawrence
See STINE, R.L.

T

TINCKNELL, Cathy

Personal
Married John Kelly (an author/illustrator).

Addresses
Home—London, England.

Career
Author and illustrator of picture books.

Awards, Honors
Blue Ribbon citation, *Bulletin of the Center for Children's Books,* 2004, for *The Mystery of Eatum Hall.*

Writings

(With husband, John Kelly) *Guess Who's Coming for Dinner?,* Templar Publishing (Dorking, Surrey, England), 2004, published as *The Mystery of Eatum Hall,* Candlewick Press (Cambridge, MA), 2004.
(With husband, John Kelly) *Scoop! An Exclusive by Monty Molenski,* Candlewick Press (Cambridge, MA), 2007.

Sidelights
Cathy Tincknell collaborates with her husband, John Kelly, to create picture books that use elaborate digital artwork to enhance the text. Tincknell's first collaboration with Kelly, *The Mystery of Eatum Hall*—published in England as *Guess Who's Coming for Dinner?*—introduces Horace and Glenda Pork-Fowler, a pig and a goose, respectively. When the Pork-Fowlers accept an invitation to a mysterious mansion for a weekend of gourmet dining, their host, Dr. Hunter, is nowhere to be seen. Happily, however, the food is plentiful and magnificent. Stuffing themselves, the Pork-Fowlers fail to notice clues in their surroundings that suggest they are being plumped for consumption themselves. *School Library Journal* contributor Lauralyn Persson liked the "look of unpolished spontaneity" in Tincknell and Kelly's book, concluding that the combination of witty puns and hidden messages hidden in the book's illustrations "will engage children on many levels." A *Kirkus Reviews* critic also cited the "digital art in an accomplished, painterly style," describing *The Mystery of Eatum Hall* "a confection, but a delicious one." According

Cathy Tincknell joins author/illustrator John Kelly to create the interactive picture-book mystery Scoop! An Exclusive by Monty Molenski.
(Illustration copyright © 2007 by John Kelly. Reproduced by permission of the publisher, Candlewick Press, Inc., Somerville, MA.)

to a correspondent for *Publishers Weekly,* with "just the right mix of horror and delight," readers of *The Mystery of Eatum Hall* "will plead to visit this eating establishment again."

Monty the mole has a problem in *Scoop! An Exclusive by Monty Molenski,* another picture-book production of Tincknell and Kelly. Monty's colleagues at the newspaper have left for a party without him, and he wants to attend. Because he is a mole—and therefore troubled by bad eyesight—Monty cannot locate the party. Worse still, his camera keeps malfunctioning, taking pictures at whim. As the pages turn, readers can see what Monty misses: aliens, mythological beasts, and even dead celebrities lurk in the shadows surrounding the befuddled mole. Nevertheless, wrote Genevieve Gallagher in *School Library Journal,* readers "will be rooting for [Monty] through his bumbling pursuits." Calling *Scoop!* "a hilarious caper," a *Kirkus Reviews* writer predicted of the book that "children aren't the only ones who will 'scoop' this up."

Biographical and Critical Sources

PERIODICALS

Horn Book, January-February, 2005, Robin Smith, review of *The Mystery of Eatum Hall,* p. 80.

Kirkus Reviews, September 1, 2004, review of *The Mystery of Eatum Hall,* p. 868; December 15, 2006, review of *Scoop! An Exclusive by Monty Molenski,* p. 1270.

Publishers Weekly, September 20, 2004, review of *The Mystery of Eatum Hall,* p. 62; February 12, 2007, review of *Scoop!,* p. 85.

School Library Journal, December, 2004, Lauralyn Persson, review of *The Mystery of Eatum Hall,* p. 112; May, 2007, Genevieve Gallagher, review of *Scoop!,* p. 100.

ONLINE

Candlewick Press Web site, http://www.candlewick.com/ (October 24, 2008), "Cathy Tincknell."*

*   *   *

TOWNSEND, Michael 1981-

Personal

Born July 1, 1981. *Education:* School of Visual Arts, degree.

Addresses

Home—Lansdale, PA.

Career

Children's book author and illustrator.

Awards, Honors

Gryphon Award, Center for Children's Books, 2008, for *Billy Tartle in Say Cheese!*

Writings

Billy Tartle in Say Cheese!, Alfred A. Knopf (New York, NY), 2007.

Sidelights

Michael Townsend's debut picture book, *Billy Tartle in Say Cheese!,* was published shortly after its author/illustrator's graduation from New York City's School of Visual Arts. Dubbed by *Curled up with a Good Kid's Book* online reviewer Zane Ewton as "silly in the best possible way," the book introduces an energetic and well-meaning young boy. Billy Tartle is looking forward to picture day at his elementary school, and the key to a fantastic picture is a fantastic haircut. The power struggle between Billy and his mom takes place at the barber shop, where Barber Ken plays mediator in the battle between a bright pink, spiky Mohawk and a tidy, good-boy haircut. When Mom wins, it is left to the resourceful Billy to find another way to shake up picture day. In *Publishers Weekly* a critic predicted that "readers with a rascally bent will likely get a kick out of Billy's overactive imagination and puckish behavior." Linda M. Kenton wrote in *School Library Journal* that Townsend's digitized comic-book art is "sharp and bright," and in *Kirkus Reviews* a contributor enjoyed the author/illustrator's "definite predilection for tomfoolery."

Biographical and Critical Sources

PERIODICALS

Bulletin of the Center for Children's Books, July-August, 2007, Deborah Stevenson, review of *Billy Tartle in Say Cheese!*

Kirkus Reviews, June 15, 2007, review of *Billy Tartle in Say Cheese!*

Publishers Weekly, July 9, 2007, review of *Billy Tartle in Say Cheese!,* p. 53.

School Library Journal, July, 2007, Linda M. Kenton, review of *Billy Tartle in Say Cheese!,* p. 86.

ONLINE

Curled up with a Good Kid's Book Web site, http://www. curledupkids.com/ (October 13, 2008), Zane Ewton, review of *Billy Tartle in Say Cheese!*

Random House Web site, http://www.randomhouse.ca/ (October 13, 2008), "Michael Townsend."*

TRUSS, Lynne 1955(?)-

Personal

Born c. 1955.

Addresses

Home—Brighton, England. *Agent*—David Higham Associates, 5-8 Lower John St., Golden Square, London W1F 9HA, England.

Career

Journalist and novelist. *Listener* magazine, literary editor, 1986-90; *Times,* London, England, television critic and sports columnist; *Daily Mail,* London, critic; *Sunday Times,* London, book reviewer. Host of British Broadcasting Corporation (BBC) Radio-4 series *Cutting a Dash.* Member of judging panel, Asham awards, 2005-06.

Awards, Honors

Named Columnist of the Year, 1996, for articles in *Women's Journal;* University College London fellowship, 2004; Book of the Year designation, British Book Awards, 2004, for *Eats, Shoots and Leaves: The Zero Tolerance Approach to Punctuation.*

Writings

Making the Cat Laugh: One Woman's Journal of Single Life on the Margins, Hamish Hamilton (London, England), 1995.

Tennyson and His Circle (biography), NPG (London, England), 1999.

Eats, Shoots and Leaves: The Zero Tolerance Approach to Punctuation, Profile Books (London, England), 2003, Gotham Books (New York, NY), 2004.

Talk to the Hand: The Utter Bloody Rudeness of the World Today; or, Six Good Reasons to Stay Home and Bolt the Door, Gotham Books (New York, NY), 2005, published as *Talk to the Hand: The Utter Bloody Rudeness of Everyday Life (or Six Good Reasons to Stay Home and Bolt the Door),* Profile Books (London, England), 2005.

The Lynne Truss Treasury: Columns and Three Comic Novels, Gotham Books (New York, NY), 2005.

A Certain Age (radio drama), Profile (London, England), 2007.

A Certain Age Volume 2: The Men's Monologues (audiobook), BBC Audiobooks (London, England), 2007.

Author of numerous comedies, dramas, and other features for BBC Radio, including *Acropolis Now, Full Circle,* and *Inspector Steine.* Contributor to *Glued to the Gogglebox: Fifty Years of British Television with Freeze-Frames,* Checkmate (Liverpool, England), 2003.

FOR CHILDREN

Eats, Shoots and Leaves: Why, Commas Really DO Make a Difference! (adapted from her adult book of the same title), illustrated by Bonnie Timmons, Putnam (New York, NY), 2006.

The Girl's Like Spaghetti: Why, You Can't Manage without Apostrophes!, illustrated by Bonnie Timmons, Putnam (New York, NY), 2007.

Twenty-odd Ducks: Why, Every Punctuation Mark Counts!, illustrated by Bonnie Timmons, Putnam (New York, NY), 2008.

ADULT NOVELS

With One Lousy Free Packet of Seed, Hamish Hamilton (London, England), 1994.

Tennyson's Gift, Hamish Hamilton (London, England), 1996.

Going Loco, Review (London, England), 1999.

Adaptations

Eats, Shoots and Leaves was adapted for audiocassette by British Broadcasting Corporation (BBC) Radio.

Sidelights

Even when Lynne Truss was a little girl, she enjoyed writing. One of her first stories, a fairy tale written at age nine, began with the dialogue: "So your the wicked

Cover of Eats, Shoots and Leaves, *Lynne Truss's well-received plea for grammatical correctness.* (Gotham Books, a division of Penguin Group USA, 2003. Reproduced by permission.)

The power of the apostrophe is illustrated by Bonnie Timmons in her artwork for Truss's entertaining **The Girl's Like Spaghetti.** (Putnam, a division of Penguin Young Readers Group, 2007. Illustration copyright © 2007 by Bonnie Timmons. Reproduced by permission.)

witch." When a sister read the story, her first comment was that Truss should have written "you're," not "your." The mistake, Truss told *USA Today* interviewer Bob Minzesheimer, left the future writer feeling "humiliated. I never finished that story, but I certainly learned the difference between *your* and *you're*." The lesson stayed with her; nearly thirty years later, Truss's love of proper grammar led to her to publish the international bestseller *Eats, Shoots and Leaves: The Zero Tolerance Approach to Punctuation.*

A journalist, critic, and novelist, Truss has reviewed books and television programs, and written about sports for the London *Times.* She is also well known to thousands of listeners of British Broadcasting Corporation (BBC)'s Radio-4 due to her dramas and comic monologues, and she has also had modest success as a novelist. It was while writing a radio program about punctuation that Truss "realized I did care, quite strongly, about these things," as she later told Bryan Alexander for *People.* Her little book on grammar, *Eats, Shoots and Leaves,* has become an international bestseller, selling millions of copies in both Great Britain and the United States and inspiring a series of related books for children.

The title *Eats, Shoots and Leaves* refers to a joke: a panda walks into a café, eats a sandwich, then shoots

an arrow into the air. When a man asks why, the panda throws him a badly punctuated nature guide and tells him to look it up. The entry for panda includes the line: "Eats, shoots and leaves." The extra comma completely changes the meaning of the sentence from a description of the panda's diet to one of a violent action. In *Eats, Shoots and Leaves,* Truss traces the history of punctuation marks like the comma, apostrophe, and semicolon. She argues that paying attention to punctuation is not being a stickler; in fact, doing so ensures correct communication. Her humor enlivens the book throughout, especially in her examples of how missing punctuation can completely change a sentence's meaning.

In 2006, Truss produced a version of her bestselling book for children, titled *Eats, Shoots and Leaves: Why, Commas Really DO Make a Difference!* In addition to the title example, Truss gives several other amusing instances of how a comma can make a difference. Cartoons help illustrate the divergent meanings of "Slow, children crossing" and "Slow children crossing." Although adapting her grammar guide for children may not seem like a natural fit, "it proves very effective, thanks to entertaining repackaging that narrows the original's broad purview to the comma," according to Jennifer Mattson in *Booklist.* A *Kirkus Reviews* critic likewise found the book to be a "clever, creative commentary on commas," adding that "the witty sentences increase in complexity (and hilarity)."

In *The Girl's Like Spaghetti: Why, You Can't Manage without Apostrophes!* Truss focuses on the power of the apostrophe, as in the difference between "those smelly things are my brother's" and "those smelly things are my brothers." "Many of the 13 scenarios successfully find the sweet spot between kid-pleasing goofiness and perfect clarity of purpose," Jennifer Mattson remarked in *Booklist*. A *Kirkus Reviews* critic commented that "some sentence pairs are whimsical while others are laugh-out-loud funny, but the entire text is easy to understand" when combined with Bonnie Timmon's illustrations. The book gives kids "wordplay or 'grammarplay' at its finest," according to Jennifer Cogan in *School Library Journal*. A third child-friendly guide, *Twenty-odd Ducks: Why, Every Punctuation Mark Counts!*, includes punctuation marks ranging from the hyphen to parentheses, quotation marks, and periods, again showing how one little change in notation can make a world of difference in meaning.

Truss continues to try to improve people's grammar, both through her books as well as by creating podcasts for use in classrooms. As she told Alexander, "I feel responsible for making others notice" poor grammar, even if it means taking a marker to badly punctuated shop signs. With her humor, she is likely to keep making converts. As Elizabeth Austin wrote in *Washington Monthly*, Truss "is a smart, engaging, perceptive, high-spirited, and paralyzingly funny writer."

Biographical and Critical Sources

PERIODICALS

Booklist, April 23, 2004, "Truss Colonises the World," p. 15; June 1, 2004, Joanne Wilkinson, review of *Eats, Shoots and Leaves: The Zero Tolerance Approach to Punctuation*, p. 1681; September 1, 2006, Jennifer Mattson, review of *Eats, Shoots and Leaves: Why, Commas Really DO Make a Difference*, p. 132; July 1, 2007, Mattson, review of *The Girl's Like Spaghetti: Why, You Can't Manage without Apostrophes!*, p. 53.

Boston Globe, March 21, 2004, Jan Freeman, review of *Eats, Shoots and Leaves*, p. C3.

Kirkus Reviews, June 15, 2006, review of *Eats, Shoots and Leaves: Why, Commas Really Do Make a Difference!*, p. 639; June 15, 2007, review of *The Girl's Like Spaghetti*.

Los Angeles Times, June 27, 2004, John Rechy, review of *Eats, Shoots and Leaves*, p. R5.

Newsweek, April 12, 2004, Elise Soukup, review of *Eats, Shoots and Leaves*, p. 12.

New Yorker, June 28, 2004, Louis Menand, review of *Eats, Shoots and Leaves*, p. 102.

New York Times Book Review, April 25, 2004, Edmund Morris, review of *Eats, Shoots and Leaves*, p. 7.

People, May 17, 2004, Bryan Alexander, interview with Truss, p. 53.

Publishers Weekly, November 29, 2004, John F. Baker, "Punctuation Princess Back," p. 8.

Reviewer's Bookwatch, November, 2004, review of *Eats, Shoots and Leaves*.

School Library Journal, August, 2004, Susan H. Woodcock, review of *Eats, Shoots and Leaves*, p. 147; July, 2007, Jennifer Cogan, review of *The Girl's Like Spaghetti*, p. 95.

Spectator, December 6, 2003, Philip Hensher, review of *Eats, Shoots and Leaves*, p. 44; January 10, 2004, Benedict le Vay, "Pluck Truss and Grieve," p. 22.

Time, May 24, 2004, Christopher Porterfield, review of *Eats, Shoots and Leaves*, p. 83.

USA Today, August 8, 2006, Bob Minzesheimer, "'Eats, Shoots, Leaves' Spelled out for Kids," p. 5D.

Washington Monthly, December, 2005, Elizabeth Austin, "Missed Manners: Lynne Truss Thinks People Are Getting Ruder. She Can Shove It," p. 42.

Washington Post, May 23, 2004, Michael Dirda, review of *Eats, Shoots and Leaves*, p. T15.

ONLINE

Eats, Shoots and Leaves Web site, http://www.eatsshootsandleaves.com/ (October 28, 2008).*

* * *

TRYON, Leslie

Personal

Daughter of Dorothy; married. *Hobbies and other interests:* Theater, dance.

Addresses

Home—Carmel Valley, CA.

Career

Author and illustrator. Former professional dancer. *Los Angeles Times Book Review*, illustrator; Air Force Art Program, creator of documentary art in Southeast Asia. Choreographed musicals and worked on a cruise ship.

Member

Society of Illustrators (president of Los Angeles chapter).

Awards, Honors

Ezra Jack Keats scholarship, Kerlan Collection; Notable Book selection, American Library Association, 1991, for *Albert's Alphabet*.

Writings

SELF-ILLUSTRATED

Albert's Alphabet, Atheneum Books (New York, NY), 1991.

Albert's Play, Atheneum Books (New York, NY), 1992.

One Gaping Wide-mouthed Hopping Frog, Atheneum Books (New York, NY), 1993.

Albert's Field Trip, Atheneum Books (New York, NY), 1993.

Albert's Thanksgiving, Atheneum Books (New York, NY), 1994.

Albert's Ballgame, Atheneum Books (New York, NY), 1996.

Albert's Christmas, Atheneum Books (New York, NY), 1997.

Albert's Halloween: The Case of the Stolen Pumpkins, Atheneum Books (New York, NY), 1998.

Albert's Birthday, Atheneum Books (New York, NY), 1999.

Patsy Says, Atheneum Books (New York, NY), 2001.

ILLUSTRATOR

Jan Gleiter and Kathleen Thompson, *Daniel Boone,* Raintree Children's Books (Milwaukee, WI), 1985.

Mary Elise Monsell, *Toohy and Wood,* Atheneum Books (New York, NY), 1992.

Alma Flor Ada, *Dear Peter Rabbit,* Atheneum Books (New York, NY), 1994.

Alma Flor Ada, *Yours Truly, Goldilocks,* Atheneum Books (New York, NY), 1998.

Alma Flor Ada, *With Love, Little Red Hen,* Atheneum Books (New York, NY), 2001.

Debbi Chocolate, *Pigs Can Fly!: The Adventures of Harriet Pig and Friends,* Cricket Books (Chicago, IL), 2004.

Alma Flor Ada, *Extra! Extra!: Fairy-tale News from Hidden Forest,* Atheneum Books (New York, NY), 2007.

Sidelights

A longtime artist, Leslie Tryon has provided illustrations for children's books by such authors as Alma Flor Ada and Debbi Chocolate. In addition, she has also written a series of self-illustrated children's books featuring a duck named Albert. Her "Albert" books are geared toward preschoolers and children up to second grade, and each volume in the series tackles a simple but realistic situation in Albert's life. In *Albert's Alphabet,* Albert, who is also the school carpenter for the Pleasant Valley school district, builds a walking path marked with all the letters of the alphabet. In *Albert's Play,* the duck directs the annual school play, offering readers a glimpse into the behind-the-scenes work that goes into putting up even a small stage production. In *Albert's Field Trip,* the duck drives a group of school children to their field trip at the apple orchard. Tryon uses this adventure to create "astute caricatures of [the animals'] . . . human counterparts" wrote a critic in *Kirkus Reviews.*

Other "Albert" adventures include *Albert's Ballgame, Albert's Christmas, Albert's Halloween: The Case of the Stolen Pumpkins,* and *Albert's Birthday.* Each of these works has been praised by critics for its bright, colorful illustrations and rhyming text, and suggested as recommended reading for both children and parents. In particular, *Booklist* contributor Shelle Rosenfeld and Gilbert Taylor praised *Albert's Birthday* as a "delightful multipurpose book" that focuses on fun as well as learning.

Tryon is also the author and illustrator of *One Gaping Wide-mouthed Hopping Frog,* an illustrated adventure set to an eighteenth-century rhyme. The simple story line, wherein a frog delivers mail to his small community of animals, is accompanied by lots of opportunities to "search out, identify, and count" in illustrations that have a "wit and charm" that are endearing, noted a *Kirkus Reviews* critic.

Additionally, Tryon has illustrated several books written by Ada, who casts familiar fairy-tale characters in such titles as *Dear Peter Rabbit* and *Yours Truly, Goldilocks.* Set in the Hidden Forest, these books feature a series of letters describing the adventures of the woodland's residents, especially their troubles with Wolfy Lupus and Fer O'Cious, a pair of ravenous cousins. Reviewing *Dear Peter Rabbit,* a *Publishers Weekly* critic described the illustrations as "delicately colored" and "lovingly detailed."

In *With Love, Little Red Hen,* another book by Ada, the title character moves into the Hidden Forest with her chicks, and with the help of her neighbors, including Little Red Riding Hood and the Three Pigs, she raises a bountiful harvest. "Tryon's detailed illustrations fit the letters perfectly," noted a contributor in *Kirkus Reviews,* and Bina Williams, writing in *School Library Journal,* commented that the pictures "depict a bucolic paradise with neighbors who look out for one another." A series of newspaper articles chronicle the latest happenings of the residents in Ada's *Extra! Extra!: Fairy-tale News from Hidden Forest.* Each edition of the *Hidden Forest News* covers the major local stories, including the sudden appearance of a large beanstalk, an Italian toymaker's search for his son, and a showdown between the Tortoise and the Hare. "Tryon's busy full-color illustrations will keep readers' attention as they search for hidden details," a *Kirkus Reviews* critic observed of the book.

Pigs Can Fly!: The Adventures of Harriet Pig and Friends, an early reader by Chocolate that features Tryon's art, contains four tales about a spirited potbellied pig. In one story, Harriet helps Penny Porcupine conquer her fear of heights, and in another she challenges Lucy Goosey to a swimming race. "Tryon brings the whole cast of likable characters to life with warm, expressive, black-and-white illustrations," Lauren Peterson stated in *Booklist,* and Lynn K. Vanca, writing in *School Library Journal,* commented that the pictures "enhance the humor of the text."

Biographical and Critical Sources

PERIODICALS

Booklist, May 1, 1994, Ilene Cooper, review of *Dear Peter Rabbit,* p. 1606; May 1, 1996, Carolyn Phelan, review of *Albert's Ballgame,* p. 1513; May 1, 1998, Ilene Cooper, review of *Yours Truly, Goldilocks,* p. 1520; October 1, 1999, Shelle Rosenfeld and Gilbert Taylor, review of *Albert's Birthday,* p. 364; September 15, 2001, Lauren Peterson, review of *With Love, Little Red Hen,* p. 229; May 1, 2004, Lauren Peterson, review of *Pigs Can Fly!: The Adventures of Harriet Pig and Friends,* p. 1561.

California Kids!, September, 2002, Patricia M. Newman, "Who Wrote That? Featuring Leslie Tryon."

Five Owls, May-June, 1992, review of *Albert's Play,* p. 69.

Horn Book, January-February, 2002, Kitty Flynn, review of *With Love, Little Red Hen,* p. 65; September-October, 2007, Kitty Flynn, review of *Extra! Extra!: Fairy-tale News from Hidden Forest,* p. 555.

Kirkus Reviews, February 1, 1993, review of *One, Gaping Wide-mouthed Hopping Frog,* p. 155; September 1, 1993, review of *Albert's Field Trip,* p. 1153; October 15, 1994, review of *Albert's Thanksgiving,* p. 1422; October 1, 2001, review of *With Love, Little Red Hen,* p. 1418; March 1, 2004, review of *Pigs Can Fly!,* p. 219; June 15, 2007, review of *Extra! Extra!*

Publishers Weekly, July 5, 1991, "Flying Starts," p. 38; February 21, 1994, review of *Dear Peter Rabbit,* p. 253; September 19, 1994, review of *Albert's Thanksgiving,* p. 27; April 22, 1996, review of *Albert's Ballgame,* p. 71; September 3, 2001, review of *With Love, Little Red Hen,* p. 89.

School Library Journal, July, 1991, Anna Biagioni Hart, review of *Albert's Alphabet,* p. 65; March, 1996, Liza Bliss, review of *Albert's Ballgame,* p. 183; September, 1998, Olga R. Barnes, review of *Albert's Halloween: The Case of the Stolen Pumpkins,* p. 184; October, 2001, Bina Williams, review of *With Love, Little Red Hen,* p. 104; May, 2004, Lynn K. Vanca, review of *Pigs Can Fly!,* p. 108; August, 2007, Julie Roach, review of *Extra! Extra!,* p. 76.*

W

WALSH, Ellen Stoll 1942-

Personal
Born September 2, 1942, in Baltimore, MD; daughter of Joseph Adolphus (a businessman) and Nell Stoll; married David Albert Walsh (a professor), August 25, 1964; children: Benjamin Martin. *Education:* Maryland Institute of Art, B.F.A., 1964; attended University of Minnesota, 1966-69.

Addresses
Home—Fairport, NY.

Career
Writer and illustrator. Houghton Mifflin, Boston, MA, freelance illustrator, 1984—. Ezra Jack Keats fellow, Kerlan Collection, University of Minnesota, 1986.

Member
Authors Guild, Society of Children's Book Writers and Illustrators.

Awards, Honors
Merit Award, Art Director's Club Fifty-ninth Annual Exhibition, and Award of Excellence, American Institute of Graphic Arts, both 1980, both for *Brunus and the New Bear;* Children's Choice selection, International Reading Association, 1982, for *Theodore All Grown Up;* Reading Magic Award, *Parenting* magazine, 1989, for *Mouse Paint;* National Outdoor Children's Book Award, 2004, for *Dot and Jabber and the Big Bug Mystery.*

Writings

SELF-ILLUSTRATED

Brunus and the New Bear, Doubleday (New York, NY), 1979.

Ellen Stoll Walsh (Photograph by Sara Koblentz. Reproduced by permission of Ellen Stoll Walsh.)

Theodore All Grown Up, Doubleday (New York, NY), 1981.
Mouse Paint, Harcourt Brace (San Diego, CA), 1989.
Mouse Count, Harcourt Brace (San Diego, CA), 1991.
You Silly Goose, Harcourt Brace (San Diego, CA), 1992.
Hop Jump, Harcourt Brace (San Diego, CA), 1993.
Pip's Magic, Harcourt Brace (San Diego, CA), 1994.
Samantha, Harcourt Brace (San Diego, CA), 1996.
Jack's Tale, Harcourt Brace (San Diego, CA), 1997.
For Pete's Sake, Harcourt Brace (San Diego, CA), 1998.
Mouse Magic, Harcourt (San Diego, CA), 2000.
Hamsters to the Rescue, Harcourt (Orlando, FL), 2005.

Mouse Shapes, Harcourt (Orlando, FL), 2007.

SELF-ILLUSTRATED; "DOT AND JABBER" SERIES

Dot and Jabber and the Great Acorn Mystery, Harcourt (San Diego, CA), 2001.

Dot and Jabber and the Mystery of the Missing Stream, Harcourt (San Diego, CA), 2002.

Dot and Jabber and the Big Bug Mystery, Harcourt (San Diego, CA), 2003.

Adaptations

Brunus and the New Bear was adapted as a filmstrip by Imperial Educational Resources, 1980; *Theodore All Grown Up* was adapted as a filmstrip by Spoken Arts, narrated by Frances Sternhagen, music by Michael Barber, 1982.

Sidelights

Children's author and artist Ellen Stoll Walsh is best known for her books *Mouse Count* and *Mouse Paint,* which help young readers master basic skills through simple texts and compelling cut-paper collage illustrations. Another book in the sequence, *Mouse Shapes,* continues to demonstrate Walsh's mastery of the beginning concept book. As Shelley B. Sutherland noted in *School Library Journal,* the "brightly colored shapes and . . . simple story line" of *Mouse Shapes* are "pitched perfectly for sharing with the youngest of listeners." Remarking on the series, a *Kirkus Reviews* writer was equally laudatory, citing the "crisp layout and well-chosen typography" characteristic of the series, as well as stories that are "clearly crafted to amuse, not frighten" young listeners.

Born in Baltimore, Maryland, Walsh grew up one of ten children in a close-knit family. "Life was often chaotic with so many people around, but there were many won-derful moments," she later recalled to *SATA.* As fond of drawing as she was of spending time outside, Walsh eventually worked as a summer-camp counselor while studying at the Maryland Institute of Art. She created her first picture book while raising her son, Ben, deciding to work with cut paper and inks. "I was amazed to find out how difficult it is to write a good children's story," she explained. "I quickly learned that no matter how nice the pictures are, if a story is not well thought out, an editor will not give it a second thought!"

In *Mouse Paint,* three white mice camouflage themselves on a piece of white paper, remaining inconspicuous to a preying cat. When they decide to venture away from their safe haven, the mice stumble upon pots of red, blue, and yellow paint. Curious, they dip their bodies into the paint, discovering that the three original primary colors form new ones (green, orange, and purple) when blended. After taking a bath to remove the paint, the mice return to their white-paper haven. *School Library Journal* contributor Karen K. Radtke described *Mouse Paint* as a "real charmer that's great fun as well as informative," and in *Horn Book* Isabel Schon wrote that Stoll's picture book is "strikingly illustrated with torn paper collage in bright primary colors."

The three mice reappear with seven new friends in *Mouse Count,* this time trying to escape a multicolored snake. The rodents find themselves trapped when the snake catches them during nap time and puts them in a jar, counting each mouse from one to ten. One of the mice deceives the snake by suggesting a place where it may find yet another mouse, and when the greedy snake departs, the mice escape from the jar. Walsh's illustrations "display a naive charm and exuberance," wrote a *Publishers Weekly* reviewer. *Horn Book* reviewer Elizabeth Watson dubbed *Mouse Count* "counting fun for two-year-olds."

Tolerance and diversity are the themes of *Hop Jump.* Here a frisky frog named Betsy is bored with hopping

In Pip's Magic *Ellen Stoll Walsh pairs her collage art with a simple nature story.* (Copyright © 1994 by Ellen Stoll Walsh. Reproduced by permission of Houghton Mifflin Harcourt Publishing Company.)

Mouse Count

Ellen Stoll Walsh

Torn-paper collage brings to life a simple concept in Walsh's popular picture book **Mouse Count.** (Copyright © 1991 by Ellen Stoll Walsh. Reproduced by permission of Houghton Mifflin Harcourt Publishing Company.)

and jumping like the other frogs, and she decides to experiment with new movements. The motion of tree leaves captivates Betsy, so she decides to pattern her own bodily rhythms after them. When her fellow frogs voice their criticism, Betsy ignores them and continues to enjoy moving in leaps and twirls. As the croaking naysayers gradually join in on the fun, one frog still protests dancing and is quickly shunned by the converts who now oppose hopping. Betsy tries to unify the lone frog and the rest of the group by promoting dancing and hopping, thus eradicating the underlying discrimination. In *School Library Journal* Nancy Seiner praised *Hop Jump* for its "large, clearly seen figures and flowing language," recommending Walsh's tale as "a popular and useful story time choice." According to a *Kirkus Reviews* contributor, *Hop Jump* is a "beautifully designed book that . . . yields new subtleties and visual delights with each reading."

Pip's Magic touches on another subject that affects many children: fear of the dark. Here Pip, an eager

salamander, hopes to combat his fear of darkness. When a group of frogs suggests he visit Old Abra, an omniscient wizard turtle, to help with his anxiety, Pip follows an obscure and lightless path to reach the turtle. Reaching Old Abra, Pip is praised and told that he has already conquered his fear by following the dark trail, gaining a little extra courage along the way. The "imaginative, boldly colored treatment of a common anxiety is [Walsh's] best work yet," declared a contributor in *Kirkus Reviews.* Elizabeth Bush, writing in *Bulletin of the Center for Children's Books,* also praised *Pip's Magic* as "brief, simple, and direct."

Walsh explores another common childhood occurrence in *Samantha.* Samantha, a young mouse, wishes her siblings would not play roughly with her. Her thoughts are acknowledged when a fairy godmother appears and acts as her guardian. The fairy godmother takes her task very seriously and becomes overly protective of Samantha, thus eliminating the little one's fun. Ultimately,

Walsh appeals to younger readers with the engaging rodent stars of her self-illustrated Dot and Jabber and the Big Bug Mystery.

the unhappy mouse drives her protector away so that she can regain her normal lifestyle. Although Samantha begins to enjoy her siblings, she is once again susceptible to harm. The young mouse ends up falling in a snowdrift, but is rescued by her fairy godmother, who never ventured far away from her tiny charge. Eunice Weech, a reviewer in *School Library Journal,* regarded *Samantha* as a "pleasing combination of a short, well-told story and simple but expressive illustrations." Deborah Stevenson asserted in *Bulletin of the Center for Children's Books* that the story will make a "cozy but not suffocating readaloud."

Other animal-centered tales are presented in *For Pete's Sake* and *Hamsters to the Rescue.* In the first-named story, Walsh introduces Pete the alligator. Pete believes he is a flamingo whose green color comes from not being "ripe" yet. A meeting with two creatures who look like him causes Pete to reassess his reality, and here "Walsh reveals her originality by not settling for the easy resolution," according to *Horn Book* critic Nancy Vasilakis. Vasilakis went on to call *For Pete's Sake* "very cleverly done," and a *Kirkus Reviews* contributor recommended the work as "a comforting, gladdening tale." In the second title, the effort of Henry and Pell to track down the owner of a lost feather leads the hamsters on a fascinating journey to the seashore. Although *School Library Journal* critic Amy Lilien-Harper found Walsh's story in *Hamsters to the Rescue* relatively tame, the "appealing hamsters and the backgrounds in [Walsh's] . . . signature cut-paper collages are easy on the eye."

Among Walsh's picture-book creations is a series featuring a pair of detective mice named Dot and Jabber.

In *Dot and Jabber and the Great Acorn Mystery* the mice try to find why a tiny oak tree is growing so far away from a big oak tree on the other side of the meadow. They know that it was started by an acorn but wonder how the acorn ended up so far away from the tree. A *Publishers Weekly* reviewer noted that "these inquisitive mice [have] an appealing, comical quality." Other reviewers cited the book for gently introducing young readers to simple science concepts, *Booklist* contributor Kathy Broderick remarking that Walsh's "graceful creatures transform the science lesson into something fun, thoughtful, and very special."

In *Dot and Jabber and the Missing Stream* the mice investigate the reasons a stream has suddenly dried up, while *Dot and Jabber and the Blue Bug Mystery* finds the rodent sleuths attempting to locate an insect that seemed to disappear before their eyes. In *School Library Journal* Be Astengo commented that in *Dot and Jabber and the Missing Stream* "Walsh successfully combines science and good storytelling" in the adventure, while Shelley B. Sutherland wrote in the same periodical that *Dot and Jabber and the Big Bug Mystery* presents young readers with an "eco-mystery" featuring "distinctive cut-paper collages" of "gentle and calming" shades of brown and green.

"The first step in making a picture book is finding a good idea for a story . . . ," Stoll once told *SATA,* in describing her creative process. "Once I have a good idea for a story, it grows so fast and in so many directions that I often have to remind myself to stop and remember what the original idea was all about. I find it almost impossible to confine myself to an outline, but write pages and pages trying to find the best way to tell my story."

"While I'm writing my stories," Walsh once explained, "I begin to imagine what the characters who move through them look like, and I want to see them on paper. Drawing my characters helps establish their personalities and makes them and my stories come alive for me. It is unwise but often difficult to resist beginning to illustrate a story before it is finished, especially since the story is still undergoing change and a favorite illustration may no longer be appropriate when the story is finished. If you have ever tried to work around a well-turned sentence or paragraph in order to save it, even though it no longer fits in with what you are writing, then you can imagine how difficult it is to edit out a favorite illustration.

"It takes weeks of writing before a story will feel right to me, and after so much writing, the story is invariably too long. I must always keep in mind what the real point of my story is as I cut and chop my favorite paragraphs and sentences. After weeks of work, I hope to end up with a story that is no more than eight hundred words long and appears to have been written effortlessly.

"After my story is finished it will take me about nine months to complete the illustrations. I will often use black-and-white photographs to establish the way a person stands or sits in my illustrations. Once the basic proportions of a figure are set down, I put the photographs aside and work from nature and my imagination."

Biographical and Critical Sources

PERIODICALS

Booklist, March 15, 1992, review of *Mouse Count,* p. 1367; November 1, 1993, Carolyn Phelan, review of *Hop Jump,* p. 532; February 15, 1996, Ilene Cooper, review of *Samantha,* p. 1027; October 15, 1998, Stephanie Zvirin, review of *For Pete's Sake,* p. 430; October 1, 2001, Kathy Broderick, review of *Dot and Jabber and the Great Acorn Mystery,* p. 330; July 1, 2007, Carolyn Phelan, review of *Mouse Shapes,* p. 66.

Bulletin of the Center for Children's Books, September, 1994, Elizabeth Bush, review of *Pip's Magic,* pp. 27-28; June, 1996, Deborah Stevenson, review of *Samantha,* p. 355.

Childhood Education, spring, 2003, review of *Dot and Jabber and the Mystery of the Missing Stream,* p. 180.

Horn Book, July-August, 1989, Karen Jameyson, review of *Mouse Paint,* p. 479; May-June, 1991, Elizabeth Watson, review of *Mouse Count,* p. 325; January-February, 1993, Margaret A. Bush, review of *You Silly Goose,* p. 104; November-December, 1993, Isabel Schon, review of *Mouse Paint,* p. 769; November,

1998, Nancy Vasilakis, review of *For Pete's Sake,* p. 722; July-August, 2007, Susan Dove Lempke, review of *Mouse Shapes,* p. 387.

Kirkus Reviews, October 15, 1993, review of *Hop Jump,* p. 1339; September 15, 1994, review of *Pip's Magic,* p. 1285; September 15, 1998, review of *For Pete's Sake,* p. 1391; August 15, 2002, review of *Dot and Jabber and the Mystery of the Missing Stream,* p. 1238; August 1, 2005, review of *Hamsters to the Rescue,* p. 860; June 15, 2007, review of *Mouse Shapes.*

New York Times Book Review, January 26, 1992, review of *Mouse Counts,* p. 21.

Publishers Weekly, February 24, 1989, review of *Mouse Paints,* p. 229; January 25, 1991, review of *Mouse Count,* p. 56; August 3, 1992, review of *You Silly Goose,* p. 70; September 20, 1993, review of *Hop Jump,* p. 70; August 22, 1994, review of *Pip's Magic,* p. 54; October 26, 1998, review of *For Pete's Sake,* p. 65; January 31, 2000, review of *Mouse Magic,* p. 105; September 3, 2001, review of *Dot and Jabber and the Great Acorn Mystery,* p. 87; September 9, 2002, review of *Dot and Jabber and the Mystery of the Missing Stream,* p. 70; September 1, 2003, review of *Dot and Jabber and the Big Bug Mystery,* p. 117.

School Library Journal, June, 1989, Karen K. Radtke, review of *Mouse Paint,* p. 96; October, 1993, Nancy Seiner, review of *Hop Jump,* p. 113; November, 1994, Joy Fleishhacker, review of *Pip's Magic,* pp. 92-93; May, 1996, Eunice Weech, review of *Samantha,* p. 101; October 26, 1998, Miriam Lang Budin, review of *For Pete's Sake,* p. 100; April, 2000, Carolyn Stacey, review of *Mouse Magic,* p. 116; September, 2001, Jody McCoy, review of *Dot and Jabber and the Great Acorn Mystery,* p. 208; November, 2002, Be Astengo, review of *Dot and Jabber and the Mystery of the Missing Stream,* p. 140; November, 2003, Shelley B. Sutherland, review of *Dot and Jabber and the Big Bug Mystery,* p. 117; October, 2005, Amy Lilien-Harper, review of *Hamster to the Rescue,* p. 131; July, 2007, Shelley B. Sutherland, review of *Mouse Shapes,* p. 87.*

*　　　*　　　*

WAYSHAK, Deborah Noyes
See NOYES, Deborah

*　　　*　　　*

WEEKS, Sarah 1955-

Personal

Born March 18, 1955, in Ann Arbor, MI; children: Gabe, Nat. *Education:* Hampshire College, B.A.; New York University, M.F.A.

Addresses

Home—New York, NY. *E-mail*—authorweeks@aol.com.

Sarah Weeks (Copyright © Sarah Weeks. Used with permission of Pippin Properties, Inc.)

Career

Singer, songwriter, and children's book author. Member of adjunct faculty, New School University, New York, NY; presenter at schools and libraries.

Awards, Honors

Texas Bluebonnet Award finalist, 2000, for *Regular Guy;* Best Book for Young Adults designation, American Library Association, and Parents' Choice Gold Award, both 2005, both for *So B. It;* Charlotte Zolotow Award Highly Recommended title, 2006, for *Overboard!*

Writings

PICTURE BOOKS

Hurricane City, illustrated by James Warhola, HarperCollins (New York, NY), 1993.

Follow the Moon, illustrated by Suzanne Duranceau, HarperCollins (New York, NY), 1995.

Red Ribbon, illustrated by Jeffrey Greene, Laura Geringer Books (New York, NY), 1995.

Noodles, illustrated by David A. Carter, Laura Geringer Books (New York, NY), 1996.

(And vocalist) *Little Factory* (includes CD), animation by Byron Barton, Laura Geringer Books (New York, NY), 1998.

Mrs. McNosh Hangs up Her Wash, illustrated by Nadine Bernard Westcott, Laura Geringer Books (New York, NY), 1998.

Splish, Splash!, illustrated by Ashley Wolff, HarperCollins (New York, NY), 1999.

Piece of Jungle, illustrated by Suzanne Duranceau, Laura Geringer Books (New York, NY), 1999.

Happy Birthday, Frankie, illustrated by Warren Linn, Laura Geringer Books (New York, NY), 1999.

Drip, Drop, illustrated by Jane Manning, HarperCollins (New York, NY), 2000.

Mrs. McNosh and the Great Big Squash, illustrated by Nadine Bernard Westcott, HarperFestival (New York, NY), 2000.

Bite Me, I'm a Shape, illustrated by Jef Kaminsky, Random House (New York, NY), 2002.

Bite Me, I'm a Book, illustrated by Jef Kaminsky, Random House (New York, NY), 2002.

My Somebody Special, illustrated by Ashley Wolff, Harcourt (San Diego, CA), 2002.

Angel Face, illustrated by David Diaz, Atheneum (New York, NY), 2002.

Oh My Gosh, Mrs. McNosh!, illustrated by Nadine Bernard Westcott, HarperCollins (New York, NY), 2002.

Two Eggs, Please, illustrated by Betsy Lewin, Atheneum (New York, NY), 2003.

(And vocalist) *Without You* (includes CD), illustrated by Suzanne Duranceau, Laura Geringer Books (New York, NY), 2003.

(And vocalist) *Crocodile Smile: Ten Songs of the Earth as the Animals See It* (songbook; includes CD), HarperCollins (New York, NY), 2003.

If I Were a Lion, illustrated by Heather M. Solomon, Atheneum (New York, NY), 2004.

Paper Parade, illustrated by Ed Briant, Atheneum (New York, NY), 2004.

Baa-Choo!, illustrated by Jane Manning, HarperCollins (New York, NY), 2004.

I'm a Pig, illustrated by Holly Berry, Laura Geringer Books (New York, NY), 2005.

Who's under That Hat? (lift-the-flap book), illustrated by David A. Carter, Harcourt (New York, NY), 2005.

Ruff! Ruff! Where's Scruff? (lift-the-flap book), illustrated by David A. Carter, Harcourt (New York, NY), 2005.

Overboard!, illustrated by Sam Williams, Harcourt (New York, NY), 2006.

Counting Ovejas, illustrated by David Diaz, Atheneum (New York, NY), 2006.

Be Mine, Be Mine, Sweet Valentine, illustrated by Fumi Kosaka, Laura Geringer Books (New York, NY), 2006.

Ella, of Course!, illustrated by Doug Cushman, Harcourt (New York, NY), 2007.

Peek in My Pocket (lift-the-flap book), illustrated by David A. Carter, Harcourt (New York, NY), 2007.

Pip Squeak, illustrated by Jane Manning, Laura Geringer Books (New York, NY), 2007.

Bunny Fun, illustrated by Sam Williams, Harcourt (New York, NY), 2008.

The Brass Bone, illustrated by Holly Berry, Laura Geringer Books (New York, NY), 2008.

Catfish Kate, illustrated by Elwood Smith, Atheneum Books (New York, NY), 2009.

Mac and Cheese, illustrated by Jane Manning, Laura Geringer Books (New York, NY), 2010.

NOVELS

So B. It (novel), Laura Geringer Books (New York, NY), 2004.

Beware of Mad Dog ("Boyds Will Be Boyds" series), Scholastic (New York, NY), 2004.

Get Well Soon, or Else! ("Boyds Will Be Boyds" series), Scholastic (New York, NY), 2004.

Danger! Boys Dancing ("Boyds Will Be Boyds" series), Scholastic (New York, NY), 2005.

Fink's Funk ("Boyds Will Be Boyds" series), Scholastic (New York, NY), 2005.

Jumping the Scratch (novel), Laura Geringer Books (New York, NY), 2006.

Oggie Cooder, Scholastic (New York, NY), 2008.

"GUY" NOVEL SERIES

Regular Guy, Laura Gerlinger Books (New York, NY), 1999.

Guy Time, HarperCollins (New York, NY), 2000.

My Guy, Laura Geringer Books (New York, NY), 2001.

Guy Wire, Laura Geringer Books (New York, NY), 2002.

Adaptations

My Guy was adapted as a feature film by Disney Studios.

Sidelights

A former singer and songwriter, Sarah Weeks is the author of picture books, illustrated songbooks, as well as middle-grade novels such as her "Guy" series. Picture books such as *Crocodile Smile: Ten Songs of the Earth as the Animals See It, Follow the Moon,* and *Without You* include recordings of her vocal performances, while *Two Eggs, Please, Bunny Fun,* and *I'm a Pig* feature lyrical rhyming texts and engaging artwork by illustrators such as Jane Manning, Holly Berry, David Diaz, Sam Williams, and Doug Cushman. Praising Weeks' "inventive" story for *If I Were a Lion,* a *Kirkus Reviews* contributor cited the book's "tremendous read-aloud possibilities," while in *Booklist* Abby Nolan dubbed the text of *Bunny Fun* "bouncy and sweet."

Mrs. McNosh Hangs up Her Wash is one of several picture-book collaborations between Weeks and artist Nadine Bernard Westcott. Another picture book, *My Somebody Special,* tells an "ultimately reassuring tale" that focuses on young children's worries over attending

Sarah Weeks' rollicking picture book **Mrs. McNosh Hangs up Her Wash** *is brought to life by humorous art by Nadine Bernard Westcott.* (Illustration copyright © 1998 by Nadine Bernard Westcott. Used by permission of HarperCollins Publishers.)

nursery school, according to *Booklist* contributor Julie Cummins. Paired with art by Ashley Wolff, Weeks' story follows an animal cast as each creature waits for the arrival of their "somebody special" at the end of the school day. In *Angel Face* a young boy wanders off while picking blackberries with his mother, prompting an aerial search by Old Crow. In *Kirkus Reviews* a contributor praised *Angel Face* as "a tribute to the unique beauty of every child," while in *Booklist* Ilene Cooper noted that the "evocative text and storybook images [by illustrator Diaz] touch the heart."

Other picture books by Weeks include *Overboard* and *Bunny Fun,* both which feature Williams' soft-toned pastel art. In *Overboard* a bunny and mouse learn about gravity by watching an assortment of objects fall, topple, and slide from high places. *Bunny Fun* finds the two animal friends spending a play day indoors, where dress-up games and pillow fights are a fine way to spend a rainy afternoon. In *Publishers Weekly* a reviewer dubbed *Overboard* a "chipper, well-observed book," while Linda M. Kenton wrote in *School Library Journal* that *Bunny Fun* provides "a winning choice for storytimes." Even more rambunctious fare is served up by Weeks in *I'm a Pig,* described by a *Publishers Weekly* critic as "an exuberant, insouciant and sublimely silly paean that brings to mind Monty Python in a less naughty moment." Weeks also appeals to those in need of a soothing bedtime tale in *Counting Ovejas,* in which Dias illustrated a bilingual story about a boy who counts a flock of colorful sheep.

Weeks introduces eleven-year-old Guy Strang in *Regular Guy,* the first book in her popular "Guy" series. Suffering the classic teen frustration of uncooperative and totally-not-with-it, hippy-era parents, Guy becomes convinced that he is actually adopted. When a nerdy schoolmate is discovered to have been born on the same day and in the same hospital, Guy decides to check the other boy's parents out, hoping for a neonatal ward mismatch. The story's "lessons in understanding emerge lightly" according to a *Horn Book* contributor, while in *Publishers Weekly* a reviewer wrote that "the climactic showdown is a virtual chain reaction of buffoonery."

Guy's frustrations mount in *Guy Time,* when his parents separate, his dad moves out of state, and the teen is left with a mom who has started dating again. With the help of best friend and coconspirator Buzz, Guy begins a letter-writing campaign that, while not causing his parents to reunite, at least brings his father closer. Meanwhile, Guy begins to have romance problems of his own in a novel that *School Library Journal* reviewer Terrie Dorio wrote "captures the intense feeling" of a young teen "trying to deal with the process of growing up." In *Publishers Weekly* a reviewer called *Guy Time* "simultaneously funny and poignant," while *Booklist* contributor Chris Sherman praised Weeks's novel as "a satisfying, funny story."

In *My Guy,* Guy's mom becomes engaged to the totally unacceptable: a professional clown who is also the fa-

ther of the meanest girl in Guy's school. *Guy Wire* finds fourteen-year-old Guy in the hospital, visiting friend Buzz following a bicycling accident and learning about the true value of friendship. Reviewing *Guy Wire* in *Booklist,* Francisca Goldsmith commended Weeks for her ability to balance a "realistic and cheerful" text with a story line that "will give thoughtful readers much to ponder."

Other middle-grade novels by Weeks includes *So B. It,* which finds twelve-year-old Heidi living with her mentally disabled mother in a tiny apartment. The pair is watched over by housebound and caring neighbor named Bernadette. When Heidi begins to question how circumstances brought her and her mom to this sad place, she finds some old photographs that prompt her to search for information about her family. Her journey takes her from her home in Nevada all the way to Liberty, New York, where she "relies on her luck, instinct, and the people she meets on the way," according to *School Library Journal* reviewer Martha B. Salvadore. In *Horn Book* Kitty Flynn called *So B. It* a "well-told story tinged with loss," while Debbie Carton praised Weeks's prose in *Booklist* as "lovely writing—real, touching, and pared cleanly down to the essentials."

In *Jumping the Scratch* fifth grader Jamie Reardon lives with his mom and Aunt Sapphy in Sapphy's trailer now that his father has abandoned the family. A brain injury has caused Sapphy to lose her short-term memory, and the daily re-explanation as to why he and his mom are now living in his aunt's home in northern Michigan gives an offbeat air to an otherwise-sad situation. When a new friend at the trailer park hypnotizes Jamie, she unlocks a recent memory that, while causing him distress, ultimately helps the preteen heal the mind of his caring aunt. Citing Weeks' "well drawn" characters and a plot that sensitively deals with sexual abuse, *Booklist* critic Ilene Cooper predicted that readers of *Jumping the Scratch* will "applaud the . . . well-deserved triumphs" of Jamie and his family, and a *Kirkus Reviews* contributor dubbed the novel "a powerful story of a child's pain."

Featuring an offbeat protagonist, *Oggie Cooder* draws readers into Oggie's unique world, where the taunts and criticism of fellow fourth graders has little effect. Oggie marches to a different drummer, and his favorite pastimes includes a kind of nibble art he calls charving— using small bites to reshape slices of American cheese into the various United States. When charving draws the interest of a television talent show, Oggie suddenly gains in popularity and aggressive classmate Donnica Perfecto pushes the reluctant boy toward television stardom. In *Oggie Cooder* Weeks "delivers a funny and fast-paced story," concluded *Booklist* contributor Todd Morning, and in *Kirkus Reviews,* a reviewer praised the story's "gentle humor" and added that "many characters will be familiar to young readers."

Weeks teams up with award-winning artist Betsy Lewin for her picture book **Two Eggs, Please.** (Illustration copyright © 2003 by Betsy Lewin. Reprinted by permission of Atheneum Books for Young Readers, an imprint of Simon & Schuster Children's Publishing Division.)

Biographical and Critical Sources

PERIODICALS

Booklist, December 1, 1994, Carolyn Phelan, review of *Crocodile Smile: Ten Songs of the Earth as the Animals See It,* p. 675; April 15, 1998, Shelley Townsend-Hudson, review of *Mrs. McNosh Hangs up Her Wash,* p. 1455; March 15, 1999, Carolyn Phelan, review of *Splish, Splash!,* p. 1339; January 1, 2000, Michael Cart, review of *Happy Birthday, Frankie,* p. 938; July, 2000, Gillian Engberg, review of *Drip, Drop,* p. 2046; August, 2000, Chris Sherman, review of *Guy Time,* p. 2142; October 1, 2000, Gillian Engberg, review of *Mrs. McNosh and the Great Big Squash,* p. 350; August, 2001, Shelle Rosenfeld, review of *My Guy,* p. 2123; February 1, 2002, Ilene Cooper, review of *Angel Face,* p. 946 May 1, 2002, Shelly Townsend-Warner, review of *Oh My Gosh, Mrs. McNosh!,* p. 1537; August, 2002, Francisca Goldsmith, review of *Guy Wire,* p. 1965, and Julie Cummins, review of *My*

Somebody Special, p. 1977; March 15, 2004, Jennifer Mattson, review of *If I Were a Lion,* p. 1311; June 1, 2004, Debbie Carton, review of *So B. It,* p. 1731; August, 2004, Hazel Rochman, review of *Baa-Choo!,* p. 1946; February 1, 2006, Ilene Cooper, review of *Jumping the Scratch,* p. 51; February 15, 2006, Carolyn Phelan, review of *Overboard!,* p. 106; June 1, 2006, Linda Perkins, review of *Counting Ovejas,* p. 90; January 1, 2008, Todd Morning, review of *Oggie Cooder,* p. 82; February 15, 2008, Abby Nolan, review of *Bunny Fun,* p. 87.

Horn Book, May, 1999, review of *Regular Guy,* p. 340; May, 2000, review of *Guy Time,* p. 323; July, 2001, review of *My Guy,* p. 462; July-August, 2004, Lolly Robinson, review of *Paper Parade,* p. 443, and Kitty Flynn, review of *So B. It,* p. 462; January-February, 2005, Martha V. Parravano, review of *Baa-Choo!,* p. 99; July-August, 2007, Betty Carter, review of *Pip Squeak,* p. 406.

Kirkus Reviews, March 1, 2002, review of *Angel Face,* p. 347; April 1, 2002, review of *My Somebody Special* and *Oh, My Gosh, Mrs. McNosh!,* p. 501; September

15, 2003, review of *Without You,* p. 1184; February 1, 2004, review of *If I Were a Lion,* p. 139; April 15, 2004, review of *Paper Parade,* p. 402; May 15, 2004, review of *So B. It,* p. 499; May 1, 2005, review of *I'm a Pig,* p. 549; February 15, 2006, review of *Overboard!,* p. 191; April 15, 2006, review of *Jumping the Scratch,* p. 418; July 1, 2006, review of *Counting Ovejas,* p. 683; March 1, 2007, review of *Ella, of Course!,* p. 233; June 15, 2007, review of *Bunny Fun;* January 1, 2008, review of *Oggie Cooder.*

Kliatt, May, 2004, Claire Rosser, review of *So B. It,* p. 15.

Publishers Weekly, August 15, 1994, review of *Crocodile Smile,* p. 27; June 19, 1995, review of *Follow the Moon,* p. 26; July 24, 1995, review of *Red Ribbon,* p. 64; November 23, 1998, review of *Little Factory,* p. 65; June 21, 1999, review of *Regular Guy,* p. 68; August 2, 1999, review of *Happy Birthday Frankie,* p. 82; December 20, 1999, interview with Weeks, p. 23; June 19, 2000, review of *Guy Time,* p. 80; February 11, 2002, review of *Angel Face,* p. 185; April 15, 2002, review of *My Somebody Special,* p. 62; November 17, 2003, review of *Without You,* p. 62; May 3, 2004, review of *So B. It,* p. 190; May 30, 2005, review of *I'm a Pig,* p. 59.

School Library Journal, June, 2000, Terrie Dorio, review of *Guy Time,* p. 155; September, 2000, Martha Topol, review of *Drip, Drop,* p. 211; December, 2000, Adele Greenlee, review of *Mrs. McNosh and the Great Big Squash,* p. 127; May, 2001, Linda Binder, review of *My Guy,* p. 160; May, 2002, Lisa Dennis, review of *My Somebody Special,* p. 130; June, 2002, Faith Brautigam, review of *Oh My Gosh, Mrs. McNosh!,* p. 114; September, 2002, Be Astengo, review of *Guy Wire,* p. 236; October, 2003, Lauralyn Persson, review of *Without You,* p. 141; April, 2004, Laurie Edwards, review of *If I Were a Lion,* p. 126; June, 2004, Roxanne Burg, review of *Paper Parade,* and Donna Marie Wagner, review of *Two Eggs, Please,* p. 121; July, 2004, Maria B. Salvadore, review of *So B. It,* p. 114; May, 2005, Robin L. Gibson, review of *I'm a Pig,* p. 103; April, 2006, Martha Topol, review of *Overboard!,* p. 120; May, 2006, Connie Tyrrell Burns, review of *Jumping the Scratch,* p. 138; June, 2006, Maria Otero-Buisvert, review of *Counting Ovejas,* p. 145; March, 2007, Kathleen Whalin, review of *Ella, of Course!,* p. 189; December, 2007, Linda M. Kenton, review of *Bunny Fun,* p. 102; February, 2008, Melinda Piehler, review of *Pip Squeak,* p. 98; March, 2008, Kathleen Meulen, review of *Oggie Cooder,* p. 179.

ONLINE

HarperChildrens Web site, http://www.harperchildrens. com/ (March 7, 2005), "Sarah Weeks."

Sarah Weeks Home Page, http://www.sarahweeks.com/ (October 15, 2008).

*   *   *

WILSON, Nathan D.
See WILSON, N.D.

WILSON, N.D. 1978-
(Nathan D. Wilson)

Personal

Born February 7, 1978; married; children: four children. *Education:* St. John's College (Annapolis, MD), M.A. *Hobbies and other interests:* Home repairs, playing with his children.

Addresses

Home—Moscow, ID. *E-mail*—contact@ndwilson.com.

Career

Educator and writer. New St. Andrews College, Moscow, ID, lecturer in English, 2001-04, fellow of literature, 2004—. Has appeared on television programs, including *Discovery Channel News, ABC World News Tonight, Good Morning, America,* and *Daily Show.*

Writings

100 Cupboards, Random House (New York, NY), 2007.
Leepike Ridge, Random House (New York, NY), 2007.

Contributor of short stories to periodicals, including *Chattahoochee Review* and *Esquire,* and of essays to *Books & Culture.*

Sidelights

N.D. Wilson's novels *100 Cupboards* and *Leepike Ridge* feature tales of suspense that are aimed at middle-school audiences. In *100 Cupboards,* twelve-year-old Henry discovers that one hundred cupboards are hidden behind the walls and locked doors of his aunt and uncle's otherwise ordinary farmhouse in Kansas. These cupboards open upon alternate worlds, some of them benign and others dangerous. When Henry and his cousin Henrietta open the one hundredth cupboard, they unlock a portal to alternate worlds from which evildoers may come to threaten them. "Fans of dark fantasy will be intrigued by the unknown realities awaiting these unsuspecting people," noted Robyn Gioia in her review of Wilson's novel for *School Library Journal.* In *Kirkus Reviews* a critic called *100 Cupboards* a "highly imaginative tale that successfully balances its hero's inner and outer struggles."

Frustrated by his widowed mother's new suitor, Tom Hammond sneaks away to float down a river on a piece of packing foam in *Leepike Ridge.* Pulled into one and then another strong current, Tom finds himself marooned inside an underwater cave, and as his mother searches for him on dry land, the boy explores the cavern and finds clues about its previous history. Rumors of hidden treasure have lured others into the cave, and

Tom is torn between his need to escape and his curiosity about the possible secrets he might find within the mountain. According to Vicky Smith in *Horn Book,* Wilson "sets the scene vividly" in a novel that the critic described as a "fast-paced adventure." In her *School Library Journal* review of *Leepike Ridge,* Kim Dare wrote that "Wilson's rich imagination and his quirky characters are a true delight" in a novel the critic dubbed "utterly captivating."

Biographical and Critical Sources

PERIODICALS

Booklist, May 15, 2007, Kathleen Isaacs, review of *Leepike Ridge,* p. 60; December 1, 2007, Cindy Dobrez, review of *100 Cupboards,* p. 38.
Bulletin of the Center for Children's Books, July-August, 2007, Elizabeth Bush, review of *Leepike Ridge,* p. 492; January, 2008, Elizabeth Bush, review of *100 Cupboards,* p. 229.
Horn Book, May-June, 2007, Vicky Smith, review of *Leepike Ridge,* p. 296; January-February, 2008, Vicky Smith, review of *100 Cupboards,* p. 98.
Kirkus Reviews, May 1, 2007, review of *Leepike Ridge;* November 15, 2007, review of *100 Cupboards.*
School Library Journal, May, 2007, Kim Dare, review of *Leepike Ridge,* p. 147; April, 2008, Robyn Gioia, review of *100 Cupboards,* p. 152.

ONLINE

N.D. Wilson Home Page, http://www.ndwilson.com (October 20, 2008).*

*   *   *

WIMMER, Mike 1961-

Personal

Born March 22, 1961, in Muskogee, OK; son of Lester Landon and Gloria Jean Hambrick (a professor) Wimmer; married Sammy Carmelita Mary Batchelor (a homemaker) June 18, 1983; children: Elijah Seth, Lauren Alexandria. *Education:* University of Oklahoma, B.F.A., 1983. *Religion:* "Nonaffiliated Christian."

Addresses

Home—Norman, OK. *Office*—I Do Art, Inc., 3905 Nicole Circle, Norman, OK 73072. *E-mail*—mike@mikewimmer.com.

Career

Illustrator, painter, and graphic designer, beginning 1983; clients include American Airlines, Disney, A T & T, Celestial Seasons Teas, Brawny, Procter & Gamble,

Mike Wimmer (Photo by Shevaun Williams. Courtesy of Mike Wimmer.)

Kimberly Clark, and major publishers. *Exhibitions:* Paintings and murals included in permanent collection at Oklahoma State Capitol.

Awards, Honors

Orbis Pictus Award for Outstanding Nonfiction, 1990, for *Flight* by Robert Burleigh; Notable Trade Book in the Field of Social Studies, National Council of Social Studies/Children's Book Council, 1991, for *Train Song* by Diane Siebert; Oklahoma Book Award for Best Illustrated Children's Book, 1995, for *All the Places to Love* by Patricia MacLachlan; Spur Award, Western Writers of America, 2003, for *Will Rogers* by Frank Keating.

Illustrator

C.S. Adler, *Split Sisters,* Macmillan (New York, NY), 1986.
Pam Conrad, *Seven Silly Circles,* Harper (New York, NY), 1987.
Pam Conrad, *Staying Nine,* Harper (New York, NY), 1988.
Doris B. Smith, *A Taste of Blackberries,* Harper (New York, NY), 1989.
Diane Siebert, *Train Song,* Harper (New York, NY), 1990.
Robert Burleigh, *Flight: The Journey of Charles Lindbergh,* Putnam (New York, NY), 1991.
Patricia MacLachlan, *All the Places to Love,* Harper (New York, NY), 1994.

Robert Burleigh, *Home Run: The Story of Babe Ruth,* Silver Whistle (San Diego, CA), 1998.

George Gershwin, *Summertime from Porgy and Bess,* Simon & Schuster Books for Young Readers (New York, NY), 1999.

Frank Keating, *Will Rogers: An American Legend,* Harcourt (New York, NY), 2002.

Frank Keating, *Theodore,* Simon & Schuster Books for Young Readers (New York, NY), 2006.

Robert Burleigh, *Stealing Home,* Simon & Schuster Books for Young Readers (New York, NY), 2007.

Robert Burleigh, *One Giant Leap,* Philomel (New York, NY), 2008.

Sidelights

Mike Wimmer is an artist and illustrator whose work brings to life a number of picture-book biographies. Beginning his illustration career in the 1980s, Wimmer found his niche creating art for books such as Diane Siebert's *Train Song* and Patricia MacLachlan's nostalgic, family-centered *All the Places to Love.* His more-recent collaboration with author Robert Burleigh has produced profiles of athletes, political figures, and other noted Americans. Reviewing Wimmer's work for MacLachlan's award-winning story, *Booklist* contributor Stephanie Zvirin wrote that the artist's "radiant, full-page paintings" for *All the Places to Love* included some images "so realistically detailed [that] they look like color photographs," while in *Publishers Weekly* a reviewer noted that in the pages of Burleigh's *Flight: The Journey of Charles Lindbergh* "Wimmer's rich oil paintings . . . saturate the pages with color and tex-

Wimmer's book illustration projects include nonfiction titles such as Robert Burleigh's Flight, a biography of Charles Lindbergh. (Illustration copyright © 1991 by Mike Wimmer. All rights reserved. Used by permission of Philomel Books, a Division of Penguin Young Readers Group, a member of Penguin Group (USA) Inc., 345 Hudson St., New York, NY 10014.)

ture." The artist's "luminous, nostalgic" images for *Train Song* were also lauded by a *Publishers Weekly* contributor for their ability to "enable readers to grasp the beauty and power" of the many trains that have become a feature of the American landscape.

Published to commemorate the fiftieth anniversary of the death of renowned athlete Babe Ruth, *Home Run: The Story of Babe Ruth* pairs a text by Burleigh with Wimmer's detailed paintings. Praising the book's informative text, a *Publishers Weekly* writer compared Wimmer's "larger-than-life oil portraits" of the beloved baseball player to the illustrations of Norman Rockwell, citing the artist's use of compelling perspective to create "marvels of realism tinged with idealism." While less enthusiastic about Burleigh's text for *Stealing Home: Jackie Robinson, Against the Odds,* Marilyn Taniguchi wrote in *School Library Journal* that the picture-book biography benefits from Wimmer's "attractive and well done" double-page oil paintings, which "capture the intense excitement . . . as the [Baseball] Hall of Famer steals home" during the 1955 World Series. In *Booklist* GraceAnne A. DeCandido dubbed the artist's "rich, thickly painted close-ups" for *Stealing Home* "simply gorgeous." *One Giant Leap,* another project with Burleigh and a companion volume to *Flight,* commemorates the "one small step for man" taken by U.S. astronaut Neil Armstrong on the surface of Earth's moon in 1969.

Collaborating with Frank Keating, the governor of his home state of Oklahoma, Wimmer produced what a *Kirkus Reviews* writer dubbed an "unabashedly reverent paean" to Theodore Roosevelt, the 26th president of the United States. In *School Library Journal* Barbara Auerbach praised the "accomplished paintings" the illustrator created for *Theodore,* while the *Kirkus Reviews* critic concluded that Wimmer captures the telling moments in the life of Roosevelt in "gorgeously lit, heroic oils." Another Keating-Wimmer project, *Will Rogers: An American Legend,* incorporates quotes and anecdotes from the life of a beloved early-twentieth-century humorist with "inarguably beautiful, accomplished, and occasionally witty" images. "Wimmer's oil paintings are striking in terms of their realism and their authenticity with regard to time period," maintained Grace Oliff, the *School Library Journal* contributor adding that while Keating's text is "confusing and disjointed," *Will Rogers* is "beautifully illustrated" and "nicely designed."

Wimmer once told *SATA:* "I have been drawing and painting since age six. Comic-book heroes and sports figures were my main subjects. I was influenced as a boy by reading and admiring the classic boy's adventures such as *Robinson Crusoe, Kidnapped, Treasure Island,* and *Swiss Family Robinson,* illustrated by such greats as N.C. Wyeth, Frank Jenny Johnson, Howard Pyle, and the realistic, fully executed stories of Norman Rockwell. I didn't know what an illustrator was, but I did know that someone painted these pictures and that I

Wimmer's paintings tap into nostalgic themes in Doris Buchanan Smith's poignant middle-grade novel **A Taste of Blackberries.** (Illustration by Mike Wimmer © 1988 by Thomas Y. Crowell. Used by permission of HarperCollins Publishers.)

wanted to be that person. I later became an all-state football player and state body-building champion. I love to paint authentic, historically researched, real-life people and events."

Biographical and Critical Sources

PERIODICALS

Booklist, June 1, 1994, Stephanie Zvirin, review of *All the Places to Love,* p. 1810; August, 1998, Helen Rosenberg, review of *Home Run: The Story of Babe Ruth,* p. 2003; August, 1999, Ilene Cooper, review of *Summertime: From Porgy and Bess,* p. 2060; September 15, 2002, Michael Cart, review of *Will Rogers: An American Legend,* p. 236; December 15, 2006, GraceAnne A. DeCandido, review of *Stealing Home: Jackie Robinson, Against the Odds,* p. 49.

Kirkus Reviews, December 1, 2005, review of *Theodore,* p. 1276.

Publishers Weekly, August 10, 1990, review of *Train Song,* p. 443; August 30, 1991, review of *Flight: The Journey of Charles Lindbergh,* p. 81; July 6, 1998, review of *Home Run,* p. 61; January 23, 2006, review of *Theodore,* p. 208; December 11, 2006, review of *Stealing Home,* p. 69.

School Library Journal, November, 2002, Grace Oliff, review of *Will Rogers,* p. 145; March, 2006, Barbara Auerbach, review of *Theodore,* p. 209; January, 2007, Marilyn Taniguchi, review of *Stealing Home,* p. 114.

ONLINE

Mike Wimmer Home Page, http://www.mikewimmer.com (October 10, 2008).

*   *   *

WOODHULL, Ann Love

Personal
Female.

Addresses
Home—Northampton, MA.

Career
Author and early-childhood educator.

Writings

This Is What We Have (poetry), March Street Press (Greensboro, NC), 2001.

(With Shelley Rotner) *Every Season,* photographs by Rotner, Roaring Brook Press (New Milford, CT), 2007.

Biographical and Critical Sources

PERIODICALS

Booklist, March 1, 2007, Gillian Engberg, review of *Every Season,* p. 87.

Horn Book, July-August, 2007, Robin Smith, review of *Every Season,* p. 384.

Publishers Weekly, May 7, 2007, review of *Every Season,* p. 59.

School Library Journal, July, 2007, Linda L. Walkins, review of *Every Season,* p. 94.*

Y-Z

YIN

Personal

Born in Brooklyn, NY; married Chris Soentpiet (an artist); children: one son. *Education:* Bachelor's degree (finance). *Hobbies and other interests:* Hiking, biking, travel, cooking.

Addresses

Home—New York, NY.

Career

Children's book author. Brown Bros. & Harriman, New York, NY, former financial writer.

Awards, Honors

Gold Award for Best Picture Book, Parents' Choice Foundation, 2001, and International Reading Association (IRA) Book Award and American Library Association Notable Book designation, both 2002, all for *Coolies;* IRA Teachers' Choice designation, 2007, for *Brothers.*

Writings

Coolies, illustrated by husband, Chris Soentpiet, Philomel Books (New York, NY), 2001.
Dear Santa, Please Come to the Nineteenth Floor, illustrated by Chris Soentpiet, Philomel Books (New York, NY), 2002.
Brothers, illustrated by Chris Soentpiet, Philomel Books (New York, NY), 2006.

Sidelights

The writer Yin focuses on the lives of Chinese immigrants of the mid-nineteenth century in her picture book *Coolies.* In a text brought to life in accompanying paint-ings by her husband, Chris Soentpiet, Yin describes the struggles and challenges faced by the many Asian men who traveled to the United States and worked to support their families back at home by engaging in the brutal labor required to establish the infrastructure of a growing nation. Through the story of Shek and his younger brother Wong, *Coolies* depicts the harsh working conditions these two young men endured in the Utah desert while laying track for the transcontinental railway. While noting that Yin portrays her protagonists as "more saintly heroes than real people," *Booklist* critic Hazel Rochman added that the presentation of "American history is powerful" in *Coolies.* In *Horn Book* Roger Sutton also had praise for the author's effort to shine a light on an overlooked aspect of America history, writing that Soentpiet's large-scale "watercolors have cinematic coloring and grandeur." Remarking on the negative connotation of the book's title, Margaret A. Chang maintained in her *School Library Journal* review that in *Coolies* Yin "transforms the familiar ethnic slur into a badge of honor."

The story of *Coolies* is continued by Yin in *Brothers,* as youngest brother Ming travels to San Francisco to help in Shek's general store and make extra money by working on a nearby farm. A friendship with a young Irishman allows Ming to learn English and then use his talents to promote his older brother's struggling enterprise. "Soentpiet's luminescent, photo-realistic paintings . . . perfectly complement Yin's thoughtful text," noted *Booklist* critic Kay Weisman, while in *School Library Journal* Barbara Scotto concluded that the "determination that drives" Shek and Ming makes *Brothers* "a good addition to stories of the immigrant experience."

Biographical and Critical Sources

PERIODICALS

Booklist, February 1, 2001, Hazel Rochman, review of *Coolies,* p. 1059; August 1, 2006, Kay Weisman, review of *Brothers,* p. 94.

Horn Book, March, 2001, Roger Sherman, review of *Coolies,* p. 204.

Kirkus Reviews, August 15, 2006, review of *Brothers,* p. 855.

School Library Journal, March, 2001, Margaret A. Chang, review of *Coolies,* p. 230; October, 2002, Maureen Wade, review of *Dear Santa, Please Come to the Nineteenth Floor,* p. 65; November, 2006, Barbara Scotto, review of *Brothers,* p. 116.

ONLINE

Chris Soentpiet Home Page, http://www.soentpiet.com/ (October 15, 2008), "Yin's Corner."*

* * *

YOLEN, Jane 1939-

Personal

Born February 11, 1939, in New York, NY; daughter of Will Hyatt (an author and publicist) and Isabelle (a social worker, puzzle-maker, and homemaker) Yolen; married David W. Stemple (a professor of computer science and ornithologist), September 2, 1962; children: Heidi Elisabeth, Adam Douglas, Jason Frederic. *Education:* Smith College, B.A., 1960; University of Massachusetts, M.Ed., 1976; completed course work for doctorate in children's literature at University of Massachusetts. *Politics:* "Liberal Democrat." *Religion:* Jewish/Quaker. *Hobbies and other interests:* "Folk music and dancing, reading, camping, politics, all things Scottish."

Addresses

Home—Phoenix Farm, 31 School St., Box 27, Hatfield, MA 01038; Wayside, 96 Hepburn Gardens, St. Andrews, Fife KY16 9LN, Scotland. *Agent*—Elizabeth Harding Curtis Brown Ltd., 10 Astor Place, New York, NY 10003. *E-mail*—janeYolen@aol.com.

Career

Saturday Review, New York, NY, production assistant, 1960-61; Gold Medal Books (publishers), New York, NY, assistant editor, 1961-62; Rutledge Books (publishers), New York, NY, associate editor, 1962-63; Alfred A. Knopf, Inc. (publishers), New York, NY, assistant juvenile editor, 1963-65; full-time professional writer, beginning 1965. Editor of imprint Jane Yolen Books for Harcourt Brace Jovanovich, 1988-98. Teacher of writing and lecturer, 1966—; has taught children's literature at Smith College. Chairman of board of library trustees, Hatfield, MA, 1976-83; member of Hatfield Arts Council.

Member

International Kitefliers Association, Society of Children's Book Writers (member of board of directors, 1974—), Science Fiction Writers of America (president,

Jane Yolen (Copyright © 2000 by Jason Stemple. Reproduced by permission.)

1986-88), Children's Literature Association (member of board of directors, 1977-79), Science Fiction Poetry Association, National Association for the Preservation and Perpetuation of Storytelling, Western New England Storyteller's Guild (founder), Bay State Writers Guild, Western Massachusetts Illustrators Guild (founder), Smith College Alumnae Association.

Awards, Honors

Boys' Club of America Junior Book Award, 1968, for *The Minstrel and the Mountain;* Lewis Carroll Shelf Award, 1968, for *The Emperor and the Kite,* and 1973, for *The Girl Who Loved the Wind;* Best Books of the Year selection, *New York Times,* 1968, for *The Emperor Flies a Kite; World on a String* named an American Library Association (ALA) Notable Book, 1968; Chandler Book Talk Reward of Merit, 1970; Children's Book Showcase of the Children's Book Council citations, 1973, for *The Girl Who Loved the Wind,* and 1976, for *The Little Spotted Fish;* Golden Kite Award, Society of Children's Book Writers, 1974, ALA Notable Book, 1975, and National Book Award nomination, 1975, all for *The Girl Who Cried Flowers and Other Tales;* Golden Kite Honor Book, 1975, for *The Transfigured Hart,* and 1976, for *The Moon Ribbon and Other Tales;* Christopher Medal, 1978, for *The Seeing Stick,* and 2000, for *How Do Dinosaurs Say Goodnight?;* Children's Choice, International Reading Association (IRA)/ Children's Book Council (CBC), 1980, for *Mice on Ice,* and 1983, for *Dragon's Blood;* Parents' LL.D., College of Our Lady of the Elms (Chicopee, MA), 1981, and

Smith College, 2003; Choice Awards, Parents' Choice Foundation, 1982, for *Dragon's Blood,* 1984, for *The Stone Silenus,* and 1989, for *Piggins* and *The Three Bears Rhyme Book; School Library Journal* Best Books for Young Adults citation, 1982, for *The Gift of Sarah Barker,* and 1985, for *Heart's Blood;* Garden State Children's Book Award, New Jersey Library Association, 1983, for *Commander Toad in Space;* CRABbery Award from Acton, MD, Public Library, 1983, for *Dragon's Blood;* Heart's Blood selected among ALA's Best Books for Young Adults, 1984; Mythopoeic Society Fantasy Award, 1984, for *Cards of Grief,* 1993, for *Briar Rose,* 1998, for "Young Merlin" trilogy; Daedelus Award, 1986; *The Lullaby Songbook* and *The Sleeping Beauty* selected among Child Study Association of America's Children's Books of the Year, 1987; World Fantasy Award, 1988, for *Favorite Folktales from around the World;* Parents' Choice Silver Seal Award, Jewish Book Council Award, and Association of Jewish Libraries Award, all 1988, Judy Lopez Honor Book, and Nebula Award finalist, both 1989, and Maude Hart Lovelace Award, 1996, all for *The Devil's Arithmetic;* Kerlan Award, 1988, for "singular achievements in the creation of children's literature" Golden Sower Award, Nebraska Library Association, 1989, and Charlotte Award, New York State Reading Association, both for *Piggins;* Smith College Medal, 1990; Skylark Award, New England Science Fiction Association, 1990; Regina Medal, 1992, for body of writing; Keene State College Children's Literature Festival award, 1995; *Storytelling World* Award, 1997, for "The World the Devil Made Up"; honorary doctorate, Keene State College, 1998; Literary Light Award, Boston Library, 1998; Nebula Award for Best Short Story, 1997, for "Sister Emily's Lightship"; Nebula Award for Best Novelette, 1998, for "Lost Girls"; Anna V. Zarrow Award, 1999; Smith College Remarkable Women designation, 1999, and honorary Ph.D., 2003; California Young Reader Medal in Young-Adult Category, 2001, and ALA Best Books and Best Books for Young Adults designations, both 2004, all for *Armageddon Summer;* National Outdoor Book Award, 2002, for *Wild Wings;* National Storytelling Network ORACLE Award, 2003; *Writer* Award, 2004. *The Emperor and the Kite* was named a Caldecott Medal Honor Book designation, 1968, for illustrations by Ed Young; *Owl Moon* received the Caldecott Medal, 1988, for illustrations by John Schoenherr.

Writings

FOR CHILDREN; PICTURE BOOKS AND FICTION

The Witch Who Wasn't, illustrated by Arnold Roth, Macmillan (New York, NY), 1964.

Gwinellen, the Princess Who Could Not Sleep, illustrated by Ed Renfro, Macmillan (New York, NY), 1965.

The Emperor and the Kite, illustrated by Ed Young, World Publishing (Cleveland, OH), 1967, reprinted, Philomel (New York, NY), 1988.

The Minstrel and the Mountain: A Tale of Peace, illustrated by Anne Rockwell, World Publishing (Cleveland, OH), 1967.

Isabel's Noel, illustrated by Arnold Roth, Funk & Wagnalls (New York, NY), 1967.

Greyling: A Picture Story from the Islands of Shetland, illustrated by William Stobbs, World Publishing (Cleveland, OH), 1968, illustrated by David Ray, Philomel (New York, NY), 1991.

The Longest Name on the Block, illustrated by Peter Madden, Funk & Wagnalls (New York, NY), 1968.

The Wizard of Washington Square, illustrated by Ray Cruz, World Publishing (Cleveland, OH), 1969.

The Inway Investigators; or, The Mystery at McCracken's Place, illustrated by Allan Eitzen, Seabury (New York, NY), 1969.

Hobo Toad and the Motorcycle Gang, illustrated by Emily McCully, World Publishing (Cleveland, OH), 1970.

The Seventh Mandarin, illustrated by Ed Young, Seabury (New York, NY), 1970.

The Bird of Time, illustrated by Mercer Mayer, Crowell (New York, NY), 1971.

The Girl Who Loved the Wind, illustrated by Ed Young, Crowell (New York, NY), 1972.

The Girl Who Cried Flowers and Other Tales, illustrated by David Palladini, Crowell (New York, NY), 1974.

The Boy Who Had Wings, illustrated by Helga Aichinger, Crowell (New York, NY), 1974.

The Adventures of Eeka Mouse, illustrated by Myra McKee, Xerox Education Publications (Middletown, CT), 1974.

The Rainbow Rider, illustrated by Michael Foreman, Crowell (New York, NY), 1974.

The Little Spotted Fish, illustrated by Friso Henstra, Seabury (New York, NY), 1975.

The Transfigured Hart, illustrated by Donna Diamond, Crowell (New York, NY), 1975, reprinted, Harcourt (New York, NY), 1997.

Milkweed Days, photographs by Gabriel Amadeus Cooney, Crowell (New York, NY), 1976.

The Moon Ribbon and Other Tales, illustrated by David Palladini, Crowell (New York, NY), 1976, 1976.

The Seeing Stick, illustrated by Remy Charlip and Demetra Maraslis, Crowell (New York, NY), 1977.

The Sultan's Perfect Tree, illustrated by Barbara Garrison, Parents' Magazine Press (New York, NY), 1977.

The Hundredth Dove and Other Tales, illustrated by David Palladini, Crowell (New York, NY), 1977.

Hannah Dreaming, photographs by Alan R. Epstein, Museum of Fine Art (Springfield, MA), 1977.

The Lady and the Merman, illustrated by Barry Moser, Pennyroyal Press, 1977.

Spider Jane, illustrated by Stefan Bernath, Coward (New York, NY), 1978.

The Simple Prince, illustrated by Jack Kent, Parents' Magazine Press (New York, NY), 1978.

No Bath Tonight, illustrated by Nancy Winslow Parker, Crowell (New York, NY), 1978.

The Mermaid's Three Wisdoms, illustrated by Laura Rader, Collins (New York, NY), 1978.

Dream Weaver and Other Tales, illustrated by Michael Hague, Collins (New York, NY), 1979, published as *Dream Weaver,* 1989.

Spider Jane on the Move, illustrated by Stefan Bernath, Coward (New York, NY), 1980.

Mice on Ice, illustrated by Lawrence DiFiori, Dutton (New York, NY), 1980.

Shirlick Holmes and the Case of the Wandering Wardrobe, illustrated by Anthony Rao, Coward (New York, NY), 1981.

The Acorn Quest, illustrated by Susanna Natti, Harper (New York, NY), 1981.

Brothers of the Wind, illustrated by Barbara Berger, Philomel (New York, NY), 1981.

Sleeping Ugly, illustrated by Diane Stanley, Coward (New York, NY), 1981.

The Boy Who Spoke Chimp, illustrated by David Wiesner, Knopf (New York, NY), 1981.

Uncle Lemon's Spring, illustrated by Glen Rounds, Dutton (New York, NY), 1981.

(Reteller) *The Sleeping Beauty,* illustrated by Ruth Sanderson, Knopf (New York, NY), 1986.

Owl Moon, illustrated by John Schoenherr, Philomel (New York, NY), 1987.

Dove Isabeau, illustrated by Dennis Nolan, Harcourt (New York, NY), 1989.

Baby Bear's Bedtime Book, illustrated by Jane Dyer, Harcourt (New York, NY), 1990.

Sky Dogs, illustrated by Barry Moser, Harcourt (New York, NY), 1990.

(Reteller) *Tam Lin: An Old Ballad,* illustrated by Charles Mikolaycak, Harcourt (New York, NY), 1990.

Elfabet: An ABC of Elves, illustrated by Lauren Mills, Little, Brown (Boston, MA), 1990.

Letting Swift River Go, illustrated by Barbara Cooney, Little, Brown (Boston, MA), 1990.

The Dragon's Boy, Harper (New York, NY), 1990.

Wizard's Hall, Harcourt (New York, NY), 1991.

Hark! A Christmas Sampler, illustrated by Tomie dePaola, music by son, Adam Stemple, Putnam (New York, NY), 1991.

(Reteller) *Wings,* Harcourt (New York, NY), 1991.

All Those Secrets of the World (autobiographical fiction), illustrated by Leslie Baker, Little, Brown (Boston, MA), 1991.

Encounter, illustrated by David Shannon, Harcourt (New York, NY), 1992.

Eeny, Meeny, Miney Mole, illustrated by Kathryn Brown, Harcourt (New York, NY), 1992.

Mouse's Birthday, illustrated by Bruce Degen, Putnam (New York, NY), 1993.

Hands, illustrated by Chi Chung, Sundance Publishing, 1993.

Honkers, illustrated by Leslie Baker, Little, Brown (Boston, MA), 1993.

Travelers Rose, Putnam (New York, NY), 1993.

Beneath the Ghost Moon, illustrated by Laurel Molk, Little, Brown (Boston, MA), 1994.

Grandad Bill's Song, illustrated by Melissa Bay Mathis, Philomel (New York, NY), 1994.

And Twelve Chinese Acrobats, (autobiographical fiction), illustrated by Jean Gralley, Philomel (New York, NY), 1994.

Good Griselle, illustrated by David Christiana, Harcourt (New York, NY), 1994.

The Girl in the Golden Bower, illustrated by Jane Dyer, Little, Brown (Boston, MA), 1994.

Old Dame Counterpane, illustrated by Ruth Tietjen Councell, Putnam (New York, NY), 1994.

(Reteller) *Little Mouse and Elephant: A Tale from Turkey,* illustrated by John Segal, Simon & Schuster (New York, NY), 1994.

(Reteller) *The Musicians of Bremen: A Tale from Germany,* illustrated by John Segal, Simon & Schuster (New York, NY), 1994.

The Ballad of the Pirate Queen, illustrated by David Shannon, Harcourt (New York, NY), 1995.

Before the Storm, illustrated by Georgia Pugh, Boyds Mills Press (Honesdale, PA), 1995.

(Reteller) *A Sip of Aesop,* illustrated by Karen Barbour, Blue Sky Press (New York, NY), 1995.

Merlin and the Dragons, illustrated by Ming Li, Dutton (New York, NY), 1995.

The Wild Hunt, illustrated by Francisco Mora, Harcourt (New York, NY), 1995.

(With daughter Heidi E.Y. Stemple) *Meet the Monsters,* illustrated by Patricia Ludlow, Walker (New York, NY), 1996.

Nocturne, illustrated by Anne Hunter, Harcourt (New York, NY), 1997.

Child of Faerie, Child of Earth, illustrated by Jane Dyer, Little, Brown (Boston, MA), 1997.

Miz Berlin Walks, illustrated by Floyd Cooper, Philomel (New York, NY), 1997.

(Reteller) *Once upon a Bedtime Story: Classic Tales,* illustrated by Ruth Tietjen Councell, 1997.

The Sea Man, illustrated by Christopher Denise, Putnam (New York, NY), 1997.

Twelve Impossible Things before Breakfast (short stories), Harcourt (New York, NY), 1997.

House, House, photographs by the Howes Brothers and son Jason Stemple, Marshall Cavendish (New York, NY), 1998.

King Long Shanks, illustrated by Victoria Chess, Harcourt (New York, NY), 1998.

(Reteller) *Pegasus, the Flying Horse,* illustrated by Ming Li, Dutton (New York, NY), 1998.

Raising Yoder's Barn, illustrated by Bernie Fuchs, Little, Brown (Boston, MA), 1998.

(Reteller) *Prince of Egypt,* Dutton (New York, NY), 1998.

(With Heidi E.Y. Stemple) *Mary Celeste: An Unsolved Mystery from History,* illustrated by Roger Roth, Simon & Schuster (New York, NY), 1999.

Moonball, illustrated by Greg Couch, Simon & Schuster (New York, NY), 1999.

How Do Dinosaurs Say Good Night?, illustrated by Mark Teague, Blue Sky Press (New York, NY), 2000.

Off We Go!, illustrated by Laurel Molk, Little, Brown (Boston, MA), 2000.

Harvest Home, illustrated by Greg Shed, Harcourt (San Diego, CA), 2000.

Boots and the Seven Leaguers: A Rock-and-Troll Novel, Harcourt (San Diego, CA), 2000.

(Editor) *Sherwood: Original Stories from the World of Robin Hood,* illustrated by Dennis Nolan, Philomel (New York, NY), 2000.

(Editor, with Heidi E.Y. Stemple, and author of introduction) *Mirror, Mirror: Forty Folktales for Mothers and Daughters to Share,* Viking (New York, NY), 2000.

(With Heidi E.Y. Stemple) *The Wolf Girls: An Unsolved Mystery from History,* illustrated by Roger Roth, Simon & Schuster (New York, NY), 2001.

Welcome to the River of Grass, illustrated by Laura Regan, Putnam (New York, NY), 2001.

The Hurrying Child, illustrated by Stephen T. Johnson, Silver Whistle (San Diego, CA), 2001.

(With Shulamith Oppenheim) *The Fish Prince and Other Stories: Mermen Folk Tales,* illustrated by Paul Hoffman, Interlink (New York, NY), 2001.

Time for Naps, illustrated by Hiroe Nakata, Little Simon (New York, NY), 2002.

(With Robert J. Harris) *Hippolyta and the Curse of the Amazons,* HarperCollins (New York, NY), 2002.

(With Robert J. Harris) *Girl in a Cage,* Philomel (New York, NY), 2002.

(Reteller) *The Firebird,* illustrated by Vladimir Vagin, HarperCollins (New York, NY), 2002.

Bedtime for Bunny: A Book to Touch and Feel, illustrated by Lynn Norton Parker, Little Simon (New York, NY), 2002.

Animal Train, illustrated by Doug Cushman, Little Simon (New York, NY), 2002.

Sword of the Rightful King: A Novel of King Arthur, Harcourt (San Diego, CA), 2003.

(With Shulamith Oppenheim) *The Sea King,* illustrated by Stefan Czernecki, Crocodile Books (Brooklyn, NY), 2003.

(With Heidi E.Y. Stemple) *Roanoke, the Lost Colony: An Unsolved Mystery from History,* illustrated by Roger Roth, Simon & Schuster (New York, NY), 2003.

My Brother's Flying Machine: Wilbur, Orville, and Me, illustrated by Jim Burke, Little, Brown (New York, NY), 2003.

Mightier than the Sword: World Folktales for Strong Boys, illustrated by Raul Colón, Harcourt (San Diego, CA), 2003.

How Do Dinosaurs Get Well Soon?, illustrated by Mark Teague, Blue Sky Press (New York, NY), 2003.

Hoptoad, illustrated by Karen Lee Schmidt, Silver Whistle (San Diego, CA), 2003.

The Flying Witch, illustrated by Vladimir Vagin, HarperCollins (New York, NY), 2003.

(With Robert J. Harris) *Prince across the Waters,* Philomel (New York, NY), 2004.

How Do Dinosaurs Count to Ten?, illustrated by Mark Teague, Blue Sky Press (New York, NY), 2004.

How Do Dinosaurs Clean Their Room?, illustrated by Mark Teague, Blue Sky Press (New York, NY), 2004.

(With Heidi Stemple) *The Barefoot Book of Ballet Stories,* illustrated by Rebecca Guay, Barefoot Books (Cambridge, MA), 2004.

Soft House, illustrated by Wendy Anderson Halperin, Candlewick Press (Cambridge, MA), 2005.

Meow: Cat Stories from around the World, illustrated by Hala Wittwer, HarperCollins (New York, NY), 2005.

How Do Dinosaurs Eat Their Food?, illustrated by Mark Teague, Blue Sky Press (New York, NY), 2005.

Grandma's Hurrying Child, illustrated by Kay Chorao, Harcourt (Orlando, FL), 2005.

Baby Bear's Chairs, illustrated by Melissa Sweet, Harcourt (Orlando, FL), 2005.

(With Adam Stemple) *Apple for the Teacher: Thirty Songs for Singing while You Work,* Harry N. Abrams (New York, NY), 2005.

(Editor) *Trot, Trot to Boston: Lap Songs, Finger Plays, Clapping Games, and Pantomime Rhymes,* illustrated by Will Hillenbrand, musical arrangements by Adam Stemple, Candlewick Press (Cambridge, MA), 2005.

(With Adam Stemple) *Pay the Piper: A Rock 'n' Roll Fairy Tale,* Starscape (New York, NY), 2006.

Baby Bear's Books, illustrated by Melissa Sweet, Harcourt (Orlando, FL), 2006.

Count Me a Rhyme: Animal Poems by the Numbers, photographs by Jason Stemple, Wordsong Press (Honesdale, PA), 2006.

Dimity Duck, illustrated by Sebastien Braun, Philomel Books (New York, NY), 2006.

(Reteller) *Fairy Tale Feasts: A Literary Cookbook for Young Readers and Eaters,* recipes by Heidi E.Y. Stemple, illustrated by Philippe Beïcha, Crocodile Books (Northampton, MA), 2006.

How Do Dinosaurs Learn Their Colors?, illustrated by Mark Teague, Blue Sky Press (New York, NY), 2006.

How Do Dinosaurs Play with Their Friends?, illustrated by Mark Teague, Blue Sky Press (New York, NY), 2006.

(With Adam Stemple) *Troll Bridge: A Rock 'n' Roll Fairy Tale,* Starscape (New York, NY), 2006.

(Editor, with Andrew Fusek Peters) *Here's a Little Poem: A Very First Book of Poetry,* illustrated by Polly Dunbar, Candlewick Press (Cambridge, MA), 2007.

Baby Bear's Big Dreams, Harcourt (Orlando, FL), 2007.

How Do Dinosaurs Go to School?, illustrated by Mark Teague, Blue Sky Press (New York, NY), 2007.

(With Robert J. Harris) *Rogue's Apprentice,* Philomel Books (New York, NY), 2007.

Shape Me a Rhyme: Nature's Forms in Poetry, photographs by Jason Stemple, Wordsong (Honesdale, PA), 2007.

(With Heidi E.Y. Stemple) *Sleep, Black Bear, Sleep,* illustrated by Brooke Dyer, HarperCollins (New York, NY), 2007.

Johnny Appleseed: The Legend and the Truth, illustrated by Jim Burke, HarperCollins (New York, NY), 2008.

Naming Liberty, illustrated by Jim Burke, Philomel Books (New York, NY), 2008.

Sea Queens: Women Pirates around the World, illustrated by Christine Joy Pratt, Charlesbridge (Watertown, MA), 2008.

My Father Knows the Names of Things, illustrated by Stepháne Jorisch, Simon & Schuster (New York, NY), 2009.

The Scarecrow's Dance, illustrated by Bagram Ibatoulline, Simon & Schuster (New York, NY), 2009.

"GIANTS" SERIES; PICTURE BOOKS

The Giants Go Camping, illustrated by Tomie DePaola, Seabury (New York, NY), 1979.

The Giants' Farm, illustrated by Tomie DePaola, Seabury (New York, NY), 1997.

"COMMANDER TOAD" SERIES; FICTION

Commander Toad in Space, illustrated by Bruce Degen, Coward (New York, NY), 1980.

Commander Toad and the Planet of the Grapes, illustrated by Bruce Degen, Coward (New York, NY), 1982.

Commander Toad and the Big Black Hole, illustrated by Bruce Degen, Coward (New York, NY), 1983.

Commander Toad and the Dis-Asteroid, illustrated by Bruce Degen, Coward (New York, NY), 1985.

Commander Toad and the Intergalactic Spy, illustrated by Bruce Degen, Coward (New York, NY), 1986.

Commander Toad and the Space Pirates, illustrated by Bruce Degen, Putnam (New York, NY), 1987.

Commander Toad and the Voyage Home, illustrated by Bruce Degen, Putnam (New York, NY), 1998.

"ROBOT AND REBECCA" SERIES; FICTION

The Mystery of the Code-carrying Kids, illustrated by Jurg Obrist, Knopf (New York, NY), 1980, illustrated by Catherine Deeter, Random House (New York, NY), 1980.

The Robot and Rebecca and the Missing Owser, illustrated by Lady McCrady, Knopf (New York, NY), 1981.

"PIGGINS" SERIES; PICTURE BOOKS

Piggins, illustrated by Jane Dyer, Harcourt (New York, NY), 1987.

Picnic with Piggins, illustrated by Jane Dyer, Harcourt (New York, NY), 1988.

Piggins and the Royal Wedding, illustrated by Jane Dyer, Harcourt (New York, NY), 1988.

"YOUNG MERLIN" SERIES; FICTION

Passager, Harcourt (San Diego, CA, 1996.

Hobby, Harcourt (San Diego, CA), 1996.

Merlin, Harcourt (San Diego, CA), 1997.

The Young Merlin Trilogy (includes *Passager, Hobby,* and *Merlin*), Harcourt (Orlando, FL), 2004.

"TARTAN MAGIC" SERIES; FICTION

The Wizard's Map, Harcourt (San Diego, CA), 1998.

The Pictish Child, Harcourt (San Diego, CA), 1999.

The Bagpiper's Ghost, Harcourt (San Diego, CA), 2002.

"YOUNG HEROES" SERIES; FICTION

(With Robert J. Harris) *Odysseus in the Serpent Maze,* HarperCollins (New York, NY), 2001.

(With Robert J. Harris) *Atalanta and the Arcadian Beast,* HarperCollins (New York, NY), 2003.

(With Robert J. Harris) *Jason and the Gorgon's Blood,* HarperCollins (New York, NY), 2004.

FOR CHILDREN; NONFICTION

Pirates in Petticoats, illustrated by Leonard Vosburgh, McKay (New York, NY), 1963.

World on a String: The Story of Kites, World Publishing (Cleveland, OH), 1968.

Friend: The Story of George Fox and the Quakers, Seabury (New York, NY), 1972, second edition, foreword by Larry Ingle, Wuaker Press of Friends General Conference (Philadelphia, PA), 2006.

(Editor, with Barbara Green) *The Fireside Song Book of Birds and Beasts,* illustrated by Peter Parnall, Simon & Schuster (New York, NY), 1972.

The Wizard Islands, illustrated by Robert Quackenbush, Crowell (New York, NY), 1973.

Ring Out! A Book of Bells, illustrated by Richard Cuffari, Seabury (New York, NY), 1974.

Simple Gifts: The Story of the Shakers, illustrated by Betty Fraser, Viking (New York, NY), 1976.

(Compiler) *Rounds about Rounds,* music by Barbara Green, illustrated by Gail Gibbons, Watts (New York, NY), 1977.

The Lap-Time Song and Play Book, musical arrangements by son Adam Stemple, illustrated by Margot Tomes, Harcourt (New York, NY), 1989.

A Letter from Phoenix Farm (autobiography), photographs by son Jason Stemple, Richard C. Owen (Katonah, NY), 1992.

Jane Yolen's Songs of Summer, musical arrangements by Adam Stemple, illustrated by Cyd Moore, Boyds Mills Press (Honesdale, PA), 1993.

Welcome to the Green House, illustrated by Laura Regan, Putnam (New York, NY), 1993.

Jane Yolen's Old MacDonald Songbook, illustrated by Rosekrans Hoffman, Boyds Mills Press (Honesdale, PA), 1994.

Sing Noel, musical arrangements by Adam Stemple, illustrated by Nancy Carpenter, Boyds Mills Press (Honesdale, PA), 1996.

Milk and Honey: A Year of Jewish Holidays, illustrations by Louise August, musical arrangements by Adam Stemple, Putnam (New York, NY), 1996.

Welcome to the Sea of Sand, illustrated by Laura Regan, Putnam (New York, NY), 1996.

Welcome to the Ice House, illustrated by Laura Regan, Putnam (New York, NY), 1998.

Tea with an Old Dragon: A Story of Sophia Smith, Founder of Smith College, illustrated by Monica Vachula, Boyds Mills Press (Honesdale, PA), 1998.

The Perfect Wizard: Hans Christian Andersen, illustrated by Dennis Nolan, Dutton (New York, NY), 2004.

FOR CHILDREN; POETRY

See This Little Line?, illustrated by Kathleen Elgin, McKay (New York, NY), 1963.

It All Depends, illustrated by Don Bolognese, Funk & Wagnalls (New York, NY), 1970.

An Invitation to the Butterfly Ball: A Counting Rhyme, illustrated by Jane Breskin Zalben, Parents' Magazine Press (New York, NY), 1976.

All in the Woodland Early: An ABC Book, illustrated by Jane Breskin Zalben, Collins (New York, NY), 1979, reprinted, Caroline House (Honesdale, PA), 1991.

How Beastly!: A Menagerie of Nonsense Poems, illustrated by James Marshall, Philomel (New York, NY), 1980.

Dragon Night and Other Lullabies, illustrated by Demi, Methuen (New York, NY), 1980.

(Editor) *The Lullaby Songbook,* musical arrangements by Adam Stemple, illustrated by Charles Mikolaycak, Harcourt (New York, NY), 1986.

Ring of Earth: A Child's Book of Seasons, illustrated by John Wallner, Harcourt (New York, NY), 1986.

The Three Bears Rhyme Book, illustrated by Jane Dyer, Harcourt (New York, NY), 1987.

Best Witches: Poems for Halloween, illustrated by Elise Primavera, Putnam (New York, NY), 1989.

Bird Watch, illustrated by Ted Lewin, Philomel (New York, NY), 1990.

Dinosaur Dances, illustrated by Bruce Degen, Putnam (New York, NY), 1990.

An Invitation to the Butterfly Ball: A Counting Rhyme, illustrated by Jane Breskin Zalben, Caroline House, 1991.

(Compiler) *Street Rhymes around the World,* Wordsong (Honesdale, PA), 1992.

Jane Yolen's Mother Goose Songbook, musical arrangements by Adam Stemple, illustrated by Rosecrans Hoffman, Boyds Mill Press (Honesdale, PA), 1992.

(Compiler) *Weather Report,* illustrated by Annie Gusman, Boyds Mills Press (Honesdale, PA), 1993.

Mouse's Birthday, illustrated by Bruce Degen, Putnam (New York, NY), 1993.

Raining Cats and Dogs, illustrated by Janet Street, Harcourt (New York, NY), 1993.

What Rhymes with Moon?, illustrated by Ruth Tietjen Councell, Philomel (New York, NY), 1993.

(Editor) *Sleep Rhymes around the World,* Boyds Mills Press (Honesdale, PA), 1993.

(Compiler and contributor) *Alphabestiary: Animal Poems from A to Z,* illustrated by Allan Eitzen, Boyds Mills Press (Honesdale, PA), 1994.

Sacred Places, illustrated by David Shannon, Harcourt (New York, NY), 1994.

Animal Fare: Zoological Nonsense Poems, illustrated by Janet Street, Harcourt (New York, NY), 1994.

The Three Bears Holiday Rhyme Book, illustrated by Jane Dyer, Harcourt (New York, NY), 1995.

Water Music: Poems for Children, photographs by Jason Stemple, Boyds Mills Press (Honesdale, PA), 1995.

(Compiler) *Mother Earth, Father Sky: Poems of Our Planet,* illustrated by Jennifer Hewitson, Boyds Mills Press (Honesdale, PA), 1996.

O Jerusalem, illustrated by John Thompson, Scholastic (New York, NY), 1996.

Sea Watch: A Book of Poetry, illustrated by Ted Lewin, Putnam (New York, NY), 1996.

(Compiler and contributor) *Sky Scrape/City Scape: Poems of City Life,* illustrated by Ken Condon, Boyds Mills Press (Honesdale, PA), 1996.

(Compiler) *Once upon Ice and Other Frozen Poems,* photographs by Jason Stemple, Boyds Mills Press (Honesdale, PA), 1997.

Snow, Snow: Winter Poems for Children, photographs by Jason Stemple, Wordsong (Honesdale, PA), 1998.

The Originals: Animals That Time Forgot, illustrated by Ted Lewin, Philomel (New York, NY), 1998.

Color Me a Rhyme: Nature Poems for Young People, Boyds Mills Press (Honesdale, PA), 2000.

(With Heidi E.Y. Stemple) *Dear Mother, Dear Daughter: Poems for Young People,* illustrated by Gil Ashby, Boyds Mills Press (Honesdale, PA), 2001.

Wild Wings: Poems for Young People, photographs by Jason Stemple, Boyds Mills Press (Honesdale, PA), 2002.

Horizons: Poems as Far as the Eye Can See, photographs by Jason Stemple, Boyds Mills Press (Honesdale, PA), 2002.

The Radiation Sonnets: For My Love, in Sickness and in Health, Algonquin Books (Chapel Hill, NC), 2003.

Least Things: Poems about Small Natures, photographs by Jason Stemple, Boyds Mills Press (Honesdale, PA), 2003.

Fine Feathered Friends: Poems for Young People, photographs by Jason Stemple, Boyds Mills Press (Honesdale, PA), 2004.

FOR YOUNG ADULTS; FICTION

(With Anne Huston) *Trust a City Kid,* illustrated by J.C. Kocsis, Lothrop (New York, NY), 1966.

(Editor) *Zoo 2000: Twelve Stories of Science Fiction and Fantasy Beasts,* Seabury (New York, NY), 1973.

The Magic Three of Solatia, illustrated by Julia Noonan, Crowell (New York, NY), 1974.

(Editor and contributor) *Shape Shifters: Fantasy and Science Fiction Tales about Humans Who Can Change Their Shape,* Seabury (New York, NY), 1978.

The Gift of Sarah Barker, Viking (New York, NY), 1981.

Neptune Rising: Songs and Tales of the Undersea Folk, (story collection), illustrated by David Wiesner, Philomel (New York, NY), 1982.

The Stone Silenus, Philomel (New York, NY), 1984.

Children of the Wolf, Viking (New York, NY), 1984.

(Editor and contributor with Martin H. Greenberg and Charles G. Waugh) *Dragons and Dreams,* Harper (New York, NY), 1986.

(Editor and contributor with Martin H. Greenberg and Charles G. Waugh) *Spaceships and Spells,* Harper (New York, NY), 1987.

The Devil's Arithmetic, Viking (New York, NY), 1988.

(Editor and contributor with Martin H. Greenberg) *Werewolves: A Collection of Original Stories,* Harper, 1988.

The Faery Flag: Stories and Poems of Fantasy and the Supernatural, Orchard Books (New York, NY), 1989.

(Editor and contributor with Martin H. Greenberg) *Things That Go Bump in the Night,* Harper (New York, NY), 1989.

(Editor and contributor) *2041 AD: Twelve Stories about the Future by Top Science-Fiction Writers,* (anthology), Delacorte (New York, NY), 1990.

(Editor and contributor with Martin H. Greenberg) *Vampires,* HarperCollins (New York, NY), 1991.

Here There Be Dragons (stories and poetry), illustrated by David Wilgus, Harcourt (New York, NY), 1993.

Here There Be Unicorns (stories and poetry), illustrated by David Wilgus, Harcourt (New York, NY), 1994.

Here There Be Witches (stories and poetry), illustrated by David Wilgus, Harcourt (New York, NY), 1995.

(Editor and contributor) *Camelot: A Collection of Original Arthurian Tales,* illustrated by Winslow Pels, Putnam (New York, NY), 1995.

(Editor, with Martin H. Greenberg, and contributor) *The Haunted House: A Collection of Original Stories,* illustrated by Doron Ben-Ami, HarperCollins (New York, NY), 1995.

Here There Be Angels (stories and poetry), illustrated by David Wilgus, Harcourt (New York, NY), 1996.

Here There Be Ghosts (stories and poetry), illustrated by David Wilgus, Harcourt (New York, NY), 1998.

(With Bruce Coville) *Armageddon Summer,* Harcourt (New York, NY), 1998.

(With Adam Stemple) *Pay the Piper,* Tor (New York, NY), 2005.

(Editor, with Patrick Nielsen Hayden) *Year's Best Science Fiction and Fantasy for Teens,* Tor (New York, NY), 2005.

"PIT DRAGON" SERIES; YOUNG-ADULT FICTION

Dragon's Blood: A Fantasy, Delacorte (New York, NY), 1982.

Heart's Blood, Delacorte (New York, NY), 1984.

A Sending of Dragons, illustrated by Tom McKeveny, Delacorte (New York, NY), 1987.

FOR ADULTS; FICTION

Merlin's Booke (short stories), illustrated by Thomas Canty, Ace Books (New York, NY), 1982.

Tales of Wonder (short stories), Schocken (New York, NY), 1983.

Cards of Grief (science fiction), Ace Books (New York, NY), 1984.

Dragonfield and Other Stories, Ace Books (New York, NY), 1985.

(Editor) *Favorite Folktales from around the World,* Pantheon (New York, NY), 1986.

Sword and the Stone, Pulphouse (Eugene, OR), 1991.

Briar Rose, Tor Books (New York, NY), 1992.

Storyteller, illustrated by Merle Insinga, New England Science Fiction Association Press (Cambridge, MA), 1992.

(Editor and contributor with Martin H. Greenberg) *Xanadu,* Tor Books (New York, NY), 1993.

(Editor and contributor with Martin H. Greenberg) *Xanadu Two,* Tor Books (New York, NY), 1994.

(Editor and contributor with Martin H. Greenberg) *Xanadu Three,* Tor Books (New York, NY), 1995.

The Books of Great Alta, St. Martin's Press (New York, NY), 1997.

(Editor) *Gray Heroes: Elder Tales from around the World,* Viking Penguin (New York, NY), 1998.

Not One Damsel in Distress, Harcourt (New York, NY), 2000.

(With Heidi E.Y. Stemple) *Mirror, Mirror,* Viking (New York, NY), 2000.

(Editor and contributor) *Sherwood: A Collection of Original Robin Hood Stories,* illustrated by Dennis Nolan, Philomel (New York, NY), 2000.

(With Robert J. Harris) *Queen's Own Fool,* Philomel (New York, NY), 2000.

"WHITE JENNA" SERIES; ADULT FICTION

Sister Light, Sister Dark, Tor Books (New York, NY), 1988.

White Jenna, Tor Books (New York, NY), 1989.

The One-armed Queen, with music by Adam Stemple, Tor Books (New York, NY), 1998.

OTHER

Writing Books for Children, Writer (Boston, MA), 1973, revised edition, 1983.

Touch Magic: Fantasy, Faerie, and Folklore in the Literature of Childhood, Philomel (New York, NY), 1981, revised edition, August House, 2000.

Guide to Writing for Children, Writer (Boston, MA), 1989.

(Author of introduction) Robert D. San Souci, reteller, *Cut from the Same Cloth: American Women of Myth, Legend, and Tall Tale,* Philomel (New York, NY), 1993.

(With Nancy Willard) *Among Angels* (poetry), illustrated by S. Saelig Gallagher, Harcourt (New York, NY), 1995.

(Author of introduction) *Best-Loved Stories Told at the National Storytelling Festival,* National Storytelling Association, 1996.

(Author of introduction) Kathleen Ragan, *Fearless Girls, Wise Women, and Beloved Sisters: Heroines in Folktales from around the World,* Norton (New York, NY), 1998.

Take Joy: A Book for Writers, Writers Books (Waukesha, WI), 2003, published as *Take Joy: A Writer's Guide to Loving the Craft,* Writer's Digest Books (Cincinnati, OH), 2006.

Also author of musical *Robin Hood,* music by Barbara Greene, produced in Boston, MA, 1967. Author of chapbook *The Whitethorn Wood.* Ghostwriter of books for Rutledge Press. Contributor to books, including *Dragons of Light,* edited by Orson Scott Card, Ace Books, 1981; *Elsewhere,* 2 volumes, edited by Terri Windling and Mark Alan Arnold, Ace Books, 1981-82; *Hecate's Cauldron,* edited by Susan Schwartz, DAW Books, 1982; *Heroic Visions,* edited by Jessica Amanda Salmonson, Ace Books, 1983; *Faery!,* edited by Windling, Ace Books, 1985; *Liavek,* edited by Will Shetterly and Emma Bull, Ace Books, 1985; *Moonsinger's Friends,* edited by Schwartz, Bluejay, 1985; *Imaginary Lands,* edited by Robin McKinley, Greenwillow, 1985; *Don't Bet on the Prince: Contemporary Feminist Fairy Tales in North America and England,* edited by Jack Zipes, Methuen, 1986; *Liavek: Players of Luck,* edited by Shetterly and Bull, Ace Books, 1986; *Liavek: Wizard's Row,* edited by Shetterly and Bull, Ace Books, 1987; *Visions,* edited by Donald R. Gallo, Delacorte, 1987; *Liavek: Spells of Binding,* edited by Shetterly and Bull, Ace Books, 1988; *Invitation to Camelot,* edited by Parke Godwin, Ace Books, 1988; *The Unicorn Treasury,* edited by Bruce Coville, Doubleday, 1988; and *Hamsters, Shells, and Spelling Bees: School Poems,* edited by Lee Bennett Hopkins, HarperCollins, 2008. Author of folk songs and lyrics.

Author of column "Children's Bookfare" for *Daily Hampshire Gazette,* c. 1970s. Contributor of articles, reviews, poems, and short stories to periodicals, including *Chicago Jewish Forum, Horn Book, Isaac Asimov's Science Fiction Magazine, Language Arts, Los Angeles Times, Magazine of Fantasy and Science Fiction, New Advocate, New York Times, Parabola, Parents' Choice, Washington Post Book World, Wilson Library Bulletin,* and *Writer.* Member of editorial board, *Advocate* (now *New Advocate*) and *National Storytelling Journal,* until 1989.

Yolen's books have been published in Australia, Austria, Brazil, China, Denmark, England, France, Germany, Greece, Japan, South Africa, Spain, Sweden, Thailand, Korea, Russia, and elsewhere.

Yolen's papers are housed at the Kerlan Collection, University of Minnesota.

Adaptations

The Seventh Mandarin was produced as a motion picture by Xerox Films, 1973; *The Emperor and the Kite* was produced as a filmstrip with cassette by Listening Library, 1976; *The Bird of Time* was adapted into a play and produced in Northampton, MA, 1982; *The Girl Who Cried Flowers and Other Tales* was released on audio cassette by Weston Woods, 1983; *Dragon's Blood* was produced as an animated television movie by Columbia Broadcasting System (CBS), 1985; *Commander Toad in Space* was released on audio cassette by Listening Library, 1986; *Touch Magic . . . Pass It On,* a selection of Yolen's short stories, was released on audio cassette by Weston Woods, 1987; *Owl Moon* was produced as a filmstrip with cassette by Weston Woods, 1988, and as both a read-along cassette and a video, 1990; *Owl Moon* was also adapted as part of the video *Owl Moon and Other Stories,* produced by Children's Circle; *Piggins* and *Picnic with Piggins* were released on audio cassette by Caedmon, 1988; *Best of Science Fiction and Fantasy* was released on audio cassette by NewStar Media, 1991; *Merlin and the Dragons* was released on audio cassette by Lightyear Entertainment, 1991, produced as a video by Coronet, 1991, and re-

leased as *What's a Good Story? Merlin and the Dragon,* with commentary by Yolen; *Greyling* was released on audio cassette by Spoken Arts, 1993; *Hands* was released on audio cassette by Sundance Publishing, 1993; *Beneath the Ghost Moon* was produced as a video by Spoken Arts, 1996; *Wizard's Hall* was released on audio cassette by "Words Take Wings," narrated by Yolen, 1997; *How Do Dinosaurs Say Good Night?* was produced as a video, Weston Woods, 2002. Recorded Books issued audio cassettes of *Briar Rose, The Devil's Arithmetic,* and *Good Griselle.*

Sidelights

A prolific and highly esteemed author, Jane Yolen is the creator of hundreds of books for children, teens, and adults. Spanning genres from fiction and poetry to biography, criticism, and books on the art of writing, Yolen is particularly well known for her history-based fiction and her fantasy novels in her "Pit Dragon" series, set in a mythological world based around cockfighting dragons on an arid planet. A folksinger and storyteller, Yolen creates works that reflect her love of music and oral folklore, such as compilations of international songs, rhymes, and stories. Several of her books are autobiographical or incorporate elements from her life or the lives of her family. Now grown, Yolen's three children also contribute to her works: daughter Heidi E.Y. Stemple as a writer and sons Adam and Jason Stemple as musical arranger and photographer, respectively. Yolen also writes both short stories and novels with her musician son.

Yolen is perhaps best known for creating original folk and fairy tales and fables that contain a surprising twist and a strong moral core. Her literary fairy tales are praised for mixing familiar fantasy motifs with contemporary elements and philosophical themes. As a fantasist, she includes dragons, unicorns, witches, and mermaids as characters, and her stories often feature shapeshifters: animals that have the ability to transform into humans or vice versa. As a writer, Yolen invests her works with images, symbols, and allusions as well as with wordplay—especially puns—and metaphors. Considered an exceptional prose stylist, her fluid, musical writing is both polished and easy to read aloud. In *Twentieth-Century Children's Writers,* Marcia G. Fuchs commented: "Faerie, fiction, fact, or horrible fantasy, Yolen's lyrical and magical tales are indeed tales to read and to listen to, to share, to remember, and to pass on."

Born in New York City in 1939, Yolen bloomed as a writer early on. A voracious reader as well as a tomboy, she played games in Central Park while being encouraged in her reading and writing by her teachers. "I was," she later recalled in *Something about the Author Autobiography Series* (*SAAS*), "the gold star star. And I was also pretty impossibly full of myself. In first or second grade, I wrote the school musical, lyrics and music, in which everyone was some kind of vegetable. I played the lead carrot. Our finale was a salad. Another gold star."

Yolen's favorite books as a child included the folk stories collected by British folklorist Allan Lang in his colored fairy books, "as well as by *Treasure Island* [by Robert Louis Stevenson] and the Louisa May Alcott books," as she once told *SATA*. "All of the Alcott books, *Jo's Boys,* and even the Alcott books that nobody else had heard of, became part of my adolescent reading. I read *The Wind in the Willows* and the Mowgli stories. We didn't have 'young adult' fiction, so I skipped right into adult books which tended to be very morose Russian novels—my Dostoevsky phase—then I got hooked on Joseph Conrad. Adventure novels or lugubrious emotional books are what I preferred. Then I went back into my fairy tale and fantasy stage. Tolkien and C.S. Lewis, metaphysical and folkloric fantasy."

In sixth grade, Yolen was accepted by Hunter, a girls' school for what were called "intelligently gifted" students. While navigating the academic challenges at Hunter, music—especially folk songs, an interest she shared with her father—became Yolen's new focus. In addition to starring as Hansel in the school production of Engelbert Humperdinck's opera *Hansel and Gretel,* she played the piano and wrote songs; she also became the lead dancer in her class at Balanchine's American School of Ballet.

In addition to her other achievements, Yolen developed an interest in writing during her early teens, and in eighth grade she penned her first two books: a nonfiction work about pirates and a novel about a trip across the West by covered wagon. She eventually described this latter work, which is seventeen pages long and includes a plague of locusts, death by snake bite, and the birth of a baby on the trail, as "a masterpiece of economy"; in fact, short stories and poetry continue to be her favored genres.

At age thirteen the high-achieving Yolen moved with her family to Westport, Connecticut, where she became captain of her high school girls' basketball team; news editor of the school paper; head of the Jewish Youth Group; vice president of the Spanish, Latin, and jazz clubs; a member of the school's top singing group; and a contributor to the school literary magazine. She also won a Scholastic essay contest called "I Speak for Democracy," and her school's English prize. Before graduation, her class named Yolen's voice to be a composite part of "The Perfect Senior." She also became close to her cousin-in-law, Honey Knopp, who sparked Yolen's lifelong interest in the Quaker faith.

After graduating from high school, Yolen attended Smith College, where she majored in English and Russian literature and minored in religion. In addition to continuing her involvement in campus activities, she also continued her writing, and saw poems published in

Poetry Digest as well as in small literary magazines. Deciding to pursue a career in journalism due to its practicality, Yolen worked as a cub reporter for a Connecticut newspaper the summer before her sophomore year. Although she continued to intern for newspapers during the next few years, she dismissed the idea of being a journalist when she found herself making up facts and writing stories off the top of her head.

After graduating from Smith College, Yolen moved to New York City and worked briefly for *This Week* magazine and the *Saturday Review* before launching her career as a freelance writer by helping her father write his book *The Young Sportsman's Guide to Kite Flying.* While living in Greenwich Village in the summer of 1960, she met her future husband, David Stemple, who was a friend of one of her roommates; the couple were married in 1962.

Several years spent working for New York City publishers followed, and then Yolen's father introduced her to the vice president of David McKay Publishing Company. Yolen's first book for children, the nonfiction title *Pirates in Petticoats,* was published by McKay in 1963; the publisher also bought Yolen's second work, *See This Little Line?,* a picture book in rhyme that was published the same year. While continuing to work in publishing, she became a ghostwriter for Rutledge Press, authoring concept and activity books published under different names. In 1963 she became an assistant editor in the children's department at Knopf, where she met authors and illustrators such as Roald Dahl and Roger Duvoisin and learned about juvenile literature.

In 1965 Yolen and her husband spent nine months traveling in Europe, Israel, and Greece. Her daughter, Heidi E.Y. Stemple was born in 1966, shortly after her parents returned to America. When David Stemple took a job at the University of Massachusetts Computer Center in Amherst, he and Yolen moved to western Massachusetts, where son Adam Stemple was born in 1968 and Jason Stemple in 1970. While raising her children, Yolen began her writing career in earnest.

The picture book *The Emperor and the Kite* was the first of Yolen's books to receive a major award. The story outlines how Djeow Seow, the youngest and smallest daughter of an ancient Chinese emperor, saves her father after he is kidnapped by sending him a kite to which is attached a rope made of grass, vines, and strands of her hair. As a reviewer in *Children's Book News* commented, "Here is a writer who delights in words and can use them in a controlled way to beautiful effect." In 1968, *The Emperor and the Kite* earned Yolen her first Lewis Carroll Shelf Award; the second would come for *The Girl Who Loved the Wind,* in 1972.

Another early award winner was 1974's *The Girl Who Cried Flowers and Other Tales,* which won the Golden Kite Award and was nominated for the National Book Award in 1975. It is a collection of five stories that, ac-

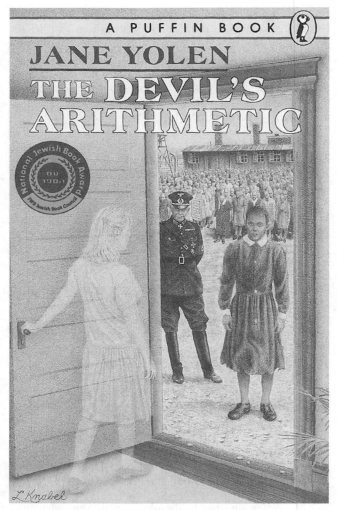

Jane Yolen focuses on the tragedies of World War II in her novel **The Devil's Arithmetic,** *featuring cover art by Lonnie Knabel.* (Copyright © 1990 by Lonnie Knabel. Reproduced by permission of Puffin Books, a division of Penguin Books USA, Inc.)

cording to a reviewer in *Publishers Weekly,* "could be called modern folk-or fairy tales, since they boast all the usual ingredients—supernatural beings, inexplicable happenings, the struggle between good and evil forces." The critic concluded that Yolen's "artistry with words . . . makes a striking book," while a critic in *Kirkus Reviews* called *The Girl Who Cried Flowers and Other Tales* a "showpiece, for those who can forego the tough wisdom of traditional fairy tales for a masterful imitation of the manner."

All in the Woodland Early: An ABC Book, one of several song books authored by Yolen, teaches the alphabet through rhyming verses. The book outlines a little boy's hunting expedition in the woods; each letter represents the animal, bird, or insect—both familiar and unfamiliar—for which he is searching. At the end of the last verse, readers discover that the boy is gathering the animals to play with him and a little girl. Yolen also provides music to go with her words. Writing in the *Washington Post Book World,* Jerome Beatty, Jr., said: "Count

on versatile Jane Yolen to invent something special and intriguing," while a reviewer for *Publishers Weekly* called *All in the Woodland Early* "an outstanding alphabet book." Other song books by Yolen include *Apple for the Teacher: Thirty Songs for Singing while You Work* and *Jane Yolen's Songs of Summer,* both of which feature music by Adam Stemple.

Other highly praised picture books by Yolen include *Harvest Home,* a story about a farm family's wheat harvest that *School Library Journal* contributor Catherine Threadgill praised as a "reflective and respectful tribute to a bygone era"; *Welcome to the River of Grass,* which introduces young children to the Florida Everglades ecosystem; *My Brothers' Flying Machine: Wilbur, Orville, and Me,* a story about the fathers of flight as told by their younger sister, Katherine; and *Sea Queens: Women Pirates around the World,* a nonfiction picture book based on an earlier work by Yolen. The writer's fascination with folk stories also extends to Russia in several books, among them *The Flying Witch,* a Baba Yaga story about an old woman who uses young children as a main ingredient in her evening meal, and *The Firebird,* a unique retelling of a classic Eastern-European fable.

More fanciful works by Yolen include *How Do Dinosaurs Get Well Soon?,* part of a series of books that finds large, bulky dinosaurs dealing with common, child-sized problems while attempting to fit into a tiny, child-sized world. Other volumes in the "How Do Dinosaurs . . . ?" series include *How Do Dinosaurs Say Good Night?, How Do Dinosaurs Clean Their Room?, How Do Dinosaurs, Eat Their Food?,* and *How Do Dinosaurs Go to School?* Dubbed a "jaunty comedy of errors" by a *Publishers Weekly* contributor, *How Do Dinosaurs Eat Their Food?* features artwork by Mark Teague that "comically captur[es] . . . the dining dinos' antics." With its focus on an average day at school for Silvasaurus, Herrasaurus, and Centrosaurus, *How Do Dinosaurs Go to School?* pairs Yolen's "easy rhymes" with Teague's "positively pop-off-the-page paintings," according to a *Kirkus Reviews* writer.

Throughout her career Yolen has ranged in her focus from books for the very young, such as *Sleep, Black Bear, Sleep* and *Baby Bear's Big Dreams,* to poetry collections like *Shape Me a Rhyme: Nature's Forms in Poetry,* to historical fiction and fantasy novels such as *Armageddon Summer,* that are geared for older readers. Her historical novels often focus on an unusual subject, as in *The Gift of Sarah Barker.* Set in a Shaker community, this story features teens Abel and Sarah. The two friends have grown up in the Society of Believers, a celibate religious community, and now find that they are sexually attracted to each other. As the young people struggle with their feelings, Yolen depicts the contradiction between the religious ecstasy of the Shakers—whose dances and celebrations gave the group their nickname—and the repressive quality of the sect's lifestyle. Sarah and Abel decide to leave the community, but not before Sister Agatha, Sarah's abusive mother, commits suicide.

Before writing *The Gift of Sarah Barker*, Yolen interviewed some of the few remaining Shakers for background information. She also used her daughter, Heidi, who was then becoming interested in boys, as the prototype for Sarah. As the author once explained to *SATA*, "I kept wondering how, in a Shaker community, you could keep the boys away from a girl like Heidi or keep Heidi away from the boys. I imagined a Romeo and Juliet story within the Shaker setting." Writing in *Children's Book Review Service*, Barbara Baker called *The Gift of Sarah Barker* "an absorbing tale" and a "jewel of a[n] historical novel," while Stephanie Zvirin noted in *Booklist:* "Into the fabric of a teenage romance [Yolen] weaves complicated and disturbing—at times violent—undercurrents that add a dimension both powerful and provocative."

Working in collaboration with Scots writer Robert J. Harris, Yolen has penned a number of novels based on Scottish history, one of Yolen's abiding interests—she makes her home in that part of Great Britain for part of each year. The first of these, *Queen's Own Fool,* recounts the tragic reign of the ill-fated Mary, Queen of Scots, from the viewpoint of her fool, Nicola. A French-born orphan, Nicola follows Mary from France to Scotland as the young queen—and half-sister of Elizabeth I of England—tries to gain her place as queen of Scotland while political power is fought over by a variety of Scottish nobles. In *Girl in a Cage* the eleven-year-old daughter of Robert the Bruce becomes a captive to the English troops her father hopes to keep out of his beloved Scotland at the turn of the fourteenth century. The story of Bonny Prince Charlie is told from the point of view of a young recruit in *Prince across the Water.* Here thirteen-year-old Highlander Duncan joins the rebels hoping to place the Scottish Prince Charles on the throne of England in the mid-1700s. He loyally follows the call of his clan and his king until the massacre of Charlie's followers by British forces at the Battle of Culloden Field dashes Scots hopes. In *The Rogues,* Yolen and Harris set their story against the backdrop of

Vlasta van Kampen teams up with Yolen to entertain very young children with basic concepts in **Sad, Mad, Glad Hippos.** (Key Porter Books, 2008. Illustration copyright © 2008 by Vlasta van Kampen. Reproduced by permission.)

the Highland clearances, a time when the Scottish lords evicted their clansmen in favor of using historic clan lands for grazing sheep.

Praising *Queen's Own Fool* in *Kliatt,* Claire Rosser wrote that Yolen "knows how to appeal to young people and keep a story moving swiftly," while in *Booklist* Anne O'Malley concluded of *The Rogues* that the story's "plot races along flawlessly in this excellent historical adventure." In *Booklist,* Carolyn Phelan praised *Prince across the Water* for its "convincing depictions of people and relationships," while in *Horn Book* Anita L. Burkham dubbed it a "well-told story set in an intriguing era that will leave readers mulling over thoughts of war and peace."

Several of Yolen's more-recent historical works have been in the area of nonfiction, as in the "Mystery from History" series, written with her daughter Heidi. In *The Wolf Girls: An Unsolved Mystery from History,* as in other volumes in the series, a fictional story is built around an actual incident that left many questions unanswered. The novel focuses on two orphaned girls living in India who, in the 1920s, were reportedly raised by wolves by missionary Joseph Singh, who ultimately gave the children a home. Noting the authors' inclusion of expert scientific evidence and a number of possible explanations for the girls' feral condition, *School Library Journal* reviewer Anne Chapman dubbed the book "tasty fodder for emerging detectives."

Other books in the series by Yolen and Stemple include *Mary Celeste: An Unsolved Mystery from History,* about a ghost ship; *Roanoke, the Lost Colony: An Unsolved Mystery from History;* and *The Salem Witch Trials: An Unsolved Mystery from History,* the last about the hysteria that gripped the Massachusetts Bay colony during its early days. Although many books have been published that detail the frenzy caused by two girls over a supposed witch in their community, *The Salem Witch Trials* "gives a different perspective" and by presenting the facts in an organized and impartial manner, lets young sleuths "evaluate the evidence and draw their own conclusions," according to *School Library Journal* contributor Elaine Fort Weischedel.

Dragon's Blood is the first volume in Yolen's "Pit Dragon" series. High fantasy for young adults that incorporates elements of science fiction, the series presents a completely realized imaginary world. *Dragon's Blood* introduces Jakkin, a fifteen-year-old slave boy. Jakkin's master is the best dragon breeder on the planet Austar IV, a former penal colony where inhabitants train and fight dragons domesticated by the early colonists. Jakkin steals a female dragon hatchling to train in secret for the gaming pits, a cockfighting ritual that contributes largely to the planet's economy. Hoping to win his freedom by raising a superior fighting dragon, the teen establishes an amazing mental link with his "snatchling," which he names Heart's Blood. The story

Cover of Yolen's middle-grade fantasy novel **Heart's Blood,** *featuring artwork by Dennis Nolan.* (Magic Carpet Books, 1996. Cover illustration copyright © 1996 by Dennis Nolan. All rights reserved. Reproduced by permission of Houghton Mifflin Harcourt Publishing Company.)

ends with the dragon's first win; Jakkin—now free—learns that his master knew about his theft and that Akki, a bond girl training in medicine whom Jakkin loves, is his master's illegitimate daughter. Writing in *Horn Book,* Ann A. Flowers called *Dragon's Blood* an "original and engrossing fantasy," while Patricia Manning wrote in *School Library Journal* that the novel provides a "fascinating glimpse of a brand new world."

In the second volume of the series, *Heart's Blood,* Jakkin is the new Dragon Master and Heart's Blood has given birth to five hatchlings. Jakkin becomes involved in Austarian politics when he is asked to infiltrate rebel forces and rescue Akki. Becoming the pawns in a deadly game, he and Akki flee with Heart's Blood into the freezing cold of night, called Dark After. Cornered by the authorities after inadvertently blowing up a major city, the trio fight for their lives. In the battle, Heart's Blood is killed. In order to survive the freezing temperatures, Jakkin and Akki enter her carcass; when they emerge, they have been given the gift of dragon's sight—telepathy—and the ability to withstand the cold of Dark After.

A Sending of Dragons finds Jakkin and Akki avoiding capture by fleeing into the wilderness with Heart's Blood's five babies. When they enter a hidden tunnel, the group encounters an underground tribe of primitives who have discovered a way to extract metals on Austar IV. Jakkin and Akki also learn that these people, who, like them, are bonded to dragons, have developed a bloody, terrifying ritual of dragon sacrifice. At the end of the novel, Akki, Jakkin, and the fledglings escape with two of the primitive community's dragons. Confronted by their pursuers from above ground, they decide to return to the city and use their new knowledge to bring about an end to the feudalism and enslavement on Austar IV.

A reviewer in *Publishers Weekly* stated that "Yolen's tightly plotted, adventurous trilogy constitutes superb storytelling. She incorporates elements of freedom and rebellion, power and control, love and friendship in a masterfully crafted context of a society sick with perversion." Writing in *School Library Journal,* Michael Cart noted that, like the two volumes preceding it, the particular strengths of *A Sending of Dragons* include "the almost encyclopedic detail which Yolen has lavished upon her fully realized alternative world of Austar IV, in her sympathetic portrayal of the dragons as both victims and telepathic partners, and in the symbolic sub-text which enriches her narrative and reinforces her universal theme of the inter-dependency and unique value of all life forms."

One of Yolen's most highly acclaimed books combines history and fantasy. *The Devil's Arithmetic,* a young-adult novel, is a time-travel fantasy that is rooted in one of the darkest episodes of history, the novel features Hannah Stern, a twelve-year-old Jewish girl who is transported from contemporary New York City to rural Poland in 1942 when she opens the door for Elijah during her family's Seder celebration. Captured by the Nazis, Hannah—now called Chaya—is taken to a death camp, where she meets Rivka, a spirited young girl who teaches her to fight against the dehumanization of the camp wherein some must live to bear witness. When Rivka is chosen to be taken to the gas chamber, Chaya, in an act of self-sacrifice, goes in her place; as the doors of the gas chamber close, Chaya—now Hannah again—is returned to the door of her grandparents' apartment, waiting for Elijah. Hannah realizes that her Aunt Eva is her friend Rivka and that she also knew her grandfather in the camp.

A critic in *Kirkus Reviews* wrote of *The Devil's Arithmetic:* "Yolen is the author of a hundred books, many of which have been praised for their originality, humor, or poetic vision, but this thoughtful, compelling novel is unique among them." Writing in *Bulletin of the Center for Children's Books,* Roger Sutton noted that

Yolen's depiction of the horrors in the camp "is more graphic than any we've seen in holocaust fiction for children before." Confirming that Yolen has brought the "time travel convention to a new and ambitious level," Cynthia Samuels of the *New York Times Book Review* concluded that "sooner or later, all our children must know what happened in the days of the Holocaust. *The Devil's Arithmetic* offers an affecting way to begin."

Yolen, who has said that she wrote *The Devil's Arithmetic* for her own children, stated in her acceptance speech for the Sydney Taylor Book Award: "There are books one writes because they are a delight. There are books one writes because one is asked to. There are books one writes because . . . they are there. And there are books one writes simply because the book has to be written."

With *Encounter,* a picture book published to coincide with the five-hundredth anniversary of the discovery of America, Yolen presented readers with what is perhaps her most controversial work. Written as the remembrance of an elderly Taino man, the story, which describes the first encounter of Native Americans with Columbus, depicts the man's experience as a small boy. The narrator awakens from a terrifying dream about three predatory birds riding the waves to see three anchored ships. Frightened yet fascinated by the strangers who come ashore, the boy tells his chief not to welcome the men, but he is ignored. The boy and several other Indians are taken aboard the ships as slaves. After he escapes by jumping overboard, the boy tries to warn other tribes, but to no avail; the Taino are wiped out.

Calling *Encounter* an "unusual picture book," Carolyn Phelan noted in *Booklist* that "while the portrayal of Columbus as evil may strike traditionalists as heresy, he did hunger for gold, abduct native people, and ultimately (though unintentionally), destroy the Taino. This book effectively presents their point of view." Writing in the *New Advocate,* James C. Junhke called *Encounter* "among the most powerful and disturbing publications of the Columbus Quincentennial." Noting the "pioneering brilliance" of the book, the critic called Yolen's greatest achievement "the reversal of perspective. This book forces us to confront what a disaster it was for the Taino people to be discovered and destroyed by Europeans. Readers young and old will fervently wish never to be encountered by such 'strangers from the sky.'"

Writing in response to Junhke's review in the same publication, Yolen said, "If my book becomes a first step towards the exploration of the meeting between Columbus and the indigenous peoples—and its tragic aftermath—then it has done its work, whatever its flaws, perceived or real." The author concluded, "We cannot change history. But we—and most especially our children—can learn from it so that the next encounters, be they at home, abroad, or in space, may be gentler and mutually respectful. It is a large hope but it is, perhaps, all that we have."

Throughout her career, Yolen has woven bits and pieces of her personal history—and that of her family and friends—into her works. Several of the author's books are directly autobiographical. For example, *All Those Secrets of the World,* a picture book published in 1991, is set during the two years the author's father was away at war. Yolen recalls how, as a four year old, she watched her father depart by ship. The next day, the fictional Janie and her five-year-old cousin Michael see some tiny specks on the horizon while they are playing on the beach; the specks are ships. Michael teaches Janie a secret of the world, that as he moves farther away, he gets smaller. Two years later, when her father returns, Janie whispers Michael's secret after he tells her that she seems bigger: that when he was so far away, everything seemed smaller, but now that he is here, she is big. A reviewer in *Publishers Weekly* wrote that "Yolen here relates a bittersweet memory from an important period in her childhood. . . . This timely nostalgic story is told with simple grace, and Janie's thoughts and experiences are believably childlike." Phyllis G. Sidorsky, in *School Library Journal,* called *All Those Secrets of the World* an "affecting piece without an extraneous word and one that is particularly timely today."

And Twelve Chinese Acrobats is a tale for middle graders that is based on family stories about Yolen's father's older brother. Set in a Russian village in 1910, the book features Lou the Rascal, a charming troublemaker who keeps getting into scrapes. When Lou is sent to a military school in Kiev, the family—especially narrator Wolf, Lou's youngest brother (and Yolen's father)—is sad. Lou is eventually expelled from military school, and months later he surprises everyone by bringing home a troupe of twelve Chinese acrobats he met while working in a Moscow circus. The acrobats fascinate the locals with their descriptions of an exotic world far removed from the little village. When the acrobats leave the shtel in the spring, Lou's father, recognizing his son's managerial ability, sends him to America to find a place for the family.

Reviewing *And Twelve Chinese Acrobats* for the *Bulletin of the Center for Children's Books,* Betsy Hearne noted that "the relationship between the two brothers . . . lends an immediate dynamic to the historical setting," and concluded that the compressed narrative, brief chapters, spacious format, large print, and Jean Gralley's "vivaciously detailed pen-and-ink illustrations dancing across almost every page make this a prime choice for young readers venturing into historical fiction for the first time, or, for that matter, considering a probe into their own family stories." A critic in *Kirkus Reviews* called *And Twelve Chinese Acrobats* a book "radiating family warmth, in words, art, and remembrance."

In an article for *Horn Book,* Yolen stated: "As a writer I am the empress of thieves, taking characters like gargoyles off Parisian churches, the ki-lin (or unicorn)

from China, swords in stones from the Celts, landscapes from the Taino people. I have pulled threads from magic tapestries to weave my own new cloth." The author concluded, "Children's literature is about growth. Just as we do not put heavy weights on our children's heads to stunt their growth, we should not put weights on our writers' heads. To do so is to stunt story forever. Stories go beyond race, beyond religion—even when they are about race and religion. The book speaks to individuals in an individual voice. But then it is taken into the reader's life and recreated, re-invigorated, re-visioned. That is what literature is about."

In her essay for *SAAS,* Yolen mused that her life, "like anyone else's is a patchwork of past and present. . . . I just want to go on writing and discovering my stories for the rest of my life because I know that in my tales I make public what is private, transforming my own joy and sadness into tales for the people. The folk."

Biographical and Critical Sources

BOOKS

Authors and Artists for Young Adults, Volume 22, Gale (Detroit, MI), 1997.

Children's Books and Their Creators, edited by Anita Silvey, Houghton Mifflin (Boston, MA), 1995, pp. 700-701.

Children's Literature Review, Gale (Detroit, MI), Volume 4, 1982, pp. 255-269, Volume 44, 1997, pp. 167-211.

Dictionary of Literary Biography, Volume 52: *American Writers for Children since 1960: Fiction,* Gale (Detroit, MI), 1986, pp. 398-405.

Drew, Bernard A., *The One Hundred Most Popular Young Adult Authors,* Libraries Unlimited, 1996.

Roginski, Jim, *Behind the Covers: Interviews with Authors and Illustrators of Books for Children and Young Adults,* Libraries Unlimited, 1985.

St. James Guide to Fantasy Writers, St. James Press (Detroit, MI), 1996.

St. James Guide to Young-Adult Writers, St. James Press (Detroit, MI), 1999.

Something about the Author Autobiography Series, Volume 4, Gale (Detroit, MI), 1987, pp. 327-346.

Twentieth-Century Children's Writers, 3rd edition, St. James Press (Detroit, MI), 1989, pp. 1075-1078.

Yolen, Jane, *Guide to Writing for Children,* Writer, 1989.

Yolen, Jane, *Touch Magic: Fantasy, Faerie, and Folktale in the Literature of Childhood,* Philomel (New York, NY), 1981.

PERIODICALS

Booklist, November 15, 1980, Judith Goldberger, review of *Commander Toad in Space,* p. 464; May 15, 1981, Stephanie Zvirin, review of *The Gift of Sarah Barker,* p. 1250; March 1, 1992, Carolyn Phelan, review of

Encounter, p. 1281; March 15, 2001, Hazel Rochman, review of *Dear Mother, Dear Daughter: Poems for Young People*, p. 1393; April 15, 2001, Gillian Engberg, review of *Odysseus in the Serpent Maze*, p 1561; July, 2001, Ilene Cooper, review of *The Wolf Girls: An Unsolved Mystery from History*, p. 2007; October 1, 2001, Connie Fletcher, review of *Welcome to the River of Grass*, p. 321; November 15, 2001, Todd Morning, review of *The Fish Prince and Other Stories: Mermen Folk Tales*, p. 562; April 15, 2002, Sally Estes, review of *Wizard's Hall*, p. 1416, and Catherine Andronik, review of *The Bagpiper's Ghost*, p. 1418; May 15, 2992, Susan Dove Lempke, review of *Wild Wings: Poems for Young People*, p. 1596; June 1, 2002, Gillian Engberg, review of *The Firebird*, p. 1732; October 15, 2002, Shelley Townsend-Hudson, review of *Harvest Home*, p. 413; January 1, 2003, Ilene Cooper, review of *How Do Dinosaurs Get Well Soon?*, p. 881; February, 1, 2003, John Peters, review of *Atalanta and the Arcadian Beast*, p. 996; March 1, 2003, Carolyn Phelan, review of *My Brothers' Flying Machine*, p. 1208; April 15, 2003, Carolyn Phelan, review of *Sword of the Rightful King: A Novel of King Arthur*, p. 1464; May 15, 2003, Karin Snelson, review of *Hoptoad*, p. 1674; July, 2003, Carolyn Phelan, review of *Roanoke, the Lost Colony: An Unsolved Mystery from History*, p. 1888; September 15, 2003, Ray Olson, review of *The Radiation Sonnets*, p. 195; October 1, 2003, Linda Perkins, review of *The Flying Witch*, p. 325; February 15, 2004, John Peters, review of *Jason and the Gorgon's Blood*, p. 1060; September 1, 2004, Ilene Cooper, review of *The Salem Witch Trials*, p. 118; November 1, 2004, GraceAnne A. DeCandido, review of *Fine Feathered Friends*, p. 478, and Ilene Cooper, review of *Barefoot Book of Ballet Stories*, p. 498; November 15, 2004, Carolyn Phelan, review of *Prince across the Water*, p. 585; July, 2005, Jennifer Mattson, review of *How Do Dinosaurs Eat Their Food?*, p. 1931; August, 2005, Jennifer Locke, review of *Meow: Cat Stories from Around the World*, p. 2033; October 1, 2005, Candace Smith, review of *How Do Dinosaurs Get Well Soon?*, p. 74; October 1, 2005, Kay Weisman, review of *Apple for the Teacher: Thirty Songs for Singing While You Work*, p. 56; November 1, 2005, Jennifer Mattson, review of *Soft House*, p. 55; April 1, 2006, Carolyn Phelan, review of *Count Me a Rhyme: Animal Poems by the Numbers*, p. 38; June 1, 2006, Carolyn Phelan, review of *Dimity Duck*, p. 90; September 1, 2006, Diana Tixier Herald, review of *Trollbridge: A Rock 'n' Roll Fairy Tale*, p. 114; November 15, 2006, GraceAnne A. DeCandido, review of *Sleep, Black Bear, Sleep*, p. 56; April 1, 2007, Randall Enos, review of *How Do Dinosaurs Go to School?*, p. 61; April 1, 2007, Hazel Rochman, review of *Here's a Little Poem*, p. 50; August, 2007, Carolyn Phelan, review of *Baby Bear's Big Dreams*, p. 81; September 15, 2007, Anne O'Malley, review of *The Rogues*, p. 63; April 15, 2008, Kay Weisman, review of *Naming Liberty*, p. 58; June 1, 2008, Thom Barthelmess, review of *Johnny Appleseed: The Legend and the Truth*, p. 104; June 1, 2008, Gillian Engberg, review of *Sea Queens: Women Pirates around the World*, p. 102.

Book Report, January-February, 2002, Anne Hanson, review of *The Fish Prince and Other Stories*, p. 74.

Bulletin of the Center for Children's Books, October, 1988, Roger Sutton, review of *The Devil's Arithmetic*, pp. 23-24; June, 1995, Betsy Hearne, review of *And Twelve Chinese Acrobats*, p. 365; September, 2003, Elizabeth Bush, review of *Roanoke, the Lost Colony* p. 40; September, 2005, Hope Morrison, review of *Meow*, p. 58.

Children's Book News, January-February, 1970, review of *The Emperor and the Kite*, pp. 23-24.

Children's Book Review Service, December, 1973, Eleanor Von Schweinitz, review of *The Girl Who Loved the Wind*, pp. 172-173; June, 1981, Barbara Baker, review of *The Gift of Sarah Barker*, p. 100.

Horn Book, August, 1982, Ann A. Flowers, review of *Dragon's Blood*, pp. 418-419; April, 1984, Charlotte W. Draper, review of *Heart's Blood*, p. 206; November-December, 1994, Jane Yolen, "An Empress of Thieves," pp. 702-705; January-February, 2003, Anita L. Burkam, review of *Girl in a Cage*, p. 86; March-April, 2003, Christine M. Hepperman, review of *How Do Dinosaurs Get Well Soon?*, p. 208; May-June, 2003, Anita L. Burkham, review of *Sword of the Rightful King*, p. 359, and Susan Dove Lempke, review of *Mightier than the Sword*, p. 362; November-December, 2004, Anita L. Burkam, review of *Prince across the Water*, p. 720; September-October, 2005, Christine M. Heppermann, review of *How Do Dinosaurs Eat Their Food?*, p. 571; July-August, 2007, Martha V. Parravano, review of *How Do Dinosaurs Go to School?*, p. 388.

Judaica Librarianship, spring, 1989-winter, 1990, Jane Yolen, transcript of acceptance speech for Sydney Taylor Book Award, pp. 52-53.

Kirkus Reviews, July 15, 1974, review of *The Girl Who Cried Flowers and Other Tales*, p. 741; August 15, 1988, review of *The Devil's Arithmetic*, p. 1248; April 15, 1995, review of *And Twelve Chinese Acrobats*, p. 564; September 15, 2991, review of *Welcome to the River of Grass*, p. 1372; January 1, 2002, review of *Hippolyta and the Curse of the Amazons*, p. 54; March 1, 2002, review of *Wild Wings* and *The Bagpiper's Ghost*, p. 349; May 1, 2002, review of *The Firebird*, p. 670; August 15, 2002, review of *Girl in a Cage* and *Harvest Home*, p. 1240; December 1, 2002, review of *How Do Dinosaurs Get Well Soon?* and *The Sea King*, p. 1776; March 15, 2003, review of *My Brothers' Flying Machine*, p. 482; April 15, 2003, review of *Mightier than the Sword*, p. 614; May 1, 2003, review of *Sword of the Rightful King*, p. 686; May 15, 2003, review of *Hoptoad*, p. 758; June 15, 2993, review of *Roanoke, the Lost Colony* p. 865; July 1, 2993, review of *The Flying Witch*, p. 917; September 1, 2003, review of *Least Things*, p. 1133; August 15, 2004, review of *The Salem Witch Trials*, p. 815; September 15, 2004, review of *Prince across the Water*, p. 923; January 1, 2005, review of *The Perfect Wizard: Hans Christian Andersen*, p. 175; July 1, 2005, review of *Meow*, p. 745; July 15, 2005, review of *Soft House*, p. 797; April 15, 2006, review of *Dimity Duck*, p. 419; June 15, 2007, review of *How Do Dinosaurs*

Go to School?; April 15, 2008, review of *Naming Liberty;* June 1, 2008, review of *Sea Queens.*

Kliatt, March, 2002, Claire Rosser, review of *Queen's Own Fool,* p. 20; May, 2003, Claire Rosser, review of *Sword of the Rightful King,* p. 15; September, 2003, Stacey Conrad, review of *Boots and the Seven Leaguers,* p. 29.

Library Journal, June 15, 1972, Janet G. Polacheck, review of *Friend: The Story of George Fox and the Quakers,* p. 2245.

New Advocate, spring, 1993, James C. Juhnke and Jane Yolen, "An Exchange on Encounter," pp. 94-96.

New York Times Book Review, November 20, 1977, Jane Langton, review of *The Hundredth Dove and Other Tales,* p. 30; November 13, 1988, Cynthia Samuels, "Hannah Learns to Remember," p. 62; November 8, 1992, Noel Perrin, "Bulldozer Blues," p. 54.

Publishers Weekly, August 14, 1967, review of *The Emperor and the Kite,* p. 50; July 22, 1974, review of *The Girl Who Cried Flowers and Other Tales,* p. 70; January 11, 1980, review of *All in the Woodland Early: An ABC Book,* p. 88; October 9, 1987, review of *A Sending of Dragons,* p. 90; March 22, 1991, review of *All Those Secrets of the World,* p. 80; April 29, 2002, review of *The Firebird,* p. 68; February, 2003, Angela J. Reynolds, review of *Atalanta and the Arcadian Beast,* p. 150; March 24, 2003, review of *My Brothers' Flying Machine,* p. 75; April 14, 2003, review of *Sword of the Rightful King,* p. 72; July 7, 2003, review of *The Radiation Sonnets,* p. 60; August 4, 2003, review of *The Flying Witch,* p. 78; November 29, 2004, review of *The Book of Ballads,* p. 24; February 21, 2005, review of *The Perfect Wizard,* p. 175; July 25, 2005, review of *How Do Dinosaurs Eat Their Food?,* p. 74; December 19, 2005, review of *Soft House,* p. 64; December 19, 2005, review of *Baby Bear's Chairs,* p. 62; December 18, 2006, review of *Sleep, Black Bear, Sleep,* p. 61.

School Librarian, December, 1983, Pauline Thomas, review of *Dragon's Blood,* p. 384.

School Library Journal, March, 1973, Marilyn R. Singer, review of *The Girl Who Loved the Wind,* p. 102; December, 1980, review of *Commander Toad in Space,* p. 66; September, 1982, Patricia Manning, review of *Dragon's Blood,* p. 146; January, 1988, Michael Cart, review of *A Sending of Dragons,* pp. 87-88; July, 1991, Phyllis G. Sidorsky, review of *All Those Secrets of the World,* p. 66; December, 2000, review of *Color Me a Rhyme,* p. 167; May, 2001, Cynthia J. Rieben, review of *Mirror, Mirror,* p. 178; July, 2001, Angela J. Reynolds, review of *Odysseus in the Serpent Maze,* p. 116; August, 2001, Anne Chapman, review of *The Wolf Girls,* p. 174; November, 2001, Margaret Bush, review of *Welcome to the River of Grass,* p. 153; March, 2002, Beth L. Meister, review of *Hippolyta and the Curse of the Amazons,* p. 240; March, 2002, Cherie Estes, review of *The Bagpiper's Ghost,* p. 240; June, 2002, Sharon Korbeck, review of *Wild Wings,* p. 127; June, 2002, Ellen Heath, review of *The Firebird,* p. 127; October, 2002, Nina Lindsay, review of *Poems as Far as the Eye Can See,* p. 152, and Starr E. Smith, review of *Girl in a Cage,* p. 178; November, 2002,

Catherine Threadgill, review of *Harvest Home,* p. 140, and Jessica Snow, review of *Time for Naps,* p. 142; February, 2003, Jody McCoy, review of *How Do Dinosaurs Get Well Soon?,* p. 126; March, 2003, Harriett Fargnoli, review of *My Brothers' Flying Machine,* p. 225; May, 2003, Miriam Lang Budin, review of *Mightier than the Sword,* p. 143; July, 2003, Margaret A. Chang, review of *Sword of the Rightful King,* p. 135; September, 2003, James K. Irwin, review of *The Flying Witch,* p. 208; October, 2003, Nancy Palmer, review of *Roanoke,* p. 157; October, 2003, Donna Cardon, review of *Least Things,* p. 157; February, 2004, Angela J. Reynolds, review of *Jason and the Gorgon's Blood,* p. 154; November, 2004, Elaine Fort Weischedel, review of *The Salem Witch Trials,* p. 174; December, 2004, Kimberly Monaghan, review of *Prince across the Water,* p. 154, and Susan Scheps, review of *Fine Feathered Friends,* and Carol Schene, review of *The Barefoot Book of Ballet Stories,* both p. 172; August, 2005, Kathleen Whalin, review of *Meow,* p. 120; August, 2005, Roxanne Burg, review of *How Dinosaurs Eat Their Food?,* p. 110; June, 2006, Joy Fleishacker, review of *Dimity Duck,* p. 130; February, 2007, Susan Weitz, review of *Sleep, Black Bear, Sleep,* p. 98; June, 2007, Neala Arnold, review of *How Do Dinosaurs Go to School?,* p. 128; July, 2008, Carol S. Surges, review of *Sea Queens,* p. 118.

Teaching and Learning Literature, November-December, 1996, Lee Bennett Hopkins, "O Yolen: A Look at the Poetry of Jane Yolen," pp. 66-68.

Washington Post Book World, April 13, 1980, Jerome Beatty Jr., "Herds of Hungry Hogs Hurrying Home," p. 10.

ONLINE

Jane Yolen Home Page, http://www.janeyolen.com (October 15, 2008).

Writers Write Web site, http://www.writerswrite.com/ (June 1, 2002), Claire E. White, interview with Yolen.

OTHER

Children's Writer at Work: Jane Yolen (film), Reel Life, 1997.*

*   *   *

ZWERGER, Lisbeth 1954-

Personal

Surname pronounced "tsvair-ger"; born May 26, 1954, in Vienna, Austria; daughter of Reinhold (a designer) and Waltraut (a medical assistant) Zwerger; married John Rowe (an artist), January 19, 1984. *Education:* Attended Hochschule für Angewandte Kunst (Vienna, Austria), 1971-74.

Addresses

Home—Vienna, Austria. *Agent*—Michael Neugebauer, Minedition, Am Gertenfeld 6, 22941 Bargteheide, Germany.

Lisbeth Zwerger (Photograph by Nancy Gorbics. Reproduced by permission of Lisbeth Zwerger.)

Career

Illustrator. Worked part-time for an insurance company. *Exhibitions:* Illustrative work has been shown in Austria, Belgium, Czechoslovakia, Germany, Italy, Japan, and the United States.

Awards, Honors

Bologna International Children's Book Fair honor, 1978, for *The Strange Child,* 1980, for *Hansel and Gretel,* 1982, for *The Swineherd,* 1986, for *The Deliverers of Their Country,* and 1987, for *The Canterville Ghost;* International Biennial of Illustration, Bratislava, honor diploma, 1979, for *Hansel and Gretel* and *The Legend of the Rose Petal,* Gold Plaquette, 1981, for *Thumbeline,* and 1983, for *The Seven Ravens* and *Little Red Cap,* and Golden Apple award, 1985, for *Selfish Giant; New York Times* Best Illustrated Books of the Year designation, 1982, for *Little Red Cap,* 1983, for *The Gift of the Magi,* 1996, for *The Wizard of Oz,* 1997, for *Noah's Ark;* Hans Christian Andersen Award for Illustration, 1990.

Writings

SELF-ILLUSTRATED

(Reteller) Pyotr I. Tchaikovsky, *Swan Lake,* translated by Marianne Martens, North-South (New York, NY), 2002.

ILLUSTRATOR

E.T.A. Hoffmann, *Das fremde Kind,* Neugebauer (Salzburg, Austria), 1977, translated as *The Strange Child,* Picture Book Studio (Boston, MA), 1984.

Clemens Brentano, *Das Maerchen von Rosenblaettchen,* Neugebauer (Salzburg, Austria), 1978, translated as *The Legend of the Rose Petal,* Picture Book Studio (Boston, MA), 1985.

Jakob and Wilhelm K. Grimm, *Hansel and Gretel,* translated by Elizabeth D. Crawford, Morrow (New York, NY), 1979.

E.T.A. Hoffmann, *Nussknacker und Mausekönig,* Neugebauer (Salzburg, Austria), 1979, adapted and translated by Anthea Bell as *The Nutcracker and the Mouse-King,* Picture Book Studio (Boston, MA), 1983, retold by Susanne Koppe and published with new illustrations as *The Nutcracker,* North-South (New York, NY), 2004.

Hans Christian Andersen, *Thumbeline,* translated by Richard and Clara Winston, Morrow (New York, NY), 1980.

Jakob and Wilhelm K. Grimm, *The Seven Ravens,* translated by Elizabeth D. Crawford, Morrow (New York, NY), 1981.

Hans Christian Andersen, *The Swineherd,* translated by Anthea Bell, Morrow (New York, NY), 1982, reprinted, Minedition (New York, NY), 2008.

O. Henry, *The Gift of the Magi,* Picture Book Studio (Boston, MA), 1982.

Jakob and Wilhelm K. Grimm, *Little Red Cap,* translated by Elizabeth D. Crawford, Morrow (New York, NY), 1983, reprinted, Minedition (New York, NY), 2006.

Oscar Wilde, *The Selfish Giant,* Picture Book Studio (Boston, MA), 1984.

Hans Christian Andersen, *The Nightingale,* Picture Book Studio (Boston, MA), 1984.

E. Nesbit, *The Deliverers of Their Country,* Picture Book Studio (San Francisco, CA), 1985.

Oscar Wilde, *The Canterville Ghost,* Picture Book Studio (Boston, MA), 1986.

Charles Dickens, *A Christmas Carol,* Picture Book Studio (Boston, MA), 1988.

Aesop, *Aesop's Fables,* Picture Book Studio (Boston, MA), 1989.

Heinz Janisch, adaptor, *Till Eulenspiegel's Merry Pranks,* translated by Anthea Bell, Picture Book Studio (Boston, MA), 1990, published as *The Merry Pranks of Till Eulenspiegel,* North-South Books (New York, NY), 2001.

Hans Christian Andersen, *Fairy Tales,* Simon & Schuster (New York, NY), 1992, published as *Hans Christian Andersen's Fairy Tales,* North-South Books (New York, NY), 2001.

Wilhelm Hauf, *Dwarf Nose,* translated by Michelle Nikly, North-South (New York, NY), 1995.

Christian Morgenstern, *Lullabies, Lyrics, and Gallows Songs,* North-South (New York, NY), 1995.

Theodor Storm, *Little Hobbin,* North-South (New York, NY), 1995.

L. Frank Baum, *The Wizard of Oz,* North-South (New York, NY), 1996.

Heinz Janisch, *Noah's Ark,* translated by Rosemary Lanning, North-South (New York, NY), 1997.

Lewis Carroll, *Alice in Wonderland,* North-South (New York, NY), 1999.

Rudyard Kipling, *How the Camel Got His Hump,* North-South (New York, NY), 2001.

Stories from the Bible, North-South (New York, NY), 2001.

Clement C. Moore, *The Night before Christmas,* Penguin (New York, NY), 2005.

Hans Christian Andersen, *The Little Mermaid,* Minedition (New York, NY), 2005.

Jakob and Wilhelm K. Grimm, *The Bremen Town Musicians,* translated by Anthea Bell, Minedition (New York, NY), 2007.

Books featuring Zwerger's illustrations have been published in many other countries, including Australia, Belgium, Denmark, England, Finland, France, Greece, Holland, Hungary, Italy, Japan, South Africa, Spain, and Sweden.

Sidelights

Lisbeth Zwerger is recognized internationally as one of the finest contemporary illustrators of children's literature. Providing the drawings for such classic holi-

Charles Dickens's classic holiday tale **A Christmas Carol** *is given a fresh look in Zwerger's paintings.* (Picture Book Studio, 1988. Illustration by Lisbeth Zwerger. Reproduced by permission of Picture Book Studio, a division of Simon & Schuster, Inc.)

day narratives as O. Henry's *The Gift of the Magi,* Clement C. Moore's *The Night before Christmas,* and Charles Dickens's *A Christmas Carol,* Zwerger has been honored by awards that include the prestigious Hans Christian Andersen Award. "Zwerger's dreamy, delicately drawn ink-and-wash illustrations shine with humanity, and are often spiced with humor," wrote Heather Frederick in describing the illustrator's appeal in *Publishers Weekly.* Zwerger's drawings are further celebrated for their ability to enhance and complement the literature they accompany. According to Frederick, the Austrian-born artist "is indisputably one of the most talented illustrators [her generation] . . . has produced."

Born in 1954 in Vienna, Austria, Zwerger grew up in a household attuned to artistic values: her father was a graphic artist and her mother, a medical assistant, had a knack for fashion design. While Zwerger relished this emphasis on art, as a child she also experienced many troubles in her schooling. "I wish I could say that by growing up in such 'colourful' surroundings my childhood was somehow different or exciting," she expressed in an essay for *Something about the Author Autobiography Series* (*SAAS*), "but sadly it was neither." In addition to her public schooling, Zwerger took private lessons, a common practice in European education. She would begin her days practicing the piano, proceed by going to school, return home for lunch, and later attend private tutoring sessions where the teachers "would do their best in trying to turn us into young Einsteins," as she later recalled.

Although Zwerger cannot remember exactly when she started drawing, she recalls being encouraged to sketch by her parents, who were talented in painting, puppetry, and photography. Zwerger and her sister engaged in many drawing projects, but Zwerger always exhibited a tendency toward illustration. Recognizing their daughter's dislike of public school, her parents eventually enrolled her at Vienna's Hochschule für Angewandte Kunst. There, under less-restrictive instruction, Zwerger enjoyed creative freedom but was disappointed at the lack of classes focusing on illustration. Discouraged by her instructors, she "seemed to drift from illustrating or drawing, until eventually things came to a sort of standstill and I lost interest all together," as she later recalled.

During the spring of 1974 Zwerger met John Rowe, an English artist then vacationing in Vienna. The two became best friends and, when Rowe decided to remain in Vienna to study, they began looking for an apartment to rent together. "This did not please my parents one little bit," Zwerger maintained in *SAAS,* In addition to marrying Rowe, the illustrator dropped out of college, deciding her time there was not time well spent. "Just when my parents had started to believe that I would be saved after all," Zwerger continued, "I brought their hopes and dreams crashing down with these two decisions. Once again I was a problem."

Financially desperate and seemingly without direction, Zwerger was inspired to illustrate again when Rowe brought home a book of illustrations by English artist Arthur Rackham; the book "was to change my whole outlook, if not my life!" declared Zwerger. "I had never seen anything like them, and as I looked through the book, something inside of me seemed to come alive. My love for illustrating returned there and then. I felt so inspired that I wanted to start again straight away."

Accustomed to drawing in black and white, Zwerger tried to imitate Rackham's style of line and color wash. Rowe showed her how to use the two-color technique at which Zwerger quickly became adept, and when her mother offered to purchase some of her illustrations the young artist begin to earn money from her craft. This new source of income helped immensely, for Zwerger and Rowe lived in a Vienna apartment with little furniture and limited funds for food.

Using the two-color technique to illustrate scenes from stories by such authors as E.T.A. Hoffmann and Hans Christian Andersen, Zwerger found modest success with her illustrations. When she showed several drawings at a private gallery, in a group exhibition including both her father and Rowe, every one of her pieces was sold.

Following this success, Zwerger and Rowe decided to move to England where they secured a tiny attic apartment; Rowe worked as a book packer and Zwerger continued to illustrate. In the meantime, Zwerger's mother was showing her daughter's drawings to various publishers in and around Vienna. Eventually, Friedrich Neugebauer, the owner of a small publishing company, took an interest in Zwerger's work, and when the artist and her husband returned to Vienna to live, she met with Neugebauer. The publisher liked her drawings for Hoffmann's *The Strange Child* and decided to have Zwerger prepare illustrations for the entire book.

Accustomed to drawing on a small scale, Zwerger adjusted to producing larger illustrations and completed the drawings for *The Strange Child* over the next year. Although surprised at the length of time Zwerger took to complete the project, Neugebauer was impressed by the work, bought the drawings, and enlisted her to illustrate three more books. Zwerger eventually began working with Neugebauer's son, Michael, when the younger man took over his father's publishing company, and under Neugebauer's guidance she has gained international recognition, particularly in the United States.

During her career, Zwerger's signature watercolors have appeared in many of the classics of children's literature—among them *Alice in Wonderland* by Lewis Carroll and *The Wizard of Oz* by L. Frank Baum—as well as in the books by some lesser-known poets and gatherers of fairy tales. Over the years she has shifted her technique from her two-color pen-and-ink and watercolor works to more opaque watercolor and gouache on colored and white papers. Reviewing *The Wizard of Oz* in *Booklist,* Ilene Cooper observed that Zwerger's "fey paintings catch the lighter elements of the story," and

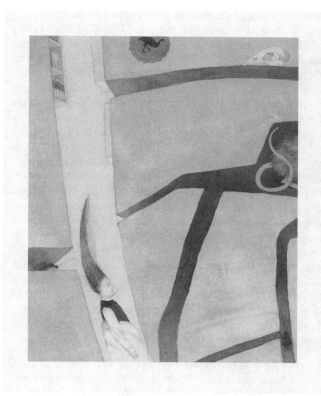

Zwerger takes a topsy-turvy view of a classic fantasy in her work for Lewis Carroll's **Alice in Wonderland.** (Minedition, an imprint of Penguin Young Readers Group, 2007. Illustration copyright © 1999 by Lisbeth Zwerger. Reproduced by permission.)

Susan Dove Lempke noted in the same periodical that her artwork for Heinz Janisch's *Noah's Ark* is, "as always . . . impeccable." Malcolm Jones, Jr., reviewing the same Bible-based picture book for *Newsweek,* concluded that "you wouldn't dream of telling Lisbeth Zwerger that the world has enough versions of *Noah's Ark,* at least not after you have seen her stylish animal catalogue." Lauren Adams, writing in *Horn Book,* also praised the book's "beautifully detailed insects and animals."

In her images for *Alice in Wonderland,* Zwerger selected an uncharacteristically vibrant palette to bring to life this childhood classic. As a contributor to *Publishers Weekly* noted, the artist's "penetrating interpretation reinvents Carroll's situations and characters and demands a rereading of the text." Noting the many who have illustrated *Alice,* from the original artist, Sir John Tenniel, through Salvador Dali and Barry Moser, *Booklist* critic Michael Cart applauded Zwerger's unique interpretation. According to the critic, her images are "uniformly lovely and, occasionally, strange and haunting in their dreamlike quality, making them a surprisingly nice match for the text." A reviewer for *Horn Book* found Zwerger's illustrations for *Alice in Wonderland* to be "so intensely realized" as to inspire the "reader's own imagination," describing Zwerger's full-page spreads as "exquisitely composed, with unexpected vantage points to give us dynamic new views of the events."

Other classics of childhood given new life in Zwerger's imaginative illustrations include *The Nutcracker* by E.T.A. Hoffman and *The Little Mermaid* by Hans Christian Andersen, both translated by Anthea Bell. Writing that the illustrator "expands her repertoire of beguilingly illustrated tales" with these books, *Booklist* contributor Jennifer Mattson added that through her study of the original elements and sources, in the case of *The Little Mermaid,* Zwerger "reinstates the tragic ending and spiritual-mystical components abandoned by Disney" in the version most familiar to U.S. readers. Hoffman's story, which Zwerger first illustrated in 1979, also benefited from her revisioning in a new 2004 edition. "Devotees of the ballet version may be surprised by the layers of fantasy and reality in this skillful distillation" of Hoffman's *Nussknacker und Mausekönig,* observed *Horn Book* critic Lolly Robinson. Another familiar story illustrated by Zwerger, *The Bremen Town Musicians* by the Brothers Grimm features "subdued watercolors" that are "infused with a sophisticated naîveté that lends them an air of gravitas even as they illustrate the story's slapstick episodes," according to *Booklist* contributor Janice Del Negro.

Incorporating what *Horn Book* reviewer Joanna Rudge Long characterized as "thoughtfully chosen selections from the King James Version," *Stories from the Bible* benefits from "powerfully expressive" illustrations by Zwerger that transcend a devout Christian perspective and "extend their meaning to a more universal human experience." Reflecting the view of several critics that Zwerger's approach might be too sophisticated for younger readers, a *Publishers Weekly* critic deemed the book's images "immaculately executed" and maintained that the artist's approach to this Christian text "will startle readers into fresh insights and appreciations."

Choosing the subject matter of her illustrations is, for Zwerger, the most enjoyable part of her work. "When I design each illustration," she once explained in *SAAS,* "I take particular pleasure in using objects, animals, and people that have some personal meaning to me. It might be a piece of furniture, or a cat, or even a picture hanging on the wall within my picture." She often incorporates details associated with people she knows; for example, her husband has appeared as several characters in her illustrations. In addition, she conducts research in order to accurately portray certain objects, characters, and time periods in her pictures.

Another aspect that Zwerger deems important in her work is determining the proper story to illustrate. "At first I was quite content to carry on illustrating the sort of stories that I knew from my childhood, all the classics from Grimm or Andersen," she disclosed, "but gradually I began to find the moral in some of them slightly degrading. The sort of stories that I mean are the ones where a beautiful, poor, but suffering girl, finally ends up marrying a prince, because deep down at heart she has been a good girl all along and in spite of all the suffering has managed to do all the right

things. . . . What's more, it became increasingly boring to always illustrate the same sort of stories. It was very refreshing to later illustrate such stories as *The Gift of the Magi* and [Oscar Wilde's] *The Selfish Giant.*"

"When I look for a story, it has to contain all the right ingredients," Zwerger explained of her work. "For a start, it has to be the right length; I like it to have a main character who is both comical and touching; it has to interest me (of course); it has to be the sort of story that my type of illustrations fit; and, last but not least, it has to have no sexist morals."

Even though Zwerger has found success with her drawings, she never finds illustration to be a simple process. "I often have the feeling that I've never drawn before in my life as I sit looking at a blank sheet of paper, wondering how I'm going to manage with this one . . . ," she admitted in *SAAS.* "It always takes a few pictures before I can settle down and get into it, and I'm often a bit bad tempered at this stage. [My husband], who is my resident critic (the only one I trust), always looks through my 'roughs,' criticizing this or that, and we always end up shouting at each other. It's a touchy time and I think we're both relieved once it's over."

Oscar Wilde's classic story **The Canterville Ghost** *reached German-language audiences paired with Zwerger's haunting art.* (North-South, 1996. Illustration by Lisbeth Zwerger copyright © 1986 by Michael Neugebauer Verlag AG, Gossau Zurich, Switzerland. Reproduced by permission of North-South Books.)

Biographical and Critical Sources

BOOKS

The Art of Lisbeth Zwerger, North-South (New York, NY), 1994.

Children's Literature Review, Volume 46, Gale (Detroit, MI), 1998.

Silvey, Anita, *Children's Books and Their Creators,* Houghton Mifflin (Boston, MA), 1995.

Zwerger, Lisbeth, *Something about the Author Autobiography Series,* Volume 13, Gale (Detroit, MI), 1991, pp. 263-272.

PERIODICALS

Booklist, May 1, 1995, Kay Weisman, review of *Dwarf Nose,* p. 1573; June 1, 1995, review of *Lullabies, Lyrics, and Gallows Songs,* p. 1779; February 1, 1996, Julie Corsaro, review of *Little Hobbin,* p. 940; October 15, 1996, Ilene Cooper, review of *The Wizard of Oz,* p. 430; December 15, 1996, Michael Cart, review of *The Canterville Ghost,* p. 722; October 1, 1997, Susan Dove Lempke, review of *Noah's Ark,* p. 323; November 1, 1999, Michael Cart, review of *Alice in Wonderland,* p. 528; April 1, 2002, Ilene Cooper, review of *Stories from the Bible,* p. 1326; January 1, 2003, Carolyn Phelan, review of *Swan Lake,* p. 886; October 1, 2004, Jennifer Mattson, review of *The Little Mermaid,* p. 328; October 15, 2005, GraceAnne A. DeCandido, review of *The Night before Christmas,* p. 58; February 15, 2007, Janice Del Negro, review of *The Bremen Town Musicians,* p. 81.

Bulletin of the Center for Children's Books, September, 2002, review of *Stories from the Bible,* p. 6; November, 2002, review of *Swan Lake,* p. 127; December, 2004, Karen Coats, review of *The Little Mermaid,* p. 159.

Horn Book, November-December, 1986, Ed Young, review of *Little Red Cap,* pp. 708-709; November-December, 1988, Mary M. Burns, review of *A Christmas Carol,* pp. 762-763; March-April, 1998 Lauren Adams, review of *Noah's Ark,* pp. 213-214; January-February, 2000, review of *Alice in Wonderland,* p. 72; July-August, 2002, Joanna Rudge Long, review of *Stories from the Bible,* p. 488; November-December, 2004, Lolly Robinson, review of *The Nutcracker,* p. 660.

Newsweek, December 1, 1997, Malcolm Jones, Jr., review of *Noah's Ark,* p. 77.

New York Times Book Review, May 11, 1980, Roger Sale, review of *Hansel and Gretel,* p. 24; April, 26, 1981, Michele Slung, *The Seven Ravens,* p. 55; November 14, 1982, Thomas Lask, review of *The Gift of the Magi,* p. 50; November 13, 1983, Thomas Lask, review of *The Nutcracker,* p. 53; December 2, 1984, Selma G. Lanes, review of *The Strange Child,* p. 53; October 19, 1986, review of *The Canterville Ghost,* p. 44; November 2, 1990, Heather Vogel Frederick, review of *The Merry Pranks of Till Eulenspiegel,* p. 10; November 17, 2002, Molly Garrett Bang, review of *Swan Lake,* p. 30.

Publishers Weekly, October 26, 1990, Heather Frederick, "A Talk with Lisbeth Zwerger," p. 42; November 16, 1992, review of *Fairy Tales,* p. 63; November 1, 1999, review of *Alice in Wonderland,* p. 84; April 1, 2002, review of *Stories from the Bible,* p. 79; November 4, 2002, review of *Swan Lake,* p. 86; September 6, 2004, review of *The Little Mermaid,* p. 62; February 5, 2007, review of *The Bremen Town Musicians,* p. 58.

School Library Journal, December, 1989, Denise Anton Wright, review of *Aesop's Fables,* p. 92; February, 1993, Karen K. Radtke, review of *Fairy Tales,* p. 92; January, 1995, Susan Scheps, review of *Dwarf Nose,* p. 118; November, 1997, Kathy Piehl, review of *Noah's Ark,* p. 84; October, 1999, Grace Oliff, review of *Alice and Wonderland,* p. 110; May, 2002, Patricia Pearl Dole, review of *Stories from the Bible,* p. 177; December, 2002, Amy Kellman, review of *Swan Lake,* p. 130; December, 2004, Susan Scheps, review of *The Little Mermaid,* p. 96; February, 2007, Margaret Bush, review of *The Bremen Town Musicians,* p. 105.

ONLINE

All Business Web site, http://www.allbusiness.com/ (September 1, 2005), Meredith E. Lewis, "New Pictures, Old Stories."

Meet Authors and Illustrators, http://www.childrenslit.com/ (October 25, 2001), Marilyn Courtot, "Lisbeth Zwerger."

Ricochet-Jeunes Web site, http://www.ricochet-jeunes.org/ (October 25, 2008), "Lisbeth Zwerger."*

DATE DUE